THE ROUTLEDGE HANDBOOK OF NONPROFIT COMMUNICATION

This handbook brings together multidisciplinary and internationally diverse contributors to provide an overview of theory, research, and practice in the nonprofit and nongovernmental organization (NGO) communication field.

It is structured in four main parts: the first introduces metatheoretical and multidisciplinary approaches to the nonprofit sector; the second offers distinctive structural approaches to communication and their models of reputation, marketing, and communication management; the third focuses on nonprofit organizations' strategic communications, strategies, and discourses; and the fourth assembles campaigns and case studies of different areas of practice, causes, and geographies.

The handbook is essential reading for scholars, educators, and advanced students in nonprofit and NGO communication within public relations and strategic communication, organizational communication, sociology, management, economics, marketing, and political science, as well as a useful reference for leaders and communication professionals in the nonprofit sector.

Gisela Gonçalves is a professor and director of the Masters in Strategic Communication program at the University of Beira Interior and associated researcher at LabCom, Portugal.

Evandro Oliveira is a Serra Húnter professor at the Autonomous University of Barcelona (UAB), Spain and researcher at LabCom, Portugal.

ROUTLEDGE HANDBOOKS IN COMMUNICATION STUDIES

THE ROUTLEDGE HANDBOOK OF POSITIVE COMMUNICATION
Edited by José Antonio Muñiz Velázquez and Cristina M. Pulido

THE ROUTLEDGE HANDBOOK OF MASS MEDIA ETHICS
Edited By Lee Wilkins and Clifford G. Christians

THE ROUTLEDGE HANDBOOK OF COMPARATIVE WORLD RHETORICS
Studies in the History, Application, and Teaching of Rhetoric Beyond Traditional Greco-Roman Contexts
Edited By Keith Lloyd

THE ROUTLEDGE HANDBOOK OF MEDIA USE AND WELL-BEING
International Perspectives on Theory and Research on Positive Media Effects
Edited By Leonard Reinecke and Mary Beth Oliver

THE ROUTLEDGE HANDBOOK OF QUEER RHETORIC
Edited by Jonathan Alexander and Jacqueline Rhodes

THE ROUTLEDGE HANDBOOK OF NONPROFIT COMMUNICATION
Edited by Gisela Gonçalves and Evandro Oliveira

THE ROUTLEDGE HANDBOOK OF INTERCULTURAL MEDIATION
Edited by Dominic Busch

THE ROUTLEDGE HANDBOOK OF CORPORATE SOCIAL RESPONSIBILITY COMMUNICATION
Edited by Amy O'Connor

THE ROUTLEDGE INTERNATIONAL HANDBOOK OF RESEARCH ON WRITING, SECOND EDITION
Edited by Rosalind Horowitz

For a full list of titles in this series, please visit www.routledge.com/series/RHCS

THE ROUTLEDGE HANDBOOK OF NONPROFIT COMMUNICATION

Edited by Gisela Gonçalves and Evandro Oliveira

NEW YORK AND LONDON

Cover image: XH4D/Getty Images

First published 2023
by Routledge
605 Third Avenue, New York, NY 10158

and by Routledge
4 Park Square, Milton Park, Abingdon, Oxon, OX14 4RN

Routledge is an imprint of the Taylor & Francis Group, an informa business

© 2023 selection and editorial matter, Gisela Marques Pererira Gonçalves and Evandro Samuel Ribeiro dos Santos Oliveira; individual chapters, the contributors

The right of Gisela Marques Pererira Gonçalves and Evandro Samuel Ribeiro dos Santos Oliveira to be identified as the authors of the editorial material, and of the authors for their individual chapters, has been asserted in accordance with sections 77 and 78 of the Copyright, Designs and Patents Act 1988.

All rights reserved. No part of this book may be reprinted or reproduced or utilised in any form or by any electronic, mechanical, or other means, now known or hereafter invented, including photocopying and recording, or in any information storage or retrieval system, without permission in writing from the publishers.

Trademark notice: Product or corporate names may be trademarks or registered trademarks, and are used only for identification and explanation without intent to infringe.

Library of Congress Cataloging-in-Publication Data
Names: Gisela Marques Pererira Gonçalves, editor. |
Evandro Samuel Ribeiro dos Santos Oliveira, editor.
Title: The Routledge handbook of nonprofit communication /
edited by Gisela Marques Pererira Gonçalves and
Evandro Samuel Ribeiro dos Santos Oliveira.
Description: 1 Edition. | New York, NY : Routledge, 2023. |
Includes bibliographical references and index.
Identifiers: LCCN 2022015704 (print) | LCCN 2022015705 (ebook)
Subjects: LCSH: Communication in organizations. |
Non-governmental organizations. | Public relations.
Classification: LCC HD30.3 .R683 2023 (print) | LCC HD30.3 (ebook) |
DDC 658.4/5—dc23/eng/20220421
LC record available at https://lccn.loc.gov/2022015704
LC ebook record available at https://lccn.loc.gov/2022015705

ISBN: 978-0-367-77177-5 (hbk)
ISBN: 978-0-367-77272-7 (pbk)
ISBN: 978-1-003-17056-3 (ebk)

DOI: 10.4324/9781003170563

Typeset in Bembo
by Apex CoVantage, LLC

CONTENTS

List of figures ... ix
List of tables ... xi
List of contributors ... xii

Introducing nonprofit communication and mapping the research field ... 1
Gisela Gonçalves and Evandro Oliveira

PART I
Democracy and civil society ... 13

1.1 Histories of the nonprofit and philanthropic sector ... 15
Thomas Davies

1.2 Communication for development and social change ... 23
Jan Servaes

1.3 NGO-ization of civil society ... 32
Sabine Lang

1.4 NGO-ization of solidarity in the digital age ... 39
Víctor Manuel Marí Sáez

1.5 Civic relations: socio-communicative collective action ... 46
Evandro Oliveira

1.6 Public interest communication: a pragmatic approach ... 55
Jane Johnston

1.7 Humanitarian communication 66
Valérie Gorin

PART II
Communication, organizations and publics 75

2.1 A constitutive approach to nonprofit communication 77
Matthew Koschmann and Matthew Isbell

2.2 Organizational listening and the nonprofit sector 85
Jim Macnamara

2.3 Integrated marketing communication management for nonprofit organizations 94
Manfred Bruhn and Anja Zimmermann

2.4 Communication monitoring and evaluation in the nonprofit sector 104
Glenn O'Neil

2.5 Fundraising and relationship cultivation 115
Richard D. Waters

2.6 Granting organizations 125
Giselle A. Auger

2.7 Communicating organizational change to nonprofit stakeholders 133
Laurie Lewis

2.8 Nonprofit and government relations 142
Bruno Ferreira Costa and Hugo Ferrinho Lopes

2.9 Companies and human right activists' engagement 150
Naíde Müller

PART III
Strategic communication, strategies and discourses 161

3.1 A conceptual approach for strategic communication: the ITNC 165
Evandro Oliveira

3.2 Internal branding in the nonprofit sector 174
Gordon Liu

3.3 Narratives and emotion in social entrepreneurship communication 182
Philip T. Roundy

3.4 Storytelling and memes: new media trends for small civil society organizations   195
     Ioli Campos

3.5 Lobbying and the nonprofit sector   203
     Ana Almansa-Martínez and Antonio Castillo-Esparcia

3.6 Open justice and court communication   215
     Jane Johnston

3.7 Semiotic analysis of environmental communication campaigns   224
     Andrea Catellani

3.8 Eco-art as discourse driver   235
     Franzisca Weder and Denise Voci

3.9 Positive communication and public relations in the nonprofit sector   246
     José Antonio Muñiz-Velázquez and Alejandro José Tapia Frade

PART IV
Nonprofit communication, campaigns and case studies   **255**

4.1 Balancing collective action and connective action in new food cooperatives: fertile ground for transformative change?   259
     Korien van Vuuren-Verkerk, Noelle Aarts and Jan Van der Stoep

4.2 Local NGO e-communication on environmental issues   269
     Valentina Burkšienė and Jaroslav Dvorak

4.3 The grassroots women water collective in India   279
     Ram Awtar Yadav and Kanshan Malik

4.4 The role of communication within a domestic violence context during a lockdown   286
     Sónia de Sá

4.5 Fundraising strategies during pandemic challenges   300
     Laura Visan

4.6 Communication and activist literacy for social change in feminist movements   307
     Alessandra Farné, Carla Cerqueira and Eloísa Nos-Aldás

4.7 Value-informed communication in nonprofit campaigns   317
     Birgit Breninger and Thomas Kaltenbacher

4.8 Identifying and classifying stakeholders in Spanish nonprofit organizations 327
María Pallarés-Renau, Lorena López-Font and Susana Miquel-Segarra

4.9 Activism and social media: case studies from Greece's economic crisis 337
Michael Nevradakis

Index *347*

FIGURES

2.3.1	Manifestations of communication in nonprofit organizations.	95
2.3.2	Overview of the different forms of integration.	98
2.3.3	Key elements of the strategic concept of integrated communication.	99
2.3.4	Concept paper of integrated communication.	100
2.3.5	Vertical and horizontal order within the system of integrated communication.	100
2.4.1	An integrated model of evaluation for strategic communication.	106
2.4.2	The World Bank's communication M&E framework.	109
2.5.1	The fundraising life cycle.	116
2.5.2	Traditional donor pyramid highlighting communication tactics and relationship cultivation strategies by donor levels.	119
2.5.3	Updated fundraising risk ladder modified from Rosso (1991)	121
2.9.1	Connections between respondents and response categories.	156
3.1.1	NGO dual management dynamic.	169
3.1.2	Conceptual model of the instigatory theory of NGO communication (ITNC).	169
3.1.3	Operational model – a cybernetic approach.	171
3.2.1	A conceptual map of internal branding research in the nonprofit-sector context.	175
3.3.1	The structure of social venture narratives research.	188
3.3.2	A micro-foundations agenda for social venture narratives research.	189
3.5.1	Phases of the communication process.	206
3.5.2	Levels of impact in communication evaluation.	208
3.5.3	NGO evolution in Transparency Register.	210
3.5.4	Category of registration.	210
3.5.5	Fields of interest.	211
3.5.6	Evolution of the top five fields of interest.	211
3.5.7	Activities.	212
3.7.1	Example of a semiotic square.	227
3.7.2	Screenshot from the website of Greenpeace.	228
3.8.1	"Die ungebrochene Anziehungskraft der Natur"/"The unending attraction of nature", Max Peintner, 1970/1971.	240
3.8.2	For Forest, Klagenfurt/Austria.	240
3.9.1	Scheme and workflow of the proposed organizational signature strengths model for nonprofit organizations.	251

Figures

4.7.1	Stimulus 22 receptionist.	322
4.7.2	Stimulus 22 receptionist.	322
4.7.3	Stimulus 22 receptionist.	323
4.7.4	Stimulus 11 UNICEF.	324
4.7.5	Stimulus 11 UNICEF.	324

TABLES

1.2.1	Major communication for development and social change approaches	29
2.2.1	Formal and informal methods and tools for organizational listening	89
2.4.1	Matrix of suggested focuses and indicators for nonprofit communication M&E	108
2.4.2	Nonprofit communication M&E matrix	110
3.1.1	Ontological principles of the ITNC	167
3.7.1	A visualization of the different layers of the generative scheme of meaning	229
3.8.1	A third way of nonprofit communication: communicatively performed problematization	238
3.9.1	The six virtues and 24 character strengths, with short descriptions	249
4.2.1	Types of bottom-up communication	270
4.2.2	Elements of research content	273
4.2.3	Differences between Salmon Diary and other NGOs	274
4.2.4	Differences in communication management	275
4.6.1	Criteria of cultural efficacy of transgressive communication	309
4.8.1	Groups detected in the reports (2018) and order of appearance of the items covered	329
4.8.2	Other groups mentioned in the reports (2018)	331
4.8.3	Proposed stakeholder reputational evaluators for the social action third sector (SATS)	333

CONTRIBUTORS

Noelle Aarts is a professor of socio-ecological interactions and director of the Institute for Science in Society (ISiS) at the Radboud University in Nijmegen. Her research focuses on interactional processes for creating space for change towards socio-ecological transformations, developing insights into the interplay between everyday conversations, and the wider structures and developments in society.

Ana Almansa-Martínez is a professor at the Department of Audiovisual Communication and Advertising, University of Málaga. She is a teacher and researcher in political communication and public relations. She holds a degree in communication from the Autonomous University of Barcelona and a PhD from the University of Malaga. She is a visiting professor at European and American universities, where she has participated in postgraduate courses and given conferences. She is the editor of the *International Journal of Public Relations*, coordinator of the Official Master's Degree in Strategic Management and Innovation in Communication and secretary of the Academic Commission in Malaga of the Interuniversity Doctorate in Communication.

Giselle A. Auger (PhD, APR) is an associate professor and chair of the Department of Communication at Rhode Island College, with a teaching specialty in public relations. She received her PhD in mass communication from the University of Florida and holds an MA in international relations and strategic studies from the University of Lancaster in England and a BA in political communication from the University of Massachusetts at Amherst. Her research interests include strategic communication of nonprofit organizations, the use of rhetoric and message structure in social media communication, and academic dishonesty.

Birgit Breninger is an associate professor at the Department of Communication Sciences at the Paris-Lodron University Salzburg. She is acting president of the InterCultural Center (ICC), a research organization at Salzburg College. In 2005 she co-founded the Intercultural College at the University of Salzburg and has led the executive graduate programs for over ten years. Dr. Breninger is chairwoman of the International Board of ICC Experts and author of the book *A Perceptual Architecture of Intercultural Competence* (2021). Her main areas of research and teaching include communication and perception, intercultural leadership, ethical decisions in multicultural contexts, and building cultural expertise.

Manfred Bruhn (Prof. Dr. Dr. h.c. mult.) spent his academic education at the University of Münster. He first had a professorship in marketing and commerce from 1983 to 1995 at the EBS University of

Economics and Law. Various calls to universities in Cologne, Jena, and Munich were rejected. Since 1995, he has held the chair of Marketing and Corporate Management at the University of Basel and is an honorary professor at the Technical University of Munich. He has received honorary doctorates from the Universities of Hohenheim and Rostock. He is the founder and partner of the strategy and marketing consultancy Prof. Bruhn & Partner AG (Basel). His main research and consulting topics are strategic marketing management, services and relationship marketing, integrated communication, sponsoring, and nonprofit marketing.

Valentina Burkšienė (Valentina Burksiene), born in 1963, received a PhD in management and administration in 2012 and a master's in recreation and tourism in 2006. She is a member of the editorial board of various scientific journals. Her scientific interests include sustainable development, sustainable organizations, strategic management, tourism and recreation, public administration, and regional development. Practical competences include private hospitality business (since 1993); head civil servant at Neringa municipality administration (2002–2011); coordinator and administration of projects funded by EU programs (since 2004); Neringa municipality council member (2015–2019); and head of a charity fund (since 2008).

Ioli Campos is a guest assistant professor at the Catholic University of Portugal and at the Nova University of Lisbon. She has a PhD in digital media from the University of Texas at Austin-Portugal Colab Program and a MA in journalism from Nova University of Lisbon. As a researcher, Campos has been focusing on journalism, media literacy, children, and media. She has also been working as a consultant in those areas for international institutions, such as OSCE and the Council of Europe (NSC). Before that, Campos worked as a journalist for 15 years for the national and foreign press.

Antonio Castillo-Esparcia is a professor at the Faculty of Communication Sciences, University of Málaga. He teaches the theory and history of public relations, political communication, communication in nongovernmental organizations (NGOs), and social movements. He holds a bachelor's and doctoral degrees from the Autonomous University of Barcelona. He is a coordinator of the master's degree in "Strategic Management and Innovation in Communication." He is a visiting professor at European and American universities, where he participates in conferences, postgraduate courses, and professional study programs. He is director of the Department of Audiovisual Communication and Advertising of the University of Malaga and president of the Association of Public Relations Researchers.

Andrea Catellani is a tenured professor of communication at the Catholic University of Louvain (UCLouvain, Belgium). He is president of the jury of the master program in communication. He leads the study and research group "Communication, Environment, Science and Society" of the French Society of Information and Communication Sciences (SFSIC). He has published various scientific articles and books, notably on environmental communication and rhetoric, discourses on the societal responsibility of organizations, the semiotic approach to organizations, ethics in communication, and the relationship between religion and communication, particularly in the digital world.

Carla Cerqueira is an assistant professor at Lusófona University and a researcher at CICANT – The Centre for Research in Applied Communication, Culture, and New Technologies. She has a PhD in communication sciences with a specialization in communication Psychology from the University of Minho, Portugal (2012). Her research interests include gender, feminisms, intersectionality, NGOs, and media studies. She is principal investigator of the project "FEMglocal – Glocal Feminist Movements: Interactions and Contradictions" and the project "Network Voices: Women's Participation in Development Processes."

Contributors

Bruno Ferreira Costa is an assistant professor at the University of Beira Interior, a researcher at Praxis – Centre of Philosophy, Politics and Culture, has a PhD in political science (University of Lisbon), and is the author of several books and articles on political science. His research interests comprise comparative politics, political participation, political systems, the European Union, and democracy. He is a member of the MPSA, APCP, and SOPCOM organizations.

Thomas Davies is a senior lecturer in international politics at City, University of London. He specializes in the history and politics of NGOs, and his publications include *NGOs: A New History of Transnational Civil Society* (2014) and the edited *Routledge Handbook of NGOs and International Relations* (2021), which was awarded the 2021 ARNOVA Award for Outstanding Book in Nonprofit and Voluntary Action Research. He is an associate editor of *Voluntaristics Review* and a fellow of the Royal Historical Society. He was educated at Magdalen College, Oxford, and his DPhil thesis was awarded the British International History Group Thesis Prize.

Sónia de Sá has a PhD in communication sciences in the inclusive television subarea. She is an assistant professor at the Department of Communication, Philosophy and Politics of the University of Beira Interior, where she teaches strategic communication at the graduate and postgraduate level. Her main research interests are gender studies; queer studies; and representations of minorities, especially Roma communities, black women and the LGBTQ+ community. She is co-author of three books and the author of several articles. In her civic action, she is a volunteer for nonprofit organizations and publishes monthly articles in the printed press on gender equality, unequal treatment of the interior of the country, and social inequalities of minorities in Portugal.

Jaroslav Dvorak, born in 1974, received a PhD in political science in 2011. He was a visiting researcher at Uppsala University (2017), Institute of Russian and Eurasian Studies, Sweden, and a visiting professor at Bialystok Technical University (2017), Poland. Jaroslav Dvorak is involved in the editorial board of international scientific journals. From December 2021 he has been chair of Council of Klaipeda nongovernmental organization.

Alessandra Farné is a lecturer of the Department of Translation and Communication of the University Jaume I (UJI) in Spain; a researcher of the Interuniversity Institute of Social Development and Peace (IUDESP) and the University Institute of Feminist and Gender Studies (IF) of the UJI; and has a PhD and MA in international studies in peace, conflict, and development and BA in public relations. Her research activity is related to social communication; equality; and information, media, and digital literacy.

Hugo Ferrinho Lopes is a PhD candidate in comparative politics at the Institute of Social Sciences, University of Lisbon (ICS-ULisboa), with a grant from the Portuguese Foundation for Science and Technology. He is also an invited teaching assistant at the University of Beira Interior (UBI), researcher at the Observatory of the Quality of Democracy (ICS-ULisboa), associate researcher at the Political Observatory (ISCSP-ULisboa), and research collaborator at the Permanent Youth Observatory (ICS-ULisboa) and PRAXIS-UBI. His research interests comprise political parties, political representation, political attitudes and behavior, and youth in politics.

Lorena López Font is a professor and contracted doctor. She currently holds the position of academic secretary of the Department of Communication Sciences at Universitat Jaume I. Her research focuses mainly on the competencies of the professional profiles of advertising and corporate communication, as well as the application of the theory of advertising and intangible assets in the film industry. She is currently a professor of theory of advertising and brand management in the degrees programs for Advertising and Public Relations and Audiovisual Communication and teaches corporate reputation in the official postgraduate course of New Trends in Communication.

Contributors

Alejandro José Tapia Frade has a PhD in marketing and works as associate lecturer and researcher at Universidad Loyola Andalucía. He is also editor-in-chief of *MLS Communication Journal* and a member of scientific committees of other journals of Mexico and Portugal. His research work joins technology and advertising in several ways, such as video games, web, and social networks.

Gisela Gonçalves is a professor at the Department of Communication, Philosophy and Politics at the University of Beira Interior (UBI – Covilhã, Portugal), where she coordinates the research group Media and Communication of LabCom – a communication research center. Currently, at UBI she is vice-president of the Faculty of Arts and director of the Master's in Strategic Communication program. She has focused her research interests on communication ethics, public relations theory, strategic communication, and political communication. Recently, she has published on topics such as government communication ethics and crises communication in the pandemic context. She is a former chair of the ECREA Strategic and Organizational Communication Section and vice-president of Sopcom, the Portuguese Association of Communication Sciences.

Valérie Gorin is a senior lecturer and researcher at the Geneva Center of Humanitarian Studies (University of Geneva and Graduate Institute) and also acts as the head of learning for the master program. A historian and media scholar, she has published extensively on humanitarian history, visual culture, and digital communication for a decade. Her most recent publications include *Making Humanitarian Crises: Emotions and Images in History* (co-edited with B. Lynn Edgar and D. Martin Moruno), Palgrave Macmillan (2022), and the special issue on "Humanitarian Action in the Age of Global Media: Visual Histories (1920s–2000s)," *Journal of Humanitarian Affairs* 3(2), 2021 (co-edited with S. Künkel).

Matthew Isbell is a professor of organizational communication at Boise State. He received a PhD from the University of Texas at Austin. His research interests are in collaboration, nonprofit organizations, and program implementation/change. As an applied scholar, Dr. Isbell works with at-risk populations around many of the intractable problems in our communities. Dr. Isbell's work is published in many top journals, including *Communication Theory*, *Communication Monographs*, *Management Communication Quarterly*, and the *American Journal of Public Health*. He is also the co-author of the award-winning book *Interorganizational Collaboration: Complexity, Ethics, and Communication*.

Jane Johnston is an associate professor of communication and PR at the University of Queensland. Her two chapters in this book represent her two key fields of scholarship: court communication and open justice and public interest communication. She has written and edited 12 books, over 70 journal articles and chapters, and many reports for Australian and international government bodies and NGOs (including the UN and law reform commissions). Her public interest research began in 2013 as a solo venture, later becoming an international collaboration with communication scholars worldwide. Her thirteenth book, on open justice and strategic communication with Cambridge, is underway.

Thomas Kaltenbacher is a senior scientist for applied linguistics at the Department of Linguistics of the Paris-Lodron University of Salzburg, Austria. He is director of the Salzburg Speech Clinic (SSC) and the Salzburg Institute for Reading Research (SIRR). Dr. Kaltenbacher specializes in psycholinguistics, neurolinguistics and clinical linguistics and works with the following methods and tools: ultrasound, lingwaves, Computerised Speech Lab (CSL – Kay-Pentax), audiometry, fMRI and eye tracking. Since 2014 he has been the acting chairman of the Austrian Clinical Linguists' Association (KLÖ).

Matthew Koschmann is an associate professor of organizational communication at the University of Colorado Boulder. He received a PhD from the University of Texas at Austin. His research focuses on nonprofit organizations and civil society collaboration. Professor Koschmann's research has been published in many top journals, including *Communication Monographs*, *Journal of Communication*, *Academy of Management Review*, and *Management Communication Quarterly*. He is co-author of *Understanding Nonprofit Work: A Communication Perspective*. Professor Koschmann is also a Fulbright scholar and worked as a visiting research professor at Ateneo de Manila University in the Philippines.

Sabine Lang is a professor of international and European politics at the Henry M. Jackson School of International Studies of the University of Washington. She directs the Center for West European Studies and the EU/Jean Monnet Center of Excellence and holds the Jean Monnet Chair for Civil Society, Inclusion, and Diversity. Her research focuses on the dynamics of inclusivity and politicization in civil society. Her publications include *NGOs, Civil Society, and the Public Sphere* (Cambridge University Press 2013) and *Gendered Mobilizations and Intersectional Challenges* (co-edited with Jill Irvine and Celeste Montoya, ECPR Press/Rowman & Littlefield 2019).

Laurie Lewis completed her PhD at the University of California at Santa Barbara. She is a professor of communication at the University of Texas at San Antonio. Her scholarly work investigates organizational collaboration, stakeholder engagement, input solicitation, and participative processes. She is author of the award-winning books *Organizational Change: Creating Change Through Strategic Communication* and *The Power of Strategic Listening in Contemporary Organizations*. She is co-editor of the *International Encyclopedia of Organizational Communication* as well as numerous academic publications on topics related to organizational change, collaboration, interorganizational communication, volunteers and nonprofits, and stakeholder communication.

Gordon Liu is a professor of marketing strategy at the Open University Business School. His work is situated at the intersection of marketing, strategy, and entrepreneurship. He has a particular interest in cause-related marketing, product innovation/new product development, strategic orientation/capabilities, and networks/strategic alliance. His work has appeared in leading academic journals, including *Entrepreneurship Theory and Practice*, *Strategic Entrepreneurial Journal*, *Journal of Product Innovation Management*, *International Journal of Operations and Production Management*, *Journal of World Business*, *Journal of Business Research*, *Journal of Business Ethics*, *Group & Organization Management*, *Nonprofit and Voluntary Sector Quarterly*, *European Journal of Marketing*, and others.

Jim Macnamara, PhD, is a distinguished professor in the School of Communication at the University of Technology Sydney (UTS). He is also a visiting professor at the London School of Economics and Political Science and the London College of Communication. He is the author of a number of books, including *Organizational Listening: The Missing Essential in Public Communication* (Peter Lang, New York, 2016) and *Evaluating Public Communication* (Routledge, UK, 2018).

Kanshan Malik is a professor at the Department of Communication, University of Hyderabad, India. She is a faculty fellow with the UNESCO Chair on Community Media and editor of the newsletter *CR News*. She obtained her PhD from the University of Hyderabad. She worked as a journalist with *The Economic Times* before pursuing a career in academics. She is co-author (with Prof. Vinod Pavarala) of the much-cited book *Other Voices: The Struggle for Community Radio in India* (Sage: 2007). Her recent co-edited book is titled *Community Radio in South Asia: Reclaiming the Airwaves* (Routledge: 2020).

Naíde Müller is a PhD candidate in communication sciences and researcher at the Center for Communication and Culture Studies at the Faculty of Human Sciences, UCP, where she also teaches in the master and degree programs in communication sciences. She was a visiting scholar at the College of Communication & Information, Kent State University (Ohio, USA). She graduated in business communication and public relations from ESCS and received a master's in integrated communication from INP. She has more than ten years of professional experience as a communication consultant and public relations advisor in corporate, nonprofit, and political projects. She investigates in the area of strategic communication, human rights activism, and media relations.

José Antonio Muñiz-Velázquez is an assistant professor and head of the Department of Communication and Education at Universidad Loyola Andalucía. He has a PhD in communication studies, a degree in advertising and public relations, and a degree in psychology, as well as an European master in relationship marketing. He is the author of multiple international publications about positive communication, persuasion, new technologies, and their relationships with happiness, human flourishing, and well-being and is the editor of *The Routledge Handbook of Positive Communication* (2019).

Michael Nevradakis (PhD, media studies, The University of Texas, 2018) is a communication instructor at Hellenic American University and at College Year in Athens, in Athens, Greece. His research interests include the public sphere and civil society, alternative media, media policy, and the media industry – primarily focusing on Greek media. His dissertation, "From the Polis to Facebook: Social Media and the Development of a New Greek Public Sphere," based on research conducted in Greece between 2012 and 2017, is being developed into a book. Dr. Nevradakis formerly produced/hosted *Dialogos Radio* and has provided journalistic content for several print and online outlets.

Eloísa Nos-Aldás is a senior professor in the area of audiovisual communication and advertising in the Department of Communication Sciences at the Universitat Jaume I of Castellón (UJI) and researcher at the Interuniversity Institute for Social Development and Peace (IUDESP at UJI) between UJI and the University of Alicante and coordinator of the research group DESPAZ (UJI). Her research deals with communication, civil society, and social change, specifically from the perspective of transformation and cultural efficacy. She has led UJI research projects in addition to national and regional ones and has participated in some others, including European ones with NGOs.

Evandro Oliveira (Dr.rer.pol, phil) is a Serra Húnter professor at the Autonomous University of Barcelona (UAB), Spain and researcher at LabCom, Portugal. His research focuses on civil society strategic communication, diversity, and intercultural communication. He has been a guest professor of nonprofit communication at various universities like the University of Mannheim, the Free University of Berlin, the University of Jena, the University of Beira Interior, and the University of Münster. He researched at the University of Leipzig with Günter Bentele and Ansgar Zerfass in Germany; and at CECS – Uminho, Portugal. He is the elected chair of the Organisational and Strategic Communication section at the European Communication Research and Education Association (ECREA). He wrote *The Instigatory Theory of NGO Communication* (Springer, 2019); has received awards from the European Public Relations Education and Research Association (EUPRERA), Public Relations and Communications Association (PRCA), and International Communications Consultancy Organisation (ICCO); and worked for over 20 years in strategic communication management, including work for NGOs like Greenpeace, Amnesty International, Salvation Army, and Doctors Without Borders.

Glenn O'Neil, PhD, is a lecturer in the Media and Communications Department at Webster University Geneva and is founder of Owl RE, an evaluation and research consultancy in Switzerland. He has been involved in some 100 reviews and evaluations in over 50 countries with a specialization in communications and advocacy for nonprofit organizations, including UN agencies, NGOs, and foundations. His research is focused on communication monitoring and evaluation, with his work published in journals such as *Evaluation and Program Planning*, *PR Review*, and *PRism*.

María Pallarés-Renau is graduated in advertising and public relations (2014) and received a PhD in communication (2021) from the Jaume I University, after obtaining the master's degree in new trends and innovation processes in communication, specializing in strategic communication management (2015). Since 2016, she has been an associate professor at the Department of Communication

Sciences at this university, and her research deals fundamentally with the evolution of the main intangibles, specifically corporate reputation (metrics, rankings, and command squares).

Philip T. Roundy is the UC Foundation associate professor of entrepreneurship at the University of Tennessee at Chattanooga. He earned his PhD in strategic management and organization theory at the University of Texas at Austin. His research focuses on the role of entrepreneurship in economic and community revitalization. He is particularly interested in entrepreneurship in struggling regions, "dying" industries, and displaced technologies. His work has appeared in *Strategic Organization*, *Journal of Management Studies*, *Journal of Business Venturing Insights*, *Academy of Management Perspectives*, and others. He serves on the editorial boards of *Strategic Entrepreneurship Journal*, *Strategic Organization*, *Small Business Economics*, and *Entrepreneurship Research Journal*.

Víctor Manuel Marí Sáez holds a PhD in journalism from the University of Seville (Spain). He is an associate professor at the University of Cadiz (Spain). Besides leading the research group Comunicación y Ciudadanía Digital (Communication and Digital Citizenship), he has published several books and papers on communication, ICTs, social movements, and social change in international journals.

Susana Miquel-Segarra is an associate professor in the Department of Communication of the Universitat Jaume I de Castellón (UJI). Since 2016, she has coordinated the Strategic Management strand of the official master's degree in "New Trends and Innovation Processes in Communication" (UJI). Her research work focuses on strategic communication, public relations, internal communication, and social media. She belongs to the Spanish Association of Communication Researchers and is an active member of the Strategic Communication Section. She maintains close ties with professional associations and is a member of the board of directors of the Valencia and Murcia branch of the Association of Communication Professionals (DIRCOM).

Jan Servaes was UNESCO chair in communication for sustainable social change at the University of Massachusetts, Amherst. He taught international communication in Australia, Belgium, China, Hong Kong, the United States, the Netherlands, and Thailand, in addition to short-term projects at about 120 universities in 55 countries. He is editor of the 2020 *Handbook on Communication for Development and Social Change*.

Jan van der Stoep (1968) is an endowed professor of Christian philosophy at Wageningen University & Research and the Theological University Kampen. He studied biology in Wageningen and philosophy at VU University Amsterdam, where he also did a PhD in political philosophy. Between 2008 and 2020, he was a professor of journalism and communication at the Ede Christian University of Applied Sciences. He is especially interested in food ethics, stewardship ethics, communication theory, political philosophy, and the philosophy of religion.

Korien van Vuuren-Verkerk (1977) is a senior lecturer in change communication at Ede University of Applied Sciences. Furthermore, she is a PhD candidate at the Institute for Science in Society of Radboud University Nijmegen. Korien is fascinated by conversational processes in (polarized) multistakeholder discussions and the transformative power of social innovations. Her research focus is on the interactional behavior that may or may not lead to constructive cooperation between people who think differently. Therefore, the central question of her PhD research is: Which interaction behavior leads to fruitful, trust-nurturing conversations and a collective approach or co-production?

Laura Visan is an adjunct faculty member of the Department of Arts, Culture and Media (ACM) at the University of Toronto Scarborough. She holds a PhD in communication and culture (York University). She researched the process of social capital formation through civic participation and networking in the case of Romanian immigrants from Toronto and co-authored an ethnographic study on Țara Făgărașului diaspora engagement in civic and philanthropic activities. Having grown up in Romania, Visan has also written about the adaptive reuse of Bucharest's socialist architecture landmarks after the 1990s and about the popular culture artifacts of the 1970s and 1980s.

Denise Voci, PhD, is senior scientist at the Department of Media and Communications of the University of Klagenfurt, Austria. She received her PhD in the field of media and communication studies with a focus on media economics and cross-border media management. Currently, besides investigating media industries, media responsibility, and sustainability, her research interests focus on environmental and sustainability communication, especially related to water scarcity issues, individual consumption choices, and institutional formal changes, as well as media sustainability, framing, and rhetoric analysis.

Richard D. Waters (PhD, University of Florida) is an associate professor in the School of Management at the University of San Francisco where he teaches strategic communication courses in the graduate programs of business, nonprofit, and public administration. His research interests include nonprofit communication, particularly in the fundraising context, and he has published more than 100 peer-reviewed journal articles and book chapters. Currently, he is the editor of *Case Studies in Strategic Communication* and serves on seven other journals' editorial review boards, including *Journal of Public Relations Research*, *Public Relations Review*, and *Journal of Philanthropy and Marketing*.

Franzisca Weder, Dr. habil, is an associate professor at the Department of Media and Communications at the University of Klagenfurt, Austria (on leave) and senior lecturer at the University of Queensland, Brisbane, Australia. She researches and teaches organizational communication and public relations specializing in sustainability communication, media ethics, and corporate social responsibility, with milestone publications like *The Sustainability Communication Reader* (Springer, 2021). She has been a guest professor and fellow at the University of Alabama, United States; University of Eichstätt-Ingolstadt, Germany; University of Waikato, New Zealand; the Royal Melbourne Institute of Technology, Australia; and University of Ilmenau, Germany. Weder is chair of the International Environmental Communication Association (IECA).

Ram Awtar Yadav is an assistant professor at the Jagran School of Journalism and Communication, Faculty of Journalism and Creative Studies, Jagran Lakecity University, Bhopal, India. He has obtained a PhD from the Department of Communication, University of Hyderabad, India. He did his master's in electronic media from Makhanlal Chaturvedi National University of Journalism and Communication, Bhopal, in 2011, after which he worked as a journalist with the *The Hitavada,* an English daily of Bhopal, for four years. He also worked as an assistant professor at the Department of Journalism and Mass Communication, Guru Ghasidas University, Bilaspur, Chhattisgarh, India, for one year.

Anja Zimmermann is a lecturer at the Lucerne School of Business and head of the Competence Center for Service and Operations Management. She studied economics and business administration at the European Business School (EBS), Germany; Regents College of Business (UK); and Universidad Argentina de la Empresa, Argentina. She worked as an academic researcher with Manfred Bruhn for several years at the University of Basel, Switzerland. Her primary areas of teaching and research focus on services marketing and integrated market communications. She is head of the Master of Advanced Studies Program Services Marketing and Management and works as a consultant and trainer for different for-profit and nonprofit organizations.

INTRODUCING NONPROFIT COMMUNICATION AND MAPPING THE RESEARCH FIELD

Gisela Gonçalves and Evandro Oliveira

In the famous book *Bowling Alone* (2000), Robert D. Putnam explained the disintegration of civic tradition in modern society because of a diminishing sense of community. He observed that despite technological developments – or because of them – people have fewer interpersonal relationships, which renders collaboration difficult to establish and maintain. As people have become isolated, they do not participate in clubs and associations, but instead, they bowl alone. The declining informal collaboration corresponds to less civic engagement, political equity, solidarity, trust, and tolerance as well as associational life (Putnam, 2000).

The NGO-ization of society (Lang, 2013), visible in the increasing number of nongovernmental organizations (NGOs) at the national and transnational level, tend to somewhat contradict Putnam's thesis. On the other hand, the number of NGOs is not per se revealing of the quality of citizen participation in those organizations. In the course of history, NGOs have been involved in different issues, namely humanitarianism, environment, gender equality, human rights, and peace (Davies, 2019). NGOs are growing faster than any other type of organization in the world, and their economy represents from 7 to 12 percent of the total workforce in some regions. The estimated number of NGOs in the world is 10 million, with India and the United States the countries with the largest numbers (Ferguson, 2018). The Yearbook of International Organizations estimates that there are more than 30,000 NGOs worldwide.[1] According to the Urban Institute report in 2019, the number of nonprofit organizations (NPOs) formally registered rose up to 1.54 million in 2016 just in the USA alone. These comprise a diverse range of sectors, including art, health, education, and advocacy; labor unions; and business and professional associations.[2] Furthermore, we can also consider foundations, aid organizations, charities, and social economy actors, like mutual and cooperatives as nonprofits – the aggregator of the typology is in fact the nonprofit-driven distinction. However, it might be useful to pursue a differentiation between civil society organizations that search for the common good and other organizations with private interests, even if they strive for the benefit of the collective.

The terms NGOS and nonprofit can be applied to the same organizational forms – some authors tend to consider the former as a type of nonprofit. Interestingly enough, in the diversity of approaches, and even definitions of this object, there is a common use of the excluding element to classify it: nongovernmental and nonprofit. This implies they are not part of the market, nor of government entities. Or, at least, they shouldn't be – NGOs that are state-controlled or that serve hidden interests, or that even defend causes that oppose human rights or democracy, should not be framed as such. How can we consider a radical group with ideologies like the Ku Klux Klan to be a nonprofit within the common understanding of it? Still, when we applied the criteria proposed by Salamon et al. (1999, p. 3), they would be considered as such. This might be the hardest angle on the way of having a consensual definition without charging the term with normative dimensions and certain values a priori. Or, we can assume the politically charged definition, especially for NGOs, as proposed before by some authors (Alvarez, 1999; Alvim & Teodósio, 2004; Aristizábel et al., 1997; Landim, 2002; Menescal, 1996; Oliveira, 2019). These authors refer to democratic values and human rights principles as a precondition for those specific organizational forms, including even internal democratic governance dynamics. The reflection is open, and we hope the discussion will go on along this book and with further research.

Some approaches, either in theory or in practice, do treat nonprofits similarly to profit organizations in a marketplace. Initially, criticisms were raised in the first research with impact on the marketization (Eikenberry & Kluver, 2004), concluding that this management approach outcome "is the potential deterioration of the distinctive contributions that nonprofit organizations make to creating and maintaining a strong civil society" (p. 138). In 2020, a case study of two NPOs revealed that one was adopting a strong entrepreneurial orientation, while the other integrated the traditional community orientation with more professionalization, confirming to partial marketization tendencies (Sandberg et al., 2020). Also, historically, the need for raising funds has been left in the hands of marketing agencies, due to the fact that activists and other volunteers were not succeeding or wanting to engage in such activities (Oliveira, 2017). That created a significant gap between the communication on advocacy and the scope of operations – with the communication within the fundraising campaigns being run by the same organization. That imprint can still be felt nowadays (Oliveira, 2017).

It is not our aim in this handbook to be prescriptive or normative, but rather to mirror the diversity that exists in nonprofit communication research and to include visions from distinct academic traditions. Nonprofit communication is a field situated at the crossroads of communication, management, marketing, organizational, and public relations studies. Furthermore, without sociological, economic, political, and other social sciences contributions, the study of communication within a nonprofit setting could be reduced to a very closed vision of these entities and of their communicative processes and dynamics.

Introducing the field

What is involved in the field of the nonprofit sector, also known as the civil society sector? Civil society has been defined as the "space of uncoerced human association and also the set of relational networks – formed for the sake of family, faith, interest and ideology – that fill this space" (Walzer, 1995, p. 7). The concept of civil society requires the precondition of the existence of public and organizational life beyond the state's administration, allowing the voluntary sector to act and intervene in the public sphere.

Deeply intertwined within civil society, NGOs provide "a practical response to problems where both the corporate, thus profit centered, and the institutional structures are absent or have failed" (Oliveira et al., 2016, p. 6). They can be considered to form a subset of the larger category of NPOs, as the latter can include a wider range of organizations such as museums, schools, or universities. One main difference between NGOs and other NPOs is the significant dedication of the former to the advocacy of public interest issues (Tkalac & Pavicic, 2009).

On the other hand, NPOs are the fabric of civil society – they can have different sizes and scopes, but all "serve some public purpose and contribute to the public good" (Salamon, 1999, pp. 10–11). To systemize the heterogeneous nature of nonprofits that operate in different countries, Salamon et al. (1999, p. 3) developed a "structural-operational definition" that includes five criteria that these organizations must share: (i) organized – institutional presence and internal structure; (ii) private – institutionally separate from government; (iii) self-governing – independent from external government or corporate influences; (iv) nonprofit-distributing – do not return profits to managers or owners; and (v) voluntary – this criteria implies that participation/membership is not compulsory, but a matter of choice.

The nonprofit sector has been strongly scrutinized in the management literature. According to Maier et al. (2016), NPOs have experienced notable changes from the 1980s onwards, rendering them more similar to profit-marketing firms. Whether or not NPOs should be more "business-like" is indeed a strong area of discussion (Dart, 2004). Often in this context, communication is approached as one more variable in the marketing mix, mainly seen as instrumental to message transmission and information sharing, contributing to the economic sustainability of the organization by securing volunteers, donors, resources, or funds. However, as NPO communication operates in a multilayered and organizationally diverse environment, it requires "looking at communication as more than a tool to achieve effectiveness" (Koschmann, 2015, p. 215).

NPO communication involves considerable complexity in terms of goals, audiences, and resources when compared to the business sector. In relation to goal setting, NPOs often have to juggle what appear to be conflicting objectives set by management needs. Communication goals related to transparency, for instance, have been considered problematic by scholars that look to NPO needs of balancing audiences' skepticism (Dethier et al., 2021). In regard to the public, nonprofit communication operates on a multilayered level, considering a diverse group of stakeholders, including donors, volunteers, minority groups, activist groups, regulatory bodies, other NPOs, and the like. At the operational level, the lack of human and material resources can have consequences on the daily life of these organizations. But it is at the social level that NPOs' legitimacy is strongly dependent on their communicative efforts to maintain high ethical standards as "servants of society" (Jeavons, 2016).

Exploring the field

When searching for journal names related to the nonprofit sector, five journals stand out – *VOLUNTAS, The Journal of Nonprofit and Public Sector Marketing, Nonprofit Management and Leadership Journal, Nonprofit and Voluntary Sector Quarterly*, and *The International Journal of Nonprofit and Voluntary Sector Marketing*. None of these journals, however, is categorized in the Web of Science (WOS) communication database category, but rather in the business category. Does this mean that research on nonprofit communication is not relevant to scholars within the field of communication? Clearly not. It means instead that nonprofit research, as an interdisciplinary field, has been addressed from diverse theoretical traditions, mainly business and organizational studies but also public relations and communication management.

Research in nonprofits can be considered an interdisciplinary field that had sociology, history, and political science as its main contributions (Hall, 1999). An analysis of knowledge production noticed an intensive advance since the 1980s, but the study of volunteering is the only core theme that could be identified (Ma & Konrath, 2018). The same analysis pointed to the main subjects and thematic clusters on network analysis, and none of them were focused on communication. Another study, which analyzed over 3,000 dissertations and 390 articles in nonprofit journals, has no mention of communication in any of the topics, despite the use of the stakeholder's theory to study NPOs, but rather within a management perspective that is not specifically communicative (Schubert et al., 2022).

Notwithstanding, over the past decade, there has been a growing interest in studying communications in the context of the nonprofit sector. A WOS search with the keywords "communication" and "nonprofit" (and similar terms[3]) in the specialized nonprofit communication literature shows a 50 percent increase in published articles, with 28 in 2012 and 56 in 2020.[4] In this period, the top five journals publishing research on nonprofit communication were the following: (i) *Public Relations*

Review, (ii) *Voluntas*, (iii) *Nonprofit and Voluntary Sector Quarterly*, (iv) *International Journal of Communication Sustainability*, and (v) *Management Communication Quarterly*.[5]

Nevertheless, and according to Koschmann et al. (2015), despite the importance of communication to the nonprofit sector, communication theory has had relatively little impact on the interdisciplinary field of nonprofit studies. A decade before, Lewis's (2005) article on the civil society sector corroborated this idea by "forwarding the claim that organizational communication scholars have not paid significant theoretical attention to nonprofit organizations" (p. 241). This means that research in this field has most often left unexamined and untested theories relating to the specific unique features of NPOs, namely social capital; mission, effectiveness, and accountability; governance and decision making; and volunteer relationships (Lewis, 2005).

In spite of that, applied research contemplates the study of an organization–public relationship, mainly in the literature on nonprofit public relations (PR) (Waters, 2015). The effective management and cultivation of complex relationships with specific stakeholders is at the core of nonprofit mission organizations. Therefore, it is not surprising that one of the most spread areas of theory-based research in nonprofit PR has been the donor–organization relationship (Sisson, 2017; Wiggill, 2014) or the organization–volunteer relationship (Bortree & Waters, 2014; Hyde et al., 2016).

Another important theme in organization–public relationships research has been the role of technology in general, and social media in particular, in engaging different audiences (Auger, 2015; Cho et al., 2014; Saxton & Waters, 2014; Xu & Saxton, 2019). The public relations dialogic theory has also been instrumental to research how charitable foundations use social media to build relationships with publics (e.g. Qu, 2020). Additionally, the diversity in fundraising roles (Waters et al., 2012; Tindall et al., 2014) and the response of NPOs to the crises that affect their reputation and relationships with key stakeholders, based on situational crisis communication theory (e.g. Sisco, 2012; Janssen et al., 2021), can be found in the literature.

Single communication issues have also been researched, including areas like trust (e.g. Gaskin, 1999; Lee et al., 2012; Sargeant & Lee, 2002; Viertmann, 2016), reputation (e.g. Liao, 1999; Sarstedt & Schloderer, 2010; Zatepilina-Monacell, 2012), social media (e.g. Buckholz, 1972; Bull & Schmitz, 1976; Callow, 2004; Dailey, 1986; Einolf & Chambré, 2011; Rodriguez, 2016; Naudé et al., 2004), branding (e.g. Abreu, 2006; Dixon, 1997; Grounds & Harkness, 1998; Hankinson, 2000; Hankinson & Rochester, 2005; Liu et al., 2014; Stride & Lee, 2007), internal communication (e.g. Liu et al., 2015; Hume & Leonard, 2014), identity (e.g. Holtzhausen, 2014), engagement and civil engagement (e.g. Jones, 2006; Shiau, 2011; Wollebæk & Strømsnes, 2008), crisis (e.g. Dixon, 1997; Frangonikolopoulos & Poulakidakos, 2015), evaluation of communication (e.g. O'Neil, 2013), media relations (e.g. Thrall et al., 2014; Powers, 2014), and volunteer communication (e.g. Hess, 2015).

Besides the issues mentioned earlier, case studies have also been carried out, including the challenges facing NGOs that work in human rights in post-Soviet states (Tsetsura, 2013); relationship building and the use of the internet for PR and advocacy in Chinese NGOs (Yang & Taylor, 2010); the study of Lynas public sentiment in Malaysia on an activist campaign (Kaur, 2015); a model for NGO media diplomacy in the internet age based on a case study of Washington Profile (Zhang & Swartz, 2009); a comparative study of NPOs' websites in Germany and Switzerland as dialogic tools (Ingenhoff & Koelling, 2010); the difference between reputation and trustworthiness in NPOs' online campaigns (Wiencierz et al., 2015); and the application of "evidence" in NGO strategic communication on war and armed conflict (Fröhlich & Jungblut, 2017). Other research proposals include a semiotic analysis of environmental NGOs' online campaigns from a business communication perspective (Catellani, 2011).

This proposed exploration of the field can serve to gather some impressions of the journal publications but has two main drawbacks. First, as an interdisciplinary area with literature coming from humanities and communication, research is typically published in a book, as already noticed by other studies (e.g. Ma & Konrath, 2018). One reason can be the format of the theoretical proposals; another the publication processes and available journals. Then, there is research published in other languages and regions that is not mirrored in WOS journals. A systematic review of NGO performance research published between 1996 and 2008 concluded that despite the large body of NGO publications and 14,469 citations identified, most of it is in gray literature and only a small number in peer-reviewed journals (Kareithi & Lund, 2012). This can be also due to the bias towards publishing only positive results for fear of losing funding or even the difficulties of performing studies in low-resourced NGO settings (Kareithi & Lund, 2012, p. 5).

Consequently, without aiming for an extensive and systematic review, we would like to mention some work that has been published on nonprofit and NGO communication in single issues, books, or chapters and in other languages or regions in order to connect dots that can add up to lines in the field map.

Recently, we can register two main works that go beyond the functionalist approach to NGO and nonprofit communication from an organizational perspective. One is *the Instigatory Theory of NGO Communication, or ITNC* (Oliveira, 2017, 2019) and the other is the book *Understanding Nonprofit Work: A Communication Perspective* (Koschmann & Sandres, 2020). Furthermore, a proposal by Jane Johnston relates public interest communication with civil society from a macro approach to PR (Johnston, 2016). Moreover, Franzisca Weder (2021) proposes reframing dissent in strategic communication with a critical perspective.

Regarding theoretical insights from other languages and countries on NPO communication, Thierry Libaert, in the French-speaking academia, has looked into distinctive elements of communication at associations, pointing to the singularity of the relationship with the publics in different conditions and concludes that "the supporter will never be a shareholder. The cause will never be a product. The recipient will never be a customer. Volunteers will never be employers" (Libaert & Pierlot, 2009, p. 6), mirroring the complexity of those relationships and the implications for communication, especially the one of transparency to promote trust and legitimation. Among German-speaking scholars, Thomas Pleil made a list of the challenges of NGO communication, highlighting its central role, as well as the fact that communication can be well-established and the central organizational goal (2005); Günter Bentele, Thobias Libert, and Michael Vogt (2001) described the *bottom-up* communication dynamic as "PR from under" and presented case studies from German civil society organizations and movements.

In South American academic literature, Sylvia Meneghetti has proposed that communication can be considered a management approach for NPOs and describes nine dimensions: organizational, institutional, humanizing, cultural, fundraising, membership capturing, accountability, lobbying, and political (9) (Meneghetti, 2001, p. 27).

Katrin Voss (2007) has researched the excellence theory by James Grunig at German and US environmental NGOs, concluding that this PR theory is only partially applicable. Voss recommends doing further research on a combined PR and NGO approach, looking at the different communicative working fields, which she identifies as PR, media relations, lobbying, and fundraising. Additionally, she discusses the issue of the participation and civil society function that is expected from NGOs (p. 291). Along the same lines, other studies have researched Steyn and Puth's normative model, which combines excellence and relationship management theories in South African NPOs (Wiggill, 2011). The model heavily focuses on communication strategy development by the communication strategist, and the research compared the original proposal with the practices of five NPOs. It was concluded that due to constraints like, for example, the nonexistence of a person dedicated to communication, a simplified model could be applied, focusing on skills training rather than on the role of the professional.

Defining NPO communication

Despite being a fruitful area of study, research based on stakeholder relationships presents a narrow managerial and functionalist perspective on communication (Koschmann et al., 2015; Koschmann, 2012), underestimating the importance of a more holistic view of NPO communication.

Framing NPO communication can be relevant to reaching a working definition. First, the context indicates that interactions between civil society organizations in postmodern environments become less physical and more symbolic toward "strategy, communication and consensus" (Pérez, 2001, p. 536). That is even more expressive when considering virtualization in online interaction. This ongoing sense-making process (Weick, 1995) from the individuals in a scaling-up[6] contributes to the ongoing constitution of the organizations in a nondirectly managed communication, but also as a conversation in the public sphere. Therefore, we can set the main communication pillars in nonprofits as the constitutive role of communication at the macro and meso levels in the interplay of modern times (Oliveira, 2017) – it comprehends the macro societal-level approach to communicative action and social change in a constitutive way and the constitutive role of communication in creating the organization. It also includes the strategic role of communication at the macro level, considering the nonprofit discourse and conversations in the public sphere. At the meso level, there is the managed communication from an organizational center perspective; and lastly, the legitimation dynamics from inside-out, setting also the primary locus of the communicative legitimation from a neo-institutionalist perspective with the citizens who are the members of the organization and, therefore, the first group that legitimizes the management and all the organization (Oliveira & Wiesenberg, 2016).

The discipline of strategic communication can also be of help, not only on their foundations and aims but also on the update of the recent reflections that call for the inclusion of the Communicative Constitution of Organizations (CCO) perspective (Oliveira, 2017; Heide et al., 2018). The discipline of strategic communication is based on five foundational assumptions (Holtzhausen & Zerfass, 2015; Frandsen & Johansen, 2018): (i) strategic communication is the "purposeful use of communication by an organization to fulfill its mission"; (ii) all types of organizations communicate to gain influence; (ii) the communicative activities of an organization can best be viewed from an integrative perspective; (iv) all communication disciplines address the same five basic issues: identification and segmentation of stakeholders, selection of media channels, behavioral outcomes, reputation management, and the agency of communication professionals; and (5) strategy is a multidimensional concept that offers alternative understandings to strategic communication, including critical and postmodern, and is not only understood as a rational decision-making process.

Trying to read NPO communication in light of strategic communication assumptions, we may underline that NPOs, like any organization, have the need to make strategic decisions and communicate strategically to attract attention, create a good reputation and trust among their stakeholders, and communicate about the subject they campaign and maintain relationships. For that, NPOs can focus on communication activities across different fields of practice such as PR, marketing communication, social marketing campaigns, or even political communication. This means that NPOs' strategic communication should look beyond disciplinary differences, searching for integration in all their strategies. The NPOs' purpose is to gain legitimacy by fulfilling their communicative role in the public sphere.

To capture the full range of possibilities of NPOs, we suggest the following working definition, based on the literature on strategic communication, PR, organizational communication, and communication management:

> Nonprofit communication is all the communicative processes enacted by an actor on behalf of a communicative entity in the public sphere and inside the collective, framed and governed polyphonically and according to formal and informal strategies.

In this definition, the communicative processes carried out by an actor include the aforementioned four pillars of communication. The actor is communicating on behalf of an entity, which can be a formal organization, a movement, or other collective entity. The communication is framed and governed polyphonically as it includes different perspectives and opinions within the group, framed within the main purpose of the collective. The formal strategy includes the set goals, purposes, and fulfillment of the mission set forth by management. Complementarily, the informal strategies refer to goals, purposes, and messages decided by ad hoc groups participating in the ongoing process in the public sphere and within the act of organizing.

Outline of the book

This handbook provides a thorough account of the theories, concepts, problems, and challenges that converge in nonprofit research in a changing and complex environment. The volume features four parts, which cover different aspects of the nonprofit communication sector.

The first part introduces metatheoretical and multidisciplinary approaches to the nonprofit sector, including the intersection of the definitions of democracy, civil society, and their dynamics. The second part offers distinctive structural approaches to communication and their models of reputation, marketing, and communication management. The third part focuses on strategy, communication, and discourses and on the relation between these organizations and their stakeholders and publics. Subsequently, the last part has a more applied focus and looks at campaigns and case studies.

We believe the handbook to have four main strengths. First, it is very diverse in terms of perspectives and theories. Second, it contains works from different continents and different schools of thought. Additionally, it covers ontogenesis, an understanding from a structural and strategic perspective, as well as new challenges in a networked society and case studies.

The *Routledge Handbook of Nonprofit Communication* aims to provide an overview of the multiple and complex approaches at micro, meso, and macro levels. NPO and communication studies, especially the applied field of communication sciences, can benefit from a handbook that brings together multiple and interdisciplinary perspectives and provides an outline of critical, structural, and strategic approaches, besides debating the new challenges, case studies, and recent trends on this social and communicational phenomenon. It is now up to you, dear reader, to see if it rises to the occasion.

An edited volume like this one only becomes as interesting and important as the contributors make it. As editors, we thus want to express our gratitude, first and foremost, to the 48 contributors who dedicated their valuable time and energy to making this book possible. Your perseverance amid a pandemic was inspiring. It has been a great pleasure to get to know and work together with you, and we are sincerely grateful for all the high-quality and original chapters.

We would also like to thank Felisa Salvago-Keyes and the staff at Routledge. We are grateful for all the consistent support we received during the process of conceiving, editing, and publishing the book.

As the chapters in this volume attest, NPO communication has become one of the most dynamic and diverse fields of study today. Although there is a rich and varied body of literature on the subject, it is hoped that this handbook will help to shed light on the many further avenues for research in this domain.

Notes

1 https://uia.org/yearbook
2 https://nccs.urban.org/publication/nonprofit-sector-brief-2019#the-nonprofit-sector-in-brief-2019
3 We searched for keywords and phrases, including "communication," "non-profit," and related words and spellings, such as "NGO," "NPO," "non-governmental," "not-for-profit," "third sector," or "voluntary sector," in the titles, abstract, and keywords of published works between 2012 and 2022. We then examined

each article of a sum of 389 to determine whether it had a close link with the topic of NPO communication from theoretical or empirical perspectives.
4 Defining what particular literature is or is not within the field of nonprofit communication can be problematic. For the sake of argument, we checked the nonprofit literature in terms of recognizable nonprofit journals indexed in WOS.
5 Other journals that publish on nonprofit communication in the last ten years, in descending order of the number of articles published, are the following: *Management Communication Quarterly, Journal of Nonprofit Education and Leadership, Corporate Communication, Journal of Nonprofit & Public Sector Marketing, Environmental Communication,* and *Journal of Communication Management.*
6 The scaling-up process is central in Communication Constitutes Organization research (e.g. Cooren & Fairhurst, 2009).

References

Abreu, M. (2006). The brand positioning and image of a religious organisation: An empirical analysis. *International Journal of Nonprofit and Voluntary Sector Marketing, 11*(2), 139–146.
Alvarez, S. E. (1999). Advocating feminism: The Latin American feminist NGO "boom". *International Feminist Journal of Politics, 1*(2), 181–209.
Alvim, F., & Teodósio, A. (2004). Gestão da Cooperação Internacional: perspectivas e desafios para as ONGs. In *Anais do XV Encontro Nacional dos Cursos de Graduação em Administração* (pp. 93–102). ANGRAD.
Aristizábal, P., Ferrero, G., & Osorio, L. (1997). *Introducción a la cooperación para el desarrollo: una propuesta curricular para la promoción de la educación al desarrollo en la universidad.* Universidad Politécnica de Valencia.
Auger, G. A. (2015). Building mutually beneficial relationships: Recommended best practices for online grant making procedures. In R. D. Waters (Ed.), *Public relations in the nonprofit sector. Theory and practice* (pp. 154–166). Routledge.
Bentele, G., Liebert, T., & Vogt, M. (Eds.). (2001). *PR für Verbände und Organisationen: Fallbeispiele aus der Praxis.* Luchterhand.
Buckholz, M. H. (1972). Volunteers and agency staff: Their different roles in policy-making bodies. *Nonprofit and Voluntary Sector Quarterly, 1*(2), 19–26.
Bull, C. N., & Schmitz, P. F. (1976). A referral agency for volunteers: Its clientele and effectiveness. *Nonprofit and Voluntary Sector Quarterly, 5*(1), 42–51.
Bortree, D. S., & Waters, R. D. (2014). Race and inclusion in volunteerism: Using communication theory to improve volunteer retention. *Journal of Public Relations Research, 26*(3), 215–234. doi:10.1080/1062726X.2013.864245
Callow, M. (2004). Identifying promotional appeals for targeting potential volunteers: An exploratory study on volunteering motives among retirees. *International Journal of Nonprofit and Voluntary Sector Marketing, 9*(3), 261–274.
Catellani, A. (2011). Environmentalists NGOs and the construction of the culprit: Semiotic analysis. *Journal of Communication Management, 15*(4), 280–297.
Cho, M., Schweickart, T., & Haase, A. (2014). Public engagement with nonprofit organizations on Facebook. *Public Relations Review, 40*(3), 565–567. doi:10.1016/j.pubrev.2014.01.008
Cooren, F., & Fairhurst, G. T. (2009). Dislocation and stabilization: How to scale up from interactions to organization. In L. L. Putnam & A. M. Nicotera (Eds.), *Buildiing theories of organization: The constitutive role of communication* (pp. 117–152). Routledge.
Dailey, R. C. (1986). Understanding organizational commitment for volunteers: Empirical and managerial implications. *Nonprofit and Voluntary Sector Quarterly, 15*(1), 19–31.
Dart, R. (2004). Being 'business-like' in a nonprofit organization: A grounded and inductive typology. *Nonprofit and Voluntary Sector Quarterly, 33*, 290–310.
Davies, T. (2019). *Routledge handbook of NGOs and international relations.* Routledge.
Dethier, F., Delcourt, C., & Willems, J. (2021). Transparency of nonprofit organizations: An integrative framework and research agenda. *Journal of Philanthropy and Marketing,* e1725. https://doi.org/10.1002/nvsm.1725
Dixon, M. (1997). Small and medium-sized charities need a strong brand too: Crisis' experience. *International Journal of Nonprofit and Voluntary Sector Marketing, 2*(1), 52–57.
Eikenberry, A. M., & Kluver, J. D. (2004). The marketization of the nonprofit sector: Civil society at risk? *Public Administration Review, 64*, 132–140. http://dx.doi.org/10.1111/j.1540-6210.2004.00355.x
Einolf, C., & Chambré, S. M. (2011). Who volunteers? Constructing a hybrid theory. *International Journal of Nonprofit and Voluntary Sector Marketing, 16*(4), 298–310.
Ferguson, D. (2018). Nongovernmental organization (NGO) communication. *The International Encyclopedia of Strategic Communication,* 1–13. https://doi.org/10.1002/9781119010722.iesc0120

Frandsen, F., & Johansen, W. (2018). Strategic communication. *The International Encyclopedia of Strategic Communication*. doi:10.1002/9781119010722.iesc0172

Frangonikolopoulos, C. A., & Poulakidakos, S. (2015). Revisiting the public profile and communication of Greek NGOs in times of crisis. *International Journal of Media & Cultural Politics*, 11(1), 119–127.

Fröhlich, R., & Jungblut, M. (2017). Between factoids and facts: The application of 'evidence' in NGO strategic communication on war and armed conflict. *Media, War and Conflict*, 11(1), 86–106. https://doi.org/10.1177/1750635217727308

Gaskin, K. (1999). Blurred vision: Public trust in charities. *International Journal of Nonprofit and Voluntary Sector Marketing*, 4(2), 163–178.

Grounds, J., & Harkness, J. (1998). Developing a brand from within: Involving employees and volunteers when developing a new brand position. *International Journal of Nonprofit and Voluntary Sector Marketing*, 3(2), 179–184.

Hall, P. D. (1999). The work of many hands: A response to Stanley N. Katz on the origins of the "serious study" of philanthropy. *Nonprofit and Voluntary Sector Quarterly*, 28(4), 522–534. doi:10.1177/0899764099284013

Hankinson, P. (2000). Brand orientation in charity organisations: Qualitative research into key charity sectors. *International Journal of Nonprofit and Voluntary Sector Marketing*, 5(3), 207–219.

Hankinson, P., & Rochester, C. (2005). The face and voice of volunteering: A suitable case for branding? *International Journal of Nonprofit and Voluntary Sector Marketing*, 10(2), 93–105.

Heide, M., Platen, S., Simonsson, C., & Falkheimer, J. (2018). Expanding the scope of strategic communication: Towards a holistic understanding of organizational complexity. *International Journal of Strategic Communication*, 12(4), 452–468. doi:10.1080/1553118X.2018.1456434

Hess, A. (2015, December 3–4). *Strategic communication of non-governmental organizations: The role of volunteers as communicators and multipliers*. Paper presented at the ECREA OSC Conference "Strategic Communication for Non-Profit Organisations: Challenges and Alternative Approaches".

Hyde, M. K., Dunn, J., Wust, N., Bax, C., & Chambers, S. K. (2016). Satisfaction, organizational commitment and future action in charity sport event volunteers. *International Journal of Nonprofit and Voluntary Sector Marketing*, 21, 148–167. https://doi.org/10.1002/nvsm.1552

Holtzhausen, L. (2014). Non-profit organizations bridging the communication divide in a complex South Africa. *Public Relations Review*, 40(2), 286–293.

Holtzhausen, L., & Zerfass, A. (2015). *The Routledge handbook of strategic communication*. Routledge.

Hume, J., & Leonard, A. (2014). Exploring the strategic potential of internal communication in international non-governmental organisations. *Public Relations Review*, 40(2), 294–304.

Ingenhoff, D., & Koelling, A. M. (2010). Web sites as a dialogic tool for charitable fundraising NPOs: A comparative study. *International Journal of Strategic Communication*, 4(3), 171–188.

Janssen, D., Beerkens, R., & Van der Vliet, S. (2021). Non-governmental organizations in crisis. *The International Journal of Humanities & Social Studies*, 9(6), 118–121.

Jeavons, T. H. (2016). Ethical nonprofit management. In D. O. Renz & R. D. Hermann (Eds.), *The Jossey-Bass handbook of nonprofit leadership and management* (pp. 188–216). John Wiley & Sons Ltd.

Johnston, J. (2016). *Public relations & the public interest*. Routledge.

Jones, K. S. (2006). Giving and volunteering as distinct forms of civic engagement: The role of community integration and personal resources in formal helping. *Nonprofit and Voluntary Sector Quarterly*, 35(2), 249–266.

Kareithi, R., & Lund, C. (2012). Review of NGO performance research published in academic journals between 1996 and 2008. *South African Journal of Science*, 108(11/12). doi:10.4102/sajs.v108i11/12.755

Kaur, K. (2015). Social media creating digital environmental publics: Case of Lynas Malaysia. *Public Relations Review*, 41(2), 311–314.

Koschmann, M. A. (2012). Developing a communicative theory of the nonprofit. *Management Communication Quarterly*, 26(1), 139–146. doi:10.1177/0893318911423640

Koschmann, M. A., Isbell, M. G., & Sanders, M. L. (2015). Connecting nonprofit and communication scholarship: A review of key issues and a meta-theoretical framework for future research. *Review of Communication*, 15(3), 200–220. https://doi.org/10.1080/15358593.2015.1058411

Koschmann, M. A., & Sandres, M. (2020). *Understanding nonprofit work: A communication perspective*. Wiley-Blackwell.

Landim, L. (2002). Múltiplas Identidades das ONGs. In S. Haddad (Ed.), *ONGs e universidades: desafios para a cooperação na América Latina* (pp. 17–50). Editora Fundação Peirópolis.

Lang, S. (2013). *NGOs, civil society, and the public sphere*. Cambridge University Press.

Lee, T., Johnson, E., & Prakash, A. (2012). Media independence and trust in NGOs: The case of postcommunist countries. *Nonprofit and Voluntary Sector Quarterly*, 41(1), 8–35.

Lewis, L. (2005). The civil society sector. A review of critical issues and research agenda for organizational communication scholars. *Management Communication Quarterly*, 19(2), 238–267. doi:10.1177/0893318905279190

Liao, M.-N. (1999). Managing reputation and dealing with public scrutiny: Issues for voluntary sector organisations. *International Journal of Nonprofit and Voluntary Sector Marketing*, 4(4), 378–381.

Libaert, T., & Pierlot, J. M. (2009). *Communication des associations*. Dunod.

Liu, G., Chapleo, C., Ko, W. W., & Ngugi, I. K. (2015). The role of internal branding in nonprofit brand management: An empirical investigation. *Nonprofit and Voluntary Sector Quarterly*, 44(2), 319–339.

Liu, G., Eng, T.-Y., & Sekhon, Y. K. (2014). Managing branding and legitimacy: A study of charity retail sector. *Nonprofit and Voluntary Sector Quarterly*, 43(4), 629–651.

Ma, J., & Konrath, S. (2018). A century of nonprofit studies: Scaling the knowledge of the field. *VOLUNTAS: International Journal of Voluntary and Nonprofit Organizations*, 29(6), 1139–1158. https://doi.org/10.1007/s11266-018-00057-5

Maier, F., Meyer, M., & Steinbereithner, M. (2016). Nonprofit organizations becoming business-like a systematic review. *Nonprofit and Voluntary Sector Quarterly*, 45(1), 64–86.

Meneghetti, S. B. (2001). *Comunicação e marketing: fazendo a diferença no dia-a-dia de organizações da sociedade civil*. Global.

Menescal, A. K. (1996). História e gênese das organizações não governamentais. In H. S. Gonçalves & A. K. Menescal (Eds.), *Organizações não governamentais: solução ou problema?* (1a ed., pp. 21–38). Estação Liberdade.

Naudé, A. M. E., Froneman, J. D., & Atwood, R. A. (2004). The use of the internet by ten South African non-governmental organizations – a public relations perspective. *Public Relations Review*, 30(1), 87–94.

Oliveira, E. (2017). *The instigatory theory of NGO communication (ITNC)*. Universidade do Minho. http://hdl.handle.net/1822/56020

Oliveira, E. (2019). *The instigatory theory of NGO communication: Strategic communication in civil society organisations*. Springer VS.

Oliveira, E., Melo, A., & Gonçalves, G. (Eds.). (2016). *Strategic communication for non-profit organisations: Challenges and alternative approaches*. Vernon Press.

Oliveira, E., & Wiesenberg, M. (2016). Von innen heraus: Vier Dynamiken der Legitimation von NGOs und Kirchen. In S. Huck-Sandhu (Ed.), *Interne Kommunikation im Wandel* (pp. 105–122). Springer VS.

O'Neil, G. (2013). Evaluation of international and non-governmental organizations' communication activities: A 15 year systematic review. *Public Relations Review*, 39(5), 572–574.

Pérez, R. A. (2001). *Estrategias de comunicación*. Ariel.

Pleil, T. (2005). Nonprofit-PR: Besonderheiten und Herausforderungen. In *Berichte aus der Forschung 5 des Fachbereichs Sozial- und Kulturwissenschaften* (pp. 1–21). FH Darmstadt.

Powers, M. (2014). The structural organization of NGO publicity work: Explaining divergent publicity strategies at humanitarian and human rights organizations. *International Journal of Communication*, 8, 18.

Putnam, R. D. (2000). *Bowling alone: The collapse and revival of American community*. Simon & Schuster.

Qu, Y. (2020). Engaging publics in the mobile era: A study of Chinese charitable foundations' use of WeChat. *Public Relations Review*, 46(1), 311–314. doi:10.1016/j.pubrev.2019.101815

Rodriguez, M., Ajjan, H., & Peterson, R. M. (2016). Social media in large sales forces: An empirical study of the impact of sales process capability and relationship performance. *Journal of Marketing Theory and Practice*, 24(3), 365–379.

Salamon, L. M. (1999). *America's nonprofit sector: A primer* (2nd ed.). Foundation Center.

Salamon, L. M., Anheier, H. K., Toepler, S., Sokolowski, S. W., & Associates. (1999). *Global civil society: Dimensions of the nonprofit sector*. Johns Hopkins Center for Civil Society Studies.

Sandberg, B., Elliott, E., & Petchel, S. (2020). Investigating the marketization of the nonprofit sector: A comparative case study of two nonprofit organizations. *Voluntas*, 31, 494–510. https://doi.org/10.1007/s11266-019-00159-8

Sargeant, A., & Lee, S. (2002). Improving public trust in the voluntary sector: An empirical analysis. *International Journal of Nonprofit and Voluntary Sector Marketing*, 7(1), 68–83.

Sarstedt, M., & Schloderer, M. P. (2010). Developing a measurement approach for reputation of non-profit organizations. *International Journal of Nonprofit and Voluntary Sector Marketing*, 15(3), 276–299.

Saxton, G. D., & Waters, R. D. (2014). What do stakeholders "like" on Facebook? Examining public reactions to nonprofit organizations' informational, promotional, and community-building messages. *Journal of Public Relations Research*, 26, 280–299.

Schubert, P., Ressler, R. W., Paarlberg, L. E., & Boenigk, S. (2022). The evolution of the nonprofit research field: An emerging scholar perspective. *Nonprofit and Voluntary Sector Quarterly*. https://doi.org/10.1177/08997640221078824

Shiau, H.-C. (2011). Engaging publics via documentaries: A typological study of advocacy functions among Taiwanese NPOs' productions. *Public Relations Review*, 37(2), 181–183.

Sisco, H. F. (2012). Nonprofit in crisis: An examination of the applicability of situational crisis communication theory. *Journal of Public Relations Research*, 24, 1–17.

Sisson, D. C. (2017). Control mutuality, social media, and organization-public relationships: A study of local animal welfare organizations' donors. *Public Relations Review*, *43*(1), 179–189.

Stride, H., & Lee, S. (2007). No logo? No way. Branding in the non-profit sector. *Journal of Marketing Management*, *23*(1–2), 107–122.

Thrall, A. T., Stecula, D., & Sweet, D. (2014). May we have your attention please? Human-rights NGOs and the problem of global communication. *The International Journal of Press/Politics*, *19*(2), 135–159.

Tindall, N. T., Waters, R. D., & Kelly, K. S. (2014). A fractured glass ceiling in fundraising? Examining the careers of minority healthcare fundraisers using role theory. In R. D. Waters (Ed.), *Public relations in the nonprofit sector. Theory and practice* (pp. 3–18). Routledge.

Tkalac, A., & Pavicic, J. (2009). Nongovernmental organizations and international public relations. In K. Sriramesh & D. Vercic (Eds.), *The global public relations handbook: Theory, research, and practice* (2nd ed., pp. 807–821). Routledge.

Tsetsura, K. (2013). Challenges in framing women's rights as human rights at the domestic level: A case study of NGOs in the post-Soviet countries. *Public Relations Review*, *39*(4), 406–416.

Viertmann, C. (2016, December 3–4). *NPO trust index*. Paper presented at the ECREA OSC Conference "Strategic Communication for Non-Profit Organisations: Challenges and Alternative Approaches".

Voss, K. (2007). *Öffentlichkeitsarbeit von Nichtregierungsorganisationen: Mittel, Ziele, interne Strukturen*. VS Verlag für Sozialwissenschaften.

Walzer, M. (1995). The concept of civil society. In M. Walzer (Ed.), *Toward a global civil society*. Berghahn.

Waters, R. D. (2015). *Public relations in the nonprofit sector. Theory and Practice*. Routledge.

Waters, R. D., Kelly, K. S., & Lee Walker, M. (2012). Organizational roles enacted by healthcare fundraisers: A national study testing theory and assessing gender differences. *Journal of communication Management*, *16*(3), 244–263.

Weder, F. (2021). Strategic problematization of sustainability reframing dissent in strategic. *Public Relations Inquiry*, 2046147X211026857.

Weick, K. E. (1995). *Sensemaking in organizations*. Sage.

Wiencierz, C., Pöppel, K. G., & Röttger, U. (2015). Where does my money go? How online comments on a donation campaign influence the perceived trustworthiness of a nonprofit organization. *International Journal of Strategic Communication*, *9*(2), 102–117.

Wiggill, M. N. (2011). Strategic communication management in the non-profit sector: A simplified model: Strategic communication management. *Journal of Public Affairs*, *11*(4), 226–235.

Wiggill, M. N. (2014). Donor relationship management practices in the South Africa non-profit sector. *Public Relations Review*, *40*(2), 278–285.

Wollebæk, D., & Strømsnes, K. (2008). Voluntary associations, trust, and civic engagement: A multilevel approach. *Nonprofit and Voluntary Sector Quarterly*, *37*(2), 249–263.

Xu, W., & Saxton, G. D. (2019). Does stakeholder engagement pay off on social media? A social capital perspective. *Nonprofit and Voluntary Sector Quarterly*, *48*(1), 28–49. doi:10.1177/0899764018791267

Yang, A., & Taylor, M. (2010). Relationship-building by Chinese ENGOs' websites: Education, not activation. *Public Relations Review*, *36*(4), 342–351.

Zatepilina-Monacell, O. (2012). High stakes: U.S. nonprofit organizations and the U.S. standing abroad. *Public Relations Review*, *38*(3).

Zhang, J., & Swartz, B. C. (2009). Toward a model of NGO media diplomacy in the Internet age: Case study of Washington profile. *Public Relations Review*, *35*(1), 47–55.

PART I

Democracy and civil society

The first part of this handbook seeks to introduce metatheoretical and multidisciplinary approaches to the nonprofit sector, mainly from a macro-level perspective, including the intersection of the definitions of democracy, civil society, and their dynamics. It centers around a reflection on the dialectic relation between citizens, association, social change, and the public sphere. Authors grounded in the field of communication, but also interdisciplinary perspectives like those from sociology, political science, and international relations, debate the history(ies) of civil society and its organizations. Major subjects are also the NGO-ization in a globalized world and communication and its task and contribution to community life and the quality of democracy. These chapters also offer insights into ongoing discussions about the concept of nonprofit communication. Furthermore, proposals made from various viewpoints such as development communication, civism, activism, public interest, and humanitarian communication are explained.

Thomas Davies from the City, University of London describes the stories of the nonprofit and philanthropic sector exploring diverse roots of associationalism (Chapter 1.1). This provides a critical and complementary standpoint to traditional narratives that have tended to concentrate on developments in Western Europe and North America. Arguing on the evolution of associationalism in three main aspects – ancient, modern, and transnational – this chapter elucidates the importance of communication across world regions to the historical development of voluntary associations.

Communication for development and social change is thematized by Jan Servaes from the University of Massachusetts, USA (Chapter 1.2). The chapter introduces the models, approaches, and ideologies of the communication for development and social change (CDSC) field by mapping and summarizing the changes and highlighting crucial issues for an understanding of CDSC in this complex world. It is proposed to distinguish between two perspectives: one that seeks to produce a common understanding among all the participants in a development initiative by implementing a policy or a development project, also called the *top-down model*, and the second as the one that emphasizes engaging the grassroots in making decisions that enhance their own lives, or the *bottom-up model*.

Chapters 1.3 and 1.4 bring two perspectives of NGO-ization, through a close look at the dynamics that are raising from this phenomenon. Sabine Lang from the University of Washington, USA and the EU/Jean Monnet Center of Excellence, postulates that NGO-ization is the most profound and ongoing structural rearrangement of civil society since the late 20th century. She describes it as a heuristic term that traces the pull of loosely networked groups from the local to the transnational level into a specific set of formalized structures. While consequences and effects of NGO-ization are disputed, Lang explains why an NGO-ized civil society has in fact become the globalized and "naturalized form" of civil society engagement. Taking it further, adding the solidarity aspect and the digital transformation, Victor Mari Sáez from the University of Cadiz, Spain, connects NGO-ization with the rise and expansion of neoliberalism (Chapter 1.4). Discussing what is named the fragmentation of organized solidarity, the chapter ascribes NGO-ization the restriction of capacity for having a political impact and influencing societal transformation at an institutional and macro-social level. Then, it also enumerates two main changes in the 21st century: an increase in private funding, which might have practical consequences for the communication of these organizations, and the momentum of the digital age, in which new communication tools and possibilities coexist alongside old reductionisms.

Chapter 1.5 discusses civic relations as socio-communicative collective action. Evandro Oliveira from the Autonomous University of Barcelona (UAB), Spain, and LabCom, Portugal, outlines this concept that emerged along the study of associative collective action within a civil society setting by performing a social origin approach. The chapter also shows how civic relations have been performed by individuals and organizations in different contexts, regions, and times: from the first Roman forms, within the religious context of the Middle Ages, and during intermediate times with the emergence of the first international non-governmental organizations in their modern form. It also compares the distinctive elements from public and civic relations from the meso-sociological level of analysis and the distinctive locus on the imperative of the common good, per se, exo organizational and communicative driven.

Considering public interest communication from a macro-sociological level of analysis in a pragmatic approach, Jane Johnston from the University of Queensland, Australia, examines in Chapter 1.6 the concept of public interest and its role in contemporary public discourse. The chapter argues that public interest is conveyed through communication, which allows ideas relating to interests to circulate and be challenged and argued in seeking answers and resolution. The chapter develops and explores the concept of "public interest communication in action," using a gay rights festival to illustrate how public interest parallels social change. In using a pragmatic theory lens, it draws on well-established theories to identify how public interest communication may be used to develop workable solutions for public problems, with a particular focus on its application to civil society and the nonprofit sector.

Part I of this handbook ends with a chapter on humanitarian communication in a critical approach by Valérie Gorin from the University of Geneva and the Geneva Center of Humanitarian Studies, Switzerland (Chapter 1.7). The chapter explores humanitarian communications for public purposes first by discussing the constraints of fundraising and aid agencies' use of public relations to build acceptance and promote a cause and progresses to the necessity for the humanitarian sector to adopt ethical codes and accountability procedures to address the donor/beneficiary relationship. Then, it focuses on operational uses, such as advocacy and negotiation, to discuss how political concerns raised publicly by humanitarian organizations challenge their neutrality. It also considers the growing use of communication technologies for relief response and their impact on life-saving communication.

1.1
HISTORIES OF THE NONPROFIT AND PHILANTHROPIC SECTOR

Thomas Davies

Introduction

Understandings of the scope of the nonprofit sector in the post–Cold War era have tended to follow the criteria put forward by Salamon and Anheier (1992, pp. 135, 130) encompassing nongovernmental associationalism that is formally organized, self-governed, and involving voluntary participation on a not-for-profit basis, with philanthropy constituting one of the sources of resources for this sector.[1] As Morris (2000) noted, definitions following these criteria miss much of the rich diversity of nonprofit-sector activities from a broader historical perspective. In order to obtain a fuller historical overview of this sector, it is necessary to take into account activities that may fall short of the ideal type of formal organization, independence from government, and voluntary participation on a nonprofit basis. Similarly, loosening these strict criteria enables better consideration of activities beyond the "Western" context in which understandings of the constitution of the nonprofit sector such as this originated.

Introductions to the history of the nonprofit sector have often focused primarily on developments in Europe and North America (Soskis, 2020), with the sector's deep historical roots frequently being traced to Jewish and Christian religious practices (Robbins, 2006) and to classical antiquity (Molnár, 2020). There has also been a tendency in related historical literatures – such as in survey histories of humanitarianism – to provide a narrative emphasizing the role of European imperialism in the global expansion of such activities (Barnett, 2011). In this chapter – by contrast – the emphasis is on the multiple histories of the nonprofit and philanthropic sector, aiming to give consideration not only to dominant narratives such as these but also to a much more geographically and socially diverse array of activities that a broader conceptualization of the sector encompasses.

Besides this broader focus, this chapter aims to shed special light on the transnational dimension of the evolution of the nonprofit and philanthropic sector. Much established scholarship has tended to be marred by methodological nationalism, with pioneering studies having tended to focus on single-country cases (Salamon et al., 1999; Heinrich & Fioramonti, 2007). This is hardly surprising, given the tendency for much of the data on the sector to be located at the national level (Anheier, 2001). Yet the transnational communications and structures that have developed in this sector have an extensive history, with transnational civil society having developed over many centuries (Davies, 2014).

Given the constraints of a short introductory chapter, a full account of the diverse multinational and transnational histories of the philanthropic sector is impossible. However, it is hoped that this chapter at least offers some indication of the plurality of histories that deserve further investigation. Voluntary action history is an emerging discipline – with its own professional societies such as the Voluntary Action History Society in the UK – but it is one that is in need of further nourishing and advancement.

Early associationalism

While there has often been scepticism as to the extent of voluntary associationalism in "pre-literate" societies (Anderson, 1971), Harris et al. (2016, p. 26) have noted that there have been efforts "to infer the extent of associational activity among preliterate societies in millennia long ago from more recent anthropological evidence." They have pointed, for example, to the formation by Tareumiut whale hunters of "voluntary associations under the leadership of an *umealiq* . . . who organises the labour necessary to acquire and maintain a large whaling boat" (Johnson & Earle, 2000, p. 177) as "evidence for the existence of different types of association among members of hunter-gatherer-fisher societies" (Harris et al., 2016, p. 25).

In subsequent periods where the historical evidence from the time is more extensive, histories of what might now be termed the nonprofit and philanthropic sector can be identified in multiple world regions. In considering the evolution of the sector in India, Joshi et al. (2001, p. 3) have asserted that "voluntarism is an integral part of Indian society, and dates back to 1500 BC when it has been mentioned in the *Rig Veda*," including the statement "May the one who gives shine most." Besides religiously motivated philanthropy, they note the significance in pre-colonial India of caste groups, professional guilds, cultural associations, efforts towards conservation of nature, and "workmen's co-operatives and guilds . . . [that] were variously called *Nigama, Sangha, Sreni, Puga* and *Nikaya*" (Joshi et al., 2001, pp. 4–5).

In considering the development of philanthropy in China, Friedrich Hirth (1912, p. 13) pointed out more than a century ago that "far from being introduced by Western missionaries, the spirit of charity to one's neighbour has originated and developed on Chinese soil itself." Yu-Yue Tsu (1912, pp. 23–24) commenced his study of Chinese philanthropy in the era of "the Five Rulers (2255–2205 BC)" when "the men of Yin" were understood to have provided nourishment to the elderly. In considering the evolution of associations in China, Ross (1976, pp. 73–78) identified a range of activities, including *she* and *hui* local-level mutual assistance and common concern associations and the *tsu*, organized around common ancestors and with the name dating to the Shang Dynasty. Research into the "long history of civil charity" in China has also noted "the Sui Dynasty's public granaries and the Song Dynasty's public farmsteads and public lands" (Wang & Xu, 2010, p. 25). The spread of Buddhism is understood to have been important in the development of voluntary associationalism in China from the fifth century onwards, while "a loss of faith in state activism" and neo-Confucianism are claimed to have played a part in the advancement of local associationalism in the Southern Song Dynasty (von Glahn, 1993, pp. 221, 246).

The evolution of associations in the classical Mediterranean has attracted the greatest attention in traditional studies. Jones (1999) emphasises the context of democratic institutions for the development of associations, or *koinoniai*, in classical Athens, as well as a law of Solon that provided for associational autonomy so long as they did not infringe on state regulations. Similarly in the early Roman republic, self-organized voluntary associations, or *collegia*, operated quite freely, but the revolutionary activities of some guilds led to a decree abolishing those against public interest in 64 BCE, leaving a "shadow . . . that was never really to lift" (Cotter, 1996, p. 76), although voluntary associationalism was to persist. This was later to include early Christian associationalism (Kloppenborg, 2019) which in the post-Constantinian era became increasingly bureaucratized and enmeshed with dominant institutions (Wilson, 1996, p. 14).

Besides religious establishments such as confraternities, associationalism in medieval Europe was to include a variety of fraternal societies and guilds, but the extent to which these were voluntary was, in some instances questionable, since as Harris et al. (2016, pp. 32–33) note, commonly "private and voluntary associations of the Middle Ages exercised powers . . . over their members . . . [that] in some settings were indistinguishable from other institutions of governance."

While dominant narratives of the evolution of associationalism and charity have emphasized Eurocentric origins such as these, there is growing attention in English-language historical literature to the diverse roots of contemporary philanthropy and associationalism around the world. Singer (2008), for example, has aimed to elucidate the history of charity in Islamic societies over the last fourteen centuries. Besides *zakat* (obligatory almsgiving), this history encompasses the role of voluntary charity (*sadaqah*) and voluntary associations.

Long-established indigenous concepts and practices shape contemporary philanthropic and voluntary associational activities in multiple world regions. For example, in South Africa the Bantu concept of *ubuntu* emphasizing "the importance of community, solidarity, caring, and sharing" and recognition that "true human potential can only be realized in partnership with others" underpins an approach to philanthropy that is "more horizontal than vertical in nature" (Mottiar & Ngcoya, 2016, p. 151). Indigenous worldviews in South America include those that have extended recognition of mutual dependence beyond humanity to include the natural environment, with, for example, the worldview of the Ashaninka of the Peruvian Amazon emphasizing that life as an *ashaninkasanori* entails caring not only for other people but also "following an ethos of conviviality in the relationship with the Earth, including respecting other-than-human beings [and] caring for the Earth through hard work" (Caruso & Sarmiento Barletti, 2019, p. 221).

Modern associationalism

An approach emphasizing responsibilities to life forms beyond other humans is to be found in multiple regional histories of voluntary associationalism. One notable aspect of late Ming associationalism in China, for example, consisted of societies promoting the liberation of animals from distress (Handlin Smith, 2009, p. 15). The Ming period of Chinese history exhibited a vast array of forms of associationalism, including charitable and welfare societies providing relief to the poor and those afflicted by disasters, micro-credit associations, and educational associations, among many other varieties of voluntary societies (Zhou & Zeng, 2006, pp. 193–202; Levy & Pissler, 2020, pp. 54–56). Especially notable are the numerous life-saving and free ferry societies on the banks of rivers and lakes, which developed practices later emulated by European "humane" societies (Evans, 2003).

As with so many other features of European modernity (Hobson, 2004), modern associationalism in Europe owed much to precedents in other continents. Besides Chinese influence on modern European humanitarianism, there was, for example, the influence of activities in the Ottoman Empire on political revolutionary associationalism in late eighteenth-century Europe, with rebellions in the Ottoman Empire being perceived as providing models to emulate in Europe (Davies, 2014, p. 25).

The expansion of voluntary associations in the late eighteenth and early nineteenth centuries also needs to be understood in the context of processes of industrialization, urbanization, and the expansion of the middle class (Morris, 1983). One British commentator noted in 1843 that there were by that time

> many institutions and associations . . . for the dispensing of every kind of good, which have arisen within the present or last generation and which have flourished most in the manufacturing towns and villages – such as mechanics institutes, literary societies, circulating

> libraries, youth's guardian societies, friendly societies, temperance societies, medical charities, clothing societies, benevolent and district visiting societies.
>
> (Edward Baines, quoted in Morris, 1983, p. 95)

At the same time, Tocqueville (1838) observed the vitality of associational life as a feature of democracy in the United States. Even in heavily regulated European states such as Russia, a diverse array of associational life was to develop by the late nineteenth century (Tumanova, 2011).

One of the most extensively studied aspects of European associationalism in the nineteenth century is its role in imperialist expansionism (Barnett, 2011). Purportedly "civilising missions" characterized the objectives of voluntary organizations such as the Holy Childhood Association, which was founded in 1843 and sought to counter infanticide in China, but which itself faced numerous accusations of infanticide, leading to the cessation of its activities in China in 1951 (Harrison, 2008).

Whereas some have viewed missionary and colonial institutions as providing part of the basis for associational activities in post-colonial states (Woodberry, 2012), far more significant were anti-imperialist associations that sought to combat these institutions. Perhaps the best-known example is Gandhian anti-imperialist associationalism and Gandhian principles such as *swaraj* (self-reliance), which in post-independence India influenced both the development of government institutions supportive of voluntary associationalism and the creation of a wide range of nongovernmental organizations explicitly drawing on Gandhian values (Sahoo, 2013, p. 44).

The historical development of modern civil society in different states exhibits significant variations depending on local context. In the case of Kenya, for example, Nasong'o and Murunga (2007, pp. 28–29) observe a significant contrast between urban-based social organizations that merely sought "to ameliorate the externalities of colonialism" and rural-based associations that "rejected out of hand colonial hegemony" and "sought to reconstruct alternative institutions or a return to African traditionalism," with the more radical approach playing a greater role in the post-imperial transition.

According to one widely circulated estimate, by 2015 there were thought to be more than 10 million nongovernmental organizations around the world (Khoo, 2018, p. 198). However, the traditional model of voluntary associationalism mediated by a hierarchical nongovernmental organizational structure has become less relevant in recent decades, especially since the development of new technologies of electronic communication. Whereas in the past, a hierarchical organizational structure may have been necessary to facilitate coordination of resources, increasingly these can be mobilized more horizontally and on an ad hoc basis through digitally mediated networks (Castells, 2013).

Transnational associationalism

One of the consequences of global digital communication has been expansion in the scope for associationalism across national borders (Frangonikolopoulos, 2012). However, transnational associationalism long precedes the technologies that facilitate its contemporary dynamics. The longest-established transnational associations are largely understood to consist of transnational religious establishments such as Roman Catholic hospitaller orders, Sufi tariqahs, and missionary societies of various faiths (Trinningham, 1998; Robert, 2009). However, cross-border performing arts societies, scientific associations, and fraternal secret societies also predate the principal waves of expansion of transnational associations from the late eighteenth century onwards (Davies, 2014, p. 20).

Besides the role of the Enlightenment, the industrial revolution, accelerated international communications, the growth of the middle class, and urbanization, the expansion of transnational civil society in the nineteenth century was facilitated through learning processes between continents. For example, one of the earliest associations to describe itself as international – the International Shipwreck Society which coordinated an international network of life-saving establishments from Paris in the 1830s and 1840s – made explicit reference to the influence of Chinese precedent (Davies, 2018).

Cosmopolitan cities served as major hubs for the development of transnational associations, notably Paris in the late eighteenth and early nineteenth centuries, London in the late nineteenth century, and Brussels and Geneva in the early twentieth century. Today, hubs of transnational associations also include Penang, birthplace of the Third World Network, and many other "Global South" transnational associations in the 1980s (Hilton, 2009): Bangkok, Johannesburg, Nairobi, Mexico City, and Buenos Aires, to name just a few examples (Taylor, 2004). The significance of cities such as Geneva and Nairobi for transnational associations reflects the presence of intergovernmental lobbying opportunities in these cities, notably the historical legacy of the establishment of the League of Nations in Geneva (White, 1968) and the opportunities provided by the UN Environment Programme in Nairobi (Livernash, 1992).

Dominant narratives of the evolution of transnational associations tend to consider their roots in late nineteenth-century Europe, with the Red Cross and International Workingmen's Association being established in Geneva and London, respectively, in the 1860s and a wide range of transnational women's, labour, humanitarian, educational, professional, and peace societies, among other sectoral associations, being established across Europe from the 1870s (Lyons, 1963; Boli & Thomas, 1999). However, similar cross-border associationalism was also to be found in other continents, notably in South America, where "republican internationalist" ideals played a significant role (Long & Schulz, 2021).

Moreover, anti-imperial and pan-regional mobilizations were to constitute significant features of transnational associationalism in the late nineteenth and early twentieth centuries. Examples of pan-regional associations include the Pan-African Association launched by Trinidadian lawyer Henry Sylvester Williams in 1897 (Geiss, 1974, pp. 176–77) and the East Asian Common Culture Association formed in Japan in 1898 (Saaler, 2007, p. 4). Anti-imperialist and Islamic revivalist objectives were advanced by transnational associations, including the Society of the Muslim Brothers, established in Egypt in 1928, which quickly expanded to other national contexts (Lia, 2006).

After former colonies gained independence, cross-regional associations to advance their common objectives were established, including the Afro-Asian People's Solidarity Organization, the creation of which in 1958 was described as

> a striking manifestation of the fundamental changes in the world, which consist in that the peoples of Asia and Africa, who but recently were oppressed, enslaved and deprived of elementary human rights, have now emerged in the world arena, have become an irresistible force that must be reckoned with.
>
> (Rashidov, 1958, p. 12)[2]

Besides exhibiting greater regional diversity, transnational associationalism in the second half of the twentieth century expanded in respect of the range of issue-area foci of mobilization, for instance, accompanying the development of "new social movements" in the late 1960s that encompassed peace, feminist, environmentalist, and many other forms of activism which were thought to be "a product of a shift to a postindustrial economy" (Pichardo, 1997, p. 412). The same period also witnessed growing professionalization of transnational associations, especially in the development aid sector (Chabbott, 1999, p. 243).

After the end of the Cold War, and accompanying the proliferation of intergovernmental conferences in the 1990s, there was thought to be a "global associational revolution" as transnational voluntary organizations greatly expanded in number, reflecting the seizing of newly expanded political opportunities in this era (Salamon, 1993). For some authors this development reflected the emergence of a "global civil society" transcending the national boundaries of the past (Kaldor, 2003).

Large-scale transnational reformist advocacy campaigns such as against landmines and for the creation of an international criminal court claimed significant successes in the immediate post–Cold War period (Price, 1998; Glasius, 2006), while more radical transnational associationalism mobilized on a remarkable scale at meetings such as those of the World Social Forum (Smith et al., 2014). At the end of the twentieth century, pan-associations such as CIVICUS were established to advance the common interests of associations around the world (CIVICUS, 1999).

Efforts to unite in coordinated action transnational associations from across the world were not without precedent. However, on each occasion they were established shortly before a period of significant associational contraction. For instance, shortly before the First World War the Union of International Associations based in Belgium sought to unify in a single organization all the world's transnational associations at the time (Union of International Associations, 1914), while in the early 1930s the International Consultative Group based in Geneva claimed to speak on behalf of transnational associations with a combined membership exceeding 100 million people (Davies, 2012, p. 415). In both cases, bold objectives of uniting transnational civil society quickly had to be abandoned.

Contemporary associationalism in historical perspective

Global associationalism has been confronted by numerous challenges in the twenty-first century, leading some to retract the optimistic assessments of the late twentieth century. Economic challenges have included the contraction of funds following the global financial crisis (Khanna & Irvine, 2018), while political challenges have included the problems of global insecurity (Irrera, 2019) and the expansion of authoritarian governance regimes (Heiss, 2019). Pressures such as these have been compounded by the repercussions of the COVID-19 crisis, with 40% of respondents to one CIVICUS survey claiming to have been "affected so severely that they expect to close down or stop activities in the near future" (CIVICUS, 2020, p. 2).

Although some have argued that recent developments may mark the reversal of the associational revolution of the late twentieth century, given financial pressures, rising authoritarianism, and new security threats, a longer-term historical perspective may lead to a less pessimistic assessment. Global associationalism has seen many previous periods of retrenchment, such as those accompanying the two World Wars and the Great Depression, and yet on each occasion it has adapted and recovered. After the First World War, a more diverse and effectively organized array of associations was to develop, seizing the opportunities provided by the new international institutions of the period (White, 1968), while the decades following the Second World War witnessed considerable diversification and growth of associations, facilitated by decolonization, democratization, and globalization processes (Davies, 2014). Moreover, consideration of the extensive voluntary associational activities even further back in human history reveals the great scope of such activities even in contexts that are extremely remote from contemporary understandings of liberal democracy.

Notes

1 It is common for academic literature on philanthropy also to follow Salamon, defining it as "the use of private resources – treasure, time and talent – for public purposes" (Phillips & Jung, 2016, p. 7).
2 AAPSO was among many "front" organizations supported by the Soviet Union in the Cold War period.

References

Anderson, R. T. (1971). Voluntary associations in history. *American Anthropologist*, 73(1), 209–222.
Anheier, H. K. (2001). Measuring global civil society. In H. K. Anheier, M. Glasius, & M. Kaldor (Eds.), *Global civil society 2001* (pp. 221–230). Oxford University Press.

Barnett, M. (2011). *Empire of humanity: A history of humanitarianism*. Cornell University Press.
Boli, J., & Thomas, G. M. (Eds.). (1999). *Constructing world culture: International non-governmental organizations since 1875*. Stanford University Press.
Caruso, E., & Sarmiento Barletti, J. P. (2019). Kametsa Asaike. In A. Kothari, A. Salleh, A. Escobar, A. Acosta, & F. Demaria (Eds.), *Pluriverse: A post-development dictionary* (pp. 220–223). Tulika Books.
Castells, M. (2013). *Networks of outrage and hope: Social movements in the internet age*. Polity.
Chabbott, C. (1999). Development INGOs. In J. Boli & G. M. Thomas (Eds.), *Constructing world culture: International nongovernmental organizations since 1875* (pp. 222–248). Stanford University Press.
CIVICUS. (1999). *Civil society at the millennium*. Kumarian.
CIVICUS. (2020, September). *COVID-19: Members views on civil society resilience and sustainability*. CIVICUS. www.civicus.org/documents/reports-and-publications/resourcing-covid-19-survey_english.pdf
Cotter, W. (1996). The collegia and Roman law: State restrictions on voluntary associations, 64BCE-200CE. In J. S. Kloppenborg & S. G. Wilson (Eds.), *Voluntary associations in the Graeco-Roman world* (pp. 74–89). Routledge.
Davies, T. (2012). A "great experiment" of the league of nations era: International nongovernmental organizations, global governance, and democracy beyond the state. *Global Governance, 18*(4), 405–423.
Davies, T. (2014). *NGOs: A new history of transnational civil society*. Oxford University Press.
Davies, T. (2018). Rethinking the origins of transnational humanitarian organizations: The curious case of the international shipwreck society. *Global Networks, 18*(3), 461–478.
Evans, C. (2003). *Rescue at sea: An international history of lifesaving, coastal rescue craft and organisations*. Conway Maritime.
Frangonikolopoulos, C. A. (2012). Global civil society and deliberation in the digital age. *International Journal of Electronic Governance, 5*(1), 1–23.
Geiss, I. (1974). *The Pan-African movement: A history of Pan-Africanism in America, Europe and Africa*. Methuen.
Glasius, M. (2006). *The international criminal court: A global civil society achievement*. Routledge.
Handlin Smith, J. (2009). *The art of doing good: Charity in Late Ming China*. University of California Press.
Harris, B., Morris, A., Ascough, R. S., Chikoto, G. L., Elson, P. R., McLoughlin, J., Muukkonen, M., Pospíšilová, T., Rokal, K., Smith, D. H., Soteri-Proctor, A., Tumanova, A., & Yu, P. (2016). History of associations and volunteering. In D. H. Smith, R. A. Stebbins, & J. Grotz (Eds.), *The Palgrave handbook of volunteering, civic participation, and nonprofit associations* (Vol. 1, pp. 23–58). Palgrave Macmillan.
Harrison, H. (2008). "A penny for the little Chinese": The French holy childhood association in China, 1843–1951. *The American Historical Review, 113*(1), 72–92.
Heinrich, V., & Fioramonti, L. (Eds.). (2007). *CIVICUS global survey of the state of civil society: Country profiles*. Kumarian Press.
Heiss, A. (2019). NGOs and authoritarianism. In T. Davies (Ed.), *Routledge handbook of NGOs and international relations* (pp. 557–572). Routledge.
Hilton, M. (2009). *Prosperity for all: Consumer activism in an era of globalization*. Cornell University Press.
Hirth, F. (1912). Introduction. In Y.-Y. Tsu (Ed.), *The spirit of Chinese philanthropy: A study in mutual aid* (pp. 7–8). Columbia University Press.
Hobson, J. M. (2004). *The Eastern origins of Western civilisation*. Cambridge University Press.
Irrera, D. (2019). NGOs and security in conflict zones. In T. Davies (Ed.), *Routledge handbook of NGOs and international relations* (pp. 573–586). Routledge.
Johnson, A. W., & Earle, T. K. (2000). *The evolution of human societies: From foraging group to agrarian state*. Stanford University Press.
Jones, N. F. (1999). *The associations of classical Athens: The response to democracy*. Oxford University Press.
Joshi, B. K., Panjani, M., & Dwivedi, S. K. (2001). *Historical background of the nonprofit sector in India*. Society for Participatory Research in Asia.
Kaldor, M. (2003). *Global civil society: An answer to war*. Polity Press.
Khanna, K., & Irvine, H. (2018). Communicating the impact of the global financial crisis in annual reports: A study of Australian NGOs. *Australian Accounting Review, 28*(1), 109–126.
Khoo, S. (2018). Development NGOs, civil society, and social change. In G. H. Fagan & R. Munck (Eds.), *Handbook on development and social change* (pp. 190–210). Edward Elgar.
Kloppenborg, J. S. (2019). *Christ's associations: Connecting and belonging in the ancient city*. Yale University Press.
Levy, K., & Pissler, K. B. (2020). *Charity with Chinese characteristics: Chinese charitable foundations between the party-state and society*. Edward Elgar.
Lia, B. (2006). *The society of the Muslim brothers in Egypt: The rise of an Islamic mass movement, 1928–1942*. Ithaca Press.
Livernash, R. (1992). The growing influence of NGOs in the developing world. *Environment: Science and Policy for Sustainable Development, 34*(5), 12–43.

Long, T., & Schulz, C. A. (2021). Republican internationalism: The nineteenth-century roots of Latin American contributions to international order. *Cambridge Review of International Affairs*, online ahead of print. doi: 10.1080/09557571.2021.1944983.

Lyons, F. S. L. (1963). *Internationalism in Europe, 1815–1914*. A. W. Sythoff.

Molnár, G. (2020). Civil society history I: Antiquity. In R. A. List, H. K. Anheier, & S. Toepler (Eds.), *International encyclopedia of civil society, living edition*. https://link.springer.com/referencework/10.1007/978-3-319-99675-2

Morris, R. J. (1983). Voluntary societies and British urban elites, 1780–1850: An analysis. *The Historical Journal, 26*(1), 95–118.

Morris, S. (2000). Defining the nonprofit sector: Some lessons from history. In *Civil society working paper 3*. London School of Economics and Political Science.

Mottiar, S., & Ngcoya, M. (2016). Indigenous philanthropy: Challenging Western preconceptions. In T. Jung, S. D. Phillips, & J. Harrow (Eds.), *The Routledge companion to philanthropy* (pp. 151–161). Routledge.

Nasong'o, S. W., & Murunga, G. R. (2007). *Prospects for democracy in Kenya*. Bloomsbury Publishing.

Phillips, S. D., & Jung, T. (2016). Introduction: A new "new" philanthropy: From impetus to impact. In T. Jung, S. D. Phillips, & J. Harrow (Eds.), *The Routledge companion to philanthropy* (pp. 5–34). Routledge.

Pichardo, N. A. (1997). New social movements: A critical review. *Annual Review of Sociology, 23*, 411–430.

Price, R. (1998). Reversing the gun sights: Transnational civil society targets land mines. *International Organization, 52*(3), 613–644.

Rashidov, S. (1958). Great assembly of Eastern peoples. In *Afro-Asian people's solidarity conference: Cairo, December 26, 1957 – January 1, 1958*. Foreign Languages Publishing House.

Robbins, K. C. (2006). The nonprofit sector in historical perspective: Traditions of philanthropy in the West. In W. W. Powell & R. Steinberg (Eds.), *The nonprofit sector: A research handbook* (2nd ed., pp. 13–31). Yale University Press.

Robert, D. L. (2009). *Christian mission: How Christianity became a world religion*. Wiley-Blackwell.

Ross, J. C. (1976). *An assembly of good fellows: Voluntary associations in history*. Greenwood Press.

Saaler, S. (2007). Pan-Asianism in Modern Japanese history: Overcoming the nation, creating a region, forging an empire. In S. Saaler & J. V. Koschmann (Eds.), *Pan-Asianism in Modern Japanese history* (pp. 1–18). Routledge.

Sahoo, S. (2013). *Civil society and democratization in India: Institutions, ideologies and interests*. Routledge.

Salamon, L. M. (1993). *The global associational revolution: The rise of the third sector on the world scene*. Johns Hopkins University.

Salamon, L. M., & Anheier, H. K. (1992). In search of the nonprofit sector. I: The question of definitions. *Voluntas: International Journal of Voluntary and Nonprofit Organizations, 3*(2), 125–151.

Salamon, L. M., Anheier, H. K., Toepler, S., Sokolowski, W., List, R., & Associates. (1999). *Global civil society: Dimensions of the nonprofit sector* (2 vols.). Johns Hopkins Center for Civil Society Studies.

Singer, A. (2008). *Charity in Islamic societies*. Cambridge University Press.

Smith, J., Karides, M., Becker, M., Brunelle, D., Chase-Dunn, C., & Della Porta, D. (2014). *Global democracy and the world social forums*. Paradigm Publishers.

Soskis, B. (2020). A history of associational life and the nonprofit sector in the United States. In W. W. Powell & P. Bromley (Eds.), *The nonprofit sector: A research handbook* (3rd ed., pp. 23–80). Stanford University Press.

Taylor, P. J. (2004). The new geography of global civil society: NGOs in the world city network. *Globalizations, 1*(2), 265–277.

Tocqueville, A. (1838). *Democracy in America*. George Dearborn.

Trinningham, J. S. (1998). *The Sufi orders in Islam*. Oxford University Press.

Tsu, Y.-Y. (1912). *The spirit of Chinese philanthropy: A study in mutual aid*. Columbia University Press.

Tumanova, A. S. (2011). *Self-organization of the Russian public in the final third of the 18th – early 20th centuries*. ROSSPEN.

Union of International Associations. (1914). *The union of international associations: A world center*. Union of International Associations.

von Glahn, R. (1993). Community and welfare: Chu Hsi's community granary in theory and practice. In R. P. Hymes & C. Schirokauer (Eds.), *Ordering the world: Approaches to state and society in sung dynasty China* (pp. 221–254). University of California Press.

Wang, M., & Xu, Y. (2010). Foundations in China. *The China Nonprofit Review, 2*(1), 19–51.

White, L. C. (1968). *International non-governmental organizations: Their purposes, methods, and accomplishments*. Greenwood Press.

Wilson, S. G. (1996). Voluntary associations: An overview. In J. S. Kloppenborg & S. G. Wilson (Eds.), *Voluntary associations in the Graeco-Roman world* (pp. 1–15). Routledge.

Woodberry, R. D. (2012). The missionary roots of liberal democracy. *American Political Science Review, 106*(2), 244–274.

Zhou, Q., & Zeng, G. (2006). *A short history of Chinese charity*. People's Press.

1.2
COMMUNICATION FOR DEVELOPMENT AND SOCIAL CHANGE

Jan Servaes

Introduction

The COVID-19 pandemic and climate change are just two of the major problems we face today. The COVID-19 pandemic forced individuals and societies to reconsider mobility and interpersonal communication practices. The potential problem of lingering health problems is huge, with isolation, lack of access and changed daily routines. In addition, the COVID-19 pandemic may cause long-term mental health issues, not to mention economic, financial and social hardship for communities and nations.

Climate change may not only lead to the permanent flooding of low-lying regions, the disruption of a potable water supply to millions around the world as the ice packs in the mountains shrink and deplete the water reserves of major population centers or to the decline in oil and gas supplies as hydrocarbon reserves peak and the price of energy increases exponentially. It also causes, directly or indirectly, deep fractures in world trade and commerce resulting in political tensions and armed conflict among religious, ethnic and cultural communities across the world. Ending extreme poverty is impossible without tackling climate change.

How do we build consensus and muster the altruistic intent of the present generation to consume less, to de-escalate conflict, to build a more just and harmonious society and to make sure that future generations inherit a habitable planet?

The tried and tested methods of agriculture extension, social mobilization and multilateral negotiation are unlikely to succeed on their own as these systemic problems grow in severity and people submit to innate human instincts for self-preservation and compete even more keenly for rapidly dwindling natural resources, ratchet up violence, hoard energy and food supplies and close markets to international commerce. We do not have appropriate strategies to begin addressing these 'new' and highly complex challenges.

At the 2012 edition of the World Economic Forum in Davos, Switzerland, the background report on the global risks our world faces clearly stated that three common, crosscutting observations emerged from the varied groups of experts consulted (World Economic Forum, 2012, p. 49):

- Decision-makers need to improve understanding of incentives that will improve collaboration in response to global risks.
- Trust, or lack of trust, is perceived to be a crucial factor in how risks may manifest themselves. In particular, this refers to confidence, or lack thereof, in leaders, in the systems which ensure

public safety and in the tools of communication that are revolutionizing how we share and digest information.
- Communication and information sharing on risks must be improved by introducing greater transparency about uncertainty and conveying it to the public in a meaningful way.

In other words, more and more, one considers communication to be crucial to effectively tackle the major problems of today. Hence, the question we need to address is: Is there a right communication strategy?

CDSC for whom and for what?

Communication for development and social change (CDSC) has started to address the specific concerns and issues such as food security, rural development and livelihood, natural resource management and environment, poverty reduction, equity and gender and information and communication technologies (ICTs). However, perspectives on sustainability, participation and culture in communication changed over time in line with the evolution of development approaches and trends and the need for effective applications of communication methods and tools to solve new issues and priorities. In other words, more analysis, discussion and research remain needed.

In the social and communication sciences, development has traditionally been associated with 'development problems' that occurred in 'developing countries.' It is only since the late 1980s and early 1990s that the concept of development was gradually replaced by 'social change' to highlight the global and universal importance of the issue.

The study of CDSC has therefore been through several paradigmatic changes. From the modernization and growth theory to the dependency approach and the multiplicity or participatory model, these new traditions of discourse are characterized by a turn toward local communities as targets for research and debate, on the one hand, and the search for an understanding of the complex relationships between globalization and localization, on the other hand.

This history has been explained and detailed in "Communication for Development. One World, Multiple Cultures" (Servaes, 1999). It distinguishes between three general development paradigms (modernization, dependency and multiplicity), which were narrowed down to two communication paradigms: diffusion versus participatory communication.

Social change (or development) can be described as a significant change of structured social action or of the culture in a given society, community or context. Such a broad definition could be further specified on the basis of a number of 'dimensions' of social change: space (micro, meso, macro), time (short, medium, long term), speed (slow, incremental, evolutionary versus fast, fundamental, revolutionary), direction (forward or backward), content (socio-cultural, psychological, sociological, organizational, anthropological, economic and so forth) and impact (peaceful versus violent) (Servaes, 2011).

The early 21st-century 'global' world, in general as well as in its distinct regional, national and local entities, is confronted with multifaceted economic and financial crises but also social, cultural, ideological, moral, political, ethnic, ecological and security crises. Previously held traditional modernization and dependency perspectives have become more difficult to support because of the growing interdependency of regions, nations and communities in our globalized world.

The conclusion that can be drawn from late 20th- and early 21st-century reconceptualizations and reorientations of development and social change is that while income, productivity and gross national product are still essential aspects of human development, they are not the sum total of human existence. Just as this has important implications for the way social change and development can be conceptualized, so too does it present opportunities for how the role and place of communication in development and social change processes can be perceived.

Sustainable development

In the last twenty years, sustainable development has emerged as one of the most prominent development paradigms. In 1987, the World Commission on Environment and Development (WCED) concluded that "sustainable development is development that meets the needs of the present without compromising the ability of future generations to meet their own needs." Sustainable development is seen as a means of enhancing decision-making so that it provides a more comprehensive assessment of the many multidimensional problems society faces. What is required is an evaluation framework for categorizing programs, projects, policies and/or decisions as having sustainability potential.

Four dimensions are generally recognized as the 'pillars' of sustainable development: economic, environmental, social and cultural.

> The essence of sustainability therefore, is to take the contextual features of economy, society, and environment – the uncertainty, the multiple competing values, and the distrust among various interest groups – as givens and go on to design a process that guides concerned groups to seek out and ask the right questions as a preventative approach to environmentally and socially regrettable undertakings.
>
> (Flint, 2007, p. IV)

Although there is no formal definition of 'sustainability,' it continues to remain popular in various political, social and economic discourses, particularly those of environmental groups, as a call to action to raise awareness around the current depletion of finite natural resources (for interesting overviews, see Agyeman, 2013; Blewitt, 2008; Dalal-Clayton & Sadler, 2014; Espinosa & Walker, 2011; Farley & Smith, 2014; Foster, 2015; McAnany, 2012; Polk, 2015; Servaes, 2013a, 2013b; Servaes & Malikhao, 2007; UN, 2012).

Recently, the term 'resiliency' has been used by a variety of researchers, policy makers and community organizers as a more relevant supplant to the term sustainability in the context of development. Hopkins (2008, p. 54) defines resilience as "the capacity of a system to absorb disturbance and reorganize while undergoing change, so as to retain essentially the same function, structure, identity and feedbacks." Zolli and Healy (2012, p. 7) confirm: "the capacity of a system, enterprise, or a person to maintain its core purpose and integrity in the face of dramatically changed circumstances." Resilience strategies almost always use feedback mechanisms to determine when a disruption is nearing. In addition, resilience is defined as

> the capacity of individuals, communities, and systems to survive, adapt, and grow in the face of stress and shocks, and even transform when conditions require it. Building resilience is about making people, communities, and systems better prepared to withstand catastrophic events – both natural and manmade – and able to bounce back more quickly and emerge stronger from these shocks and stresses.
>
> (Rockefeller Foundation, 2013)

This refers to three dimensions: the ability to resist, cope and bounce back in the face of disturbance; the capacity to adapt to change and uncertainty; and the capacity for transformation (Brown, 2016, pp. 10–11). Thus, strategies of resilience might be developed for economic, social and ecologic systems. There is no doubt that current global problems such as climate change and the economic crises make the call for sustainability and resiliency from different groups more urgent. The Thai philosopher and monk Phra Dhammapidhok (Payutto, 1998) points out that sustainable development in a Western perspective lacks the human development dimension. He states that the Western ideology emphasizes 'competition.' Therefore, the concept of 'compromising' is used in the WCED definition. Compromising means lessening the needs of all parties. If the other parties do not want to compromise, you have to compromise your own needs, and that will lead to frustration. Development won't be sustained if people are not happy. He consequently reaches the conclusion that the Western perception of and road to sustainability, based on Western ethics, leads development into a cul-de-sac.

From a Buddhist perspective, sustainability concerns ecology, economy and evolvability. The concept 'evolvability' means the potential of human beings to develop themselves into less selfish persons. The main core of sustainable development is to encourage and convince human beings to live in harmony with their environment, not to control or destroy it. If humans have been socialized correctly, they will express the correct attitude towards nature and the environment and act accordingly. Dhammapidhok argues that

> a correct relation system of developed mankind is the acceptance of the fact that human-beings are part of the existence of nature and relate to its ecology. Human-beings should develop themselves to have a higher capacity to help their fellows and other species in the natural domain; to live in a harmonious way and lessen exploitations in order to contribute to a happier world.
>
> (Payutto, 1998, p. 189)

This holistic approach of humans relates to cultural development in three dimensions (Sivaraksa, 2010):

- Behaviors and lifestyles which do not harm nature;
- Minds in line with (Eastern) ethics, stability of mind, motivation, etc., to see other creatures as companions;
- Wisdom includes knowledge and understanding, attitude, norms and values in order to live in harmony with nature.

No universal development model

Different perspectives – based on both 'Western' and 'Eastern' philosophical starting points – have resulted in a more holistic and integrated vision of sustainable development or social change. A unifying theme is that there is no universal development model. Development is an integral, multi-dimensional and dialectic process that differs from society to society, community to community, context to context. In other words, each society and community must attempt to delineate its own strategy to sustainable development, starting with the resources and 'capitals' available (not only physical, financial and environmental but also human, social, institutional, etc.), and considering the needs and views of the people concerned.

Sustainable development implies a participatory, multistakeholder approach to policy making and implementation; mobilizing public and private resources for development; and making use of the knowledge, skills and energy of all social groups concerned with the future of the planet and its people.

Pursuit of this kind of sustainable development requires:

- A political system that secures effective citizen participation in decision-making;
- An economic system that provides for solutions for the tensions arising from disharmonious development;
- A production system that respects the obligation to preserve the ecological base for development;
- A technological system that fosters sustainable patterns of trade and finance;

- An administrative system that is flexible and has the capacity for self-correction;
- A communication system that gets this organized and accepted by all parties concerned at all levels of society.

Within this framework, communication and culture play a strategic and fundamental role by (a) contributing to the interplay of different development factors, (b) improving the sharing of knowledge and information and (c) encouraging the participation of all concerned.

Empowerment

Development is shaped and done by people – not for people. In order for people to be able to do so, they need to understand 'how the system works.' Therefore, development or social change should be equated with empowerment: the ability of people to influence the wider system and take control of their lives (Friedman, 1992).

It's obvious that people cannot do this entirely on their own. It also requires effort on the part of development change partners (agencies and agents) to help solve some of the dysfunctions in the system and create the enabling conditions. Therefore, one argues that communication needs to be explicitly built into development plans and social change projects to ensure that a mutual sharing/learning process is facilitated. Such communicative sharing is deemed the best guarantee for creating successful transformations.

The new starting point is thus examining the processes of 'bottom-up' change, focusing on self-development of local communities. The basic assumption is that there are no countries or communities that function completely autonomously or completely self-sufficiently, nor are there any nations whose development is exclusively determined by external factors. Every society is dependent on the other in one way or another, both in form and in degree.

Consequently, we have defined CDSC as:

> Communication for development and social change is the nurturing of knowledge aimed at creating a consensus for action that considers the interests, needs and capacities of all concerned. It is thus a social process, which has as its ultimate objective sustainable development at distinct levels of society. Communication media and ICTs are important tools in achieving social change, but their use is not an end in itself. Interpersonal communication, traditional, group and social media must also play a fundamental role.

The resiliency and sustainability of CDSC processes

The field of communication for social change is vast, and the models supporting it are as different as their underlying ideologies. Generally speaking we see two approaches: one aims to produce a common understanding among all the participants in a development initiative by implementing a policy or a development project, that is, the top-down model. The other emphasizes engaging the grassroots in making decisions that enhance their own lives, or the bottom-up model. Despite the diversity of approaches, there is a consensus in the early 21st century on the need for grassroots participation in bringing about change at both social and individual levels (Besette, 2004; Servaes et al., 1996).

We have subdivided communication strategies for development and social change into five levels (see Servaes, 2007b, 2013b, 2020; Servaes & Malikhao, 2017):

(a) Behavior change communication (BCC) (mainly interpersonal communication);
(b) Mass communication (MC) (community media, mass media, online media and ICTs);

(c) Advocacy communication (AC) (interpersonal and/or mass communication);
(d) Participatory communication (PC) (interpersonal communication, community media and social media);
(e) Communication for structural and sustainable social change (CSSC) (interpersonal communication, participatory communication, mass communication and ICTs).

Interpersonal communication and MC form the bulk of what is being studied in the mainstream discipline of communication science and the subdiscipline of health communication (Malikhao, 2012, 2016). BCC is mainly concerned with short-term individual changes in attitudes and behavior. It can be further subdivided into perspectives that explain individual behavior, interpersonal behavior and community or societal behavior.

BCC, MC, and AC, though useful in themselves, will not be able to create sustainable development. Therefore, PC and CSSC are more concerned about long-term sustained change at different levels of society.

Looking at desired or expected outcomes, one could think of four broad headings:

(a) Approaches that attempt to change attitudes (through information dissemination, awareness raising, public relations, etc.);
(b) Behavioral change approaches (focusing on changes of individual behavior, interpersonal behavior and/or community and societal behavior);
(c) Advocacy approaches (primarily targeted at policy-makers and decision-makers at all levels and sectors of society);
(d) Communication for structural and sustainable change approaches (which could be top-down, horizontal or bottom-up).

At each level different perspectives on the role and place of information and CDSC may apply. No single media is better than the other. Often multimedia approaches are considered the most effective. However, change is seldom the result of exposure to media alone. Each type of media has to be assessed in its specific cultural context and has strengths and weaknesses. Therefore, each type should be assessed on a case-by-case basis: interpersonal communication versus mass media use; 'old' versus 'new' media; the role and place of community media; the role and impact of ICTs; etc.

As mentioned, the first three approaches, though useful by themselves, are in isolation not capable of creating sustainable development. Sustainable social change can only be achieved in combination with and incorporating aspects of the wider environment that influences (and constrains) structural and sustainable change.

These aspects include structural and conjunctural factors (e.g., history, migration, conflicts); policy and legislation; service provision; education systems; institutional and organizational factors (e.g., bureaucracy, corruption); cultural factors (e.g., religion, norms and values); socio-demographic factors (e.g., ethnicity, class); socio-political factors; socio-economic factors; and the physical environment.

All these aspects need to be transformed through policy, legislative, institutional and cultural processes, which may lead to structural and sustainable change at the levels of the public and private/commercial sector and civil society. Each society and community must attempt to delineate its own strategy to sustainable development starting with the resources and 'capitals' available (not only physical, financial and environmental but also human, social, institutional, etc.) and considering needs and views of the people concerned.

Thirteen major CDSC approaches

We counted (see Servaes, 2007a, 2007b, 2008, 2013a) thirteen different CDSC approaches which currently remain used and applied (see Table 1.2.1). Some of these are more traditional, hierarchical and linear, some more participatory and interactive. Most contain elements of both. From an

Table 1.2.1 Major communication for development and social change approaches

1. Extension/diffusion of innovations as a development communications approach
   Modernization
   Diffusion
   Top-down

   To inform the audience or to persuade a behavioral change in a predetermined way

2. Network development and documentation
   Modernization
   Diffusion
   Top-down

   Computerized satellite telecommunication Internet
   Distance education

3. Information and communication technologies for development (ICT4D)
   Modernization/dependency
   Diffusion
   Top-down

   Internet
   Telecenters
   Digital divide (ITU)

4. Training/education and capacity building/strengthening
   Modernization/dependency
   Diffusion
   Top-down

   Professional/institutional development
   Technical assistance

5. Social marketing
   Modernization/dependency
   Diffusion
   Top-down

   Social applications of commercial marketing techniques

6. Edutainment (EE)
   Modernization/dependency/multiplicity
   Diffusion/participatory
   Top-down

   Hybrid forms of education/information and entertainment
   From awareness to attitude change

7. Health communication
   Modernization/dependency/multiplicity
   Diffusion/participatory
   Top-down/horizontal

   From cure to prevention (WHO)
   Mixed strategies determined by the problem and context (UNICEF, UNAIDS)

8. Information, education and communication (IEC)
   Modernization/dependency/multiplicity
   Diffusion/participatory
   Top-down/horizontal

   Population and family planning (UNFPA)
   From attitude to behavior change

9. Institution building
   Modernization/dependency/multiplicity
   Diffusion/participatory
   Top-down/horizontal

   Infrastructure building
   Policy and planning (UNESCO)
   Advocacy

10. Knowledge, attitudes and practices (KAP)
    Modernization/dependency/multiplicity
    Diffusion/participatory
    Top-down/horizontal

    Knowledge and attitude in enabling environments

11. Development support communication (DSC)
    Modernization/dependency/multiplicity
    Diffusion/participatory
    Top-down/horizontal/bottom-up

    Needs assessment/information gathering
    Decision-making/strategy development
    Implementation
    Evaluation (FAO, UNICEF)

12. HIV/AIDS community approach
    Modernization/dependency/multiplicity
    Diffusion/participatory
    Top-down/horizontal/bottom-up

    UNAIDS
    Contextual, integrated strategic approach

13. Community participation
    Dependency/multiplicity
    Participatory
    Horizontal/bottom-up

    Sustainable and resilient development
    Active participation/advocacy
    Structural change

epistemological and ontological perspective, that doesn't always make sense, but in practice that seems to be a given.

It should also be emphasized that any of these CDSC approaches have to be carefully assessed for a specific context and particular cultural environment.

In sum

CDSC theory and practice have been changing over time in line with the evolution of development approaches and trends and the need for effective applications of communication methods and tools to solve new issues and priorities.

At the end of the 1980s the multiplicity and participatory approach became a key feature in the applications of communication for sustainable development. In line with this vision, CDSC is about dialogue, participation and the sharing of knowledge and information. It takes into account the needs and capacities of all concerned through the integrated and participatory use of communication processes, media and channels. It works by:

- Facilitating participation: giving a voice to different stakeholders to engage in the decision-making process.
- Making information understandable and meaningful. It includes explaining and conveying information for the purpose of training, exchange experience and sharing know-how and technology.
- Fostering policy acceptance: enacting and promoting policies that increase rural people's access to services and resources.

Within this framework, communication is viewed as a social process that is not just confined to media or to messages. CDSC methods are appropriate in dealing with the complex issues of sustainable development in order to:

- Improve access to knowledge and information to all sectors of society and especially to vulnerable and marginalized groups.
- Foster effective management and coordination of development initiatives through bottom-up planning.
- Address equity issues through networking and social platforms influencing policy-making.
- Encourage changes in behavior and lifestyles, promoting sustainable consumption patterns through sensitization and education of large audiences.
- Promote the sustainable use of natural resources, considering multiple interests and perspectives and supporting collaborative management through consultation and negotiation.
- Increase awareness and community mobilization related to social and environmental issues.
- Ensure economic and employment opportunities through timely and adequate information.
- Solve multiple conflicts ensuring dialogue among different components in a society.

References

Agyeman, J. (2013). *Introducing just sustainabilities. Policy, planning, and practice*. Zed Books.
Besette, G. (2004). *Involving the community: A guide to participatory development communication*. Southbound/IDRC.
Blewitt, J. (Ed.). (2008). *Community, empowerment and sustainable development*. Green Books.
Brown, K. (2016). *Resilience, development and global change*. Routledge.
Dalal-Clayton, B., & Sadler, B. (2014). *Sustainability appraisal. A sourcebook and reference guide to international experience*. Routledge/Earthscan.
Espinosa, A., & Walker, J. (2011). *A complexity approach to sustainability. Theory and application*. Imperial College Press.

Farley, H., & Smith, Z. (2014). *Sustainability. If it's everything, is it nothing?* Routledge.
Flint, W. (2007). *Sustainability manifesto. Exploring sustainability: Getting inside the concept*. Retrieved July 21, 2021, from www.eeeee.net/sd_manifesto.htm
Foster, J. (2015). *After sustainability. Denial, hope, retrieval*. Routledge/Earthscan.
Friedmann, J. (1992). *Empowerment: The politics of alternative development*. Blackwell.
Hopkins, R. (2008). *The transition handbook: From oil dependency to local resilience*. Green Books.
Malikhao, P. (2012). *Sex in the village. Culture, religion and HIV/AIDS in Thailand*. Southbound & Silkworm Publishers.
Malikhao, P. (2016). *Effective health communication for sustainable development*. Nova Publishers.
McAnany, E. G. (2012). *Saving the world: A brief history of communication for development and social change*. University of Illinois Press.
Payutto, P. (1998). *Sustainable development*. Buddhadham Foundation.
Polk, E. (2015). *Communicating global to local resiliency. A case study of the transition movement*. Lexington Books.
Rockefeller Foundation. (2013). *100 resilient cities*. Retrieved March 29, 2016, from www.100resilientcities.org/#/-_/
Servaes, J. (1999). *Communication for development: One world, multiple cultures*. Hampton.
Servaes, J. (2007a). Harnessing the UN system into a common approach on communication for development. *The International Communication Gazette, 69*(6), 483–507.
Servaes, J. (Ed.). (2007b). *Communication for development. Making a difference – A WCCD background study*. World Congress on Communication for Development: Lessons, Challenges and the Way Forward, World Bank, pp. 209–292.
Servaes, J. (Ed.). (2008). *Communication for development and social change*. Sage.
Servaes, J. (2011). *Social change*. Oxford Bibliographies Online (OBO), Oxford University Press. www.oxfordbibliographiesonline.com/display/id/obo-9780199756841-0063
Servaes, J. (Ed.). (2013a). *Sustainable development and green communication. African and Asian perspectives*. Palgrave.
Servaes, J. (Ed.). (2013b). *Sustainability, participation and culture in communication. Theory and praxis*. Intellect-University of Chicago Press.
Servaes, J. (Ed.). (2020). *Handbook on communication for development and social change* (Vols. 1 + 2). Springer.
Servaes, J., Jacobson, T., & White, S. (Eds.). (1996). *Participatory communication for social change*. Sage.
Servaes, J., & Malikhao, P. (2007). *Communication and sustainable development*, FAO, Communication and sustainable development: Selected papers, FAO, pp. 1–38.
Servaes, J., & Malikhao, P. (2017, September–December). The role and place of communication for sustainable social change (CSSC). *International Social Science Journal, LXV*, 217/218, 171–184. Wiley & UNESCO. ISSN: 0020–8701.
Sivaraksa, S. (2010). *The wisdom of sustainability. Buddhist economics for the 21st century*. Silkworm Books.
United Nations Secretary-General's High-Level Panel on Global Sustainability. (2012). *Resilient people, resilient planet: A future worth choosing*. UN. ISBN: 978-92-1-055304-9.
World Commission on Environment and Development (WCED). (1987). *Our common future*. Published as Annex to General Assembly document A/42/427, Development and International Co-operation: Environment. UN.
World Economic Forum. (2012). *Global risks 2012* (7th ed.). An Initiative of the Risk Response Network. WEF.
Zolli, A., & Healy, M. (2012). *Resilience: Why things bounce back*. Free Press.

1.3
NGO-IZATION OF CIVIL SOCIETY

Sabine Lang

Introduction

A diverse and active civil society is frequently invoked as the most important guarantor of late-modern democracies. Publicly engaged citizens and civil society organizations are perceived to be the most potent shields against hollowing out democratic institutions and shifts towards illiberalism. What parties were to the 20th century, civil society is credited to be to the 21st – a democratizing force that holds power accountable, organizes citizen participation, and in the process fortifies democracy. Likewise, in authoritarian and totalitarian regimes, civil society is perceived to be the single most pronounced threat to regime survival. As substantial responsibility rests on a functioning civil society, however, its essential support structure, its internal dynamics, and its direct and indirect effects remain the object of academic debates and political controversy.

Most generally, civil society serves as a blanket term for activities undertaken in a sphere between the state, the economy, and citizens' private lives. Ideally, in this civic space, citizens form associations that work towards a common good. Neither the notion of associations nor that of a common good are, however, well-defined and settled concepts. The kinds of associations that dominate civil society have been changing over the course of the 20th century (Skocpol, 2003), moving from early century membership-based organizations to more "managed' organizational forms without members. With the advent of web-based civic mobilizations in the early 21st century, moreover, engagement in and with associations has moved increasingly online, resulting in more targeted and fluctuating forms of engagement while at the same time widening audiences and increasing civil spaces for voice and activism. This ambivalent trend has led to worries that civil society erodes and gives way to fractured and inward-looking civic bubbles, resulting in publics that resemble reified echo chambers instead of associative and communicative spheres. The idea of a common good, likewise, faces challenges as late modern societies, for example, harbor contested notions of human rights and their Northern- and Western-centric normative underpinnings. Along similar lines, what is civil about civil society is disputed, manifesting, for example, in the tension between hate speech and free speech. An additional site of contestation is the presumed independence of civil society: While civil society is conceived of as an arena of nonstate, noneconomic, and nonprivate communication and negotiation about how citizens live together in their polity, it does receive considerable funding from governments, business, and private donors, and its actors increasingly look towards business models in order to advance their public-facing goals (Mitchell et al., 2020; Prakash & Gugerty, 2009).

The most profound and ongoing structural rearrangement of civil society since the late 20th century is its NGO-ization (Lang, 1997, 2013). Following the social movement decades of the 1960 and 1970s, NGO-ization refers to a process "by which social movements professionalize, bureaucratize, and institutionalize in vertically structured policy-outcome-oriented organizations that focus on generating issue-specific and, to some degree, marketable expert knowledge or services" (Lang, 2013, p. 64). NGO-ization thus is a heuristic term that describes the pull of loosely networked groups from the local to the transnational level into a specific set of formalized structures. While consequences and effects of NGO-ization are disputed, an NGO-ized civil society has in fact become the globalized and naturalized form of civil society engagement.

In the following, I will first address the NGO-ization of civil society conceptually, then discuss the logics that emanate from NGO-ization. Third and finally, I will present current challenges to NGO-ization and an assessment of its consequences for nonprofit communication.

The NGO-ization of civil society: a conceptual framework

The NGO-ization of civil society involves two parallel and mutually reinforcing processes by which (1) civil society is becoming equated with the nongovernmental sector and (2) civically engaged groups experience a functional pull to institutionalize, professionalize, and bureaucratize in order to organize their survival (Lang, 1997). Broadly aligning with the post–Cold War era in the global North when civil society was perceived to be the widely acclaimed guarantor for liberal democracies, NGO-ization as a "sensitizing concept" acknowledges that nonprofits have a key role in what the Westminster Foundation in 1992 described as "creating civil society. Their focus on mobilizing resources, providing services, undertaking research and public education, while also providing advocacy for membership organizations and people's associations, gives NGOs an unparalleled liaison role between civil society and government" (op. cit. Henderson, 2003, p. 74).

Civic engagement has scaled up from mostly local and national sites to transnational forms of mobilizations as international organizations such as the United Nations or the World Health Organization have created discursive arenas for input from nongovernmental actors. At the same time, NGOs experienced an increased need to secure funding and organize influence. Thus, social movements 'learned' to reduce or abandon traditional movement repertoires that involved loosely organized and horizontally dispersed actors and public contestations. Instead, movements started to redefine their engagement practices along professionalized, bureaucratized, and institutionalized lines of work. Incentives for NGO-ization were multifaceted: Professionalization occurred as the authority of civil society expertise received recognition vis-à-vis the authority of ethical or moral positions. At the same time, receiving monetary compensation for substantial work and time commitments appeared only logical in increasingly neoliberal settings where many functions of the welfare state were offloaded to organized civil society. Thus, involvement in movement activism turned into professionalized careers. Activists turned into NGO workers whose expertise was much sought after. At the same time, project-based funding produced precarity (Ana, 2019; Krause, 2014). Bureaucratic pull factors came on the heels of professionalization: As social movements interacted with governments and private donors in order to receive funding for specific projects, the pull to legally incorporate and operate in hierarchical structures became stronger. Bureaucratized and vertical structures needed to be in place that allowed for smooth operations and effective organizational practices. Tax exemptions incentivized incorporations as a legal charity, but also resulted in NGOs establishing particular modes of governance. Finally, the pull to NGO-ize had an institutional dimension, as governments increasingly relied on civil society expertise and invited groups to the table in extended governance settings. Having a formal structure in place that allowed for consistent messaging and continuity in representation of civic interests thus presented itself as a logical consequence of successfully raising social movement voice.

In sum: As NGO-ized civil societies reoriented their priorities towards meeting the needs of funders more than those of supporters, they faced demands to adopt business-style logics of operation, resulting in a rationalized organization, bureaucratized forms of budgeting and reporting, as well as hierarchical internal structures. NGO-ization was not cost-neutral to social mobilizations. It affected strategies and techniques of advocacy and redefined relationships with publics, turning from a reliance on activist involvement and/or membership to a mix of internal structural fortification combined with more fluid and issue-based outreach, facilitated by social media. This move from collective to connective action (Bennett & Segerberg, 2013) also brought about particular modes of accountability and legitimacy of NGOs, gearing accountability towards funders and drawing legitimacy from participation in institutional policy settings.

Effects of an NGO-ized civil society

The effects of NGO-ized civil societies have been studied globally from West and East-Central Europe (Lang, 2013; Jacobsson & Saxonberg, 2013; Ana, 2019) to the Americas (Alvarez, 2009), the Middle East (Herrold, 2016), and Africa and in policy fields ranging from women's and LGBTQ mobilizations (Lang, 1997; Paternotte, 2016) to development studies (Chandhoke, 2003) and community-based natural resource management (Crosman et al., 2022) and many other policy fields (Banks et al., 2015; Thiel, 2017). Concern with the limited capacity of the NGO sector as the primary actor in, and carrier of, civil society focuses primarily on the organizational dynamics that a project-based civil society cultivates, on the sector's relationship with donors and their effects on accountability and legitimacy, and on relationships with their publics.

Project culture–based civil society

NGOs have learned to adapt their goals to institutional norms of feasibility within their respective field's knowledge, language, and overall terms of trade (Lang, 2013, p. 72; Banks et al., 2015). Managerial practices established within a shared social space lead to the production of what Monika Krause calls "the good project" as a commodity that NGOs sell and in which the beneficiaries "become part of" this commodification of civil society (Krause, 2014, p. 4). As donors and other stakeholders provide funds only for specific projects, showcasing short-term results becomes paramount, and admitting to failure is not an option. Project-based NGO work increasingly relies on particular internal and operational mechanisms that are captured in process tracing techniques such as the logframe (Krause, 2014, p. 70) or in other new public management operational modes (Sanchez Salgado, 2010, p. 527). The logframe suggests a form of rationality and dependability on clear outcome criteria that NGO work on the ground often defies. It projects results-based management strategies and compatibilities in outcome evaluation that wants to make civil society development 'measurable', but in the process often reduces measurability to quantifiable, mostly economic or government-led social data points. Accountability thus becomes directly related to the "marketiziation of the nonprofit sector" (Eikenberry & Kluver, 2004, also Sandberg et al., 2020). Broader and more radical social change goals that would address systemic and institutional factors of inequalities, climate change, or other pressing social challenges tend not to fit this project-based logic. Within a market of projects, moreover, NGOs are pitted against each other in competing for grants and in effect are often forced to operate highly individualized. While this increases survival anxiety and makes organizational reproduction a central internal goal, it at the same time leads to 'association overload' – "the creation of civic landscapes that display layers of NGOs, alliances, and networks" that often replicate each other's work (Lang, 2021, also Herrold & Atia, 2016). NGOs thus are forced to calibrate their mission in terms of a set of factors that are not necessarily aligned well with the needs of their constituencies or with the broader goal of empowering civil society.

Relationship to donors and stakeholders

NGOs produce their projects as 'products' in a setting in which donors are turned into their prima facie consumers (Krause, 2014, p. 4). Thus, private and public donor demands become central to the operational logics of NGOs (Heiss & Kelley, 2017). Broader economic and political constraints lead to a "principled instrumentalism" in which NGOs "pursue their principled objectives within the economic constraints and political opportunity structures imposed by their external environments" (Mitchell & Schmitz, 2014, p. 489). The European Union funding structures for civil society is a case in point: Top-down EU funding calls for proposals, and tenders structure NGO work in three ways: shaping priorities, project goals, and public outreach. First, they narrow civil society engagements of NGOs to a specific set of intergovernmental priorities that are defined by EU institutions and member states. Second, the funds that are available for a specific sector spark its growth and "[lead] to goal-displacement at the micro-level" (Sanchez Salgado, 2010, p. 526). Engholm et al. identify it as a "*property*, a resource that must be gained from the external environment and that is of strategic importance for an organization's survival" (Engholm et al., 2020, p. 6). This focus on donor rationales, thirdly, prevents "citizen's appropriation of the policy process" (ibid, p. 527) and minimizes active citizen engagement. Thus, the impetus of NGOs in Western democracies is to contribute to democratic societies "by performing civic relations as well as maintaining the values of democracy, liberty, equality, diversity, participation and solidarity" (Oliveira, 2017, p. 325). Performing NGO means situating your organization within power struggles in which donor and institutional stakeholder rationales tend to prevail over constituencies and publics.

Relationship to constituencies and publics

Being a legitimate voice at the table of governance processes involves a professionalized habitus that is able to reframe systemic social, economic, and political challenges into solvable problems. Civil society organizations that lack interest in or the capability to do such constant reframing are frequently marginalized (Lang, 2013, p. 200). Communication strategies based on expertise, however, while they might bolster institutional legitimacy, could come at the expense of organizing broader public engagement and political activism.

NGOs' focus on donors, moreover, also incentivizes a reorientation of communication from publicity to public relations, both in an organization's web-based presentation and in its attempt to be present in legacy media. Whereas only very few highly visible NGOs in the 1990s made it into the legacy media, professionalized news operations with trained communication staff altered the landscape around the turn of the millennium. NGO communication professionalized as they are forced to increase communication and deliver different types of communication (policy reports, press releases, donor reports) to different audiences (Powers, 2018, p. 7). Managing their brand (ibid.) became an area of increasing attention of the NGO sector. Focus on self-image and on favorable media portrayals, however, binds resources that deter from public outreach in a more inclusive and participatory sense. Organizing publicness by making issues known to wider audiences and organizing these audiences into powerful citizen voices are thus the most pressing challenges for an NGO-ized civil society, and all too often they are the ones that are least 'fundable' in the eyes of donors. The call for rethinking NGOs' role in public engagement processes thus has become louder across policy fields (f.e. Tortajada, 2016; Crosman et al., 2022).

NGO-ization and nonprofit communication: the path ahead

Nonprofit communication takes place in an increasingly fractured public sphere. Today's civil society actors need to signal not just to the traditional tripartite of government/business, media, and individual supporters, but they operate in a complex communication environment where audiences are fragmented, fluctuating, and fickle. As traditional membership bases have eroded and clicktivism challenges continuities of investment in social justice causes, NGOs have come to see donors as their prime audience, and they have reoriented communication practices accordingly.

There are, however, multiple indicators that this shift has run its course. The path ahead for civil society demands NGOs critically engage with their image and identity as professionalized and donor-oriented actors in a shrinking civic space. Countering the limiting effects of NGO-ization by way of (1) utilizing new technologies to democratize outreach and build buy-in from audiences; (2) politicizing the limitations of donor and government accountabilities and instead organizing public engagement accountabilities; and (3) building alliances across NGOs to upend the donor-driven logics of competition will allow the NGO sector to engage in what its civic mission is: to organize associative spaces in which we can envision and develop transformative agendas for social and political change – in other words: be political citizens.

Using technology for building publics

Technological changes, and in particular the rise of social media, have helped the NGO sector to diversify communication strategies, but at the same time web-based technology has massively altered the relationship of NGOs with their publics. The question of how to control their brand while at the same time signaling inclusivity and organizing interactive and participatory modes is confounding NGO communication strategists. On the upside, new technologies and social media allow NGOs to transcend the straitjacket of purely donor- and donation-oriented modes of communication. Crowd-sourced campaigns, such as Amnesty International's efforts to harness the competence of volunteers in order to document human rights violations in Darfur (Amnesty International, 2016) – in which on the first day alone some 4500 digital volunteers analyzed over 33,000 square kilometers of satellite imagery – speak to the potential of social media in helping NGOs with their outreach to publics and with democratizing advocacy. Here, the NGO (Amnesty International) deliberately embraced stepping into a coordinating role and used the digital media expertise of their supporters to drive the political message. At the same time, the NGO built its supporter base by asking not for money, but for skills, time, and commitment to the cause. It is with campaigns like this that NGOs can counter the challenges emanating from single-instance clicktivism campaigns and use the political engagement of Generation Z to reinvigorate civil society.

Replacing donor and government accountabilities with public accountabilities

One of the issues in highly NGO-ized civil societies is that formal incorporation as a civil society actor comes with strings attached, usually in the form of limits to political action in order to not threaten the organization's status as a charity (Lang, 2013, p. 98). While some evidence shows that "nonprofits that foster nonpolitical civic participation are extending those activities in political directions" (Suarez, 2020, p. 498), the basic limitation remains that nonprofit law restricts NGO operations across the globe to nonpolitical activities and sanctions transgressions. In illiberal democracies and (semi-)authoritarian regimes, incorporation as an NGO goes hand-in-hand with government surveillance and increasingly rigid restrictions on 'foreign donations'. Most illiberal or autocratic states have passed new NGO laws over the past decade that curtail cooperation with 'foreign agents', add bureaucratic layers to NGO reporting, and ultimately limit the NGO workforce to the task of institutional reproduction (Herrold & Atia, 2016). And while donors occasionally reflect critically on past practices of financial allocations and offer to embrace stronger political messaging and methods for social justice, what is needed is a paradigm shift from donor accountability to public accountabilities, including funding mechanisms that "support, rather than erode, the political roots of civil society organizations" (Banks et al., 2015, p. 715). In particular, as governments and legislators lose credibility, the NGO sector needs to capitalize more on its identity as a trusted and somewhat 'selfless' source of information and advocacy (Powers, 2018, p. 8). NGOs still harbor the reputation of building "civic relations as a social communicative function" in which "the civic exercise of pursuing and seeking the common good" is performed (Oliveira, 2017, p. 324). NGO-ization thus could be used by NGOs themselves to articulate and politicize the very institutional logics that prevent or limit them from exercising their work towards the common good and from fulfilling their public accountabilities.

Building alliances across NGOs to help grow democratic publics

The NGO sector has been challenged in recent years by a flurry of seemingly 'direct democratic' organizational forms such as Avaaz or MoveOn.org that offer individuals ways to support causes without commitment to a particular NGO. While these platforms undoubtedly are able to mobilize effectively for some causes, they are a double-edged civic 'sword': As they ask for citizens' signature and/or money, they feed into neoliberal individualistic modes of the narcissistic self that bypasses organizational commitments and spreads its attention (and support) across myriad causes on the spur of a moment. The effect is detrimental to civil society: Instead of empowering NGOs to tackle global challenges such as institutional breakdown, party collapse, widening inequalities, and social injustice, these platforms provide surrogate empowerment in a 'civil society of ones' and feed the competitive race of established NGOs to get supporters' attention.

On the output side of successful campaigns, there is evidence that NGOs increasingly seek collaborators in order to provide the sustenance and institutional memory for long-term policy change. The Latin American experience suggests that as NGO-ized civil society "revealed limits for actually implementing hard-won policy gains, which requires public pressures, secured through changes in public opinion, not just through policy monitoring" (Alvarez, 2009, p. 178), the search for cross-sector and cross-movement collaborations increased. Frustration with the limited success of institutional advocacy of environmental NGOs also spurred new youth movements such as Fridays for Future – leading to NGOs collaborating and engaging in distributed activism with groups on the ground or youth movements (Vera & Herranz de la Casa, 2020).

The path forward of NGO-ized civil societies thus entails radical change. NGOs need to build and cultivate new membership bases, fight for being able to have a political voice, and replace donor and government accountability with innovative designs to strengthen public accountabilities. This is no verdict on NGOs' principled stance for equality. But it is an acknowledgment of the embeddedness of the sector's projects in global neoliberal alignments in which civil society has become accustomed to being managed in a highly individualized, commercialized, and semi-privatized form. If NGOs do not challenge their own embeddedness in these civil society structures, they will "remain unable to engage with transformative agendas that seek large-scale redistribution and the re-ordering of wealth and privilege" (Banks et al., 2014, p. 715). Today, the NGO operations of the richest men (this gendered term is valid here) globally have more financial capital and intervention power in the fields of health, education, development, and social justice than most public entities. NGO-ized civil society actors from local to transnational levels know best how dependence on preconfigured agendas distorts their operations and their vision for the future. Their future communicative agenda will need to include voicing those distortions.

References

Alvarez, S. (2009). Beyond NGO-ization? Reflections from Latin America. *Development, 52*(2), 175–184. https://doi.org/10.1057/dev.2009.23

Amnesty International. (2016, October 13). *Digital volunteers to expose Darfur human rights violations in 'revolutionary' crowd sourcing project*. www.amnesty.org/en/latest/news/2016/10/digital-volunteers-to-expose-darfur-human-rights-violations/

Ana, A. (2019). *The NGO-ization of social movements in neoliberal times: Contemporary feminisms in Romania and Bulgaria* (Ph.D. Thesis). Scuola Normale Superiore.

Banks, N., Hulme, D., & Edwards, M. (2015). NGOs, states, and donors revisited: Still too close for comfort? *World Development, 66*, 707–718. https://doi.org/10.1016/j.worlddev.2014.09.028

Bennett, W. L., & Segerberg, A. (2013). *The logic of connective action. Digital media and the personalization of contentious politics*. Cambridge University Press.

Chandhoke, N. (2003). *The conceits of civil society*. Oxford University Press.

Crosman, K. M., Singh, G. G., & Lang, S. (2022). Confronting complex accountability in conservation with communities. *Frontiers in Marine Science, 8*. doi:10.3389/fmars.2021.709423

Eikenberry, A. M., & Kluver, J. D. (2004). The marketization of the nonprofit sector: Civil society at risk? *Public Administration Review, 64*(2), 132–140. https://doi.org/10.1111/j.1540-6210.2004.00355

Engholm, L., Heyse, L., & Mourey, D. (2020). Civil society organization: The site of legitimizing the common good – a literature review. *VOLUNTAS, 31*, 1–18. https://doi.org/10.1007/s11266-019-00171-y

Heiss, A., & Kelley, J. (2017). Between a rock and a hard place: International NGOs and the dual pressures of donors and host governments. *Journal of Politics, 79*(2), 732–741. https://doi.org/10.1086/691218

Henderson, S. L. (2003). *Building democracy in contemporary Russia: Western support for grassroots organizations*. Cornell University Press.

Herrold, C., & Atia, M. (2016). Competing rather than collaborating: Egyptian nongovernmental organizations in turbulence. *Nonprofit Policy Forum, 7*(3), 389–407. https://doi.org/10.1515/npf-2015-0033

Jacobsson, K., & Saxonberg, S. (2013). *Beyond NGO-ization. The development of social movements in Central and Eastern Europe*. Ashgate.

Krause, M. (2014). *The good project. Humanitarian relief NGOs and the fragmentation of reason*. University of Chicago Press.

Lang, S. (1997). The NGOization of feminism. In J. W. Scott, C. Kaplan, & D. Keates (Eds.), *Transitions, environments, translations: Feminism in international politics* (pp. 101–120). Routledge.

Lang, S. (2013). *NGOs, civil society, and the public sphere*. Cambridge University Press.

Lang, S. (2021). Civil society as a public sphere. In J. S. Ott & L. A. Dick (Eds.), *The nature of the nonprofit sector* (4th ed., pp. 101–120). Routledge.

Mitchell, G., & Schimtz, H. (2014). Principled instrumentalism: A theory of transnational NGO behaviour. *Review of International Studies, 40*(3), 487–504. https://doi.org/10.1017/S0260210513000387

Mitchell, G. E., Schmitz, H. P., & Vijfeijken, T. B. (2020). *Between power and irrelevance. The future of transnational NGOs*. Oxford University Press.

Oliveira, E. (2017). *The instigatory theory of NGO communication. Strategic communication in civil society organizations*. Springer Publ.

Paternotte, D. (2016). The NGOizaation of LGBT activism: ILGA-Europe and the treaty of amsterdam. *Social Movement Studies, 15*(4), 388–402. doi:10.1080/14742837.2015.1077111

Powers, M. (2018). *NGOs as newsmakers. The changing landscape of international news*. Columbia University Press.

Prakash, A., & Gugerty, M. (Eds.). (2009). *Rethinking advocacy organizations: A collective action perspective*. Cambridge University Press.

Sanchez Salgado, R. (2010). NGO structural adaptation to funding requirements and prospects for democracy: The case of the European union. *Global Society, 24*(4), 507–527. https//10.1080/13600826.2010.508986

Sandberg, B., Elliott, E., & Petchel, S. (2020). Investigating the marketization of the nonprofit sector: A comparative case study of two nonprofit organizations. *VOLUNTAS: International Journal of Voluntary and Nonprofit Organizations, 31*, 494–510. https//10.1007/s11266-019-00159-8

Skocpol, T. (2003). *Diminished democracy. From membership to management in American civic life*. University of Oklahoma Press.

Suarez, D. (2020). Advocacy, civil engagement, and social change. In W. W. Powell & P. Bromley (Eds.), *The nonprofit sector – a research handbook* (pp. 491–506). Stanford University Press.

Thiel, M. (2017). *European civil society and human rights advocacy*. University of Pennsylvania Press.

Tortajada, C. (2016). Nongovernmental organizations and influence on global public policy. *Asia and the Pacific Policy Studies, 3*(2), 266–274. https://doi.org/10.1002/app5.134

Vera, J. M., & Herranz de la Casa, J. M. (2020). How influential are international NGOs in the public arena? *The Hague Journal of Diplomacy, 15*, 624–635. https//10.1163/1871191X-bja10040

1.4
NGO-IZATION OF SOLIDARITY IN THE DIGITAL AGE

Víctor Manuel Marí Sáez

Introduction

The phenomenon of the NGO-ization of society has been an object of study since the rise and expansion of neoliberalism. It is a process characterized by the fragmentation of organized solidarity, which restricts its capacity for having a political impact and for transforming society at an institutional and macrosocial level. This "bottom-up" neoliberalism (Petras, 1999) has consequences for the communication dimension of nongovernmental organizations (NGOs), a specific type of nonprofit body. It leads to a technocentric perspective of communication (McQuail, 1987) whose principal aim is to achieve a media impact that positions a nongovernmental organization in the competitive market of solidarity (Sogge et al., 1996), while leaving any attempt to transform society structurally by the wayside. The NGO-ization of society and communication has new features in the twenty-first century. This is due, among other things, to (1) an increase in private funding, which obviously has practical consequences for the communication of these organizations (Wilkins & Enghel, 2013), and (2) to the momentum of the digital age, in which new communication tools and possibilities coexist alongside old reductionisms. These two aspects have important consequences in the field of communication. When blindly adopting the language of donors, NGOs assume hegemonic strategies for framing solidarity. By the same token, the tendency to reproduce the same strategies implemented in commercial or political communication in solidarity communication means that the full potential of digital tools for dialogic and transformative communication is not leveraged.

What is NGO-ization?

The NGO-ization of society (Álvarez, 2009; Banks et al., 2015; Choudry & Kapoor, 2012) refers to the process that, with special intensity, has developed since the 1980s, when neoliberal policies were imposed in many countries the world over. These tensions between the globalization and fragmentation of solidarity action can also be observed in the previous waves of transnational civil society (Davies, 2013; Laqua, 2011). Against this backdrop, state and public social policies were attacked *from above* (by international bodies like the World Bank and the International Monetary Fund), while the state was eroded *from below* (Petras, 1999), with the collaboration or exploitation of NGOs, a specific type of body within the broad group of nonprofit organizations (Salamon & Anheier, 1997).

The NGO-ization of society thus involves a sort of fragmentation of transformative collective action and a shift of emphasis towards technical management in politics. For authors like Sonia E.

Álvarez (2009), the field of feminist social movements in Latin America was one of the first in which this NGO-ization process was observed – a process, it warrants noting, brought about by the de-politicization of feminist agendas resulting from their combination with their neoliberal counterparts in the implementation of "social adjustment" policies. Accordingly, NGO-ization "entailed national and global neo-liberalism's active promotion and official sanctioning of particular organizational forms and practices among feminist organizations and other sectors of civil society" (p. 176).

With time, the NGO-ization process was extended to other social movements and regions. Thus, for example, this concept was revisited to analyze the role of social movements and NGOs in Eastern-Central Europe following the fall of the Berlin Wall (Jacobsson & Saxonberg, 2015; Kováts, 2017), India (Mosse & Nagappan, 2020; Ramanath, 2016; Roy, 2015), South Africa (Sinwell, 2013), and Palestine (Jad, 2008). As a rule, one could say that it is characterized by a fragmentation of organized solidarity which restricts its capacity for political impact and societal transformation at institutional and macro-social levels. It has to do with the tendency of certain social movements to become institutionalized in the shape of NGOs and, in this way, enmeshed in the logics of dependence on private foundations and governments. This institutionalization obliges solidarity organizations to create mechanisms for professionalization and management which, together with other factors, can lead to their de-politicization and competition with other NGOs jockeying for position in the competitive "solidarity market" (Sogge et al., 1996).

Consequently, Choudry and Kapoor (2012) suggest that NGO-ization leads to the professionalization of dissent and knowledge colonization for capital. In this context, the "non-governmental" character of organizations of this type, as Revilla (2002) observed, can be expressed in two ways: on the one hand, as going against the grain of neoliberal policies, conceiving NGOs as anti-establishment actors; and, on the other, considering that these organizations also participate in the production of the public sphere, albeit in a supplementary and different way from the state (cited in Monge & Boza, 2010, p. 84).

NGO-ization and communication for social change in the digital age

The NGO-ization of society has reappeared time and again since the turn of the century, especially as a result of major cyclic crises, like that in 2008 and the most recent one triggered by the COVID-19 pandemic. In a way, the history of neoliberalism (Harvey, 2007) is also that of NGO-ization.

Whenever it reappears, the phenomenon shares features with previous periods, together with other new ones or ones that have a new dimension. The context imposed by digital (Schiller, 2000; Fuchs & Mosco, 2015) and platform capitalism (Srnicek, 2017) has had an enormous impact on the social and nonprofit sector. This has given rise to a philanthrocapitalism (Thorup, 2013; McGoey, 2012) in which the so-called "development industries" (Wilkins & Enghel, 2013; Mediavilla & Garcia-Arias, 2019) and the nonprofit corporate complex (Gurcan, 2015; Rodríguez, 2007) establish the strategic lines along which the communication of solidarity and nonprofit organizations flows.

There are several levels at which the communication analysis of the NGO-ization of solidarity occurring in the twenty-first century – namely, in the digital age – can be organized. The first allows for establishing a correlation between the main funding sources of NGOs and the type of communication that they practice. In this respect, it is possible to talk about the incorporation of a "global policy language" by NGOs (Mannan, 2015), which allows for connecting their work with the strategic lines of development not only implemented by governments but also, above all, by the major global social foundations so as to guarantee the success of their efforts to attract funding. As Banks et al. (2015) remark, "professionalised NGOs have the advantage of being able to express their objectives and impact in the same terminology used by donors" (Crack, 2019).

The fact that governments and public bodies have recently been cutting funding for development and solidarity, while the major private foundations have been increasing it, has obliged NGOs to readapt their strategies and languages. This phenomenon, together with the increase in private funding through micro-subsidies granted by donors (with stable quotas and, moreover, with sporadic contributions), influences actions and communication practices, which tend to be aimed at solidarity projects and initiatives that obtain immediate and easily measurable results. On the contrary, those initiatives that place the accent on societal transformations at a macro level yield less tangible results. In addition, those initiatives that challenge the interests of economic, political and media power groups are less likely to receive funding from major foundations. As observed by a series of US feminist social movements in 2007, the revolution will not be funded (INCITE!, 2017).

In short, a historical problem has yet again arisen in cooperation and solidarity action, namely, that of the tendency to pay more attention to the effects of poverty than to its causes. In other words, the illusion of efficient communicative action conceals the inability to get to the root of the problems engendering global inequalities. This situation brings to mind the old debate in the field of communication for development (Servaes, 1999) and communication for social change (hereinafter CSC) (Gumucio-Dagron & Tufte, 2006) between a mainstream communication focusing on campaign logic and another more process-oriented communication (Marí, 2020b), with the subsequent political, communicative and methodological options for each one of them. In view of the empirical knowledge and experience accumulated in CSC, it has been confirmed that a communication aimed at addressing and resolving the causes behind social inequalities would have to give priority to the communication processes that affect political and economic structures and institutions in order to transform them.

Be that as it may, the majority of nongovernmental development organizations (NGDOs) have not adopted these communication proposals emerging from CCS. On the contrary, as Waisbord (2011, p. 144) notes, "As they have uncritically adopted the conventions of journalism, NGOs tacitly endorse the politics of manufactured publicity and political marketing that dominate contemporary mediated politics."

Accordingly, hegemonic strategies for framing the solidarity actions performed by NGOs have gained relevance (Iranzo, 2017; Darnton & Kirk, 2011; Nos et al., 2012). In this regard, the experts refer to two types of conflictive frames: one that is hegemonic and of a charitable nature, and the other that is alternative and of a transformative character. According to this scheme, in the dominant paradigm

> a relationship is established between the powerful donor and the grateful recipient, who blames poverty on the domestic problems of the countries suffering from it and appeals for low-intensity public commitment, which manages to increase donations, but not the quality of that commitment. Versus this paradigm, the authors defend an alternative, grounded in an authentic process of transformation geared to social change, aware that financial aid is not a long-term solution and that there is a need for a deep commitment to the citizenry.
> (Iranzo, 2017, p. 68, based on Darnton & Kirk, 2011)

The research performed by Chouliaraki (2006, 2013), especially her concept of post-humanitarian communication, whose aim is to define campaigns that break with the aesthetic conventions and moral mechanisms characterizing their conventional counterparts, such as "shock effect" and "positive imagery," points in a similar direction.

In the digital age, the dominant paradigm for framing solidarity communication is highlighted in a special way when NGOs attempt to make their messages go viral. In a process that some have called "humanitarian virality" (Kurasawa, 2019), the idea is to reproduce, in the field of solidarity, the same communication strategies implemented in commercial and political communication in order to achieve the widespread dissemination of messages. However, it warrants noting – besides the dysfunctionality between the means and the ends resulting from the reproduction of hegemonic frames in solidarity communication – that the strategies for using and appropriating social networking sites implemented by nonprofit organizations tend to have certain defects, which means that they do not make the most of the opportunities that the new digital communication environment offers them.

By and large, solidarity organizations do not fully leverage the interactive and participatory potential of digital devices (Armstrong & Butcher, 2018; Guo & Saxton, 2013; Hamelink, 1999; Marí, 2006; Waters et al., 2009). Thus, for example, it had been observed that, although nonprofits are open and transparent with their Facebook profiles, they are not using them to their full potential to inform others and to involve them in organizational activities, whereby nonprofits need to do more to enhance their information dissemination and involvement strategies (Waters et al., 2009, p. 106).

On the other hand, Guo and Saxton (2013) found that the majority of the tweets analyzed in their study were aimed at providing stakeholders with information, followed by building an online community, and then calling that community to action. Therefore, it is possible to talk about an information capital generated by solidarity organizations which, in the main, situates their digital communication actions at the most basic level – the transmission of information – but which hinders their efforts to reach more sophisticated levels – that is, the construction of knowledge for social change (Marí, 2006).

In order to overcome these limitations, when designing their digital communication strategies NGOs would be well advised to leverage some of the lessons learned by social movements in the cycle of protests beginning in 2011 with the so-called "Arab spring," plus other similar processes that got underway around the same time (such as the "indignados" movement in Spain and Occupy Wall Street in the United States). In this connection, Bennett and Segerberg (2012) have coined the term "connective logic" to refer to the communication and organizational developments of the aforementioned movements. For these authors, the centrality of communication promoted by the formal structures of a specific social or political (collective action) organization is supplemented and, on occasion, gradually gives way to that generated by the citizenry around the same cause, without the control or campaign guidelines emanating from that organization. This involvement of the citizenry in communication – through memes, viral messages, blog entries and so forth – who feel linked to a cause (connective action) plays a leading role in expanding the scope of influence of collective action and centralized communication. In this way, solidarity organizations make the most of the dialogic potential of these technical devices, based on more horizontal, two-way and participatory communication models, thus generating dialogues that allow for overcoming contradictions and social inequalities (Fuchs, 2021; Gonçalves, 2020; Marí, 2020b; van Dijck, 2013; Waisbord, 2020).

Beyond NGO-ization

As has been seen, NGOs are already constructing alternatives to the NGO-ization of solidarity action, proposals that are also reflected in the field of communication. Certainly, these measures, albeit a minority, are viable and not the product of good intentions that are impossible to achieve.

These measures involve the design of public policies relating to strategic issues for societal life, such as development communication or cooperation. In the sense that the public goes beyond governmental or institutional initiatives, including these terms while expanding them, a significant number of NGOs and social movements are becoming involved in new and broader conceptions of the public sphere. Thus, the fragmentation and atomization inherent to neoliberalism and NGO-ization can be reversed by processes of social reorganization.

In this vein, Fenton (2008) claims that, versus the postmodern celebration of fragmentation, difference and diversity, it is crucial to create a viable political community in which solidarity can be mediated through new communication technologies. The real challenge, though, is to combine online politics with actual movements and struggles on the ground. As a result, NGOs can take advantage of their traditional strengths to build bridges between grassroots organizations and local and national structures and processes, applying their knowledge of local contexts to strengthen their roles in empowerment and social transformation (Banks et al., 2015). In their ambivalence, just as NGOs can further the fragmentation inherent to neoliberalism, so too can they show the way to constructing alternative alliances to the neoliberal project, particularly in times of crisis and polarization.

In the realm of digital communication practices, the challenge of going beyond NGO-ization involves opting for alternative contexts when framing solidarity actions aimed at social change at three levels: personal, micro-social and structural (Marí, 2020a). As to the normal strategies and appropriation of digital communication devices, the difference between techno-centric and media-centric approaches, noted by McQuail (1987), is still valid. While the former are of a reductionist character, with a deterministic orientation towards technological development, the latter allow for placing the accent on processes of social change at whose service technological devices are placed. Lastly, another line of work involves leveraging the digital environment's potential for dialogue, participation and collective knowledge construction, so as to go beyond strategies for transmission and to give more importance to dialogic approaches.

Furthering the alternatives to NGO-ization is not an easy task, something of which the volunteers working in solidarity organizations are fully aware. For many of them, the promotion of social justice is an endeavor akin to breaking rocks (Samimi & de Herrera, 2020). Notwithstanding the structural and institutional barriers to the alternatives to neoliberalism, a significant group of volunteers and activists are persisting in this adverse environment, relying on their personal experience in the field of social justice and on an untraditional vision of self-care, thus enabling them to believe that change is indeed possible (op. cit.). In these approaches it is possible to detect the words of the sociologist W. Mills who, in his classic *The Sociological Imagination* (1959), claimed that sociological imagination allows us to become aware of history and biography and the relationship between both in society. "This is its task and promise [. . .]. No social study that does not come back to the problems of biography, of history and of their intersections within a society has completed its intellectual journey" (p. 18). The construction of alternatives to NGO-ization involves, first and foremost, believing that they are possible and viable in order to avoid a colonization of imagination that aborts any attempt to imagine and construct other possible worlds.

Acknowledgements

This research has been carried out in the framework of the AEI (State Research Agency, Spain) project entitled, "Digital Solidarity Communication" PID2019–106632GB-I00/AEI/10.13039/501100011033. PI: Víctor Manuel Marí Sáez. It has also been possible thanks to a subsidy for the requalification of the Spanish university system (2021–2023) (UCA/R155REC/2021), awarded by the Ministry of Universities and NextGenerationEU.

Thanks to Thomas MacFarlane for translating the article into English.

References

Álvarez, S. (2009). Beyond NGOization? Reflections from Latin America. *Development*, 52(2), 175–184. doi:10.1057/dev.2009.23
Armstrong, C., & Butcher, C. (2018). Digital civil society: How Nigerian NGOs utilize social media platforms. *International Journal of Politics, Culture and Society*, 31, 251–273. doi:10.1007/s10767-017-9268-4
Banks, N., Hulme, D., & Edwards, M. (2015). NGOS, states, and donors revisited: Still too close for comfort? *World Development*, 66, 707–718. doi:10.1016/j.worlddev.2014.09.028
Bennett, W. L., & Segerberg, A. (2012). The logic of connective action: Digital media and the personalization of contentious politics. *Information, Communication & Society*, 15(5), 739–768. doi:10.1080/1369118X.2012.670661
Choudry, A., & Kapoor, D. (2012). *NGOization: Complicity, contradictions and prospects*. Zed Books.

Chouliaraki, L. (2006). *The spectatorship of suffering*. Sage Publications.
Chouliaraki, L. (2013). *The ironic spectator: Solidarity in the age of post-humanitarianism*. Polity Press.
Crack, A. (2019). Language, NGOs and inclusion: The donor perspective. *Development in Practice, 29*(2), 159–169. doi:10.1080/09614524.2018.1546827
Darnton, A., & Kirk, M. (2011). *Finding frames: New ways to engage the UK public in global poverty*. Oxfam, Department for International Development (DFID).
Davies, T. (2013). *NGOs: A new history of transnational civil society*. Hurst & Company.
Fenton, N. (2008). Mediating solidarity. *Global Media and Communication, 4*(1), 37–57. doi:10.1177/1742766507086852
Fuchs, C. (2021). *Social media. A critical introduction*. Sage.
Fuchs, C., & Mosco, V. (2015). *Marx in the age of digital capitalism*. Brill.
Gonçalves, G. (2020). Are hospitals our friends? An exploratory study on the role of Facebook in hospital organizations' dialogic communication. *Health Marketing Quarterly, 37*(53), 1–15. doi:10.1080/07359683.2020.1805898
Gumucio-Dagron, A., & Tufte, T. (Eds.). (2006). *Communication for social change anthology: Historical and contemporary readings*. CFSC Consortium.
Guo, C., & Saxton, G. D. (2013). Tweeting social change: How social media are changing nonprofit advocacy. *Nonprofit and Voluntary Sector Quarterly, 43*(1), 57–79. doi:10.1177/0899764012471585
Gurcan, E. (2015). The nonprofit-corporate complex. An integral component and driving force of imperialism in the phase of monopoly-finance capitalism. *Monthly Review, 66*(11), 37–53. doi:10.14452/MR-066-11-2015-04_4
Hamelink, C. (1999). Language and the right to communicate. *Media Development, XLVI*(4), 14–17.
Harvey, D. (2007). *A brief history of neoliberalism*. Oxford University Press.
INCITE! (2017). *The revolution will not be funded*. Duke University Press.
Iranzo, A. (2017). La comunicación de las ONGD: la lenta erosión del enfoque caritativo dominante. *Disertaciones, 10*(1), 66–83. doi:10.12804/revistas.urosario.edu.co/disertaciones/a.4910
Jacobsson, K., & Saxonberg, S. (Eds.). (2015). *Social movements in post-communist Europe and Russia*. Routledge.
Jad, I. (2008). *The demobilization of women's movements: The case of Palestine*. AWID (Association for Women's rights In Development).
Kováts, E. (Ed.). (2017). *The future of the European union. Feminist perspectives from East-Central Europe*. Friedrich-Ebert-Stiftung.
Kurasawa, F. (2019). On humanitarian virality: Kony 2012, or, the rise and fall of a pictorial artifact in the digital age. *Visual Communication, 18*(3), 399–423. doi:10.1177/1470357219851807
Laqua, D. (Ed.). (2011). *Internationalism reconfigured: Transnational ideas and movements between the world wars*. Tauris.
Mannan, M. (2015). *BRAC, global policy language, and women in Bangladesh: Transformation and manipulation*. State University of New York Press.
Marí, V. M. (2006). Communication, networks and social change. In A. Gumucio-Dagron & T. Tufte (Eds.), *Communication for social change anthology: Historical and contemporary readings* (pp. 1009–1013). CFSC Consortium.
Marí, V. M. (2020a). Institutionalization and implosion of communication for development and social change in Spain: A case study. In J. Servaes (Ed.), *Handbook of communication for development and social change* (pp. 1311–1323). Springer. doi:10.1007/978-981-10-7035-8_65-2
Marí, V. M. (2020b). Lessons on communication, development, and evaluation from a Freirean perspective, *Development in Practice, 30*(7), 862–873. doi:10.1080/09614524.2020.1755232
McGoey, L. (2012). Philanthrocapitalism and its critics. *Poetics, 40*(2), 185–199. doi:10.1016/j.poetic.2012.02.006
McQuail, D. (1987). *Mass communication theory: An introduction* (2nd ed.). Sage.
Mediavilla, J., & Garcia-Arias, J. (2019): Philanthrocapitalism as a neoliberal (development agenda) artefact: Philanthropic discourse and hegemony in (financing for) international development. *Globalizations, 16*(6). doi:10.1080/14747731.2018.1560187
Mills, C. W. (1959). *The sociological imagination*. Oxford University Press.
Monge, L., & Boza, E. (2010). La función política ideológica de las ONG en el escenario de la (contra) reforma estatal. *Reflexiones, 89*(1), 77–86.
Mosse, D., & Nagappan, S. B. (2020). NGOs as social movements: Policy narratives, networks and the performance of Dalit rights in South India. *Development and Change, 52*(1), 134–167. doi:10.1111/dech.12614
Nos, E., Iranzo, A., & Farné, A. (2012). La eficacia cultural de la comunicación de las ONGD: los discursos de los movimientos sociales actuales como revisión. *CIC Cuadernos de Información y Comunicación, 17*, 209–237. doi:10.5209/rev_ciyc.2012.v17.39265

Petras, J. (1999). NGOs: In the service of imperialism. *Journal of Contemporary Asia*, *29*(4), 429–440. doi:10.1080/00472339980000221

Ramanath, R. (2016). Defying NGOization? Lessons in livelihood resilience observed among involuntarily displaced women in Mumbai, India. *World Development*, *84*, 1–17. doi:10.1016/j.worlddev.2016.04.007

Revilla, M. (Ed.). (2002). *Las ONG y la política. Detalles de una relación*. Istmo.

Rodríguez, D. (2007). The political logic of the nonprofit industrial complex. In INCITE! (Ed.), *The revolution will not be funded: Beyond the nonprofit industrial sector* (pp. 21–22). South End Press.

Roy, S. (2015). The Indian women's movement: Within and beyond NGOization. *Journal of South Asian Development*, *10*(1), 96–117. doi:10.1177/0973174114567368

Salamon, L. M., & Anheier, H. K. (Eds.). (1997). *Defining the nonprofit sector: A cross-national analysis*. Manchester University Press.

Samimi, C., & De Herrera, C. (2020). Picando Piedras: Picking at the rocks of social justice under the nonprofit industrial complex. *Journal of Progressive Human Services*, 1–18. doi:10.1080/10428232.2020.1734426

Schiller, D. (2000). *Digital capitalism: Networking the global market system*. MIT press.

Servaes, J. (1999). *Communication for development. One world, multiple cultures*. Hampton Press.

Sinwell, L. (2013). From radical movement to conservative NGO and back again? A case study of the democratic left front in South Africa. In A. Choudry & D. Kapoor (Eds.), *NGOization: Complicity, contradictions and prospects* (pp. 102–117). Zed Books.

Sogge, D., Biekart, K., & Saxby, J. (Eds.). (1996). *Compassion and calculation: The business of private foreign aid*. Pluto Press.

Srnicek, N. (2017). *Platform capitalism*. Polity Press.

Thorup, M. (2013). Pro bono? On philanthrocapitalism as ideological answer to inequality. *Ephemera: Theory & Politics in Organization*, *13*(3), 555–576.

van Dijck, J. (2013). *The culture of connectivity: A critical history of social media*. Oxford University Press.

Waisbord, S. (2011). Can NGOs change the news? *International Journal of Communication*, *5*, 142–165.

Waisbord, S. (2020). Family tree of theories, methodologies, and strategies in development communication. In J. Servaes (Ed.), *Handbook of communication for development and social change* (pp. 93–132). Springer. doi:10.1007/978-981-15-2014-3_56

Waters, R., Burnett, E., Lamm, A., & Lucas, J. (2009). Engaging stakeholders through social networking: How nonprofit organizations are using Facebook. *Public Relations Review*, *35*(2), 102–106. doi:10.1016/j.pubrev.2009.01.006

Wilkins, K., & Enghel, F. (2013). The privatization of development through global communication industries: Living proof? *Media, Culture and Society*, *35*(2), 165–181. doi:10.1177/0163443712468606

1.5
CIVIC RELATIONS
Socio-communicative collective action

Evandro Oliveira

Introduction

While the ideal of symmetric public relations from James Grunig (1992) puts a societal demand of the organizations at the center to legitimize their action by complying with the collective expectations from society in a dialogic way, corporate social responsibility stems from the possibility of organizations to go further and do more than they have to in the benefit of the society and the planet (Carroll, 1991). Those ethical compensations or commitments,[1] associated with communication management and a public relations (PR) agenda, comprehend a societal dimension of the exercise, resembling the European origin of public relations – the *Öffentlichkeitsarbeit* – as a work in favor of the public sphere (Bentele, 1997). Considering PR as a form of public communication, similar to journalism, this understanding sets an ethical dimension from a macro-sociological level of understanding of PR. Kindred with a systemic approach to PR, we can consider the role of PR in society and the impact of its exercise, while considering PR at the meso-social level – the organization – and setting the *locus* on that actor form and its relations and implications. Nevertheless, there is a communication form that is set as a collective action for the *common good*, beyond the organizational form and the interests of its members, which comes from between and involves the micro, meso and macro levels of social analysis. We can find this type of communication in collectives forms, which can also be called civil-society organizations or collective actors, while they communicate in the public sphere. Therefore, it cannot be considered equal to PR in an organizational-centered perspective due to this multilevel communication dynamics interdependence; neither can it be considered equivalent to systemic macro-approaches.

This communicative action starts from the individual private interest on an issue (micro), finds echo in collective forms and distills it into the public sphere. Those actors communicate from the *bottom up* (Bentele et al., 2001). Furthermore, this communication can aim at socio-communicative processes involving other organizations, institutions or governments with a socio-political-communicative component. In an effort to incorporate some of these actors into international socio-political processes with an institutionalization dimension, the UN charter called for some of those actors' nongovernmental organizations (NGOs) (UN, 1945, article 71). Whereas for some, this might have been an advantage, due to the institutionalization aspect, the denomination of these organizations might have obstructed their own perception, projecting a multiplicity of definitions and understandings within all the disciplines, including social sciences and, more specifically, communication sciences. Despite this, not all the collective actors involved have the characteristics of NGOs.

The questions remain: If they are not governmental, what are they? Where do they come from? If they do more than PR from a communication standpoint, what is it that they do? If they are outside the market and don't have a product or the ability to generate intrinsic monetary value, what are their goals? And how can we frame this socio-communicative process?

If we consider the condition of a citizen and the civil society as a group of citizens, we might have to go back in time to the first democracy and observe it through a socio-origin approach (Salamon & Anheier, 1998), thus capturing the *ontos* of this phenomenon. Therefore, the definition of *civic relations* (Oliveira, 2019;)[2] as a socio-communicative multidimensional concept is a proposal to include its distinctive aspects. This chapter draws elements from a possible *parcours* that starts at the origins of democracy and citizenship and aims to expose the argument and the dimensions that the definition comprehends.

Collective action as citizen participation

The collective action within a democratic setting is done by people in their condition as citizens of a certain governing system in their right or duty to participate and associate. This can be traced back to the individual dimension of engaging in collective action towards the public good, without being directly paid for it, as the ontological pre-condition of this engagement and, therefore, by doing the analysis of traces on both individual (including certain iconic individualities as archetypes for the respective governmental systems) and on semi-organized or organized forms over time. Public good[3] can be considered as "those goods that serve all members of a given community and its institutions, and, as such, includes both goods that serve no identifiable particular group, as well as those that serve members of generations not yet born" (Etzioni, 2015, p. 1).

In classical times, the Greek definition of citizenship emphasized the activity of collective self-rule, while the Roman conception considered that legal status and privilege were in the middle (Pocock, 1995). In the former, citizenship was, as mentioned by Aristotle, *zoon politikon*, a political animal from the *civis*, while the other was a legal man from the *polis* who had a legal relationship with the government (Pocock, 1995, p. 38). The concepts were related to forms of collective action for the common good in both scenarios. Citizenship comprised the active social meaning of participation in public life (Manville, 1997, p. 5). This participation was on itself through communication in forms of public discussions and debates in the Greek culture and saw the need of intermediaries in the Roman culture. Therefore, we can argue that the collective consequences of the citizen discussions were already absorbed by the direct democracy rules.

In ancient Athens, during the 4th century, ideas about individual liberty were connected to citizens' obligations to the state (*polis*) and the community – also called civic obligations (Liddel, 2007). In this case, the notion of equality was less important than liberty, as equality's effects were believed to be able to be nullified or even turned to the advantage of the common benefit (Liddel, 2007). These negotiations of obligations involved piety and adherence to an oath with values related to sharing and reciprocity, as well as euergetic[4] behavior (Liddel, 2007). On the other hand, Hellenic queens and other prominent women were engaged in public goods, and female euergetism contributed to a different idea of the female citizen as involved in communal life (James et al., 2010). These are two iconic examples of forms of effective individual pursuit of the common good.

On the Aristotelian-driven concept of the man as a political animal, man can only completely fulfil his own nature and live with the happiness – *eudaimonia* – while part of a city that aims to achieve the common good, as well as cultivate friendship.[5,6] For Aristotle, "For even if the good is the same for an individual as for a city, that of the city is obviously a greater and more complete thing to obtain and preserve. For while the good of an individual is a desirable thing, what is good for a people or for cities is a nobler and more godlike thing" (NE, I, 1, 1094b). The common good, the good of the polis, is thus explained in contrast to the exclusive good of the individual, which is inferior. Following that line, the individual good as citizen is the pursuit of virtue of balancing his interests and also his commitments to the common good (Guyette, 2012). Using a nautical analogy, Aristotle is illustrating different tasks on a ship as the different duties of every citizen, but still being the "overall success of the ship's voyage" (Guyette, 2012, p. 113) or "the salvation of the community" (1276b 25–30, as cited in Guyette, 2012, p. 113), the more comprehensive good.

An interpretation of Plato by Jonathan Culp points that in *The Republic*, Plato defends that the happiness of the city will be left to nature[7] if we take an individual perspective, but the rulers should look after the civic functioning (Culp, 2015). Therefore, "the rulers will not directly concern themselves with the happiness of individual citizens or groups of citizens" (Culp, 2015, p. 207). This is making a distinction between individual versus collective happiness and excluding the interest of groups. The holistic perspective proposed by some scholars like Culp is in contrast with the reductionist interpretation that the happiness of the whole can be identical to the happiness of the citizenry. Although this cannot be totally excluded from the interpretation of parts of the text, according to the work of Jonathan Culp, the passages supporting the quality of the civic functioning as the collective happiness are more abundant (2015, p. 211).

Besides the individual part of the common good, the *polis* as it existed before the 4th century BC can be considered as a kind of voluntary association itself (Peterson & Peterson, 1973, p. 5). This conclusion comes after a review of the forms of individual voluntary associations in Ancient Greece and is also in line with other scholars who see the ancient cities as "freely-willed associations" or "confederated fraternity of associations", or even later as "territorial corporation" (Peterson & Peterson, 1973, p. 5). In this case, the model of government and citizenship included the inherent common good at its core, which is why it is considered that the most ancient Athenian associations were "expressive", meaning "associations geared to the satisfaction of participating members" (Peterson & Peterson, 1973, p. 13), except the "social hetaery as a political club", which can be considered an instrumental association, defined by Peterson, as "associations for the achievement of some social purpose". Despite that, we cannot exclude the idea that some certain common good intentions, actions or dynamics were not present in these organizations, even if it is not evident, or at least they did not surpass the own members' good.

Only a few centuries later (ca. 168 BC) there were clubs during the Achaean League against Rome that had clear political intentions, like the "men united to uphold the constitution of their fathers" (Peterson & Peterson, 1973, p. 13). Among the reasons for that practical inexistence of "social influence groups", Peterson and Peterson point out direct and personal participation in politics, so those organizations were not needed. Another reason is that citizens did not distrust the government and felt no anxiety about what government would do (Peterson & Peterson, 1973, p. 14).

Given that, we see the need of an organized collective action in the form of two steps: the first on a micro-level of communication, and the second from a meso-level as intermediary to the governmental structures. For the Ancient Roman philosophers, the concept of common good was inherent to the concept of *republic* or *people*, as a group of people that agree in terms of what justice is and have a partnership for the common good (Etzioni, 2015, p. 1). However, in Roman times, the contract with the law was the tie with the citizen. That already divided the dynamics themselves, as the people who were establishing the law had a different influence in the process.

Therefore, there was, on the one hand, a need to include non-exclusive neoclassical or market economics notions in economic thought. In Roman economic policy, there were *euergetic* impulses, which they called *benefia* (Vivenza, 1998, p. 323). This characteristic was attributed to the nature of the emperor, but mostly with non-objective criteria, with concepts like friendship and benevolence (Vivenza, 1998, p. 324). For Vivenza, that shows "a contractual attitude which considered partners as equals, and the second with an aristocratic, munificent attitude, which clearly involved marked social inequality" (1998, p. 324).

It is in this context that we see the emergence of the right to private associations, or voluntary organizations, as we would call them, including the idea that they are "the ideal vehicle for defending the democratic principle of liberty and pluralism" (Kloppenborg, 1996, p. 2). Even if they cannot be seen entirely in this way, Kloppenborg, who analyzed voluntary associations in the Roman world, recorded some "modest amount of political activity", which also used ways of drawing attention to issues such as strikes or threats to stop work (Kloppenborg, 1996, p. 2). He also points out that associations suspected of "harboring socially disruptive elements" were banned. In that sense, he concludes that "they were nevertheless a collective attempt to assert influence on the course of political affairs", also highlighting that associations often became part of the establishment they set out to challenge (Kloppenborg, 1996, p. 3). On this, attention has to be drawn to the distinctive feature of an NGO compared to other organizations: an NGO never aims to become elected or be part of the power and is independent from governments themselves. However, I consider those associations as participants in the sense of pursuing the common good. The Roman philosopher Cicero also included partnership for the common good in all these senses in his definition of "people" or "republic" (Etzioni, 2015, p. 1), without being specific about the forms or actors involved.

Despite roots in ancient times, in a study about the history of transnational civil society, Thomas Davies understands that we can only consider the first development of modern international non-governmental organizations (INGOs) as taking place after the late 18th century (2014, p. 20). Nonetheless, some human societies, namely for lifeguarding and rescue purposes, were founded in the 13th century in China and can also be understood as international civil society participants. Those associations proliferated over time and the first one in Europe was created in Amsterdam in 1767 as "the society for recovery of the drowned" (Davies, 2014, p. 25).

Searching the common good within religious environments

Some notions of the common good can also be found in religious thought. Since Augustine, for example, Christian theologians have referred to the need to pursue the common good. Aquinas defines it as "the good of the whole universe", making a distinction between private interest and good associated with sin and selfishness and the common good with God (Etzioni, 2015, p. 2). In the medieval period in Europe, the concept of citizenship was not of major importance (Heater, 2004, p. 42). Reasons for that may include the encroachment of Christianity, so values were of a religious order, although we can consider that the Aristotelian principle was present and, except for Italy, status was anchored in a city or town and not in a state. There was therefore a new administrative organization with authority given to bishops, and this became important when installed in Roman "cities", which they called "dioceses". The civil and ecclesiastical orders coincided, and when the Roman Empire collapsed, bishops played a political role as well. With cities' growth and maturation, the citizenry became impatient and demanding and created their own lay civic institutions. Although Aquinas tried in the 13th century to tie the principle of citizenship to Christianity, the same was not done by Augustine. For him, in his book *The City of God*, prayer, rather than civic duties, was what made a good man. On the other hand, the idea of corruption in this world versus the good life in heaven also weakened the main premises of the good citizen (Heater, 2004, pp. 43–44).

Within this scenario, we can, during this period, consider that the pursuit of the common good could only be rooted in religious organizations and that they paved the way for the development of other non-profit organizations in the form that we know today (Stoecker, 2000, p. 64; Curbach, 2009, p. 35). Therefore, to recognize the civic duties within those organizations, we must follow the proposed path and not be blinded by structures and names, and instead focus on the social agents.

The Order of Malta was created in 1048 and can be considered one of the oldest international organizations (Krethlow, 2001, p. 34) that is still operating. After being founded in 1048 in Jerusalem (Palestine), where it kept its headquarters until 1291, the organization moved to Cyprus, Rhodes and Malta. From 1798 to 1917, it was based in Russia, and then in the United States until 1976. Since then, it has been in Malta and remains there today. The Order of Malta is now present in 21 countries to care for the sick and the poor (*Yearbook of International Organizations 2015*–2016, 2015).

In 1099 the Order of St. John was founded by the Roman Catholics, while the Church of the East in Asia started to spread from the 6th century, as did Sufi tariqahs like the Naqshbandiyyah in the 12th century in the Islamic world. All of these orders played a crucial role in the development of horizontal relationships among people in various contexts before the emergence of the public sphere. They were in the roots of later organizations like the independent Order of Good Templars and other charitable organizations, and later on the Quakers – the Religious Society of Friends – which were crucial in the development of transnational activism (Davies, 2014, p. 21).

International organizations were not the only ones in the realm of the search for the common good. In religion we can also find sainthoods awarded to queens who pursued and defended the common good against the orders of their husbands and kings, distributing bread to the poor and performing charitable actions. We can find two records in history in particular, both from the same family: one is St. Elisabeth Von Ungarn (1207–1235) and the other Queen Saint Isabel of Portugal (1271–1336), great-grandchild of the former and also named after her. Like the Greek concept of female euergetism, the two queens embodied civic relations. The most iconic story about both is the legend of the roses. In the telling of St. Elisabeth Von Ungarn, it is said that she was surprised by her husband, Louis IV, Landgrave of Thuringia, during one of the charitable acts that he often chided her for. The moment they met, the loaves of bread she was carrying miraculously changed into roses and that convinced him of the worthiness of her kindness (Saint Elizabeth of Hungary – Princess of Hungary, n.d.). This tale finds parallels with today's civil society organizations, calling governments' attention to the societal issues and the weak who need assistance.

Despite the religious aspects related to both queens, the socio-political dimension of Queen Saint Elizabeth has been researched in document analysis, and it has been revealed that she was highly engaged in social challenges and problems, and even in international politics (Gimenez, 2005, p. 174). Throughout communication, mostly in letters, she performed a highly intensive diplomatic role all her life, as well as forming hospitals and providing assistance to the poor. This goes against the common hagiographies that state that she completely dedicated herself to religious affairs and that she lived in a nunnery after the death of D. Diniz. (Gimenez, 2005, p. 177). We can consider that the civic relations performed by those queens were in the same tradition as the Franciscan order that itself performed duties similar to NGOs and became institutionalized in 1982 in the United States with Franciscans International, an INGO that has an advocacy focus on peace, extreme poverty and the environment – which they call "an integrated human rights-based approach".[8]

The examples provided show that most societal forms and structures that pursued the common good had their roots in religion. Civic relations were performed by many actors, collectively or individually and in various religions. It is not this chapter's goal to carry out a systematic analysis of this phenomenon, but rather to demonstrate the path followed in order to collect the ontological features.

Associativism in modern times

In early modern times (1500–1750), associations like the Scientific Society in 1560 or the Ladies of Charity in 1617 were founded (Davies, 2014, p. 20). By the end of the 16th century, the number of INGOs related to the Roman Catholic religion had risen to 90 (Davies, 2014, p. 21). However, it was with the start of the mid-modern period (around 1750) that we find the final transitions from religious and secret societies to multiple-issue INGOS (Davies, 2014, p. 23). In 1775, for instance, the Society for the Relief of Free Negroes Unlawfully Held in Bondage and the Society of Universal Good-Will, the International Association for Peace in 1834 and the Aborigines Protection Society in 1837 are other examples (Davies, 2014, p. 24). Anti-Slavery International began in the UK in 1787 (Davies, 2014, p. 32).

The 19th century and societal changes, as well as forms of civic culture, may be considered the "golden age" of philanthropic activity in society (Hilton et al., 2012, p. 14). However, civil humanism, inspired by the classical period, also appeared in Italy during the first half of the 15th century (Zamagni, 2008, p. 467) and had repercussions all over Europe. Referring to philanthropic activity in Europe, this kind of society activity is considered to be different from the activity done in the United States (Hoffmann, 2003, p. 269), mostly known from the travelogue of Alexis de Tocqueville, published in 1835 and 1840.

Alternatively, for many scholars, including those that take the approach of INGOs as a recent phenomenon with greater expansion since the 1980s, despite the constitutive journey of collective action and the described examples of what is considered the first INGO and the evidence from the time, I postulate that we can only research this area by taking an untraveled path. This "new" story and thesis were uncovered by Thomas Davies, who considers the modern era until 1914 to be the first wave of a cyclical process, with the consolidation of that wave taking place between 1870 and 1900 (Davies, 2014, p. 44). He approaches this development in the context of the "second Industrial Revolution", as well as technological developments. Until the First World War, transnational civil society at the beginning of the 20th century was visible and represented by INGOs (Davies, 2014, p. 65).

The period between the two wars is usually depicted as a stagnant time (Hoffmann, 2006, p. 82), although recent works show alternative views of the often overlooked period (Laqua, 2011; Davies, 2014). After the analysis of the authors' writings about international affairs, it can be concluded that "the scale of transnational associational life that developed from the First World War until the early 1930s surpassed that which preceded the conflict" (Davies, 2014, p. 77). It is during this period, in 1919, that the Paris Peace Conference was held and "was an unprecedented opportunity for NGOs to influence governments" (Davies, 2014, p. 81). Refusing a linear pattern, Davies suggests a cyclical pattern with peaks at the beginning of the 20th century, the early 1930s and after the 1990s (Davies, 2014, p. 176). In sum, NGOs or other civil society organizations and their communication are not a recent phenomenon and have roots in various social and political contexts like those described in this chapter.

If we analyze the action of those civil society organizations and their social offspring, we see at the core communication, as well as a crucial organizational goal, allowing the intervention to fulfill their missions, which was also observed by Pleil (2005, p. 9). In light of the need to embed it in the communication sciences, civil society can be seen as "the organized expression of the values and interests of society" (Castells, 2008, p. 78) and the public sphere in three different ways. The first is as "the space of communication of ideas and projects that emerge from society and are addressed to the decision makers in the institutions of society" (Castells, 2008). The second is in a Habermasian sense, in line with the redefinition proposed by Jensen, postulating a reintroduction of the concepts of the public sphere in public relations theory, as "the discursive processes in a complex network of persons, institutionalized associations and organizations" (Jensen, 2002, p. 136), in which those "discourses are a civilized way of disagreeing openly about essential matters of common concern" (Jensen, 2002, p. 136). The third is as a public sphere with dominant characteristics like collapses in structural constraints in the communication sphere in "a network of points of interest", with communicators considered to be those points (Bentele & Nothhaft, 2010, p. 112).

Conclusion

Civil society organizations like NGOs can be considered native organizational forms of both civil society and one of the main communicative actors in the public sphere, since they concentrate expression on societal challenges, after filtering and following internal discourse from the private sphere through the actors of civil society (associations, organizations and movements) in a Habermasian sense (Habermas, 1962, 1990; Habermas, 2001, pp. 366–368; Oliveira & Wiesenberg, 2016, p. 117).

In the origins of democracy, in ancient Athens, the government structures had some characteristics of modern civil society organizations, and a concern with the public good was at the heart of this, as already shown. But if instead of a participative democracy we look at other forms of government, like the Roman model, we find a need for association as an intermediate function of exercising citizenship for the common good. Besides, there were also other ways of addressing this, like the normative *euergetic* notion of the imperator, also found in economic principles.[9] In that sense, Oliveira (2019) notes that the *ontos* relies on a need for structures or organizational forms, like civil society organizations, which allow for broader participation in democracy, among other reasons, to balance powers in the creation of laws, but also to exercise influence according to the views of groups that are voluntarily organized by citizens and that reflect on the public good. Therefore, it is argued that "the civic exercise of *zoon politikon* is fulfilled in *eudaimonia* when individuals participate in public life as a referential at personal level" (Oliveira, 2019, p. 24), considering it from a political, philosophical and socio-communicative perspective as civic relations.

During history and in different parts of the globe, civic relations have been performed by individuals and organizations in different contexts: from the first Roman forms, within the religious context of the Middle Ages or during intermediate times with the emergence of the first INGOs in their modern form. First, in an ideal situation, NGOs are set in a democratic context, from citizens with rights to congregate and express their opinions. Second, scientific, technological, environmental, economic, social, political and organizational factors contribute to that path. But the ontological realm remains constant in the pursuit of the common good and is also embodied in a social communicative function that proposes the central definition of civic relations as "a social communicative function of an agent that directly or indirectly performs the civic exercise of pursuing and seeking the common good" (Oliveira, 2019, p. 24). Their endeavors can be undertaken at the "individual, group, formal organization, movement, network or other level" (Oliveira, 2019, p. 25). First, communication is crucial during the process of exercising political life while striving for consensus in the Habermasian sense,[10] as the discussion is ongoing in the public sphere and the communicative action is leading a social-political process. Second, communication plays a role in its performative dimension as a constitutive part of social reality. Third, communication around the subject, either strategically or uncoordinated, will contribute to gather information about the subject for other citizens and social actors, or even to facilitate setting agendas and influencing public agendas (Oliveira, 2019).

Notes

1 There are proposals that even call for a balanced company as corporate integrity (see e.g. Smith, 2003).
2 Parts of this chapter include components of previous work by the author.
3 I use the term public good, but this can also be called common good, the public interest or public goods.
4 *Euergetism* is derived from the Greek word "εὐεργετέω" and means "doing good deeds".
5 Bruni and Zamagni (2016, p. 70) show with a text and argument analysis that Aristotle's eudaimonia is a vision of happiness connected with civil happiness. That includes civil, social and political spheres. This comprehends also the value of the relational and civil life: "Surely it is strange, too, to make the supremely happy man a solitary; for no one would choose the whole world on condition of being alone, since man is a political creature and one whose nature is to live with others. Therefore, even the happy man lives with others; for he has the things that are by nature good. And plainly it is better to spend his days with friends and good men than with strangers or any chance persons. Therefore, the happy man needs friends" (NE, IX, 9, 1169b).
6 The concept of friendship also encompasses reciprocal relationships. That is pointing out of a second dimension of the happiness within a private sphere, related to an *euergetic* behavior or reciprocity.

7 "Socrates (doesn't) affirmatively declare that nature will make each class as happy as it can be when they are properly civically formed. He does not say what quality or degree of happiness nature will distribute. Perhaps the greatest support for holism in this passage is that Socrates speaks here as though it is possible to make a city happy as a whole without being directly concerned with the happiness of the parts, which suggests that the happiness of the city is something other than and even independent of the happiness of the citizenry" (Culp, 2015, p. 207)
8 Vision and Mission. (n.d.). Retrieved February 1, 2015, from http://franciscansinternational.org/Vision-Mission.118.0.html
9 The expression intermediary or "bridging" role was introduced by the anthropologist Thomas Carrol after a multicountry study on NGOs and development (Carroll, 1992). The same expression can be found in the context of civil society and the function of NGOs as communities of interpretation (Berger & Luckmann, 1995).
10 I refer here to the critical process of public communication (see Hebermas, 1962, 1990).

References

Bentele, G. (1997). PR-Historiographie und funktional-integrative Schichtung. Ein neuer Ansatz zur PR-Geschichtsschreibung. In P. Szyszka (Ed.), *Auf der Suche nach Identität: PR-Geschichte als Theoriebaustein* (pp. 67–84). Vistas.

Bentele, G., Liebert, T., & Vogt, M. (Eds.). (2001). *PR für Verbände und Organisationen: Fallbeispiele aus der Praxis.* Luchterhand.

Bentele, G., & Nothhaft, H. (2010). Strategic communication and the public sphere from a European perspective. *International Journal of Strategic Communication*, 4(2), 93–116. doi:10.1080/15531181003701954

Berger, P. L., & Luckmann, T. (1995). *Modernität, pluralismus und sinnkrise: Die orientierung des modernen menschen.* Bertelsmann Stiftung.

Bruni, L., & Zamagni, S. (2016). The challenges of public hapiness: An historical-methodological reconstruction. In J. Sachs, L. Becchetti, & A. Annett (Eds.), *World happiness report 2016, special rome edition* (Vol. II, pp. 66–87). Sustainable Development Solutions Network.

Castells, M. (2008). The new public sphere: Global civil society, communication networks, and global governance. *The ANNALS of the American Academy of Political and Social Science*, 616(1), 78–93. doi:10.1177/0002716207311877

Carroll, A. B. (1991, July/August). The pyramid of corporate social responsibility: Toward the moral management of organizational stakeholders. *Business Horizons*, 34, 39–48. doi:10.1016/0007-6813(91)90005-G

Carroll, T. F. (1992). *Intermediary NGOs: The supporting link in grassroots development.* Kumarian Press.

Culp, J. (2015). Happy city, happy citizens? The common good and the private good in Plato's Republic. *Interpretation A Journal of Political Philosophy*, 41(3), 201–226.

Curbach, J. (2009). *Die corporate-social-responsibility-bewegung.* VS Verlag für Sozialwissenschaften.

Davies, T. R. (2014). *NGOs: A new history of transnational civil society.* Oxford University Press.

Etzioni, A. (2015). Common good. In M. Gibbons (Ed.), *The encyclopedia of political thought* (pp. 1–7). John Wiley. doi:10.1002/9781118474396

Gimenez, J. C. (2005). *A rainha Isabel nas estratégicas políticas da peninsula: 1280–1336.* Universidade Federal do Paraná.

Grunig, J. E. (1992). *Excellence in public relations and communication management.* Lawrence Erlbaum Associates.

Guyette, F. (2012). Friendship and the common good in aristotle. AGATHOS. *An international Review of the Humanities and Social Sciences*, 3(2), 107–121.

Habermas, J. (1990 [1962]). *Strukturwandel der Öffentlichkeit. Untersuchungen zu einer Kategorie der bürgerlichen Gesellschaft.*

Habermas, J. (2001). *Between facts and norms: Contributions to a discourse theory of law and democracy.* MIT Press.

Heater, D. (2004). *A brief history of citizenship.* New York University Press.

Hilton, M., Crowson, N., Mouhot, J.-F., & McKay, J. (2012). *A historical guide to NGOs in Britain: Charities, civil society and the voluntary sector since 1945.* Palgrave Macmillan.

Hoffmann, S. (2003). Democracy and associations in the long nineteenth century: Toward a transnational perspective. *The Journal of Modern History*, 75(2), 269–299.

Hoffmann, S.-L. (2006). *Civil society.* Palgrave Macmillan.

James, S. L., Castner, C. J., James, S. L., Milnor, K., Connors, C., & Neils, J. (2010). *The Oxford encyclopedia of Ancient Greece and Rome* (Vol. 7). Oxford University Press.

Jensen, I. (2002). Public relations and emerging functions of the public sphere: An analytical framework. *Journal of Communication Management*, 6(2), 133–147.

Kloppenborg, J. S. (Ed.). (1996). *Voluntary associations in the Graeco-Roman world* (1. publ.). Routledge.
Krethlow, C. A. (2001). *Der Malteserorden: Wandel, Internationalität und soziale Vernetzung im 19*. Lang.
Laqua, D. (Ed.). (2011). *Internationalism reconfigured: Transnational ideas and movements between the world wars*. Palgrave Macmillan.
Liddel, P. P. (2007). *Civic obligation and individual liberty in ancient Athens*. Oxford University Press.
Manville, P. B. (1997). *The origins of citizenship in Ancient Athens*. Princeton University Press.
Oliveira, E. (2019). *The instigatory theory of NGO communication: Strategic communication in civil society organisations*. Springer VS.
Oliveira, E., & Wiesenberg, M. (2016). Von innen heraus: Vier Dynamiken der Legitima-tion von NGOs und Kirchen. In S. Huck-Sandhu (Ed.), *Interne Kommu-nikation im Wandel* (pp. 105–122). Springer VS.
Peterson, S., & Peterson, V. A. (1973). Voluntary associations in Ancient Greece. *Nonprofit and Voluntary Sector Quarterly*, *2*(1), 2–15.
Pleil, T. (2005). Nonprofit-PR: Besonderheiten und Herausforderungen. In *Berichte aus der Forschung 5 des Fachbereichs Sozial- und Kulturwissenschaften* (pp. 1–21). FH Darmstadt.
Pocock, J. G. A. (1995). The ideal of citizenship since classical times from "Theorizing citizenship." In R. Beiner (Ed.), *Theorizing citizenship* (pp. 29–52). State University of New York Press.
Saint Elizabeth of Hungary – Princess of Hungary. (n.d.). www.britannica.com/biography/Saint-Elizabeth-of-Hungary
Salamon, L. M., & Anheier, H. K. (1998). Social origins of civil society: Explaining the nonprofit sector cross-nationally. *Voluntas: International Journal of Voluntary and* Nonprofit *Organizations*, *9*(3), 213–248.
Smith, F. I. (2003). The balanced company: A theory of corporate integrity. *Academy of Management Perspectives*, *17*, 136–137.
Stoecker, F. W. (2000). *NGOs und die UNO: die Einbindung von Nichtregierungsorganisationen (NGOs) in die Struk-turen der Vereinten Nationen*. Lang.
UN. (1945). *United nations charter*. www.un.org/en/about-us/un-charter/full-text
Vivenza, G. (1998). Roman thought on economics and justice. In S. T. Lowry & B. Gordon (Eds.), *Ancient and medieval economic ideas and concepts of social justice* (pp. 269–332). Brill.
Yearbook of International Organizations 2015–2016. (2015). *Vol. Yearbook set of 6 volumes*. Brill.
Zamagni, S. (2008). Pursuing the common good: How solidarity and subsidiarity can work together. *Pontifical Academy of Social Sciences, Acta 14*. www.pass.va/content/dam/scienzesociali/pdf/acta14/acta14-zamagni.pdf

1.6
PUBLIC INTEREST COMMUNICATION
A pragmatic approach

Jane Johnston

Introduction

Public interest communication brings together two powerful elements – public interest and communication – which when combined, provide a potent tool for use by the nonprofit sector. While the concept of the public interest comes from a long-established and often-debated political theory (sometimes used interchangeably with 'public good'), public interest communication (PIC) has emerged as a more recent theory about how communication both constructs understanding of public interest and is in a dialectical relationship with all public interest–forming practices (Johnston & Pieczka, 2018). PIC is a theoretical and practical approach to communication that may be applied to different social contexts, public problems and contested situations. In essence, PIC demands ideas be allowed to circulate, be challenged and debated in seeking resolution (Johnston & Pieczka, 2018). Workable solutions may then be incorporated into social and political structures. At the same time, not all interest conflicts can or will be resolved. Indeed, this is precisely why communication is so vital to the management and stewardship of what constitutes public interest because it "accentuates the role of judgement and discretion required by decision makers in determining concrete decisions and outcomes" (Johnston & Pieczka, 2018, p. 12). In so doing, the expectation of normative commitments to consensus or dissensus are discarded in favour of a pragmatic approach to communication as the "coordination of practical activities through discourse and reflexive inquiry" (Craig, 2007, p. 136; see also Johnston & Pieczka, 2018).

This chapter builds on earlier work on PIC by Johnston and Pieczka (2018) and others (see Carah, 2018; Fessman, 2016; Heath & Waymer, 2018; Ihlen et al., 2018; Johnston, 2020; Johnston & Gulliver, 2022) and recalibrates the focus to more fully place PIC as a *pragmatic theory of communication*. In so doing, the chapter will continue to build the theory of PIC while providing practical examples and contexts of how PIC is enacted within different sectors of society, with particular attention to civil society and the nonprofits. Using a pragmatic lens, the chapter draws on the work of Dewey, Peters, Flathman, Habermas and others in sorting through the many layers of first, the public interest as the root concept and second, how it is circulated and enabled through communication. This advances communication scholarship on pragmatic communication (e.g. Craig, 2007; Peters, 1999; Russill, 2008) that has historically focussed attention on the "problem-oriented dimension" of pragmatism (Russill, 2008, p. 479), seeing communication as fundamentally a "political and ethical problem rather than a semantic one" (Peters, 1999, p. 30). Arguments for pragmatic communication thus share much in common with PIC, which further integrates elements of publics, inquiry, problematization and action.

The chapter also considers the material spaces in which PIC occurs: so-called "public arenas of debate" (Cefaï, 2016), as described by pragmatic sociologists, or "discourse arenas" (Heath & Waymer, 2018) from communication theory. Located in public meetings, media and exhibitions as part of deliberative action, these arenas unfold around problematic or contested interest-centred situations and the publics involved. "In this sense, public interest communication contributes to research that has engaged with the idea of *the public* . . . and, through it, conceptually embedded with the nature of social change" (Johnston & Pieczka, 2018, pp. 9–10; see also Cefaï, 2018: Dewey, 1927; Habermas, 1984; Johnston, 2020). The chapter outlines key elements in this pragmatic and reflexive process, incorporating the analytical PIC framework proposed by Johnston and Pieczka (2018), which when considered in *time* and *context*, provide the communication environment in which solutions may be sought and social change may be enabled.

Positioning public interest communication

Simply put, PIC articulates, invokes or debates public interest in relation to a problem, issue or contested situation. But what is public interest? For us to fully explore the scope and potential of PIC, it is necessary to first unpack this fundamental concept. Public interest is best known as a political and public administration concept, yet it has no single, canonical definition or operational meaning (thus leading to criticism of its very existence). It is nevertheless thought to be a "cornerstone of democratic governance, a touchstone for public policy and a matter of practical consequence and activity" (Johnston & Pieczka, 2018, p. 9). Wheeler explains its enigmatic nature: "While it is one of the most used terms in the lexicon of public administration, it is arguably the least defined and least understood" (2013, p. 34). Yet paradoxically, this elusive nature is also said to be "understood in construction" (Mitnick, 2008, p. 1735), as public interest takes its meaning within the context of the interests that come into consideration, often weighed against each other. As political science scholar E. Pendleton Herring noted: "Its abstract meaning is vague but its application has far-reaching effects" (Herring, 1968, p. 170). This application is deeply embedded within political, social, legal and media discourse, seen in a wide range of legislation, case law, policy, regulation, governance and administrative documentation within democratic systems of government. Accordingly, claims to public interest are fundamentally based on sets of values and norms within political systems that have wider merit than satisfying private or individual needs or wants (Bozeman, 2007; Dewey, 1927; Flathman, 1966; McQuail, 1992).

Public interest has been described as "a staple of American political thought", a concept that the framers of the American Constitution employed "with relatively little reflection" due to the assumption that the term was transparent and apparently not in need of any detailed or precise elaboration (Rogers, 2012, p. 5). More recently, legal and political discourse surrounding public interest finds it to be in a constant state of review. As one famous legal case before the UK House of Lords heard: "The categories of the public interest are not closed, and must alter from time to time whether by restriction or extension as social conditions and social legislation develop" (D v National Society for the Prevention of Cruelty to Children, 1978). As such, legal scholars Carter and Bouris (2006) note how legislators and policy makers view the public interest as changing over time, according to the circumstances of each situation in which it is applied. Take, for example, the following:

> 50 years ago it was assumed that there was a public interest in knowing that an MP was gay, but little or no public interest in whether he drove home drunk, hit his wife or furnished his house using wood from non-sustainable sources. Now, obviously, it's the other way round. Society does – and should – constantly redefine what the public interest entails.
> (Sparrow, 2012 in Elliott, 2012 n.p.)

Johnston notes how at the national and international level public interest is often balanced against individual rights or national sovereignty. For example, the Human Rights Act 1988 (UK), the European Convention for the Protection of Human Rights and Fundamental Freedoms (2010) and the Canadian Human Rights Act (2004) aim to strike this balance (Meyerson, 2007, cited in Johnston, 2016). The European Court of Human Rights, for instance, examines whether a decision "is likely to be effective in achieving the government's purpose, whether there are less restrictive ways of achieving the purpose, and whether the cost to the right is justified by the public interest or public benefit" (Meyerson, 2007, pp. 4–5, cited in Johnston p. 5).

Therefore, while public interest has a utilitarian function, what is equally important is how it can act as a mechanism for representing the rights and struggles of marginalized or minority publics (Johnston & Pieczka, 2018; Sorauf, 1957). At a public administration level, this has been likened to a 'hair shirt' function, essentially intended to remind public officials and citizens of the need to recognize the "unorganized, unrepresented or underrepresented" lest they be ignored or forgotten due to their lack of social or political power (Sorauf, 1957, p. 639). This orientation has a clear fit for the nonprofit sector and its communication, which may include cause-related endeavours, advocacy and activism, pro bono service and other noncommercial (or less commercial) emphases on individual rights, social values and public responsibility. As Hall (1987) suggests, the nonprofits exist either to provide a service or further a cause, which sees PIC fitting their purpose, as the chapter now explores.

A multi-faceted concept

There is not one theory or view of how we can know what 'the public interest' is, who it should represent or who should benefit from it. However, to help scaffold our understanding, it is useful to consider how, over the years, scholars have placed public interest theory into certain typologies that align with how interests are decided, applied and understood. The first of these is the *abolitionist* approach, which proposes ignoring or removing the public interest from public discourse due to its vague nature and nonscientific meaning. The second is the *normative* approach, which sees the public interest as synonymous with the common good or seeking a substantive value. Third, the *communitarian* or *consensualist* approach highlights consensus found in certain types of societies that are more community oriented and less individualist. Fourth, the *process or procedural* approach sees the public interest derived as it is operationalized and as accommodating of pluralism or as an aggregate of many individual interests. Fifth, the *critical* approach argues for the need to pay fuller attention to power (differences), access, equality and agency of publics and decision makers. Finally, the *pragmatic* approach highlights the role of judgement and discretion required by decision makers in determining problem-centred decisions and outcomes (see Bozeman, 2007; Cochran, 1974; Johnston, 2016; Johnston & Pieczka, 2018; Flathman, 1966).

However, these categories are rarely discrete or siloed; indeed, they merge and bleed across boundaries. For example, the idea of pluralism and communitarianism can be combined in a sort of "civic pluralism" (Kalantzis, 2000), which can form a social contract that creates social cohesion by negotiating diversity. Early public interest scholar Richard Flathman (1966) and others (e.g. Bozeman, 2007) debunked the notion of any single public interest. Flathman warned against the idea of a summation of interests resulting in ideas of '*the* public interest' – what he called the Benthamite position. He argued: "When combined with an insistence upon the universality of government action and with social and political conflict, this summation was not merely difficult but (if we take the word summation literally) logically impossible" (1966, p. 21). With these categories in mind, I argue pragmatism, inclusive of its focus on pluralism and process, provides a most logical theory for further exploring PIC.

Prioritizing pragmatism

Pragmatism, for all its many theoretical variations, has been described as essentially about "the constitution of public problems" (Ogien, 2014, p. 422; see also Bozeman, 2007; Dewey, 1927). Moreover, the core of pragmatism is arguably about how action is applied (or not applied) (Heubner, 2016) and how this leads to or is driven out of inquiry. As such,

> if there is one thesis to which all of pragmatism can adhere, it is that which asserts that when individuals have to solve the problems that result from the essential incompleteness of action, they engage in an "inquiry" and implement experimental procedures in order to find a practical solution to it.
>
> (Ogien, 2014, p. 418)

In other words, pragmatism sees a problem and seeks to find a solution through inquiry and action. John Dewey's seminal work on the *Public and Its Problems* (1927) positions public interest as a pragmatic theory that considered these core elements, while others – Jürgen Habermas, for instance – adapted and developed pragmatism to a specific theory of communication action (Ogien, 2014; Habermas, 1984, 1998; Johnston, 2016). In his work, Dewey was concerned with how public problems could be managed through public reason and open public debate in deliberative democracies. As such, he said public interest can never be known in any real way in the absence of social enquiry, public discussion and debate (Bozeman, 2007; Dewey, 1927). Dewey and others in the pragmatist tradition argued that pragmatism should thus call on "the power of collective mobilisations that assert their autonomy, while calling out to governmental bodies from which they expect actions of recognition, reparation and regeneration" (Cefaï, 2018, para 43). Yet Dewey was under no illusions that all publics and interests could be accommodated by pragmatic decision making, famously noting: "Of course, there *are* conflicting interests; otherwise there would be no social problems" (1991, p. 81 original emphasis). Following Dewey, Bozeman describes public interest as a field of "pragmatic idealism", which calls for "keeping in mind an ideal of the public interest . . . moving toward that ideal, making the ideal more concrete as one moves toward it" (2007, p. 13).

Dewey's focus on democracy and dialectical problems thus opens the scope for other theoretical connections. The associated field of deliberative inquiry, for instance, considers how deliberation can be used to address practical problems while generating new possibilities for action (Barge & Craig, 2009; see also Carcasson & Sprain, 2016). Carcasson and Sprain note that deliberative inquiry's central mission is to "enhance local democracy through improved public communication and community problem solving" (2016, p. 44). By necessity, this calls for input from the citizenry. This was richly illustrated at the national level in Ireland's 2015 marriage equality referendum, which was initiated by the country's Constitutional Convention. Also called a 'citizen's assembly', the Convention of 66 members of the public, 33 elected representatives and an independent chair saw Ireland as the first country to vote for same-sex marriage by referendum (Farrell, 2015, n.p.). While:

> there were concerns that the conciliatory tone of the Convention had altered to become a battleground of interest-focused rhetoric prior to the Referendum. . . . It successfully put a social movement onto its country's political agenda, exposed it to national debate, and let the people decide what they believed was in the public interest.
>
> (Johnston, 2016, p. 157)

Thus, when we look at how public interest is practised in democratic systems, we may see it as a *process* aiming to achieve an *outcome* (Wheeler, 2013, 2018). In this way, it is best achieved by using a three-stage process:

- firstly, identification of the relevant population – the 'public' whose interests are to be considered in making a decision;
- secondly, identification of the public interests applicable to an issue or decision; and
- thirdly, assessment and weighing of each applicable public interest, including the balancing of conflicting or competing public interests. (Wheeler, 2013, p. 18)

At the same time, Wheeler argues what is more important than finding solutions for the public administrator "is that a conscientious attempt is made to find appropriate answers, and that the decision-maker is able to demonstrate that the appropriate approach was followed and all relevant matters were considered" (Wheeler, 2013, p. 48). However, Russill argues the "tests for handling different interests are less important than the vision of public participation they underwrite" (2008, p. 492). This participatory focus – seen through different lenses – is in keeping with Dewey's, which calls for inquiry to be public-centred. Dewey's method was to respond to problematic situations by deferring to the public or publics involved, arguing that those who wear the shoes "[know] best that it pinches and where it pinches" (Dewey, 1927, p. 207). Peters points out that Dewey is an exemplar of theorizing about "communication as partaking" (1999, p. 18), with the emphasis on inclusion and interaction. For the nonprofits, which prioritize the idea of collective action (Powell & Clemens, 1998), this can mean enabling voices, often through partnerships, alliances or collaborations.

Discourse arenas

Accordingly, the pragmatic approach proposes that debate should occur in public, material spaces – so-called "arenas of public debate" described by sociologists (Cefaï, 2016) or "discourse arenas" described by public relations and communication scholars (Heath & Waymer, 2018). For PIC these form a crucial nexus between public interest and communication because they are the discursive places – both physically and mediated – in which public interest is debated. Discourse arenas or public arenas of debate can take many forms – they include physical public sites such as streets or parks, community and meeting halls and parliamentary chambers and courtrooms. They also include media channels in many forms (print, broadcast, online, social, news, ambient) plus other forms of deliberative action such as citizen councils, juries and associations that may be held in various locations (Badouard et al., 2016; Carcasson & Sprain, 2016; Cefaï, 2016; Chwalisz, 2019; Johnston, 2020). These 'arenas' represent the places and activities that members of civil society use to circulate and challenge ideas, discuss, listen and argue, championing social causes and airing problems for public audiences. They take physical form through, for example, rallies, protests, public meetings and private lobbying. Arenas may be strengthened by formal or informal partnerships, alliances and networks through which shared value systems, goals and objectives bring organizations and individuals together to work toward a common public interest or cause. Sociologists note that these arenas "possess their own cultures of debate" that include particular ways through which issues are proposed for discussion and where exchanged arguments are considered to be valid or not (Badouard et al., 2016, p. 4). Within deliberative democracies, public arenas provide members of civil society with spaces to air public problems, placing pressure on government organizations to see the problem and take ownership of it (Johnston, 2020). These in turn can see new regulations, public services and public policies created to address public problems (Cefaï, 2016). If we return to Ireland's marriage equality referendum as an example, there were many discourse arenas – both mediated and face to face. On the grander scale, the Constitutional Convention was itself an arena. More directly was the social media campaign based around the slogan #hometovote that brought many members of the Irish diaspora home to deliver a high voter turnout (Johnston, 2016).

Heath and Waymer (2018) describe discourse arenas as "public interest battlegrounds" (2018, p. 40) that work as "layered networks of interlocking relationships, interests, and dialectically voiced viewpoints" (2018, p. 41). They argue that mutual benefit can be attained by engagement in these arenas which work in dialectic fashion, buffeting against one another, which thus enable PIC in three ways. First, to provide forums for advocacy and counter-advocacy; second, for collaborative decision making as a form of deliberative democracy; third, in redefining issues as competing perspectives (Heath & Waymer, 2018, p. 41–42). Through this process, facts, values, policies and issues will be better understood (Heath & Waymer, 2018). However, the reality is that discourse arenas can also go off course and divert the focus from public interests to hidden or vested interests (Heath & Waymer, 2018). This is what Habermas calls "systematically distorted communication" (1998, p. 168). Practices such as astroturfing and green washing illustrate this, where obfuscation and fake news prevail. And so, where one-sided communication represses alternative views, such as in war-time propaganda or the subjugation of protest views, communication cannot be argued to be of a public interest nature (Johnston & Gulliver, 2022). Heath and Waymer caution against strategic management seeking a favourable power distribution in discourse arenas when they are pitted against less powerful voices. They use the example of organized disinformation campaigns used by the oil sector in the climate change debate where "discord benefits enterprise and weakens the agency of society" (2018, p. 43). Among the checks and balances of discourse arenas are the investigative media, political competition, watchdog civic organizations and institutions, critical scholarship and public policy intelligentsia (Heath & Waymer, 2018; Mitnick, 2008).

PIC in action

The chapter now develops the concept of 'public interest in action', as expressed by Bozeman (2007), to the more targeted concept of 'public interest *communication* in action'. This follows the Deweyan observation that social and political knowledge is not an innate possession, but rather it is a "function of association and communication" (Dewey, 1927, p. 158). This is premised on shared language. As Wheeler explains:

> Acting in the public interest will always require public discussion about what matters and why. . . . Language is a public possession and what the public understands by certain words and phrases is not mere semantics, especially when the public interest needs to be set out in words.
>
> (2018, p. 64)

These shared understandings allow for clear interpretations and the capacity to offer counter-assertions, or counter-narratives, which can only be achieved through publicness, deliberation and discovery (Dewey, 1927; Flathman, 1966; Habermas, 1998). For Dewey, deliberation as part of social inquiry was seen to promote discovery of new courses of action, sometimes revealing underlying shared interests that can emerge from confrontation or even conflict. This confirms the importance of time and context in providing the cultural and political landscape for discourse and discovery to take place and social change to occur. Let us take an example.[1]

The Sydney Gay and Lesbian Mardi Gras (Mardi Gras) is widely celebrated as a global, cultural event. First held in Sydney in 1978 and run annually since then, it has become known not only for championing social tolerance but also for its artistic accomplishments, economic success and grand scale (Kates, 2003). The story of Mardi Gras centres on social and political change, underpinned by ongoing forms of participation and publicity. Mardi Gras began as a small protest for gay rights, resulting in violence and police arrests in its first year (Sydney Gay and Lesbian Mardi Gras, 2022). By the second year, however, the legislation that had allowed the arrests to be made had been repealed (Sydney Gay and Lesbian Mardi Gras, 2022). From that time onward the event moved from strength to strength, with participation, inclusivity and partnerships acting as central pillars in its success and longevity. The festival presented then, as now, a collection of social and political narratives, using a wide range of discourse arenas – from street marches, to media, in coffee shops and entertainment centres (Johnston, 2020). Willett outlines how a "complex network of media . . . businesses . . . professional services . . . political and cultural organizations run by and for lesbians and gay men" developed over time (2000, p. 183).

So, too, the legislative, social and political landscape was to irrevocably change shape during the life of Mardi Gras. When it began in 1978, Australia had yet to reform its homosexual laws; by the 1980s all but one state had decriminalized homosexuality, with decriminalization legislated nationally in 1994 (Bartle, 2020). As stated in its strategic plan: "Much has been achieved by LGBTQI communities since early activists took to the streets" (Sydney Gay and Lesbian Mardi Gras, 2019). The event's themes over five decades illustrate the shifting social and political focus: from *Power in the Darkness* in 1979, to *Fearless* 40 years later in 2019, and *United We Shine* in 2022.

As it nears half a century of history, Mardi Gras is in a constant state of reflection and renewal, discussed and debated, with attention to the conflicts between its political, commercial and celebratory dimensions (Johnston, 2020; Lewis & Markwell, 2022; Markwell & Waitt, 2009). Notwithstanding its decades of success, there have been ongoing struggles and dialectic tensions within Mardi Gras' highly diverse participant base, highlighted in 2022 by the decision to move the parade away from Sydney's Oxford Street "Gaybourhood" to the Sydney Cricket ground due to COVID-19 (Lewis & Markwell, 2022).

> Oxford Street provides the parade and its exuberant participants with a connection to what is arguably Australia's LGBTIQ+ imagined homeland – and the struggles and celebrations of past generations. . . . It is not surprising the shift to the Sydney Cricket Ground . . . was not accepted by all LGBTIQ+ people.
>
> (Lewis & Markwell, 2022, n.p.)

In considering its foundational roots, Lewis and Markwell note how for many, "a protest is only a protest if it disrupts the everyday routines of public life" (2022).

Over the years, members, organizers, venue hosts and other stakeholders have had to reconcile:

- the rising corporatization of the event "especially where in the view of the movement's radicals . . . the interests of capitalism and of gay liberation were incompatible" (Willet, 2000, p. 173);
- the shift from a 'movement' (and protest) to a 'community' (and festival) underwritten by commerce;
- changing the timing of the event from winter in Australia (June), in line with US gay-rights Stonewell riots, to February/March because "Sydney is a summer city" (Marsh & Galbraith, 1995, p. 303); and
- COVID-19 considerations, which raised tensions between the "pilgrimage" status of early years to the more sanitized, controlled environment of 2022 (Lewis & Markwell, 2022).

Mardi Gras must therefore "continue to balance its historic and future aims and different stakeholder needs, in a constant (re)negotiation of its *raison d'être*" (Johnston, 2020).

PIC in action can incorporate public discourse arenas, including media and public events, public-private partnerships and large-scale participation and, in the case of Mardi Gras, can challenge not only social and political conventions but legal ones as well. Dewey saw this when he observed: "Social change is here as a fact . . . changes that are revolutionary in effect are in process in every phase of life. . . . Flux does not have to be created. But it does have to be directed" (1991, 61). In turn, this direction needs to be communicated, and this must be done "out in the open" (Dewey, 1927, p. 81), which is why access to arenas, in a range of forms, is so important. This provides the oxygen for issues, problems and causes to be debated; to evolve; and, in the case of Mardi Gras, to succeed in many ways and contribute to public interest of LGBTIQ+ rights internationally. In turn, this sees public interest served at both the minority and wider community levels as public opinion acts as "the squeaky wheel" to government, law and policy makers (Johnston, 2016, p. 154).

Often embedded in decades of protest and lobbying, movements such as LGBTIQ+ rights, brought to life in Mardi Gras, show how civil society can effect change through ongoing protest, publicity and debate. Likewise, "movements opposed to war, racial injustice, global warming, animal cruelty and child labor have . . . been instrumental in initiating changed laws reflecting shifts in community values and attitudes" (Johnston, 2016, p. 155). As Cefaï notes, "The distinctive feature of the public [in the previous case, the LGBTIQ+ community] is to bring forth its audiences, its issues, its factions and battle lines" (2018, para 30). And in bringing this forth, publics can raise awareness through effective communication and action that reach the ears and eyes of decision makers and the wider community. As Russill points out, pragmatic communication enables learning, which can then make a range of solutions possible (2008).

Developing PIC theory

As PIC develops as a theoretical and practical concept, it has clear application for nonprofits and civil society, which act as both a response and a complement to public and private sectors (Powell & Clemens, 1998). As the chapter has explored, PIC is inherently public; that is, it must be acted out and debated in the open for ideas to be communicated, contested and, potentially, resolved or agreed upon, which may or may not require compromise or consensus. Here then we see the first of the dimensions proposed by Johnston and Pieczka (2018) for a PIC framework – *publicness*. Following this, PIC must also be *accessible* in both physical and semiotic senses to the relevant publics – we see this in how discourse arenas function with cultural and linguistic understanding. Through this, language is used for coordinating action (Habermas, 1984), and *action* is a central part of the process of PIC. Johnston and Pieczka (2018) note how "the whole point of eliciting a shared sense of where the public interest lies in any given case is to make it possible for practical action to follow legitimately, be it policy or specific practices". Underpinning this, as the chapter has explored, is ongoing *deliberation*, *inquiry* and *discovery*.

A pragmatic approach to PIC thus pays attention to how communication is involved in the "coordination of practical activities . . . [and] judged by its consequences" (Craig, 2007, p. 136). This will usually occur throughout the PIC process, crucially providing reasons given for decisions made. Thus, while public interest has no conclusive meaning, its descriptive meaning is found through reasoned discourse that attempts to relate to changeable community values and is open to listening to differing community perspectives. Drawing on the work of leading public interest scholar Richard Flathman (1966, p. 40), PIC thus "performs a logic" that will influence the kinds of policies adopted and rejected and the overall character of society. Yet at the same time its limitations in modern society – in both democracies and other systems of government – are apparent. Not all individuals or publics have access to public debate – public arenas do not magically open up to everyone. Even after combining forces in partnerships, alliances and other collaborations, all voices and the interests they represent may be repressed, ignored or represent risk associated with speaking out (Johnston & Gulliver, 2022). Here, we are reminded that public interest must also acknowledge a critical theory dimension in which it is acknowledged that power is unevenly divided, where access and agency are not automatic and where minority or marginalized voices are not guaranteed the opportunity to rise up. Dewey's approach of "pragmatic idealism" (see Bozeman, 2007, p. 13) comes to mind in reconciling the messy realities of the social and political world.

Communication in the public interest may end up characterized as what Peters calls an "imperfect fit that chafes the stump" (1999, pp. 30–31) in much the same way as political theorist Frank Sorauf called the public interest itself "a hair shirt" for decision makers (1957, p. 639). These metaphors point to the need for pragmatic thinking and a recognition by government, business and civil society of the complexity and difference within society which must be considered for effective PIC to occur.

Acknowledgements

My work on PIC began as an amazing joint venture with Magda Pieczka and a stellar lineup of international scholars, published in our 2018 book. It has been foundational for my ongoing work in this field, most recently with Robyn Gulliver in an open-access pressbook of the same name (Johnston & Gulliver, 2022).

Note

1 An earlier analysis of this event is examined in Johnston, 2020.

References

Badouard, R., Mabi, C., & Monnoyer-Smith, L. (2016). Arenas of public debate: On the materiality of discussion spaces. PUN – Editions universitaires de Lorraine. *Questions de Communication*, *30*, 1–15. http://questionsdecommunication.revues.org/11000

Barge, J. K., & Craig, R. (2009). Practical theory in applied communication scholarship. In L. Frey & K. N. Cissna (Eds.), *Routledge handbook of applied communication scholarship* (pp. 55–78). Routledge.

Bartle, J. (2020). *The historical offence of homosexuality in Australia, Sydney City lawyers*. www.sydneycriminallawyers.com.au/blog/the-historical-offence-of-homosexuality-in-australia/?utm_source=Mondaq&utm_medium=syndication&utm_campaign=LinkedIn-integration

Bozeman, B. (2007). *Public values and public interest: Counterbalancing economic individualism*. Georgetown University Press.

Canadian Human Rights Act. (2004). https://laws-lois.justice.gc.ca/eng/acts/H-6/section-16.html

Carah, N. (2018). Commercial media platforms and the challenges to public expression and scrutiny. In J. Johnston & M. Pieczka (Eds.), *Public interest communication: Critical debates and global contexts* (pp. 92–110). Routledge.

Carcasson, M., & Sprain, L. (2016). Beyond problem solving: Reconceptualizing the work of public deliberation as deliberative inquiry. *Communication Theory*, *26*, 41–63. doi:10.1111/COMT.12055

Carter, M., & Bouris, A. (2006). *Freedom of information: Balancing the public interest* (2nd ed.). The Constitution Unit-University College.

Cefaï, D. (2016). Publics, public problems, public arenas: The teachings of pragmatism. *Communication Matters*, *2*(30), 25–64. http://doi.org/10.4000/questionsdecommunication.10704

Cefaï, D. (2018, February 26). Publics and publicity: Toward a pragmatic inquiry. *Politika*. www.politika.io/index.php/en/notice/publics-and-publicity-towards-a-pragmatist-enquiry

Chwalisz, C. (2019, November 26). A new wave of deliberative democracy. *Carnegie Europe*. https://carnegieeurope.eu/2019/11/26/new-wave-of-deliberative-democracy-pub-80422

Cochran, C. E. (1974). Political science and the public interest. *The Journal of Politics*, *36*(2), 327–355. https://doi.org/10.2307/2129473

Craig, R. T. (2007). Pragmatism in the field of communication theory. *Communication Theory*, *17*, 125–145.

D v National Society for the Prevention of Cruelty to Children, [1978] AC 171, at 230.

Dewey, J. (1927). *The public and its problems*. H. Holt & Co.

Dewey, J. (1991). *Liberalism and social action*. Prometheus.

Elliott, C. (2012, May 21). The readers' editor . . . how should we define the public interest. *The Guardian*. www.theguardian.com/commentisfree/2012/may/20/open-door- definition-public-interest

European Convention for the Protection of Human Rights and Fundamental Freedoms. (2010). *European Convention on Human Rights*. https://www.echr.coe.int/Documents/Convention_ENG.pdf

Farrell, D. (2015, May 17). Constitutional Convention 'brand' is in jeopardy. *The Irish Times*. www.irishtimes.com/opinion/david-farrell-constitutional-convention-brand-is-in-jeopardy-1.2142826

Fessmann, J. (2016). The emerging field of public interest communications. In E. Oliveira, A. D. Melo, & G. Goncalves (Eds.), *Strategic communication in nonprofit organisations: Challenges and alternative approaches* (pp. 13–34). Vernon Press.

Flathman, R. E. (1966). *The public interest: An essay concerning the normative discourse of politics*. John Wiley & Son.

Habermas, J. (1984). *The theory of communicative action. Vol. I: Reason and the rationalization of society*. Beacon Press.

Habermas, J. (1998). *On the pragmatics of communication*. Polity.

Hall, P. D. (1987). A historical overview of the private nonprofit sector. In W. W. Powell (Ed.), *The nonprofit sector: A research handbook* (pp. 3–26). Yale University Press.

Heath, R. L., & Waymer, D. (2018). Terministic dialectics of individual and community agency: Co-creating and co-enacting the public interest. In J. Johnston & M. Pieczka (Eds.), *Public interest communication: Critical debates and global contexts* (pp. 32–47). Routledge.

Herring, P. (1968). Public interest. In D. L. Sills (Ed.), *International encyclopedia of the social sciences* (p. 170). Macmillan Co and Free Press.

Heubner, D. A. (2016). History and social progress: Reflections on mead's approach to history. *European Journal of Pragmatism and American Philosophy*, VIII-2. doi:10.4000/ejpap.637. http://journals.openedition.org/ejpap/637

Ihlen, O., Raknes, K., Somerville, I., Valentini, C., Stachel, C., Lock, I., Davidson, S., & Seele, P. (2018). Framing 'the public interest': Comparing public lobbying campaigns in four European states. *Journal of Public Interest Communications*, 2(1), 107–127.

Johnston, J. (2016). *Public relations & the public interest*. Routledge.

Johnston, J. (2020). Where public interest, virtue ethics and pragmatic sociology meet: Modelling a socially progressive approach for communication. *Westminster Papers in Communication and Culture*, 15(2), 79–94. https://doi.org/10.16997/wpcc.355

Johnston, J., & Gulliver, R. (2022). *Public interest communication*. University of Queensland.

Johnston, J., & Pieczka, M. (Eds.). (2018). *Public interest communication: Critical debates and global contexts*. Routledge.

Kalantzis, M. (2000). Multicultural citizenship. In W. Hudson & J. Kane (Eds.), *Rethinking Australian citizenship*. Cambridge University Press.

Kates, S. M. (2003). Producing and consuming gendered representations: An interpretation of the Sydney Gay and Lesbian Mardi Gras. *Consumption, Markets and Culture*, 6(1), 5–22. http://doi.org/10.1080/10253860302699

Lewis, C., & Markwell, K. (2022, May 22). Homage, pilgrimage and protest: Why Sydney's Mardi Gras Parade should go back to the street. *The Conversation*. https://theconversation.com/homage-pilgrimage-and-protest-why-sydneys-mardi-gras-parade-should-go-back-to-the-streets-171820

Markwell, K., & Waitt, G. (2009). Festivals, space and sexuality: Gay pride in Australia. *Tourism Geographies*, 11(2), 143–168. http://doi.org/10.1080/14616680902827092

Marsh, I., & Galbraith, L. M. (1995). The political impact of the Sydney Gay and Lesbian Mardi Gras. *Australian Journal of Political Science*, 30, 300–320.

McQuail, D. (1992). *Media performance: Mass communication and the public interest*. Sage.

Mitnick, B. (2008). The public interest. In R. W. Kolb (Ed.), *Encyclopedia of business ethics and society* (Vol 5, pp. 1887–1802). Sage.

Ogien, A. (2014). Pragmatisms and Sociologies. *Revue Française de Sociologie*, 55(3), 414–428. https://doi.org/10.4000/ejpap.371

Peters, J. D. (1999). *Speaking into the air*. University of Chicago Press.

Powell, W. W., & Clemens, E. S. (Eds.). (1998). *Private action and the public good* (pp. 20–35). Yale University Press.

Rogers, M. L. (2012). Introduction. In *Dewey, the Public and Its Problems*. Pennsylvania State University.

Russill, C. (2008). Through a public darkly: Reconstructing pragmatist perspectives in communication theory. *Communication Theory*, 18, 478–504. doi:10.1111/j.1468-2885.2008.00331.x

Sorauf, F. J. (1957). The public interest reconsidered. *The Journal of Politics*, 19(4), 616–639.

Sydney Gay and Lesbian Mardi Gras. (2019). *Strategic plan: 2018/19–2020/2021*. www.mardigras.org.au/images/uploads/images/mg19-strategic-plan-flipbook.pdf

Sydney Gay and Lesbian Mardi Gras. (2022). *Partners*. www.mardigras.org.au/partners

Wheeler, C. (2013). The public interest revisited – We know it's important but do we know what it means? *AIAL Forum, 48*, 1–25. www.researchgate.net/publication/282853660_The_Public_Interest_Revisited_-_We_know_it's_important_but_do_we_know_what_it_means

Wheeler, C. (2018). Public interest as an accountability test. In T. Frame (Ed.) *Who defines the public interest?* Connor Court.

Willett, G. (2000). Australian gay activists: From movement to community. *Radical History Review, 76*, 169–187. http://doi.org/10.1215/01636545-2000-76-169

1.7
HUMANITARIAN COMMUNICATION

Valérie Gorin

Introduction

In 2015, the Dutch nongovernmental organization (NGO) Cordaid announced that its 2007 campaign "Little Money, Big Difference" was going viral. Found somehow on the Internet after eight years, the images Saatchi and Saatchi created to draw consumers' attention to drought-affected areas were shared on Twitter by 9 million people, from Canada to India.[1] After ten years of work in Kenya with local organizations to build resilience in farming and entrepreneurship projects, Cordaid collaborated with the public relations (PR) agency to design a responsible campaign to raise funds and awareness, with the Samburu nomadic people posing in the ads with consumer goods. Reversing the codes of fashion magazines so people would confront their consumer behavior, the campaign aligned with new, post-humanitarian representations NGOs adopted a decade ago, focusing on irony and self-reflection instead of pity (Chouliaraki, 2013). Yet the combination of fundraising, educational purposes and ethical considerations uniquely reflects some of the fundamental components and paradoxes of humanitarian communication. Communication in the aid sector has primarily been studied in the field of social marketing, highlighting the adoption of business-like concepts and methods in the humanitarian industry. A growing body of knowledge has also focused on the critique of humanitarian representations, showing the shortcomings of fundraising campaigns and the need to apply more integrative approaches from communication sciences. Humanitarian communications are multiple, instead, as they overlap with other communication fields, such as political communication, corporate social responsibility or crisis reporting (Chouliaraki & Vestergaard, 2022).

The professionalization of communication in the humanitarian sector has developed throughout the 20th century at the same time that mass media and communication have been revolutionized to enable large-scale humanitarian operations. Strictly limited by ethical guidelines and grounded in humanitarian principles, humanitarian communications also involve educational, promotional, accountability, awareness and advocacy purposes to reach multilayered target audiences, such as civil society, opinion leaders, political and military authorities and donors. Yet the adoption of professional communication techniques has prompted controversies about the moral ambiguities of the visual politics of aid, collaboration with attention- and profit-driven actors (the media and publicity agencies) and political engagement. Although aid agencies are also concerned with issues related to internal communication, in this chapter, I will explore humanitarian communications by distinguishing its two main sectors of activity: public communication and operational communication. First, I examine the constraints of fundraising and aid agencies' use of public relations to build acceptance and promote a cause. Second, I discuss the humanitarian sector's adoption of ethical codes and accountability procedures to face criticism and address the donor/beneficiary relationship. Finally, I focus on advocacy, negotiation and life-saving communication, whose operational uses have been neglected in the literature despite the shift to a human rights–based approach in the humanitarian discourse since the 1970s and the growing use of new communication technologies for relief response.

Communicating for profit

Despite their not-for-profit nature, humanitarian communications share close boundaries with marketing, as they look to generate symbolic capital as well as funds. Aid agencies have a *doxa* – saving lives and alleviating suffering – even though the neoliberal logic driving humanitarian fundraising departs from the philosophical altruistic ideals of humanitarian sentiments born in the 19th century. Similarly to news media outlets and enterprises, humanitarian organizations have competed for the same resource: publicity in its broad sense, i.e. the need to raise public attention, have a public image, make oneself known and advertise (Gorin, 2021a). Humanitarian communications have adopted market-driven models for fundraising, purchasing and accounting ever since NGOs hired their first publicists in the 1920s. Asking for donations from the public and private sectors, aid agencies today use all the communication means available, including direct mailing, sponsoring, social media solicitations, street fundraising, telethons and merchandise sold at public venues or concerts. Two major humanitarian crises have hastened the shift from amateur activism to professional communication: the Nigerian Civil War (1967–1970) and the Ethiopian famine (1984–1985). In both cases, civilian suffering was largely brought home to Western audiences through television and news magazines in an increasingly visual world. *Live Aid*, the huge charity show for Ethiopia broadcast to 2 billion people on 13 July 1985, also redefined celebrity fundraising and endorsement, with many international artists participating in charity songs. Although the political dimensions of the conflicts and the instrumentalization of the relief response by local governments were often ignored in the media coverage of both humanitarian crises, the civil society response in the West was so intense that it redefined humanitarian communication, with many aid agencies adapting their strategies with media training and by hiring consultants or experts in public relations, marketing and journalism (Franks, 2013).

Yet the use of publicity has generated ethical dilemmas and resistance among aid agencies, who dealt with the intrinsic paradox of selling suffering (Kennedy, 2009). Instead of selling goods, they sell the promotion of Good linked to an ethos of compassion (Albuquerque, 2016) toward deserving others presented as beneficiaries, to the extent that humanitarian organizations have been called "merchants of morality" (Bob, 2002). To make suffering more palatable, humanitarian organizations have massively used all media formats to eliminate the distance between affected populations and benefactors to turn the spectacle of suffering into a moral obligation to care beyond borders. "Regarding the pain of others," to quote Susan Sontag's (2003) seminal work, therefore implies a moral ambivalence and an unequal relationship between those who are fortunate enough in the so-called Global North to observe those who are unfortunate in the Global South (Boltanski, 1999). Studies in social psychology and marketing have largely emphasized that distant suffering – whether geographical, racial, emotional or psychic – plays a role in soliciting audiences' affects and donations (Mittelman & Dow, 2018; Orgad & Seu, 2014; Small & Loewenstein, 2003). Charitable giving is related to the intensity of media coverage, as well as the geographical or cultural proximity with the country affected by the crisis; the geometry of compassion is thus determined by geopolitics and economic interests rather than global solidarity (Eckel et al., 2007; Olsen et al., 2003).

Researchers in history, postcolonial critique and semiotics have also explored the visual economies of aid since the 1980s. First, the commodification of suffering through miserable and paternalistic clichés showcases the idealized and neocolonial image of the White savior. Whereas communities affected by disasters and conflicts are undeniably the first responders in times of catastrophes, they have most often been stereotyped and rendered voiceless, anonymous or helpless in aid imagery. Humanitarian communications are therefore partially responsible for turning relief into a form of assistance to match the rationales of institutional donors rather than to display global equality or humanity (da Silva Gama et al., 2013; Dogra, 2012; Nolan & Mikami, 2013). Images of children in humanitarian appeals have received much attention because they embody innocence, dependence and vulnerability altogether, and they trigger donations and moral support from adult viewers who react as missing caregivers (Burman, 1993; Malkki, 2010; O'Dell, 2008). As the use of children often infantilizes and reduces complex humanitarian emergencies, it also acts as a "brand logo that advertises NGOs' encoded humanitarian principles" (Manzo, 2008, p. 635). Similarly, the visual politics in humanitarian portrayals of refugees show how much they have been dehumanized and racialized, subordinated "to the 'Western self' and state interests" (Ongenaert & Joye, 2019, p. 478; see also Malkki, 1996).

A second body of critics targets the "charity business" and this market-driven model's shortcomings in the last few decades (Sargeant, 1999). The bureaucratization and market saturation have led to limited solicitations of donors in a very competitive sector, public distrust of NGOs due to financial scandals and corruption and gross exaggerations in aid's impact. The independence of aid organizations, albeit one of the core humanitarian principles, should be more nuanced considering NGOs' and multilateral agencies' growing reliance on public subsidies and the private sector.[2] Whereas the legislation varies between countries to categorize the status of NGOs, they have become less distinguishable from enterprises and other welfare organizations (Missoni & Alesani, 2013). The extent of so-called compassion fatigue (Moeller, 1999) has also pushed aid agencies to address the ethical challenges their communications raise.

Communicating for social capital

With the charity sector's incredible growth after World War II, aid organizations enhanced their identity and visibility. Public, corporate and organizational communications have developed among aid agencies to build trust among donors/beneficiaries, enhance the organizations' public profiles, exalt common affects for the benefits of humanity and communicate ethically for impact (Daccord, 2005). Reflecting on the surge of emergency medical NGOs since the 1970s, MSF France's former director Rony Brauman (2004) emphasized the difference with faith-based charity groups; if organizations such as World Vision, Islamic Relief and the Joint Distribution Committee can rely on transnational religious groups and diasporas, secular NGOs emerging from civil society need to broaden their public support base. They all have to build social capital and recruit the general public to support their cause.

Dijkzeul and Moke's (2005) classification of NGOs and United Nations (UN) organizations according to the fundamental humanitarian principles – neutrality, independence and impartiality – shows how these principles constitute a unique feature in their public communications. They shape not only their mandate and core beliefs but also their communication policies in ways that commercial communication does not encounter. Communicating about these principles, therefore, is crucial in the aid agencies' engagement with other stakeholders, specifically to recruit volunteers, raise awareness and influence decision makers; negotiate with armed groups; and, above all, provide credibility and legitimacy when they engage with affected communities. As a consequence, the need to promote a recognizable visual identity and a unique set of values has pushed humanitarian organizations to brand themselves (Slim, 2003; Vestergaard, 2009). This form of neoliberal humanitarianism also involves celebrities in campaigns to endorse merchandise, such as the RED products, through claims of ethical consumerism (Davis, 2010).

Principled public communication raises critical challenges at two levels. First, when the humanitarian identity and mandate are jeopardized, a clash of values is triggered. MSF Belgium notoriously published a fundraising poster in 1991 stating, "We also help the Blacks and the Arabs. If this bothers you, don't give us money". The poster demonstrated political antagonism after the far-right party's victory in the Belgian general elections and the call to the population to fight discrimination and xenophobia. In the same vein, Action Against Hunger released a poster in the aftermath of the US coalition's 2003 Iraq invasion, stating, "You don't improvise yourself a humanitarian", with a picture of a military helmet full of rice. The campaign was a blatant reminder of the blurring identity resulting from increasing humanitarian military interventions since the 1990s (as in Somalia or Kosovo) while NGOs had complained about the security risks they faced if seen as allies to the military (Fassin & Pandolfi, 2010). Second, public communication in the aid sector highlights the vital yet complex relationship with the news media. Humanitarian organizations have become news providers that influence crisis reporting and media-driven humanitarian assistance (Abbott, 2015). Although sudden-onset disasters make the news more often than chronic conflicts, aid agencies challenge time and resource allocations in global reporting by promoting their own "forgotten crises" in the news and by forming public relations with journalists and media outlets that can increase their social and financial capital (Cottle & Cooper, 2015). Researchers explored this relationship in many media analyses after the failure of the international community and the media to stop the 1994 genocide in Rwanda (Girardet, 1995). Mutual critiques have been raised: media practices include selective news coverage, regional disparities, Western-centrism, lack of specialist knowledge and formulaic scripts and sensationalism, and journalists see the aid industry as corporate, patronizing and not really open to public scrutiny or willing to discuss their malpractices (CARMA International, 2006; Magee, 2014).

Communicating with principles

With the need to address public and media scrutiny, the adverse effects of fundraising as well as ethical controversies have forced humanitarian organizations to adopt deontological guidelines. Critiques of image-based fundraising have consistently been made in the last few decades, particularly over what has been labeled "poverty porn" and the lack of dignified representations in the aid sector, including in non-Western NGOs (Benthall, 1993; Bhati & Eikenberry, 2016). A proliferation of codes of conduct regarding images and messages was a direct result of such public controversies, forming another peculiar aspect of humanitarian communication. A majority of them, such as the DOCHAS code, adopted in 1989 (2006), address dignity, equality, fairness, solidarity and justice and provide strict standards to sensitize new volunteers, journalists and publicity agencies for collaborations with a stronger ethical responsibility in a quickly evolving media environment. They also show the need to evaluate more systematically perceptions of the aid sector and how humanitarian representations are produced, circulated, experienced and understood among general audiences, journalists, communication officers and image makers (Dencik & Allan, 2017). Insights reveal the ambivalence of NGOs preferably seen as "good Samaritans" rather than as "marketers" (Seu & Orgad, 2017). Because of a lack of time, tools and collaborations with the academy, aid agencies are still reluctant to focus more on reception studies despite timid attempts to introduce a socio-anthropological lens to understand perceptions among beneficiaries of MSF medical emergency care or people used in the images of Save the Children (Abu-Sada, 2012; Warrington & Crombie, 2017). The emergence of non-Western media outlets and the intensification of dialogue on digital social platforms have also opened channels for alternative, more inclusive representations (Hallas, 2012). The necessity to adapt to the new media ecology of Internet-based communication has pushed NGOs to adopt new practices, such as association with social influencers (Pantti, 2015), which has also brought into question ordinary people's legitimacy in raising awareness of sensitive issues.

Parallel with ethical guidelines, accountability procedures aimed toward donors and recipients have been an essential tool of humanitarian management and communications for fifteen years. Without establishing proper customer services, aid agencies are seen as service providers with the adoption of feedback and complaint mechanisms, and accountability is part of the new "engagement with affected communities". This participatory approach has been reviewed essentially from the point of view of practitioners (Bryant, 2020; HPN, 2019), but engagement with communities would assume a fair and balanced distribution of power between clients who have consumers' choice and NGOs who act as deliverers. This assumption is very questionable in the humanitarian ecosystem, where power dynamics are reversed for the benefit of aid organizations. This unequal relationship would explain why it is often difficult for beneficiaries to raise concerns against organizations that provide life-saving services in the fear that they might be excluded from aid distribution. Nevertheless, accountability and engagement aim at integrating people of concern in decision-making processes while opening lines of inquiry to assess the impact and efficiency of aid. Humanitarian organizations are still very reluctant to discuss publicly their professional misconduct in terms of behaviors and attitudes, however, as the way Oxfam and Save the Children mismanaged allegations of sexual exploitation in 2018 made clear (Scurlock et al., 2020).

Communicating for access

The need to speak out in sensitive contexts and in front of violence has therefore challenged the limits humanitarian principles have imposed on aid organizations when they venture into political communication. Somehow ignored in the literature until ten years ago (Bowden & Metcalfe-Hough, 2020; Bridges, 2010), advocacy has become a new trend to improve humanitarian access. Access can be understood in two ways: to speak on behalf of others or raise their voices so they can gain access to humanitarian assistance or to limit obstacles to humanitarian assistance by facilitating access to populations affected by conflicts. Consequently, advocacy overlaps with the identity of aid agencies because it questions the boundaries of humanitarianism, either narrowed down to the action of treating symptoms (alleviating suffering) or broadened to address the root causes of suffering (global justice). Humanitarian advocacy is often an all-encompassing concept with "interchangeable terms" (DuBois, 2008, p. 12) that refer to campaigning, face-to-face dialogue, behind-the-door bilateral or multilateral diplomacy with techniques borrowed from lobbying and full public and international mobilization through street protest or petitioning.

Raising political concerns publicly therefore intersects with the politics of aid. For a long time, NGOs in particular seemed to have been lost on how to become channels to politicize their concerns, and they would pass the responsibility for political action into the hands of citizens. The legislation that defines the status of NGOs can also restrain aid charities from political activism or calling governments to change policies, as with the Charity Act in the UK. In this case, aid agencies are confronted with the limits of neutrality, from not taking sides to speaking out. Therefore, advocacy strategies and political communication will depend on the organization's identity, its relationship with donor governments and its activities. The International Committee of the Red Cross, acting as a custodian of the Geneva Conventions and whose main activities involve visits to detention places, must maintain close relationships with the states and prefers to remain silent most of the time (Kellenberger, 2004), whereas MSF has gained a tradition of bearing witness and speaking out when facing human rights abuses or violations of the humanitarian space, such as when the organization denounced the government's forced resettlement policy during the Ethiopian famine, which led to its expulsion from the country (Gorin, 2021b).

NGOs opened their first advocacy units in the 1970s, and two schools have since predominated: educational advocacy is mainly practiced by British NGOs and focuses on a transformative agenda to promote global solidarity and justice through the mobilization of the civil society to put an end to poverty or hunger, for example, whereas political advocacy is more related to French NGOs and seeks to increase protection of civilians in emergency settings, using more persuasion or denunciation techniques to target states, governments and armed groups in priority (Edwards, 1993; Gorin, 2018). The relationships developed with PR agencies or journalists since the 1980s have increased humanitarian organizations' ability to mobilize the public sphere around a specific issue at a specific time, as the popular "International Days or Weeks," which the UN introduced, did. Coupled with fundraising events, they participate in shaping global awareness and policies by focusing on political, social, cultural and economic agendas. To double such campaigns' impact, the UN has also borrowed from celebrity endorsement techniques by naming sports or arts celebrities as "goodwill ambassadors." More recently, celebrity advocacy has become a field of research considering the links between the philanthropic and diplomatic sectors, as well as such ambassadors' global outreach, especially their legitimacy and credibility as a soft power (Cooper, 2008).

At the operational level, humanitarian advocacy is used for protection and involves negotiation skills and techniques. The use of humanitarian negotiation (Mancini-Griffoli & Picot, 2004; Radice, 2016) attests to the growing insecurity in the aid sector. For a long time, the idea persisted that aid organizations were protected by their purpose of "doing good" and acting as impartial and neutral intermediaries, but the increased number of attacks against humanitarian staff since September 11 shows how much they are now targeted on purpose. The humanitarian space is politicized and instrumentalized by armed groups who have understood the symbolic, ideological and financial value of NGOs, particularly international NGOs operating from the West. As Hugo Slim (2004) frames it, humanitarian organizations have to pay particular attention to the way they look, as their public image can generate hostile perceptions. As such, humanitarian negotiation participates in humanitarian communications to improve the staff's and civilians' security and protection and manage trusted relationships with all parties to the conflict to support basic humanitarian programming and expand the humanitarian principles.

Communicating to save lives

The focus on operational communication in humanitarian contexts has also been emphasized by the need to explore how affected populations communicate and use information. Under the motto "Communication is aid", the aid sector has developed a form of risk communication that aims at preventing, preparing and mitigating harm by educating communities for behavior change (Bradley et al., 2014; Romo-Murphy et al., 2011). The use of social networking platforms like Facebook during large-scale disasters since 2005 demonstrates the importance of disseminating life-saving information, sometimes in a 72-hour span, as well as the impact of big data that virtual volunteers can aggregate for crisis mapping (Norris, 2020). In parallel, the involvement of media development agencies (i.e. BBC Media Action) and telecommunication companies in life-saving communication has fostered technological support, such as the distribution of mobile phones and better Internet access after the 2010 Haiti earthquake. It emphasizes the growing interdependence of the charity sector to foundation-funded projects in the field of communication technologies and innovations.

Life-saving communication is not unique to the humanitarian sector because similar approaches exist in other nonprofit communication, such as that about peace, the environment and development. It focuses on communication in times of armed conflicts and natural disasters to increase coordination and connectedness; learn how people communicate; and adapt content that can save, educate and promote trust and resilience among affected communities. Although many more evaluations are needed, life-saving communication offers opportunities to enhance capacity-building programs; alter risk perception; promote dialogue, reconciliation and conflict resolution; and counter misconceptions and rumors (Baú, 2019). One recent example is the Federation of Red Cross and Red Crescent Societies and UNICEF's co-production of *The Story of Ebola* under the leadership of

Global Health Media, a nonprofit media organization that produces easy-to-use digital resources and educational material for frontline health workers, to be used also in remote places. The movie provided trusted information to dispel myths about the chain of infection and counter misinformation about the disease in West Africa in 2015, and the choice to use animation allowed viewers to focus on highly sensitive and intimate stories in an ethical way. The initiative was so successful (almost 70 million viewers since 2015) that it was reproduced for the *Story of Coronavirus* in 2021, in the midst of the pandemics and available at this time in 44 languages.[3]

Conclusion

Three main areas of concern have been raised regarding the aid sector's communication practices: 1) the moral ambiguity of the relations between aid agencies and PR or publicity agencies, as well as the challenging collaboration with news media outlets to attract public attention; 2) ethical concerns over visual messages in humanitarian appeals that sell suffering; and 3) the limits of political communication when aid agencies raise concerns about belligerents' attitudes or obstacles to the distribution of aid, which question the fundamental humanitarian principles, particularly neutrality. These grounded principles perhaps constitute the unique features of humanitarian communications for organizations that focus on the same mission and values despite their diverse range of activities, including emergency relief, child protection, women's education and climate change. Yet "path dependence" remains between philanthropy, politics and NGOs that "interact with established mechanisms of institutional production (start-up costs, feedback effects, knowledge accumulation) to explain why NGOs continue to persist in media-centered publicity strategies despite new technological possibilities" (Powers, 2016, p. 490).

If new communication technologies can be seen as a tool to create more direct, two-way communication between beneficiaries and humanitarian organizations, it is still unclear how the aid sector will address the digital gap to reduce power asymmetries and give people opportunities to make their voices heard (Madianou et al., 2015). Essentially explored from the perspective of social marketing and crisis reporting, humanitarian communications would benefit from studies that can explore the intersection with other communication fields, such as risk and crisis communication, conflict resolution and persuasive communication. The contexts in which humanitarian communications operate, as well as the limitations of humanitarian activities and the local and global audiences targeted, should be considered to discuss the connection of the humanitarian sector with development, peace or human rights.

Notes

1. For more information on the campaign's impact and design, see Cordaid's website: www.cordaid.org/en/news/how-samburu-models-went-viral/
2. Although Médecins Sans Frontières (MSF) is considered one of the most independent NGOs, with more than 90% of its funding coming from individual donors and private institutions, the Bill & Melinda Gates Foundation is the second largest contributor to the World Health Organization.
3. Both movies are available for free on YouTube.

References

Abbott, K. (2015). How NGOs became the new(s) reporters. In S. Cottle & G. Cooper (Eds.), *Humanitarianism, communications and change* (pp. 183–197). Peter Lang.

Abu-Sada, C. (Ed.). (2012). *In the eyes of others. How people in crises perceive humanitarian aid*. MSF, Humanitarian Outcomes, NYU Center on International Cooperation.

Albuquerque, C. (2016). The 'ethos of compassion' in contemporary social intervention: The Janus faces of humanitarian action proposals. *European Journal of Multidisplinary Studies*, 2(1), 51–58.

Baú, V. (2019). Re-designing the media in humanitarian interventions. Communicating with Communities at times of crisis. In I. S. Shaw & S. Selvarajah (Eds.), *Reporting human rights, conflicts, and peacebuilding: Critical and global perspectives* (pp. 67–81). Springer International Publishing.

Benthall, J. (1993). *Disasters, relief and the media*. Sean Kingston Publishing.

Bhati, A., & Eikenberry, A. M. (2016). Faces of the needy: The portrayal of destitute children in the fundraising campaigns of NGOs in India. *International Journal of Nonprofit and Voluntary Sector Marketing, 21*(1), 31–42.

Bob, C. (2002). Merchants of morality. *Foreign Policy, 129*, 36–45.

Boltanski, L. (1999). *Distant suffering: Morality, media and politics*. Cambridge University Press.

Bowden, M., & Metcalfe-Hough, V. (2020). *Humanitarian diplomacy and protection advocacy in an age of caution* (HGP Briefing Note). Humanitarian Policy Group.

Bradley, D., McFarland, M., & Clarke, M. (2014). The effectiveness of disaster risk communication: A systematic review of intervention studies. *PLoS Currents Disasters, 6*.

Brauman, R. (2004). Entretien: La communication des ONG, une affaire d'Etats? *Revue Internationale et Stratégique, 56*, 109–115.

Bridges, K. (2010). Between aid and politics: Diagnosing the challenge of humanitarian advocacy in politically complex environments – The case of Darfur, Sudan. *Third World Quarterly, 31*(8), 1251–1269.

Bryant, J. (2020). *ReliefWatch. Designing a new accountability service for people affected by humanitarian crises* (HPG Report). Humanitarian Policy Group – ODI.

Burman, E. (1993). Innocents abroad: Western fantasies of childhood and the iconography of emergencies. *Disasters, 18*(3), 238–253.

CARMA International. (2006). *The CARMA report on Western media coverage of humanitarian disasters*. Carma International.

Chouliaraki, L. (2013). *The ironic spectator: Solidarity in the age of post-humanitarianism*. Wiley.

Chouliaraki, L., & Vestergaard, A. (2022). *Routledge Handbook of humanitarian communication*. Routledge.

Cooper, A. (2008). *Celebrity diplomacy*. Paradigm Publishers.

Cottle, S., & Cooper, G. (Eds.). (2015). *Humanitarianism, communications and change* (Vol. 19). Peter Lang.

da Silva Gama, C. P., Pellegrino, A. P., de Rosa, F., & de Andrade, I. (2013). Empty portraits – Humanitarian aid campaigns and the politics of silencing. *International Journal of Humanities and Social Science, 3*(19), 39–50.

Daccord, Y. (2005). ICRC communication: Generating support. *International Review of the Red Cross, 87*(860), 693–706.

Davis, L. (2010). Feeding the world a line? Celebrity activism and ethical consumer practices from live aid to product red. *Nordic Journal of English Studies, 9*(3), 89–118.

Dencik, L., & Allan, S. (2017). In/visible conflicts: NGOs and the visual politics of humanitarian photography. *Media, Culture & Society, 39*(8).

Dijkzeul, D., & Moke, M. (2005). Public communication strategies of international humanitarian organizations. *International Review of the Red Cross, 87*(860), 673–691.

DOCHAS. (2006). *Code of conduct on images and messages*. Dochas Development Education Working Group.

Dogra, N. (2012). *Representations of global poverty: Aid, development and international NGOs*. I. B. Tauris.

DuBois, M. (2008). Civilian protection and humanitarian advocacy: Strategies and (false?) dilemmas. *Humanitarian Exchange Magazine, 39*, 12–15.

Eckel, C., Grossman, P., & Milano, A. (2007). Is more information always better? An experimental study of charitable giving and Hurricane Katrina. *Southern Economic Journal, 74*(2), 388–411.

Edwards, M. (1993). Does the doormat influence the boot? Critical thoughts on UK NGOs and international advocacy. *Development in Practice, 3*(3), 163–175.

Fassin, D., & Pandolfi, M. (Eds.). (2010). *Contemporary states of emergency: The politics of military and humanitarian interventions*. Zone Books.

Franks, S. (2013). *Reporting disasters: Famine, aid, politics and the media*. Hurst.

Girardet, E. (Ed.). (1995). *Somalia, Rwanda, and beyond: The role of international media in wars and humanitarian crises*. Crosslines.

Gorin, V. (2018). Advocacy strategies of Western humanitarian NGOs from the 1960s to the 1990s. In J. Paulmann (Ed.), *Humanitarianism and media. 1900 to the present* (pp. 201–221). Berghahn Books.

Gorin, V. (2021a). When "seeing was believing". Visual advocacy in the early decades of humanitarian cinema. *Journal of Humanitarian Affairs, 3*(2), 18–27.

Gorin, V. (2021b). Witnessing and témoignage in MSF's advocacy. *Journal of Humanitarian Affairs, 3*(2), 28–33.

Hallas, R. (2012). Photojournalism, NGOs, and the new media ecology. In M. McLagan & Y. McKee (Eds.), *Sensible politics: The visual culture of nongovernmental activism* (pp. 95–114). Zone Books.

HPN. (2019). Communication and community engagement in humanitarian response. *Humanitarian Exchange Magazine, 74*.

Kellenberger, J. (2004). Speaking out or remaining silent in humanitarian work. *International Review of the Red Cross*, *86*(855), 593–609.

Kennedy, D. (2009, February 28). Selling the distant other: Humanitarianism and imagery – Ethical dilemmas of humanitarian action. *The Journal of Humanitarian Assistance*. https://sites.tufts.edu/jha/archives/411

Madianou, M., Longboan, L., & Ong, J. C. (2015). Finding a voice through humanitarian technologies? Communication technologies and participation in disaster recovery. *International Journal of Communication*, *9*, 19.

Magee, H. (2014). *The aid industry – What journalists really think*. IBT.

Malkki, L. (1996). Speechless emissaries: Refugees, humanitarianism, and dehistoricization. *Cultural Anthropology*, *11*(3), 377–404.

Malkki, L. (2010). Children, humanity, and the infantilization of peace. In I. Feldman & M. Ticktin (Eds.), *In the name of humanity: The government of threat and care* (pp. 58–87). Duke University Press.

Mancini-Griffoli, D., & Picot, A. (2004). *Humanitarian negotiation. A handbook for securing access, assistance and protection for civilians in armed conflict*. Center for Humanitarian Dialogue.

Manzo, K. (2008). Imaging humanitarianism: NGO identity and the iconography of childhood. *Antipode*, *40*(4), 632–657.

Missoni, E., & Alesani, D. (2013). *Management of international institutions and NGOs: Frameworks, practices and challenges*. Routledge.

Mittelman, R., & Dow, D. (2018). Biases in charitable giving to international humanitarian aid. The role of psychic distance. *Journal of Macromarketing*, *38*(4), 1–17.

Moeller, S. (1999). *Compassion fatigue. How the media sell disease, famine, war and death*. Routledge.

Nolan, D., & Mikami, A. (2013). 'The things that we have to do': Ethics and instrumentality in humanitarian communication. *Global Media and Communication*, *9*(1), 53–70.

Norris, W. (2020). Digital humanitarians. Citizen journalists on the virtual front line of natural and human-caused disasters. In M. Wall (Ed.), *Mapping citizen and participatory journalism in newsrooms, classrooms and beyond*. Routledge.

O'Dell, L. (2008). Representations of the 'damaged' child: 'Child saving' in a British children's charity ad campaign. *Children & Society*, *22*, 383–392.

Olsen, G. R., Carstensen, N., & Hoyen, K. (2003). Humanitarian crises: What determines the level of emergency assistance? Media coverage, donor interests and the aid business. *Disasters*, *27*(2), 109–126.

Ongenaert, D., & Joye, S. (2019). Selling displaced people? A multi-method study of the public communication strategies of international refugee organisations. *Disasters*, *43*(3), 478–508.

Orgad, S., & Seu, B. I. (2014). 'Intimacy at a distance' in humanitarian communication. *Media, Culture & Society*, *36*(7), 916–934.

Pantti, M. (2015). Grassroots humanitarianism on YouTube: Ordinary fundraisers, unlikely donors, and global solidarity. *International Communication Gazette*, *77*(7), 622–636.

Powers, M. (2016). NGO publicity and reinforcing path dependencies: Explaining the persistence of media-centered publicity strategies. *The International Journal of Press/Politics*, *21*(4), 490–507.

Radice, H. (2016). The responsibility to protect as humanitarian negotiation: A space for the 'politics of humanity'? *International Politics*, *53*, 101–117.

Romo-Murphy, E., James, R., & Adams, M. (2011). Facilitating disaster preparedness through local radio broadcasting. *Disasters*, *35*(4), 801–815.

Sargeant, A. (1999). Charitable giving: Towards a model of donor behaviour. *Journal of Marketing Management*, *15*(4), 215–238.

Scurlock, R., Dolsak, N., & Prakash, A. (2020). Recovering from scandals: Twitter coverage of Oxfam and save the children scandals. *VOLUNTAS: International Journal of Voluntary and Nonprofit Organizations*, *31*(1), 94–110.

Seu, B. I., & Orgad, S. (Eds.). (2017). *Caring in crisis? Humanitarianism, the public and NGOs*. Palgrave Macmillan.

Slim, H. (2003, May). *Marketing humanitarian space: Argument and method in humanitarian persuasion*. Humanitarian Negotiators Network.

Slim, H. (2004, April 21). *How we look: Hostile perceptions of humanitarian action*. Conference on Humanitarian Coordination, Montreux.

Small, D., & Loewenstein, G. (2003). Helping a victim or helping the victim: Altruism and identifiability. *The Journal of Risk and Uncertainty*, *26*(1), 5–16.

Sontag, S. (2003). *Regarding the pain of others*. Farrar, Strauss and Giroux.

Vestergaard, A. (2009). Identity and appeal in the humanitarian brand. In L. Chouliaraki & M. Morsing (Eds.), *Media, organisations and identity* (pp. 168–184). Palgrave Macmillan.

Warrington, S., & Crombie, J. (2017). *The people in the pictures. Vital perspectives on Save the Children's image making*. Save the Children.

PART II

Communication, organizations and publics

This second part of the handbook offers distinctive approaches to communication and organization by deepening the reflections about the challenging interplay of nonprofit organizations (NPOs) with specific subjects and publics, including communication management, evaluation and relationships with donors, volunteers, meta-organizations and their complex dynamics in society. NPOs are communicative entities characterized by their explicit commitment to promoting political, cultural or social missions, but they can also be studies in communication in their constitutive understanding. Different perspectives such as integrated marketing communication management, stakeholder relationship management and fundraising or organizational listening are hereafter at the center of the debate among the chapters. Two case studies close this part of the handbook. The first is focused on government–NPO relationship potential to enhance democratic values, and the second proposes a reflection about possible symbiotic relationships between companies and human rights activists.

Matthew Koschmann and Matthew Isbell, from the University of Colorado Boulder and Boise State University (USA), respectively, open the second part of the handbook. They defend a constitutive approach to nonprofit communication as an alternative perspective on communication and interaction. In contrast with the transmission or informational model of communication, a constitutive approach is based on the broad idea that communication *constitutes*, or *makes*, our social realities rather than merely *reflects* or *represents* them. The main contribution of this perspective is to allow questioning the existence of NPOs, i.e., their structure, forms of power, principles and norms of operations not as "natural," but as something that came into existence via specific communication processes. Through this lens, ways of communicating that lead to more favorable outcomes for more people can be explored.

Another relevant lens for studying the communication of the nonprofit sector is presented by the theory of organizational listening, authored by Jim Macnamara from the University of Technology Sydney. Chapter 2.2 reviews contemporary research on organizational listening, including listening to those beyond the limited sphere of real-time aural listening, and how organizational listening processes and systems can enhance the effectiveness of NPOs. The chapter starts with a brief debate about what constitutes listening, vis-a-vis concepts as hearing, dialogue, consensus and agreement and their benefit to individuals, organizations and societies. Then, the formal and informal methods and tools for organizational listening are systematized and exemplified. The main conclusion is that with active listening, NPOs can increase trust and reputation, as well as a more equitable representation of interests, better understanding of diversity, more political engagement by citizens and better understanding of community concerns and needs.

Chapter 2.3 brings the integrated marketing communication management approach to the study of strategic planning in NPOs. Manfred Bruhn, professor at University of Basel, and Anja Zimmermann, from Lucerne School of Business, Switzerland, reflect on how professional management can support NPOs and brands to achieve a differentiating strategic positioning in the market. The authors claim that the coordination of all communication instruments and activities contribute to the creation of a strong image in the minds of stakeholders.

Understanding how stakeholders evaluate communication efforts is of paramount importance to any organization, as well as monitoring the ongoing communicator activities. This theme is brought to the center of our attention by Glenn O'Neil, from the Webster University Geneva. Chapter 2.4 reflects on how to adjust for-profit communication monitoring and evaluation (M&E) models to the nonprofit realm. The author stresses that to increase the uptake of communication M&E, nonprofit communicators should engage with the latest developments in methods and tools while recognizing the value of even small-scale and low-cost M&E.

Richard D. Waters, professor at the University of San Francisco, authored the chapter on fundraising and relationship cultivation (Chapter 2.5). The author discusses how fundraising strategies depend on the donor's level of involvement with the nonprofit, the giving history with the organization and the fundraising life cycle. He argues that successful relationship cultivation builds emotional outcomes with donors, as they trust the fundraisers they work with and become committed to the organization. Apart from donors, granting organizations, usually foundations, are also important stakeholders that provide funding to others to fulfill their mission and purpose by addressing one or more social issues. Giselle A. Auger, from Rhode Island College, USA, presents different types of granting organizations, such as private, independent, family, corporate or community foundations; public charities; and governments (Chapter 2.6). In addition, types of grants, the grant-making process and changes to grant making as a result of the coronavirus pandemic are also critically discussed.

Organizational change in the nonprofit field is debated by Laurie Lewis, from the University of Texas at San Antonio (Chapter 2.7). Bearing in mind the multiple stakeholders surrounding NPOs – clients/patrons/members/participants, employees, volunteers, donors, board members, national affiliates, local partners, government agencies and neighborhoods/communities – the chapter provides an overview of key processes of nonprofit change, including how change is triggered, stakes and stakeholders during change, challenges in NPO change and key communication dynamics throughout the implementation of change in NPOs.

Bruno Ferreira Costa and Hugo Ferrinho Lopes from University of Beira Interior (Portugal) discuss the main challenges of promoting democracy through NPOs. Theoretically, Chapter 2.8 focuses on nonprofits' relations with governments and the external pressure for democracy, transparency and accountability. Based on the case of Transparency International (TI), they conclude that nonprofits may be democratic linking mechanisms for governments by pushing legislation and engaging with government officials to promote democratic indicators. However, TI's case also revealed dubious relations with governments, as it was criticized for not securing intraorganizational transparency and accountability. Intriguingly, the more TI communicates on democratic issues, the more trust in political institutions tends to decrease, and TI only engages with other nonprofits when such a movement is advantageous to them.

The last chapter in this second part of the handbook proposes a reflection about the complex interplay between companies and human rights activists. Through an ethnographic approach, Naíde Müller from the Catholic University of Lisbon presents the case study of a nonprofit NGO, GAT – Portuguese Activist Group for HIV/AIDS – that advocates for legal and political changes within the scope of the United Nations 2030 Agenda for Sustainable Development (Chapter 2.9). She argues that, despite the strong cultural resistance to this kind of partnership in this social environment, this is a future communication trend that can be likewise an opportunity for both activists and companies to advance causes. To achieve that, companies are required to know how to position wisely on critical and complex social issues.

2.1
A CONSTITUTIVE APPROACH TO NONPROFIT COMMUNICATION

Matthew Koschmann and Matthew Isbell

Introduction[1]

Communication is central to nonprofit organizations and the activities of the nonprofit sector. Volunteer management and board governance, fundraising and donor relations, collaboration and cross-sector partnerships, client relationships, and service delivery – all involve dynamic processes of human interaction, symbol use, and language. Thus, scholars have developed a considerable amount of empirical and applied research on nonprofit communication. Much of the field of communication has converged on a meta-theoretical approach to communication centered on *constitution*, or the idea that communication is *constitutive* of our social realities. A broad claim, to be sure, and one that manifests differently across various subfields of communication. But this constitutive approach has enabled communication scholarship to overcome some of the fragmentation that plagued the discipline in the past and afforded more substantive contributions in a variety of interdisciplinary spaces, including the area of nonprofit studies. Our purposes in this chapter are to trace these developments and explain the implications and applications of a constitutive approach to nonprofit communication.

Communication scholars have made notable contributions to the conventional nonprofit literature in recent years (e.g., Atouba & Shumate, 2015; Sanders, 2015; Shumate et al., 2017), and there is a recognizable contingency of communication scholars committed to nonprofit issues in their research and teaching. This is especially true in the subfield of organizational communication (our disciplinary home), as evidenced by conference panels and preconference workshops (2010, National Communication Association), special issue forums of key journals (*Management Communication Quarterly*, 2012, 2021), edited volumes (Kramer et al., 2012, 2013), recent book projects (Heath & Isbell, 2017; Koschmann & Sanders, 2020), and other notable publications (Koschmann et al., 2015; Smith & Kramer, 2015).

A *constitutive approach* to communication and communication research came into prominence throughout the late 1990s and early 2000s. Briefly, a constitutive approach to communication (also referred to as *communicative constitution*) is rooted in the broad idea that communication *constitutes* or *makes* our social realities rather than merely *reflects* or *represents* them. It is often defined in contrast with a *transmission* or *informational* model of communication, where communication is conceptualized as merely the sending and receiving of messages versus a more robust process of producing and reproducing shared meanings. Craig's (1999) influential essay in *Communication Theory* fully articulates this constitutive principle and labels it a "meta-model" for the field of communication, claiming it can provide conceptual coherence across a variety of first-order communication theories, leading to an overall "communicational perspective" on social reality to define the scope and purpose of the communication discipline. This approach has resonated with many communication scholars, leading many to recognize communicative constitution as the discipline's "distinguishing principle," "overarching premise," and "the field's major contribution thus far" (Ashcraft et al., 2009, p. 1–2, 4).

Constitutive thinking has been part of organizational communication scholarship for decades (if somewhat implicitly), particularly in studies of culture, power, and networks (Ashcraft et al., 2009). But since the early 2000s some scholars have coalesced around a more explicit articulation of constitutive communication under the moniker *communicative-constitution-of-organization*, or CCO for short. A handful of distinct schools of CCO thought have emerged that formulate different conceptions and applications of constitutive communication (Schoeneborn & Blaschke, 2014), but all are aligned with the basic idea that organizations and organizational realities are constituted in and through communicative action.

As a framework, constitutive communication certainly influenced communication scholars who were interested in the nonprofit sector – recognizing that nonprofit organizations were not simply interesting or convenient contexts to study conventional communication phenomena, but rather the nonprofit sector is fundamentally communicative, and therefore we should seek to understand nonprofit organizations "communicationally," or from a perspective that is distinctly "communicational." Conversely, we are likely to miss important aspects of the nonprofit if we are not thinking from a communication perspective, and we limit our ability to account for the role of human interaction in creating and sustaining the social realities of nonprofit organizing.

The remainder of this chapter is devoted to looking at what exactly is a constitutive approach to communication, where it came from, and how is it different from alternative approaches to communication.[2] More importantly, we unpack how a constitutive approach to communication has been taken up in nonprofit studies and what it contributes to our understanding of the nonprofit sector and nonprofit organizations. Our goal is to provide the sufficient background and intellectual justification for a constitutive approach to communication, enabling us to articulate a distinct "communication perspective" on nonprofit studies and distinguish this from perspectives in other fields.

The emergence of a constitutive approach to communication

To begin, it is important to note that a constitutive approach to communication is not a specific theory per se, but rather a general orientation towards human interaction and the social world(s). And since it emerged in response to more traditional approaches to communication centered on message transmission and information exchange, it is often helpful to understand constitutive communication in contrast to the functionalism and instrumentalist orientations that underwrite more conventional approaches. This is especially relevant for understanding nonprofit communication, which to date has largely reflected these functional and instrumental assumptions about communication.

Although communication *scholarship* has not always been well-represented in the nonprofit literature, the *topic* of communication certainly has. This literature generally presents an instrumental approach to communication that is focused on message transmission and information sharing – communication used as a tool to achieve some notion of effectiveness (see Koschmann et al., 2015 for a review). We see this in studies about email communications (Seshadri & Carstenson, 2007), nonprofit communications planning (Henley, 2001), and nonprofit organizational communications (Hoffmann, 2011), for example. Also prevalent is an emphasis on information communication technologies (Burt & Taylor, 2003) and communication channels (Dumont, 2013), which reinforces assumptions about message transmission and functionality.

This instrumental approach prevailed as the dominant conception of communication throughout the 20th century in large part due to Claude Shannon's work in information theory. His *Mathematical*

Theory of Communication (1948) offered communication scholars an early quantitative model for explaining human interaction, and thus the scientific respectability needed for institutional support and research funding. Shannon's work focused on the efficiency of information transmission between senders and receivers, with the goal of enhancing channel capacity through appropriate encoding and decoding systems. Although Shannon's theory emphasized impersonal processes of technical systems, his work provided communication scholars a vocabulary to articulate a scientific model of communication for social systems and a conceptual framework to quantify human interaction. Consequently, "information" became the central concept in the academic study of communication, with "message effects" as the primary dependent variable (Rogers, 1994). Thus, a broad notion of *functionalism* emerged as the prevailing intellectual paradigm for the discipline of communication during these formative decades and has persisted as the main paradigm through which other disciplines understand the academic study of human communication.

However, this move was fraught with complications from the beginning. Most importantly, Shannon always claimed that his model did not apply to human communication. His model was designed for static, technical systems that involved intentional, formal, explicit, and logical transmission of information. Things like nonverbal communication, unintentional messages, and interpretive differences had no place in Shannon's model – these were all considered "noise" that interfered with channel capacity and the efficient transmission of information. Accordingly, the primary critique of a functionalist approach to communication is that it fails to account for the complexities of human interaction that are essential to most communicative events. People communicate for so many more reasons than to transmit information, and communication is rarely just a linear process that can be assessed solely in terms of message effects. Also, communication is filled with intricacies such as nonverbal behavior, unintended messages, multiple interpretations, conflicting motivations, and changing contexts that cannot be explained in terms of a sender-message-channel-receiver model of communication (even if we include components like noise and feedback).

At a deeper level, the problem with a functionalist approach is that it depicts communication as a relatively neutral "conduit" (Axley, 1984) that transmits already-formed realities – inner psychological states that await expression through communication. Communication from this perspective is seen as separate from realities themselves and not significantly involved in their production. This renders communication as epiphenomenal, a surface-level manifestation that is driven by other structural mechanisms or the "natural" order of events (Kuhn & Putnam, 2014). Communication is seen as the way we transmit pre-existing meanings between people, but those meanings are formed and reside elsewhere – and thus understood psychologically, sociologically, or even biologically, but not communicatively. However, this ignores how meaning is fundamentally a social process, created and sustained through our interactions with other people.

The problem is that meaning and information are not synonymous, and any approach that reduces the complex processes of meaning making through human interaction (communication) to the mere transmission or exchange of information (functionalism) is troublesome. Thus, Wittgenstein (1953) famously said, "Nothing is more wrong-headed than calling meaning a mental activity" (p. 172). The point here is that the social world is mainly about what things *mean*, not simply what they *are*, and we are mistaken if we think that meaning is just something mental we figure out on our own and then straightforwardly transmit to other people through our communication. Instead, the very process of communicating with people is what creates meaning and where meaning resides – meaning is "in" the interaction, not simply in our heads.

Added to all this were other intellectual developments in the social sciences that were sweeping across the academy. The most notable for the field of communication was the so-called linguistic turn in social theory, which depicts language as producing (not merely reflecting) social reality (Rorty, 1992). Thus, language replaced consciousness as the core philosophical problem to be investigated (Deetz, 1994). The upshot of these developments was that more hermeneutic and cultural approaches began to dominate the landscape of communication theory and research (even though functionalism was still the main paradigm taught in undergraduate classes and disseminated through workshops and the popular press literature). Consequently, throughout the 1980s and 1990s communication scholars wrestled with the implications of the linguistic turn in social theory to develop alternative conceptions based on meaning, interpretation, and social construction. This led to the articulation of the *constitutive approach* as a meta-theoretical model to account for these developments and provide a more unified orientation for the field of communication.

Given this foundational understanding, what are the implications of constitutive communication for understanding the nonprofit sector and nonprofit work? We submit that a constitutive approach entails three major "rethinkings" of communication and nonprofit scholarship. Together, these implications form what we suggest is an overall *communication perspective* to enhance our understanding of the nonprofit sector and nonprofit organizations.

Rethinking communication as a mode of explanation

The most significant implication of a constitutive approach is elevating communication from a unit of analysis to a mode of explanation. This means that communication is not just a phenomenon to be explained, but rather provides an explanatory framework from which to understand a host of other social phenomena. Traditionally communication has been understood as a unit of analysis – instances of talk and message exchange that happen in certain contexts, resulting in different "kinds" of communication (e.g., superior-subordinate communication, instructional communication, family communication, crisis communication, volunteer communication) but which are formed and explained from other perspectives (e.g., psychologically, sociologically, economically). Conversely, a constitutive approach to communication reverses the explanatory direction: studying psychological, sociological, or economic phenomena as formed and explained "communicatively" or "communicationally." Deetz (1994, p. 571) clarifies this idea:

> What we need is an understanding of disciplines as holistic but complementary. Disciplines are attempts at explaining a totality: There are not psychological or sociological things; there are things that are constituted by thinking and talking about things psychologically or physiologically.

He goes on to say:

> If psychological explanations explain individual behavior using goals, reinforcements, needs, and drives, and sociological explanations explain collective action using economic class difference, social structures, and forms of integration, then communication explanations explain [social] practice by showing how goals, needs, reinforcements, drives, economic class, social structures, and forms of integration are produced and reproduced in interaction.
>
> (Deetz, 1994, p. 577)

This is how we are conceptualizing communication, as a mode of explanation – not simply a "thing" to be explained, but rather a way of explaining multiple aspects of human behavior and organizational life.

For nonprofit scholarship, this relates to how we theorize and explain the nonprofit sector and the operations of nonprofit organizations. Most nonprofit theorizing is influenced by economic thinking, which attempts to explain why nonprofits exist and how they function in a market economy (Anheier, 2014). However, economics represents only one way to understand the nonprofit sector,

A constitutive approach

and assuming the primacy of the market economy to develop theoretical explanations has notable limitations (Dempsey, 2012). Instead, why not start from different assumptions about the nature of collective experience to understand and explain certain aspects of the nonprofit sector? This is what a constitutive approach to communication can provide. Lohmann (1989, p. 200) argues that the central economic facts of the nonprofit sector are "episodes of communicative interaction" because services are primarily "social acts and not physical objects." If this is the case, then we should also pursue communicative explanations of nonprofit organizations and the nonprofit sector to complement economic theorizing.

There already exists an extensive body of research and writing from several disciplines – particularly economics, sociology, and psychology – that composes most of the nonprofit scholarly literature, so what does a communication perspective offer that we don't already know? How is a communication perspective different from these other perspectives? What does it contribute? The wrong way to answer these questions is to focus simply on objects of study. That is, economics studies the economy; sociology studies society; psychology studies the human psyche; and consequently, the field of communication studies, well, communication. But that puts us right back to a message-centered, transmissional understanding of communication that we critiqued earlier. Plus, it doesn't account for what these areas of study are actually doing in their research or how they seek to shape our understanding of the nonprofit. Instead, we want to differentiate a communication perspective from other fields of study in terms of their modes of explanation.

For example, people are obviously biological creatures, but there are limits to biological explanations – you simply cannot comprehend and appreciate the fullness of the human experience through biological dissection and classification. Just like you cannot fully understand poetry through analyzing the chemical composition of the ink and paper. Likewise, when we reduce the nonprofit to a singular perspective, we then paint ourselves into a corner of having to explain all phenomena from this perspective. Nonprofits are certainly legal, financial, and economic entities, but they are also fundamentally communicative, and surely we miss something important if we forgo a communication perspective and are likely to gain much from incorporating a communication perspective. Our concern here is reductionism and the insights we lose if we insist on shoehorning all phenomena into a particular framework or perspective.

Rethinking core concepts

A second and related implication of a constitutive approach to communication involves challenging the taken-for-granted, or "natural," character of nonprofit concepts and phenomena. We often take for granted terms like volunteer, nonprofit, mission, faith-based, and sector. A functionalist approach to communication (where social realities are pre-existing and exchanged/transmitted as information) lures us into accepting these concepts as given or natural, when in fact they are quite fragile, artificial, political, and arise from very particular social circumstances. A constitutive approach to communication helps us see that language matters because it calls into being specific social realities that enable or restrict social action with real material consequences – it is not just a matter of perception. Volunteers, for example, do not simply "exist," but rather are created and sustained through how we use this term.

A constitutive approach to communication helps us see how the social realities we often take for granted are actually created, sustained, and/or transformed depending on how people interact with each other. One area where this is especially relevant is the ongoing discussions in the literature about whether or not nonprofits should be more "business-like" (Dart, 2004). Terms like "efficiency," "bottom line," or "effectiveness" may have common dictionary definitions, but they do not refer to a neutral or natural state of affairs. Instead, they are used in practice to constitute particular social realities that may favor certain interests and marginalize others. Taking a "communication perspective" towards various nonprofit phenomena means exploring the processes and patterns of human interaction that constitute specific social realities and not just accepting them as given or inevitable. Sanders' (2015) study of the mission-market tension facing many nonprofits does just this. As he describes, "The notion of being business-like in the nonprofit sector can be understood as a communicative construction whose meaning is not fixed but is negotiated and transformed in practice" (p. 206). This demonstrates the value of a communication perspective for understanding important aspects of the nonprofit sector and exemplifies scholarship grounded in a constitutive approach to communication.

Rethinking organizations *as* communication

A final implication involves reconsidering what nonprofit organizations "are" in the first place. In the common vernacular, we talk about communication that happens *within* organizations, which is consistent with an informational approach to communication that emphasizes message transmission inside pre-existing systems. This "container metaphor" (Putnam & Boys, 2006) implies that communication "flows" depend on the literal or figurative shape of the organization. The key is that communication is seen as something existing separately from the organization itself. Yet this is problematic because it requires us to account for the ontological status of organizations apart from human interaction (Kuhn, 2008). In contrast, a constitutive approach to communication encourages us to think about organizations *as* communication.

We know that organizations are not the physical structures or material resources we encounter in their operations, nor are they merely the corporate charters that give them a virtual existence in our legal system. What makes an organization truly an organization are specific processes, practices, and procedures that set them apart from other collections of people. An organization is basically an ongoing assemblage of interactions, decisions, interpretations, symbols, negotiations, agreements, contracts, relationships, and so forth – what communication scholar Pearce (2009) called "temporary configurations of a continuous process" (p. 49). These processes are made visible in temporary structures, which often take so much time, effort, and attention that it's hard not to want them to be permanent. Yet few people experience nonprofit organizations as financial entities, and the most fundamental aspects of the nonprofit sector cannot be reduced to legal abstractions. For most people what constitutes their experience of nonprofit organizations is fundamentally social, relational, interactive, and meaningful – in short, *communicative*. We cannot fully account for what a nonprofit organization is by just reading its articles of incorporation, reviewing its organizational chart, or going through its financial statements. That misses the true character of the organization and tells us nothing about the actual experience of being part of the organization as a volunteer, employee, client, or donor (Koschmann, 2012). The spirit of the nonprofit sector is grounded in social entrepreneurship, civic and political engagement, service delivery, and religious faith/values (Frumkin, 2005), and these essential aspects of the nonprofit sector are created and sustained through ongoing patterns of human interaction.

Conclusion

A constitutive approach to nonprofit communication emphasizes the production of meaning and social reality, rather than the mere transmission of information to increase effectiveness. Researchers who bring a communication perspective to nonprofit studies will explain a variety of nonprofit phenomena through a framework of human interaction, they will explore how important nonprofit concepts are constituted communicatively and the different interests represented in those processes, and they will examine how the communicative existence of nonprofit organizations shapes the lived experiences of key stakeholders – all of which promise to add valuable insights to the nonprofit literature and complement other fields that compose the interdisciplinary study of the nonprofit sector.

The point is that a constitutive view of organizations as communication enables us to question and investigate key organizational realities, not just accept them as given. We can question the existence of nonprofit organizations – their structures, forms of power, guiding assumptions, norms of operations, and so on. If these features are not "natural," but rather came into existence through specific communication processes, then we can examine the implications of those communication processes and explore ways of communicating that lead to more favorable outcomes for more people. We can examine, for example, how certain patterns of interaction give rise to norms of conflict resolution, or how the taken-for-granted values of a particular industry or sector shape the practice of leadership, or how interpersonal dynamics affect the success of an organizational change initiative. We can look at how certain views of masculinity or femininity are connected to communication practices, like how certain professions become "gendered" based on how we talk about them and our cultural assumptions about who is "supposed" to do certain kinds of work (like demeaning comments about male nurses or the ways we distinguish between "accountants" [masculine] and "bookkeepers" [feminine] in professional discourse). We can also explore how our very identities are often created and sustained through organizational communication and how certain occupations appear to be "natural" fits for certain kinds of people and improbable for others (e.g., how people who are mistaken as janitors tend to fit a particular profile, while those mistaken as managers fit another). We can uncover hidden forms of power and control that are embedded within communication processes. We can explore ways to make organizations more equitable and representative by surfacing alternative voices. We can figure out how to make nonprofit more productive, adaptive, and responsive through communication that encourages innovation and collaboration. Whatever the case, a constitutive view of organizations as communication provides a valuable explanatory framework to analyze and understand the complexities of nonprofit organizing and communicating.

Notes

1 Portions of this chapter are adapted with permission from the following sources: Koschmann, M., Isbell, M., & Sanders, M. (2015). Connecting nonprofit and communication scholarship: A review of key issues and a meta-theoretical framework for future research. *Review of Communication, 15*(3), 200–220; Koschmann, M., & Sanders, M. (2020). *Understanding nonprofit work: A communication perspective.* Wiley-Blackwell.
2 A longer explanation of this background is provided in Koschmann et al. (2015).

References

Anheier, H. K. (2014). *Nonprofit organizations: Theory, management, policy.* Routledge.
Ashcraft, K. L., Kuhn, T. R., & Cooren, F. (2009). Constitutional amendments: "Materializing" organizational communication. *Academy of Management Annals, 3*(1), 1–64. https://doi.org/10.5465/19416520903047186
Atouba, Y. C., & Shumate, M. (2015). International nonprofit collaboration: Examining the role of homophily. *Nonprofit and Voluntary Sector Quarterly, 44*(3), 587–608. https://doi.org/10.1177/0899764014524991
Axley, S. R. (1984). Managerial and organizational communication in terms of the conduit metaphor. *Academy of Management Review, 9*(3), 428–437. https://doi.org/10.5465/amr.1984.4279664
Burt, E., & Taylor, J. (2003). New technologies, embedded values, and strategic change: Evidence from the UK voluntary sector. *Nonprofit and Voluntary Sector Quarterly, 32*(1), 115–127. https://doi.org/10.1177/0899764002250009
Craig, R. T. (1999). Communication theory as a field. *Communication Theory, 9*(2), 119–161. https://doi.org/10.1111/j.1468-2885.1999.tb00355
Dart, R. (2004). Being "business-like" in a nonprofit organization: A grounded and inductive typology. *Nonprofit and Voluntary Sector Quarterly, 33*(2), 290–310. https://doi.org/10.1177/0899764004263522
Deetz, S. A. (1994). Future of the discipline: The challenges, the research, and the social contribution. *Annals of the International Communication Association, 17*(1), 565–600. https://doi.org/10.1080/23808985.1994.11678904

Dempsey, S. E. (2012). Nonprofits as political actors. *Management Communication Quarterly*, *26*(1), 147–151. https://doi.org//10.1177/0893318911424375

Dumont, G. E. (2013). Nonprofit virtual accountability: An index and its application. *Nonprofit and Voluntary Sector Quarterly*, *42*(5), 1049–1067. https://doi.org/10.1177/0899764013481285

Frumkin, P. (2005). *On being nonprofit: A conceptual and policy primer*. Harvard University Press.

Heath, R. G., & Isbell, M. G. (2017). *Interorganizational collaboration: Complexity, ethics, and communication*. Waveland Press.

Henley, T. K. (2001). Integrated marketing communications for local nonprofit organizations: Developing an integrated marketing communications strategy. *Journal of Nonprofit & Public Sector Marketing*, *9*(1–2), 141–155. https://doi.org/10.1300/J054v09n01_08

Hoffmann, J. (2011). In the triangle of civil society, politics, and economy: Positioning magazines of nonprofit organizations. *Voluntas: International Journal of Voluntary and Nonprofit Organizations*, *22*(1), 93–111. https://doi.org/10.1007/s11266-010-9141-9

Koschmann, M. A. (2012). Developing a communicative theory of the nonprofit. *Management Communication Quarterly*, *26*(1), 139–146. https://doi.org/10.1177/0893318911423640

Koschmann, M. A., Isbell, M. G., & Sanders, M. L. (2015). Connecting nonprofit and communication scholarship: A review of key issues and a meta-theoretical framework for future research. *Review of Communication*, *15*(3), 200–220. https://doi.org/10.1080/15358593.2015.1058411

Koschmann, M. A., & Sanders, M. L. (2020). *Understanding nonprofit work: A communication perspective*. John Wiley & Sons.

Kramer, M. W., Lewis, L. K., & Gossett, L. M. (Eds.). (2012). *Volunteering and communication: Studies from multiple contexts*. Peter Lang.

Kramer, M. W., Lewis, L. K., & Gossett, L. M. (Eds.). (2013). *Volunteering and communication volume 2: Studies in international and intercultural contexts*. Peter Lang.

Kuhn, T. R. (2008). A communicative theory of the firm: Developing an alternative perspective on intra-organizational power and stakeholder relationships. *Organization Studies*, *29*(8–9), 1227–1254. https://doi.org/10.1177/0170840608094778

Kuhn, T. R., & Putnam, L. L. (2014). Discourse and communication. In *The Oxford handbook of sociology, social theory, and organization studies* (pp. 414–446). Oxford University Press.

Lohmann, R. A. (1989). And lettuce is nonanimal: Toward a positive economics of voluntary action. *Nonprofit and Voluntary Sector Quarterly*, *18*(4), 367–383. https://doi.org/10.1177/089976408901800407

Pearce, W. B. (2009). *Making social worlds: A communication perspective*. John Wiley & Sons.

Putnam, L. L., & Boys, S. (2006). Revisiting metaphors of organizational communication. *The Sage Handbook of Organization Studies*, *2*, 541–576.

Rogers, E. M. (1994). *History of communication study*. Free Press.

Rorty, R. (Ed.). (1992). *The linguistic turn: Essays in philosophical method*. University of Chicago Press.

Sanders, M. L. (2015). Being nonprofit-like in a market economy: Understanding the mission-market tension in nonprofit organizing. *Nonprofit and Voluntary Sector Quarterly*, *44*(2), 205–222. https://doi.org/10.1177/0899764013508606

Schoeneborn, D., & Blaschke, S. (2014). The three schools of CCO thinking: Interactive dialogue and systematic comparison. *Management Communication Quarterly*, *28*(2), 285–316. https://doi.org/10.1177/0893318914527000

Seshadri, S., & Carstenson, L. (2007). The perils of e-mail communications in nonprofits. *Nonprofit Management and Leadership*, *18*(1), 77–99. https://doi.org/10.1002/nml.172

Shannon, C. E. (1948). A mathematical theory of communication. *The Bell System Technical Journal*, *27*(3), 379–423. https://doi.org/10.1002/j.1538-7305.1948.tb01338.x

Shumate, M., Cooper, K. R., Pilny, A., & Pena-y-lillo, M. (2017). The nonprofit capacities instrument. *Nonprofit Management and Leadership*, *28*(2), 155–174. https://doi.org/10.1002/nml.21276

Smith, J. M., & Kramer, M. W. (Eds.). (2015). *Case studies of nonprofit organizations and volunteers*. Peter Lang Incorporated, International Academic Publishers.

Wittgenstein, L. (1958). *Philosophical investigations. 1953. Trans. GEM Anscombe*. Blackwell.

2.2
ORGANIZATIONAL LISTENING AND THE NONPROFIT SECTOR

Jim Macnamara

Introduction

In Book 1 of his *Politics*, Aristotle wrote that "Nature . . . has endowed man[1] alone among the animals with the power of speech" and identified speaking as a key attribute that defines humans (as cited in Haworth, 2004, p. 43). Voice and speaking have been studied and celebrated since the early Western civilizations of ancient Greece and Rome where rhetoric – the art of speaking persuasively – was recognized as one of the foundational liberal arts based on the writings of Plato, Aristotle, Cicero, and Quintilian (Atwill, 1998; Kennedy, 1994). Rhetoric also was developed as an 'art' as early as 500 BCE in Islamic societies of North Africa (Bernal, 1987) and in China (Lu, 1998).

Renaissance philosopher Thomas Hobbes echoed Aristotle's trope in *Leviathan*, saying "the most noble and profitable invention of all others was that of speech" (Hobbes, 1946, p. 18). John Durham Peters refers to communication as "the natural history of our talkative species" (1999, p. 9).

However, as contemporary communication studies scholar Robert Craig (2006) succinctly reminds us, communication requires "talking and listening" (p. 39). In writing about the importance of voice, sociologist Nick Couldry (2009) describes voice as "the implicitly linked practices of speaking and listening" (p. 580). It is significant that Couldry notes that listening is implicit, not explicit. Despite attempts by some such as Back (2007) to highlight the importance of listening, Fiumara noted that listening has often been "a secondary issue" (1995, p. 6).

These are highly pertinent comments, particularly for those living and working in democracies. Democracy is founded on the principle of *vox populi* – the voice of the people (the *demos*) being able to influence decisions and policy exercised by those with power and authority (the *krátos*). However, voice has no effect or value without listening.

Notwithstanding, throughout the twentieth and into the twenty-first century, organizations of all types – government, corporate, nongovernment, and many nonprofits – have been misled by theories and models that conceptualize communication as one-way transmission of information and seduced by the growing global industries of advertising, marketing, public relations, and promotion that focus on rhetoric and persuasion. So-called theories of communication, such as the *mathematical theory of communication* of Shannon and Weaver (1949) and the similar *source, message, channel, receiver* (SMCR) model of Berlo (1960), that are still widely used represent information transmission, not human communication.

DOI: 10.4324/9781003170563-12

Rediscovering communication and dialogue

While the term 'communication' and its common abbreviation 'comms' are used widely to denote the creation and distribution of information such as through publications, website content, videos, and social media posts, the English term communication is derived from the Latin root *communis*, meaning common or public, and the related noun *commūnicātiō*, which denotes "sharing or imparting", and the verb *communicare*, which means to "share or make common" (Peters, 2015, p. 78).

Thus, while imparting information is one element in the process of human communication, it is not complete without sharing and achieving some common position or view with others. Contemporary scholars therefore associate communication with meaning making and sharing meaning. Dictionaries define communication as "exchange" (Merriam-Webster, 2021) and refer to "discussing, debating", and "conferring" (Etymonline, 2021).

Communication is therefore a *two-way* process and is closely linked with dialogue. However, even dialogue is commonly misunderstood, with many assuming that the Greek term *dia* means two. In fact, *dia* means 'through', with *logos* meaning speech, logic, and reasoning or argument. In reality, dialogue can be no more than two or more parties speaking, with each paying little attention or giving little consideration to others. Based on extensive research, this chapter argues that, instead of attempting to communicate primarily *dia logos* (through speech, logic, and argument), society needs more engagement *dia akouó* – through hearing and listening. It suggests that this is particularly relevant for nonprofit organizations (NPOs) that perform important representative and agency roles in society.

Hearing, listening, consensus, agreement

This leads to an important juncture of identifying what constitutes listening. In particular, a question asked by many is whether listening necessarily results in 'common ground' such as consensus or agreement.

First, a clear distinction must be understood between hearing and listening. Hearing in humans involves sound waves striking the eardrum. The organizational equivalent is the receipt of correspondence, telephone calls, research data, and so on. It is well known that much of what people hear is ignored or quickly forgotten – and the same occurs in the case of information, requests, and reports received by organizations (see Macnamara, 2017, pp. 26–27).

Glenn (1989) identified 50 definitions of listening in a literature review in the *International Journal of Listening*, which focus on interpersonal listening. Drawing on this literature, as well as political science, psychology, psychotherapy, and ethics, "seven canons" of listening were identified in Macnamara (2016, pp. 41–43) that apply to both individuals and organizations. These are (1) *recognition* of others as having rights to speak and be treated with respect (Honneth, 2007; Husband, 2009); (2) *acknowledgement* (Schmid, 2001); (3) giving *attention* to what is said (Bickford, 1996; Honneth, 2007; Husband, 2009); (4) *interpreting* what others say fairly and receptively, such as avoiding stereotyping and overcoming reactance and cognitive dissonance; (5) trying as far as possible to achieve *understanding* of others' views and context (Bodie & Crick, 2014; Husband, 1996, 2000); (6) giving *consideration* to what others say (Honneth, 2007; Husband, 2009); and (7) *responding* in an appropriate way (Lundsteen, 1979; Purdy & Borisoff, 1997).

At no point does the literature identify agreement or compliance with all requests, suggestions, or recommendations as a requirement of listening. Studies in relation to human communication, democratic politics, and ethics note that listening requires an active and authentic attempt to reach a shared or common position. But sociology, cultural studies, and democratic political science also advocate acceptance of difference and even dissent. In many cases, there are good reasons that people and organizations cannot agree or comply with requests or recommendations. In such cases, an explanation should be provided. Response is essential to close the 'communication cycle'. William James (1952), the founder of American pragmatism, stated that ignoring someone is the most "fiendish" way to deal with another.

The emerging theory of organizational listening

Beyond the important and extensive literature on interpersonal listening, of which a summary is provided in *The Sourcebook of Listening Research* (Worthington & Bodie, 2017), Burnside-Lawry (2011) is one of the few who have attempted a definition of *organizational listening*. In her study of listening competency of employees, she drew on the research of Flynn et al. (2008) in relation to listening in business to say:

> Organizational listening is defined as a combination of an employee's listening skills and the environment in which listening occurs, which is shaped by the organization and is then one of the characteristics of the organizational image.
>
> (Burnside-Lawry, 2011, p. 149)

This definition is useful in several respects. First, it notes that skills are required for listening and suggests that these are different from the skills of speaking and presenting information. Second, it draws attention to the organizational environment, which includes culture, policies, structure, and other elements. Third, by focusing on employees, it identifies that ultimately it is people in organizations who listen – or don't listen. While communication is the basis of human organization and *communication constitutes organizations* (CCO theory), as identified by Vásquez and Schoeneborn (2018) and Schoeneborn et al. (2019, p. 475), organizations themselves are inanimate entities.

However, three key characteristics distinguish organizations in terms of the capability and capacity for listening to occur in them. First, there is the issue of *scale* – what Dobson (2014) refers to as the problem of "scaling up" from interpersonal and small-group communication (pp. 75, 124). Organizations typically need to be able to listen to hundreds and often thousands, or even hundreds of thousands, of people who are stakeholders (Freeman, 1984),[2] as well as those who some refer to as *stakeseekers* (Heath, 2002; Spicer, 2007).

The issue of scale leads to the second key characteristic of organizational listening – *delegation*. To engage with a large number and range of stakeholders, organizations typically delegate listening to functional units such as customer or member relations, research departments, social media monitoring teams, public relations, and human resources (HR) for listening to employees.

Scale, in addition to distanciation in space and time that occurs in the case of organizations operating in multiple locations and even internationally, leads to the third key factor to be addressed in organizational listening – *mediation*. The 'voice' of stakeholders is commonly expressed to organizations through correspondence such as letters and emails, written complaints, online comments, submissions to consultations, phone calls to call centres, and other mediated means.

Delegation and mediation mean that, in order to influence decisions and policies, the voice of stakeholders needs to be interpreted and articulated by various functional units and teams in order to reach and be considered by decision makers and policy makers. These factors, along with Burnside-Lawry's observations, led to the concept of an *architecture of listening* (Macnamara, 2013, 2015, 2016) as an essential prerequisite for effective listening in organizations. Five years of research in The Organizational Listening Project (Macnamara, 2013, 2015, 2016) involving more than 100 organizations on three continents concluded that recognition of an architecture of listening enables organizations to design effective listening into their operations, rather than ineffective add-on attempts such as conducting periodic 'listening tours' or 'listening posts' or relying on a software application.

The architecture of listening proposed for organizations is based on eight key principles and elements as follows:

1. An organizational *culture* that is open to listening, as defined by Honneth (2007), Husband (1996, 2009), and others – that is, one that *recognizes* others' right to speak, pays *attention* to them, and tries to *understand* their views.
2. Addressing the *politics of listening*, such as selective listening to certain individuals or groups, while others are ignored and marginalized, as discussed by Dreher (2009, 2010) and Bassel (2017).
3. *Policies* that specify and require listening in an organization.
4. *Systems* that are open and interactive, such as websites that allow visitors to post comments and questions.
5. *Technologies* that aid listening, such as monitoring tools or services for tracking media and online comments, automated acknowledgement systems, and analysis tools for sense-making. Such technologies are further discussed in the following section.
6. *Resources*, including staff to operate listening systems and do the *work of listening* (Macnamara, 2013, 2015), such as establishing forums and consultations; inviting comment; and monitoring, analyzing, and responding to comments and questions.
7. *Skills/competencies* for large-scale organizational listening, such as textual analysis and social media analysis.
8. *Articulation* of what is said to an organization to policy making and decision making. Unless there is a link to policy making and decision making for consideration of what is said to an organization, voice has no value, as Couldry (2010) notes.

A 2016 definition of listening emphasized the eight elements of an architecture of listening and the 'seven canons' of listening, stating:

> Organizational listening is comprised of the culture, policies, structure, processes, resources, skills, technologies, and practices applied by an organization to give recognition, acknowledgement, attention, interpretation, understanding, consideration, and response to its stakeholders and publics.
>
> (Macnamara, 2016, p. 52)

Listening systems

In addition to arguing that listening has to be designed into an organization – not simply 'bolted on' to an existing structure – because effectiveness is dependent on organizational culture, politics, policies, and skills, the third stage of The Organizational Listening Project identified that large-scale listening by organizations is substantially aided by a range of specialist practices and technologies. While organizations typically have sophisticated systems for speaking, such as website development teams, media production departments, and advertising and public relations units or agencies, they often lack specific methods and tools for listening.

Listening systems do not replace face-to-face and other forms of interpersonal communication such as meetings, telephone calls, and video conferencing, which are emphasized by many researchers (e.g., Bassel, 2017; Bodie & Crick, 2014). But they are essential for delegated, mediated listening by organizations at scale. Table 2.2.1 identifies some common formal and informal methods and tools for organizational listening.

As shown in Table 2.2.1, organizational listening requires and depends on systematic *analysis* of data, not simply collections of data such as research reports, submissions, and feedback. Too often vast quantities of information from stakeholders such as submissions to consultations, online

Table 2.2.1 Formal and informal methods and tools for organizational listening

Research-related methods of listening	Other methods of organization listening
Quantitative analysis of responses to surveys (including open-ended comments)	Analysis of the minutes of meetings of advisory boards and committees
Qualitative analysis of transcripts of interviews (e.g., coding and textual analysis)	Recording and analyzing public dialogues
Qualitative analysis of transcripts of focus groups	Capturing and analyzing feedback such as website comments and 'suggestion boxes' (digital and physical)
Content analysis of media reporting, opinion columns, and letters to the editor	Recording notes or minutes of all key stakeholder engagements and meetings
Content analysis of social media comments by relevant stakeholders	Journal notes during field visits and tours
Textual analysis of recordings of forums and discussion groups	Crowdsourcing initiatives in developing policies and plans
Textual analysis of written submissions to consultations	Systematically reviewing petitions
	Citizen juries
Textual analysis of written correspondence, including complaints (e.g., over the period of several months or a year to identify consistent topics, messages, and patterns)	Study circles
Textual analysis of digitally recorded phone calls to call centres enabled by voice-to-text (VTT) software	
Use of research methods such as participatory action research (PAR), deliberative polling, and appreciative inquiry that involve high levels of participation and input from stakeholders	
Behavioral insights analysis	
Sense-making methodology	

feedback, and call centre recordings remain unread and unused. For example, the second stage of The Organizational Listening Project focussed on listening by government organizations found 127,400 public submissions on health topics had not been analyzed because the department had no natural language processing (NLP) textual analysis software or staff with the necessary training to undertake such a task (Macnamara, 2017, pp. 26–27).

Table 2.2.1 also shows that organizational listening needs to extend beyond quantitative methodologies that focus on statistics. People speak and write in words, not numbers. Therefore, textual analysis and related analysis methods such as content analysis are essential skills for a listening organization. Specialist software applications are available and often needed as part of listening systems.

In addition, Table 2.2.1 identifies that, as well as employing traditional quantitative and particularly qualitative research methods such interviews and focus groups, organizational listening can be implemented through a number of advanced research and engagement methods including *deliberative polling* (Fishkin, 2011); *participatory action research* (PAR); *sense-making methodology* (Dervin & Foreman-Wernet, 2013); *appreciative inquiry* (Cooperrider et al., 2008); *behavioral insights* (Thaler & Sunstein, 2008); and *customer journey mapping* (Court et al., 2009), which can be adapted to studying the 'touchpoints' of stakeholders interacting with NPOs.

The rapidly growing field of *data analytics* is another systematic way that the voices of stakeholders can be accessed and considered, and digital technologies such as voice-to-text (VTT) software enables recorded phone calls to be transferred to text for textual analysis that can identify common messages, themes, and patterns.

Organizations are also adopting artificial intelligence (AI) tools such as *chat bots* to 'listen' to users of web pages and respond with relevant information, as well as learning algorithms based on NLP and machine learning code that respond to users' data entry and selections (Macnamara, 2019).

Some object to such technologies being described as listening systems, and it is acknowledged that these bring with them limitations as well as some serious concerns and questions. Critical technosocial and technocultural scholars such as Gillespie (2018), Landau (2017), and Napoli (2014) express concern about *digital surveillance* and the effects of algorithms such as *algorithmic filtering* (Caplan, 2018). As Caplan says, in many if not most online platforms, algorithms decide "the inclusion or exclusion of information" (Caplan, 2018, p. 564). Algorithms can lead to *filter bubbles*, a term that refers to recipients of information receiving only what they are disposed to receive from those whom they are disposed to receive it from – also referred to as *echo chambers*.

Based on recent research trialling and evaluating a range of advanced systems and methods of listening in organizations, the following expanded definition of organizational listening was published in a leading international communication journal:

> Organizational listening comprises the creation and implementation of scaled processes and systems that enable decision makers and policy makers in organizations to actively and effectively access, acknowledge, understand, consider and appropriately respond to all those who wish to communicate with the organization or with whom the organization wishes to communicate interpersonally or through delegated, mediated means.
>
> (Macnamara, 2019, 5191)

The costs of not listening

Political scientist Susan Bickford (1996) was one of the first to observe serious negative consequences in society caused by a lack of effective listening by organizations on which citizens depend or place expectations. More recently, a number of researchers have warned that many countries are facing a "democratic deficit" (Norris, 2011) and even a "crisis of democracy" (Przeworski, 2019; Van der Meer, 2017).

At an individual level, research shows that when people are not listened to, they disengage from politics and civic life (Bennett et al., 2011; Coleman, 2013); they become unrepresented and marginalized (Dreher, 2009, 2010), and many plummet into a "spiral of silence" (Noelle-Neumann, 1974). Dobson calls for "*listening out for*" as well as "listening to" people (2014, p. 34) [original emphasis], particularly in relation to "otherwise unheard voices" (p. 22), which draws attention to the need for *active* listening, not simply passive processing of what is received. Such calls are particularly relevant to NPOs.

Two recent case studies demonstrate that a failure of organizations to effectively listen can even be a matter of life and death. The 2013 report of the Mid Staffordshire NHS Foundation Trust Public Inquiry into deaths in UK hospitals concluded:

> Building on the report of the first inquiry, the story it tells is first and foremost of appalling suffering of many patients. This was primarily caused by a serious failure on the part of a provider Trust Board. It did not listen sufficiently to its patients.
>
> (Her Majesty's Stationery Office, 2013)

Even more recently, the tragic 2017 Grenfell Tower fire in London, which claimed more than 70 lives and injured many more, has been directly attributed to a "failure to listen" (Ghelani, 2017, para. 1). Warnings of inadequate fire safety standards were reportedly posted on the website of the

Grenfell Action Group four years before the disaster (Ghelani, 2017, para. 5), and reports identifying the dangers of combustible cladding on buildings were submitted to the UK Parliament as early as 1999 (House of Commons, 1999).

Listening by NPOs

Some NPOs have established quite sophisticated listening methods and systems. For example, after originally focussing on interpersonal communication, the Public Dialogue Consortium (PDC) in the United States (https://publicdialogue.org) has expanded its activities to include training and facilitation of dialogue, particularly in relation to government–community consultation. The PDC employs some advanced communication techniques to support public leaders in assessing organizational and community readiness to co-design and deliver engagement processes and provides training for organization staff, officials, and community members in communication with a focus on dialogue. Despite limited funds, many other NPOs make substantial efforts to engage in two-way communication with their stakeholders.

However, many NPOs, as well as communication and social marketing guides for NPOs, ignore or place little focus on listening. For instance, under the heading 'Best non-profit communication strategies', one online guide places priority on identifying "target audiences" – audiences being receivers of information – and the main sections focus on "Tell the organization's story" and "Lead the conversation" (Queens University of Charlotte, 2021). Similarly, on the *Non-profit PRO* website, a guide titled 'Effective marketing communication strategies for non-profits' says that nonprofits can "build connection through storytelling" (Alameda, 2020, para. 3) – 'telling' being the focus that this chapter challenges.

The benefits of listening

Active listening by organizations offers many benefits to individuals, organizations, and society. While commercial organizations gain benefits such as increased customer loyalty; increased employee morale, motivation, and productivity; and increased insights into market needs (Jenkins et al., 2013; Leite, 2015), NPOs can achieve increased and more equitable representation of interests; better understanding of diversity; increased social and political engagement by citizens; and even improved mental and physical health and well-being through increased understanding and reflection of community concerns, fears, anxieties, and needs. Research also shows that all organizations can gain increased trust and reputation through listening (Leite, 2015; Tomlinson & Mayer, 2009).

Notes

1 Gendered term in original text.
2 Stakeholders is a term proposed by R. Edward Freeman (1984) in his book *Strategic Management: A Stakeholder Approach* to denote "any group or individual who can affect or is affected by the achievement of the organization's purpose and objectives" (Freeman, 1984, p. 6).

References

Alameda, L. (2020). Effective marketing communication strategies for non-profits. *Non-profit PRO*. www.non-profitpro.com/article/effective-marketing- communication-strategies-for-non-profits
Atwill, J. (1998). *Rhetoric reclaimed: Aristotle and the liberal arts tradition*. Cornell University Press.
Back, L. (2007). *The art of listening*. Berg.
Bassel, L. (2017). *The politics of listening: Possibilities and challenges for democratic life*. Palgrave Macmillan.
Bennett, W., Wells, C., & Freelon, D. (2011). Communicating civic engagement: Contrasting models of citizenship in the youth Web culture. *Journal of Communication*, *61*(5), 835–856. https://doi.org/10.1111/j.1460-2466.2011.01588.x

Berlo, D. (1960). *The process of communication: An introduction to theory and practice*. Harcourt/Holt, Rinehart & Winston.
Bernal, M. (1987). *Black Athena: The Afroasiatic roots of classical civilisation*. Rutgers University Press.
Bickford, S. (1996). *The dissonance of democracy: Listening, conflict and citizenship*. Cornell University Press.
Bodie, G., & Crick, N. (2014). Listening, hearing sensing: Three modes of being and the phenomenology of Charles Sanders Peirce. *Communication Theory*, 24(2), 105–123. https://doi.org/10.1111/comt.1203
Burnside-Lawry, J. (2011). The dark side of stakeholder communication: Stakeholder perceptions of ineffective organisational listening. *Australian Journal of Communication*, 38(1), 147–173.
Caplan, R. (2018). Algorithmic filtering. In P. Napoli (Ed.), *Mediated communication* (pp. 561–583). De Gruyter.
Coleman, S. (2013). *How voters feel*. Cambridge University Press.
Cooperrider, D., Whitney, D., & Stavros, J. (2008). *Appreciative inquiry handbook* (2nd ed.). Crown Custom.
Couldry, N. (2009). Commentary: Rethinking the politics of voice. *Continuum: Journal of Media & Cultural Studies*, 23(4), 579–582. https://doi.org/10.1080/10304310903026594
Couldry, N. (2010). *Why voice matters: Culture and politics after neoliberalism*. Sage.
Court, D., Elzinga, D., Mulder, S., & Vetvik, O. (2009, June). The consumer decision journey. *McKinsey Quarterly*. www.mckinsey.com/business-functions/marketing-and-sales/our-insights/the-consumer-decision-journey
Craig, R. (2006). Communication as a practice. In G. Shepherd, G. St John, & T. Striphas (Eds.), *Communication as . . . Perspectives on theory* (pp. 38–49). Sage.
Dervin, B., & Foreman-Wernet, L. (2013). Sense-making methodology as an approach to understanding and designing for campaign audiences. In R. Rice & C. Atkin (Eds.), *Public communication campaigns* (4th ed., pp. 147–162). Sage.
Dobson, A. (2014). *Listening for democracy: Recognition, representation, reconciliation*. Oxford University Press.
Dreher, T. (2009). Listening across difference: Media and multiculturalism beyond the politics of voice. *Continuum: Journal of Media & Cultural Studies*, 23(4), 445–458. https://doi.org/10.1080/10304310903015712
Dreher, T. (2010). Speaking up or being heard? Community media interventions and the politics of listening. *Media, Culture and Society*, 32(1), 85–103. https://doi.org/10.1177/0163443709350099
Etymonline.com. Communication. (2021). *Online etymology dictionary*. www.etymonline.com/word/communication
Fishkin, J. (2011). *When the people speak: Deliberative democracy and public consultation*. Oxford University Press.
Fiumara, G. (1995). *The other side of language: A philosophy of listening*. Routledge.
Flynn, J., Valikoski, T., & Grau, J. (2008). Listening in the business context: Reviewing the state of research. *International Journal of Listening*, 22(2), 141–151. https://doi.org/10.1080/10904010802174800
Freeman, R. (1984). *Strategic management: A stakeholder approach*. Pitman.
Ghelani, D. (2017, June 22). Grenfell tower: "There are only the deliberately silent, or the preferably unheard". *Media Diversified*. https://mediadiversified.org/2017/06/22/grenfell-tower-there-are-only-the-deliberately-silent-or-the-preferably-unheard
Gillespie, T. (2018). *Custodians of the internet: Platforms, content moderation, and the hidden decisions that shape social media*. Yale University Press.
Glenn, E. (1989). A content analysis of fifty definitions of listening. *The International Journal of Listening*, 3(1), 21–31. https://doi.org/10.1207/s1932586xijl0301_3
Haworth, A. (2004). *Understanding the political philosophers: From ancient to modern times*. Routledge.
Heath, R. (2002). Issues management: Its past, present and future. *Journal of Public Affairs*, 2(2), 209–214. https://doi.org/10.1002/pa.114
Her Majesty's Stationery Office. (2013). *Report of the Mid Staffordshire NHS foundation trust public inquiry*. www.midstaffspublicinquiry.com/sites/default/files/report/Executive%20summary.pdf
Hobbes, T. (1946). *Leviathan*. Basil Blackwell. (Original work published 1651)
Honneth, A. (2007). *Disrespect*. Polity.
House of Commons. (1999). *Potential risk of fire spread in building via external cladding systems*. Select Committee on Environment, Transport and Regional Affairs First Report. https://publications.parliament.uk/pa/cm199900/cmselect/cmenvtra/109/10907.htm
Husband, C. (1996). The right to be understood: Conceiving the multi-ethnic public sphere. *Innovation: The European Journal of Social Sciences*, 9(2), 205–215. https://doi.org/10.1080/13511610.1996.9968484
Husband, C. (2000). Media and the public sphere in multi-ethnic societies. In S. Cottle (Ed.), *Ethnic minorities and the media* (pp. 199–214). Open University Press.
Husband, C. (2009). Commentary: Between listening and understanding. *Continuum: Journal of Media & Cultural Studies*, 23(4), 441–443. https://doi.org/10.1080/10304310903026602
James, W. (1952). *The principles of psychology*. Dover Publications.
Jenkins, H., Ford, S., & Green, J. (2013). *Spreadable media: Crating value and meaning in a networked culture*. New York University Press.

Kennedy, G. (1994). *A new history of classical rhetoric*. Princeton University Press.
Landau, S. (2017). *Listening in*. Yale University Press.
Leite, E. (2015, January 19). *Why trust matters in business*. Address to the World Economic Forum, Davos-Klosters, Switzerland. https://agenda.weforum.org/2015/01/why-trust-matters-in-business
Lu, X. (1998). *Rhetoric in ancient China fifth to third century BCE: A comparison with classical Greek rhetoric*. University of South Carolina Press.
Lundsteen, S. (1979). *Listening: Its impact on language and the other language arts*. ERIC Clearing House on Reading and Communication Skills.
Macnamara, J. (2013). Beyond voice: Audience-making and the work and architecture of listening. *Continuum: Journal of Media and Cultural Studies*, *27*(1), 160–175. https://doi.org/10.1080/10304312.2013.736950
Macnamara, J. (2015). The work and 'architecture of listening': Requisites for ethical organization-public communication. *Ethical Space: Journal of the Institute of Communication Ethics*, *12*(2), 29–37. http://journals.communicationethics.net
Macnamara, J. (2016). *Organizational listening: The missing essential in public communication*. Peter Lang.
Macnamara, J. (2017). Creating a 'democracy for everyone': Strategies for increasing listening and engagement by government. *The London School of Economics and Political Science*. www.lse.ac.uk/media-and-communications/assets/documents/research/2017/MacnamaraReport2017.pdf
Macnamara, J. (2019). Explicating listening in organization-public communication: Theory, practices, technologies. *International Journal of Communication*, *13*, 5183–5204. https://ijoc.org/index.php/ijoc/article/view/11996/2839
Merriam-Webster. (2021). Communication. In *Merriam-webster dictionary*. www.merriam-webster.com/dictionary/communication
Napoli, P. (2014). Automated media: An institutional theory perspective on algorithmic media production and consumption. *Communication Theory*, *24*(3), 340–360. https://doi.org/10.1111/comt.1203
Noelle-Neumann, E. (1974). The spiral of silence: A theory of public opinion. *Journal of Communication*, *24*(2), 43–51. https://doi.org/10.1111/j.1460-2466.1974.tb00367.x
Norris, P. (2011). *Democratic deficit: Critical citizens revisited*. Cambridge University Press.
Peters, J. Durham (1999). *Speaking into the air. A history of the idea of communication*. The University of Chicago Press.
Peters, J. (2015). Communication: History of the idea. In W. Donsbach (Ed.), *The concise encyclopedia of communication* (pp. 78–79). Wiley-Blackwell. https://onlinelibrary.wiley.com/doi/abs/10.1002/9781405186407.wbiecc075
Przeworski, A. (2019). *Crisis of democracy*. Cambridge University Press.
Purdy, M., & Borisoff, D. (1997). *Listening in everyday life: A personal and professional approach* (2nd ed.). University of America Press.
Queens University of Charlotte. (2021). *Best Non-profit communication strategies*. https://online.queens.edu/resources/article/non-profit-communication-strategies
Shannon, C., & Weaver, W. (1949). *The mathematical theory of communication*. University of Illinois.
Schmid, P. (2001). Acknowledgement: The art of responding: Dialogical and ethical perspectives on the challenges of unconditional relationships in therapy and beyond. In J. Bozarth & P. Wilkins (Eds.), *Rogers' therapeutic conditions: Evolution, theory and practice* (Vol. 3, pp. 155–171). PCCS Books.
Schoeneborn, D., Kuhn, T., & Kärreman, D. (2019). The communicative constitution of organization: Organizing and organizationality. *Organization Studies*, *40*(4), 475–496. https://doi.org/10.1177/0170840618782284
Spicer, C. (2007). Collaborative advocacy and the creation of trust: Toward an understanding of stakeholder claims and risks. In E. Toth (Ed.), *The future of excellence in public relations and communication management: Challenges for the next generation* (pp. 27–40). Lawrence Erlbaum.
Thaler, R., & Sunstein, C. (2008). *Nudge: Improving decisions about health, wealth, and happiness*. Yale University Press
Tomlinson, E., & Mayer, R. (2009). The role of causal attribution dimensions in trust repair. *Academy of Management Review*, *34*, 85–104. https://doi.org/10.5465/amr.2009.35713291
Van der Meer, T. (2017). Political trust and the crisis of democracy. In *Oxford research encyclopedia of politics*. Oxford University Press.
Vásquez, C., & Schoeneborn, D. (2018). Communication as constitutive of organization. In R. Heath & W. Johansen (Eds.), *The international encyclopedia of strategic communication* (pp. 1–12). John Wiley & Sons.
Worthington, D., & Bodie, G. (Eds.). (2017). *The sourcebook of listening research: Methodology and measures*. Wiley-Blackwell.

2.3
INTEGRATED MARKETING COMMUNICATION MANAGEMENT FOR NONPROFIT ORGANIZATIONS

Manfred Bruhn and Anja Zimmermann

Communication challenges for nonprofit organizations

With their social, cultural, or societal missions, nonprofit organizations make an essential and valuable contribution to the public good and wellbeing. The economic contribution of nonprofit organizations is clearly evidenced, and an increasing professionalization of the sector can be observed in the field of business management (Golensky & Hager, 2020; Powell & Bromley, 2020; Helmig & Boenigk, 2019; Andreasen & Kotler, 2014). Nevertheless, marketing and the associated notion of applying principles of commercial marketing to one's own nonprofit organization still encounter concerns and fears, even rejection (Zimmermann, 2018). Communication as a sub-discipline of marketing is also affected by this. Professional marketing and communication work is not part of the management's self-evident tasks in all nonprofit organizations, especially not in smaller institutions. The broadening and deepening of the concept of marketing (Kotler, 1972), and thus the transfer of professional marketing thinking to the nonprofit as well as the public sector, which was already developed by Kotler in the early 1970s and known as the generic concept of marketing, is more and more required today (Bruhn & Herbst, 2022; Grau, 2021; Bennett, 2019; Andreasen & Kotler, 2014). The deepening discussion of marketing by nonprofit organizations is receiving new attention, especially communication, due to the increasing diversity of online communication channels. Research on nonprofit communication is extensive (Souder, 2016).

Looking at the current developments and trends nonprofit organizations are facing, the need for professional marketing communication will continue to increase in the future, as competitive pressure is rising from various sides. Changing legal framework conditions, especially in social legislation, declining support for nonprofit organizations from public funds due to tight public finances, as well as the decreasing solidarity principle or the decreasing willingness for voluntary work are some of the central factors that increase the pressure on nonprofit organizations. They must increasingly position and differentiate themselves in markets (sourcing and offering) not only in relation to other nonprofit organizations but also in relation to private providers who are increasingly entering the nonprofit sector. To be able to convince in competition, they must be perceived as a brand and trigger preferences among stakeholders through strong brand positioning (Beger, 2018, p. 637ff.).

Such communication work by nonprofit organizations not only has to consider the perspective of external, market-oriented communication. In many organizations, the service itself is provided as a service to people or as interaction with society, so interactive communication is also important and often even much more effective than external communication. A prerequisite for

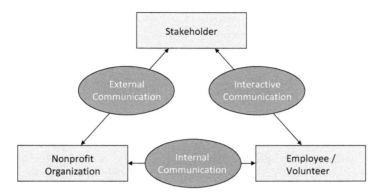

Figure 2.3.1 Manifestations of communication in nonprofit organizations.

convincing external and interactive communication in this context is internal communication with full-time employees and volunteers. These different manifestations of communication are shown in Figure 2.1.1. Within strategic communication planning they should be considered together as an entity and not in isolation.

Peculiarities in communication for nonprofit organizations

A simple one-to-one transfer of professional communication concepts to the nonprofit sector cannot be the means of choice, despite the competitive conditions that are becoming increasingly like those in traditional markets. Rather, the specific characteristics and contextual factors of nonprofit organizations must be taken into consideration.

The primary task of nonprofit organizations is to convince. The immaterial task is directed at the organization's own employees, at customers of services, at political bodies and institutions, and at sponsors, donors, members, and volunteers, as well as at society as a whole and its relevant sub-publics. For nonprofit organizations, due to their mostly intangible, content-related objectives, initial difficulties become apparent in the question of identifying and describing their market and their "customers", followed by challenges in the use of communication policy, but also other marketing instruments. Due to the often-intangible services, hurdles arise e.g., in pricing and thus "value perception", as well as a multitude of specific challenges and peculiarities in communication.

The heterogeneity and diversity of the stakeholder groups with which nonprofit organizations interact is one of the key challenges for communication. Different stakeholders have different needs, sometimes conflicting objectives, resulting in a wide range of messages and many communication channels. Against the backdrop of scarce resources, these diverse requirements often cannot be met adequately in terms of communication. A focus on "low-cost" and individual means of communication is not seldom the result, and individual stakeholder groups are only considered to a limited extent or not at all. Moreover, the significance of marketing communication in nonprofit organizations has been disputed for years and is still disputed today. As a result, professionalization in communication is limited. A lack of awareness of the importance and necessity of professional communication, coupled with scarce financial resources and simultaneous pressure for legitimacy, result in low internal acceptance for external communication campaigns – they are sometimes even regarded as a wrong investment, with the comment that the budget should be invested more sensibly in the core mission of the institution. Generally scarce personnel resources in nonprofit organizations, and thus often personnel bottlenecks in the field of marketing and communication, also hinder the completion of communication tasks. The democratization of decision-making processes in many organizations leads to problems in the centralized and decentralized coordination of communication processes. Above all, internal skepticism about topics such as branding and the frequently low awareness of the need for strategic planning of communication overlook the central importance of brand positioning for sustainable support, market position, and thus the long-term success of the nonprofit organization.

Finally, the characteristics of the nonprofit services themselves lead to specific peculiarities of communication policy, as it must consider the intangible nature of services. Nonprofit organizations have a variety of internal and external communication instruments at their disposal. However, due to the immateriality of the service, the overall tendency can be observed that interactive communication between service provider and service recipient, as well as internal employee communication, is becoming particularly important for success. Due to the role of employees in the process of service creation, they must be considered as credible multipliers in the communication process when focusing on a holistic approach to communication. Due to the intangibility of services, it is also the task of communication to make the service itself tangible, as well as to build up and maintain the image as a central trust anchor in the usage decision process. Furthermore, it is essential to positively control and shape the encounter and interaction of the service recipient and the service provider in the process of using the service through communication (Bruhn & Herbst, 2022).

Necessity of integrating the communication of nonprofit organizations

The complexity of the communication work of a nonprofit organization arises from a diverse network of relationships with heterogeneous stakeholders. It is also characterized by increasing efficiency and competitive pressure in the sourcing and demanding markets. A major battlefield is taking place in the market for attention and affection. These challenges force organizations to plan and structure their communication work professionally. An organization's communications work should not be satisfied with simply serving individual stakeholders with singular communication tools such as press releases or brochures, which are often not coordinated with each other. Instead, what is needed is holistically planned and managed communication work that conveys a uniform and consistent image of the organization and combines different communication tasks. The concept of integrated communication offers such a holistic management approach for nonprofit organizations.

For decades, managers and academics have been looking for ways to coordinate their diverse communication activities to increase efficiency and effectiveness. The demand for integration of the growing number of communication instruments and measures in an increasingly fragmented communication environment is evident and undisputed. Inconsistent, however, are the various understandings and interpretations of integrated communication as a claim and concept. The concept itself has gained importance over the last three decades, and with it, a variety of concepts and definitions have emerged (Tafesse & Kitchen, 2016; Bruhn, 2014; Duncan & Caywood, 1996). There is an ongoing debate to reach consensus about the meaning of the concept (e.g., Bruhn & Schnebelen, 2017; Kliatchko & Schultz, 2015; Kerr et al., 2008; Kitchen et al., 2008; Kliatchko, 2008, 2005; Low, 2000; Bruhn, 1998).

Integrated communication can be defined as a strategic and operational process, which involves analysis, planning, organizing, implementing, and monitoring and which aims to communicate a coherent and consistent image of a company, institution, or reference object by integrating the company's distinctive sources of different forms of communication (Bruhn, 2014, p. 38).

The need for an integrated communication concept arises for nonprofit organizations for various reasons in addition to the increasing competition already outlined. They can be divided into external and internal drivers of integrated communication.

Key internal reasons for integrated communication in nonprofit organizations are as follows:

- In many nonprofit organizations, clear responsibilities, tasks, and roles for communication with internal and external stakeholders are not defined.
- The importance and role of communication work for the success of one's own organization are often not consciously perceived, and the ideas of how a communication concept can be professionally designed vary greatly.
- Communication activities are often not coordinated but designed as selective individual measures. Coordination does not take place consistently and universally, which prevents individual communication measures from working synergistically.
- Externally contradictory and inconsistent communication measures not only threaten the credibility of the organization vis-à-vis the outside world but are also a burden on identity and identification internally.
- Internal communication towards volunteers or employees and external communication show discrepancies; often these communication levels are not well coordinated.
- Marketing and communication budgets are usually tight in nonprofit organizations; thus, making efficient and effective use of resources is even more essential.

The necessity of integrating the communication work of a nonprofit organization also arises from external developments, above all driven by the changing and increasing demands of stakeholders and competition.

The main reasons for managing communication in a holistic and integrated manner are many and varied:

- Expectations regarding communication and information by nonprofit organizations are constantly increasing. Transparency and legitimacy of the work, as well as the use of allocated financial resources, are important requirements that nonprofit organizations must fulfill to ensure trust and support.
- Reputational crises, e.g., due to mismanagement of donations or allegations of corruption, have significantly heightened awareness and perception of the work of nonprofit organizations and produced media sensitization.
- Contradictory statements due to uncoordinated communication processes and, as a result, irritation can be avoided vis-à-vis stakeholders and, above all, the attentive media through professionally managed integrated communication.
- The number of nonprofit organizations is increasing and with it the danger of not generating a clear profile in the perception of the stakeholders.

In view of the competition, the following reasons call for integrated communication:

- It is precisely the low significance and the restraint in the use of professional communication that lead to a great similarity in the communicative appearance of nonprofit organizations. This means that they are unable to establish a clear profile against their competitors.
- A lack of appreciation of the benefits of strong branding, and thus a low level of awareness of nonprofit organizations, also frequently makes these organizations losers in the battle for attention and financial donations. Personal engagement and willingness to donate within local communities are also influenced by communication (Wenlin & Nah, 2020).
- The problem of weak brand personalities subsequently also influences the ability of nonprofit organizations to acquire and retain professional employees based on an attractive employer brand.

The reasons outlined here, which clearly speak to the use of integrated communication in nonprofit organizations, are not conclusive, but represent the central arguments why especially nonprofit organizations should strive more consciously and professionally for an irritation-free, differentiating, and internally convincing communication management in the sense of integrated communication.

Strategic planning of integrated communication

In comparison to other concepts like corporate identity or corporate communication, the integrated communication approach focusses on the management process for integrating internal, interactive, and external communication. It goes far beyond a mere formal integration of communication with a consistent corporate design. Real integration is more extensive, comprising formal integration, the question of timing, and – this is the most challenging aspect – the integration of messages and content in communication relations. Figure 2.3.2 gives an overview of these forms of integration, their underlying targets, and tools.

To be successfully managed, integrated communication needs to be planned at different levels simultaneously, i.e., strategic planning at the corporate level, and the integrative strategic planning of each single communication activity or program at the level of maybe even different functional departments like public relations, internal communication, and events within the nonprofit organization. To build an "entity" which can be easily identified by the organization's main stakeholders and target groups, it is essential to define a strategic concept of communication at the organizational level. This strategic concept, which is illustrated in Figure 2.3.3, delivers a common framework for the planning and execution of any single communication activity, programme, or tool. It comprises three basic elements: the strategic positioning as the most important strategic communication goal of the organization; the key message as a central marketing idea or claim; and the key communication tool to be employed, which is in lead for the realization of the strategic communication aims and which therefore has a dominant role against other instruments.

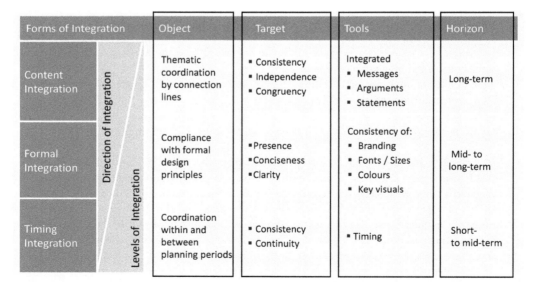

Figure 2.3.2 Overview of the different forms of integration. (Bruhn, 2014, p. 144)

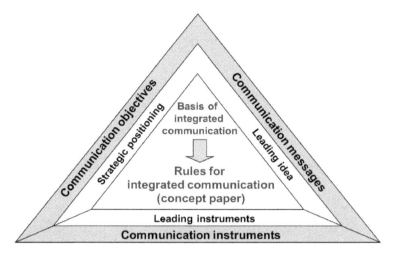

Figure 2.3.3 Key elements of the strategic concept of integrated communication.

With these three strategic decisions, which must be taken by the management of the nonprofit organization, the strategic framework is fixed and serves as a fundament for all communication activities. However, it is far too abstract and conceptual to be used or implemented in a corporation as a daily foundation. Therefore, it must be translated top-down and made operational for the purposes of a single department, programme, or activity.

Realizing integrated communication

The application of the strategic communication concept, and thus the integration of communication activities throughout the organization, can be supported by establishing a set of common guidelines and rules (see Figure 2.3.4), which build the basis for the realization of an integrated communication concept and which enable departments to implement strategic decisions at their level. These conceptual rules are intended to clarify the communication strategy to everybody concerned and involved within the organization and to give the strategic concept a binding character. These guidelines thus enable and control the implementation of an integrated communication concept. A closer look at Figure 2.3.4 and the described rules reveals the principle of this approach. Integration is realized by a hierarchization of:

- Communication objectives.
- Messages.
- Communication tools.

For instance, at the level of the message platform, the key message as a central claim provides a message that is valid for the entire nonprofit organization or the organizational brand (e.g., WWF as a brand). This guiding concept or focal message must be translated into more specific core messages that are developed and designed with respect to the different target groups and stakeholders (e.g., employees, volunteers, donors, clients, suppliers, and partners), whereas single arguments and patterns of argumentation prove the core messages by supplying messages with traceable evidence. This creation of hierarchies is not to be seen as a strict "prescription" of content or messages, but rather as a serving guideline that enables different organizational units to define their communication contents so that these reinforce each other without contradiction.

I. Strategy Paper
1. Strategy of Integrated Communications   Definition of the strategic positioning, leading idea or claim and leading instrument at organizational level

II. Communication Rules
2. Target platform   Specification of strategic positioning, objectives at stakeholders / target group level and goals at the level of communication acitivities
3. Message platform   Specification of the leading idea or claim, core message for different target groups and arguments to prove the core message
4. Instrument platform   Specification of the instruments in lead for achieving the strategic position, definition of corporate design and determination of the role of further instruments and media.

III. Organization Rules
5. Rules for Cooperation and Coordination   Specification of the organization responsibilities and the structure of communications, single operations and processes. Rules of cooperation and coordination between departments or people in charge.

Figure 2.3.4 Concept paper of integrated communication (Bruhn, 2014, p. 262).

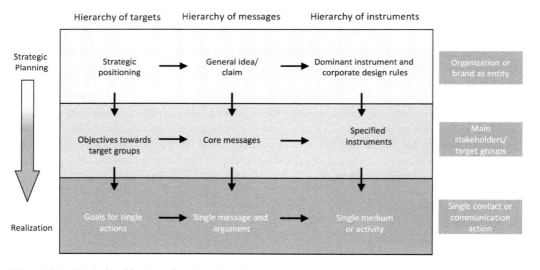

Figure 2.3.5 Vertical and horizontal order within the system of integrated communication (Bruhn, 2014, p. 294).

This outlined approach for integrated communication has been implemented many times by German and Swiss companies making integration manageable (see the best practice cases in Bruhn, 2014, pp. 515–674). Also, in the nonprofit and public sector, the concept has been realized successfully. Figure 2.3.5 provides an overall view of the procedural order of the integrated communication activities that are necessary for achieving targets, messages, and instruments in terms of strategic hierarchy.

Regardless of this structuring approach, the actual content task of communication remains a challenge for many nonprofit organizations when it comes to pointing out problems, grievances, dangers, and risks and making stakeholders aware of them, using the right message forms, such as narratives. (Cadet & Carroll, 2019).

Implementation of integrated communication in nonprofit organizations

The development of a concept for integrated communication is a strategic planning task. This is the prerequisite for a long-term and consistent communication of a nonprofit organization with its relevant stakeholders and the foundation for a concise and sustainable communication appearance internally and externally. In addition to the planning work, it is primarily the implementation of a communication concept that represents the real hurdles when attempting to professionalize the communication effort (Bruhn, 2014; Ots & Nyilasy, 2015). In the following, therefore, two vital aspects of organizational and personnel implementation in nonprofit organizations should be highlighted, in particular organizational implementation and personal implementation.

Organizational implementation

Communication work in nonprofit organizations sometimes fails because it does not experience an organizational home and a clear assignment of responsibility. The topic of communication is often not clearly anchored in either in the organizational structure or the process organization. It is frequently assigned to a public relations department or a press spokesperson, who is often unable to fulfill the complexity of communication work in their function. If one wants to successfully initiate, plan, and implement integrated communication in a nonprofit context, the work urgently requires the claim of a management task. Integrated communication must be established as a controlled management process that cannot be delegated to a specialist department, but initially requires the attention and the weight of top management. Above all, the development of the identity of the brand and the associated brand elements is a task for the top management, which should, however, actively involve the employees of the organization, the volunteers, and representatives of the stakeholder groups. The strategic elements of an integrated communication concept must also be interpreted as a management task, initiated top-down but supported and shaped bottom-up. The formation of a cross-functional project team for the implementation of the tasks of integrated communication has proven successfully in practice.

Personal implementation

One of the biggest barriers in the implementation of integrated communication is personal resistance, both in management and in the operational units in nonprofit organizations. This resistance can be based on created structures and subcultures, but it can also be an expression of resistance to change, fear of losing power, or a lack of understanding of the need for professional, integrated communication work. The sense of integrated communication and the development of an awareness of the brand and its impact internally and externally must therefore be created by the management and consolidated by a sustained discourse within the company. Central to this is involving internal stakeholders – employees as well as volunteers – in communication processes not just once, but on an ongoing basis, to do justice to their importance as communicators (Andersson, 2019; Sadrabadi et al., 2018; Cervellon & Lirio, 2017). Internal brand clarity, internal relational communication, and internal brand presence are key factors influencing the success of branding in a nonprofit context (Ramjaun, 2021).

A simple but vital rule here is to always conduct internal communication before external communication. This can also raise awareness among employees of their role as brand ambassadors because employees are among the most credible communicators of an organization. Therefore, internal marketing is of special relevance in the context of nonprofit organizations (Liu et al., 2015; Piehler et al., 2015). Especially in the age of digital communication and the importance of social communication channels and cross-media communication relationships, the employees of a nonprofit organization are challenged as communication and brand ambassadors (Svensson et al., 2015). Internal branding is significant to marketing success and should therefore be considered in strategic brand communication efforts (Iyer et al., 2018). Individual and personal enabling, as well as targeted further training for communication in social media, are increasingly important. This allows employees to assume their role within a community-based communication, which has an impact on nonprofit participation behaviour in the form of giving and volunteering (Wenlin & Nah, 2020). The differentiated, distinctive perception of a nonprofit organization is made possible by an existing congruence between its external communication appearance, its interaction with stakeholders, and its actions.

Integrated communication is a valuable communication concept for nonprofit organizations that is more than simply the coordination and standardization of communication instruments: It comprises a strategic planning built upon a defined strategic positioning of the organization, as well as managerial, organizational, and individual tasks and must focus on relationship communication (Finne & Grönroos, 2009). The balancing between the inside-out perspective (i.e., communication generated by the organization and its representatives) and the outside-in perspective (i.e., integration of stakeholder-generated content, for example, in online channels) will be one of the challenges integrated communication has to face in the future (Bruhn & Schnebelen, 2017).

References

Andersson, R. (2019). Employees as ambassadors: Embracing new role expectations and coping with identity-tensions. *Corporate Communication: An International Journal*, 24(4), 702–716. https://doi.org/10.1108/CCIJ-04-2019-0038.

Andreasen, A. R., & Kotler, Ph. (2014). *Strategic marketing for nonprofit organisations* (7th ed.). Pearson.

Beger, R. (2018). *Present-day corporate communication*. Springer International.

Bennett, R. (2019). *Nonprofit marketing and fundraising: A research overview*. Routledge.

Bruhn, M. (1998). Integrated marketing communication: The German perspective. *Journal of Integrated Marketing Communication*, 8(1997/98), 37–43.

Bruhn, M. (2014). *Integrierte Unternehmens- und Markenkommunikation. Strategische Planung und operative Umsetzung* (6th ed.). Schäffer-Poeschel.

Bruhn, M., & Herbst, U. (2022). *Marketing für Nonprofit-Organisationen: Grundlagen – Konzepte – Instrumente*. Kohlhammer Edition Marketing (in print).

Bruhn, M., & Schnebelen, St. (2017). Integrated marketing communication – from an instrumental to a customer-centric perspective. *European Journal of Marketing*, 51(3), 464–489.

Cadet, F. T., & Carroll, R. (2019). Nonprofit organization communication: Risky business. *Review of Business*, 39(1), 1–14.

Cervellon, M.-C., & Lirio, P. (2017). When employees don't 'like' their employers on social media. *MIT Sloan Management Review*, 58(2), 63–70.

Duncan, T., & Caywood, C. (1996). The concept, process, and evolution of integrated marketing communication. In E. Thorson & T. Moore (Eds.), *Integrated communication: Synergy of persuasive voices* (pp. 13–34). Psychology Press.

Finne, Å., & Grönroos, C. (2009). Rethinking marketing communication: From integrated marketing communication to relationship communication. *Journal of Marketing Communication*, 15(2/3), 179–195.

Golensky, M., & Hager, M. A. (2020). *Strategic leadership and management in nonprofit organizations: Theory and practice* (2nd ed.). Oxford University Press.

Grau, S. L. (2021). *Marketing for nonprofit organizations: Insights and innovations* (2nd ed.) Oxford University Press.

Helmig, B., & Boenigk, S. (2019). *Non profit management* (2nd ed.).Vahlen.

Iyer, P., Davari, A., & Paswan, A. (2018). Determinants of brand performance: The role of internal branding. *Journal of Brand Management*, 25(3), 202–216.

Kerr, G., Schultz, D., Patti, Ch., & Kim, I. (2008). An inside out approach to integrated marketing communication. *International Journal of Advertising*, 27(4), 511–548.

Kitchen, P. J., Kim, I., & Schultz, D. E. (2008). Integrated marketing communication: Practice leads theory. *Journal of Advertising Research*, 48(4), 531–546.

Kliatchko, J. (2005). Towards a new definition of IMC. *International Journal of Advertising*, 24(1), 7–34.

Kliatchko, J. G. (2008). Revisiting the IMC construct – a revised definition and four pillars. *International Journal of Advertising*, 27(1), 133–160.

Kliatchko, J. G., & Schultz, D. E. (2015). Twenty years of IMC. *International Journal of Advertising*, 33(2), 373–390.

Kotler, Ph. (1972). A generic concept of marketing. *Journal of Marketing*, 36(2), 46–54.

Liu, G., Chapleo, Ch., Ko, W., & Ngugi, I. K. (2015). The role of internal branding in nonprofit brand management: An empirical investigation. *Nonprofit and Voluntary Sector Quarterly*, 44(2), 319–339.

Low, G. S. (2000). Correlates of IMC. *Journal of Advertising Research*, 40(1), 27–39.

Ots, M., & Nyilasy, G. (2015). Integrated marketing communication: Why does it fail? An analysis of practitioner mental models exposes barriers of IMC implementation. *Journal of Advertising Research*, 55(2), 132–145.

Piehler, R., Hanisch, S., & Burmann, C. (2015). Internal branding. Relevance, management and challenges. *Marketing Review St. Gallen*, 32(1), 52–61.

Powell, W. W., & Bromley, P. (2020). *The nonprofit sector: A research handbook* (3rd ed.) Stanford University Press. https://ebookcentral.proquest.com/lib/hslu-ebooks/detail.action?docID=6124191.

Ramjaun, T. A. (2021). Corporate brand management in a charity context: The internal communication challenge. *Corporate Communication*, 26(2), 296–310.

Sadrabadi, A. N., Saraji, M. K., & Monshi Zadeh, M. (2018). Evaluating the role of brand ambassadors in social media. *Journal of Marketing Management and Consumer Behavior*, 2(3), 54–70.

Souder, L. (2016). A review of research on nonprofit communication from mission statements to annual reports. Voluntas. *International Journal of Voluntary and Nonprofit Sector Organizations*, 27(6), 2709–2733.

Svensson, P. G., Mahoney, T. Q., & Hambrick, M. E. (2015). Twitter as a communication tool for nonprofits: A study of sport-for-development organizations. *Nonprofit and Voluntary Sector Quarterly*, 44(6), 1086–1106.

Tafesse, W., & Kitchen, P. J. (2016). IMC – an integrative review. *International Journal of Advertising*, 36(2), 210–226. www.tandfonline.com/doi/full/10.1080/02650487.2015.1114168.

Wenlin, L., & Nah, S. (2020). Community attachment, communication mediation, and nonprofit participation: An integrated community communication approach. *Voluntas Manchester*. https//doi.org/10.1007/s11266-020-00276-9.

Zimmermann, A. (2018). Marketing. In J. Krummenacher, C. Buerkli, P. Bürkler, & A. Schnyder (Eds.), *Management von non profit organisationen* (pp. 141–160). Seismo-Verlag.

2.4
COMMUNICATION MONITORING AND EVALUATION IN THE NONPROFIT SECTOR

Glenn O'Neil

Introduction

Increasingly communicators working for businesses, government – and nonprofit organizations – are under pressure to show the results of their communication activities as budgets rise, communication channels multiply and the role of communication becomes more strategic (Macnamara, 2006; Zerfass et al., 2017). Across all activities, including communication, nonprofit organizations have also faced increased pressure from funders and stakeholders to monitor and evaluate their results (Harlock & Metcalf, 2016; Bach-Mortensen & Montgomery, 2018). This has been reinforced by the adoption of results-based management (RBM) systems by nonprofit organizations that emphasize monitoring and evaluation (M&E) (Mayne, 2007).

As communicators seek solutions, there has been an increased focus on communication M&E in the past decades (Gregory, 2020; Likely & Watson, 2013; Macnamara, 2018). Positively, this has meant that resources such as articles, textbooks and guidelines have been developed and are available for supporting communicators in carrying out M&E activities (Lindenmann, 2003; Macnamara & Likely, 2017; Watson & Noble, 2014). For communicators working in nonprofit organizations, the International Association for Measurement and Evaluation of Communication (AMEC), an industry body, has an active not-for-profit group for communicators, established since 2013, that holds regular exchanges and has dedicated sessions on M&E for nonprofit communication as part of the annual AMEC summit (AMEC, n.d.). The Communications Consortium Media Center (CCMC, 2004) has also issued guidelines for evaluating nonprofit communication efforts.

For the purpose of this chapter, it is helpful to define what is meant by M&E. Monitoring is an ongoing activity that collects data and information to provide communicators and their managers (and possibly donors, sponsors and supporters) with indications of their progress in meeting their objectives (OECD-DAC, 2002). For communication, monitoring tends to focus on the tracking of predefined indicators or metrics, such as presence in the media, interactions on social media or changes in the public's attitudes. Evaluation is the systematic and objective assessment of an ongoing or completed initiative in order to determine if it met its objectives, in addition to its relevance, coherence, effectiveness, efficiency, impact and sustainability (OECD-DAC, 2002). Evaluation is carried out at a point in time, such as the end of planning or funding cycle (e.g. two years) or conclusion of a series of activities. Communication M&E should also take place prior to communication activities, commencing in order to set benchmarks or baselines as a starting point for the communication (Gregory, 2020; Watson & Noble, 2014). The importance of communication M&E to improve the overall effectiveness of the communication activities is also emphasized (Stacks & Michaelson, 2010; Watson & Noble, 2014).

Challenges and current practices of nonprofit communication M&E

Communicators in general have faced challenges and barriers for implementing M&E, including availability of resources and budget, the lack of competencies and know-how, limited management demand, support and access to methodologies or tools and incoherent industry models and standards (Gilkerson et al., 2019; Macnamara, 2020; Volk & Buhmann, 2019). Lack of staff, time and budget has been particularly highlighted by nonprofit communicators (Lim, 2019). The inability to find a single "silver bullet" measure for communication has undoubtedly disappointed communicators seeking simple solutions to what are complex matters (Gregory, 2020).

Yet these challenges have been largely addressed, and communicators today *are* monitoring and evaluating their activities (Lim, 2019; Macnamara, 2020). The boxes featured later provide two examples of the diversity of nonprofit organizations carrying out communication M&E: the global international nongovernmental body the Organisation for Economic Co-operation and Development (OECD) that promotes social and economic growth and the Nigerian civic organization BudgIT that supports citizens in advocating for transparency in public spending.

Nevertheless, sector-wide studies indicate that communication M&E is not yet fully anchored in nonprofit organizations. A 2016 survey of 339 nonprofit communicators reported 71% conducted some type of measurement (Lim, 2019). A 2017 survey of 1,601 communicators in 40 European countries confirmed that communication M&E was consistently lower for nonprofit organizations compared to businesses (Zerfass et al., 2017). It has been estimated that this lower level is not only due to a lack of resources but also because of the complexity of nonprofit communication and the limited presence of M&E in the design of nonprofit communication initiatives (O'Neil, 2013).

Distinction of nonprofit communication M&E

The main distinction with communication M&E for nonprofit organizations and for for-profit organizations is related to the fundamental difference between these two types of organizations, notably that nonprofit organizations do not have a profit motivation, i.e. selling products or services (Eagle et al., 2020). Therefore, nonprofit organizations as drivers of social change and development often have a broader range of objectives and are often seeking attitude, behavior and societal changes that are harder to measure than financial transactions such as sales of products or services. Further, the results of communication activities can be difficult to separate from the other social change strategies being implemented (CCMC, 2004; Eagle et al., 2020; Oliveira et al., 2016).

At the same time, it must be recognized that for-profit organizations have increasingly moved from a singular shareholder approach to a broader stakeholder approach, and consequently their communication today has broader goals beyond the profit margin, even if their sincerity is debatable (Donaldson & Preston, 1995; Freeman, 2001). Although nonprofit organizations do not have communication objectives aimed to contribute to a profit margin, many do have communication objectives in support of raising funds to finance their organizations from members of the public or institutional donors, such as governments, companies and foundations (Lim, 2019; Van Dyk, 2016).

Therefore, it follows that the nonprofit communication M&E is not fundamentally different from for-profit communication M&E; more so that the approaches, models and methods need to be adjusted, bearing in mind the earlier distinctions. A further distinction identified by O'Neil (2013) was that when evaluation was carried out by international nonprofit organizations, it tended to focus on the outcome rather than the output level, whereas the for-profit organizations tended to focus on the output level. An explanation offered was the adoption of RBM systems by nonprofit organizations and an increasing interest in outcome-level evaluation from institutional donors that fund many of these organizations. As these RBM systems and M&E frameworks are adopted across all nonprofit activities, this also allows communication M&E to be part of these broader systems and mechanisms, as seen in the case of BudgIT (see box feature later).

What nonprofit communication M&E measures

Communication scholars and practitioners have developed a range of models (or frameworks) for communication M&E that mostly all follow a similar approach of measurement along a continuum (Macnamara, 2018; Watson & Noble, 2014). The most well-known models include Macnamara's pyramid model (1992), Lindenmann's effectiveness yardstick model (1993), the United Kingdom's Government Communication Service (GCS) Evaluation Framework (GCS, 2018), the European Commission's communication evaluation model (European Commission, 2015) and AMEC's integrated evaluation framework (2016). These models provide guidance for communicators on levels or steps that can be measured, most commonly labelled as inputs, activities, outcome and impact (Gregory, 2020; Macnamara, 2020).

Macnamara (2018) created an expanded evaluation model for strategic communication (see Figure 2.4.1), integrating the best features of previous models and adding some missing features, such as the two-way nature of communication and interaction with stakeholders, publics and society; explicitly linking organizational objectives with SMART (specific, measurable, achievable, relevant and time-bound) communication objectives; recognizing the overlapping nature of the different levels from input to impact; and including the importance of context and unintended impacts (Macnamara, 2018). This model is also well suited to provide guidance for nonprofit communication M&E.

In general M&E offers the possibility to measure the levels or steps of an initiative from the initial inputs to the eventual impact. The same approach can be used for nonprofit communication M&E, where at each level, indicators (or metrics) are determined to indicate progress. As seen in Figure 2.4.1, the reference point should always be the communications objectives that guide the results sought at each level. Mapping the pathway of change from inputs to impact in a "program logic" or "theory of change" can also be useful (Macnamara & Likely, 2017; O'Neil, 2020). Although program logic and theory of change have been found to be largely absent from communication M&E and planning (Macnamara & Likely, 2017), they are very much present in nonprofit M&E and planning in general (Benjamin, 2021), and therefore will be familiar to most nonprofit communicators. Based on the five levels found in Figure 2.4.1, a (nonexhaustive) matrix

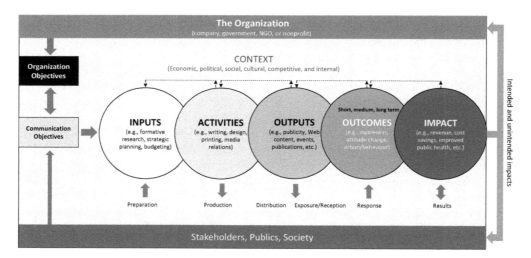

Figure 2.4.1 An integrated model of evaluation for strategic communication. © Macnamara, 2018, reproduced with permission.

of higher-level focuses and indicators for nonprofit communication M&E is found in Table 2.4.1, drawn from a range of sources (CCMC, 2004; European Commission, 2015; Gilkerson et al., 2019; Gregory, 2020; Macnamara, 2016; O'Neil, 2020; Romenti & Murtarelli, 2020; Zerfass et al., 2017).

The guidance provided in Table 2.4.1 would have to be further refined and adapted depending upon the focus on the nonprofit organization. An example of how nonprofit organizations select and prioritize their focuses can be seen in the example of the World Bank's communication M&E framework (Figure 2.4.2), where they indicated their priorities for M&E at each level with the keywords stated.

As seen in Table 2.4.1, the impact level for nonprofit communication is aimed towards long-term social change and contribution to development goals. This is a challenging level to measure, given the broad changes sought, and would only be possible through broad studies that examine the contribution of the whole efforts of the nonprofit organization to the society and development changes desired. Some organizations, such as the World Bank, also interpret impact at two levels: first, contribution to broad communication goals and second, to the mission of the organization that is focused on society and development change (see Figure 2.4.2). Given the challenges to measure impact, it has been recognized that communicators should focus on evaluating outcomes, which are not as significant as impact but much more so than outputs (Gregory, 2020; O'Neil, 2020).

In selecting what should be measured for nonprofit communication, it is also important to distinguish between what will be measured through monitoring and what will be measured through evaluation. Nonprofit communicators should be monitoring indicators to track their progress, and this would normally include output-level indicators, such as number of people reached, media coverage received and possibly some outcome-level indicators, such as level of engagement (e.g. actions taken online or changes to audiences' attitudes). Evaluation, which is carried out at a point in time, would normally incorporate all monitoring data collected and carry out additional data collection to provide an overall assessment of success. Further, evaluation may also look at broader and more process-based questions such as how the communication activities were managed and implemented, were they relevant and coherent, etc., with an aim to improve the overall effectiveness of communication (Stacks & Michaelson, 2010; Watson & Noble, 2014). Although evaluation is often carried out by external experts commissioned by nonprofit organizations, there is also great value in nonprofit communicators "stepping back" and assessing their own success annually, biennially or at the conclusion of a communication initiative.

How nonprofit communication M&E measures

Once it has been determined what level and indicators will be measured, the next step is to determine which methods are best suited to measure these levels and indicators. Considering that a range of outputs and outcomes will be the focus of the nonprofit communication M&E, it implies that multiple quantitative and qualitative methods are used, essentially a "mixed methods" approach (Stacks & Michaelson, 2010; Watson & Noble, 2014). For inputs and activities, specific methods are normally not needed to monitor their implementation, in that it is more so good project management to ensure that budgets and plans are in place (inputs) and the various activities are carried out. Measuring impact is much more complex as described earlier, and thus the focus on outcomes and outputs (to a lesser extent) is recommended.

Quantitative methods gather from larger groups and use statistical analyses for numerical data collected; qualitative methods examine opinions and ideas in depth (Stacks & Michaelson, 2010). A given method can usually measure multiple indicators, for example, a survey of audiences can measure reach, awareness, attitude and behavior change indicators.

Table 2.4.1 Matrix of suggested focuses and indicators for nonprofit communication M&E

Level	Inputs	Activities	Outputs	Outcomes	Impact
Main focus	Preparation of communication plan, baseline, objectives and budget	Production and implementation of communication activities	Reach, exposure and reception by target audiences	Changes in knowledge, attitudes and behavior of target audiences; changes to target organizations	Long-term social change and contribution to development goals
Example metrics/indicators	- Budget designed and secured - Communication objectives developed - Communication plan in place - Baseline data obtained - Pre-testing of material carried out	- Communication activities carried out - Communication content/materials produced - Partnerships/coalitions established/joined	- Number of person with opportunities to see - Number of persons reached - Quantity/favorability of media coverage - Quantity/favorability of social media content - Share of voice on media and social media compared to like-minded organizations	- Changes to level of knowledge and/or attitudes of audiences - Changes to behavior of audiences - Level of engagement on social media and websites - Changes to policies and practices of target organizations	- Changes to society norms and values - Improvement of the well-being of people - Changes to political and legal frameworks - Changes to the context and environment - Attainment of development goals

Figure 2.4.2 The World Bank's communication M&E framework. © World Bank, 2019, reproduced with permission.

It is important to ensure that there is no "substitution problem" (Broom, 2009, p. 358), that is, where a measure at one level is used as a higher level, for example, measuring the quantity of media coverage (an output) as an alleged outcome (Macnamara, 2018). In this respect, it is helpful for each communication initiative to match its communication objectives to outputs, outcomes, indicators, methods and a sampling frame in an M&E matrix, as seen in the example found in Table 2.4.2.

Following is a brief description of the most commonly used methods for the output and outcome levels for nonprofit communication evaluation.

Output methods

Outputs typically use quantitative methods, such as variations of content analysis and/or interactions that can measure indicators such as opportunities to see, reach, share of voice, etc. Increasingly these indicators can be measured using automated tools. For example, websites and social media platforms often have integrated statistical usage modules that provide such data. Automated tools are also available that monitor, extract, compile and analyze across media and social media, providing the ability to estimate total input indicators, such as opportunity to see, reach, etc. (Romenti & Murtarelli, 2020). It must be recognized that these automated tools that measure across media and social media are commercial products and mostly subscription-based, which may make them out of reach for smaller nonprofit organizations. Other methods used include simple mechanisms to track the number of people attending events or partners signing up to participate, as seen in the example found in Table 2.4.2.

Most of these output methods should be deployed on an ongoing basis, for example, in real time or on a monthly basis as part of a monitoring approach to support nonprofit communicators in assessing performance and making necessary adjustments to activities. The previously mentioned automated tools also provide the possibility to calculate the level of financial efficiency of the inputs until the level of outputs. For example, to calculate the cost per impression by channel or the cost of opportunities to see using social media channels compared to traditional media (Romenti & Murtarelli, 2020).

Outcome methods

Outcomes typically require a combination of qualitative and quantitative methods to measure changes to knowledge, attitudes and behavior. Methods that can capture such changes include surveys, focus groups, interviews, case studies and ethnographic and observational studies (O'Neil,

Table 2.4.2 Nonprofit communication M&E matrix

Communication objectives	Indicators	Methods	Sampling frame
In 2022, citizens of city A become more actively engaged in "greening" their city	Output: Number of citizens with opportunities to see information on "greening" campaign" (target: 60% of citizens) Outcome: Number of citizens who report carrying out recommended "greening" actions such as cycling to work, using a compost, joining a community garden, increasing recycling, etc. (target: 20% of citizens)	Monitoring of media and social media Survey of citizens Tracking mechanism of "greening" actions, e.g. recycling and compost records, cycling levels as monitored by city	Main media and social media used in city A Representative sample of citizens of city A Available records and monitoring data across all of city A
In 2022, community-based organizations (CBOs) of city A become more actively engaged in "greening" their city	Output: Number of CBOs signing up to become "greening" campaign partners (target: 10 CBOs) Outcome: Number of "greening projects" proposed by CBOs (target: 5 projects)	CBOs' campaign partnering statistics Tracking of CBOs' "greening" project proposals	50 CBOs (potential campaign partners)

2020). The automated tools described under outputs can also be used for some outcome indicators, for example, for measuring online behavior such as "engagement", normally defined as the number and type of comments made and referrals of online content (O'Neil, 2020; Romenti & Murtarelli, 2020).

Most methods to measure outcomes would be carried out at a given point of time, such as for an evaluation, as many nonprofit organizations could not afford to survey or interview audiences regularly, even as useful as it could be. However, some methods can be used more regularly as part of a monitoring approach, including the previously mentioned automated tools, low-cost surveying and tracking mechanisms to monitor change to policies (O'Neil, 2020).

The use of quasi-experimental methods, such as randomized control trials, is much less seen in nonprofit communication M&E. But it is feasible to use such methods in certain situations, such as seen in the case of an evaluation of a communication campaign for potential migrants in Senegal by the International Organization for Migration (Dunsch et al., 2019). For this evaluation, surveying was done with audiences before and after they were exposed to campaign messages and to a parallel ("control") group who were not exposed to the messages. Normally, costs, complexity and the issue of "contamination", where communication messages are difficult to isolate, make the use of quasi-experimental methods challenging for communication initiatives (Flay & Cook, 1981; Lim, 2019).

Analysis and reporting of nonprofit communication M&E

The analysis of data and information involves sorting, arranging and processing to "make sense" of it, using appropriate qualitative and quantitative techniques (Stacks & Michaelson, 2010; Watson & Noble, 2014). The analysis should refer to the purpose of M&E in general, that is, assessing progress, measuring success and seeking improvements. Assessing progress is mostly straightforward, i.e. are indicators and their targets being met, such as number of people reached. The measure of success, the extent to which communication objectives are being achieved, is more complex. It may be straightforward; for example, if an objective focuses on the number of people to reach, then output-level data will provide a clear response. Where an objective focuses on changes to knowledge, attitudes and behavior, this would involve looking at data from multiple methods at the outcome level, such as surveys, interviews, focus groups and tracking mechanisms. The communicator would then need to make a judgement as to what the triangulation of data indicates about the level of achievement seen. Other broader questions may also have to be answered such as how were the communication activities managed, were they relevant and coherent, etc., as described earlier.

This also brings one to the thorny question as to what extent did the communication activities contribute to any changes seen (Lim, 2019). In the example provided earlier of the randomized control trial, the communicator would have solid evidence as to their campaign's influence compared to other potential contributions. However, in most cases, nonprofit communicators will not have such data available. More so, they need to make an assessment and judgement based on the data and information they have available while considering the limitations of the research (O'Neil, 2020).

Reporting means putting the M&E findings into formats accessible to those who need them for learning and decision-making. Findings provided in summary formats can support rapid comprehension, such as in dashboards and scorecards (Watson & Noble, 2014), as used by the OECD (see highlighted box later). For some findings, such as an evaluation at the conclusion of a communication initiative, a report would be needed to summarize the findings, conclusions and recommendations (O'Neil, 2020).

The use of nonprofit communication M&E findings

M&E is of little use if the findings are not known and acted upon. Although there is a considerable body of research on how M&E findings in general are used (Johnson et al., 2009), little attention has been paid to how the findings of communication M&E are used, both in not-for-profit and for-profit organizations. One exception was a 2018 study of two communication campaigns where the authors returned four years after their evaluation to see how the nonprofit organizations had used the evaluation findings (O'Neil & Bauer, 2018). The authors concluded that "evaluation findings were used to improve efficacy of future campaigns, and mostly so in a surprising way, opportunistic ways and often delayed in time. . . . Evaluation findings proved to be of value to communication staff, even if not applied directly and to the letter" (p. 87).

Conclusion

The key approach proposed in this chapter for nonprofit communication M&E – essentially breaking down communication into measurable elements and matching them to data collection methods – is not without its critics. This approach potentially simplifies complex communication initiatives and their audiences where results can be unpredictable and occur in a nonlinear fashion (Lennie & Tacchi, 2013; Lim, 2019). One mitigation strategy is to map out fully the pathway from inputs to impact in a theory of change, as described earlier, and build flexibility into M&E to cope with complexity and capture unexpected results (Macnamara, 2018; O'Neil, 2020).

In the future, communication M&E can be advanced considerably by engaging with the wealth of studies, guidance and methods available from other disciplines: with predictive modelling, behavioral insights and sense-making methodology being the latest developments highlighted among others (Lim, 2019; Macnamara, 2020a, 2020b). At the same time, nonprofit communicators should not always aim to adopt advanced methods and meet academic levels of rigor for their M&E; as Watson and Noble (2014) stated, "Much useful information can be gathered using low-cost, small-sample research" (p. 50). Nonprofit communicators should be encouraged to collect and use what they can within their means for M&E.

Communication M&E never occurs in a vacuum and ideally should be integrated within the design of all communication initiatives. To increase the likelihood of its success, a holistic approach is needed that aligns M&E with the communication and organizational priorities, supported by the required investment, together with an organizational culture conducive to utilizing communication M&E findings (Gilkerson et al., 2019). Further, many goals of nonprofit organizations are focused on communication, and a greater recognition of these goals would also place more emphasis on their measurement and consequent integration of findings within the communication management process. In these ways, M&E can support nonprofit organizations in understanding and recognizing the value of communication.

BudgIT integrated communication M&E

BudgIT, the Nigerian civic organization working across West Africa, has communication objectives and indicators integrated within its overall M&E approach. BudgIT uses technology to support citizen mobilization for greater accountability for public spending, and communication activities are central to their initiatives, combined with budget analysis; technical assistance; and capacity building for citizens, civil society partners and government officials. For example, BudgIT has in place a project-tracking tool (Tracka) that allows Nigerians to post pictures of government projects in their communities, monitor their progress and advocate for their completion. For each initiative, BudgIT sets out SMART objectives with output and outcome indicators that are part of an M&E matrix that is monitored throughout an initiative's duration. Communication-specific indicators that are monitored for most initiatives include opportunities to see, reach, media coverage, citizen mobilization, partnerships established and policy/budget changes secured. These complement the noncommunication indicators that are monitored such as the number of budget datasets analyzed, the number of government projects tracked, the number of community advocates ("champions") active and the level of presence of BudgIT in the states of Nigeria. An automated tool supports data collection, in addition to tracking policy changes, participation statistics and constantly monitoring feedback from citizens. Every year, BudgIT collates and publishes the results of its monitoring across its initiatives in its annual report. For example, in 2020, BudgIT reported it had over 1,200 mentions in print and online newspapers, reached over 183,000 citizens through offline engagement (output indicators) and had seen major policy change on budget transparency in 22 states (outcome indicator) (BudgIT, 2020). As BudgIT is supported by institutional donors, it also carries out in-depth evaluations of initiatives as a complement. The ability of BudgIT to set and monitor a series of integrated communication and noncommunication indicators provides the organization with a comprehensive overview of its success and feedback for the organization to improve its effectiveness.

OECD Communications Impact Framework

The OECD has established a "Communications Impact Framework" to provide guidance to measure and evaluate their communication activities. The framework sets out the pathways from inputs to impact, with key indicators defined at each level that are monitored regularly and reported on annually in an "OECD Impact

Scorecard". Output indicators measure the quantity of content produced, with short-term outcome indicators measuring audience size and extent of engagement. Long-term outcome indicators measure awareness and perception among citizens; initiatives with partners; recognition and "share of voice" in media (coverage compared to like-minded organizations); and decision-maker and institutional outcomes such as number of key references and mentions of OECD in policies, laws, parliamentary debates and reports. Impact indicators (under development in early 2022) measure the number of OECD recommendations, laws, regulations and policies adopted and reference the OECD "Better Life" index (www.oecdbetterlifeindex.org) where applicable. The Intelligence and Impact team of the Public Affairs and Communications Directorate uses a range of tools and methods to measure these key indicators, including digital monitoring tools, eye tracking software (for optimizing online content), surveys and policy tracking mechanisms. The team emphasizes the learning aspect of their monitoring and evaluation by carrying out a range of bespoke analyses to produce insights for immediate improvements to communication actions, such as which social media channels are the most effective for engagement, how OECD's share of voice has changed on an issue it is campaigning on and where OECD policy recommendations are seeing greatest uptake (or not). The Impact Scorecard also provides a rapid overview of the communications results for OECD staff and management. This holistic approach provides the Public Affairs and Communications Directorate with a comprehensive assessment of their progress with learnings as to how their communications activities could be more effective and illustrates clearly their contribution to providing an enabling environment for policy change within OECD member states.

References

AMEC (International Association for Measurement and Evaluation of Communication). (n.d.). *About AMEC not for profit group.* https://amecorg.com/join-amec/nonprofit-membership/

Association of Measurement and Evaluation of Communication (AMEC) (2016). *Integrated evaluation framework.* London, UK: AMEC

Bach-Mortensen, A. M., & Montgomery, P. (2018). What are the barriers and facilitators for third sector organisations (nonprofits) to evaluate their services? A systematic review. *Systematic Reviews*, 7(1), 1–15.

Benjamin, L. M. (2021). Beyond programs: Toward a fuller picture of beneficiaries in nonprofit evaluation. In P. Dahler-Larsen (Ed.), *A research agenda for evaluation* (pp. 81–105). Edward Elgar Publishing.

Broom, G. (2009). *Cutlip & center's effective public relations* (10th ed.). Pearson.

BudgIT. (2020). *Impact in unprecedented times, annual report 2020.* https://yourbudgit.com/wp-content/uploads/2021/05/annual-report-FA2-web.pdf

CCMC. (2004). *Guidelines for evaluating nonprofit communications efforts.* Communications Consortium Media Center. www.pointk.org/resources/files/Eval_comm_efforts.pdf

Donaldson, T., & Preston, L. E. (1995). The stakeholder theory of the corporation: Concepts, evidence, and implications. *Academy of Management Review*, 20(1), 65–91.

Dunsch, F., Tjaden, D., & Quiviger, W. (2019). *Migrants as messengers: The impact of peer-to-peer communication on potential migrants in Senegal.* Impact Evaluation Report. International Organization for Migration. https://publications.iom.int/system/files/pdf/migrants_as_messengers_senegal.pdf

Eagle, L., Czarnecka, B., Dahl, S., & Lloyd, J. (2020). *Marketing communications.* Routledge.

European Commission. (2015). *Toolkit for the evaluation of communication activities.* Brussels. http://ec.europa.eu/dgs/communication/about/evaluation/documents/communication-evaluationtoolkit_en.pdf

Flay, B., & Cook, T. (1981). Evaluation of mass media prevention campaigns. In R. Rice & W. Paisley (Eds.), *Public communication campaigns* (pp. 239–264). Sage.

Freeman, R. E. (2001). A stakeholder theory of the modern corporation. In W. M. Hoffman, R. E. Frederick, & M. S. Schwartz (Eds.), *Business ethical: Readings and cases in corporate morality* (pp. 38–48). McGraw-Hill.

GCS (Government Communication Service). (2018). *Evaluation framework.* Cabinet Office, HM Government. https://gcs.civilservice.gov.uk/guidance/evaluation/toolsand-resources

Gilkerson, N. D., Swenson, R., & Likely, F. (2019). Maturity as a way forward for improving organizations' communication evaluation and measurement practices: A definition and concept explication. *Journal of Communication Management*, 23(3), 246–264.

Gregory, A. (2020). The fundamentals of measurement and evaluation of communication. In V. Luoma-aho & M. Canel (Eds.), *The handbook of public sector communication* (pp. 367–382). Wiley-Blackwell.

Harlock, J., & Metcalf, L. (2016). Measuring impact: Prospects and challenges for third sector organisations. *Voluntary Sector Review*, 7(1), 101–108.

Johnson, K., Greenseid, L. O., Toal, S. A., King, J. A., Lawrenz, F., & Volkov, B. (2009). Research on evaluation use a review of the empirical literature from 1986 to 2005. *American Journal of Evaluation*, 30(3), 377–410.

Lennie, J., & Tacchi, J. (2013). *Evaluating communication for development: A framework for social change*. Routledge.

Likely, F., & Watson, T. (2013). Measuring the edifice: Public relations measurement and evaluation practices over the course of 40 years. In K. Sriramesh, A. Zerfass, & J-N. Kim (Eds.), *Public relations and communication management: Current trends and emerging topics* (pp. 143–162). Routledge.

Lim, J. R. (2019). *Nonprofits' Public Relations Measurement and Evaluation*. Institute for Public Relations. https://instituteforpr.org/wp-content/uploads/nonprofits_comm_measurement_jungkyurhysLim.02.28.pdf

Lindenmann, W. (1993). An 'effectiveness yardstick' to measure public relations success. *Public Relations Quarterly*, 38(1), 7–9.

Lindenmann, W. (2003). *Guidelines and standards for measuring the effectiveness of PR programs and activities*. Institute for Public Relations. www.instituteforpr.org/wp-content/uploads/2002_MeasuringPrograms.pdf

Macnamara, J. (1992). Evaluation of public relations: The Achilles Heel of the public relations profession. *International Public Relations Review*, 15(2), 19–25.

Macnamara, J. (2006). Two-tier evaluation can help corporate communicators gain management support. *PRism*, 4(2). https://citeseerx.ist.psu.edu/viewdoc/download?doi=10.1.1.673.2796&rep=rep1&type=pdf

Macnamara, J. (2016). *A taxonomy of evaluation: Towards standards*. AMEC. https://amecorg.com/amecframework/home/supporting-material/taxonomy/

Macnamara, J. (2018). A review of new evaluation models for strategic communication: Progress and gaps. *International Journal of Strategic Communication*, 12(2), 180–195.

Macnamara, J. (2020a). Embracing evaluation theory to overcome "stasis": Informing standards, impact and methodology. *Corporate Communications: An International Journal*, 25(2), 339–354.

Macnamara, J. (2020b). Public sector communication measurement and evaluation. The handbook of public sector communication. In V. Luoma-aho & M. Canel (Eds.), *The handbook of public sector communication* (pp. 361–365). Wiley-Blackwell.

Macnamara, J., & Likely, F. (2017). Revisiting the disciplinary home of evaluation: New perspectives to inform PR evaluation standards. *Research Journal of the Institute for Public Relations*, 2(2), 1–21.

Mayne, J. (2007). *Best practices in results-based management: A review of experience: A report for the United Nations Secretariat, Volume 1: Main report, July 2007*. www.focusintl.com/RBM043-2007%2007%20UN%20Best%20Practices%20in%20Results-Based%20Management.pdf

OECD- DAC. (2002). *Evaluation and aid effectiveness, glossary of key terms in evaluation and results based management*. www.oecd.org/dac/evaluation/2754804.pdf

Oliveira, E., Melo, A. D., & Gonçalves, G. (Eds.). (2016). *Strategic communication for nonprofit organisations: Challenges and alternative approaches*. Vernon Press.

O'Neil, G. (2013). Evaluation of international and non-governmental organizations' communication activities: A 15 year systematic review. *Public Relations Review*, 39, 572–574.

O'Neil, G. (2020). Measuring and evaluating audience awareness, attitudes, and response. In V. Luoma-aho & M. Canel (Eds.), *The handbook of public sector communication* (pp. 405–416). Wiley-Blackwell.

O'Neil, G., & Bauer, M. W. (2018). Pathways to use of communication campaigns' evaluation findings within international organizations. *Evaluation and Program Planning*, 69, 82–91.

Romenti, S., & Murtarelli, G. (2020). Measuring and evaluating media: Traditional and social. In V. Luoma-aho & M. Canel (Eds.), *The handbook of public sector communication* (pp. 383–403). Wiley-Blackwell.

Stacks, D., & Michaelson, D. (2010). *A practitioner's guide to public relations research, measurement and evaluation*. Business Expert Press.

Van Dyk, L. (2016). Perceptions from the bottom up: Relationships between nonprofit organisations and their corporate donors. In E. Oliveira, A. D. Melo, & G. Gonçalves (Eds.), *Strategic communication for nonprofit organisations: Challenges and alternative approaches* (pp. 121–145). Vernon Press.

Volk, S. C., & Buhmann, A. (2019). New avenues in communication evaluation and measurement (E&M): Towards a research agenda for the 2020s. *Journal of Communication Management*, 23(3), 162–178.

Watson, T., & Noble, P. (2014). *Evaluating public relations: A best practice guide to public relations planning, research & evaluation* (3rd ed.). Kogan Page.

World Bank, (2019). *A guide for the measurement and evaluation of communications at the world bank*. World Bank.

Zerfass, A., Verčič, D., & Volk, S. C. (2017). Communication evaluation and measurement: Skills, practices and utilization in European organizations. *Corporate Communications: An International Journal*, 22(1), 2–18.

2.5
FUNDRAISING AND RELATIONSHIP CULTIVATION

Richard D. Waters

Introduction

Although it is a major component of fundraising, soliciting donors is far from the majority of work that a fundraiser does. Many leading practitioners and scholars argue that soliciting gifts is less than 10% of the work that fundraisers perform (Wood, 1997; Kelly, 2001; Sargeant & Shang, 2010). Instead, as colloquial as it may sound, the true work behind fundraising is friend-raising (Fourie, 2001). Relationship cultivation is at the heart of fundraising. Yet many of those involved in the nonprofit sector want little to do with fundraising because of a misunderstanding of how fundraising works.

Nonprofit board members often look away when an organization's executive director calls for volunteers to serve on the development committee, while program staff and volunteer coordinators in small nonprofits shy away from taking on small tasks connected to fundraising. Schroeder (2018) argues that the board members with the best intentions simply don't understand what is behind fundraising. Indeed, Weisman (2002) finds that most within organizations only see fundraising as the solicitation of donations. Fundraisers work with an organization's existing donors and potential prospects for charitable gifts, and there is no secret on either side of the nonprofit organization–donor relationship that a solicitation is eventually going to happen. There is considerable work, however, to understand those individuals' interest in the organization, its mission, and its programs before "the ask" is going to occur.

Fundraisers understand that the pool of potential donors for a particular nonprofit cause is somewhat limited, especially considering competing nonprofits. Therefore, they must focus their time, energy, and resources on pursuing donors in a way that increases the likelihood that a donation will be made to the organization once the donor relationship has been developed. Even though donors vary in the size of the charitable gifts they may make, fundraisers work to cultivate relationships with donors at all levels. From the e-philanthropy donor who makes a recurring $10 gift automatically through monthly giving programs to the annual giving donor who writes a $500 check to a nonprofit in response to the year-end direct mail letter, these donors are just as valuable as the major gift donor who donates $10,000 and more annually.

The nonprofit organization–donor relationship

Fundraisers are focused on investing in these donors by educating them about the organization's past successes and future plans for expansion. Sargeant (2001a) suggests that nonprofits must look

Figure 2.5.1 The fundraising life cycle.

at donors as long-term partners. Rather than seeing donors as short, quick fixes to budget deficits, nonprofits need to evaluate donors based on their lifetime value. Fundraisers work to keep donors involved in the fundraising cycle. As shown in Figure 2.5.1, prospects are invited to become involved with the nonprofit organization. This may be direct through targeted outreach, such as an invitation to volunteer as part of a civic group or through a request for their involvement in advocacy work (e.g., signing a petition), or through indirect outreach, such as exposure to social media postings or public service announcements. Once that invitation is extended and acted on by the individual, the nonprofit jumps into action to educate individuals about who they are, what they do, and how successful they are. Additionally, the organization shares information about how they can contribute as a volunteer, an online advocate who shares information about the organization, or possibly as a participant in programs. As the involvement with the nonprofit grows, the organization will ultimately ask for a donation as part of its fundraising efforts. If a gift is received, nonprofits should thank donors within 48 hours with a genuine thank-you note signed by someone from the development team. Fundraisers must continue communication with these donors, as well as those who did not give when they were asked so they can keep them engaged to learn more through future updates. Based on how individuals respond to the solicitation request and other interactions with nonprofit staff, the opportunities to learn about the organization and ways they can contribute will become tailored based on donors' interests. The goal of fundraising is not only the donation but to keep the relationship maturing in a way that promotes the development of trust and commitment to the nonprofit.

Marketing and public relations have both claimed that they are the academic home of studying fundraising. While the two disciplines have different approaches to understanding its practice, they both agree that fundraising is performed best when it focuses on relationship cultivation and management. Marketing scholars have said that fundraising follows a relationship marketing approach rather than being focused on a sales orientation (Sargeant, 2001b; MacMillan et al., 2005), and public relations scholars have examined fundraising using its relationship management theory (Hall, 2002; Waters, 2010a).

The relationship marketing approach to fundraising and public relations' relationship management theory have regularly found that trust is a key component of the nonprofit organization–donor relationship, though its place in the relationship cultivation process varies. Marketing scholars have advocated that donors who feel a sense of trust in the organization's work lead to long-term relationship commitment with the organization (Sargeant & Lee, 2004). Public relations scholars, on the other hand, propose that trust and commitment are developed simultaneously as emotional outcomes that result from relationship cultivation (Hon & Grunig, 1999; Waters, 2010a).

Relationship cultivation strategies defined

Applying the relationship management theory from public relations to fundraising argues that once an invitation for a potential donor to become involved with the nonprofit is extended, the fundraisers have an obligation to incorporate a variety of relationship cultivation strategies into their outreach. Research initially applied strategies that were adapted from interpersonal communication literature (Canary & Stafford, 1994). Strategies from interpersonal relationships can be applied to organizational relationships, where both sides stand to benefit from mutual involvement with one another. Specifically, six strategies have been regularly examined in relationship with nonprofit publics, including donors (Waters, 2010a), members (Pressgrove et al., 2017), and volunteers (Waters & Bortree, 2012).

Organizational relationship cultivation strategies that have been adapted from interpersonal relationship literature include access, assurances, networking, openness, positivity, and sharing of tasks. Access focuses on whether organizations provide stakeholders with access to organizational decision-making processes and the leaders that make those decisions and vice versa. Both sides of the relationship should be willing to communicate with the other during good times and bad, rather than ignoring their counterparts or expressing negative reactions toward them. Assurances are attempts by the two parties in the relationship that their concerns are legitimate and being addressed; these actions are attempts to demonstrate that they are committed to maintaining the relationship. Networking involves developing formal and informal coalitions with similar groups as their nonprofits' stakeholders do. Transparency is at the root of openness. Stakeholders and nonprofit representatives are open about their thoughts, feelings, and actions when a relationship is healthy. Positivity focuses on anything that an organization or stakeholder may do to make the relationship more enjoyable for all parties involved. Finally, sharing of tasks describes ways that organizational representatives and stakeholders can work together to resolve conflict and address common ground issues. Structural equation modeling has been used to find that these relationship cultivation strategies have a positive impact on how annual giving and major gift donors evaluate their relationships with nonprofits (Waters, 2010b).

These strategies, however, are not the only ones that have been proposed as key actions to consider when developing relationships with donors. Kelly (2001) proposed a conceptualization of stewardship that was grounded in her professional fundraising work in higher education. She suggested that there were four key dimensions of stewardship: reciprocity, responsibility, reporting, and relationship nurturing. Reciprocity is offering genuine demonstrations of gratitude to donors for their involvement with the organization. Pressgrove (2017) further went to operationalize that reciprocity consisted of regard, thanking donors for their involvement and recognition, and acknowledging donors either privately or publicly depending on the size and impact of charitable gifts. The second dimension of stewardship focused on organizations keeping their promises to donors; responsibility comes in many forms, whether it is applying a donation to a specific program as requested by a donor or following up on requests made by stakeholders. Kelly (2001) argues that it is not enough for fundraisers to be responsible and keep promises made to their donors and prospects. Reporting back to donors holds fundraisers accountable to the donors and prospects that they are interacting with because it requires follow-up communication to inform people about what work was done on their behalf. The final dimension of stewardship is relationship nurturing. Kelly (2001) viewed this dimension as a catch-all for all relationship cultivation activities that were not outlined with the other three dimensions of stewardship; however, it has been further defined to focus on actions taken by fundraisers to serve as the organizational conscience of the organization (Waters, 2009). Fundraisers often voice the concerns and feelings of their donors during organizational meetings so that decisions are not made without considering these important stakeholders.

In a classic test of theory and practice, Waters (2010b) examined which approach to relationship cultivation had the stronger ability to predict relationship outcomes for annual giving and major gift donors. For both groups of donors, both relationship cultivation strategies derived from interpersonal relationship literature and stewardship derived from fundraising practice were found to have positive impacts on creating feelings of trust, commitment, and satisfaction with the nonprofit organization–donor relationship. Overall, the four stewardship strategies slightly outperformed the interpersonal relationship strategies.

Greenfield (2013) proposed that the Donor Bill of Rights, which was adopted in 1993, and the e-Donor Bill of Rights that followed approximately 20 years later outlined the best practices that nonprofits could incorporate into their donor cultivation plans. The Donor Bill of Rights was created by the Association of Fundraising Professionals, the Association for Healthcare Philanthropy, the Council for Advancement and Support of Education, and the Giving Institute in response to a number of early 1990 nonprofit scandals. The e-Donor Bill of Rights was created in response to the growing rise of e-philanthropy to ensure that online donors would have greater confidence in organizations' ability to manage online donor relations safely.

These two documents were designed to complement the fundraising associations' codes of ethics, but they also intersect the relationship cultivation strategies proposed by scholars. Examining the two bills of rights reveals some obvious overlap with Kelly's (2001) stewardship dimensions, specifically reporting (e.g., "To be assured their gifts will be used for the purposes for which they were given" [AFP, 2015, Right #4]) and reciprocity (e.g., "To receive appropriate acknowledgement and recognition" [AFP, 2015, Right #5]). There is even greater overlap with the relationship cultivation strategies derived from interpersonal relationship scholarship. Access (e.g., "To have access to the organization's most recent financial statements" [AFP, 2015, Right #3]), assurances (e.g., "To be assured that information about their donations is handled with respect and with confidentiality to the extent provided by law" [AFP, 2015, Right #6]), openness (e.g., "To be informed of the identity of those serving on the organization's governing board" [AFP, 2015, Right #2]), and positivity (e.g., "To feel free to ask questions when making a donation and to receive prompt, truthful and forthright answers" [AFP, 2015, Right #10]) are represented conceptually by the documents.

Through the use of the co-orientation methodology, fundraisers' and their donors' views on cultivation strategies were compared to see whether they viewed the use of these strategies in the relationship similarly. Measured on a 9-point modified Likert scale, the stewardship strategies were viewed as important ones to maintain a healthy nonprofit organization–donor relationship by both sides of that relationship; however, all four measures were viewed as being more important by the fundraisers than the donors (Waters, 2010a). The donors in this study also expressed that they thought the fundraisers placed greater value in the stewardship strategies than donors did. This result indicated that while these relationship cultivation strategies were important, they were not the only elements of the relationship that were important to donors.

Nonprofit organizations have regularly expressed a desire to diversify their fundraising staff so that it is representative of the community and donors they serve (Jung, 2015; Pettey & Wagner, 2007). Given that donors interact with the development team more often than any other representative of the nonprofit, it is important the team reflects the diversity of the community. Having

Fundraising and relationship cultivation

a homogeneous fundraising team can cause doubt among donors as to whether the organization is able to serve diverse clientele. Gasman and Bowman (2013) suggest that hiring diverse fundraising staff is not only good for the nonprofit, as it allows new perspectives and voices to be brought into the organization, but it is also a good relationship cultivation strategy for donors, as it expands the range of staff who donors may connect with. While a donor's relationship with a fundraiser remains professional, the personal connection is also important, as it is often necessary for the donor to feel comfortable enough to communicate why they are involved with the nonprofit organization and their connection to the bigger mission. This connection grows as the relationship cultivation efforts become more customized as they move up the various levels of the donor pyramid.

Relationship cultivation and the donor pyramid

Nonprofit organizations use a wide range of communication approaches to cultivate relationships with donors and drive loyalty to the organization (Macedo et al., 2021). The donor pyramid shown in Figure 2.5.2 combines the typical donor categories with examples of communication tactics that are used to reach those individuals. The base level of the pyramid represents the starting point of the relationship cultivation for donors, and this grouping has the largest number of donors for all nonprofit organizations. These donors are the ones who are making their first cycle through the life cycle of fundraising presented in the first figure in this chapter. These individuals typically respond to communication outreach targeting mass audiences. They donate online as a result of peer-to-peer giving or social media campaigns after learning about the nonprofit's work. These donors may also be introduced to the nonprofit through special events or generic direct mail that is written for purchased mailing lists. Communication that is directed to these donors is designed to identify those who have an interest in the mission the nonprofit addresses so that they can be targeted for future cultivation efforts.

When donors make it through their first round of the fundraising life cycle and decide to continue their involvement with the nonprofit, they are elevated to the annual giving level of the

Figure 2.5.2 Traditional donor pyramid highlighting communication tactics and relationship cultivation strategies by donor levels.

pyramid. Whether a second gift is made to the nonprofit is considered to be the key factor that determines whether that donor is going to remain with the organization (Love, 2017). Nonprofits pay close attention to ensuring as many second gifts from first-time donors as possible because that is an indication that the individual is not only committed to the mission that the nonprofit addresses but that they are also pleased with the engagement they have had with that nonprofit. The general messaging that people often respond to with their first gift begins to be customized for annual giving donors. It begins with the personalized thank-you note following the first gift, and nonprofits may even have a personal phone call to express gratitude for the gift. As the donor moves through the second round of the fundraising life cycle, the development team is watching donors' behaviors to see how they respond to different topics. Emails are monitored to see which topics are deleted from inboxes immediately and which topics are opened and clicked through to the organization's website. This helps prepare more tailored direct mail, which begins to transition from general topics written to introduce the nonprofit to the donor to messaging that highlights specific aspects of the nonprofit that the donor has expressed an interest in. Depending on the size of the gift, the length of time being an annual giving donor, or their personal connection with employees and leadership within the organization, the development team may reach out with personalized phone calls to get to know the donor even more.

Fundraisers actively seek out information through donor research to determine which donors have the financial capacity and interest to invest in the organization through recurring major gifts or with a special gift during capital or endowment campaigns. While there is no set definition of what constitutes a major gift, it is generally accepted that these gifts are at least $10,000 annually (Kelly, 1998). At the major gift level, donors have considerable access to the nonprofit organization when they have questions or concerns. As opposed to lower-tier donors who might have to call the main phone number, send an inquiry to a general organization-wide email address, or submit a form via the nonprofit's website, major gift donors have the ability to send a text message or call a specific member of the development team or possibly even email members of the executive leadership teams. As a result of getting to know the major gift donor through one-on-one meetings and phone calls designed to update the individual on the organization's progress on their work, the development teams cultivate these significant relationships with a great amount of interpersonal attention. It's not uncommon for development staff to send birthday or get-well cards that also include brief updates about the nonprofit when appropriate to these donors. If the organization is carrying out a capital or endowment campaign, it's possible that these donors may also receive a tailored proposal that highlights how their involvement and their gifts can propel the organization in its growth and expansion efforts.

The pinnacle of the nonprofit organization–donor relationship is leaving the organization a gift as part of their will or estate-planning arrangements. Naming a nonprofit as a recipient of part of a donor's estate is an act that anyone can do. Annual donors who weren't financially able to make a major gift during their lifetimes regularly leave gifts to nonprofits they are loyal to after their death. For this reason, nonprofits often develop marketing collateral about the benefits of a planned gift and make them available to donors through their website. Development staff may even hold a one-on-one informational meeting with donors who inquire about planned giving options. But because of potential conflicts of interest in helping a donor set up the planned gift and the complexity of the legal structure of these gifts, development staff rarely are involved in establishing planned gifts. Instead, fundraisers offer lists of estate planning attorneys and other individuals who aren't affiliated with the nonprofit that can offer their services to interested donors. Even though the development team isn't involved with developing the planned gift mechanism, there is a considerable amount of interpersonal communication with donors to educate them about different possible avenues to make the gift and who can help them make the ultimate investment in the nonprofit.

Fundraising and relationship cultivation

Nonprofit organization–donor communication

Across the levels a wide range of communication tactics are used, and development staff must be comfortable using mass-mediated, organization-controlled, and interpersonal strategies. The need to message a large number of prospects and new donors in the early stages of the fundraising life cycle always remains as the fundraising team takes on more customized and interpersonal techniques as they make subsequent rounds through the life cycle. As relationship cultivation grows, the amount of personal attention and interpersonal communication increases significantly due to the differences in the proportion of donor types and the size of the gifts the different donor types make. Although they represent a smaller percentage of the overall donor database, major gift and planned giving donors give significantly larger gifts than first-time or annual giving donors. Scholars have suggested that the fundraising is a prime example of Pareto's principle, which argues that 80% of an outcome comes from just 20% of the causes. Applying it to fundraising, major gifts and planned giving donors may represent only 20% of the donor database, yet they provide 80% of the charitable gifts made to the nonprofit. First-time and annual giving donors are considerable in proportion to the database and quantity of gifts, but the gifts are smaller in size (Aldashev et al., 2014).

Rosso (1991) proposed that fundraisers must be prepared to use a wide range of communication strategies and tactics in their work because of the different nature of annual giving and major gift fundraising. Specifically, he focused his discussion about communication around a "risk ladder." The ladder, shown in Figure 2.5.3, uses a combination of personalization and risk to calculate the overall effectiveness of a solicitation. At the bottom rung of the ladder, advertising (e.g., billboards and public service announcements) and mass media efforts (e.g., news coverage and media interviews) are broadcast to audiences with requests for support. These efforts have little personalization involved in the request and little potential for risk for embarrassment of being told no by the potential donor. Moving up the rungs of the ladder increases the amount of personalization needed to use the different forms of communication in the relationship cultivation efforts with a donor. That interpersonal connection also increases the level of risk that the fundraiser must be comfortable with. Recent research examined different forms of communication and found that more personalized

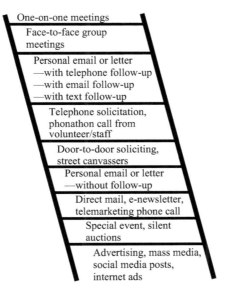

Figure 2.5.3 Updated fundraising risk ladder modified from Rosso (1991).

communication resulted in greater levels of public support based on donations, volunteering, and advocating for a nonprofit (McKeever et al., 2019). This signals that the middle and higher rungs of the risk ladder must be incorporated into fundraising communication as often as possible to have a strong impact on relationship cultivation efforts. Considerable research has been done to demonstrate the increasing power of the website (Ingenhoff & Koelling, 2009) and social media (Bhati & McDonnell, 2020; Xiao, 2021) as successful drivers of relationship cultivation in early stages of the nonprofit organization–donor relationship, but more personal phone calls and face-to-face meetings are the most successful communication techniques to understand what motivates donors (Das et al., 2008; Spears, 2002).

Ethical issues with relationship cultivation

Given the close relationship that develops between fundraisers and the donors they work with, it is important to address two key ethical issues to ensure lasting, mutually beneficial relationships for the organization and the donor. Payton (2006) says that nonprofits must be active in overseeing donor relationships. While interaction occurs between the fundraiser and the donor, the fundraiser is acting on behalf of the organization. As the relationship grows and cultivation efforts increase, more personal, one-on-one communication is used with donors. Fundraisers must remember that the relationship with the donor – while genuine in nature – is truly a relationship with the organization. If the fundraiser leaves the nonprofit for another job opportunity, they must work with the donor to transition the relationship to another member of the development staff. Fundraisers need to leave the donor's contact information and research about the donor behind as they move to another fundraising role at a nonprofit. Whether that new nonprofit is a competitor to their previous employer or not, the fundraiser ethically cannot reach out to the donors they previously worked with in an effort to get them to donate to their new organization.

Additionally, the close nature of the nonprofit organization–donor relationship can result in uncomfortable situations for fundraisers who may be exposed to situations involving sexual harassment. In wake of the #MeToo movement, fundraisers spoke out about their experiences and demanded improved policies from their employers (Beaton et al., 2021). These policies give fundraisers the ability to say no to meeting with donors one-on-one and often forbid meeting with donors outside business hours to avoid uncomfortable situations. If sexual harassment occurs, nonprofits have an obligation to remove the fundraiser from involvement in that donor relationship – if the relationship continues. Ethical nonprofits should sever ties with donors that sexually harass nonprofits. That being said, nonprofits that face immediate financial challenges may find it difficult to cease involvement with these donors due to their need for donations. Additionally, leadership may object to ending a relationship with a donor based on the time and resources poured into developing that relationship. However, nonprofits must consider both sides of the relationship – fundraiser and donor – to determine whether relationship cultivation will continue, because the fundraising process can only be successful if the nonprofit organization–donor relationship is healthy for both parties.

References

Aldashev, G., Marini, M., & Verdier, T. (2014). Brothers in alms? Coordination between nonprofits on markets for donations. *Journal of Public Economics*, *117*, 182–200. https://doi.org/10.1016/j.jpubeco.2014.04.009

Association for Fundraising Professionals. (2015). *A donor bill of rights*. https://afpglobal.org/sites/default/files/attachments/2018-10/DonorBillofRights.pdf

Beaton, E. E., LePere-Schloop, M., & Smith, R. (2021). "Whatever it takes": Sexual harassment in the context of resource dependence. *Journal of Public Administration Research and Theory*, *31*(4), 617–633. https://doi.org/10.1093/jopart/muab005

Bhati, A., & McDonnell, D. (2020). Success in an online giving day: The role of social media in fundraising. *Nonprofit and Voluntary Sector Quarterly, 49*(1), 74–92. doi:10.177/0899764019868849

Canary, D. J., & Stafford, L. (1994). Maintaining relationships through strategic and routine interaction. In D. J. Canary & L. Stafford (Eds.), *Communication and relational maintenance* (pp. 3–22). Academic Press.

Das, E., Kerkhof, P., & Kuiper, J. (2008). Improving the effectiveness of fundraising messages: The impact of charity goal attainment, message framing, and evidence on persuasion. *Journal of Applied Communication Research, 36*(2), 161–175. https://doi.org/10.1080/00909880801922854

Fourie, I. (2001). Fundraising and friend-raising on the web. *Online Information Review, 25*(2), 131–141. https://doi.org/10.1108/oir.2001.25.2.131.4

Gasman, M., & Bowman III, N. (2013). *Engaging diverse college alumni: The essential guide to fundraising.* Routledge.

Greenfield, J. M. (2013). Rights of donors. In J. G. Pettey (Ed.), *Nonprofit fundraising strategy: A guide to ethical decision making and regulation for nonprofit organizations* (pp. 35–52). John Wiley & Sons.

Hall, M. R. (2002). Building on relationships: A fundraising approach for community colleges. *Community College Journal of Research and Practice, 1*(1), 47–60. https://doi.org/10.1080/106689202753365007

Hon, L. C., & Grunig, J. E. (1999). *Guidelines for measuring relationships in public relations.* Institute for Public Relations.

Ingenhoff, D., & Koelling, A. M. (2009). The potential of Web sites as a relationship building tool for charitable fundraising NPOs. *Public Relations Review, 35*(1), 66–73. https://doi.org/10.1016/j.pubrev.2008.09.023

Jung, Y. (2015). Diversity matters: Theoretical understanding of and suggestions for the current fundraising practices of nonprofit art museums. *The Journal of Arts Management, Law, and Society, 45*(4), 255–268. https://doi.org/10.1080/10632921.2015.1103672

Kelly, K. S. (1998). *Effective fund-raising management.* Lawrence Erlbaum.

Kelly, K. S. (2001). ROPES: A model of the fund-raising process. In J. M. Greenfield (Ed.), *The nonprofit handbook: Fundraising* (pp. 96–116). John Wiley & Sons, Inc.

Love, J. (2017, September 7). *Just how important is a donor's second gift.* https://bloomerang.co/blog/just-how-important-is-a-donors-second-gift/

Macedo, J., Gonçalves, M., & Sousa, B. B. (2021). Relationship marketing and communication as a driver of fundraising loyalty and success in non-profit organizations: A theoretical perspective. In M. D. Olivera-Lobo, J. Gutierrez-Artacho, I. Rivera-Trigueros, & M. Diaz-Millon (Eds.), *Innovative perspectives on corporate communication in the global world* (pp. 52–77). IGI Global.

MacMillan, K., Money, K., Money, A., & Downing, S. (2005). Relationship marketing in the not-for-profit sector: An extension and application of the commitment – trust theory. *Journal of Business Research, 58*(6), 806–818. https://doi.org/10.1016/j.jbusres.2003.08.008

McKeever, B. W., McKeever, R., Pressgrove, G., & Overton, H. (2019). Predicting public support: Applying theory to prosocial behaviors. *Journal of Communication Management, 23*(4), 298–315. https://doi.org/10.1108/JCOM-02-2019-0030

Payton, R. L. (2006). The ethics and values of fundraising. In D. Elliott (Ed.), *The kindness of strangers: Philanthropy and higher education* (pp. 109–119). Rowman & Littlefield.

Pettey, J. G., & Wagner, L. (2007). Introduction: Union gives strength – diversity and fundraising. *International Journal of Educational Advancement, 7*(3), 171–175. https://doi.org/10.1057/palgrave.ijea.2150059

Pressgrove, G. N. (2017). Development of a scale to measure perceptions of stewardship strategies for nonprofit organizations. *Journalism & Mass Communication Quarterly, 94*(1), 102–103. https://doi.org/10.1177/1077699016640221

Pressgrove, G. N., McKeever, R., McKeever, B., & Waters, R. D. (2017, May). *Redefining stakeholder support: Connecting perceptions of the organization-public relationship, communicative action, and behavioral intentions.* Paper presented to the Public Relations Division of International Communication Association Annual Conference.

Rosso, H. A. (1991). *Achieving excellence in fundraising.* Jossey-Bass.

Sargeant, A. (2001a). Using donor lifetime value to inform fundraising strategy. *Nonprofit Management & Leadership, 12*(1), 25–38. doi.org/10.1002/nml.12103

Sargeant, A. (2001b). Relationship fundraising: How to keep donors loyal. *Nonprofit Management and Leadership, 12*(2), 177–192. https://doi.org/10.1002/nml.12204

Sargeant, A., & Lee, S. (2004). Trust and relationship commitment in the United Kingdom voluntary sector: Determinants of donor behavior. *Psychology & Marketing, 21*(8), 613–635. doi.org/10.1002/mar.20021

Sargeant, A., & Shang, J. (2010). *Fundraising principles and practice.* Jossey-Bass.

Schroeder, T. (2018). Address board member objections to fund development. *Successful Fundraising, 26*(5), 7. https://doi.org/10.1002/sfr.30917

Spears, L. A. (2002). Persuasive techniques used in fundraising messages. *Journal of Technical Writing and Communication, 32*(3), 245–265. https://doi.org/10.2190/BE4V-QJNC-Q97H-DFXN

Waters, R. D. (2009). Measuring stewardship in public relations: A test exploring impact on the fundraising relationship. *Public Relations Review*, *35*(2), 113–119. doi.org/10.1016/j.pubrev.2009.01.012

Waters, R. D. (2010a). Increasing fundraising efficiency through evaluation: Applying communication theory to the nonprofit organization-donor relationship. *Nonprofit and Voluntary Sector Quarterly*, *40*(3), 458–475. doi.org/10.1177%2F0899764009354322

Waters, R. D. (2010b). The value of relationship and communication management in fundraising: Comparing donors' and practitioners' views of stewardship. *PRism*, *7*(1).

Waters, R. D., & Bortree, D. S. (2012). Improving volunteer retention efforts in public library systems: How communication and inclusion impact female and male volunteers differently. *International Journal of Nonprofit and Voluntary Sector Marketing*, *17*(2), 92–107. https://doi.org/10.1002/nvsm.438

Weisman, C. (2002, July/August). Getting comfortable with the f word: Fundraising and the nonprofit board member. *Nonprofit World*, *20*(4), 10–15.

Wood, E. W. (1997). The four Rs of major gift fundraising, developing major gifts. *New Directions for Philanthropic Fundraising, Indiana University Center on Philanthropy/Jossey Bass*, *16*, 5.

Xiao, A., Huang, Y., Bortree, D. S., & Waters, R. D. (2021). Designing social media fundraising messages: An experimental approach to understanding how message concreteness and framing influence donation intentions. *Nonprofit and Voluntary Sector Quarterly*. doi.org/10.1177/2F08997640211022838

2.6
GRANTING ORGANIZATIONS

Giselle A. Auger

Introduction

Granting organizations are those organizations, usually foundations, that provide funding to others to fulfill their mission and purpose addressing one or more social issues. According to the Council on Foundations (2021), the term *foundation* has no precise meaning but is defined "as an entity that supports charitable activities by making grants to unrelated organizations or institutions or to individuals for scientific, educational, cultural, religious, or other charitable purposes" (*What is a foundation?* n.p.). Among the various types of granting organizations are private foundations, corporate foundations, family foundations, and community foundations.

Herrington (2017) refers to granting organizations as facilitators; in other words, they do not directly reduce the burden of government by providing services, but rather facilitate the activities of other nonprofit organizations that he refers to as doers. This facilitator/doer relationship is a special kind of organization–public relationship (OPR) based on mutual benefit, yet it is often challenging as granting organizations seek to identify appropriate nonprofit partners and those potential partners navigate the grant process (Auger, 2014). Despite the challenges, granting organizations need nonprofit partners to do the work towards addressing social issues of importance to the grantor, and the nonprofit 'doer' needs the support of the granting organization to carry out that work. As Revere (2016) says:

> In recent years, we seem to have forgotten that philanthropy succeeds only when foundations and nonprofit have strong partnerships that recognize the complexity of the problems we seek to solve and the need for solid, sophisticated, and sustainable nonprofit institutions to envision a better future and carry out the work.
>
> (para. 1)

According to the *Global Philanthropy Report* (Johnson, 2018), approximately 260,000 granting organizations in 39 countries spend the equivalent of $150 billion U.S. every year providing resources to advance the public good. The location of foundations is highly concentrated, with 95% of such organizations located in Europe and North America; however, the predominant type of organization varied by region, with corporate foundations predominant in Latin America, family foundations in Africa, independent foundations in Europe and North America, and government-ed foundations in Saudi Arabia and the UAE (Johnson, 2018).

Among the issues of greatest interest to grantors, education was highest, with significant resources also allocated to human services and social welfare, arts and culture, and health. Latin American foundations were more invested in Sustainable Development Goal (SDG) areas than other regions.

History of granting organizations

Globally, foundations or similar organizations play a large role in the world of philanthropy. Interestingly, philanthropy derives from *philanthropa* in Ancient Greek that means 'to love people' and today refers to the act of voluntary giving to other individuals or organizations for the benefit of the common good (Philanthropy New York, 2008). In the United States modern philanthropy began in the early 1900s when big industrialists like Andrew Carnegie and John D. Rockefeller began to give away some of their accumulated wealth, obtained at a time when the country did not have income tax. Later, Frederick Goff established the first community foundation in Cleveland, where individuals bequeathed funds to the foundation for disbursement rather than establishing their own foundation (Fritz, 2019).

Types of granting organizations

Private foundations

Private foundations are nongovernmental nonprofit organizations that are generally funded from a single source, for example, from an individual, a family, or a corporation. Such organizations are also sometimes referred to as independent foundations, and they are established to aid specific issues of importance to that individual, family, or corporation, for example, issues affecting the environment, arts and culture, or poverty. Such issues can be social, educational, or religious and global, local, or national. Most often such issues are clearly stated in the foundation's mission. Support for the organizations addressing these issues is primarily provided through grant making. Private foundations are established either as nonprofit corporations or as charitable trusts, and they are designated as either a private (operating) foundation or as a nonoperating private foundation.

Private operating foundations develop programs to achieve their charitable goals directly, rather than providing grants to outside organizations. Though they may provide grants occasionally, private operating foundations are not governed by the distribution requirement of nonoperating private foundations in the United States, but must spend a certain portion of their assets on charitable activities (COF, 2021; Fritz, 2019). The J. Paul Getty Trust is an example of a private operating foundation. The trust was established with some of the fortune made by J. Paul Getty through oil prospecting and, according to Fritz (2019), funds from the trust are used "to promote understanding and preservation of the visual arts, especially in California. The Trust funds The J Paul Getty Museum, Research Institute, Conservation Institute, and the Getty Foundation. The Institute is one of the five most wealthy foundations in the US" (*Operating Private Foundations*, n.p.).

Nonoperating private foundations are the foundations generally recognized for grant making. They realize their charitable goals by providing funding to outside nonprofit organizations whose mission and goals align. These nonoperating foundations are the organizations to which nonprofit grant writers send their grant proposals. Nonoperating private foundations can also be corporate or family foundations. As Fritz (2019) notes, the Bill & Melinda Gates Foundation is perhaps the best known nonoperating private foundation. It is also the largest foundation in the United States and a family foundation. The Gates Foundation is known for providing grants related to the issue areas of poverty and health.

Prior to 1969, private foundations in the United States were subject to looser regulatory standards than they are today. The 1969 Private Foundation Law provided stricter, extensive rules for private foundations than for public charities (COF, 2021). Troyer (1999) notes that "the concerns of Congress at which the law struck had roots reaching back for more than two decades, and its core restrictions on the personal use and financial practices of foundations had solid policy justification" (p. 2). The new rules included restrictions on the amount of stock private foundations may hold in any one company; the amount they are allowed to pay out for operating costs, grants, and charitable programs; compensation of staff and board members; and financial transactions between the foundation and its largest contributors and officers (COF, 2021).

The law also imposed the so-called 'distribution requirement', which requires nonoperating private foundations to distribute a minimum of 5% each year. Troyer (1999) provides a historical analysis of the origins and underpinning rationale of the 1969 law for those who are interested in more in-depth information.

Independent foundations

Unlike family or corporate foundations, independent foundations are not governed by the benefactor, the benefactor's family, or a corporation (COF, 2021), yet they may be established by an individual, family, or corporation. They are considered an independent foundation rather than a family foundation, providing the benefactor, their family, or the corporation do not govern the foundation. Independent foundations are generally established and funded by endowments from an individual or other single source or a group of individuals.

Family foundations

Family foundations are established and maintained with funds from a single family. To be considered a family foundation, at least one family member must continue as the donor and serve as an officer or on the board of the foundation. Moreover, according to Fritz (2019), the family member is expected to provide a significant role in the governance and management of the foundation. Family foundations may be big, like the Bill & Melinda Gates Foundation, or small. Like all nonoperating private foundations, family foundations may focus on a single issue or several. Most are run by family members who volunteer as trustees or directors without compensation, while other family foundations hire others to run the foundation.

Corporate foundations

The Council on Foundations (2021) defines corporate foundations as "philanthropic organizations that are created and financially supported by a corporation" (*Corporate Foundations*, n.p.). Such foundations derive their grant-making funds primarily from a profit-making business. Though corporate foundations are separate legal entities from the business, the company often maintains a close relationship with the foundation (Fritz, 2019). Corporate foundations often have their own endowments and are usually set up as private foundations and are subject to the same rules and regulations as other private foundations. However, in circumstances where they will be largely publicly supported, they can sometimes be established as a public foundation.

Corporate foundations are usually established to support issues related to their corporate activities, to support the communities in which they operate, or to support the communities in which their employees live. As the Council on Foundation notes, "Companies establish foundations and giving programs to have a positive impact on society" (*Corporate Foundations*, n.p.). Two large and well-known corporate foundations are the Walmart Foundation and the Ford Motor Company Fund.

According to *Giving in Numbers 2020* (CECP, 2020) $24.8 billion was contributed to corporate social investment in that year through matching gift programs, employee volunteer hours, and cash awards. The report also highlighted a 49% increase in international end recipients for 2020 (CECP, 2020).

Community foundations

The first community foundation in the United States was founded by Frederick H. Goff in 1914 in Cleveland. Since then, Goff's model has been replicated to the extent that there are approximately 800 community foundations in the United States and 1,800 worldwide (Cleveland Foundation, 2021).

Goff's vision was

> to pool the charitable resources of Cleveland's philanthropists, living and dead, into a single, great, and permanent endowment for the betterment of the city. Community leaders would then forever distribute the interest that the trust's resources would accrue to fund "such charitable purposes as will best make for the mental, moral, and physical improvement of the inhabitants of Cleveland".
>
> (Candid, 2021b)

Community foundations are like public charities in that they seek financial support from the public, and yet they are like nonoperating private foundations because they provide grants to other organizations. Community foundations are made up of permanent funds provided by many separate donors who do not want to establish their own foundations but wish to provide for the long-term benefit of area residents. Typically, community foundations serve an area no larger than a state (University of Southern California, 2021).

Public charities

Public charities are usually grant seekers and not grant makers. However, there is a subset of public charities whose primary purpose is to provide grants to others, and they are referred to as public foundations. Though these organizations receive most of their funding from the public, they function as funders to others. The most widely recognized type of public foundation are community foundations. As noted, some corporate foundations may be established as public foundations.

Government

National and local governments provide grants to nonprofit organizations that can address issues of importance to their people. In the United States, there are four major categories of federal grants – competitive, formula, continuing, and pass-through (eCivis, 2020). Competitive, or discretionary, funding refers to the process where organizations submit proposals for review, competing with other organizations for funding. Reviewers then determine which proposals best fit the requirements set forth in the proposal guidelines. Recipients of competitive funding are not predetermined, but are selected on the merits of their proposal. Formula funding is noncompetitive and provided to predetermined organizations that meet eligibility requirements, for example, based on census criteria. All applicants that meet the minimum requirements are entitled to receive funds. Continuing grants are provided to organizations with current grant funding to extend their funding period. Finally, pass-through grants are federal grant funds provided to states, who then pass it on to organizations within their states.

Types of grant funding

Candid, a U.S. 501(c)3 nonprofit organization,[1] was created to combine two centers of information for grantors and grantees – The Foundation Center and GuideStar – who joined forces in 2019. The organization conducts and compiles research on both granting organizations and nonprofit organizations, providing tools to allow effective collaboration by connecting those with the funds to those who need the funds to address important global issues.

According to Candid (2021a) there are several key issue areas of interest to funders, for example, arts and culture, diversity, the environment, and community building. Other important issues include human rights, heath, civic engagement, and peace and conflict. Issues affecting youth or those related to emergencies and disasters are also major granting areas.

Nonprofit organizations and individuals wishing to obtain grants should seek grants from funders whose stated mission and issue areas most closely resemble and are most relevant to their funding request. Research is an important first step in the grant-making process, or cycle (Funding for Good, 2017).

There are six broad types of grant making.

General operating grants

These types of grants are valued by grantees, as they involve unrestricted funds. For example, funds can be used for operating expenses and administrative costs, two items that are often restricted from other types of grants. While many grants will often allow some small percentage for administrative costs, funds for operating expenses are quite rare. (Pattison, 2021).

Program and project grants

Program and project grants are the most common type of grant award, where funds are restricted for use towards the program or project described in the grant proposal. The funds can be used to create new programs or projects or to support or expand existing programs or projects. According to Pattison (2021) "Grantmakers prefer to give this type of grant because (a) the projects they fund are more likely to align to grantmaker's own mission, and (b) it is easier to evaluate the impact of the grant award" (*Programs and Project Grants*, n.p.).

Capacity-building grants

Capacity-building grants provide funding for organizations that seek to expand their overall potential. Improving potential could mean, for example, improving internal systems, increasing staffing, providing training for employees, or evaluating their overall effectiveness to determine future direction.

Capital grants

Organizations that wish to construct new facilities, renovate existing space, purchase costly equipment, or make large technological improvements often embark on capital campaigns. Such campaigns generally involve a multipronged strategy to seek donors as well as grants. Grants made for such activities are called capital grants or, sometimes, brick-and-mortar grants (Pattison, 2021).

Endowment grants

Endowment grants are funds distributed from the interest earned on an endowment's capital. The principal remains intact, and a percentage of the interest is used to fund organizations as intended by the purpose designated at the creation of the endowment fund. Organizations must follow guidelines spelled out by the endowment when applying for a grant.

Matching or challenge grants

If a donor offers to give a large sum of money to a nonprofit organization, if that organization can raise the same amount from other sources, the organization can attempt to gather those funds by applying for matching grants from granting organizations. Conversely, organizations can seek the initial funds for a matching gift fundraising program from a granting organization. These types of grants are called challenge grants. Both types of grant help stimulate giving by providing donors with the opportunity to double the impact of their contribution (Pattison, 2021).

The grant-making process

The grant application process can be an area of frustration in the grantor–grantee relationship. Auger (2014) found grant application information to be extremely variable, with few exemplar organizations that provided clear information and easy-to-use website interfaces for nonprofit grantees to navigate. Moreover, Allen et al. (2021) suggest that "Many foundations ask grantees and prospective grantees to jump through hoops that take up too much of their precious time, are out of proportion to the size of the grants, and don't produce valuable insights" (para. 13).

Experts suggest tactics for both the granting organizations and the recipient nonprofits to ease the frustration of the grant-making process. For example, Revere (2016) suggests that granting organizations treat their nonprofit grantees as experts in their issue area, connect them to others who may be able to help them be more effective, and refrain from questioning management decisions. They also urge grantors to provide general operating grants, adequate overhead funds, and sufficient duration, preferably for between three and five years. Moreover, granting organizations should have open processes for soliciting proposals to hear from a wide variety of organizations and diversity of ideas. Finally, grantors should consider grants that strengthen the nonprofit recipient, as well as grants to support programs provided by those organizations (Revere, 2016).

As for the nonprofit grantees, Flynn (2019) advocates that grant writers carefully read the full application, guidelines, and eligibility requirements. They should research the granting organization to identify their priorities and granting strategies and to ensure that they are a good fit. Applicants should gather all the required data, plans, and supporting documentation, as well as a clearly detailed budget that is in line with the program plan described. Applicants should ensure that all questions have been answered completely, then review the entire package before submitting. Finally, grant writers should make sure to represent the good work the organization is doing and what they need, but they should do so genuinely. According to Mento (2020) granting organizations want clear information, but they also want to hear genuine, authentic voices, not overly curated marketing copy.

Changes in grant making: COVID-19 and beyond

Historically, granting organizations have failed to cover nonprofits' actual costs, which leaves the recipient organization financially weak and less effective (Allen et al., 2021); however, the coronavirus pandemic and social unrest such as the Black Lives Matter (BLM) movement have led to significant changes in granting behavior that may be long-lasting (Allen et al., 2021; Falik, 2021; Mento, 2020).

The Council on Foundations (COF) led a challenge that asked granting organizations to make a philanthropic pledge to assist nonprofits to survive the economic consequences of the pandemic.

According to Allen et al. (2021) more than 800 organizations signed the pledge, and the most frequent changes made in their granting were to loosen or eliminate grant restrictions, make new grants as unrestricted as possible, and reduce what was being asked from the grantees.

The pandemic also highlighted the importance of relationships. "Many big donors say they feel an extra weight of responsibility to do more than at any other time in their lives and to push other philanthropists to do the same" (Mento, 2020, para 20), but they must make hard decisions about where to direct those funds. When making those decisions, they are likely to turn to organizations with whom they have a trusted relationship. As Falik (2021) said, "Donors stepped up their support, with fewer strings attached. 'I see you and I trust you', they seemed to say. It was liberating – and I hope it's here to stay" (para. 25).

The pandemic also led to bold new visions and practices in philanthropy, for example, MacKenzie Scott's promise to give billions of dollars, unsolicited, to organizations she and her team identified, without the constraints of the traditional grant-making process. Jack Dorsey also revolutionized giving by making his grant-making process 100% transparent through a Google spreadsheet (Falik, 2021).

Whether these new philanthropic practices and ways of giving will continue is uncertain; however, it is likely that some will endure. Granting organizations and their nonprofit partners will need to find a balance between the many needs of society, from the pandemic to racial inequality, social injustice, and climate change and its resulting catastrophes such as famine, wildfires, flooding, and the like. As Holk and Kasper (2020) say, "Grant makers will need to find the right balance across these very different – and often competing – types of societal needs, and their choices will have increasingly important consequences for their grantees, partners, and communities" (para. 20).

Note

1. U.S. Internal Revenue Tax Code 501(c) has 29 categories under which organizations can seek exemption from federal tax requirements. Section 501(c)3 is specific to charitable, nonprofit, religious, and educational organizations and provides federal tax-exempt status for those that meet its requirements.

References

Allen, T., Enright, K., & Pennington, H. (2021). How grant makers can commit to meaningful changes a year after Covid. *Chronicle of Philanthropy, 33*(6), 30–31.

Auger, G. A. (2014). Improving foundation-nonprofit efficiency: Best practices for online grant making procedures. In R. Waters (Ed.), *Public relations in the nonprofit sector: Theory and practice* (pp. 154–166). Routledge.

Candid. (2021a). *Grant craft.* https://grantcraft.org/?_gl=1*13eafar*_ga*MTE2OTY2NjMwLjE2MjcxNTk3NzQ.*_ga_5W8PXYYGBX*MTYyNzE1OTc3My4xLjEuMTYyNzE2MDAzMi4w&_ga=2.107646146.1183702476.1627159775-116966630.1627159774

Candid. (2021b). *What is a community foundation? Where can I learn more about them?* https://learning.candid.org/resources/knowledge-base/community-foundations/

Chief Executives for Corporate Purpose (CECP). (2020). *Giving in numbers 2020 edition.* CECP. https://cecp.co/home/resources/giving-in-numbers/?tid=1398

Cleveland Foundation, The. (2021). *History.* www.clevelandfoundation100.org/?utm_source=100&utm_medium=redirect&utm_campaign=centennial

Council on Foundations. (2021). *Foundation basics.* www.cof.org/content/foundation-basics#what_is_a_foundation

eCivis. (2020, May 20). Law enforcement grants: The four main types of grant funding. *eCivis.* www.ecivis.com/blog/bid/48460/law-enforcement-grants-the-four-main-types-of-grant-funding

Falik, A. (2021). Covid-19 has reshaped fundraising: Let's hope it lasts. *Chronicle of Philanthropy, 33*(5), 30–31.

Flynn, N. (2019). 5 steps to filling out a grant application. *Cielo 24.* https://cielo24.com/2019/05/5-steps-to-filling-out-a-grant-application/

Fritz, J. (2019, May 30). The history and types of foundations. *The Balance Small Business.* www.thebalancesmb.com/the-history-and-types-of-foundations-2502444

Funding for Good. (2017, November 30). *7 things to know for successful grant research.* https://fundingforgood.org/7-things-to-know-before-conducting-grant-research/

Herrington, J. B. (2017). *Nonprofits as policy solutions to the burden of government.* Walter de Gruyter Inc.

Holk, J., & Kasper, G. (2020). Nonprofits must plan for multiple futures in this time of calamities. *Chronicle of Philanthropy, 33*(1), 34–35.

Johnson, P. (2018). *Global philanthropy report: Perspectives on the global foundation sector.* Hauser Institute for Civil Society at Harvard University. https://cpl.hks.harvard.edu/files/cpl/files/global_philanthropy_report_final_april_2018.pdf

Mento, M. D. (2020). What big donors are thinking: Three philanthropists talk about their approaches to giving in the time of Covid, racial unrest, and economic devastation. *Chronicle of Philanthropy, 32*(12), 22–25.

Pattison, J. (2021). 6 common types of grant awards. *The Resourceful Community.* https://theresourcefulcommunity.com/blog/6-common-types-grant-awards

Philanthropy New York. (2008). *History of U.S. Philanthropy.* https://philanthropynewyork.org/sites/default/files/resources/History%20of%20Philanthropy.pdf

Revere, E. (2016). After 25 years of grant making, I worry we have lost sight of nonprofit struggles. *Chronicle of Philanthropy, 28*(11), 28–31.

Troyer, T. A. (1999). *The 1969 private foundation law: Historical perspective on its origins and underpinnings.* Council on Foundations.

University of Southern California. (2021). *Types of grant funding.* https://libguides.usc.edu/c.php?g=411183&p=2803568

2.7
COMMUNICATING ORGANIZATIONAL CHANGE TO NONPROFIT STAKEHOLDERS

Laurie Lewis

Organizations of all types and sectors experience organizational change. Change is a prominent feature of organizational and civic life and a frequent topic of scholarly and popular discourse. Nonprofit change can serve as a means to address many important challenges, such as those related to distribution of rights and resources; challenges of efficiency and effectiveness; and challenges hinged on shared values, understanding, and cooperation. Change can also be wrongheaded, faddish, unnecessary, and a waste of resources. This chapter provides an overview of key processes of nonprofit change, including how change is triggered, stakes and stakeholders during change, challenges in nonprofit organization (NPO) change, and key communication dynamics throughout the implementation of change in NPOs.

Triggers for nonprofit change

Classic models of organizational change depict a linear path rooted in individual ingenuity that leads to organizational change and ultimately spreads to the environment (Rogers, 1995). That is, changes are presumed to be generated through accidental or intentional innovation processes. A new idea is created and deemed potentially useful or "good." Sometimes the innovation of a given organization is diffused through the local or larger networks. Although the rational depiction of invention–selection–diffusion is prevalent in some of the change literature, there is increasing acknowledgement that oftentimes change is thrust upon an organization rather than selected for potential "innovativeness." For example, in the case of regulatory change, organizations are compelled to adopt new practices and processes (Verbruggen et al., 2011). NPOs may change due to the reprioritization or requests of major funders (Seo, 2020).

Further, external trends and fads can also trigger change. Zorn et al. (1999) make the case that "change for change's sake" (p. 4) can become a managerial fashion which results in constant change in organizations. This constant change can at times lead to disastrous outcomes, including ill-considered timing of change, dysfunctional human resource management practices, exhaustion from repetitive cycles of change, and loss of benefits that stem from stability and consistency.

In many sub-sectors of the nonprofit sector, change comes about because of a mandate, regulatory ruling, legal requirement, funding opportunity, or other coercive mechanism. Changes in political leadership at local, state, or federal levels may result in reprioritization of resources; change in the priorities of benefactors, donors, patrons, or even volunteers can create necessity for nonprofits to alter practices, programs, services, and/or resource allocations. One common coercive mechanism for NPO change comes from social pressure. In a study of the adoption of websites, Flanagin (2000) found evidence that NPOs' self-perceptions of their status and leadership position in their field were positively correlated with adoption decisions. They ascribed this pattern in part to the felt pressures to stay on the leading edge. Lewis (2015) states:

> As more and more organizations in a local area or within a sector or sub-sector adopt a specific innovation, the pressure mounts for those who do not have that innovation to mimic the adopters. In contrast, if powerful stakeholders eschew an idea or find they desire other alternatives, pressure to drop or discontinue a new idea may mount.
>
> (p. 506)

In case studies of NPOs in New Zealand, Zorn et al. (2013) found evidence that talk within professional networks influences the ways in which new technologies are viewed, as well as the initial enthusiasm to use them. However, they also found that organizational resource issues (e.g., time, money, infrastructure) play a part in determining use, especially the dual pressures and enticements of internal and external environments.

Thus, triggers for change may stem from communication among key stakeholders who take notice of internal or external environmental features that lead them to make a case for a change and/or to develop an innovative response. Decision makers often work through the adoption of a change by comparing their understandings and sense of "what is going on" with that of competitors, regulators, customers, industry partners, and internal stakeholders, such as employees, volunteers, and affiliated national organizations (Lewis, 2015).

Stakes and stakeholders in NPO change

As organizations move through change processes, individuals and groups may perceive threats and opportunities to their stakes in that organization. A stake in an organization may take any number of forms, including finances, information access, goods/services, reputation, relationships, environmental conditions, and mission loyalty, among others.

> No matter the type, size, scope, or age of an organization, there will be sets of stakeholders who depend on the organization or hope to derive benefit (or avoid harm) related to the organization's operation. When an organization changes in some significant way, stakes are invoked and often are cast into uncertainty.
>
> (Lewis, 2021, p. 250)

There are many types of stakeholders surrounding NPOs. These include clients/patrons/members/participants, employees, volunteers, donors, board members, national affiliates, local partners, government agencies, and neighborhoods/communities. There are complexities in defining specific groups of stakeholders for any organization or organizational change (Lewis, 2021). As NPOs change, these individuals, groups, and organizations are likely to be impacted in many visible and invisible ways. Communities and individuals can gain or lose resources; volunteers may see new or fewer opportunities to participate; donors may become energized by or disenchanted with the organization; and partners may find themselves feeling threatened or re-engaged.

As we think about potential costs and benefits of change in NPOs, we need to keep in mind these various stakes and stakeholders' perspectives. We should view the perception of stakes as fluid across a change process. Individual stakeholders or groups of stakeholders may come to see their stakes competing or complementary with others' stakes. Researchers have documented that the talk surrounding a change (frequently in the form of framing and stories) helps clarify these perceptions.

> Storytelling and interactional framing clearly influence the perceptions that stakeholders have about their changing stakes in the organization and potential for threat or opportunity related to those stakes. The collective sensemaking may make individuals aware of competing and/or complementary stakes among stakeholder groups, and the cases made to support or resist the change.
>
> (Lewis, 2021, p. 259)

As stakeholders engage with one another during a change process, they may discover ways to engage allies or to compete with rivals. Shelly Bird's (2007) investigation of a group of women coping with organizational change illustrates the alliance building that occurs during some changes. Bird found that elaborated and joint storytelling helped the women cope with uncertainty and to support each other through it. Lewis (2019) argues that as we work through stories and concerns that these stories invoke, we may "discover attractions to some and repulsions from others that ultimately shape our social network in the context of change. In short, we come to see shared fate with some stakeholders and see distance or even antagonistic goals with others" (p. 273–4).

Challenges in nonprofit change

Stakeholders during change will have a variety of reactions, responses, and perspectives that are likely to be fluid and, at times, unpredictable. The context and triggers for the change (perceived and real), the implementation processes, and the likely mixed reactions of various stakeholder groups will all come to influence how stakeholders come to accept, resist, or opt out of change. Some of the particularly challenging aspects of nonprofit change include coping with regulatory or other mandated changes; managing change with few slack resources; resisting mission drift as a consequence of changes to responding to external trends and pressures; and effectively communicating to a variety of stakeholders with diverse views about the change.

A case study of the Australian Meals and Wheels (MoW) program (Oppenheimer et al., 2014) offers a good example of challenges with externally mandated change. The regulatory change brought about a new reality for this program's management. Under national food safety standards introduced in 2008, organizations regularly producing or processing food to be served to vulnerable populations, including MoW recipients, had to have an auditable, documented food safety plan. The cost of developing and maintaining an auditable food safety program, including training staff, upgrading equipment, and regulatory audit fees, was part of the changes required of the NPOs involved as service providers. These changes ultimately came to influence the role of volunteers in some negative ways, including raising demands on reporting and other paperwork.

> Some of the demands, and the skills and knowledge required in the regulatory environment, now go beyond what should reasonably be expected of a volunteer. As one senior manager stated, "You can't expect volunteers to be willing to deal with all the training that's required, and the paperwork and all the reporting that's required, it should be a paid job. It's not a volunteer role any longer. And that's because of the legislation."
>
> (p. 1562)

In cases of changes brought about through regulatory and other coercive mechanisms, NPOs may not be able to simply give up on the change when it is not received well by key stakeholders. They must develop communication strategies that support coping with new regulatory change without debating the changes themselves.

The Australian MoW case also illustrates another critical issue for many NPOs whose changes are mandated from some outside source – the lack of slack resources to make and sustain changes. As one senior leader in the MoW case study reported, the costs associated with implementing mandated audits was beyond what they could afford.

> Audits commenced in 2012, and already there are concerns about the cost of regularly conveying an auditor to small services located across such a large State in remote regions. A senior staff member said that the sheer expense of being audited could make it impossible for such services to continue: You're talking about $1000 for a roundtrip flight to one of the smaller airfields in the middle of the Pilbara, then potentially a three hour drive there and back, and accommodating and feeding them, and paying for the time it takes. And it all comes from the organization's pockets.
>
> (p. 1560)

Another potential consequence of imposed or coercive change in NPOs is the possibility of mission drift. As organizations respond to the favored priorities of funding agencies; significant donor organizations; or priorities of local, state, or federal initiatives, they may risk sacrificing the needs and preferences of key stakeholders and the core mission as they chase resources. In other words, leaders can be faced with choices between sticking with the core mission and making do with fewer resources. Volunteers, small-dollar donors, clients/patrons/members, and community members may find mission drift to be unacceptable while not always appreciating the financial squeeze that many NPOs experience. Fitzgerald et al.'s (2014) case study of a large nonprofit human services organization in Australia highlights how mission drift is driven by rationalization, outsourcing, and competition for funding in the increasingly business-like sector. However, these authors conclude that managers can counterbalance these changes through leadership, good governance, adequate resources, and a strong commitment to vision and mission. Although the mission drift problem has been feared as a major concern for nonprofits who adapt to changing environments, recent evidence suggests it is rarer than generally thought (Auer et al., 2011).

A major challenge in implementing change in nonprofits relates to the widely diverse stakeholder groups that are impacted by and have a desire to impact the change process. As noted earlier, there can be a vast array of potential groups who hold a stake in an NPO and in any specific change effort. Akingbola et al. (2019) argue that "organizational members are concerned about how change impacts their particular interests, values, and identity" (p. 210) and further cite a research study (Solebello et al., 2016) examining a membership organization that illustrates this point. Members of this trade and professional association resisted or withheld support from diversity initiatives that were perceived as threats to their access to membership incentives or their control over and power of the association and ability to dictate their sense of identity. A study of efforts to garner the support of NPO employees (Chad's, 2016) offers another example. Akingbola et al. (2019) summarizes the study's results:

> Examining corporate rebranding as a change management process, tensions were identified at several points in the process when employees were only informed of the rebranding activities or had received details after their clients. Chad argues that given the strong ethos driving nonprofit employees, this principle of attaining internal support in rebranding is more relevant in the nonprofit – than the for-profit – context.
>
> (p. 202)

Nonprofits and change implementers who are charged with steering change processes must contend with the multiple demands of various stakeholders. As noted earlier, these stakeholders may have competitive or complementary demands. NPOs will likely be challenged by the alliances among stakeholder groups, who may put pressure on NPOs to make decisions supporting their goals. They may also be challenged by conflicts that arise during a change process when groups desire opposing goals.

Communication during NPO change

Given the significant challenges that many NPOs deal with as the implement changes, especially those triggered by environmental pressures or demands, managers and leaders must develop significant communication strategies and tactics to ease the stress of change, frame the change, and involve key stakeholders throughout the change.

As leaders and change implementers form strategy about how they will introduce a change to stakeholders and manage a change process, it is important that they recognize that stakes will change during the process and that stakeholders' perceptions of their stakes will likely be quite fluid throughout the life of the change. As Lewis (2021) argues:

> A part of this process is co-creating an understanding of which stakes are in play and in what ways an individual's stakes are advantaged or threatened. As stakes are reassessed and uncertainty is built and resolved, stakeholders' perceptions of their own stakes and stakes of other groups and individuals evolve. Changing perceptions and valuing of stakes is influenced through the sensemaking and strategic interactions among stakeholders. As information is shared, concerns are fomented, and stories are weaved, and stakeholders' understandings of the change and what is at stake are formed and altered.
>
> (p. 257)

The ways in which stakeholders assess, form, and reform their stakes and the stakes of others is through the communication they have with each other and with implementers. Stakeholder groups will share stories and rumors, ask and answer questions, provide and consume information, state and hear opinions, and give and receive supportive messages. Dewulf et al. (2009) argue that stakeholders use interactional frames to make collective sense of a situation. As they communicate with each other, they categorize and arrange ambiguous events in meaningful ways. These are the conversations where people figure out "what is going on here," "what this means," and "why this is happening."

Leaders and implementers need to appreciate the complexity of sense making and communication that is happening among stakeholders and within and between stakeholder groups as they form strategy for their own communication about change. Key in their strategic choices need to be plans for managing resistance, disseminating information, and soliciting input.

Communicating through resistance. Coping with resistance to change is a key challenge in most organizations going through widespread change processes that touch on the stakes of many groups of stakeholders. As change implementers consider how to approach communication strategies to bring change processes along, they need to consider the important power (formal and informal) that various stakeholder groups have.

Silver et al. (2006) examined a pre- and post-change survey study comparing comparable change in an NPO and for-profit organization (FPO). They found that the FPO effort was successful while the NPO failed. The NPO made initial progress towards achieving a culture change, but subsequently began to lose its focus on empowerment-related efforts of the culture change. The change effort reached a plateau due to a lack of middle managerial leadership to support and role-model practices of empowerment. As Akingbola et al. (2019) summarize:

> [T]he NPO failed to involve the senior team and use employee feedback systematically. . . . In contrast, the for-profit organization focused broadly on fostering learning and sustained progress on leadership development and empowerment, with managers applying these concepts within their areas with staff.
>
> (p. 209)

Volunteers are another stakeholder group who play a key role in success and resistance to change in NPOs, as seen in the earlier example of Oppenheimer et al.'s (2014) case study of the Australian MoW. The engagement of long-standing volunteers became a key challenge in managing change and required taking their concerns seriously.

Information dissemination. Change implementers typically focus on communication that they have designed to engage stakeholders in positive ways and to limit resistance (Lewis, 2021). The organizational change literature has documented that stakeholders prefer that implementers be honest and open, and research suggests that these characteristics produce subsequent cooperativeness and enhanced ability of stakeholders to cope with change (Lewis, 2015). Implementers will oftentimes attempt to sell change to stakeholder groups in an effort to gain their faith that the change is necessary, beneficial, well timed, and supported by key organizational leaders. For example, Applequist et al.'s (2016) study of the implementation of a model for patient-centered care within 20 medical practices found evidence of the effectiveness of three overarching themes: (1) open, consistent communication that encourages active listening and feedback; (2) appropriate reinforcement techniques; and (3) a clearly identifiable patient centered medical home "champion" or change implementer.

Although information acquisition can help stakeholders reduce uncertainty during change, research and theory also suggest that uncertainty is managed in other ways than merely information accumulation (Brummans & Miller, 2004). For example, Kramer et al. (2004) examined uncertainty in the context of an airline acquisition. Their study found that individuals differed in the degrees to which they sought out information. Some who were less actively seeking information managed their uncertainty internally and discounted the available information. They found the information available to be potentially inaccurate, misleading, or unavailable and therefore not worth the effort to gather. The study also found that a majority of the pilots sought information to create comfort, share rumors (even if they were thought to be false), and seek mutual support.

Input solicitation. Accumulating evidence supports soliciting input as a way to lower resistance to change, increase the satisfaction of participants, and increase stakeholders' feelings of control (cf. Bordia et al., 2004; Sagie & Koslowsky, 1994). Further, consequences of poor or absent genuine input-seeking on the part of implementers are potentially dire for change efforts (Sahay, 2021). In the realm of public-sector innovation, Nyhan (2000) and Page (2003) maintain that public entrepreneurs should encourage collaboration, participation, and inclusive decision-making processes that engender trust in their work settings.

Research also suggests that organizations tend to emphasize downward dissemination of information over soliciting stakeholder input (Doyle et al., 2000; Lewis, 1999, Lewis et al., 2003). When input is sought, the opportunities for voice are rarely equal (Lewis et al., 2003; Lewis & Russ, 2012), and determining whom to invite to the conversation is often difficult (Barge et al., 2008). And oftentimes, stakeholder input that is invited may not be used in a genuine way to shape the change or make substantive decisions (Neumann, 1989; Sahay, 2021).

Lewis (2019) argues that a common approach to requesting feedback during change consists of asking nonmanagerial employees for opinions, feedback, and reactions regarding the change in question. However, as Lewis cautions, input is not always used as a resource by the organization and may simply be collected to enhance stakeholders' commitment to the change. As Sahay (2021) notes, "[T]his latter type of symbolic solicitation may begin with honest, authentic intentions, but may be rendered inauthentic over the course of the change" (p. 2).

Another problematic habit of input solicitation concerns managers' desire to only consider input that appears to have significant shared support (Lewis & Russ, 2012; Sahay, 2021). Sahay's (2021) study included interviews with chief operating officers (COOs) about their approach to input solicitation during change. One COO expressed a common theme reflecting this issue, "One executive said, 'I ask the consultants or managers to bring me problems that have been vetted. If they hear the same concerns over and over again, then we must know about it'" (p. 7). Input providers who were interviewed in the same study emphasized that their unique concerns were often ignored because they were perceived as lacking credibility and support. As posited by a health care employee, "I spoke about the issues, but it was just me. So, they ignored it'" (p. 7). Ignoring outliers and their unique information can have devastating consequences in organizations in general, but particularly during major organizational change (Clarke & Eddy, 2017; Lewis, 2019, 2020). Individuals or groups who hold unique perspectives or key bits of information unknown to others can provide insights that, when ignored, may lead to catastrophic outcomes. Lewis (2019) summarizes their findings:

> The Cassandras were "often ignored, their warnings denigrated, disregarded, or given only inadequate, token responses" (p. 4). Clarke and Eddy explore the specific events. . . . What is clear from these analyses is that often flawed processes; biases in how evidence, data, and cautionary signals are processed; and the lack of listening are responsible for preventable and sometimes tragic failures in organizations.
>
> (p. xi)

Lewis (2019) posits some of the causes of poor listening during organizational change: "Those tasked with gathering input may be strongly motivated to report up the chain only good news, solvable problems, and positive reactions" (p. 51). As Lewis notes, major organizational change is often marked by conflict and risk, as well as perceived threat or loss. Change may trigger stakeholders to focus on the organizations with new intensity, and this may cause leaders to eschew listening to naysayers and those considered to be resistant. In the worst cases, perceived resistors even may be actively silenced.

Conclusion

Change in nonprofits shares many pitfalls and stressors that present to all organizational types and sectors. However, the types and diversity of stakeholders and stakes bring additional complexity. Further, while most any organization may find itself coerced into a change it does not want or can afford to implement, this is far more common in the NPO sector. Further, the level of public scrutiny faced by NPOs is often more intense and potentially harmful for these organizations, who can easily lose substantial resources if they are not able to meet the demands of donors/patrons/members, employees, volunteers, and communities. Managing these complex demands as they ebb and flow over a change process is quite demanding. Deft change communication necessitates appreciating the multistakeholder context; effectively reducing uncertainty among stakeholders; and navigating equitable, effective, quality listening and input gathering.

References

Akingbola, K., Rogers, S. E., & Baluch, A. (2019). Implementing change in nonprofit organizations. In *Change management in nonprofit organizations*. Palgrave Macmillian.

Applequist, J., Miller-Day, M., Cronholm, P. F., Gabbay, R. A., & Bowen, D. S. (2016). In principle we have agreement, but in practice it is a bit more difficult: Obtaining organizational buy-in to patient-centered medical home transformation. *Qualitative Health Research*, *27*(6), 909–22.

Auer, J. C., Twombly, E. C., & De Vita, C. J. (2011). Social service agencies and program change. *Public Performance & Management Review*, *34*(3), 378–396.

Barge, J. K., Lee, M., Maddux, K., Nabring, R., & Townsend, B. (2008). Managing dualities in planned change initiatives. *Journal of Applied Communication Research*, *36*(4), 364–390.

Bird, S., (2007). Sensemaking and identity: The inter-connection of storytelling and networking in a women's group of a large corporation. *Journal of Business Communication*, *44*(4), 311–339.

Bordia, P., Hobman, E., Jones, E., Gallois, C., & Callan, V. (2004). Uncertainty during organizational change: Types, consequences, and management strategies. *Journal of Business and Psychology*, *18*(4), 507–532.

Brummans, B., & Miller, K. I. (2004). The effect of ambiguity on the implementation of a social change initiative. *Communication Research Reports*, *21*(1), 1–10.

Chad, P. (2016). Corporate rebranding: An employee-focused nonprofit case study. *Journal of Nonprofit & Public Sector Marketing*, *28*(4), 327–350.

Clarke, R. A., & Eddy, R. P. (2017). *Warnings: Finding Cassandras to stop catastrophes*. HarperCollins.

Dewulf, A., Gray, B., Putnam, L. L., Lewicki, R., Aarts, N., Bouwen, R., & Van Woerkum, C. (2009). Disentangling Approaches to framing in conflict and negotiation research: A meta-paradigmatic perspective. *Human Relations*, *62*, 155–193.

Doyle, M., Claydon, T., & Buchanan, D. (2000). Mixed results, lousy process: The management experience of organizational change. *British Journal of Management*, *11*(S1), S59–S80.

Fitzgerald, S., Rainnie, A., Goods, C., & Morris, L. (2014). The restructuring of WA human services and its implications for the not-for-profit sector. *Australian Journal of Social Issues*, *49*(4), 509–528.

Flanagin, A. (2000). Social pressures on organizational website adoption. *Human Communication Research*, *26*(4), 618–646.

Kramer, M., Doughtery, D. S., & Pierce, T. A. (2004). Managing uncertainty during a corporate acquisition: A longitudinal study of communication during an airline acquisition. *Human Communication Research*, *30*(1), 71–101.

Lewis, L. K. (1999). Disseminating information and soliciting input during planned organizational change: Implementers' targets, sources and channels for communicating. *Management Communication Quarterly*, *13*, 43–75.

Lewis, L. K. (2015). Organizational change and innovation. In L. L. Putnam & D. K. Mumby (Eds.), *The new handbook of organizational communication* (pp. 503–524). Sage.

Lewis, L. K. (2019). *Organizational change: Creating change through strategic communication* (2nd ed.). Wiley-Blackwell.

Lewis, L. K. (2020). *The power of strategic listening in contemporary organizations*. Roman & Littlefield.

Lewis, L. K. (2021). Stakeholder model of change. In M. S. Poole & A. H. Van de Ven (Eds.), *Handbook of organizational change and innovation* (pp. 250–274). Oxford University Press.

Lewis, L. K., Richardson, B. K., & Hamel, S. A. (2003). When the stakes are communicative: The lamb's and the lion's share during nonprofit planned change. *Human Communication Research*, *29*, 400–430.

Lewis, L. K., & Russ, T. (2012). Soliciting and using input during organizational change initiatives: What are practitioners doing? *Management Communication Quarterly*, *26*(2), 267–294.

Neumann, J. E. (1989). Why people don't participate in organizational change? In R. W. Woodman & W. A. Pasmore (Eds.), *Research in organizational change and development* (Vol. 3, pp. 181–212). JAI Press.

Nyhan, R. (2000). Changing the paradigm: Trust and its role in public sector organizations. *American Review of Public Administration*, *30*(1), 87–109.

Oppenheimer, M., Warburton, J., & Carey, J. (2014). The next 'new' idea: The challenges of organizational change, decline and renewal in Australian meals on wheels. *Voluntas*, *26*, 1550–1569.

Page, S. (2003). Entrepreneurial strategies for managing inter-agency collaboration. *Journal of Public Administration Research and Theory*, *13*(3), 311–340.

Rogers, E. M. (1995). *Diffusion of innovations* (4th ed.). Free Press.

Sagie, A., & Koslowsky, M. (1994). Organizational attitudes and behaviors as a function of participation in strategic and tactical change decisions: An application of path-goal theory. *Journal of Organizational Behavior*, *15*(1), 37–47.

Sahay, S. (2021). Organizational listening during organizational change: Perspectives of employees and executives. *International Journal of Listening*. doi:10.1080/10904018.2021.1941029

Seo, J. (2020). Resource dependence patters, goal change, and social value in nonprofit organizations: Does goal change matter in nonprofit management? *International Review of Administrative Sciences*, *86*(2), 368–387.

Silver, S., Randolph, W. A., & Seibert, S. (2006). Implementing and sustaining empowerment: Lessons learned from comparison of a for-profit and a nonprofit organization. *Journal of Management Inquiry*, *15*(1), 47–58.

Solebello, N., Tschirhart, M., & Leiter, J. (2016). The paradox of inclusion and exclusion in membership associations. *Human Relations*, *69*(2), 439–460.

Verbruggen, S., Christiaens, J., & Milis, K. (2011). Can resource dependence and coercive isomorphism explain nonprofit organizations' compliance with reporting standards? *Nonprofit and Voluntary Sector Quarterly*, *40*(1), 5–32.

Zorn, T. E., Christensen, L. T., & Cheney, G. (1999). *Do we really want constant change*. Berret-Koehler Communications.

Zorn, T. E., Grant, S., & Henderson, A. (2013). Strengthening resource mobilization chains: Developing the social media competencies of community and voluntary organizations in New Zealand. *Voluntas: International Journal of Voluntary and Nonprofit Organizations*, *24*(3), 666–687. http://www.jstor.org/stable/42629832

2.8
NONPROFIT AND GOVERNMENT RELATIONS

Bruno Ferreira Costa and Hugo Ferrinho Lopes

Introduction

The role of civil society in contemporary democracies has been extensively studied in the broader context of social sciences. It derives from the growing importance of framing the evolution of democracy based on the public and private actors involved in social organization. The bridge between these two sectors lies in the very idea of civil society resulting from political culture and collective values (Roniger, 1994). It allows the collaboration between different actors involved in structuring society and implementing a hierarchy of political values (priorities established by civil society).

The concept of civil society presupposes the existence of public and organized life beyond the state's administration, allowing the private and voluntary sectors to act and intervene in the public sphere. In this multi-structural organization, the role of nonprofit organizations (NPOs) is crucial to understand the dynamics underlying the promotion of democratic values. They have a vital role in several sectors (economic, cultural, social, political). These organizations may be considered both an expression of civic society (Rothschild & Whitt, 1986; Roniger & Güneş-Ayata, 1994) and political institutions – in the form of recognized norms, rules, procedures, and routines (Ghosh, 2009). And as an alternative mechanism to traditional (i.e., mere electoral) political participation. From this perspective, NPOs are pivotal agents in a multi-dynamic society, wherein the responsibility for building the democratic project does not rely only on traditional institutions or political officials (Clarke, 1998).

If the construction of the pillars of society is carried out with the contribution of multiple political and social actors, the action of NPOs deserves a careful look. The nonprofit sector is an institutional response to unmet demand resulting from limitations on the governmental provision of public goods (Weisbrod, 1986). NPOs perform critical political functions, not only in contributing to strengthen democracy (Rothschild & Stephenson, 2009) and political representation as a form of indirect democracy (Guo, 2007; Guo & Musso, 2007) but also human rights (van Boven, 1989; van Tuijl, 1999), participation (Mosley, 2015), and public interest communication (Bonk et al., 2008; Patterson & Radtke, 2009; Oliveira et al., 2016; Gonçalves et al., 2018). However, communication and provision of public goods through NPOs also pose challenges to governments, namely, understanding citizens' perception of responsibility for action between political and public institutions (Lecy et al., 2012).

This raises two central questions. First, in the face of the competition concerning the exercise of public functions, why do NPOs continue to be essential for stabilizing the system and promoting democracy? Second, to what extent are their problems associated with providing public goods through NPOs, mainly with the advancement of democracy, transparency, and accountability? This research aims to discuss the costs and benefits of NPOs' activities in promoting democratic values. Specifically, we investigate relations between NPOs and governments and their contribution to democracy, transparency, and accountability while assuring, or not, the internal maintenance of those values and external communication mechanisms (i.e., improving its brand). The chapter further studies the case of Transparency International (TI) by assessing its advantages and problems in disseminating democratic values. The issue derives from its monopoly in promoting such matters and being an NPO dealing with the issue of transparency, assuming a dual role in the consolidation of democratic rules. This goal is achieved by integrating online collected data and qualitative interviews, contributing to a broader discussion on the nonprofit sector, political systems, quality of democracy, and strategic communication.

The following section reviews the literature on nonprofit communication and the promotion of democracy. Then, the role of NPOs in actual global governance is surveyed. The third section analyses the critical elements behind TI's action and examines its costs and benefits. Finally, we discuss the implications of the results considering the theoretical background and suggest pathways for future investigations.

Nonprofit organizations and promotion of democracy

Democracy builds on a wide range of civil, political, and social rights. Nonprofit communication is relevant to promoting democratic values and rights, complementing governmental functions, and strengthening the relationship between state and citizens (King & Griffin, 2019). This perspective follows Robert Dahl's (1998) idea of an independent process to form democracies and the ability to reinvent regimes.

Democracy, however, being considered a "common good," lacks an interdisciplinary, multi-organizational analysis to guarantee a complete interpretation of social organization (Gotchev, 1998; Kim & Moon, 2003). This implies a specific look at organizations that promote democratic values. The nonprofit sector fits here as a central object of study, since it serves as a counterpoint to the excessive power of the public sector (Bucholtz, 1998). This covers a dichotomic debate, with some perspectives supporting a deep separation from the political sphere and others establishing the idea that civil society is part of the public sphere (Bucholtz, 1998).

The implementation and consolidation of democracy is a "continuing and endless process of sociopolitical development" (Ghosh, 2009, p. 481) involving the whole political system: rules, civil society, institutions, and overall citizenship. In this context, NPOs act as political institutions (Ghosh, 2009) deriving from the empowerment of individuals and the ability to pressure traditional political institutions. They serve as critical elements of communication between citizens and political actors. Therefore, the analysis of the NPO's role leads to the interdependence between all aspects of the political system, replacing some traditional functions performed by political institutions and ensuring some control over the decision- and policy-making processes, as NPOs exert influence over those in power (e.g., through lobbying).

In this strategy of disseminating democracy, "the message is the heart of efforts to reach target audiences" (Patterson & Radtke, 2009, p. 87). Identifying each organization's mission allows for establishing the most effective communication strategy, according to the characteristics of the message to be sent and the ones concerning the global audience (citizens). Strategic communication allows the audience to discuss different ideas, being fundamental for the organization to achieve its mission (Patterson & Radtke, 2009). This communication maximizes the action of NPOs and their respective role within society. Their communication strategy aggregates "a plan, goals, practices and tools which a [NPO] sends consistent messages about its mission values, and accomplishments" (Patterson &

Radtke, 2009, p. 7). Considering this goal, the mission of an NPO in democratic societies "is to articulate their values clearly so that people can relate to the mission, connect to the underlying values and commit to taking action to support the organization" (Patterson & Radtke, 2009, p. 8).

The contribution of NPOs thus fits into a model of public policy development and reconciliation society with governments (Marwell & Brown, 2020). The action of NPOs is both complementarity and competition about government (Najam, 2000), but at the same time control and accountability of the latter. NPOs are often perceived as schools of democracy, enabling them to equip citizens with tools and skills that prepare them for broader civic participation (King & Griffin, 2019). However, at the same time, they also face the demands of internal democracy, accountability, and transparency, as well as a set of means and financial constraints to act as legitimate substitutes of traditional political institutions in a hyper-competitive global scenario to intervene in democracy promotion (Salamon & Geller, 2008, p. 1).

Building on this framework, NPOs act alongside state and public actors, decisively shaping democracy. Given that transparency and accountability are two core indicators to measure the quality of democracy (Schmitter & Karl, 1991; Diamond & Morlino, 2004), we pick these two indicators to analyze the promotion of democracy through NPOs, discussing its advantages and challenges, and choose a case study that acts on both transparency and accountability. That is the case with TI, which deals with transparency and accountability, working in legal procedures associated with public decisions. Therefore, we need to review the role of NPOs in global governance and examine the specific functioning of TI.

Global governance and nonprofit organizations

Political, economic, and cultural globalization brings several global and domestic governance issues. It has contributed to the rapid spread of liberal democracies and the substitution of the Keynesian state by a regulatory state. Nonetheless, conventional political institutions face declining levels of trust and participation (Norris, 2011). They are more permeable to new trends, such as corruption, illiberal and anti-globalization discourses, hatred, and overall loss of support for democracy (de Sousa et al., 2014). From this perspective, the state is increasingly under pressure at the national level due to its lack of capacity to respond to problems affecting the lives of citizens, many of which derive from the impact of global developments.

The idea of governance (including civil society) emerges as a response to these issues, merging communication through a new range of policy networks wherein NPOs help to fill the governments' gaps (Rhodes, 1997). International NPOs (INPOs) play a crucial role in fighting global challenges such as global warming, nuclear and water crises, pandemics such as COVID-19, terrorism, financial crises, inequality, migrations, corruption, and lack of transparency. As part of civil society, based on its assumption on public organized life and associations beyond the state's sphere, they are a linking mechanism between elites and citizens (Roniger, 1994) and challenge the winners rather than the losers of globalization.[1] However, as Chandhoke (2005) calls to attention: To whom are NPOs accountable? Which issues are "worthy" of their attention? Who decides whose interests they should emphasize most?

As Rothschild and Stephenson state, "newer grassroots non-governmental and nonprofit enterprises and social movement organizations reject outright the image of hierarchy and bureaucracy that was so central to the modernist project. Instead, they favor an image of the organization that is, at its core, collectivist and egalitarian" (2009, p. 801). Nonetheless, if NPOs assume public functions, they must be subject to political accountability – i.e., the more NPOs assume public functions, the more scrutinized they shall be (van Tuijl, 1999, p. 506). Can the democracy, transparency, and accountability that they (externally) promote be simultaneously internally secured? The following section investigates a case study working on those issues to examine this question.

The case of transparency international

The previous discussion establishes a puzzling pattern on the trade-off between the costs and benefits of promoting democracy through NPOs. This section analyzes the extent to which NPOs do so while simultaneously ensuring internal democracy, transparency, and accountability. We survey the literature and mix the results obtained from online collected data by the authors and qualitative data from the research project *Transparency International and the Problem of Corruption*.[2] This allows for an in-depth exploratory analysis to answer the research question. To guarantee data protection, statements from the project's interviews are anonymized.

The rise of anti-corruption agencies – the "integrity warriors" – in the 1990s marks the most innovative feature of the transparency movement of the last decades (de Sousa, 2010). They are "public (funded) bodies of a durable nature, with a specific mission to fight corruption and reduce the opportunity structures propitious for corruption occurrence in society through preventive and/ or repressive measures," being often "regarded by governments, donors and international governmental organizations as the ultimate institutional response to corruption" (de Sousa, 2010, pp. 5–6). One of those NPOs deserves a particular glance: Transparency International. As an "independent, non-governmental, not-for-profit" organization, TI has filled a gap like no other organization before and is nowadays the most important "civil society 'corruption fighter' at the global level" (de Sousa, 2009, p. 186). Consequently, TI's relevance as a case study derives from its dual role in the consolidation of democratic values, i.e., the double circumstance of being an unavoidable INPO dealing with the issue of transparency and accountability.

TI was founded in 1993 by high-level officials to curb corruption and promote transparency, accountability, and integrity.[3] It is based in Berlin, sponsored by other INPOs, and plays a significant role in mobilizing civil society and pressuring decision-makers to adopt transparency policies. TI combines a broad coalition involving governments, the private sector, and civil society and acts at the national level through its national chapters (NCs), pushing national integrity systems. Other NPOs approach corruption and transparency, but TI has a clear monopoly: it has led to the adoption of two international conventions by the Organisation for Economic Co-operation and Development (OECD) and the United Nations (UN). TI now has a worldwide representation, with NCs in more than 100 countries, comprising most European member states.

TI's action builds upon the following key elements: engagement with key government officials; pressure for democracy, transparency, accountability; and its brand's improvement. This comprises complex state–society relations and the boost on internal and external communication: a constant search for "a constituency (legitimization and representation factors) and the need to consolidate the brand (the marketing factor)" (de Sousa, 2009, p. 189). However, TI also faces tensions and dilemmas when pursuing these three elements.

First, regarding its relations with governments. TI is funded by many donors, including government agencies, multilateral institutions, foundations, and the private sector.[4] Governments, specifically, provide more than half of TI's income, whereas other NPOs and research institutions contribute with only 3.9%.[5] If government agencies support TI's work, can the organization be free from the government's interests? Furthermore, there are "different kinds of nonprofit"[6] activism in TI's grassroots: many NCs' board members are – or have come to be – politicians or government officials.[7] If there is no unclouded barrier between civil society's pressure groups and politicians, how may this NPO be free from government demands?

To avoid agency losses and ensure that NPOs contribute to collective goals, governments have to bear the costs of monitoring and expend scarce resources on selective incentives to punish and reward NPOs collaborating with them to achieve governments' goals (see Cox & McCubbins, 2007). Although governments recognize the need for a shared vision in the construction of democratic values and the institutional pillars of society, the progressive transfer of responsibilities from the formal sector (mainly political authorities) to NPOs can be considered an opportunity but also a failure in the prosecution of state functions. They are harder to punish, since the tools used to control governmental agencies often fail with NPOs: even if governments retrieve the funding or resources from one NPO to another, the new organization will have the same incentive to "cheat" (Gates & Hill, 1995). Furthermore, on the one hand, despite resulting in the adoption of massive anti-corruption packages, they have had limited effects since legislators have no integrated view about transparency (de Sousa, 2010). On the other hand, at the very least, TI has been able to "make governments reconceptualize the costs and benefits of corruption and to take the issue of corruption seriously" (Wang & Rosenau, 2001, p. 42).

Second, there are recurrent tensions between TI's secretariat in Berlin and NCs. From one's perspective, it demands more bottom-up accountability; from the latter, the rejection of a top-down approach to agenda setting. Can TI promote transparency, accountability, and democracy while simultaneously ensuring intra-organizational democratic values? Results suggest otherwise. TI is not cohesive and lacks collective action. Although there is pressure on governments for openness to democratic values, TI's internal relations and communication mechanisms have failed to ensure those values.

From the elites' perspective, the grassroots have failed to comply with TI's principles. Most NCs started from informal contacts by the two "fathers" of TI, Peter Eigen and Jeremy Pope, following a "catch-all membership" that preceded the organization's consolidation. TI then needed to address national and transnational corruption problems, but they lacked grassroots support or experience in transparency (de Sousa, 2009). This raises issues on the quality of NCs' activity and their purposes. NCs have different agendas regardless of the global principles of the organization (Kimeu, 2014). The results of NCs' actions are heterogeneous, and even questionable, with an obscure picture in countries such as the United States (Wang & Rosenau, 2001). Two TI officials considered that NCs "also have to be more accountable and there should be a set of standards by which it [accountability] is done,"[8] and that despite the fact that NCs "are the masters," calling the "shots," "some just come to meetings, nothing happens in between."[9]

Nonetheless, this has a reverse side. Once gaining worldwide expansion, TI faced increasing demands for more internal democracy, transparency, and accountability (de Sousa, 2009). From the grassroots perspective, TI must be more inclusive, not "more bureaucratic," and do not treat NCs as a "colony," even competing with them for funding.[10] This has led NCs to no longer be interested in being part of Berlin's initiated projects.[11] Many act as independent organizations that are only formally connected to TI. The most feasible solution may be the complete separation of powers: TI operating at the international level and NCs at the national level.[12] This separation has also been acknowledged by one of TI's officials.[13]

Third, regarding the marketing brand and TI's external communication. On the one hand, despite communication being less than 5% of TI's official budgets, other significant investments are channeled to "the outside,"[14] improving the brand. The consolidation of TI and the widespread franchising through the NCs led to the communication of transparency, accountability, and corruption-related issues wherein the Corruption Perception Index (CPI), the Global Corruption Barometer (GCB), and the Anti-Corruption Knowledge Hub emerge as fundamental tools due to the relevance of data in the presentation of the role of NPOs in the democratic archetype. TI uses these barometers to get to a broader audience and gain credibility (see, for this communication strategy, Gutterman, 2014). However, communicating these problems to civil society may often decrease trust in political institutions if no adequate measures are applied (de Sousa, 2010). In effect, the more anti-corruption marketing increases, the more salience corruption gets, thus leading citizens to reevaluate their attitudes towards general democracy. Corruption is one of the most critical issues for electors (e.g., Eurobarometer or Gallup International Annual surveys results). Therefore, external communication efforts may lead to increased political disaffection and the decline of trust in political institutions, affecting the overall quality of democracy.

Finally, external tensions also exist besides its somewhat dubious relations with governments and the TI–NCs tensions. Several other interviewees state that TI should engage more with additional pressure and civil groups. TI has felt that it was the only legitimate actor, not being coalitional enough.[15] Collaboration between TI and other international nongovernmental organizations only occurs after considering the costs and benefits and whenever it facilitates TI's power or funding (de Sousa, 2009). If TI has "fulfilled its objectives" and "was not clear [enough] about its role," the remaining question is TI's ability to move on: the challenge of its "value added."[16]

Closing remarks

The growing relevance of NPOs as the bridge between state and society opens a broad multidisciplinary field of study. Nonprofit communication, in particular, allows a holistic view of society and the promotion of democracy outside the traditional axis of political organizations. In effect, this chapter discusses and describes the main challenges of promoting democracy through the nonprofit sector. To answer the research questions and to expand the understanding of the strategy, the mechanisms, and the means of promoting democracy through such organizations, it is focused on NPOs and their relations with governments, its external pressure for democratic values while internally securing them, and the improvement of its communication brand.

The relationship between the nonprofit sector and political entities is marked by either complementarity or competitiveness in pursuing a significant set of public goods. Findings reveal that delivering public functions through NPOs brings advantages in response to government failures. NPOs are relevant in performing several public positions, thus helping political institutions answer citizens' demands. They act as pivotal agents in current political systems for two main reasons: a space for citizens' political participation and a complementary mechanism to democratic development. The scope of the collaborative work between multiple entities allows reinforcement of the bases for democratic functioning, understood as a standard and foundational asset of a significant number of states. Consequently, NPOs present a specific structure, action, and communication model, based on each entity's objectives and missions. This process occurs alongside the progressive dissatisfaction with democracy and the growth of anti-globalization and populist movements, which are constraining the functioning of democracies.

However, results also reveal tensions and costs to global and domestic governance. On the one hand, NPOs are increasingly performing public functions because of the weariness of political institutions in providing it themselves. There is a lack of engagement capability between politicians and citizens. On the other hand, there are a set of constraints to the action of NPOs due to the environment of high competition in the public sphere. These constraints relate to the division of responsibilities and the identification of roles assigned to political institutions or NPOs. The central aspect of this competition is as follows: if NPOs assume a relevant and prominent role in the public sphere, control mechanisms must be created to scrutinize their actions. In this broad debate, it is essential to bear in mind the role that each NPO plays and the process of defining thematic priorities that each ends up listing or enhancing.

The case of TI's affirmation corresponds to a growing interest in the phenomenon of corruption. Its action is marked by promoting transparency and ensuring greater accountability for the public agents' actions. First, TI has pushed several mechanisms to increase transparency and mobilizes civil society towards a significant global, national, and local governance goal. It has undoubtedly contributed to the increase of good government. Second, however, TI is centralized, with some dubious relationships between NCs and governments or private corporations that narrow its autonomy. It is criticized for not being able to secure intra-organizational transparency and accountability. Third, the more TI communicates on democratic issues, the more the trust in political institutions tends to decrease. Lastly, the assumption of TI's legitimacy is more dependent on its communication – namely, how the audience sees its role – than on TI's example (Gutterman, 2014). These results have important implications for democratic consolidation and nonprofit–government relations, namely for the "linking mechanism" they perform.

This chapter launches several pathways for future investigations on this and other organizations that compete with the state in responding to the needs of civil society. Researchers should expand the scope of the analysis to test different types of methods. This permits one to unpack cross-organizational and cross-national variation. For example, a comparison between NCs would improve on recent knowledge by providing a better understanding of how good practices may be replicated in different contexts and how to adopt a set of standards to prevent questionable actions by NCs' members such as seen in this chapter. Moreover, scholars should expand by comparing the results with other NPOs. Large-N and comparative methods may confirm or reject the generalization of these results and describe the main benefits and costs of the government–NPO relationship in the current global and multi-level governance system.

Acknowledgements

This research is partially supported by FCT PhD Research Grant number 2020.07270.BD.

Notes

1. For a distinction between winners and losers of globalization, see Kriesi et al. (2008).
2. Research project funded by the Australian Research Council (ARC), coordinated by Barry Hindess and Peter Larmour (2005) (Ref.: ARC Discovery Grant CI DPO 344125). More information at: http://purl.org/au-research/grants/arc/DP0344125.
3. More information about the "founding fathers" and TI's history is available at www.transparency.org/en/about. Accessed 30 May 2021.
4. www.transparency.org/en/the-organisation/who-supports-us.
5. www.transparency.org/en/the-organisation/who-supports-us.
6. Interviewee A.
7. The example of Kenya.
8. Interviewee A.
9. Interviewee B.
10. Interviewee B.
11. Interviewee C.
12. Interviewee D.
13. Interviewee B.
14. Information retrieved from TI's budgets available at www.transparency.org/en/the-organisation/our-operating-budget.
15. Interviewee E.
16. Interviewee E.

References

Bonk, K., Tynes, E., Griggs, H., & Sparks, P. (2008). *Strategic communications for nonprofits. A step- by-step guide to working with the media second edition* (2nd ed.). Jossey-Bass.

Bucholtz, B. K. (1998). Reflections on the role of nonprofit associations in representative democracy. *Cornell Journal of Law and Public Policy*, 7(2), 555–604.

Chandhoke, N. (2005). How global is global civil society? *Journal of World-Systems Research*, 355–371.

Clarke, G. (1998). Non-governmental organizations (NGOs) and politics in the developing world. *Political Studies*, 46(1), 36–52.

Cox, G. W., & McCubbins, M. D. (2007). *Legislative leviathan*. University of California Press.

Dahl, R. (1998). *On democracy*. Yale University Press.

de Sousa, L. (2010). Anti-corruption agencies: Between empowerment and irrelevance. *Crime, Law and Social Change*, 53(1), 5–22.

de Sousa, L., Hindess, B., & Larmour, P. (Eds.). (2009). *Governments, NGOs and anti-corruption. The new integrity warriors*. Routledge.

de Sousa, L., Magalhães, P. C., & Amaral, L. (2014). Sovereign debt and governance failures: Portuguese democracy and the financial crisis. *American Behavioral Scientist, 58*(12), 1517–1541.

Diamond, L. J., & Morlino, L. (2004). The quality of democracy: An overview. *Journal of Democracy, 15*(4), 20–31.

Gates, S., & Hill, J. (1995). Democratic accountability and governmental innovation in the use of nonprofit organizations. *Review of Policy Research, 14*(1–2), 137–148.

Ghosh, S. (2009). NGOs as political institutions. *Journal of Asian and African Studies, 44*(5), 475–495.

Gonçalves, G., Somerville, I., & Melo, A. D. (2018). *Organisational and strategic communication research: European perspectives*. LabCom Books.

Gotchev, A. (1998). *NGOs and promotion of democracy and civil society in east-central Europe, NATO research fellowships programme, 1996/1998*. www.nato.int/acad/fellow/96-98/gotchev.pdf

Guo, C. (2007). Government funding and community representation on nonprofit boards: The bargain we strike. *Nonprofit Quarterly, 14*(4), 70–76.

Guo, C., & Musso, J. A. (2007). Representation in nonprofit and voluntary organizations: A conceptual framework. *Nonprofit and Voluntary Sector Quarterly, 36*(2), 308–326.

Gutterman, E. (2014). The legitimacy of transnational NGOs: Lessons from the experience of transparency international in Germany and France. *Review of International Studies, 40*(2), 391–418.

Hindess, B., & Larmour, P. (2005). *Research project on transparency international and the problem of corruption, funded by the Australian Research Council (ARC)*. Ref.: ARC Discovery Grant CI DPO 344125. http://purl.org/au-research/grants/arc/DP0344125

Kim, P. S., & Moon, J. (2003). NGOs as incubator of participative democracy in South Korea: Political, voluntary, and policy participation. *International Journal of Public Administration, 26*(5), 549–567.

Kimeu, S. (2014). Corruption as a challenge to global ethics: The role of transparency international. *Journal of Global Ethics, 10*(2), 231–237.

King, D., & Griffin, M. (2019). Nonprofit as schools for democracy: The justifications for organizational democracy within nonprofit organizations. *Nonprofit and Voluntary Sector Quarterly, 48*(5), 910–920.

Kriesi, H., Grande, E., Lachat, R., Dolezal, M., Bornschier, S., & Frey, T. (2008). *West European politics in the age of globalization*. Cambridge University Press.

Lecy, J. D., Schmitz, H. P., & Swedlund, H. (2012). Non-governmental and not-for-profit organizational effectiveness: A modern synthesis. *Voluntas, 23*, 434–457.

Marwell, N., & Brown, M. (2020). Towards a governance framework for government-nonprofit relations. In W. W. Powell & P. Bromley (Eds.), *The nonprofit sector: A research handbook*. Stanford University Press.

Mosley, J. E. (2015). Nonprofit organizations' involvement in participatory processes: The need for democratic accountability. *Nonprofit Policy Forum, 7*(1), 77–83.

Najam, A. (2000). The Four-C's of Third sector-government relations: Cooperation, confrontation, complementarity, and co-optation. *Nonprofit Management and Leadership, 10*(4), 375–396.

Norris, P. (2011). *Democratic deficit: Critical citizens revisited*. Cambridge University Press.

Oliveira, E., Melo, A. D., & Gonçalves, G. (2016). *Strategic communication for nonprofit organisations. Challenges and alternative approaches*. Vernon Press.

Patterson, S. J., & Radtke, J. M. (2009). *Strategic communications for nonprofit organizations. Seven steps to creating a successful plan*. John Wiley & Sons.

Rhodes, R. A. (1997). *Understanding governance: Policy networks, governance, reflexivity and accountability*. Open University.

Roniger, L. (1994). Civil society, patronage and democracy. *International Journal of Comparative Sociology, 35*(3–4), 207–220.

Roniger, L., & Güneş-Ayata, A. (1994). *Democracy, clientelism, and civil society*. Lynne Rienner Publishers.

Rothschild, J., & Stephenson, M. (2009). The meaning of democracy in nonprofit and community organizations: Charting the currents of change. *American Behavioral Scientist, 52*(6), 800–806.

Rothschild, J., & Whitt, J. A. (1986). *The cooperative workplace: Potentials and dilemmas of organizational democracy and participation*. Cambridge University Press.

Salamon, L. M., & Geller, S. L. (2008). Nonprofit America: A force for democracy? *Communiqué* (9).

Schmitter, P. C., & Karl, T. L. (1991). What democracy is . . . and is not. *Journal of Democracy, 2*(3), 75–88.

van Boven, T. (1989). The role of non-governmental organizations in international human rights standard-setting: A prerequisite of democracy. *California Western International Law Journal, 20*, 207–227.

Van Tuijl, P. (1999). NGOs and human rights: Sources of justice and democracy. *Journal of International Affairs, 52*(2), 493–512.

Wang, H., & Rosenau, J. N. (2001). Transparency international and corruption as an issue of global governance. *Global Governance: A Review of Multilateralism and International Organizations, 7*(1), 25–49.

Weisbrod, B. A. (1986). Toward a theory of the voluntary nonprofit sector in a three-sector economy. In S. Rose-Ackerman (Ed.), *The economics of nonprofit institutions*. Oxford University Press.

2.9
COMPANIES AND HUMAN RIGHT ACTIVISTS' ENGAGEMENT

Naíde Müller

Introduction[1]

According to the United Nations (UN) SDG Progress Report 2020,[2] the COVID-19 pandemic affected the Sustainable Development Goals (SDGs) social indicators by reversing several positive trends and increasing several inequalities within and between countries. The pandemic challenge reinforced the reality that a global collaborative response from governments, the private sector, civil society, and the general public is needed to achieve the goals.

Several contextual conditions have led to the emergence of "hybrid multifunctional voluntary organizations" with an activist culture that can mobilize resources and obtain commitments (Hasenfeld & Gidron, 2005), like GAT – Portuguese Activist Group for HIV/AIDS[3] – which is the object of this study.

The engagement between private institutions and nonprofit associations to advance specific causes is well known, mainly in terms of corporate social responsibility (CSR). However, cases of corporate political advocacy (CPA), such as the support of Ben & Jerry's for the Black Lives Matter movement (Ciszek & Logan, 2018); the support of Starbucks, Google, Microsoft, and Ben & Jerry's for the legalization of same-sex marriage in the United States (Wettstein & Baur, 2016); and Gillette's videos about toxic masculinity in response to the #MeToo movement (DiRusso, 2021), are not so common.

This form of CPA or corporate activism is one new dimension of influence management, with all the ingredients to become a relevant area for demonstrating companies' CSR and reputation (Monaghan & Monaghan, 2014; Peterson & Pfitzer, 2009). These trends present an organizational reality that public relations practitioners may eventually have to deal with (Ciszek & Logan, 2018, p. 118).

Through an ethnographic approach to GAT organizational dynamics and the consultation of 12 communication and public relations experts, this research analyzes the engagement between private companies and human rights activists. It begins with a literature review that addresses activism's significance to public relations theory and practice in different organizational contexts. Next the methodology is described, followed by the findings that suggest that, beyond the strong cultural resistance that still exists about this kind of partnership in Portugal, this is a future trend that can be an opportunity for activists to advance causes within the scope of human rights and the 2030 Agenda and for companies if they know how to position wisely on these issues.

Public relations and activism in different organizational contexts

Because strategic communication is fundamental to promote social change, its applicability in an organizational context is relevant for activist movements. Strategic communication helps establish a common understanding of initiatives for social change, creating the basis for common action. Strategic communication plans and activities empower the various stakeholders in these projects with knowledge and information that can be applied to effective decision-making, responsible management, social and political mobilization, individual behavior change, and collective growth (Mozammel & Schechter, 2005, p. 1). Likewise, communication and the strategic use of a variety of media by citizens within the scope of policies and practices for development and social change not only allows the inclusion of different voices for a pluralist policy. Citizens' communicative approaches to the media contribute to social and cultural construction processes, redefining norms and power relations and allowing people to remodel the spaces in which their voices find expression (Pettit et al., 2009). Ciszek (2017) analyzed a transnational activist network for LGBT rights in 15 regions, concluding that activists are producers of strategic communication for social change and that activism and public relations are not antagonistic, but occupy a fluid space influenced by cultural and economic forces.

Various forms of activism through history have contributed to the appearance of "hybrid multifunctional voluntary organizations" (Hasenfeld & Gidron, 2005) that fought for social change, challenging dictatorships, protecting workers from exploitation, protecting the environment, promoting equality for women, opposing racism, helping vulnerable communities, and being actively involved with many other issues. Depending on their legal nature and the causes they advocate, interest groups within the third sector[4] and the organizations they establish to achieve their objectives can vary substantially, showing territories where third-sector organizations mix with social movements (Ferreira, 2004; Hasenfeld & Gidron, 2005; Martins, 2003).

Just as private organizations co-create relationships with each other and their surroundings to achieve their business goals, activists' organizations also do that to achieve their advocated social change (Taylor & Botan, 2006). Holtzhausen (2000, 2012) and Holtzhausen and Voto (2002) have claimed that although public relations can create, maintain, and reproduce powerful, dominant discourses, they can also resist and disrupt such discourses. These assumptions have been addressed by different authors of the critical school of public relations (Adi, 2020; Coombs and Holladay (2012a, 2012b), Demetrious (2006, 2013), Edwards and Hodges (2011), L'Etang (2006, 2016), and O'Brien (2018, 2020). Assuming that advocacy[5] is a central function of public relations that involves several practices, most practitioners know this function, in itself, is neither good nor bad. Instead, it is how the function is performed that makes the difference (Edgett, 2002).

In the corporate, private organizational context, while some corporations are engaging in socially responsible initiatives related to their businesses or benefiting their communities, other companies have advanced further in this area, supporting controversial causes related, or not, to their core business. Researchers Florian Wettstein and Dorothea Baur from the University of St. Gallen's Institute for Business Ethics label this activism "corporate political advocacy" (CPA). This perspective argues that businesses should publicly communicate their positions on sociopolitical issues and try to engage different public types on complex subjects (Wettstein & Baur, 2016). CPA is a public relations initiative and implies the acceptance that not all stakeholders will agree with the ideologies and values advocated by an organization (Ciszek & Logan, 2018; DiRusso, 2021).

Although it is not an easy decision for companies, CPA is emerging as a new and dynamic communication trend. It suggests that implied political values on behalf of companies are likely to precipitate divergent consumer reactions. This practice causes simultaneously "disapproval and boycotts from those that oppose the company's position, but approval and boycott from those that support the company's position" (Hydock et al., 2019, p. 76).

This type of advocacy requires that companies are not just concerned about doing no harm but speak out publicly, which can be critical to advancing human rights and the 2030 Agenda. However, a company must be careful about the choices of issues to advocate. The criteria to make this selection are (a) consistency – the issue must be consistent with the values of the company; (b) plausibility – the topic chosen must be part of a long-term commitment to specific causes or issues; and (c) authenticity – supporting a cause implies more concrete actions than words. Only within these criteria will a company's cause advocacy be credible (Wettstein & Baur, 2016, p. 211). Furthermore, an experiment by DiRusso (2021) provided several key takeaways for companies planning CSA communication, pointing to the utility of negatively toned CSA communication about highly salient social issues.

This communication landscape addresses significant change confronting public relations with corporate activism, that is, corporations taking public stances on political (Wettstein & Baur, 2016) and social (Dodd & Supa, 2014) issues.

Methodology

In this investigation, it is intended to articulate the data with the existing theories about the phenomena under observation. The study's analytical approach was based on two data collection stages and analysis – case study and expert interview. In the first moment, we resorted to an ethnographic immersion in the organizational dynamics of GAT using participant observation, interviews, informal conversations with the different members of the team, social media monitoring, and analysis of documents, compiled in a field diary (a document in which all the interactions and information are noted daily). Ethnography has been presented as a method that brings relevant developments to public relations research, namely within the scope of sociocultural traditions (Everett & Johnston, 2012; L'Etang et al., 2012; Xifra, 2012). L'Etang (2006) argued that placing research in public relations more broadly as "cultural and ideological practice involved in complex intercultural processes and away from technocratic concerns can help in developing an understanding of public relations work in international society and its relations with the world of life and the public sphere" (p. 393). Although it is not yet a frequently used method, when investigators are looking for descriptive inferences to identify the interactions between an organization's culture and its social environment, ethnography has been identified as a methodological imperative in public relations (Everett & Johnston, 2012). In public relations research, ethnography will examine how a group understands and experiences its environment and how it seeks to adapt to that environment (Sutton & Anderson, 2004; Winthrop, 1991).

In a second stage, we interviewed experts from 12 communication and public relations agencies associated with APECOM – Portuguese Association of Council Companies in Communication and Public Relations – to understand their position on the topic under study. We focused on the interviewees' designated "expert position" (Demo, 1995), and we asked all 12 experts the same question:

> Some authors talk about a new type of corporate activism that presupposes that companies take a public stand in defense of specific causes (for example, the support of Starbucks, Google, Microsoft, and Ben & Jerry's for the legalization of marriage between people of the same sex in the US in 2015). What is your perspective on associations of this type between private companies and human rights activist organizations/2030 Agenda in Portugal, mainly concerning the so-called controversial sociopolitical issues?

Through those two moments of data collection and analysis, we intended to answer the following research question: Can the public endorsement by private companies of human rights activist groups on controversial sociopolitical issues, like homophobia, racism, xenophobia, and women's rights (Guterres, 2021), be seen as a communication trend in Portugal?

Case study

GAT is a nonprofit nongovernmental organization (NGO) based in Portugal and founded in 2001. This organization works with groups of people infected by HIV or at risk (migrants, prisoners, sex workers, drug users, gay men, and others). GAT advocates for legal and political changes within the scope of human rights and the 2030 Agenda, namely the third objective of the UN SDGs: ensure healthy lives and promote well-being for all at all ages. GAT activity highlights the territories where third-sector organizations mix with social movements (Ferreira, 2004). GAT's mission is to advocate and work with other stakeholders for social changes that positively affect the health, rights, and quality of life of people living with HIV-associated diseases, especially those from the most vulnerable groups.

Data sampling and sources

Within ethnography, the amount of time the researcher should spend in the field has not been established, but some authors have defined a period from three months to two years depending on the research design (Fetterman, 1998; Hammersley & Atkinson, 2007; Johnston & Everett, 2012). This study's data were collected over three months – January to March 2021. The methods used for data collection were adapted to the organization's reality and the interviewees, considering the confinement and restrictions imposed by the COVID-19 pandemic during the observation period. GAT's teams and the interviewees worked from home, communicating through videoconferences on platforms like Zoom. GAT does not have a formal communication team. People who currently do some communication tasks are scattered throughout project coordination. In this sense, the field diary was fed through online meetings and conversations (Zoom platform) with these persons, and the monitoring of GAT actions was done via Facebook (the only social media platform where the organization is currently active) and through attending their online events, like live talks and conferences on different topics. We also analyzed GAT's 2021 activity plan and other documents. As in the study of Johnston and Everett (2012), we used a qualitative method for data collection based on "participant observation (experiencing), interviewing (enquiring) and studying materials prepared by others (examining)" (Wolcott, 1994, p. 10), paying attention to the details in the expressions of culture, framed in their context (Ybema et al., 2009).

Ethical considerations, mainly related to managing the observer–participant relationship, need to be addressed during all the ethnographic research stages (Fetterman, 1998). We addressed this issue by making the researcher role explicit through all the interactions and asking for permission to record the conversations and quote the people involved. The researcher's role and the investigation's objectives were explained in the document of informed, clarified, and free consent to participate in the study signed by the executive director of GAT.

Data analysis and reduction

Case study and expert consultation

Through ethnographic immersion and interviews, a very high volume of data was obtained. It required a careful selection process of meaning units. Converting data through description, analysis, and interpretation is not a linear process in ethnographic approaches (Wolcott, 1994). In the first stage of description, fieldwork observation data was documented in the field diary, and all recorded interviews were transcribed as they were undertaken (Baszanger & Dodier, 2004). To select the relevant information from the ethnographic approach to GAT, two main selection criteria/categories (obtained from the literature review) were used: (a) type of activism, according to the typology of activism proposed by Harrebye (2016, p. 3), and (b) position on private-sector companies' support for activist causes (Ciszek & Logan, 2018; Wettstein & Baur, 2016).

In order to analyze the responses of the communication experts Nvivo software (12) was used.[6] The data treatment started by reading, identifying, and classifying codes suggested by the data rather than collected from the literature (Lansisalmi et al., 2004). Coding was operationalized as nodes (meaning structures) and managed by computer-assisted qualitative data analysis.

Findings

Ethnographic immersion GAT: type of activism

According to the typology of activism proposed by Harrebye (2016, p. 83), GAT presents a type of "professional" activism whose "fundamental logic" is based on "lobbying," that is, on the pressure and influence of decision makers to adopt measures that benefit the communities with which they work. Their most "typical activities" are "campaigns and meetings," and their "intended objectives" are the "reform" of the system. The "types of slogan" that these activist groups use most are "we are going to commit ourselves all in writing to the real reduction of carbon emissions." The case of a similar slogan used in a campaign during the period of observation is "to end the HIV and AIDS epidemic as a public health problem in the city of Lisbon by 2030, by improving access to the various responses available" (Campaign #ZERODISCRIMINATION, Lisbon Without AIDS), in partnership with the Lisbon City Council.[7] Concerning the "dominant perception of institutional agents (police, politicians, media)," these types of activists are considered "impertinent specialists (the relationship is appreciated, but often ignored)."

Position on the support of private-sector companies for activist causes

On partnerships with the private sector to advance activist causes, GAT Executive Director Ricardo Fernandes said that

> it is a complex issue since many activism movements in Portugal (which is not the case with GAT) have strong links to leftist movements and there is an ideology related to what a company stands for – capitalism – that does not welcome sponsorships by companies and brands for activist events. In some cases in which these sponsorships occur, namely within the scope of the LGBTI+ community, there are even strong internal divisions between activists since some consider that the communication strategies oriented to the promotion of institutions, countries, people, products, or companies, invoking their sympathy for gay-friendly territories are a form of "pinkwashing" [appropriation of causes to improve public image].

Ricardo Fernandes explained that "GAT has several donors, including the pharmaceutical industry, who have a vested interest in having us testing for HIV; the more we test, the more people consume their products." Margarida Santos, one of the coordinators of the "MORE PARTICIPATION, better health"[8] project (in partnership with GAT), with whom we had an informal conversation via Zoom, explained that "GAT is certainly critical of the pharmaceutical industry, but it knows that it depends partly on its funding." She clarified that there must be a shared interest and responsibility between the government and private entities in funding activism.

In the most relevant communication moments, companies from the pharmaceutical industry with which GAT collaborates provide their communication and public relations agencies' services. Ricardo Fernandes explained that

> the main difficulty in these partnerships with the private sector is that it is not systematic, there is no continuity. It is when the organization has availability, but this does not always coincide with our communication needs. I think that if an organization wants to move forward, it must have a mixed regime. We have to use what is in the community, but we need to find internal resources to do things for us.

Expert consultation

Regarding the interviews with communication experts from APECOM-associated agencies, Figure 2.9.1 shows the connections between respondents and the response categories. The data obtained through these interviews allowed the creation of the following categories (by order of highest frequency with which they were mentioned):

- **Companies and Brands Public Positioning**. All experts agreed that this kind of public positioning is not "innocent." Despite the differences of views on whether they advised their clients or not to engage in this type of more ideological involvement, the majority of the participants agreed that if it happens, "this positioning must already be part of an organization's DNA" and "what is essential is that it is something genuine, transparent; otherwise, it is a very dangerous path."
- **Future Trends**. Nine of the 12 experts believed that the organizations' purposes are being redefined and the involvement of companies in social issues, considered controversial, has been growing globally. They agreed that this is a communication trend that will also reach Portugal, although later than in other cultures.
- **Business Interest and Objectives**. Seven of the consulted experts agreed that this type of positioning is a marketing and communication strategy. These companies said that they agree with specific causes because most people are also in agreement, which serves their business interests. One of the respondents said that if activist groups "explain and show Portuguese companies that their market segment, their audience has a high percentage of people who belong to or defend certain causes, they may be interested in these causes and even finance them."
- **Culture**. Six experts reported that the Portuguese business culture is not yet prepared for this type of positioning. One respondent highlighted that "I think that in Portugal we do not have the business maturity for this path. Our leadership and CEOs do not get involved at this level. We do not have that kind of strength, neither in large companies nor in smaller ones." Another explained that "Portuguese companies do not want to get involved in controversies . . . there is a big difference in how we walk the talk here compared with Anglo Saxon companies."
- **Causes**. Six experts agreed that this kind of endorsement in Portugal depends on the causes. Within the scope of their social responsibility actions, Portuguese companies are more oriented toward solidarity on universally accepted values such as charity.
- **Kind of Activism**. The experts' responses also showed that very aggressive and unreasonable communication styles do not work well in the context of business partnerships. One of the interviewees highlighted that "activists often have to use the classic tools of capitalism to achieve their goals."

Naíde Müller

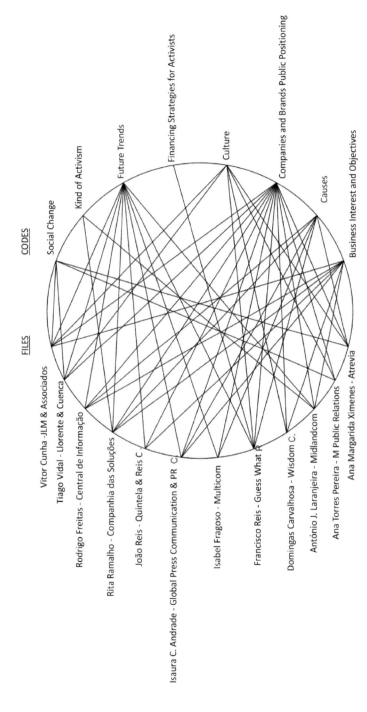

Figure 2.9.1 Connections between respondents and response categories. Created by the author at NVivo Software.

- **Social Change**. On current social changes, it was mentioned that "societies are changing, young people ask for another type of communication and this activist communication, more interventional, reaches both young people and older people."
- **Financing Strategies for Activists**. One of the interviewees analyzed this issue from an interesting perspective for activists: "I think it is a smart choice and one that should be sought. For all of what we are talking about, it does take some money, even if some work can be offered, some things will always need money and companies have money, and therefore, it is a source that must be explored."

Discussion and conclusion

This study analyzed private companies and human rights activists' engagement through two distinct but related organizational perspectives. It observed the relevance of the public relations function within the scope of activities by "hybrid multifunctional voluntary organizations" such as GAT (Hasenfeld & Gidron, 2005). Through the ethnographic approach, it was possible to observe how activism and social movements can be considered a form of public relations work concerned with advocacy, promotion, events, public interest, lobbying, and public affairs, communicating with a wide range of audiences, clearly oriented toward social change and for the realization of idealized objectives. In this way, public relations can be understood as an intervention directed toward collective action (L'Etang, 2016).

The observation also allowed us to perceive the distrust that some activist groups in Portugal have concerning companies due to political ideologies. Nevertheless, one of the main challenges activist groups face is the scarce financial resources available. As the communication experts mentioned, structured partnerships with the private sector to advance causes can be a strategic option for these organizations within the framework of human rights and the 2030 Agenda. GAT presents a pragmatic view of its organizational objectives, characteristic of strategic planning in public relations, focusing more on the win–win advantages that these partnerships can bring to the causes and less on ideological divisions that may not have concrete consequences for their mission. In this case, the pharmaceutical companies that support GAT do not practice corporate political advocacy. It is recognized that pharmaceutical companies' support for associations such as GAT is fundamentally related to their core business and commercial objectives. This is, the companies do not publicly take a stand on the defense of human rights causes, nor do they get engaged in GAT's advocacy for breaking stereotypes that affect people infected by HIV or at risk (migrants, prisoners, sex workers, drug users, gay men, and others). They are limited to classic forms of financial support like donors or sponsorship. Nonetheless, they are important partners in terms of financing GAT's activity. Furthermore, that support does not prevent GAT from having a critical social voice, if necessary, about the pharmaceutical industry.

However, strategic partnerships between human rights activists and companies are not common in Portugal. On the one hand, this is due to the suspicions that exist from several activist groups toward companies based on political and cultural oppositional traditions. On the other hand, Portuguese culture in general, and business culture in particular and its leaders, do not have the maturity for this positioning in progressive causes such as gay marriage. In answer to this study's research question, the public endorsement by private companies for human rights activist groups on controversial sociopolitical issues is not currently a practice that is followed in Portugal. The communication experts consulted expressed doubts about the specific contexts in which this may occur. However, they also agreed that this scenario is changing. Portuguese companies will have to adapt to these new trends and choose wisely what causes and groups to support. This can present an opportunity for activists in the human rights scope and the 2030 Agenda.

Lidl supermarket, for example, recently launched a campaign that quickly went viral on social media.[9] To present its toy suggestions for the Portuguese Christmas 2020 campaign, the company decided to break gender stereotypes, reversing the roles generally associated with girls and boys (Imagens de Marca, 2020). Several commentators applauded this initiative and underlined the importance of steps like this in breaking stereotypes. Portuguese Member of European Parliament Maria Manuel Leitão Marques congratulated the company's decision on Twitter, stressing that any help to dismantle gender stereotypes, as "one of the main barriers to equal opportunities," is "welcome."

A recent study from Parcha and Kingsley (2020) revealed that a "corporate statement on a controversial social issue is effective in changing an individual's attitude toward the issue depending on how much the issue is relevant to the individual's goals and/or if the corporate statement is supported by other corporations" (p. 350). Apparently "corporations are making conscious efforts to improve their social responsibility by taking stands on controversial social issues," but "corporate social irresponsibility is still occurring" (Parcha & Kingsley, 2020, p. 377). Although human rights defenders are key civil society actors and protecting them should be considered a "pre-competitive" issue in everybody's interest to find solutions, "company engagement to respect and support human rights defenders is still far too rare" (UN Working Group on Business and Human Rights, 2017, p. 3–5[10]).

Regarding future research concerns, there are important questions about the balances and imbalances resulting from this attribution and/or appropriation of, even more, powers of social intervention to corporations. In the face of growing social polarization, the tendency is for companies to adopt more explicit positions concerning specific political or ideological issues. In the context of the struggle for human rights and the 2030 Agenda, these circumstances can represent an opportunity for strategic communication and public relations.

Notes

1. This research was supported by the Portuguese national funding agency for science, research and technology, Foundation for Science and Technology (FCT) Grant Nr. SFRH/BD/144467/2019.
2. UN SDG Progress Report, 2020. https://unstats.un.org/sdgs/report/2020/The-Sustainable-Development-Goals-Report-2020.pdf
3. GAT. Grupo de Ativistas em Tratamentos. www.gatportugal.org
4. The "third sector" is a field of study that is difficult to define. The term refers to very different types of organizations that are designated as nonprofit, voluntary, intermediary, nongovernmental (NGOs), social economy, civil society, etc., and that do not fall under the first sector (public/state) or in the second sector (private/market) (Corry, 2010: 11–20; Ferreira, 2004).
5. Advocacy is defined as "the act of publicly representing an individual, organization, or idea with the objective of persuading targeted audiences to look favorably on – or accept the point of view of – the individual, the organization, or the idea" (Edgett, 2002, p. 1).
6. QSR International. (1999). NVivo Qualitative Data Analysis Software. www.qsrinternational.com/nvivo-qualitative-data-analysis-software/home
7. Campaign #ZERODISCRIMINATION. www.lisboa.pt/lisboasemsida
8. www.participacaosaude.com
9. Imagens de Marca, 2020. Lidl quebra estereótipos de género em campanha viral, November 24, 2020, at www.imagensdemarca.pt/artigo/lidl-quebra-estereotipos-de-genero-em-campanha-viral
10. UN Working Group on Business and Human Rights, 2017. "Human rights defenders and civic space – the business & human rights dimension", Informal summary of workshop convened by the UN Working Group on Business and Human Rights (Geneva, 11 May 2017), at www.ohchr.org/Documents/Issues/Business/Session18/WorkshopSummaryConsultationHRDefenders.pdf

References

Adi, A. (2020). *Protest public relations – Communicating dissent and activism* (1st ed.). Routledge.
Baszanger, I., & Dodier, N. (2004). Ethnography: Relating the part to the whole. In D. Silverman (Ed.), *Qualitative research: Theory, method and practice* (2nd ed.). Sage Publications.

Ciszek, E. L. (2017). Activist strategic communication for social change: A transnational case study of lesbian, gay, bisexual, and transgender activism. *Journal of Communication, 67*(5), 702–718. https://doi.org/10.1111/jcom.12319

Ciszek, E. L., & Logan, N. (2018). Challenging the dialogic promise: How Ben & Jerry's support for Black Lives Matter fosters dissensus on social media. *Journal of Public Relations Research, 30*(3), 115–127. doi:10.1080/1062726X.2018.1498342

Coombs, T. W., & Holladay, S. J. (2012a). Fringe public relations: How activism moves critical PR toward the mainstream. *Public Relations Review, 38*(5), 880–887, https://doi.org/10.1016/j.pubrev.2012.02.008

Coombs, T. W., & Holladay, S. J. (2012b). Privileging an activist vs. A corporate view of public relations history in the US. *Public Relations Review, 38*, 347–353, https://doi.org/10.1016/j.pubrev.2011.11.010

Corry, O. (2010). Defining and theorizing the third sector. In R. Taylor (Ed.). *Third sector research* (pp. 11–20). Springer.

Demetrious, K. (2006). Active voices. In J. L'Etang & M. Pieczka (Eds.), *Public relations: Critical debates and contemporary practice* (pp. 93–107). Lawrence Erlbaum Associates.

Demetrious, K. (2013). *Public relations, activism, and social change: Speaking up*. Routledge

Demo, P. (1995). *Metodologia científica em ciências sociais*. Atlas.

DiRusso, C. (2021). *Strategies for sharing corporate social advocacy messages on social media*. The Institute for Public Relations (IPR). https://instituteforpr.org/strategies-for-sharing-corporate-social-advocacy-messages-on-social-media

Dodd, M. D., & Supa, D. W. (2014). Conceptualizing and measuring "corporate social advocacy" communication: Examining the impact on corporate financial performance. *Public Relations Journal, 8*(3), 2–23. https://prjournal.instituteforpr.org/wp-content/uploads/2014DoddSupa.pdf

Edgett, R. (2002). Toward an ethical framework for advocacy in public relations. *Journal of Public Relations Research, 14*(1), 1–26. doi:10.1207/S1532754XJPRR1401_1

Edwards, L., & Hodges, C. E. M. (2011). *Public relations, society & culture: Theoretical and empirical explorations*. Routledge.

Everett, J. L., & Johnston, K. A. (2012). Toward an ethnographic imperative in public relations research. *Public Relations Review, 38*(4), 522–528. https://doi.org/10.1016/j.pubrev.2012.05.006

Ferreira, S. (2004). *O papel de movimento social das organizações do terceiro sector em Portugal*. Atas dos ateliers do V° Congresso Português de Sociologia, Sociedades Contemporâneas: Reflexividade e Acão Atelier: Classes, Movimentos e Lutas Sociais. https://estudogeral.sib.uc.pt/handle/10316/44071

Fetterman, D. M. (1998). *Ethnography step by step*. Sage.

Guterres, A. (2021). *Secretary-general's message to the opening of the 46th regular session of the human rights council*. United Nations. www.un.org/sg/en/content/sg/statement/2021-02-22/secretary-generals-message-the-opening-of-the-46th-regular-session-of-the-human-rights-council-delivered-scroll-down-for-all-english-and-french

Hammersley, M., & Atkinson, P. (2007). *Ethnography: Principles in practice* (3rd ed.). Routledge.

Harrebye, S. F. (2016). *Social change and creative activism in the 21st century: The mirror effect*. Palgrave Macmillan.

Hasenfeld, Y., & Gidron, B. (2005). Understanding multi-purpose hybrid voluntary organizations: The contributions of theories on civil society, social movements and nonprofit organizations, *Journal of Civil Society, 1*(2), 97–112. doi:10.1080/17448680500337350

Holtzhausen, D. R. (2012). *Public relations as activism*. Routledge.

Holtzhausen, D. R. (2000). Postmodern values in public relations. *Journal of Public Relations Research, 12*(1), 93–114. https://doi.org/10.1207/S1532754XJPRR1201_6

Holtzhausen, D. R., & Voto, R. (2002). Resistance from the margins: The postmodern public relations practitioner as organizational activist. *Journal of Public Relations Research, 14*(1), 57–84. https://doi.org/10.1207/S1532754XJPRR1401_3

Hydock, C., Paharia, N., & Weber, T. J. (2019). The consumer response to corporate political advocacy: A review and future directions. *Customer Needs and Solutions, 6*(3–4), 76–83. doi:10.1007/s40547-019-00098-x

Imagens de Marca. (2020). *Lidl quebra estereótipos de género em campanha viral*. Retrieved from www.imagensdemarca.pt/artigo/lidl-quebra-estereotipos-de-genero-em-campanha-viral

Johnston, K. A., & Everett, J. L. (2012). Employee perceptions of reputation: An ethnographic study. *Public Relations Review, 38*(4), 541–554. https://doi.org/10.1016/j.pubrev.2012.05.007

L'Etang, J. (2006). Public relations and propaganda: Conceptual issues, methodological problems, and public relations discourse. In J. L'Etang & M. Piecska (Eds.), *Public relations: Critical debates and contemporary practice* (pp. 23–40). Lawrence Erlbaum.

L'Etang, J. (2016). History as a source of critique. In J. L'Etang, D. McKie, N. Snow, & J. Xifra (Eds.), *The Routledge handbook of critical public relations*. Routledge.

L'Etang, J., Hodges, E. M., & Pieczka, M. (2012). Cultures and places: Ethnography in public relations spaces – Editorial. *Public Relations Review, 38*(4), 519–521. http://dx.doi.org/10.1016/j.pubrev.2012.05.013

Lansisalmi, H., Peiro, J., & Kivimake, M. (2004). Grounded theory in organizational research. In C. Cassell & G. Symon (Eds.), *Essential guide to qualitative methods in organizational research*. Sage.

Martins, S. da Cruz. (2003). Novos associativismos e tematizações na sociedade portuguesa. *Sociologia, Problemas e Práticas, 43,* 103–132. www.scielo.mec.pt/scielo.php?script=sci_arttext&pid=S0873-65292003000300009&lng=en&tlng=

Monaghan, P., & Monaghan, P. (2014). *Lobbying for good: How business advocacy can accelerate the delivery of a sustainable economy*. Greenleaf Publishing – Routledge.

Mozammel, M., & Schechter, G. (2005). *Strategic communication for community-driven development*. World Bank.

O'Brien, M. (2018). Nonprofit issues management: A new approach to resist the label of "risk." In N. Garsten & I. Bruce (Eds.), *Communicating causes: Strategic public relations for the non-profit sector* (pp. 41–54). Routledge.

O'Brien, M. (2020). Activists as pioneers in PR: Historical frameworks and the suffragette movement. In A. Adi (Ed.), *Protest public relations – Communicating dissent and activism* (1st ed.). Routledge.

Parcha, J. M., & Kingsley Westerman, C. Y. (2020). How corporate social advocacy affects attitude change toward controversial social issues. *Management Communication Quarterly, 34*(3), 350–383. https://doi.org/10.1177/0893318920912196

Peterson, K., & Pfitzer, M. (2009, Winter). Lobbying for good. *Stanford Social Innovation Review*.

Pettit, J., Salazar, J. F., & Dagron, A. G. (2009). Citizens' media and communication. *Development in Practice, 19*(4 & 5), 443–452.

Sutton, M. Q., & Anderson, E. (2004). *Introduction to cultural ecology*. Altamira Press.

Taylor, M., & Botan, C. H. (2006). *Global public relations: Application of a cocreational approach*. 9th International Public Relations Research Conference, "Changing Roles and Functions in Public Relations," South Miami, Florida, 9–12 March 2006. Institute for Public Relations. http://195.130.87.21:8080/dspace/bitstream/123456789/742/1/Global%20Public%20Relations-Application%20of%20a%20Cocreational%20Approach.pdf

UN Working Group on Business and Human Rights. (2017). *Workshop Summary Consultation*. Retrieved from www.ohchr.org/Documents/Issues/Business/Session18/WorkshopSummaryConsultationHRDefenders.pdf

Wettstein, F., & Baur, D. (2016). Why should we care about marriage equality? Political advocacy as a part of corporate responsibility. *Journal of Business Ethics, 138*(2), 199–213. https://doi.org/10.1007/s10551-015-2631-3

Winthrop, R. H. (1991). *Dictionary of concepts in cultural anthropology*. Greenwood Press.

Wolcott, H. F. (1994). *Transforming qualitative data: Description, analysis, and interpretation*. Sage.

Xifra, J. (2012). Public relations anthropologies: French theory, anthropology of morality and ethnographic practices. *Public Relations Review, 38*(4). https://doi.org/10.1016/j.pubrev.2012.05.003

Ybema, S., Yanow, D., Wels, H., & Kamsteeg, F. (Eds.). (2009). *Organizational ethnography*. Sage.

PART III

Strategic communication, strategies and discourses

The third part of the Handbook focuses on NPOs' strategic communication, strategies and discourses. The key principle of strategic communication is the achievement of organizational goals, and so several chapters use different NPO environments to propose specific theories and approaches, such as the instigatory theory of NGO communication, the NPO branding and strategic management theory or the social venture narrative communication. Furthermore, particular subjects are discussed, as the use of communication strategies that involve innovative tools like memes or storytelling; open justice discourses and PR; the proposal of positive communication approach within nonprofit and lobbying strategies. Regarding the environmental issue, there are also two contributions that concentrate into the discursive level, one from a semiotics and the other from a socio constructivist discursive approach.

Evandro Oliveira from the Autonomous University of Barcelona, Spain; and LabCom, Portugal, epitomizes in the instigatory theory of NGO communication (ITNC) (Chapter 3.1). After framing the presence of NGOs in the global public sphere and discussing an integrated social sciences NGO definition, the chapter outlines the main components of the theory. The ITNC is based on the theorization process of collecting the so-called *ontological principles* as an outcome of the indagations about the distinctive socio-communicative features of those organizations. Following a historical-anthro pological, communicational, sociological, economical and managerial perspectives, the ITNC proposes both an applied communication management conceptual model and a cybernetic operational model. It addresses not only a possibility of understanding and framing communication, but also gives insights on how to manage the strategic communication of those civil society organizations.

From a strategic marketing perspective, Gordon Liu from the Open University Business School, UK, looks at Internal Branding distinctive dynamics in the case of nonprofit organizations (Chapter 3.2). This chapter describes a conceptual map that identifies the key internal branding elements that emerged: organizational brand-building behaviors, internalization, employee brand-building behaviors, internalization facilitators, environmental/contextual conditions and consequences. Among them, the former four elements reflect the NPO's internal branding processes. The synthesis of this diverse research provides a deeper insight into the proposed understanding of internal branding in the nonprofit sector.

Chapter 3.3 discusses narratives and emotion in social entrepreneurship communication. Philip Roundy from the University of Tennessee, USA, provides a state-of-the-literature review that synthesizes research on social entrepreneurship communication with an emphasis on how entrepreneurs create social venture narratives to communicate with their stakeholders. The main insights from the literature are organized to create multi-stage and multi-level frameworks that explain how the content of social venture narratives influences communication practices and outcomes. The frameworks can help social entrepreneurs to develop persuasive narratives and assist scholars in identifying research opportunities within social entrepreneurship communication.

Ioli Campos from the Nova University of Lisbon introduces storytelling and memes within advocacy communication (Chapter 3.4). The chapter researches common affordances and differences between those two formats and it argues that small CSOs with limited resources may take advantage of these new trends by including both formats in transmedia or cross-media communication strategies. The chapter is based on a critical literature review and guided by two consulting assignments for CSOs as the empirical data setting: a workshop on the use of storytelling by small CSOs and an evaluation of a transnational social media campaign that used memes.

Ana Almansa-Martínez and Antonio Castillo-Esparcia from the University of Malaga, Spain, analyse NGOs and their lobbying strategies (Chapter 3.5). After discussing the concepts of participation and state, arguing that one main social and political function is to translate demads into the political system, the chapter describes social engagement with a direct action and an indirect action components. Moreover, the discussion of strategic planning and strategic communication in nonprofit, to introduce the lobbying activities within the European Union as an example. The analyse of the registered NGOs reveals that they are the main interest group, ahead of business and professional advocacy groups. Likewise, the centres in which they act indicate a preponderance of parliamentarians over civil servants; the development of actions in social networks; and the defense of issues related to the environment, education and training, research and innovation.

Jane Johnston from the University of Queensland introduces the subject of open justice and court communication (Chapter 3.6). This chapter explores the theory and practice of open justice in a range of countries, finding support for the principle in legislation and case law, from local to national Supreme Courts, and from the United Nations to the European Union. It examines the role played by public relations in facilitating open justice. In recent decades, this public relations role has brought new agency to the practice of open justice and has been instrumental in transitioning court communication into the 21st century. The chapter explores how the culture, traditions and history of courts make this field of nonprofit government communication and public relations quite unique in both theoretical and practical ways.

A specific version of semiotics and its application to the analysis of environmental communication campaigns is proposed by Andrea Catellani from the UCLouvain, Belgium (Chapter 3.7). This chapter introduces theoretical elements of a particular school of semiotics related to the contribution of Algirdas Greimas. After, it developed examples, focusing on the hybridization of semiotics with other approaches, such as the contribution of Michel Foucault and rhetorical analysis. It introduces a method of analyzing multimodal communication materials that combine text, images, and other forms of signs from a semiotic point of view. Along the chapter, a recent campaign by Greenpeace France against a company is put into these lenses of analysis.

Franzisca Weder from the University of Queensland and Denise Voci from the University of Klagenfurt, Austria, propose a look into eco-art as a discourse driver (Chapter 3.8). In this chapter, social movements, participatory community projects, interventions and art are debated as "intermediary" type of organization, with their potential to thematize, problematize and therefore "diffuse" and "normalize" new norms like sustainability in a different way. With a case study of an eco-art-intervention in Central Europe, supported by interviews with key stakeholders, it explores how much nonprofit-communication's unique character lays in *problematization* and creating resonance for a new narrative of the future, like the one of sustainability.

The proposal of positive communication as a strategic asset for nonprofit organization is bought by José Antonio Muñiz Velázquez and AlejandroTapia Frade and closes the third part of the handbook

(Chapter 3.9). As a framework for a desirable corporate behavior, it suggests the development of a simplified, four-step system of positive communication management, drawing inspiration from Peterson and Seligman's model of 24-character strengths and considering Grunig & Hunt's symmetrical Public Relations model. It argues alongside that communication can be positive in a double sense. First, because of its ultimate purpose, namely, to help the non-profit organization in bettering the world; and second, because it would intend to nurture certain character strengths of publics in the short and medium term.

3.1
A CONCEPTUAL APPROACH FOR STRATEGIC COMMUNICATION
The ITNC

Evandro Oliveira

Introduction[1]

During the last few years, new disruptive organization forms have entered the global public sphere to address eminent issues in communicative processes. The so-called hashtags movements, like #FFF – Fridays for Future or #MeToo, set some new dynamics that add to the portfolio of civil society collective action and which can still be framed within strategic communication (Oliveira, Ruiz-Mora & Zeler, 2021; Rodriguez-Amat et al., 2021). Despite that, other organizational forms, like nongovernmental organizations (NGOs), pursue and have an active role in sociocommunicative political processes for similar subjects. For example, despite the mediatic relevance of #FFF and the online discussion it gave rise to, the number of NGOs present in the International Climate Negotiations of the United Nations Framework Convention on Climate Change (UNFCCC) as observers is constantly rising. If in 1995, there were 163 admitted NGOs, in 2021 there were 2,902 NGOs participating in COP 26 in Dublin.[2] Despite the mediatic visibility of the new actors, NGOs are still increasing their participation in activity and number.

In a mass-mediated and digital society, those organizations developed a constant presence in the public sphere towards defending the *common good* and special perspectives, such as human rights issues (Amnesty International) or environmental issues (Greenpeace or 350.org). Civil society organizations' communication challenges reveal a complex agglomerate of questions from both conceptual understandings and the strategic and operational communication management. Some of them remain more challenging than ever for institutionalized NGOs, especially due to recent changes in civil society, most notably, complementary collective action aggregational forms, like the aforementioned hashtags movements and the digital transformation of society. The challenges can be grouped into four themes: (i) the usual split between media relations or communication and fundraising; (ii) not focusing on volunteer communication and on other publics that formed the organization; (iii) the gap between the need to obtain media attention or presence and also discursively addressing the issues; and (iv) understanding dynamics in communication processes from a holistic perspective.

Although most of the theory of communication management and strategic communication disciplines has been empirically tested and has developed with a focus on for-profit organizations while trying to consider nonprofit organizations as well, it cannot be said that research has been done on communications management within NGOs from a holistic perspective (Liu, 2012). Even with the professionalization of NGOs (Clarke, 1998, p. 36) and the spread of "modern managerial practices" as a consequence of globalization (Roberts et al., 2005, p. 1845), especially since the 1980s (Martens, 2002, p. 271) and two academic journals on the management of NGOs, communication in NGOs had only been researched at an operational, nonconceptual level until the publication of the instigatory theory of NGO communication (ITNC) (Oliveira, 2019).

Nevertheless, Matthew Koschmann had already addressed the need for the development of a communicative theory in the nonprofit context (2012), pointing out three tenets: "(a) lived experiences, (b) language and discourse, and (c) communicative constitution" (Koschmann, 2012, p. 141). In 2020, the same author, together with Matthew Sanders, proposed a communicative perspective that in some ways was in line with the ITNC proposals on the communicative aspect. He underlined that "the nonprofit is *fundamentally communicative*, and therefore we should seek to understand the nonprofit 'communicationally,' from a perspective that is distinctly 'communicational'" (Koschmann & Sandres, 2020, p. 2). Even though the ITNC is going beyond the communicational aspect, including the communication management perspective as well as the social and political process, along with an alternative economic frame that set the relational approach to the question of fundraising, it should be noted that the ITNC has been proposed for NGOs specifically and not for all nonprofits, although sometimes both terms are used for the same kind of organizations (Priller & Zimmer, 2001) or used even in the United States as a synonym (Lang, 2014, p. 11). However, "there is little agreement as to what exactly an NGO is", says Thomas Davies in the *Routledge Handbook of NGOs and International Relations* (2021, introduction). Therefore, along the theorization process of the ITNC, an integrated NGO definition within the social sciences context is hereby proposed.

Despite Martens' aim of an inclusive, comprehensive sociological, and juridical definition (Martens, 2002), it is argued that it lacks three aspects with sociopolitical and communicative nuances. The first has to do with the use of the expression "common goals" as public goods. The civic relations component, which is regarded as a distinctive element of what is considered in this chapter to be the social origins – or ontology – of NGOs, is not fully reflected (Oliveira, 2019). The use of the expression *common good* or *civic relations* could introduce the civic society and public sphere dimensions of the term not only in an international studies and political science perspective, as considered by Lang (2014, p. 11), but also in the previously mentioned understanding of a communication sciences approach to both concepts.

Reflections by Iberian and Latin American scholars (Alvarez, 1999; Alvim & Teodósio, 2004; Aristizábal et al., 1997; Landim, 2002; Menescal, 1996) and Herbert de Souza indicate the direction of a social sciences approach. De Souza makes a clear distinction of NGOs due to their "positive" political vocation, the aim of developing a democratic society, and their focus on the values of democracy – liberty, equality, diversity, participation, and solidarity (Souza, 1992). This approach reveals what is considered to be the second shortcoming in the definition: the development of the democratic society and corresponding values. Lastly, there is the distinction between an association and an NGO in the sense that the former pursues the interests of its members and the latter the interests of nonmembers (Heins, 2002, p. 46).

NGOs can be considered "one specific possible form of collective action and human community" from an anthropological perspective (Fisher, 1997, p. 459). This definition also matches the same expression in the context of civil society and the function of NGOs as communities of interpretation (Berger & Luckmann, 1995), as well as the role attributed to them as civil society actors that "distill and transmit (. . .) [private sphere] reactions in amplified form" (Habermas, 2001, p. 366). That exercise, which not only includes bottom-up inputs but also top-down approaches, includes intermediaries between individuals and political decision-makers (Bastgen, 2016, pp. 48–50). The intermediaries' system of special interest transmission from a political communication perspective has also been proposed with a traditional and mediatized model. In that model, associations and social movements are described as mediators between political decision-makers and citizens (Jarren & Donges, 2011).

An integrated social sciences definition aiming at contributing to the definitional imperatives of the term NGO has been proposed as follows:

> Non-governmental organizations are formal, independent, societal, voluntary and civic groups of people that pursue the common good for the interests of non-members. NGOs are driven by an interpretation dynamic as an intermediary actor of civil society. They aim to develop a democratic society by performing civic relations, as well as maintaining the values of democracy: liberty, equality, diversity, participation and solidarity.
>
> (Oliveira, 2019, p. 37)

The instigatory theory of NGO communication

The ITNC is based on the theorization process of collecting the so-called *ontological principles* (OPs) (Table 3.1.1) as an outcome of the indagations about the distinctive sociocommunicative features of

Table 3.1.1 Ontological principles of the ITNC

1.	Civic relations are a social communicative function of an agent that directly or indirectly performs the civic exercise of pursuing and seeking the common good.
2.	Nongovernmental organizations (NGOs) are formal, independent, societal, voluntary and civic groups of people that pursue the common good for the interests of nonmembers.
3.	NGOs are driven by an interpretation dynamic as an intermediary actor of civil society. They aim to develop a democratic society by performing civic relations, as well as maintaining the values of democracy: liberty, equality, diversity, participation and solidarity.
4.	NGO strategic communication is the practice of symbolic social action (communication) to reach set goals, create the organization, perform civic relations and fulfil its mission.
5.	NGOs are booming agents focusing on reflexive self-identity and overcoming the sense of fragmentation and dispersal.
6.	NGOs have a link with coordinated engagement on a global level. NGOs drive the post-scarcity system.
7.	NGOs are collective actors, and when individual actors reproduce the structure, they are at the same time communities of interpretation.
8.	NGOs are communities of social integration and perform reflexive self-regulation of the system.
9.	NGOs are innate system integrators and constitute entities of social change – they are the natives of social change. They are the being, the doing and the acting.
10.	NGOs can be framed within the concepts of substantivism and within an actor analysis of NGOs as collectivities and individuals acting in the name of an organization, falling into one of three categories: market, redistribution and reciprocity.
11.	NGOs can be framed within market, nonmarket and nonmonetary economies and act in the interplay of that triad.
12.	NGOs are economic collectives contributing to the prevention of a market society, meaning they keep alive the idea that the nature of the earth is not produced by mankind, as labor cannot be stored or detached from life, and that money is a creation of banking and state finance and is fictitious.
13.	Donating, volunteering, participation, involvement in political questions and advocacy are key dimensions of prosocial behavior by individuals.
14.	Division between the act of donating once and donations that are given under relational premises demand a breakdown of the stakeholders' monetary donors.
15.	The distinction between a supporter or volunteer who only donates time, support and money and a person who only makes the transaction in terms of the value they receive in return calls for a division of the group of stakeholders that are donors in a broad sense into different subgroups.
16.	Donations are social facts moved by conviction, such as beliefs, values and attitudes that encourage altruism, and by community, such as social pressure and solicitations for contributions.

Source: Oliveira, 2017

those organizations. A social constructivist approach is followed by aiming at the identification of anthropological, economic and sociopolitical elements based on an anti-positivist, also called interpretive, tradition. Following historical-anthropological, communicational, sociological, economical and managerial perspectives, the ITNC proposes an applied communication management conceptual model and a cybernetic operational model for understanding and managing communication at NGOs. Those models were tested using a mixed-method research design, composed of a worldwide quantitative study on international human rights NGOs and qualitative elite interviews (Oliveira, 2017).

It is named instigatory theory because the common thread identified in the OPs is the sense of instigation in the private and moving to the public in an intermediary role. Moreover, as an instigator, NGO communication perpetrates and triggers social change. This communication is wider than the organization itself and driven by the cells that form the organization – citizens. They are focused on enactment and stimulate the process of improving social life within democratic settings, driven by the urge to find solutions for the communicative process and action. Communication, meant in the postmodern sense, is integrated into an "organic concept within the bounds of strategic communication" (Smith, 2013a, p. 77). Since a postmodern vision of communication and worldview guides the approach to communication, with concepts like co-creation of meaning, flexibility of interpretation and spontaneity, the theoretical foundations here, guided by a functional management perspective, might present a contradiction at first sight. Still, empirical research shows that both principles are at work (Smith, 2013a). Communication professionals also serve as activists, and this fits with Giddens's theoretical concept of duality of (communicative) action and structure (Smith, 2013a; Giddens, 1984).

Logics and management

Focusing on communication in NGOs, on one side, there should be introduced the concept of management logic, driven from the concept of dominant logic by Prahalad and Bettis (1986), framed in Weick's sense-making processes as (i) identity construction, (ii) retrospective, (iii) enactive of sensible environments, (iv) social, (v) driven by plausibility, (vi) focused on and by extracted cues and (vii) ongoing (1995, p. 17, 18). This logic is the worldview that is introduced in the conceptual model. On the other side, NGOs have varying administrative forms of governance and management, but often have a professionalized structure and a volunteer governance or surveillance structure. Oliveira (2019) called this the *NGO dual management dynamic*, due to the fact that both also have an ongoing process with donors, members and supporters (as illustrated in Figure 3.1.1). It is therefore advanced that there are two dominant coalitions in a constant process of sense-making and negotiation between themselves, but also with the other stakeholders.

Perspectives of communication

Some main ideas outlining the ITNC from a communicative perspective are worth discussing. The first is to see organizing as communication, as Karl Weick defines it, "the communication activity is the organization" (Weick, 1995, p. 75); the second is understanding organizational communication as a distinctive proposal, with the absolute center of the study being concerned with the organization as a communicative system, in a coherent community of interest and shared understanding before being framed within a management proposal perspective (Taylor, 1993). At the center of the communication management component is a partially normative conceptual model. The model comprises five levels: communication perspectives, a conceptual division of communication areas, stakeholders/publics and the identification of organizational goals and specific/operational communication goals. Figure 3.1.2 gives an overview.[3]

A conceptual approach for strategic communication

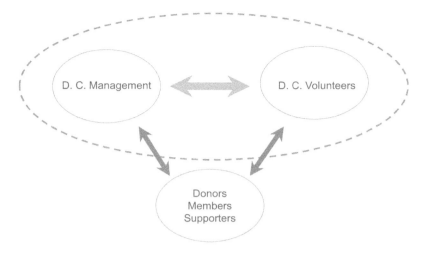

Figure 3.1.1 NGO dual management dynamic.

Source: Oliveira, 2017.

Note: D.C. stands for dominant coalition, in this case referring to a formal or informal structure. The management logic is defined in a governance sense by both coalitions, in a constant exchange with organizational shareholders – the donors, members and supporters.

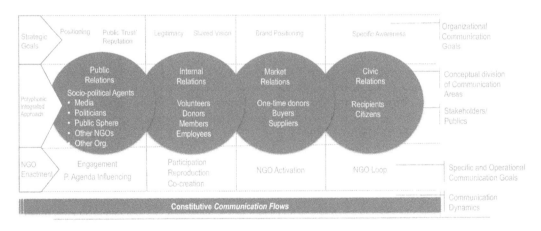

Figure 3.1.2 Conceptual model of the instigatory theory of NGO communication (ITNC).

Source: Oliveira, 2017.

More than communication, it is argued that the organization builds, maintains and develops relations through communication. Let us recall that the features of the public relations and communication management definition from a European approach are (i) managerial, (ii) operational, (iii) reflective and (iv) educational (Ruler & Verčič, 2012). The first one is framed within the management of relationships, the second as the preparation of communication and supporting members to formulate communication, the third is in the sense of environmental scanning and input and the last is the role of increasing its members' communication competence. As illustrated in the model, it is suggested dividing this into public relations, internal relations, market relations and civic relations. These areas are to be seen only as a simplification and are not mutually exclusive.

By public relations it is meant the relationships with the political and social spheres. The strategic goals are reputation and trust, as well as the positioning of the organization. They generate sociopolitical potential and the primary "license to operate".

Trust as an organizational goal includes two dimensions: one is trust as "the willingness of a party to be subject to the actions of another party based on the expectation that the other will perform a particular action important to the trustor, irrespective of the ability to monitor or control that other party" (Mayer et al., 1995, p. 712) and the *public trust* as mediated trust.

By positioning, the public sphere and the expression of the organizational identity in society is meant. This includes taking stances related to relevant issues in society, even if not directly related to the cause. As described before, NGOs congregate action in the public sphere and with that, they occupy a position as a collective actor.

In terms of operative goals, engagement and public agenda have an influence. The first can be divided into initial engagement and further engagement. The definition of engagement used here is a citizen getting to any level of involvement with the NGO. It can be symbolic, by supporting the cause or the NGO in informal communication, it can be any other action requested by the NGO, like signing a petition, subscribing to a newsletter or participating in a street demonstration. Engagement is a continuum and will then develop into other, deeper forms of relationship that are described in the operative goals as part of internal relations. The public agenda–influencing goal is driven by media presence and the concept of agenda setting from McCombs and Shaw (1972). In the case of an NGO, depending on campaigns, agenda setting or influencing of certain perspectives may be crucial for guaranteeing the achievement of its goal. We can describe the example of human rights in a certain country that requires a change to increase protection. The NGO needs to first search for agenda-setting methods and then make efforts to influence the public agenda also in terms of content. Besides the mediated public sphere, it could also be argued that public agenda influencing can take place within the intermediary system.

Internal relations consider the organization members and the organization's strategic communication goals, legitimacy and shared vision. By shared vision, it is meant that there is an ongoing process of identity negotiation and vision that also constantly changes in the organization and is not implemented by the management as a fully defined one. It may also be the adaptation or negotiation of a previously established vision and identity.

Stakeholders and publics include employees and also volunteers, donors and members. Donors are long-term, regular donors. They are differentiated from one-time donors. The operative goals are participation, reproduction and co-creation of the organization. Participation means a regular bond with the organization that is formalized and therefore different from engagement. Reproduction means the mechanism of a citizen activating another citizen to engage or participate. Co-creation is the input from various stakeholders to the development of the organization as well as the process of identity negotiation.

In terms of market relations, it is proposed here, in accordance with Zerfaß (2004), as relationships with suppliers and also relationships with buyers and one-time donors. We consider that, for those, the strategic goal of brand positioning guarantees the generation of income potential and optimized resource acquisition. We can compare the act of buying with the one-time donor. With regard to buyers, it is possible for some NGOs to sell goods and services as a way of raising funds, and some of them use merchandising articles. In terms of operative goals, NGO activation is framed within this category. By that, the superficial contact that one citizen has with an NGO through a simple donation or buying a product or service, or even service providers supplying special conditions to NGOs, is meant. This is not to be confused with NGO enactment, which is defined as the process achieved through engagement, public agenda influencing, participation, reproduction and co-creation, NGO activation and NGO loop. In terms of brand positioning, the brand personality elements of functional attributes (the cause) and symbolic values (brand values) are included (Hankinson, 2000, p. 211).

A conceptual approach for strategic communication

Civic relations is the last conceptual area of communication within NGOs and addresses the specific communication that is done from the citizens' perspective and according to what is described throughout the theory. The strategic goal is specific awareness about the main subjects or causes that an organization might have. This communication can be framed or driven within an organization, and goals can be set for contributing to that awareness. Communication in the public sphere and other communication settings regarding the subject contribute to that. The operative communicational goal is to support the NGO loop, defined as the possibility of activating other citizens to join the cause or civic relations process. Citizens here are the general public, together with the beneficiaries, as those helped in case of operational NGOs. They are distinguished by one having a more active role and the other a more receptive role. The fact that beneficiaries are positioned within civic relations is supported by understanding the plural economies and reciprocity as the constant process of restoring balance, especially multilateral reciprocity, framed within substantivism (Polanyi, 1957, 2001).

Fundraising can be considered communication within one department or part of the organization or as a function that is centralized and coordinated alone. But this would mean reducing a complex process and multidimensional social phenomenon to a mechanistic approach to social reality. The same would be the case if fundraising within an NGO was isolated. Therefore, the proposal is to see it as a crosscutting function, integrated and diffused in terms of operations and contributions.

Conceptualization of the operational model was done using a cybernetic approach, considering a journey as a meaning-based reproduction at the micro level but also at the group level within an organization. It was also considered at the macro level, since the formal and informal groups are active in the public sphere and civil society (see Figure 3.1.3). At another analytical level,

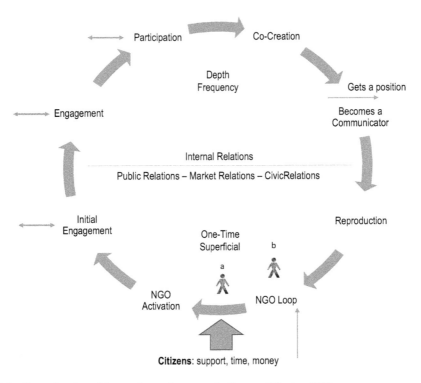

Figure 3.1.3 Operational model – a cybernetic approach. Source: Oliveira, 2017.

communication is a supporting process for the citizen's journey, meaning that the relationship is driven and maintained by a structural system of support. The circular journey in abstract terms includes dimensions of depth and frequency and is influenced by individual characteristics and motivation to be a member of an organization, as well as expectations and other circumstantial life-related parameters.

Conclusion

This chapter describes the ITNC as a conceptual proposal from both strategic and operational communication management standpoints. *Management logic* and *dual management dynamic* are two key concepts in the ITNC, and the conceptual model allows strategic communication management understanding and practice. By considering fundraising as an integrated cross-function in a balanced perspective, a new proposal in this field is put forward. Additionally, the operational model and the cybernetic approach to communication can provide insights into the processes of engaging with citizens.

The main components of the ITNC consider logic and management, OPs, and perspectives of communication, i.e., manageable communication, nondirect management communication, communication dynamics, public communication and legitimation dynamics.

Despite the fact that the ITNC has been developed for NGOs in particular, most aspects of it might be transferable to other civil society organizational forms. Future research could usefully explore this applicability in a theoretical exercise, and a more empirical approach could be equally fruitful for other civil society organizations that share similar dynamics but differ in scope when compared to the studies of the original proposal.

Notes

1 Portions of this chapter are adapted from the original theory manuscript (Oliveira, 2017).
2 Source: https://unfccc.int/process-and-meetings/parties-non-party-stakeholders/non-party-stakeholders/statistics#eq-2
3 There is also an illustration of the constitutive communication flows and the communication dynamics, including the CCO and the constitutive role of communication. Please see Oliveira, 2019, p. 94–104 for detailed description.

References

Alvarez, S. E. (1999). Advocating feminism: The Latin American feminist NGO "boom". *International Feminist Journal of Politics*, 1(2), 181–209.
Alvim, F., & Teodósio, A. (2004). Gestão da Cooperação Internacional: Perspectivas e desafios para as ONGs. In *Anais do XV Encontro Nacional dos Cursos de Graduação em Administração* (pp. 93–102). ANGRAD.
Aristizábal, P., Ferrero, G., & Osorio, L. (1997). *Introducción a la cooperación para el desarrollo: una propuesta curricular para la promoción de la educación al desarrollo en la universidad*. Universidad Politécnica de Valencia.
Bastgen, S. (2016). *Die Demokratisierungspotenziale europäischer NGOs: Zwischen Professionalisierung und Linkage*. Springer VS.
Berger, P. L., & Luckmann, T. (1995). *Modernität, Pluralismus und Sinnkrise: die Orientierung des modernen Menschen*. Bertelsmann Stiftung.
Clarke, G. (1998). Non-Governmental Organizations (NGOs) and politics in the developing world. *Political Studies*, 46(1), 36–52. doi:10.1111/1467-9248.00128
Davies, T. R. (2021). *The Routledge handbook of NGOs and international relations*. Routledge.
Fisher, W. F. (1997). Doing good? The politics and antipolitics of NGO practices. *Annual Review of Anthropology*, 26, 439–464. doi:10.1146/annurev.anthro.26.1.439
Giddens, A. (1984). *The constitution of society: Outline of the theory of structuration*. University of California Press.
Habermas, J. (2001). *Between facts and norms: Contributions to a discourse theory of law and democracy*. (1. MIT Press ed., 4. Printing). MIT Press.

Hankinson, P. (2000). Brand orientation in charity organisations: Qualitative research into key charity sectors. *International Journal of Nonprofit and Voluntary Sector Marketing, 5*(3), 207–219.

Heins, V. (2002). *Weltbürger und Lokalpatrioten: eine Einführung in das Thema Nichtregierungsorganisationen*. Bayerische Landeszentrale für Politische Bildungsarbeit.

Jarren, O., & Donges, P. (2011). Strukturen des intermediären Systems der Interessenvermittlung. In O. Jarren & P. Donges (Eds.), *Politische Kommunikation in der Mediengesellschaft* (3rd ed., pp. 119–128). VS Verlag für Sozialwissenschaften.

Koschmann, M. (2012). Developing a communicative theory of the nonprofit. *Management Communication Quarterly, 26*(1), 139–146. doi:10.1177/0893318911423640

Koschmann, M., & Sandres, M. (2020). *Understanding nonprofit work: A communication perspective*. Wiley-Blackwell.

Landim, L. (2002). Múltiplas Identidades das ONGs. In S. Haddad (Ed.), *ONGs e universidades: desafios para a cooperação na América Latina* (pp. 17–50). Editora Fundação Peirópolis.

Lang, S. (2014). *NGOs, civil society, and the public sphere* (1st ed.). Cambridge University Press.

Liu, B. (2012). Toward a better understanding of nonprofit communication management. *Journal of Communication Management, 16*(4), 388–404. http://dx.doi.org/10.1108/13632541211279012

Martens, K. (2002). Mission impossible? Defining nongovernmental organizations. *Voluntas: International Journal of Voluntary and Nonprofit Organizations, 13*(3), 271–285.

Mayer, R. C., Davis, J. H., & Schoorman, F. D. (1995). An integrative model of organizational trust. *The Academy of Management Review, 20*(3), 709–734.

McCombs, M. E., & Shaw, D. L. (1972). The agenda-setting function of mass media. *Public Opinion Quarterly, 36*(2), 176.

Menescal, A. K. (1996). História e gênese das organizações não governamentais. In H. S. Gonçalves & A. K. Menescal (Eds.), *Organizações não governamentais: solução ou problema?* (1a ed., pp. 21–38). Estação Liberdade.

Oliveira, E. (2017). *The instigatory theory of NGO communication (ITNC)*. Universidade do Minho. http://hdl.handle.net/1822/56020

Oliveira, E. (2019). *The instigatory theory of NGO communication: Strategic communication in civil society organisations*. Springer VS.

Oliveira, E., Ruiz-Mora, I., & Zeler, I. (2021, November). *#FridaysForFuture ¿Comunicación estratégica? Análisis de las pautas de una conversación*. Paper presented at the IV Move.net. Congreso Internacional sobre Movimientos Sociales y TIC. University of Sevilla, Andalucia, Spain.

Polanyi, K. (1957). *Trade and market in the early empires: Economies in history and theory*. Free Press.

Polanyi, K. (2001[1944]). *The great transformation the political and economic origins of our time*. Beacon Press.

Prahalad, C. K., & Bettis, R. A. (1986). The dominant logic: A new linkage between diversity and performance. *Strategic Management Journal, 7*(6), 485–501.

Priller, E., & Zimmer, A. (Eds.). (2001). *Der dritte Sektor international: mehr Markt – weniger Staat?* Edition Sigma.

Roberts, S. M., Jones, J. P., & Fröhling, O. (2005). NGOs and the globalization of managerialism: A research framework. *World Development, 33*(11), 1845–1864.

Rodriguez-Amat, R., Oliveira. E., & Ruiz-Mora, I. (2021, September). *Strategic communication beyond organizations. The case of Fridays for future*. Paper presented at the 8th ECREA European Communication Conference. Braga and Virtual.

Ruler, B., & Verčič, D. (2012). Public relations and communication management in Europe: Challenges and opportunities. *Comunicação e Sociedade*. doi:8.179.10.17231/comsoc.8(2005).1189

Smith, B. G. (2013a). The internal forces on communication integration: Co-created meaning, interaction, and postmodernism in strategic integrated communication. *International Journal of Strategic Communication, 7*(1), 65–79.

Souza, H. (1992). As ONGs na década de 90. In I. Santiago (Ed.), *Desenvolvimento, cooperação internacional e as ONGs* 1o. Encontro Internacional de ONGs e o Sistema de Agências das Nações Unidas. IBASE.

Taylor, J. R. (1993). *Rethinking the theory of organizational communication: How to read an organization*. Ablex

Weick, K. E. (1995). *Sensemaking in organizations*. Sage.

Zerfaß, A. (2004 [1996]). *Unternehmensführung und Öffentlichkeitsarbeit: Grundlegung einer Theorie der Unternehmenskommunikation und Public Relations* (2nd ed.). VS Verlag für Sozialwissenschaften.

3.2
INTERNAL BRANDING IN THE NONPROFIT SECTOR

Gordon Liu

Introduction

An organization's brand can be expressed through its name, logo, symbol, or other unique features that allow the public to identify one organization from another. It has long been considered one of the most critical assets of a nonprofit organization (NPO). The typical route to develop an NPO's brand involves utilizing marketing tools (e.g., advertising) and the media (e.g., newspaper) to communicate directly to the public and influence their thoughts, feelings, perceptions, images, experiences, beliefs, and attitudes toward the NPO (Daw et al., 2010; Sepulcri et al., 2020). Internal branding represents an alternative route of brand development for NPOs. More specifically, internal branding focuses on persuading NPO members (e.g., employees, volunteers) to buy in to the organization's brand promise and allow it to influence their behaviour (Liu et al., 2015; Nogueira et al., 2020). The successful execution of internal branding will transform an NPO's members into the organization's "brand ambassadors"[1] when interacting with customers, donors, beneficiaries, and other stakeholders (Laidler-Kylander & Simonin, 2009; Liu *et al.*, 2017). This will ultimately contribute to the NPO's overall efforts to shape the public perception of the organization's brand.

Over the past decade, there has been a growing interest in studying internal branding in the context of the nonprofit sector. The purpose of this chapter is to review the literature on this area. We used the EBSCO database, ABI/Inform, and Google Scholar to search for published articles. We searched for keywords and phrases, including *internal branding*, *brand building*, *brand ambassadors*, *brand champions*, *brand citizenship*, *employee brand*, and *brand representatives* in the titles, keywords, or abstracts of published works. We then examined each article to determine whether or not it had a close link with the topic of internal branding. Further, this chapter focuses on internal branding activities in the nonprofit sector.[2] Therefore, we exclude studies that focus on private-sector organizations.

As a result of our review, we identified six different elements concerning internal branding in the nonprofit sector. "Organizational brand-building behaviors" reflect NPO engagement in brand orientation and re-branding. "Internalization" discusses the processes whereby NPO members accept the promise of the organization's brand and transform it into their personal value. "Internalization facilitators" describes the two key organizational functions – internal marketing and management functions – supporting the internalization processes. "Employee brand-building behaviours" focus on two specific NPO members' acts as brand builders: in-role behaviours and extra-role behaviours. These four elements represent an NPO's internal branding processes. The key "consequences" derived from the internal branding processes are marketing and human resource management

Internal branding in the nonprofit sector

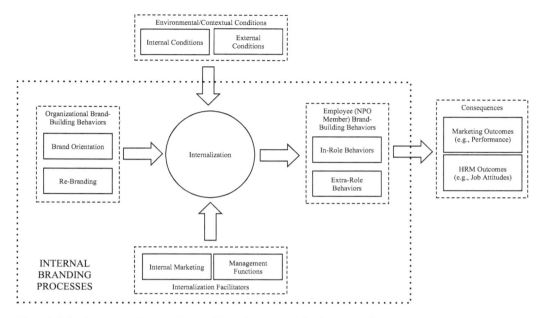

Figure 3.2.1 A conceptual map of internal branding research in the nonprofit-sector context.

(HRM) outcomes. Furthermore, the environmental/contextual conditions that can influence the internal branding processes include various internal and external factors. Figure 2.1 provides a conceptual map of the internal branding research in the nonprofit sector context. We will discuss each part in detail in the following sections.

Organizational brand-building behaviours

The internal branding processes start with organizational brand-building behaviours. Organizational brand-building behaviours describe an NPO's efforts to develop and manage its brand at the organizational level. Building on a review of the prior literature, we identify two major research themes concerning organizational brand-building behaviours: 1) brand orientation and 2) re-branding. Many researchers have investigated the meaning (and practices) of brand orientation in the context of internal branding in the nonprofit sector. One prominent example is Ewing and Napoli (2005)'s work, which suggests that brand orientation in NPOs consists of three dimensions of activities: orchestration (the key stakeholders have a clear perception of the brand portfolio and related marketing activities), interaction (there is a dialogue with the key stakeholders about the organization's brand that responds to changes in the environment), and affect (understanding key stakeholders' likes/dislikes about the organization's brand and the reasons for these). Others, such as Hankinson, point out that brand orientation comprises three essential practices, such as "brand understanding," "brand communication," "the strategic use of the brand," and other factors concerning the managerial responsibilities for an NPO's brand (Hankinson, 2000, 2001a, 2001b). Mulyanegara conceptualizes brand orientation as uniqueness (distinctive characteristics), reputation (image in the community), and orchestration (integrated marketing activities) (Mulyanegara, 2011a, 2011b). Baumgarth (2009) further differentiates between cultural (value – the role of the brand in business strategy development; norms – rules that determine the basic operations of the brand management; artefacts – perceptible symbols that reflect the brand) and behavioural (actions to communicate the brand) aspects of brand orientation when studying art museums. Despite these differences in conceptualization, scholars agree that the central premise of brand orientation reflects a focus on building an NPO's brand promise (Casidy, 2013, 2014; da Silva et al., 2020).

Whereas brand orientation efforts focus on creating and developing an NPO's brand, re-branding emphasizes making changes to the brand in alignment with the changes in the business environment. Many studies have investigated what happens when an NPO re-brands itself and the process of this in the context of internal branding in the nonprofit sector. For example, Lee (2013) explores re-branding in the context of NPOs and suggests practical guidelines for NPO managers to deal with the tensions that may arise during the process, including 1) aligning image and identity, 2) managing multiple stakeholders' dialogues and access, and 3) balancing the marketing requirements with the organizational identity. Lee and Bourne (2017) identify different types of re-branding strategies and managers' inputs to justify, re-vision, and influence in order to reduce the emerging tensions during the re-branding process by conducting case studies of ten NPOs. Chad (2016) explores the employees' feelings about the re-branding process and identifies the management principles to facilitate the various phases of the process. Hankinson and Lomax (2006) conducted a quantitative survey of 465 staff from ten large UK charities that shows that re-branding efforts can update the staff's knowledge about the organization's brand but that this occurs unevenly across different levels of seniority. Clark et al. (2020) suggest that successful rebranding practices should include internal engagement, a launch event, consultation, awareness among managers, and a sustained launch. In general, these studies highlight the role of re-branding in shaping the NPO members' (e.g., employees, volunteers) experience of the organization's brand.

Internalization

Once an NPO develops or repositions its brand via organizational brand-building behaviours, the next step in internal branding is for the NPO members (e.g., employees, volunteers) to accept the brand and identify with it (Hankinson, 2004; Sujchaphong et al., 2015). This process can be described as "internalization." Scholars have studied internalization from different perspectives in the context of internal branding in the nonprofit sector. For example, Liu *et al.* (2015) consider internalization as one-way process-oriented mechanisms and suggest that an NPO's engagement in brand orientation can affect the staff's emotional brand attachment (how strongly the NPO members feel about the brand) and subsequently staff service involvement (how strongly the NPO members perceive that the services provided by the brand are personally relevant to them). Alternatively, Dean et al. (2016) consider internalization to be a series of loops (discovering the brand, living the brand, learning the brand, representing the brand, [re]discovering the brand, living the brand, learning the brand, representing the brand) that enable the NPO members to co-create the brand meaning (promise) and accept it as their own value. Even from different perspectives, internalization generally represents the process of transforming an NPO's brand promise into the members' own personal value.

Internalization facilitators

Internalization involves the NPO members coming to accept the brand and identifying with it. Previous studies have discovered two categories of practices – "internal marketing" and "management functions" – that can help to facilitate the internalization movement and ensure that NPO members successfully become brand representatives. Internal marketing focuses on using marketing techniques to instill organizational values and brand promise into an NPO's internal "customers" (e.g., NPO members – employees, volunteers) (Bennett & Barkensjo, 2005; Mitchell & Taylor, 1997). Among researchers who studied internal marketing, Yu et al. (2018) suggest that successful internal marketing requires three key features: 1) internal information collection (understanding the NPO members' current and future needs), 2) internal communication (informing the NPO members), and 3) responsiveness (giving feedback to and participation by NPO members). Mitchell and Taylor (1997) suggest that the application of internal marketing in the nonprofit sector needs to incorporate several key issues: membership (i.e., fit/appropriateness), socialization (i.e., the process of understanding an NPO's value system), identity (i.e., understanding the roles within the NPO), structural (i.e., rules), interpersonal (i.e., relationship interactions), and environmental (i.e., the organizational context). Hume and Hume (2015) propose that the successful implementation of internal marketing should focus on ensuring the personal relevance of the marketing messages and the use of socialization strategies (e.g., workgroup meetings) to deliver the messages with the support of internal communication channels (newsletters, etc.). From these perspectives, the NPO managers need to focus not only on the communication of the brand promise to the NPO members but also on "how" the NPO is communicating the messages about the brand via internal marketing as a tool for facilitating internal branding in the nonprofit sector. These studies enhance our understanding of internal marketing in the nonprofit sector in supporting an NPO's overall internal branding efforts.

Studies of internal branding in the nonprofit context have identified several management functions that can facilitate internalization movements. Several scholars have pointed out the importance of leadership in providing guidance and governance mechanisms in supporting internalization (e.g., Chad, 2016; Chapleo, 2015). Notably, Liu *et al.* (2015) argue that charismatic leadership (inspiring subordinates to mimic the leader's attitudes and behaviour) increases the strength of the linkage among brand orientation, staff emotional brand attachment, and staff service involvement. Sujchaphong *et al.* (2015) highlight the role of transformational leadership (encouraging one's followers to work hard) in providing space for intellectual stimulation and the consideration of individuals in influencing employees' behaviours to accept universities' brand promises. In addition to leadership, Chapleo (2015) states that a supportive organizational culture can help employees to buy into an organization's brand promises. Hankinson (2004) highlights the senior management's role in ensuring that employees fully understand the different components of a charity brand, including the functional (charity purpose), symbolic (charity values), behavioural (managerial practice), and experiential ("feel" of the working environment) components. Others point to the importance of employee training and orientation events, along with internal communication (marketing), to help employees internalize their role identity as brand representatives (Dean *et al.*, 2016; Liu *et al.*, 2017; Mitchell & Taylor, 1997).

Employee (NPO member) brand-building behaviours

Internal branding aims to translate NPO members into representatives of the NPO's brand by stimulating their brand-building behaviours (Laidler-Kylander & Simonin, 2009; Liu *et al.*, 2017). There are two types of employee brand-building behaviours. In-role employee brand-building behaviours happen when the NPO members meet the standard of reflecting the NPO's brand promises when interacting with external stakeholders (customers, donors, etc.). For example, a volunteer from an environmental NPO brings his or her own reusable shopping bags to the grocery store and refuses to use the store's plastic bags. Such behaviours align with the NPO's brand promise to "protect the environment" and "engage in recycling," which can be described as in-role brand-building behaviours. Extra-role employee brand-building behaviours refer to the NPO members' actions beyond the prescribed brand promises to benefit the NPO's brand when interacting with external stakeholders. Using the same example, when an environmental NPO's volunteer actively passes external stakeholders' feedback back to the NPO to support the brand management's efforts or spread positive word of mouth to their relatives or friends about the NPO's brand, these actions go beyond the prescribed role of acting according to the brand promises. They can be considered extra-role brand-building behaviours.

Many studies investigate these two types of employee brand-building behaviours as the results of internal branding processes in a nonprofit context. For example, Liu *et al.* (2017) examine the processes whereby brand orientation affects both the in-role and extra-role employee brand-building behaviours in UK-based NPOs. Yu *et al.* (2018) suggest that UK universities' internal branding efforts can ultimately lead to the development of brand-supportive behaviours – actual behaviours that extend beyond the formal role requirements in support of the university brand (i.e., extra-role brand-building behaviours). Nogueira *et al.* (2020) adopt a mixed-methods approach to study Portuguese volunteers' brand citizenship behaviors – employees' consistent, spontaneous, and genuine behaviours regarding the brand promise (i.e., in-role brand-building behaviors) and positive word of mouth about the brand (i.e., extra-brand-building behaviors) and their antecedents. Laidler-Kylander and Simonin (2009) propose a nonprofit brand equity model and urge nonprofit managers to embrace internal branding efforts to encourage internal brand ambassadors to be passionate and excited about internally promoting the brand beyond their job context (extra-role build-building behaviors). Overall, this line of research highlights employee brand-building behaviors as crucial outcomes of the internal branding processes.

Environmental/contextual conditions

As mentioned earlier, the internal branding processes are often concerned with the combination of organizational brand-building behaviors, internalization, employee brand-building behaviors, and internalization facilitators elements. However, these four elements do not operate in isolation. Previous studies have identified several internal and external environmental/contextual conditions that can influence internal branding processes' effectiveness. Regarding internal conditions, Clark et al. (2020) suggest that managers should provide consultation to employees during re-branding processes. Hankinson (2001a) advises managers to pay attention to the recruitment practices and ensure the fit between NPO members and the brand in order to support the organization's brand orientation efforts. Chapleo (2015) points out the importance of allocating appropriate budgets and equipping appropriate information technology systems, as well as having necessary managerial experience and operational routines (i.e., organizational capabilities) to perform the tasks concerning external and internal marketing research and communication for supporting internal branding efforts. In terms of the external conditions, Hankinson (2001a) finds that changes in the environmental setting are an important driver of an NPO's brand orientation efforts. Similarly, Lee and Bourne (2017) point out that the presence of market and alliance opportunities are important drivers of the re-branding practices of an NPO. Although the quantitative studies have not directly investigated the impacts of internal and external environmental/contextual conditions, they have controlled several important conditions (such as NPO size, NPO age, social sectors, employee age, employee gender, and employee social status) during the data analysis in studying an NPO's internal branding processes (e.g., Casidy, 2014; Gross & Rottler, 2019; Liu *et al.*, 2017). In other words, these scholars have acknowledged the influence of internal and external environmental/contextual conditions on an NPO's internal branding processes

Consequences

Previous studies have identified several important aftereffects of implementing internal branding in the nonprofit sector. The impact of the internal branding processes on an NPO's marketing outcomes (translated into different types of performance) as the primary consequences has received scholarly interest (e.g., Liu *et al.*, 2015). It is also important to note that many studies have not adopted the process-oriented approach to assess the connections between internal branding (processes) and performance. Instead, they examine the effects of different factors (e.g., brand orientation, internal marketing) within the internal branding processes on performance but build their arguments from the perspective of internal branding. For example, Baumgarth (2009) examined the impact of brand orientation (culture and behaviour) on art museums' market and culture performance. Gross and Rottler (2019) studied 140 volunteers in a German arts organization and found that internal marketing can influence volunteers' behaviours through improving their satisfaction and experience in voluntary work (volunteer performance). Napoli (2006) and Hankinson (2002) examined the direct relationship between brand orientation and NPO performance. Both scholars developed their arguments concerning brand orientation engagement that allows an NPO to effectively develop the brand and leverage its brand to fulfill a range of organizational performance objectives.

Another important consequence of the internal branding processes relates to the HRM outcomes (e.g., recruitment and retention, job satisfaction). Like the studies of the marketing outcomes of internal branding processes, a few studies adopt the process-oriented view to examine the impact of internal branding (processes) on this type of consequence (e.g., Nogueira et al., 2020). Most of the studies examine the effects of different factors within the internal branding processes on HRM outcomes and adopt the logic of internal branding to develop their arguments. For example, Hankinson (2000) suggests the connection between brand orientation and the success of recruitment practices in the UK charity sector. Hankinson (2004) points out the important role played by senior managers in implementing internal branding (HR/managerial functions) to unify the workforce around a common purpose. Bennett and Barkensjo (2005) surveyed 91 volunteers across five regional offices of a large UK charity and found a strong effect of internal marketing on job satisfaction and organizational commitment. Modi and Sahi (2018) studied 370 NPOs and found that the implementation of internal marketing can help to improve the staff retention rate. Mitchell and Taylor (1997) proposed that an NPO's internal marketing efforts can help to support volunteer recruitment, volunteer retention, and voluntary group cohesiveness. This research line helped draw attention to the importance of understanding the internal branding processes as an important mechanism for developing the brand that the members desire and improving the HRM outcomes.

Discussion and concluding remarks

Unlike private-sector organizations, with abundant resources to engage in traditional marketing activities (e.g., paid advertising) for the purpose of increasing brand awareness, many NPOs have turned to internal branding strategies to turn their employees (NPO members) into brand ambassadors to achieve the same objective (Dean et al., 2016; Hankinson, 2004; Liu et al., 2017). The primary purpose of this chapter was to assess the literature concerning internal branding in the nonprofit sector. We identified six key internal branding elements that have emerged through this research stream: organizational brand-building behaviours, internalization, employee brand-building behaviours, internalization facilitators, environmental/contextual conditions, and consequences. We then incorporated these elements into a conceptual map that illustrates the internal brand processes (an interactive set of organizational brand-building behaviours, internalization, employee brand-building behaviours, and internalization facilitators) and contingent factors (environmental/contextual conditions) and concluded with the improvement in marketing and HRM outcomes (consequences).

More specifically, for an NPO, the internal branding will start with the engagement in activities (i.e., brand orientation and re-branding) that develop the organizational brand. A strong, meaningful organizational brand makes it easy for the NPO members to accept the brand promises and identify themselves with the brand (internalization). To facilitate this procedure, an NPO can pursue internal marketing to communicate the brand promises to its members or utilize the management functions to create a favourable organizational atmosphere that supports internalization. The NPO members' in-role and extra-role (brand) behaviours represent the fact that they have become the ambassadors for the NPO's brand. The connection between these activities represents the processes that transform an NPO's brand promises into a reality, which we refer to as "internal branding processes." Such implementation of internal brand processes will lead to several marketing and HRM outcomes. Furthermore, several internal and external environmental/contextual conditions dictate the effectiveness of an NPO's internal branding processes. Altogether, this work provides a general overview of the up-to-date research on the topic of internal branding in the nonprofit sector.

Notes

1. The nonprofit literature employs several related terms interchangeably, such as brand ambassadors, brand champions, employee brand, brand citizenship, and brand representatives (Laidler-Kylander & Simonin, 2009; Liu et al., 2017; Nogueira et al., 2020).
2. We define an NPO broadly as any legal entity that organizes and operates according to its mission and focus on making a contribution to society (Ciconte & Jacob, 2008). Therefore, we include studies of the internal branding activities of charities, social enterprises, universities, churches, and other nonbusiness entities.

References

Baumgarth, C. (2009). Brand orientation of museums: Model and empirical results. *International Journal of Arts Management*, *11*(3), 30–45.

Bennett, R., & Barkensjo, A. (2005). Internal marketing, negative experiences, and volunteers' commitment to providing high-quality services in a UK helping and caring charitable organization. *Voluntas: International Journal of Voluntary and Nonprofit organizations*, *16*(3), 251–274.

Casidy, R. (2013). The role of brand orientation in the higher education sector: A student-perceived paradigm. *Asia Pacific Journal of Marketing and Logistics*, *25*(5), 803–820.

Casidy, R. (2014). Linking brand orientation with service quality, satisfaction, and positive word-of-mouth: Evidence from the higher education sector. *Journal of Nonprofit & Public Sector Marketing*, *26*(2), 142–161.

Chad, P. (2016). Corporate rebranding: An employee-focused nonprofit case study. *Journal of Nonprofit & Public Sector Marketing*, *28*(4), 327–350.

Chapleo, C. (2015). Brand 'infrastructure' in nonprofit organizations: Challenges to successful brand building? *Journal of Marketing Communications*, *21*(3), 199–209.

Ciconte, B. L., & Jacob, J. (2008). *Fundraising basics: A complete guide*. Jones & Bartlett Publishers.

Clark, P., Chapleo, C., & Suomi, K. (2020). Branding higher education: An exploration of the role of internal branding on middle management in a university rebrand. *Tertiary Education and Management*, *26*(2), 131–149.

da Silva, L. C., Mainardes, E. W., Teixeira, A. M. C., & Júnior, L. C. (2020). Brand orientation of nonprofit organizations and its relationship with the attitude toward charity and donation intention. *International Review on Public and Nonprofit Marketing*, *17*(3), 353–373.

Daw, J., Cone, C., Erhard, A., & Merenda, K. D. (2010). *Breakthrough nonprofit branding: Seven principles to power extraordinary results*. John Wiley & Sons.

Dean, D., Arroyo-Gamez, R. E., Punjaisri, K., & Pich, C. (2016). Internal brand co-creation: The experiential brand meaning cycle in higher education. *Journal of Business Research*, *69*(8), 3041–3048.

Ewing, M. T., & Napoli, J. (2005). Developing and validating a multidimensional nonprofit brand orientation scale. *Journal of Business Research*, *58*(6), 841–853.

Gross, H. P., & Rottler, M. (2019). Nonprofits' internal marketing and its influence on volunteers' experiences and behavior: A multiple mediation analysis. *Nonprofit and Voluntary Sector Quarterly*, *48*(2), 388–416.

Hankinson, P. (2000). Brand orientation in charity organisations: Qualitative research into key charity sectors. *International Journal of Nonprofit and Voluntary Sector Marketing*, *5*(3), 207–219.

Hankinson, P. (2001a). Brand orientation in the charity sector: A framework for discussion and research. *International Journal of Nonprofit and Voluntary Sector Marketing*, *6*(3), 231–242.

Hankinson, P. (2001b). Brand orientation in the Top 500 fundraising charities in the UK. *Journal of Product & Brand Management*, *10*(6), 346–360.

Hankinson, P. (2002). The impact of brand orientation on managerial practice: A quantitative study of the UK's top 500 fundraising managers. *International Journal of Nonprofit and Voluntary Sector Marketing*, *7*(1), 30–44.

Hankinson, P. (2004). The internal brand in leading UK charities. *Journal of Product & Brand Management*, *13*(2), 84–93.

Hankinson, P., & Lomax, W. (2006). The effects of re-branding large UK charities on staff knowledge, attitudes and behaviour. *International Journal of Nonprofit and Voluntary Sector Marketing*, *11*(3), 193–207.

Hume, C., & Hume, M. (2015). The critical role of internal marketing in knowledge management in not-for-profit organizations. *Journal of Nonprofit & Public Sector Marketing*, *27*(1), 23–47.

Laidler-Kylander, N., & Simonin, B. (2009). How international nonprofits build brand equity. *International Journal of Nonprofit and Voluntary Sector Marketing*, *14*(1), 57–69.

Lee, Z. (2013). Rebranding in brand-oriented organisations: Exploring tensions in the nonprofit sector. *Journal of Marketing Management*, *29*(9–10), 1124–1142.

Lee, Z., & Bourne, H. (2017). Managing dual identities in nonprofit rebranding: An exploratory study. *Nonprofit and Voluntary Sector Quarterly*, *46*(4), 794–816.

Liu, G., Chapleo, C., Ko, W. W., & Ngugi, I. K. (2015). The role of internal branding in nonprofit brand management: An empirical investigation. *Nonprofit and Voluntary Sector Quarterly*, *44*(2), 319–339.

Liu, G., Ko, W. W., & Chapleo, C. (2017). Managing employee attention and internal branding. *Journal of Business Research*, *79*(1), 1–11.

Mitchell, M. A., & Taylor, S. L. (1997). Adapting internal marketing to a volunteer system. *Journal of Nonprofit & Public Sector Marketing*, *5*(2), 29–41.

Modi, P., & Sahi, G. K. (2018). The meaning and relevance of internal market orientation in nonprofit organisations. *Service Industries Journal*, *38*(5–6), 303–320.

Mulyanegara, R. C. (2011a). The relationship between market orientation, brand orientation and perceived benefits in the nonprofit sector: A customer-perceived paradigm. *Journal of Strategic Marketing*, *19*(5), 429–441.

Mulyanegara, R. C. (2011b). The role of brand orientation in church participation: An empirical examination. *Journal of Nonprofit & Public Sector Marketing*, *23*(3), 226–247.

Napoli, J. (2006). The impact of nonprofit brand orientation on organisational performance. *Journal of Marketing Management*, *22*(7), 673–694.

Nogueira, M., Santarém, F., & Gomes, S. (2020). Volunteer brand equity? Exploring the adoption of employee brand equity (EBE) dimensions to understand volunteers' contributions to build nonprofit organizations' brands. *Journal of Nonprofit & Public Sector Marketing*, *32*(1), 73–104.

Sepulcri, L. M. C. B., Mainardes, E. W., & Belchior, C. C. (2020). Nonprofit branding: A bibliometric analysis. *Journal of Product & Brand Management*, *29*(5), 655–673.

Sujchaphong, N., Nguyen, B., & Melewar, T. C. (2015). Internal branding in universities and the lessons learnt from the past: The significance of employee brand support and transformational leadership. *Journal of Marketing for Higher Education*, *25*(2), 204–237.

Yu, Q., Asaad, Y., Yen, D. A., & Gupta, S. (2018). IMO and internal branding outcomes: An employee perspective in UK HE. *Studies in Higher Education*, *43*(1), 37–56.

3.3
NARRATIVES AND EMOTION IN SOCIAL ENTREPRENEURSHIP COMMUNICATION

Philip T. Roundy

Introduction

Social entrepreneurs pursue innovative opportunities to address societal problems through revenue-generating activities (Miller et al., 2012; Saebi et al., 2019). In creating new products, technologies, programs, and initiatives, social entrepreneurs balance designing financially viable business models with addressing conditions harmful to society, such as poverty, pollution, human trafficking, and animal abuse (Kickul & Lyons, 2020; Wry & York, 2017). To use the marketplace as an engine for social impact (Rawhouser et al., 2019), social entrepreneurs create hybrid ventures that are legally incorporated as for-profit or nonprofit organizations and allow entrepreneurs to pursue a social mission without exclusively relying on donations, public funding, grants, or volunteer labor (Guan et al., 2021). However, founding and scaling social ventures require entrepreneurs to manage the tensions between market-based logics focused on efficiency, competition, and value capture and community logics focused on community needs, cooperation, and value creation (Bruneel et al., 2016). The novel organizational dynamics that social entrepreneurs face, along with their unique motivations, opportunities, legal structures, stakeholders, and performance outcomes, make social entrepreneurship a phenomenon that is different from both conventional entrepreneurship and traditional nonprofit organizations and, thus, a distinctive subject of academic inquiry (Austin et al., 2006; Cohen et al., 2019).

Although most early-stage organizations face communication challenges (e.g., Wiesenberg et al., 2020), the differences between social ventures, traditional nonprofit organizations, and conventional for-profit businesses have implications for social entrepreneurship communication. Most notably, in creating and growing their ventures, social entrepreneurs mobilize resources (i.e., the tangible and intangible assets that enable entrepreneurs to exploit opportunities; Clough et al., 2019) from stakeholders that span organizational, industry, and sectoral boundaries and are more varied than the stakeholders of purely commercial or social-purpose organizations (Austin et al., 2006; Raith & Starke, 2017). For instance, unlike conventional entrepreneurs who communicate a business-oriented message and have customers as their primary demand-side stakeholders (Priem et al., 2012), many social entrepreneurs seek to satisfy two distinct demand-side groups: beneficiaries, who are the focus of a venture's prosocial behaviors, and consumers, who purchase a social venture's goods and services, thereby generating revenue (Roundy, 2017). In addition to communicating with beneficiaries and consumers, social entrepreneurs must gain the support of other groups in their ecosystems, such as investors, employees, volunteers, and co-founders (Muñoz & Kimmitt,

2019). However, the business and social-impact messages of social entrepreneurs, combined with the hybrid structures of their ventures that blur business and nonprofit categories, make it difficult for stakeholders to evaluate social entrepreneurs (e.g., Lortie et al., 2022; Moss et al., 2018). If social entrepreneurs cannot craft persuasive communication, they will struggle to acquire financial, social, and human capital and other resources (e.g., legitimacy) (Ruebottom, 2013).

Most social entrepreneurship research has focused on a specific form of entrepreneurial communication – narratives – and its influence on social venture stakeholders (e.g., Lewis et al., 2021; Margiono et al., 2019). A social venture narrative is *communication about a social venture that has temporality and a plot and enables sense-making and sense-giving* (Roundy, 2014b).[1] Social venture narratives communicate who social entrepreneurs are, why their ventures were founded, how they produce economic and social value, what their business models and social missions are, and why stakeholders should support them (Roundy, 2014c; Zamantılı Nayır & Shinnar, 2020). Because of the complexity of these messages, social entrepreneurs often struggle to craft and communicate persuasive narratives. Smith (2011) summarized these challenges:

> in a world where social enterprise[2] isn't well understood and people think in pretty black and white terms about charity and business, how do you balance your social and business message? Which comes first, and does it really matter whether people understand your social mission at all? [. . .] "[g]etting the message right is going to be vital for social enterprise. But what should the message be and how should it be delivered?"

In the decade since Smith posed these fundamental questions about social entrepreneurship, scholars have made significant progress in understanding how social venture narratives are created and used in organizational communication.

This chapter provides a state-of-the-literature review that synthesizes research on social entrepreneurship communication with an emphasis on how entrepreneurs create social venture narratives to communicate with their stakeholders. The main insights from the literature are organized to construct multi-stage and multi-level frameworks that explain how the content of social venture narratives influences communication practices and outcomes. The frameworks can help social entrepreneurs develop narratives that are more persuasive and assist scholars in identifying research opportunities in social venture communication.

Narratives and resource acquisition in conventional entrepreneurship

Narratives play a critical role in the traditional (i.e., nonsocial) entrepreneurship process (Downing, 2005). Entrepreneurs use narratives "internally" to construct and make sense of their identities and the opportunities they pursue (Garud & Giuliani, 2013; Liubertė & Dimov, 2021; Roundy, 2021). Entrepreneurs also use narratives "externally" in communication with stakeholders and, particularly, in interactions with audiences who have the resources needed to found and scale new ventures (Martens et al., 2007). The narratives told by and about entrepreneurs can help to create favorable evaluations of the wealth-creating possibilities of new ventures, thus increasing the likelihood that entrepreneurs mobilize resources (Lounsbury & Glynn, 2001). Narratives influence stakeholders' perceptions and their resource allocation decisions, in part, by creating and legitimating a new venture's identity and reducing stakeholders' information asymmetries about social entrepreneurs and their ventures. For instance, Martens and colleagues (2007) used a mixed-methods approach to study the role of narratives in the resource acquisition efforts of high-technology entrepreneurs during their initial public offerings (IPOs). Martens et al. found that influential narratives construct unambiguous identities for new ventures, elaborate how the ventures will attenuate risk, and invoke familiar elements to ground venture characteristics that are less familiar to audiences.

A challenge entrepreneurs face in mobilizing resources is that they often must convince stakeholders to lend support and provide resources to risky projects amidst uncertain future outcomes (Suddaby et al., 2021). Entrepreneurs can overcome this challenge by communicating a compelling vision of the future through narratives. Suddaby et al. contend that this form of narrative communication is difficult because entrepreneurs must communicate in a way that unites stakeholders who have different perceptions and expectations about the risks of a venture and the uncertainty of its future. Suddaby et al. argue that entrepreneurs can navigate this issue by developing a "diegetic narrative model of stakeholder enrollment," which communicates how entrepreneurs embed their "vision of the future in a coherent and collectively held narrative of the past" (p. 1).

Although research has made strides in explaining how conventional entrepreneurs use narratives to communicate with their stakeholders, social entrepreneurs differ from conventional entrepreneurs in key ways, which suggests that insights developed from studying conventional entrepreneurs do not necessarily apply to social entrepreneurs (Saebi et al., 2019). For this reason, scholars have sought to identify the unique dynamics of social entrepreneurship narrative communication. In the next sections, this research is synthesized to develop a framework describing the content, communication practices, moderating factors, and outcomes of social venture narratives.

Narratives and social venture communication

The content of social venture narratives

Studies of social entrepreneurship communication have focused on identifying the content of social venture narratives. Understanding narrative content is important because it constitutes social venture communication and describes the characteristics, events, and actions of social entrepreneurs. For instance, in a study of 121 individuals in the United States involved in social entrepreneurship (entrepreneurs, investors, and ancillary supporters), Roundy (2014b) developed a content-based typology of social venture narratives. Social entrepreneurs communicated three narratives to stakeholders: *personal narratives*, which are compilations of social entrepreneurs' experiences, attributes, significant life events, and founding stories; *social-good narratives*, which focus on the characteristics of the social problem being addressed; and *business narratives*, which contain descriptions of a venture's products, customer value proposition, revenue model, and the "business case" for why the venture should receive financial investment and other resources. These narratives, and their elements (e.g., themes, characters, events), are the building blocks for social entrepreneurs' communication about their ventures and for the narrative practices used to acquire resources (described later).

In a case study of a social venture in Mexico, Suarezserna's (2020) dissertation research confirmed the presence of the three-narrative typology outside the US context. Suarezserna found evidence that personal, social-good, and business narratives operate alongside a fourth narrative element: region-specific information (e.g., regional characteristics and values). Ruebottom (2013) also examined the linkages between narrative content and venture outcomes (legitimacy). In a comparative case study of 10 social ventures, Ruebottom found that social venture narratives were built from distinct content, such as problematizing statements, vocabulary sets (i.e., specific groups of words commonly used together), and protagonist and antagonist themes.

Other research has refined what constitutes the content of social venture narratives. In a comparative case study of Indonesian and UK-based social ventures, Margiono et al. (2019) identified several important elements of social entrepreneur narratives and how the narratives are received by audiences: the main characters, the storytellers' role identity, the storyline (plot), the narrative medium (verbal or visual), the familiarity of the story-receiver (i.e., audience) with the characters and issues, narrative transportation, and story-receiver actions. Margiono et al.'s model aligns with the extended transportation-imagery model (cf. Van Laer et al., 2014), which explains how compelling narrative content causes audiences to enter mentally constructed worlds evoked by stories. Based on their findings, Margiono et al. develop a conceptual framework explaining how social venture narrative elements (e.g., characters, plot) influence audiences' narrative transportation, empathy, and psychological empowerment, which in turn, influence audiences' evaluations of social venture legitimacy.

In more recent studies of narrative content, Lewis et al. (2021) studied the mission statements of 100 UK-based social ventures to understand if the content might indicate how social entrepreneurs reconciled tensions between social and financial objectives. Lewis et al. treated mission statements as "micro-narratives" that could reveal how "the competing logics of social mission and financial sustainability are being articulated and prioritized, and the linguistic turn and utilization of rhetoric to communicate purpose" (Lewis et al., 2021: 3). They found that mission statements contained nine vocabulary sets corresponding to common themes, such as the values of the organization; its business and social benefits; and its connection to a specific community, space, and place (Lewis et al., 2021). Lewis and colleagues also identified three content strategies in social entrepreneurs' micro-narratives corresponding to ethos, logos, and pathos Aristotelian rhetorics.

In an experimental study that manipulated the content of social venture narratives, Waldner (2020) examined how information about social entrepreneurs influenced stakeholders' emotions and their evaluations of venture reputation. In the experimental conditions, Waldner changed three aspects of narrative content: if (1) written information or (2) images were focused on the venture or the social entrepreneur, and if (3) descriptions of social entrepreneur traits focused on a societal orientation or were business-oriented. Waldner found that focusing communication content (text or images) on social entrepreneurs rather than organizations did not influence venture reputation. However, ventures were perceived as having better reputations if descriptions of social entrepreneurs' traits were society-oriented rather than business-oriented. Waldner concluded that: "By presenting a story of a social entrepreneur as a role model for societal change, [social entrepreneurs] are able to trigger positive emotions among stakeholders (Roundy, 2014a), which in turn signals their ability to meet the stakeholders' expectations." In sum, social venture narratives are composed of a complex set of elements, which form the basis for the communication practices that social entrepreneurs use with stakeholders.

Social venture narrative practices

Social entrepreneurs communicate narratives to diverse groups, including beneficiaries, customers, policy makers, volunteers, partner organizations, and the media (Cohen et al., 2019). In a qualitative study of eight UK-based social ventures, Di Domenico et al. (2010) found that narratives are used to persuade different types of resource providers. Social entrepreneurs took steps to convince resource providers of the "business case" for their ventures and clearly articulated why entrepreneurs' plans for social impact and value creation should be given legitimacy.

Some social entrepreneurs adapt their narratives to different stakeholder groups. For instance, Bandyopadhyay and Ray (2019) suggest that social entrepreneurs who are focused on fair trade and organic products balance their dual objectives by using one narrative to communicate with producers and a different narrative to encourage customers to buy their products. Bandyopadhyay and Ray (2019) also contend that social entrepreneurs must align their narratives with the local cultures of target communities.

Roundy (2014b) labeled these communication practices *narrative tailoring* – adapting the emphasis of a narrative (or using different narratives) to match the interests of a particular audience. In a qualitative study comparing social entrepreneurs who received angel or venture capital investment with those that did not, Roundy (2014b) found that social entrepreneurs who received investment tailored their communication to emphasize a business narrative with investors and a social good narrative with noninvestor resource providers (e.g., the media, customers). Social entrepreneurs receiving investment also used elements of their personal narratives in communication with both investor and noninvestor groups.

Building on Roundy's (2014b) findings about business, social-good, and personal narratives and narrative tailoring, Ryder and Vogeley (2018) used framing theory (and the concepts of keying and anchoring) and critical discourse analysis to understand how social entrepreneurs tailored their stories in online communication on a digital impact investing platform. They studied the communication interactions between a Balinese social enterprise (East Bali Cashews) and a Singaporean impact investment exchange that connected social entrepreneurs with mission-aligned impact investors. Ryder and Vogeley found that funding was more likely to flow to social entrepreneurs when their stories were "narratives leveraging personal, social good, and business sub-strands" and when they "strategically engage[d] specific frames, a mix of pathos and logos (with an emphasis on the latter), and a select set of New Critical and rhetorical tools" (p. 16). Ryder and Vogeley point to the importance of narrative "multiplexity" – when narratives contain multiple potential ties to more than one stakeholder group (Roundy, 2014c). Related to this work, Roundy (2014c) used the three-narrative typology (i.e., business, social-good, personal narratives) to examine the higher-order tactics, characteristics, and evolution of social venture narratives. He found that social entrepreneurs who communicate *multiplex* and *linked* narratives are more likely to receive funding than other entrepreneurs. Narrative linking is a communication practice that involves connecting more than one narrative theme (e.g., business and social-good themes).

Zamantılı Nayır and Shinnar (2020) also found evidence of narratives communicating a social venture's "business case" and "social case" and of narrative tailoring. They studied 19 social entrepreneurs in Istanbul, Turkey, and found that entrepreneurs engaged in rhetorical strategies to establish social venture legitimacy. To gain cognitive legitimacy, social entrepreneurs communicated the business case for their ventures while also making the argument that their ventures were distinct from other businesses in the same industry. Social entrepreneurs' second communication strategy involved establishing moral legitimacy by focusing on the venture's social impact. A third practice was gaining legitimacy by using narratives that appealed to a higher authority or established the social entrepreneur as an authority on the problem being addressed. Social entrepreneurs' final communication strategy was tailoring their messages to their audiences and communicating different narratives to different stakeholder groups, including investors and potential customers.

Social entrepreneurs' communication practices influence stakeholders, in part, through emotion-invoking mechanisms. Narrative's ability to generate an affective, emotional response in audiences is a defining feature of narrative communication (Miall, 1988; Keen, 2006) and a fundamental means by which narratives influence audiences (Dunlop et al., 2008; Escalas & Stern, 2003). In a qualitative study of 62 entrepreneurs, investors, consultants, media members, attorneys, and marketing professionals in the US social entrepreneurship sector, Roundy (2014a) examined if social entrepreneurs used narratives to influence the emotional reactions of stakeholders. Based on the study's findings, Roundy developed a conceptual model of the role of emotion in social venture communication. The model suggests that, compared to other ventures, social ventures that communicate emotional narratives are more likely to capture the attention of stakeholders, form connections with stakeholders, and inspire stakeholder action. These effects were moderated by two factors: direct- vs. indirect-benefit business models and communicating a business narrative. Social ventures with direct-benefit business models (i.e., selling a product or service linked directly to a single beneficiary) were more able to construct emotional narratives than ventures with indirect-benefit models (i.e., not directly involving beneficiaries in the venture's supply chain). Communicating about a compelling business model increased the impact of emotional narratives on stakeholders.

Barberá-Tomás et al. (2019) also focused on how social entrepreneurs elicit emotions in their audiences. They contend that stimulating emotions is important for convincing others "to identify with [the social entrepreneur's] cause and to enact it in their daily lives" (p. 1790). Barberá-Tomás et al. found that social entrepreneurs engaged in what they termed "emotion-symbolic work" – i.e., "making a conscious, intended try at altering feeling" (Hochschild, 1979: 560). This activity involved "using visuals and words to elicit negative emotions through moral shock, and then transforming those emotions into emotional energy for enactment" (p. 1789). To understand emotion-symbolic work, Barberá-Tomás et al. conducted an inductive, longitudinal study of social entrepreneurs who were trying to convince audiences that they were responsible for plastic pollution and that they should join the social entrepreneurs' efforts to promote "refusing" (rather than simply recycling) plastic products. Barberá-Tomás et al. (2019) found that social entrepreneurs' narratives included visual images that evoked moral shock and negative emotions, such as sadness, despair, and rage towards plastic pollution. These emotions fueled audience involvement in social entrepreneurs' causes. Barberá-Tomás et al.'s findings encourage scholars to go beyond studying narrative texts and draw attention to the emotion-invoking images in narrative communication.

The outcomes of social venture narratives

Early work on social entrepreneurship acknowledged that "it is critical for the social entrepreneur to develop a large network of strong supporters, and an ability to communicate the impact of the venture's work *to leverage resources outside organizational boundaries that can enable them to achieve their goals*" (Austin et al., 2006: 12; emphasis added). Combining the content of their social venture narratives with communication practices (described in the previous sections) enables social entrepreneurs to influence stakeholders and acquire the tangible and intangible resources they need.

The narratives communicated by social entrepreneurs can influence their ability to acquire early-stage financial investment from professional investors (Roundy, 2014a, 2014b, 2014c). Most research has focused, however, on how social entrepreneurs use narratives to gain nonfinancial resources, particularly legitimacy (e.g., Bandyopadhyay & Ray, 2019; Margiono et al., 2019). Ruebottom (2013) analyzed the rhetorical strategies that social entrepreneurs use to build legitimacy for their social change initiatives and found that social entrepreneurship communication influenced organizational legitimacy through distinct practices. Specifically, entrepreneurs communicated narratives that framed their social ventures as protagonists and those who challenged entrepreneurs' attempts at social change as antagonists.

Social venture narratives also influence legitimacy by communicating social entrepreneurs' identities. For instance, in a qualitative study based on interviews with the leaders of 21 UK-based social ventures, Granados and Rosli (2020) found that "communication is critical for [social entrepreneurs] to make sure stakeholders understand why they are there, and also to make them aware of their identity" (164). Rich, content-laden narratives help to reduce information asymmetries between social entrepreneurs and their stakeholders (Raith & Starke, 2017). In related work, in a study of four Danish social ventures, Schmeltz (2020) focused on "strategic identity communication" and examined how social entrepreneurs communicate venture identity through corporate communication. Schmeltz used institutional theory, a legitimacy lens, and a value systems theoretical framework to study the extent to which social entrepreneurs create alignment between the value systems associated with their corporate identities, typically embodied in traditional business values, and their social responsibility value systems, which are tied to being a social venture. Schmeltz claimed that the hybrid nature of social ventures makes it necessary for social entrepreneurs to find alignment between corporate values and corporate social responsibility (CSR) values and that communication with a high degree of alignment between the two value systems enables social entrepreneurs to

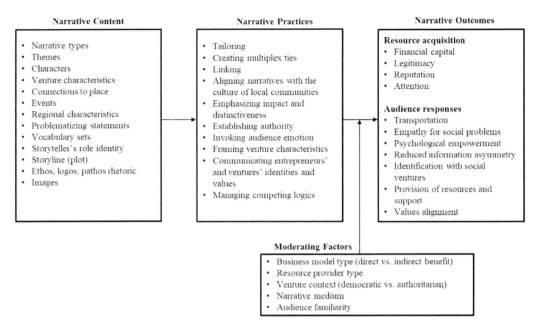

Figure 3.3.1 The structure of social venture narratives research.

convey a clear identity, which increases their legitimacy. Schmeltz studied the communication contained in organizations' websites and found that social entrepreneurs focused on competence-based, business values when presenting who they are and on social values when presenting their mission, vision, and responsibilities. Schmeltz concluded that, in pursuing legitimacy, social entrepreneurs' narrative content differed depending on if their objective was to describe the venture's business identity or its social mission and vision.

Neuberger et al. (2021) called attention to the fact that social ventures pursue legitimacy in different contexts. Not all social entrepreneurs operate in environments characterized by democratic systems; some social entrepreneurs pursue their missions in authoritarian contexts. To explore the ramifications of these contextual differences, Neuberger et al. studied how a disability rights social venture in post-revolutionary Egypt navigated distinct challenges created by authoritarianism to gain legitimacy for their activities. They found that the social venture "achieve[d] optimal assimilation by balancing protective disguise with harmonious advocacy." In this process, the social entrepreneurs used narratives to evoke emotions in nondisabled audiences, which motivated them to pursue the venture's mission of promoting disability rights. Figure 3.3.1 provides a framework that summarizes the social venture narratives literature.

Discussion

The goal of this chapter was to organize research on social venture narratives and make this work more accessible to scholars and practitioners. Despite the progress made in prior research on social entrepreneurship communication, much remains to be learned. This chapter concludes by proposing an agenda for studying social venture narrative communication. To organize the proposed research agenda, a micro-foundations framework (cf. Felin et al., 2015) is used, which draws attention to the mechanisms, connections, and relationships linking micro (entrepreneur), meso (social venture), and macro (ecosystem) levels of analysis (Figure 3.3.2).

Narratives and emotion

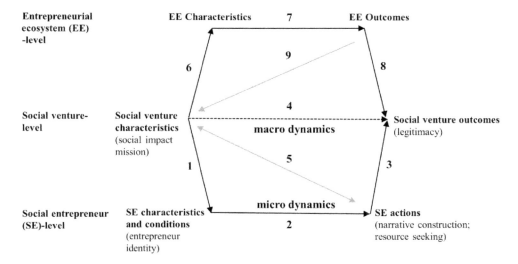

Figure 3.3.2 A micro-foundations agenda for social venture narratives research.

Opportunities for future research

How do "internal" and "external" narrative practices interact?

This chapter has primarily focused on how entrepreneurs construct social venture narratives based on their personal and venture characteristics (Figure 3.3.2, arrows 1 and 2) and how these narratives are used in external communication to influence social venture outcomes (arrow 3). However, narratives have other functions in social entrepreneurship and operate at different levels of analysis.

There is a burgeoning research that takes a "life-story" approach to analyze the narratives of social entrepreneurs and focuses on how narratives are used by entrepreneurs as sense-making tools to understand their lives (Cohen et al., 2019; Jeong et al., 2020). This work seeks a rich understanding of the interplay between social entrepreneurs' characteristics (e.g., their experiences and personal identities) and how they construct narratives (arrow 2). For instance, in a study of 11 social entrepreneurs in the Twin Cities (Minneapolis/St. Paul) region of the United States, Jeong et al. (2020) explored how social entrepreneurs used narratives to structure the meaning of their professional experiences.

Research is also beginning to study how individual sense-making and identity construction can influence venture characteristics (arrow 5). For example, Seanor et al. (2013) studied how social entrepreneurs talk about – and make sense of – the social and business aspects of their ventures. Seanor et al.'s findings illustrate how social entrepreneurs use narratives to construct venture, rather than individual, identities (Cornelissen et al., 2021) and how narratives operate across organizational levels (Feldner & Fyke, 2016).

Opportunities also exist for researchers to combine their focus on social entrepreneurs' "internal" use of narratives as sense-making devices with narratives' "external use" as sense-giving tools in stakeholder communication. Such research could cast light on how social entrepreneurs narrate their personal experiences, which influences how they construct organizational narratives and, in turn, their attempts to acquire resources from audiences (arrows 2–3). Related to this topic, important questions remain about what specific micro-level characteristics, personal attributes, and individual differences are associated with effective social venture narrative construction and communication. For instance, Cohen et al. (2019) suggested that extraversion may make entrepreneurs more effective leaders and, in turn, more persuasive communicators. Research is needed to understand if other individual-level characteristics make some social entrepreneurs better "storytellers" than others.

How can conceptions of social venture narratives and their outcomes be expanded?

Opportunities exist for future research to develop an expanded conceptualization of social venture narratives and their outcomes. For instance, as reviewed, most research has focused on the link between social venture narratives and a single organizational outcome, venture legitimacy (Figure 3.3.2, arrow 3.3). While legitimacy is critical to the success of early-stage ventures, entrepreneurs require an array of resources (cf. Clough et al., 2019). In exploring other outcomes related to venture success, more research is needed that directly studies social venture narratives rather than relying primarily on social entrepreneurs' assessments of resource providers.

Moreover, Mattson (2021, p. 30) has argued that scholars should "shift from inspirational identity narratives that assume an individualist and instrumentalist model of communication to fellowship narratives that assume a collective and participatory model." In other work, Mattson (2018) notes that scholars have tended to focus on narrative models emphasizing senders and receivers, but that scholars should expand this conceptualization to consider a performative model of communication in which actions and messages are interwoven. These points suggest that opportunities exist to expand the boundaries of the model of social venture narratives developed in this chapter (and illustrated in Figure 3.3.1).

What are the ties between social venture narratives and social venture marketing?

Strong, but largely unexplored, connections exist between social entrepreneurship communication and the characteristics of social ventures (Figure 3.3.2, arrow 5). For instance, it is not clear how social venture narratives influence the organizational marketing of social ventures (Bandyopadhyay & Ray, 2019; Srivetbodee et al., 2017). Sutton et al. (2018), for example, examined how higher education institutes used an accreditation indicator, the "Social Enterprise Mark." They found that the mark could be a valuable marketing tool for communicating an organization's social agenda and demonstrating to stakeholders that the organization puts the interests of people and the environment before financial gains. Likewise, Roundy (2017) examined how social entrepreneurs market their ventures to consumers and sought to address three questions: to what extent is marketing necessary for social entrepreneurs; do social entrepreneurs face unique marketing challenges and opportunities; and how do social entrepreneurs interact with, understand, and educate consumers? Roundy (2017) found that social entrepreneurs described one of their main marketing activities as crafting compelling narratives that communicate the value their ventures create for consumers and beneficiaries. Developing this complex narrative involved communicating both business- and social-oriented messages persuasively and succinctly to customers.

Bandyopadhyay and Ray (2019) considered the communication channels social entrepreneurs use to market their ventures and found that social media and online marketing platforms provide a low-cost medium for social entrepreneurs to communicate with their target customers and sell their products at a low cost (also cf. Madill & Ziegler, 2012). Social entrepreneurs tend to adopt a low-cost communication and marketing approach and work through their contacts and networks instead of investing extensive resources into formal brand-building activities. These studies suggest there are deep connections between narrative construction and how a venture is marketed and that promising areas of future research exist at the marketing and social venture communication interface.

What is the impact of local entrepreneurial ecosystems on social venture narratives?

Opportunities also exist to study how the narratives that social entrepreneurs communicate influence, and are shaped by, their local communities (Figure 3.3.2, arrows 6–9). An emerging stream of research builds on the "contextual turn" in entrepreneurship research (Welter, 2011) and focuses on how social entrepreneurs interact with the ecosystems in which they are embedded (e.g., Hazenberg et al., 2016). These studies acknowledge that a holistic understanding of social entrepreneurship requires acknowledging that social entrepreneurs are influenced by place-based and context-specific forces in the cities and regions in which they pursue opportunities. For instance, Samuel et al. (2022) examined how "Social Enterprise Places" (SEPs), a UK program focused on raising awareness, promoting, increasing validity, and building markets for social entrepreneurs at local levels, influences the legitimacy of social entrepreneurship. Samuel et al. found that SEPs influence social entrepreneur legitimacy, in part, by providing place-based language that can be used in resource mobilization and communication about common social goals. Other work has hinted at the linkages between social entrepreneurs' communication practices and the characteristics of their local ecosystems (Díaz-González & Dentchev, 2021; Pathak & Mukherjee, 2021; Wiesenberg et al., 2020). For instance, compelling narratives about social entrepreneurs and their ventures can influence their recognition and visibility in their local ecosystems (Díaz-González & Dentchev, 2021; Roundy, 2016), which can increase their likelihood and ease of mobilizing resources. However, research is needed that explicitly examines how social entrepreneurs' narratives are influenced by the elements (cf. Stam & Van de Ven, 2021) and the functioning of their local entrepreneurial ecosystems. Studies could also explore how the narratives that social entrepreneurs communicate influence ecosystem activities, for instance, by encouraging other ecosystem participants to pursue social entrepreneurship and garnering resources for local ecosystems.

Conclusion

Mobilizing the collective efforts of diverse groups to address social problems requires continuous communication among entrepreneurs and their stakeholders to "build trust, assure mutual objectives, and create common motivation" (Kania & Kramer, 2013: 1). However, social entrepreneurs' dual missions and the hybridity of their ventures (Battilana & Lee, 2014) create unique communication challenges. Further complicating these challenges, conceptual and practical agreement about social entrepreneurship and its boundaries has yet to be reached (Jeong et al., 2020; Choi & Majumdar, 2014), which makes it difficult for entrepreneurs to communicate clear and persuasive organizational narratives because the underlying phenomenon remains contested in the minds of some audiences. The desire to understand how social entrepreneurs overcome these communication issues is the basis for most of the research reviewed in this chapter and underscores the importance of the continued study of the content, practices, and outcomes of social venture narratives.

Notes

1. The definition of social venture narratives encapsulates both structuralist perspectives, which focus on narratives' temporal and causal features, and functionalist perspectives, which focus on how narratives are used.
2. In this chapter, the terms "social venture" and "social enterprise" are used synonymously.

References

Austin, J., Stevenson, H., & Wei – Skillern, J. (2006). Social and commercial entrepreneurship: Same, different, or both? *Entrepreneurship Theory and Practice*, *30*(1), 1–22.

Bandyopadhyay, C., & Ray, S. (2019). Social enterprise marketing: Review of literature and future research agenda. *Marketing Intelligence & Planning, 38*(1), 121–135.

Barberá-Tomás, D., Castelló, I., De Bakker, F. G., & Zietsma, C. (2019). Energizing through visuals: How social entrepreneurs use emotion-symbolic work for social change. *Academy of Management Journal, 62*(6), 1789–1817.

Battilana, J., & Lee, M. (2014). Advancing research on hybrid organizing – Insights from the study of social enterprises. *Academy of Management Annals, 8*(1), 397–441.

Bruneel, J., Moray, N., Stevens, R., & Fassin, Y. (2016). Balancing competing logics in for-profit social enterprises: A need for hybrid governance. *Journal of Social Entrepreneurship, 7*(3), 263–288.

Choi, N., & Majumdar, S. (2014). Social entrepreneurship as an essentially contested concept: Opening a new avenue for systematic future research. *Journal of Business Venturing, 29*(3), 363–376.

Clough, D. R., Fang, T. P., Vissa, B., & Wu, A. (2019). Turning lead into gold: How do entrepreneurs mobilize resources to exploit opportunities? *Academy of Management Annals, 13*(1), 240–271.

Cohen, H., Kaspi-Baruch, O., & Katz, H. (2019). The social entrepreneur puzzle: The background, personality and motivation of Israeli social entrepreneurs. *Journal of Social Entrepreneurship, 10*(2), 211–231.

Cornelissen, J. P., Akemu, O., Jonkman, J. G., & Werner, M. D. (2021). Building character: The formation of a hybrid organizational identity in a social enterprise. *Journal of Management Studies, 58*(5), 1294–1330.

Díaz-González, A., & Dentchev, N. A. (2021). Ecosystems in support of social entrepreneurs: A literature review. *Social Enterprise Journal, 17*(3), 329–360.

Di Domenico, M., Haugh, H., & Tracey, P. (2010). Social bricolage: Theorizing social value creation in social enterprises. *Entrepreneurship Theory and Practice, 34*(4), 681–703.

Downing, S. (2005). The social construction of entrepreneurship: Narrative and dramatic processes in the coproduction of organizations and identities. *Entrepreneurship Theory and Practice, 29*(2), 185–204.

Dunlop, S., Wakefield, M., & Kashima, Y. (2008). Can you feel it? Negative emotion, risk, and narrative in health communication. *Media Psychology, 11*(1), 52–75.

Escalas, J. E., & Stern, B. B. (2003). Sympathy and empathy: Emotional responses to advertising dramas. *Journal of Consumer Research, 29*(4), 566–578.

Feldner, S. B., & Fyke, J. P. (2016). Rhetorically constructing an identity at multiple levels: A case study of social entrepreneurship umbrella organizations. *International Journal of Strategic Communication, 10*(2), 101–114.

Felin, T., Foss, N. J., & Ployhart, R. E. (2015). The microfoundations movement in strategy and organization theory. *Academy of Management Annals, 9*(1), 575–632.

Garud, R., & Giuliani, A. P. (2013). A narrative perspective on entrepreneurial opportunities. *Academy of Management Review, 38*(1), 157–160.

Granados, M. L., & Rosli, A. (2020). 'Fitting in' vs. 'Standing out': How social enterprises engage with stakeholders to legitimize their hybrid position. *Journal of Social Entrepreneurship, 11*(2), 155–176.

Guan, S., Tian, S., & Deng, G. (2021). Revenue diversification or revenue concentration? Impact on financial health of social enterprises. *Public Management Review, 23*(5), 754–774.

Hazenberg, R., Bajwa-Patel, M., Mazzei, M., Roy, M. J., & Baglioni, S. (2016). The role of institutional and stakeholder networks in shaping social enterprise ecosystems in Europe. *Social Enterprise Journal, 12*(3), 302–321.

Hochschild, A. R. (1979). Emotion work, feeling rules, and social structure. *American Journal of Sociology, 85*(3), 551–575.

Jeong, S., Bailey, J. M., Lee, J., & McLean, G. N. (2020). "It's not about me, it's about us": A narrative inquiry on living life as a social entrepreneur, *Social Enterprise Journal, 16*(3), 263–280.

Kania, J., & Kramer, M. (2013). Embracing emergence: How collective impact addresses complexity. *Stanford Social Innovation Review*, 1–8.

Keen, S. (2006). A theory of narrative empathy. *Narrative, 14*(3), 207–236.

Kickul, J., & Lyons, T. S. (2020). *Understanding social entrepreneurship: The relentless pursuit of mission in an ever changing world* (3rd ed.). Routledge.

Lewis, K. V., Henry, C., & Roy, M. J. (2021, In press). Tethering mission to context? Exploring narratives underpinning the competing social and financial imperatives of social enterprise. *Journal of Social Entrepreneurship*.

Liubertė, I., & Dimov, D. (2021). "One tiny drop changes everything": Constructing opportunity with words. *Journal of Business Venturing Insights, 15*, e00242.

Lortie, J., Cox, K. C., & Roundy, P. T. (2022). Social impact models, legitimacy perceptions, and consumer responses to social ventures. *Journal of Business Research, 144*, 312–321.

Lounsbury, M., & Glynn, M. A. (2001). Cultural entrepreneurship: Stories, legitimacy, and the acquisition of resources. *Strategic Management Journal, 22*(6–7), 545–564.

Madill, J., & Ziegler, R. (2012). Marketing social missions – adopting social marketing for social entrepreneurship? A conceptual analysis and case study. *International Journal of Nonprofit and Voluntary Sector Marketing, 17*(4), 341–351.

Margiono, A., Kariza, A., & Heriyati, P. (2019). Venture legitimacy and storytelling in social enterprises. *Small Enterprise Research, 26*(1), 55–77.

Martens, M. L., Jennings, J. E., & Jennings, P. D. (2007). Do the stories they tell get them the money they need? The role of entrepreneurial narratives in resource acquisition. *Academy of Management Journal, 50*(5), 1107–1132.

Mattson, C. E. (2018). *Rethinking communication in social business: How re-modeling communication keeps companies social and entrepreneurial*. Lexington Books.

Mattson, C. E. (2021). Woo-woo for gainful good? A critical examination of social entrepreneurs and spiritually invested storytelling. *Journal of Communication & Religion, 44*(1), 30–49.

Miall, D. S. (1988). Affect and narrative: A model of response to stories. *Poetics, 17*(3), 259–272.

Miller, T. L., Grimes, M. G., McMullen, J. S., & Vogus, T. J. (2012). Venturing for others with heart and head: How compassion encourages social entrepreneurship. *Academy of Management Review, 37*(4), 616–640.

Moss, T. W., Renko, M., Block, E., & Meyskens, M. (2018). Funding the story of hybrid ventures: Crowdfunder lending preferences and linguistic hybridity. *Journal of Business Venturing, 33*(5), 643–659.

Muñoz, P., & Kimmitt, J. (2019). Social mission as competitive advantage: A configurational analysis of the strategic conditions of social entrepreneurship. *Journal of Business Research, 101*, 854–861.

Neuberger, I., Kroezen, J., & Tracey, P. (2021, In press). Balancing "protective disguise" with "harmonious advocacy": Social venture legitimation in authoritarian contexts. *Academy of Management Journal*.

Pathak, S., & Mukherjee, S. (2021). Entrepreneurial ecosystem and social entrepreneurship: Case studies of community-based craft from Kutch, India. *Journal of Enterprising Communities: People and Places in the Global Economy, 15*(3), 350–374.

Priem, R. L., Li, S., & Carr, J. C. (2012). Insights and new directions from demand-side approaches to technology innovation, entrepreneurship, and strategic management research. *Journal of Management, 38*(1), 346–374.

Raith, M. G., & Starke, C. (2017). Negotiating the organizational effectiveness of social ventures among multiple stakeholders. *VOLUNTAS: International Journal of Voluntary and Nonprofit Organizations, 28*(4), 1473–1499.

Rawhouser, H., Cummings, M., & Newbert, S. L. (2019). Social impact measurement: Current approaches and future directions for social entrepreneurship research. *Entrepreneurship Theory and Practice, 43*(1), 82–115.

Roundy, P. T. (2014a). Doing good by telling stories: Emotion in social entrepreneurship communication. *Journal of Small Business Strategy, 24*(2), 41–68.

Roundy, P. T. (2014b). The stories of social entrepreneurs: Narrative discourse and social venture resource acquisition. *Journal of Research in Marketing and Entrepreneurship, 16*(2), 200–218.

Roundy, P. T. (2014c). The tactics and evolution of social entrepreneurial storytelling. *Journal of Business and Entrepreneurship, 26*(2), 117–152.

Roundy, P. T. (2016). Start-up community narratives: The discursive construction of entrepreneurial ecosystems. *The Journal of Entrepreneurship, 25*(2), 232–248.

Roundy, P. T. (2017). Doing good while serving customers: Charting the social entrepreneurship and marketing interface. *Journal of Research in Marketing and Entrepreneurship, 19*(2), 105–124.

Roundy, P. T. (2021). On entrepreneurial stories: Tolkien's theory of fantasy and the bridge between imagination and innovation. *Business Perspectives and Research, 9*(1), 31–45.

Ruebottom, T. (2013). The microstructures of rhetorical strategy in social entrepreneurship: Building legitimacy through heroes and villains. *Journal of Business Venturing, 28*(1), 98–116.

Ryder, P., & Vogeley, J. (2018). Telling the impact investment story through digital media: An Indonesian case study. *Communication Research and Practice, 4*(4), 375–395.

Saebi, T., Foss, N. J., & Linder, S. (2019). Social entrepreneurship research: Past achievements and future promises. *Journal of Management, 45*(1), 70–95.

Samuel, A. J., White, G. R. T., Peattie, K., & Thomas, R. (2022). Social enterprise places: A place-based initiative facilitating syntactic, semantic and pragmatic constructions of legitimacy. *Journal of Macromarketing, 42*(1), 51–70.

Schmeltz, L. (2020). Heartcore business? A study of how social enterprises, as organizations crossing traditional sectorial borders, communicate their corporate identity. *Globe: A Journal of Language, Culture and Communication, 9*, 15–28.

Seanor, P., Bull, M., Baines, S., & Ridley-Duff, R. (2013). Narratives of transition from social to enterprise: You can't get there from here! *International Journal of Entrepreneurial Behavior & Research, 19*(3), 324–343.

Smith, C. (2011). *For social enterprises: How your mission can help your sales*. http://wejungo.wordpress.com/2011/04/25/for-social-enterprises-how-your-mission-can-help-your-sales/

Srivetbodee, S., Igel, B., & Kraisornsuthasinee, S. (2017). Creating social value through social enterprise marketing: Case studies from Thailand's food-focused social entrepreneurs. *Journal of Social Entrepreneurship, 8*(2), 201–224.

Stam, E., & Van de Ven, A. (2021). Entrepreneurial ecosystem elements. *Small Business Economics, 56*, 809–832. https://doi.org/10.1007/s11187-019-00270-6

Suarezserna, F. (2020). *Once upon a time . . . How stories strengthen brands* [Doctoral dissertation, EGADE Business School, Instituto Tecnologico y de Estudios Superiores de Monterrey (Mexico)].

Suddaby, R., Israelsen, T., Mitchell, J. R., & Lim, D. S. (2021, In press). Entrepreneurial visions as rhetorical history: A diegetic narrative model of stakeholder enrollment. *Academy of Management Review.*

Sutton, E., McEachern, M., & Kane, K. (2018). Communicating a social agenda within HEIs: The role of the social enterprise mark. *Social Enterprise Journal, 14*(3), 328–347.

Van Laer, T., De Ruyter, K., Visconti, L. M., & Wetzels, M. (2014). The extended transportation-imagery model: A meta-analysis of the antecedents and consequences of consumers' narrative transportation. *Journal of Consumer Research, 40*(5), 797–817.

Waldner, C. J. (2020, In press). In the centre of attention: How social entrepreneurs influence organisational reputation. *Journal of Social Entrepreneurship*, 1–23.

Welter, F. (2011). Contextualizing entrepreneurship – conceptual challenges and ways forward. *Entrepreneurship Theory and Practice, 35*(1), 165–184.

Wiesenberg, M., Godulla, A., Tengler, K., Noelle, I. M., Kloss, J., Klein, N., & Eeckhout, D. (2020). Key challenges in strategic start-up communication: A systematic literature review and an explorative study. *Journal of Communication Management, 24*(1), 49–64.

Wry, T., & York, J. G. (2017). An identity-based approach to social enterprise. *Academy of Management Review, 42*(3), 437–460.

Zamantılı Nayır, D., & Shinnar, R. S. (2020). How founders establish legitimacy: A narrative perspective on social entrepreneurs in a developing country context. *Social Enterprise Journal, 16*(3), 221–241.

3.4
STORYTELLING AND MEMES
New media trends for small civil society organizations

Ioli Campos[1]

Introduction

Civil society organizations (CSOs) often present powerful social media campaigns on multiple platforms, using a variety of formats to tell complex stories in a simplified, accessible, and engaging way. This chapter examines two media constructs that could be placed at the core of a cross-media or transmedia communication strategy: storytelling and memes.

Cross-media and transmedia definitions refer to delivering narratives across platforms, but to a different extent. While Boumans' (2007) notion of cross-media refers to one story in various platforms, Jenkins' (2006) conceptualization of transmedia foresees diverse stories within the same narrative universe. "A transmedia story unfolds across multiple media platforms, with each new text making a distinctive and valuable contribution to the whole. In the ideal form of transmedia storytelling, each medium does what it does best" (pp. 95–96). This mix of narratives in various platforms is related to the idea of convergence culture, which was also introduced by Jenkins (2006) to describe the communication flow between message distribution across new media platforms, audiences, and industries.

In an experiment with 219 participants, Voorveld et al. (2011) identified two main psychological processes that increase media effects in cross-media campaigns. The first is "forward encoding", which refers to the teaser or priming effect; it involves repetition and elements that arouse curiosity. These elements increase the audience's motivation to keep following the campaign. The second process is "multiple source perception", which is related to the power of synergy. The authors explain that "acquiring information from different sources can enhance the persuasive power of the message because the different media are seen as independent sources" (p. 73). To put it bluntly, the research shows that campaign synergy is more effective than the sum of their parts (Naik & Raman, 2003). Nevertheless, the implementation of cross-media and transmedia campaigns may seem to require vast resources, skills, and knowledge. Thus, one could wonder if the effort of developing such new formats is worth the cost, especially in the case of CSOs with limited resources.

While studying the CSOs' communication strategies about LGBTQ on Facebook, Mazid (2020) concluded that "advocacy strategies and tactics appeared as significant predictors of virality" (p. 115). It is challenging for CSOs to attain media access and make their voices heard in an information-saturated world. When CSOs approach conventional mass media to reach the public, they compete with many other newsworthy stories (Gregory, 2006). Therefore, good storytelling and memes could be an "ideal strategy" for CSOs. On the contrary to what one may think, in the current media landscape, those formats are affordable to produce, and they can reach a broad audience (Leiser, 2019; Yea & Chou, 2019).

This chapter contributes to the literature by researching those two media trends: storytelling and memes. This analysis relied on a critical literature review. A critical approach implies an attitude and strategic thinking that highlights power issues based on a rationale supporting social change. Such an approach includes an inquiry process challenging prevailing assumptions and privileging marginalized groups of people (Swaminathan & Mulvihill, 2017). Two consulting assignments inspired this critical review: a tailor-made workshop to teach CSOs how they could use storytelling and an evaluation of a transnational campaign that incorporated the use of memes.

The broader research question that guided this inquiry was: How can CSOs benefit from a transmedia or cross-media communication strategy that includes storytelling and memes? In particular, this chapter examines the following sub-questions: What characteristics does storytelling have that may contribute to improving CSOs' communication strategies? What features do memes have that may improve CSOs' communication strategies? What common affordances do storytelling and memes have to strengthen CSOs' communication strategies when used together in a transmedia or cross-media campaign? What challenges may CSOs face when creating a cross-media or transmedia campaign that uses storytelling and memes?

Storytelling

Storytelling is one of the most natural and oldest ways of communicating. Ancient oral tradition meant that stories would be told again and again. The current digital environment facilitates such repetition and dissemination. Storytelling entails an interpretative representation of reality. It is usually associated with sharing a narrative and passing knowledge on to others. It is also an effective mechanism for telling complex stories in an accessible way. Furthermore, "storytelling can transform dull knowledge into an engaging narrative" while conveying valuable information (Yea & Chou, 2019, p. 277). Stories help individuals understand change by creating order and resisting contradictory information (van Wessel, 2018). Therefore, in interpreting human experiences, stories help to create meaning. More importantly, they may help counter dominant narratives (Moyer et al., 2020; Trevisan, 2017).

For all those reasons, storytelling has been adopted in advocacy to communicate with the broader public and stakeholders. Indeed, its target audience may be the community, other activists, legal decision-makers, policymakers, opinion formers, broad Internet audiences, general audiences, or professional media and journalists (Cizek, 2006). Similarly, storytelling goals for advocacy may vary. The story may be used in a social media campaign to attract more volunteers or raise awareness; in an annual report to show funders how their money was spent and attract more funding; and as a piece of evidence in human rights commissions, courts, or tribunals (Cizek, 2006).

Looking into story structure in classical literature models or Hollywood blockbuster movies, or even in long-form nonfiction, it becomes apparent that stories usually contain some sort of conflict or drama. Stories usually show people overcoming a problem, which can be physical or just a conflict of interests, personalities, or ideas (Cizek, 2006). In advocacy communication, one may be dealing with a problem that has not been overcome yet. However, there is usually an idea of what the solutions could be, which is the focus of the work of CSOs. Therefore, in line with overall CSOs' goals, a fundamental difference in stories for advocacy is that they usually end with a call for action (Cizek, 2006).

Unsurprisingly, CSOs have been using stories in their communication strategies for quite some time, with various levels of complexity. Sometimes, CSOs invest in making large and complex video projects; other times, they publish a small blog post with a few pictures. Regardless of the budget, the technical equipment, and the professional expertise available, storytelling is accessible to all kinds of CSOs precisely because it can be approached in various forms. Several institutions have issued guidelines to help small CSOs incorporate a storytelling culture into their organizations (Rockfeller Foundation et al., 2014).

To tell a good story, it is crucial to have access. Often, activists are on the field gathering stories first-hand. When that is not possible, they may provide a platform for people to send their own stories instead. Thanks to the participatory paradigm, crowdsourcing for storytelling is becoming increasingly common among grassroots movements (Trevisan et al., 2020). Opening a platform for people to upload their own stories may facilitate access. Simultaneously it may help smaller CSOs, with fewer resources, gather information more cost-effectively.

It is often said that stories connect people. Stories are persuasive in advocacy communication because they help create empathy and emotional resonance with the characters and situations. Empathy brings human beings closer to each other. Proximity is one of the main elements of newsworthy stories too. This is true not only of geographical proximity but also of emotional closeness. Ultimately, raising empathy is an essential component of a call for action.

Not surprisingly, various authors claim that stories can win public debates (Trevisan et al., 2020). As primatologist and activist Jane Goodall (2019) said in an interview, if one wants leaders to truly listen, take action, and make a change, one should tell them a story. This power stems from the fact that stories help mobilize people by bringing them into collective action (Trevisan et al., 2020). Accordingly, various studies have demonstrated the effectiveness of advocacy storytelling in multiple fields, such as racial equity and educational justice (Moyer et al., 2020) and environmental mobilization (Gladwin, 2020).

In short, stories seem to have transformative power. That power can be even greater if local activists and minorities are empowered to collect and tell stories themselves, doing so instead of trained media professionals (Gregory, 2006). Even before social networks were standard, the documentary film *Seeing Is Believing* by Wintonick and Cizek (2002) already showed such transformative power in action as ordinary people picked up handycams and started to record. That sort of mobilization contributes to the authenticity of stories too. It contributes to the process of liberation forged with the oppressed, as argued by Freire (1968 rpt. 2014). Finally, studies have also shown that the participatory process can be therapeutic "when coupled with an altruistic opportunity to help others through story sharing" (D'Cruz et al., 2019, p. 1409).

Memes

A meme is a unit of cultural transmission, which is spread by replication, according to Richard Dawkins (1976), who first coined that expression. "Memes carry information, are replicated, and are transmitted from one person to another, and they have the ability to evolve, mutating at random and undergoing natural selection, with or without impacts on human fitness" (Rogers, n.d.).

Among the contemporary online community, memes rely on a picture and a sort of punchline. However, contrary to what one might think, memes are not necessarily simplistic. In fact, some authors consider memes as complex structures to convey humour (Moussa et al., 2020). Meme creators reinterpret reality also by expressing irony or sarcasm over a visual base. To assimilate that reinterpretation, it is essential that the creator and community share at least some knowledge about the issue (Ross & Rivers, 2019).

While stories usually have three parts – a beginning, a middle, and an end – jokes typically have only two parts – a beginning and a middle (Hannah Gadsby, 2018). Therefore, if memes are viewed as jokes, a difference in structure can easily be recognized. They lack the ending, but as mentioned before, in the context of advocacy, stories are usually still unfolding as their conclusion is subject to change.

Memes are technically easy to create, and there are even meme-generating sites. Hence, their creation is accessible to CSOs with few resources. The biggest challenge may be finding the correct wording and punchline. The research shows that advocacy memes use various frames: convinced logic, sceptical, impact, and actions to be taken (Ross & Rivers, 2019). While evaluating a campaign to counter hate speech in five Eastern European countries, I found that advocacy memes can also use the contrast between oppressor and oppressed to raise awareness of unjust social situations (Campos, 2019).

Another characteristic of memes is that the message they carry usually remains in the memory of its recipient (Patrick, 2012). "According to its duration, it will have more power to infect other recipients of the message" (Flecha Ortiz et al., 2021, p. 171). This notion of memes as a contagious condition is also shared by Knobel and Lankshear (2007). While spreading from human to human like a virus, memes gain the power to change a social group's mentality and lead its members to a change in action (Knobel & Lankshear, 2007). In other words, memes can influence the ending of real stories.

At the same time, memes can act as a form of civic expression (Mihailidis, 2020). Furthermore, they can also be considered what Freire called an act of rebellion, given their subversive tone (Moussa et al., 2020; Williams, 2020). Indeed, various studies have shown the effectiveness of memes in reversing the power dynamics concerning racial equality against white supremacy (Williams, 2020), in reversing climate change scepticism (Ross & Rivers, 2019), in promoting marriage equality in the United States (Waddock et al., 2020), and in promoting LGBTQ+ activism against the Russian state (Baker et al., 2020).

Additionally, various authors argue that memes can have a therapeutic effect in some situations. After analysing the use of memes during COVID-19 in Puerto Rico, Flecha Ortiz et al. (2021) concluded that memes helped reach out to mainstream media and mitigate the stressful effects of social events through collective coping.

Even before memes were common in online communities, Surman and Reilly (2003) recommended that CSOs embrace the open-source culture and experiment and broaden their online presence. Going back to the ideas of involvement, empowerment, and the therapeutic effect, inviting the community to develop their memes may have its advantages.

Again, as with any other advocacy communication strategy, it is crucial to know the goal and target group. Memes and hashtags are relevant among online communities and, often, among young people (Mihailidis, 2020). But they may only reach specific publics if they become viral and get to the mainstream media. However, not all memes will become viral. Why some become viral while others do not is a line of study that requires further development. Even so, studies already show that the reason may be related to influencer nodes (Leiser, 2019). Therefore, a good dissemination strategy may be crucial for meme efficacy.

Common affordances

Storytelling and memes share several affordances when used in advocacy communication despite being two different formats. It may be helpful to consider the common affordances when planning a transmedia or cross-media campaign that uses both formats. For that reason, four common affordances found in this critical literature review are highlighted next.

First, because they are spread through digital media, they have the power to go beyond national borders and bring a local story to a global audience. In other words, they facilitate broader media access to smaller CSOs in the current media landscape.

Second, they are media constructions that can be disseminated across various platforms that target different groups of people. While reaching bigger audiences, these two formats may become viral. When they become viral, they can change power narratives and public discourse (Moussa et al., 2020). In part, that is why Bozkuş (2016) considers memes a new kind of digital social capital.

Third, the inherently participatory nature of storytelling and memes can serve as a venue of expression for the oppressed. In that sense, storytelling and memes are two powerful communication tools that may liberate the oppressed by working with them instead of working for them, as Freire (1968 rpt. 2014) advocated. "Only power that springs from the weakness of the oppressed will be sufficiently strong to free both" (Freire, 1968 rpt. 2014, p. 43). Storytelling and memes may give media access to the oppressed, who usually struggle to have their voices heard precisely because they are oppressed. In that sense, these two formats are powerful tools to counteract dominant narratives and ideologies while empowering minorities to express themselves. Still following Freire's framework, if we consider the media as a setting for informal education, storytelling and memes made by or with the oppressed could also work as a pedagogy of the oppressed.

That would be in line with a fourth common affordance: the therapeutic effect various authors attribute to storytelling and memes (D'Cruz et al., 2019; Flecha Ortiz et al., 2021). Ultimately, storytelling and memes can help communities cope with their struggles by sharing their stories and participating in their production.

These common affordances make storytelling and memes valuable in the context of advocacy communication. Nonetheless, there are various limitations and challenges in their use by CSOs, which should also be considered.

The ethical challenges

There are several challenges in the use of stories and memes for advocacy. Here I will focus on the ethical dimension of those challenges, as technical constraints may be more easily overcome.

On the one hand, it can be argued that it may be difficult to find the right balance in the appropriation of suffering and in the choice of the right imagery. However, I would insist that the focus should not be on victimization; it should be on the solutions. That may not always come easily, as Tony Quinlan, founder of Narrate Consulting, a UK-based firm that helps collect stories for non-governmental organizations (NGOs), highlighted in an interview.

> There was a time five years ago I can remember having a conversation with UNICEF. It was a heated conversation, where they would determine that for fundraising, they have to tell negative stories. They had to tell stories that scared their potential donors, that says, "Oh this is dreadful. I must donate".
>
> (Quinlan, 2014)

However, Quinlan's advice for the United Nations and for CSOs is: "tell their stories, not yours" (Quinlan, 2014). To which I would add: empower them to participate in the process too.

On the other hand, Durham (2018) argues that memes have opposing ethical concerns to those of photojournalism when it comes to the representation of vulnerable bodies. The author says that photojournalism relies on the "ethics of care to generate empathy", while memes disrupt those affective connotations (p. 240). Regardless of whether one agrees with Durham's view of photojournalism or not, his general view on memes is pertinent. In the case of advocacy memes, I would argue that that characteristic is precisely what makes them helpful in countering dominant narratives. However, it can be a double-edged sword. Digital media are powerful institutions for youth expression, socialization, participation, and mobilization, and memes have also been used as propaganda tools for radicalization and recruitment (DeCook, 2018).

When it comes to using storytelling and memes for advocacy, several lines of study still need further development. One of those is related to the evaluation of the effectiveness of storytelling and memes in advocacy communication, which is a hard endeavour given the multiple symbolic meanings and the difficulty in establishing casual relations (van Wessel, 2018).

Conclusion

This chapter set out to research how CSOs could benefit from a transmedia or cross-media communication strategy, incorporating storytelling and memes. It has done so by critically reviewing the characteristics and affordances of storytelling and memes in the context of advocacy communication.

One of the key ideas is that storytelling may be an important communication tool for CSOs because when CSOs tell authentic stories that are still unfolding, the audience can shape the ending of such stories in real life. Additionally, stories contribute to raising empathy and helping simplify complex issues. Hence, storytelling may be an effective mechanism to engage donors, stakeholders, and the broader public in meaningful action. Memes can also contribute to meaningful action. Some could say that memes are too simple, not serious enough, and not in line with the tone that CSOs seek to emphasize in their messages.

However, memes have proven to be powerful and engaging communication tools. Some CSOs have moved beyond the stigma of silliness associated with them and found promising results in their use (Campos, 2019). While some CSOs may still resist the idea of using humour to talk about serious issues, Cizek (2006) argues that "it's fine to be funny" because "humour can help subjects. Humour is often an expression of resilience and coping. Humour can also help ease the pain" (pp. 76–77).

That brings us back to the initial question of this chapter. Given that transmedia campaigns are more than the sum of their parts (Naik & Raman, 2003), memes and storytelling may be two critical components that can be used to complement one another. Applying the concepts of "forward encoding" and "multiple source perception" of Voorveld et al. (2011), one can argue that the combined use of storytelling and memes in an advocacy campaign may increase media effects. Where memes could ignite, storytelling could explain and connect.

Note

1 The revision of this chapter was funded by FCT – Fundação para a Ciência a Tecnologia; reference UIDB/05021/2020.

References

Baker, J. E., Clancy, K. A., & Clancy, B. (2020). Putin as gay icon? Memes as a tactic in Russian LGBT+ activism. In R. Buyantueva & M. Shevtsova (Eds.), *LGBTQ+ activism in central and eastern Europe* (pp. 209–233). Palgrave Macmillan.

Boumans, J. (2007). *Cross-media: An operational term for city and regional development policy*. Paper presented at the 1st International Conference on Crossmedia Interaction Design at Hemavan, Sweden.

Bozkuş, Ş. B. (2016). Pop polyvocality and Internet memes: As a reflection of socio-political discourse of Turkish youth in social media. *Global Media Journal: Turkish Editions*, *6*(12), 44–74.

Campos, I. (2019). *Evaluation of counter hate speech campaigns*. Retrieved from Minority Rights Group Europe; co-funded by the Rights, Equality and Citizenship Programme of the European Union. http://stories.minorityrights.org/freedom-from-hate/wp-content/uploads/sites/23/2019/08/MRGE_Evaluation_Report_FINAL.pdf

Cizek, K. (2006). Storytelling for advocacy: Conceptualization and preproduction. In S. Gregory, G. Caldwell, R. Avni, & T. Harding (Eds.), *Video for change: A guide for advocacy and activism* (pp. 74–121). Pluto Press.

Dawkins, R. (1976). *The selfish gene*. Oxford University Press.

D'Cruz, K., Douglas, J., & Serry, T. (2019). Narrative storytelling as both an advocacy tool and a therapeutic process: Perspectives of adult storytellers with acquired brain injury. *Neuropsychological Rehabilitation*, *30*(8), 1409–1429. https://doi.org/10.1080/09602011.2019.1586733

DeCook, J. R. (2018). Memes and symbolic violence: #proudboys and the use of memes for propaganda and the construction of collective identity. *Learning, Media and Technology*, *43*(4), 485–504. https://doi.org/10.1080/17439884.2018.1544149

Durham, M. G. (2018). Resignifying Alan Kurdi: News photographs, memes, and the ethics of embodied vulnerability. *Critical Studies in Media Communication, 35*(3), 240–258. https://doi.org/10.1080/15295036.2017.1408958

Flecha Ortiz, J. A., Santos Corrada, M. A., Lopez, E., & Dones, V. (2021). Analysis of the use of memes as an exponent of collective coping during COVID-19 in Puerto Rico. *Media International Australia, 178*(1), 168–181. https://doi.org/10.1177/1329878X20966379

Freire, P. (1968 rpt. 2014). *Pedagogy of the oppressed: 30th anniversary edition:* Bloomsbury Publishing.

Gadsby, H. (Producer). (2018). *Nanette.* www.netflix.com/title/80233611?trackId=13752289&trackIdJaw=13752289&trackIdEpisode=13752289&trackIdTrailer=13752289&dpLeftClick=1

Gladwin, D. (2020). Digital storytelling going viral: Using narrative empathy to promote environmental action. *Media Practice and Education, 21*(4), 275–288. https://doi.org/10.1080/25741136.2020.1832827

Goodall, J. (2019). Jane Goodall: If you want leaders to truly listen, use the power of storytelling/interviewer: A. Gibbs. *CNBC.* www.cnbc.com/2019/01/29/wef-2019-jane-goodall-on-the-power-of-storytelling-and-activism.html

Gregory, S. (2006). Transnational storytelling: Human rights, WITNESS, and video advocacy. *American Anthropologist, 108*(1), 195–204.

Jenkins, H. (2006). *Convergence culture: Where old and new media collide.* New York University Press.

Knobel, M., & Lankshear, C. (2007). Online memes, affinities, and cultural production. In M. Knobel & C. Lankshear (Eds.), *A new literacies sampler* (Vol. 29, pp. 199–227). Peter Lang.

Leiser, A. (2019). *Spreadable media, citizens, and participatory culture: Uses and effects of political internet memes* [PhD, Bremen International Graduate School of Social Sciences, Bremen]. http://nbn-resolving.de/urn:nbn:de:gbv:46-00107495-14

Mazid, I. (2020). Virality of social change messages on Facebook: A study of advocacy and relationship building strategies of LGBTQ advocacy organizations. *International Journal of Strategic Communication, 14*(2), 105–121. https://doi.org/10.1080/1553118X.2020.1730377

Mihailidis, P. (2020). The civic potential of memes and hashtags in the lives of young people. *Discourse: Studies in the Cultural Politics of Education, 41*(5), 762–781. https://doi.org/10.1080/01596306.2020.1769938

Moussa, M. B., Benmessaoud, S., & Douai, A. (2020). Internet memes as "tactical" social action: A multimodal critical discourse analysis approach. *International Journal of Communication, 14,* 5920–5940.

Moyer, J. S., Warren, M. R., & King, A. R. (2020). "Our stories are powerful": The use of youth storytelling in policy advocacy to combat the school-to-prison pipeline. *Harvard Educational Review, 90*(2), 172–194. https://doi.org/10.17763/1943-5045-90.2.172

Naik, P. A., & Raman, K. (2003). Understanding the impact of synergy in multimedia communications. *Journal of Marketing Research, 40*(4), 375–388. https://doi.org/10.1509/jmkr.40.4.375.19385

Patrick, D. (2012). The language of internet memes. In M. Mandiberg (Ed.), *The social media reader* (pp. 120–134). New York University Press.

Quinlan, T. (2014). 'Chief storyteller' to UN, NGOs: Tell their story, not yours/interviewer: J. L. Ravelo. *Devex.* www.devex.com/news/chief-storyteller-to-un-ngos-tell-their-story-not-yours-85020

Rockefeller Foundation, Hattaway Communications, & Timshel. (2014). *Digital storytelling for social impact.* www.rockefellerfoundation.org/wp-content/uploads/Digital-Storytelling-for-Social-Impact.pdf

Rogers, K. (n.d.). meme. *Encyclopedia Britannica.* www.britannica.com/topic/meme

Ross, A. S., & Rivers, D. (2019). Internet memes, media frames, and the conflicting logics of climate change discourse. *Environmental Communication, 13*(7), 975–994. https://doi.org/10.1080/17524032.2018.1560347

Surman, M., & Reilly, K. (2003). *Appropriating the internet for social change: Towards the strategic use of networked technologies by transnational civil society organizations.* Information Technology and International Cooperation Program. https://marksurman.commons.ca/wp-content/uploads/sites/2/Surman_2003_Appropriating_Internet_Social_Change.pdf

Swaminathan, R., & Mulvihill, T. M. (2017). *Critical approaches to questions in qualitative research.* Taylor & Francis.

Trevisan, F. (2017). Crowd-sourced advocacy: Promoting disability rights through online storytelling. *Public Relations Inquiry, 6*(2), 191–208. https://doi.org/10.1177/2046147X17697785

Trevisan, F., Bello, B., Vaughan, M., & Vromen, A. (2020). Mobilizing personal narratives: The rise of digital "story banking" in US grassroots advocacy. *Journal of Information Technology Politics, 17*(2), 146–160. https://doi.org/10.1080/19331681.2019.1705221

van Wessel, M. (2018). Narrative assessment: A new approach to evaluation of advocacy for development. *Evaluation, 24*(4), 400–418. https://doi.org/10.1177%2F1356389018796021

Voorveld, H. A., Neijens, P. C., & Smit, E. G. (2011). Opening the black box: Understanding cross-media effects. *Journal of Marketing Communications, 17*(02), 69–85. https://doi.org/10.1080/13527260903160460

Waddock, S., Waddell, S., & Gray, P. S. (2020). The transformational change challenge of Memes: The case of marriage equality in the United States. *Business & Society*, *59*(8), 1667–1697. https://doi.org/10.1177/0007650318816440

Williams, A. (2020). Black memes matter: #LivingWhileBlack with Becky and Karen. *Social Media+ Society*, *6*(4), 1–14. https://doi.org/10.1177/2056305120981047

Wintonick, P., & Cizek, K. (Writers). (2002). Seeing is believing: Handicams, human rights and the news. In F. Miquet, K. Cizek, & P. Wintonick (Producers), *Canada: Necessary illusions*.

Yea, C. C., & Chou, W. H. (2019). Promoting social advocacy through digital storytelling: The case of ocean acidification. *World Academy of Science, Engineering and Technology. International Journal of Humanities and Social Sciences*, *13*(3). https://doi.org/10.5281/zenodo.2643585

3.5
LOBBYING AND THE NONPROFIT SECTOR

Ana Almansa-Martínez and Antonio Castillo-Esparcia

Introduction

Complexity is one of the main characteristics of contemporary societies, as a multitude of social and individual interests coexist in the social ecosystem. These interests are organized and structured through numerous social associations that are the expression of civic society.

In this sense, social relationships are elements that connect individuals, allowing to produce through them effective social and political interrelationships. In the social ecosystem, relationships are essential and can be a direct product of it or can emerge through social associations. In this sense, social networks (in sociological terms) are one of the main mechanisms of intersubjective relationships. Increasingly, however, these networks are projected through associations that bring together individuals with a certain interest and serve as a common space between people.

The starting point for the analysis of groups in social and political life comes from the research carried out by Bentley (1983) on the different social manifestations, where he points out:

> The main work in the study of all forms of social life is the analysis of groups, which is much more than a classification. When groups are properly defined, everything is defined. And when I say everything, I mean each and every thing.
>
> (1983: p. 256)

Bentley's contribution initiated a rational shift in the perception of political activity in static, legal, and formalistic terms, to give way to a dynamic vision of social and political life, based on the numerical richness of groups as organizations that formally structure individuals and bring them together based on their multiple interests. In this sense, the diversity of interests for Burdeau (1982: p. 164) increases with the complexity of a society, a situation that facilitates the increase of more concrete and contradictory interests.

The increase in social complexity and the natural tendency to seek the condition of equilibrium, in which the interests of some groups may cause others to react because they have conflicting or similar interests (Truman, 1968; Ward, 1978 and Salisbury, 1969; Tu, 2021; Drelich-Skulska & Domiter, 2020), are two interrelated social processes that lead to group formation.

This complexity is the result of enlargement and specialization, which also has the effect of further segmenting groups to better articulate their own needs. Thus, people join various organizations that welcome, integrate, listen to them, take on their demands, and become their spokespersons.

These organizations often take on numerous affiliations and are the contemporary expression of their interests and their relations with the political sphere. Numerous studies have analyzed how these intersubjective relationships (between individuals) are produced through social associations (Kwaunick, 1970; Castles, 1973; Gray & Lowery, 1993).

Therefore, individuals have their main mechanism of social expression in associations, since they connect people with common interests and could project those interests on other individuals, society, or the political system, generating spaces for coexistence and mutual understanding (Sørensen, 2013).

This proliferation of citizens' associations is growing. Walter (1983, p. 394) pointed out that half of the professional groups had been created between 1850 and the Second World War. In the case of citizen groups, it was from 1960 onwards that half the current number appeared. This sociological trend has been emphasized by the emergence and generalization of social media, which make it possible for any citizen to become a manager and producer of content.

In this respect, nongovernmental organizations (NGOs) are social organizations that bring people together to achieve certain objectives, without governmental links and devoid of a profit-making purpose. Their income comes from various sources, whether their own (membership fees, sale of products, organization of events) or external (donations, subsidies, or public or private aid), enabling them to achieve their organizational objectives.

Some aspects that characterize citizen associations with respect to other types of organizations that participate in the political dynamics are the following:

- Their ability to detect and respond to social needs and demands more quickly than official bodies (Brinkerhoff & Brinkerhoff, 2002).
- They offer a greater capacity to provide outlets and solutions that are closer, more innovative, and more creative than the bureaucratic structure.
- From the internal point of view, they have less bureaucratization, which allows them to acknowledge issues and act on them in an accelerated manner.
- An initial informality, which allows them to face social problems in a more effective way, due to their better relationship and connection with the social base.
- Closeness to the population, which means better two-way communication flows.

Society, state, and participation

In the interrelationship between society and state, different positions coexist between the power of one and the other, but the degree of relationship is conditioned by the involvement of the state in the social fabric and the consequent social response. In an arrangement in which the state participates intensely in society, it is presented as normal that society tries to influence and act on the state since the decisions of the state affect it to a great extent (Mongentau, 1970; Fogarty, 1990; Whiteley & Winyard, 1984).

In this sense, one of the social and political functions of social organizations is the translation of citizens' demands into the political system. Almond and Powell (1972, p. 19) point out that they have functions of articulation and aggregation of interests, since they act as organizations that articulate social interests and transfer them to the institutional sphere. All this is due to a greater and better interrelation with individuals, who participate in politics through the social organizations to which they belong. Therefore, one of their main functions is that social articulation takes the form of becoming specialized channels, which transfer social demands, since individuals do not have the contacts, relationships, knowledge, time, or capacity to become political actors (Shamsul Haque, 2020; Teegen et al., 2004; Batley, 2011; Eliantonio, 2018).

This perception of citizen associations has been widely discussed by numerous researchers, who have emphasized this regulatory role of social demands (Burchell & Cook, 2011; Fogarty, 2011;

Doh & Guay, 2006). Hence, analyzing how citizens participate in the political sphere involves, to a large extent, analyzing which social groups people are integrated into and what social and political role these associations play.

This research postulates that citizens participate in politics through citizen associations and that these associations transfer citizen demands to the political system (Schmitter, 1977; Andersen & Eliassen, 1991; Greenwood & Ronit, 1994; Bowler & Farrell, 1995). It is a perspective that the political dynamics themselves have been emphasizing through the increasing participation of the state in the resolution of social problems and conflicts, such as economic or health crises.

Korten's (1990) classification of how the functions of NGOs have evolved clearly establishes two typologies of organizations:

a) The first is that in which organizations focus on solving social problems and carrying out activities and actions of assistance, emergency, or transfer of resources to society. In this case, they would correspond to what are called first-generation or welfare NGOs and second-generation or developmental NGOs.
b) On the other hand, new models of citizen participation have emerged through NGOs since the 1970s. In this sense, these social organizations carry out actions of political participation and advocacy, focused on social denunciation and the necessary modification of regulations that affect social dynamics. In this way, they become active political actors who carry out communication campaigns and direct action aimed at those in power (meetings, interviews, presentation of documentation) to influence institutional decisions, but they also develop communication actions aimed at their affiliates and sympathizers.

Citizenship and social engagement

In the democratic system, to influence public opinion is to influence political power indirectly. Every power adds a degree of difficulty to its activity when the measures it intends to adopt have an unfavorable public opinion. Thus, the political game is organized and structured on public opinion in its modern aspect, and the political struggle tends to be increasingly reduced to a battle to win public support.

In this symbolic struggle, each actor seeks and intends to monopolize and triumph his singular vision of the social order and to impose it as just and true on the greatest number of subjects. These new activities imply the capacity to be interlocutors between the social and the political systems, transferring citizens' demands to the political sphere that are related to their organizational objectives. To be able to participate in these political instances, associations structure their activities in two main actions:

a) Direct action on public decision-makers, through participation in legislative or governmental commissions, interventions in government advisory bodies, official meetings with government representatives, meetings in the legislative arena, presentation of documents to elaborate governmental or legislative regulations, meetings with political parties, and attendance at working groups in the legislative arena. All these activities allow them to establish a relationship with all institutionalized actors and become spokespersons for individuals who are affiliated with their own organizations and who serve them as a support and source of legitimization of their political demands (Johnston, 2015; Allan & Hadden, 2017).
b) Indirect action on the political system, through communication campaigns aimed at promoting, raising awareness, educating, and sensitizing public opinion on the issues defended by the association. Thus, one of the fundamental elements of democracies is the role of public opinion, which is why they aim to show social support for their demands. To this end, they resort to

strategies aimed at achieving media presence. They also resort to campaigns to mobilize their supporters on social media as a communication strategy that allows the involvement of members who become prescribers and who play an essential role in social media (Herrero-Jiménez et al., 2018; Castillo-Esparcia et al., 2015).

Communication and the nonprofit sector

Communication plays an essential role in nonprofit organizations, as it allows them to reach spaces of relationship with citizens in order to disseminate their objectives and obtain social support for their demands. Thus, communication flows in these organizations through strategic planning, which must structure, organize, implement, and evaluate communication objectives. For this, planning needs to integrate four macro-processes: research, planning, implementation, and evaluation (see Figure 3.5.1).

Research

Research should be done on target audiences, focusing, among other aspects, on how they perceive the organization. To do this, the organization must work on the following sections:

- Analyzing the characteristics of the audiences the organization is going to address, knowing their values, their perceptions, how they consume information, how they manage their information and communication needs, how they interact with their peers, or how they access information. With these, the organization can select the most efficient and effective media, messages, and processes for communication. In this sense, if the organization wants to target a young audience, they must bear in mind that a very significant part of their information sources consists of social media and not the traditional mass media.

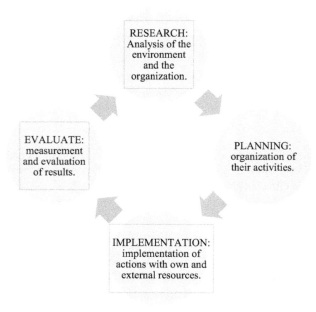

Figure 3.5.1 Phases of the communication process. Source: Own elaboration.

- To study the social perception of the nonprofit sector in society, to find out what values are associated with the sector and what social image it has.
- To find out the image that the organization has among citizens and political actors (institutions, political parties, media, etc.). In this sense, studies on prestige and notoriety can help to plan communication campaigns.

Planning

Review the material, economic, and personal resources available in order to know whether a campaign can be carried out in-house or whether it will be necessary to resort to external support. One example was the initiative taken in some European countries back when the euro was introduced as a currency. Thus, some NGOs planned to collect the country's now obsolete physical currency, but this required collection and transport infrastructures. For this reason, hotels, pharmacies, and restaurants were contacted, in which a container was placed for customers to deposit physical currencies that were no longer in use. In turn, to collect and transport all these deposit boxes, the collaboration of security companies was requested. In this way, several thousands of coins were collected and used to finance the activities of the NGOs.

Implementation

In order to implement the campaign, a process of managing people, resources, and time is needed through organizational systems such as the Gantt chart or the Program Evaluation and Review Technique (PERT) method.

Evaluation

The last step is measurement and evaluation. Measuring is not evaluating, since evaluation is the process that allows us to know to what extent we have achieved the objectives of the campaign. To do so, it uses a series of measurements.

- Outputs correspond to the analysis of the immediate results of a particular action or activity. To measure them, the following can be used: analysis of the materials published in the media, online presence, the quantity and quality of those attending an event, promotional material distributed, incidents and behavior of guests, public opinion polls, etc.
- Outtakes consist of the analysis of the reception, attention, and real understanding or comprehension of messages among key audiences.
- Outcomes are the most sophisticated objectives to measure because they explore changes in the opinion, attitude, and behavior of audiences who have received the same messages. For this measurement, it is suggested to resort to social science research tools (focus groups, surveys, and ethnographic studies, among others) and to types of social research (quantitative and qualitative).

In this sense, the evaluation of communication should address both impact objectives (in the short term) and image and prestige objectives of organizations (in the long term), as shown in Figure 3.5.2.

In this context, organizations have communication departments that enable them to carry out the process (Almansa-Martínez & Fernández-Souto, 2020). As Almansa-Martínez (2005, p. 123) points out, this department "is an organized structure, reporting directly to senior management, which coordinates and brings together all communication actions (internal and external) to create, maintain or improve the image of the organization in the eyes of all its audiences."

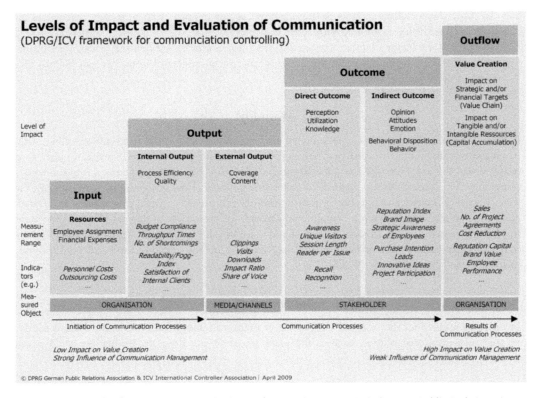

Figure 3.5.2 Levels of impact in communication evaluation. Source: DPRG German Public Relations Association & ICV International Controller Association (April 2009).

Citizen social networks

Nowadays, citizen organizations have the tendency to increasingly undertake actions aimed at dramatizing what they are and do, determined to exhibit themselves in the communicative ecosystem (Gitlin, 1980; Ericson; Baranek & Chan, 1987; Junk, 2015; Trong Duong, 2017). As Molotoch and Lester (1974: p. 110) assert, to produce the news movement, members must gather at an inappropriate time and in an inappropriate place to engage in inappropriate activity.

The instrument that has traditionally allowed these organizations to connect with the public has been the media, under four pretensions:

- Educating the population about the problems of individuals.
- Mobilizing people to increase the degree of participation and intersubjective involvement.
- Sensitizing individuals to focus their attention on certain social issues.
- Legitimizing organizations, as they present themselves as valid interlocutors between individuals and the political system.

There is a duality among associations, since in the face of an increase in their number, only a few stand out for their capacity for participation due to their growing professionalization. On one hand, there are organizations that maintain a constant grassroots attitude with specialized and hired personnel and, on the other hand, there are others that develop an episodic, limited, and intermittent activity (Youmans & York, 2012; Trong Duong, 2017; Chalmers, 2012).

From this perspective, we can catalog two major typologies of organizations:

- Proactive strategy – This planned and strategic capacity allows them to be co-creators of public policies, co-participants in their elaboration, and codifiers of knowledge and acceptance for the recipients. In essence, they are one of the actors in the political process, which implies a permanent, updated, and professional structure. All this implies links with decision-makers and a constant capacity to listen to and monitor public policies and legislative agendas.
- Reactive strategy – The main function of a reactive strategy is to react to initiatives of other actors without participating in the proposal, but instead mobilizing only when their interests are affected.

In this sense, associations mobilize their members and sympathizers to act socially through communication and grassroots strategies in which they propitiate a series of actions aimed at public opinion, the media, and public decision-makers to show a strong and potent social power with citizen support for the association's proposals (Connor & Yerbury, 2018).

These activities can take place in various scenarios, such as:

- Citizen presence in public spaces, through demonstrations, protests, collection of signatures, or social posters.
- Media activity based on the use of tools for relations with the media (Sommerfeldt et al., 2012; Waters & Jamal, 2011; Krøvel, 2012).
- Generating spaces in the digital sphere through the creation of web spaces, blogs, and social network profiles to reach a wide layer of citizens. Digital campaigns can be generated through virality (García-Galera et al., 2019; Connor & Yerbury, 2018; Takahashi et al., 2015).

One of the most relevant aspects from the point of view of the strategic communication of citizens' associations is the control of information and message content (Castillo-Esparcia et al., 2020). Thus, the organization becomes a spokesperson for its interests and encourages its members and supporters to generate messages in support of the demands and interests defended by the organization. However, some research indicates that associations want to maintain control of communication flows and message content, so they basically generate unidirectional communication strategies, in which they are the ones who manage the information content (Comfort & Hester, 2019; Hestres, 2014: Lovejoy et al., 2012).

NGO lobbying in the European Union

The evolution of NGOs in the European Union register has been very positive, as they have been increasing since 2013, with peaks in 2016 and 2019, when the number of NGOs increased significantly compared to the previous year (see Figure 3.5.3). This is influenced by the growing involvement of the European Union in national regulations due to the development of laws, both from the European Commission and the European Parliament, which must be transposed into the legislation of the member states (Almansa-Martínez et al., 2022).

The specific peak in 2016 may have been due to the entry into force of The Paris Agreement on climate change in that year. As it is an international treaty, legally binding for the countries that sign it, it was necessary to develop regulations within the European Union. NGOs wanted to actively participate in this process by contributing their proposals to the regulations, and to do so, they had to be registered in the Transparency Register.

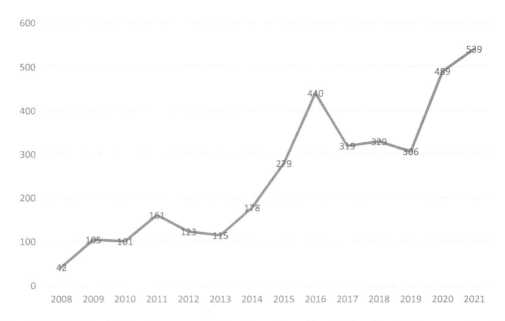

Figure 3.5.3 NGO evolution in Transparency Register. *Source*: Own elaboration based on the Transparency Register.

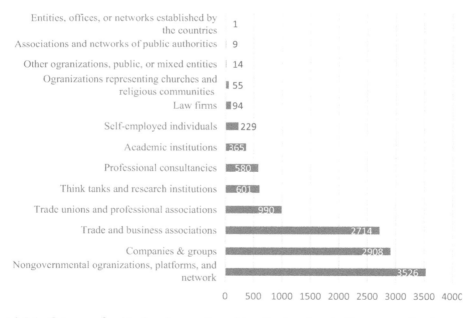

Figure 3.5.4 Category of registration. Source: Own elaboration based on the Transparency Register.

The Paris Agreement was a milestone in the multilateral climate change process because, for the first time, a binding agreement brought all countries together through a common cause to undertake ambitious efforts to combat climate change and adapt to its effects.

In terms of the types of registration in the European Union, the organizations with the highest number of entries are NGOs, followed by companies and groups and trade and business associations (see Figure 3.5.4).

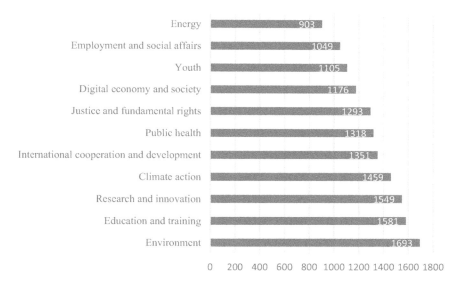

Figure 3.5.5 Fields of interest. Source: Own elaboration based on the Transparency Register.

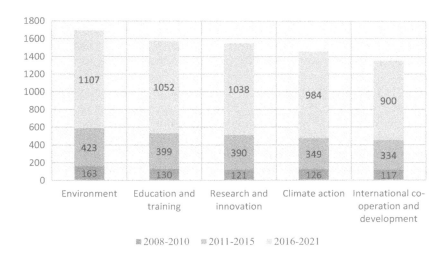

Figure 3.5.6 Evolution of the top five fields of interest. Source: Own elaboration based on the Transparency Register.

This means that the presence of NGOs in the processes of proposing, drafting, and approving community regulations is high due to the significance that these laws have on national regulations. This is a sign of the presence of social organizations in lobbying processes (Castillo-Esparcia et al., 2022).

The main field of interest of the NGOs registered in the Transparency Register is the environment, with 48.01% devoting a very significant part of their efforts to this issue. In second place comes education and training, with 44.835% of NGOs showing interest in this subject. In third, research and innovation, with 43.93%. In fourth place, climate action, with 41.37%, and in fifth place, international cooperation and development, with 38.31%. If we add up the different interests, we can see that issues directly related to the environment are the main lines of interest of NGOs in the European Union (see Figure 3.5.5).

Figure 3.5.7 Activities. Source: Own elaboration based on the Transparency Register.

When we analyze the five largest NGO fields of interest, we see that their growth has been very homogeneous since the creation of the Transparency Register in 2008 (see Figure 3.5.6). This means that the issues on which the NGOs are actively participating have not changed in the last 15 years.

The NGOs in the European Union focus their actions on the European Parliament, since of the 3,526 registered NGOs, 769 (21.80%) actively participate in the groups that are organized in the Parliament to discuss the regulations to be approved. In contrast, only 547 (15.51%) maintain an active presence in the discussion groups of the European Commission (see Figure 3.5.7). These data points show that the presence in participation formats with Members of European Parliament is greater than with the European Commission, due to the fact that the processes of interaction, mobilization, and discussion are swifter and the people working on them are elected by citizens.

References

Allan, J. I., & Hadden, J. (2017). Exploring the framing power of NGOs in global climate politics. *Environmental Politics*, 26(4), 600–620. https://doi.org/10.1080/09644016.2017.1319017

Almansa-Martínez, A. (2005). Relaciones públicas y gabinetes de comunicación. *Anàlisi*, 32, 117–132.

Almansa-Martínez, A., & Fernández-Souto, A.-B. (2020). Professional public relations (PR) trends and challenges. *Profesional De La Información*, 29(3). https://doi.org/10.3145/epi.2020.may.03

Almansa-Martínez, A., Moreno-Cabanillas, A., & Castillo-Esparcia, A. (2022). Political communication in Europe. The role of the lobby and its communication strategies. In Á. Rocha, D. Barredo, P. C. López-López, & I. Puentes-Rivera (Eds.), *Communication and smart technologies. ICOMTA. Smart innovation, systems and technologies* (Vol. 259). Springer. https://doi.org/10.1007/978-981-16-5792-4_24

Almond, G. A., & Powell, G. B. (1972). *Política comparada*. Editorial Paidos.

Andersen, S., & Eliassen, K. (1991). European community lobbying. *European Journal of Political Research*, 20(2), 173–187.

Batley, R. (2011). Structures and strategies in relationships between non-government service providers and governments. *Public Administration and Development*, 31(4), 306–319. https://doi.org/10.1002/pad.606

Bentley, A. (1983). *Il Processo di Governo. Uno studio delle Pressione Sociali*. Giuffrè.

Bowler, S., & Farrell, D. (1995). The organizing if the European parliament: Committees, specialization and co-ordination. *British Journal of Political Science*, *25*(2), 219–244.

Brinkerhoff, J., & Brinkerhoff, D. (2002). Government – nonprofit relations in comparative perspective: Evolution, themes and new directions. *Public Administration and Development*, *22*(1), 3–18. https://doi.org/10.1002/pad.202

Burchell, J., & Cook, J. (2011). Banging on open doors? Stakeholder dialogue and the challenge of business engagement for UK NGOs. *Environmental Politics*, *20*(6), 918–937. https://doi.org/10.1080/09644016.2011.617176

Burdeau, G. (1982). *Traité de Science Politique* (Tom III, La Dynamique Politique) (Vol. I, Les Forces Politiques). Librairie Géneérale de Droit et Jurisprudence.

Castillo-Esparcia, A., Almansa-Martínez, A., & Gonçalves, G. (2022). Lobbies: The hidden side of digital politics. In B. García-Orosa (Ed.), *Digital political communication strategies*. The Palgrave Macmillan Series in International Political Communication. Palgrave Macmillan. https://doi.org/10.1007/978-3-030-81568-4_5

Castillo-Esparcia, A., Almansa-Martínez, A., & Smolak-Lozano, E. (2015, October 1). East European think tanks in social media – towards the model of evaluation of effective communication/PR strategies: Case study analysis, *Catalan Journal of Communication & Cultural Studies*, *7*(2), 231–250(20). https://doi.org/10.1386/cjcs.7.2.231_1

Castillo-Esparcia, A., Castillero-Ostio, E., & Castillo-Díaz, A. (2020). The think tanks in Spain. Analysis of their digital communication strategies. *Revista Latina de Comunicación Social*, (77), 253–273. https://doi.org/10.4185/RLCS-2020-1457

Castles, F. G. (1973). The political functions of organized groups. *Political Studies*, *XXI*(1), 26–34.

Chalmers, A. W. (2012). Trading information for access: Informational lobbying strategies and interest group access to the European Union. *Journal of European Public Policy*, *20*(1), 39–58. https://doi.org/10.1080/13501763.2012.693411

Comfort, S. E., & Hester, J. B. (2019). Three dimensions of social media messaging success by environmental NGOs. *Environmental Communication*, *13*(3), 281–286. https://doi.org/10.1080/17524032.2019.1579746

Connor, M., & Yerbury, H. (2018). Information provision and active citizenship: An NGO's information-based interactions. *Journal of the Australian Library and Information Association*, *67*(2), 82–95. https://doi.org/10.1080/24750158.2018.1463076

Doh, J. P., & Guay, T. R. (2006). Corporate social responsibility, public policy, and NGO activism in Europe and the United States: An institutional-stakeholder perspective. *Journal of Management Studies*, *43*(1), 47–73. https://doi.org/10.1111/joms.2006.43.issue-1

Drelich-Skulska, B., & Domiter, M. (2020). The European Union as a platform for the European NGOs' operations: Market versus democracy. In M. Bilgin, H. Danis, E. Demir, & U. Tony-Okeke (Eds.), *Eurasian Economic Perspectives. Eurasian Studies in Business and Economics*, *15*(1), 155–167. Springer. https://doi.org/10.1007/978-3-030-48531-3_11

Eliantonio, M. (2018). The role of NGOs in environmental implementation conflicts: 'Stuck in the middle' between infringement proceedings and preliminary rulings? *Journal of European Integration*, *40*(6), 753–767. https://doi.org/10.1080/07036337.2018.1500566

Ericson, R., Baranek, P., & Chan, J. (1987). *Visualizing deviance: A studi of news organization*. University of Toronto Press.

Fogarty, E. A. (2011). Nothing succeeds like access? NGO strategies towards multilateral institutions. *Journal of Civil Society*, *7*(2), 207–227. https://doi.org/10.1080/17448689.2011.573670

Fogarty, M. (1990). Efficiency and democracy in large voluntary organizations. *Policy Studies*, *11*(3), 42–48.

García-Galera, M. C., Fernández Muñoz, C., & Del Olmo Barbero, F. (2019). NGOs' communication and youth engagement in the digital ecosystem. Social network analytics computational research methods and techniques. In N. Dey, S. Borah, R. Babo, & A. Ashour (Eds.), *Social network analytics* (pp. 227–247). Social Academic Press. https://doi.org/10.1016/B978-0-12-815458-8.00012-8.

Gitlin, T. (1980). *The whole world is watching*. University of California Press.

Gray, V., & Lowery, D. (1993). The diversity of State Interest Group Systems. *Political Research Quarterly*, *46*(1), 81–98.

Greenwood, J., & Ronit, K. (1994). Interest groups in the EC (European Community): Newly emerging dynamics and forms. *West European Politics*, *17*(1), 31–52.

Herrero-Jiménez, B., Arcila Calderón, C., Carratalá, A., & Berganza, R. (2018). The impact of media and NGOs on four European Parliament discourses about conflicts in the Middle East. *Media, War & Conflict*, *11*(1), 65–84. https://doi.org/10.1177/1750635217727310

Hestres, L. E. (2014). Preaching to the choir: Internet-mediated advocacy, issue public mobilization, and climate change. *New Media and Society*, *16*(2), 323–339. https://doi.org/10.1177/1461444813480361

Johnston, K. (2015). Public governance: The government of non-state actors in 'partnerships'. *Public Money & Management*, *35*(1), 15–22. https://doi.org/10.1080/09540962.2015.986860

Junk, W. M. (2015). Two logics of NGO advocacy: Understanding inside and outside lobbying on EU environmental policies. *Journal of European Public Policy*, *23*(2), 236–254. https://doi.org/10.1080/13501763.2015.1041416

Korten, D. (1990). *Getting to the 21th century: Voluntary action and the global agenda*. Kumarian Press.

Krøvel, R. (2012). Setting the agenda on environmental news in Norway. *Journalism Studies*, *13*(2), 259–276. https://doi.org/10.1080/1461670X.2011.646402

Kwaunick, D. (1970). Pressure group demands and the struggle for organizational status: The case of organized labour in Canadá. *Canadian Journal of Political Science*, *3*, 56–72.

Lovejoy, K., Waters, R. D., & Saxton, G. D. (2012). Engaging stakeholders through Twitter: How nonprofit organizations are getting more out of 140 characters or less. *Public Relations Review*, *38*(2), 313–318. https://doi.org/10.1016/j.pubrev.2012.01.005

Molotoch, H., & Lester, M. (1974). News as purposive behavior. *American Sociological Review*, (39), 101–112.

Morgentau, H. J. (1970). The new Feudalism. In H. S. Kariel (Ed.), *The political ordre* (pp. 317–336). Random House.

Salisbury, R. (1969). An exchange theory on interest groups. *Midwest Journal of Political Science*, *13*(1), 1–32.

Schmitter, P. C. (1977). Modes of interest intermediation and models of social change in Western Europe. *Comparative Political Studies*, *10*, 7–38.

Shamsul Haque, M. (2020). A critique of the role of NGOs as partners in governance. *Asia Pacific Journal of Public Administration*, *42*(1), 17–32. https://doi.org/10.1080/23276665.2020.1748960

Sommerfeldt, E. J., Kent, M. L., & Taylor, M. (2012). Activist practitioner perspectives of website public relations: Why aren't activist websites fulfilling the dialogic promise? *Public Relations Review*, *38*(2), 303–312. https://doi.org/10.1016/j.pubrev.2012.01.001

Sørensen, E. (2013). Institutionalizing interactive governance for democracy. *Critical Policy Studies*, *7*(1), 72–86. https://doi.org/10.1080/19460171.2013.766024

Takahashi, B., Edwards, G., Timmons, R., & Duan, R. (2015). Exploring the use of online platforms for climate change policy and public engagement by NGOs in Latin America. *Environmental Communication*, *9*(2), 228–247. https://doi.org/10.1080/17524032.2014.1001764

Teegen, H., Doh, J., & Vachani, S. (2004). The importance of noNGOvernmental organizations (NGOs) in global governance and value creation: An international business research agenda. *Journal International Business Studies*, *35*, 463–483. https://doi.org/10.1057/palgrave.jibs.8400112

Trong Duong, H. (2017). Fourth generation NGOs: Communication strategies in social campaigning and resource mobilization. *Journal of Nonprofit & Public Sector Marketing*, *29*(2), 119–147. https://doi.org/10.1080/10495142.2017.1293583

Truman, D. (1968). *The governmental process political interest and public opinion*. Alfred A. Knopf.

Tu, X. (2021). Understanding the role of nonprofit organizations in the provision of social services in China: An exploratory study. *Voluntas: International Journal of Voluntary and Nonprofit Organizations*. https://doi.org/10.1007/s11266-021-00375-1

Walter, J. (1983). The origins and maintenance of interest groups in America. *The American Political Science Review*, *77*(2), 390–406.

Ward, J. (1978). Arthur Bentley´s philosophy of social science. *American Journal of Political Science*, *22*(3), 595–603.

Waters, R. D., & Jamal, J. Y. (2011). Tweet, tweet, tweet: A content analysis of nonprofit organizations' Twitter updates. *Public Relations Review*, *37*(3), 321–324. https://doi.org/10.1016/j.pubrev.2011.03.002

Whiteley, P. F., & Winyard, S. J. (1984). The origins of the new poverty lobby. *Political Studies*, *XXXII*(1), 32–54.

Youmans, W. L., & York, J. C. (2012). Social media and the activist toolkit: User agreements, corporate interests, and the information infrastructure of modern social movements. *Journal of Communication*, *62*(2), 315–329. https://doi.org/10.1111/j.1460-2466.2012.01636.x

3.6
OPEN JUSTICE AND COURT COMMUNICATION

Jane Johnston

Introduction

Courts around the world have been relatively late adopters of professional communication and public relations (Davey et al., 2010; Fife-Yeomans, 1995; Greenhouse, 1996; Johnston, 2017, 2018a; Moran, 2014; Peleg & Bogoch, 2014). With few exceptions, courts have very short histories of appointing specialist communication and public relations staff (court-PR)[1] to assist in the core activities of explaining what they do and building relationships and trust with key stakeholders. While there was some early development in this sector, with the Supreme Court in the United States making what appears to be the world's first appointment in 1935 (Davis, 1994), this was not the norm. Courts elsewhere, such as the Netherlands, began appointing specialist 'press judges' in the 1970s whose primary purpose was to liaise with the news media while also working with a small cohort of communication specialists within the courts. Australia's first court-PR position was appointed in the 1980s, following other arms of government (the legislature and the executive arms), with the trend only becoming mainstream in the 1990s and 2000s (Gleeson, 1998; Johnston, 2018b). Elsewhere, in Britain for instance, momentum was slow, with the first appointment to the UK Supreme Court[2] in 2012 (Owen, 2017).

Early court-PR was typically seen to work behind the scenes, at most facilitating access to materials and documents already in the public domain, not intended to raise the visibility of the sector. As such, experts argued that courts had a "limited requirement for publicity" (Ericson et al., 1989, p. 54.). Somewhat paradoxically, however, courts in many liberal democracies have worked under a broad legal principle of 'open justice' that dates back at least to the 17th century (Nettheim, 1984). This principle is intended to ensure "court proceedings are subjected to public and professional scrutiny" (Australian Law Reform Commission, 2015, para 10.43) by keeping courts physically open to the public and the media on the public's behalf.

The chapter will examine the intersections and associations between court-PR and open justice, focussing on how the professional communication and public relations role within courts has been instrumental in transitioning open justice from its original legal understanding to a crucial part of modern courts and government. This transition has included a focus on media relations, the adoption of social media, the development of diverse storytelling practices, and attention to the role of community outreach. Finally, the chapter will consider the synergies between court-PR and the judiciary, which are bonded through the principle of open justice and how this reflects the evolving professional status of public relations more broadly. As PR and strategic communication scholars

DOI: 10.4324/9781003170563-26

examine their ethical and professional place in the world, the principles that guide open justice may provide insights and perspectives into the value of publicness, openness, and ultimately, the importance of public confidence by the people within the polity.

The principle of open justice

Yale law professor Judith Resnik describes courts in liberal democracies as an "obligatorily open institution" (2013, p. 78). With some early discussion from the 17th century, the most influential writing about this important democratic and constitutional principle was in the early 19th century by English philosopher Jeremy Bentham. Bentham saw the practice of open courts as an important check on the performance of judges. "Deeply suspicious of the only arm of democratic government not to be held publicly accountable through elections. . . . He reasoned that judges would only act in a fair, unbiased and just manner if their actions were subject to public review and criticism" (Warren, 2014, p. 46). In turn, the public nature of courts was seen to transfer authority back to the public, enabling them to check on the probity of the actions of judges through their own observations (Resnik, 2013; Warren, 2014). As such, Bentham's ideas of open justice have been described as a "comprehensive, relentless, and unavoidable *public* oversight" (Postema, 2014, p. 43, original italics). While there are exceptions to holding courts openly for public viewing, with these varying across jurisdictional borders, there are nevertheless fundamental principles that see open courts as "immutable" and an "essential aspect" of judicial character (Wilson, 2015, p. 20).

A reading of Bentham's famous treatise *Works* finds 'open justice' or 'openness' in courts used interchangeably with the term 'publicity' (Bentham, 1843; see also Nettheim, 1984; Resnik, 2013; Stoker & Rawlins, 2005). Here, it is necessary to take a brief detour to consider these words in ensuring they are understood as Bentham meant them. Publicity, as he described it, was an honorary pursuit. He argued, "Without publicity, all other checks are fruitless" (Bentham, 1843, p. 317). His use of the term was in the context of "making things public" and open to scrutiny as "the fittest law for securing the public confidence" (Bentham, 1843, ch. 2). In this original use, according to Bentham and others of this era such as Immanuel Kant, publicity acted as a conceptual framework for determining whether an action would hold up to public scrutiny, thereby providing a test for the legitimacy or justness of public policy (see Johnston, 2018a; Luban, 1998; Stoker & Rawlins, 2005).

In more recent times the concept of publicity has changed quite dramatically, nowadays better understood for the promotion of a point of view and a strategic communication function (Stoker & Rawlins, 2005; Johnston, 2018a). Journalism scholars Stoker and Rawlins (2005; see also Johnston, 2018a) found that the Benthamite and Kantian understanding of openness, as *reflecting* public opinion, began changing around the start of the 20th century, to become a function of *shaping public opinion*. The earlier was said to shed broad light on a subject, the latter to direct attention through a selective narrow prism (Stoker & Rawlins, 2005). While further analysis of this change is beyond the scope of this chapter, it is important to acknowledge this shift when reading early work on open justice and publicity. For Bentham and other early writers, the press was the champion of publicity and therefore the purveyors of open justice.

Today, the principle of open justice is threaded through international law and policy standards. It is articulated in the legal concept of "due process" in the International Covenant on Civil and Political Rights (ICCPR), the Universal Declaration of Human Rights (UDHR) (Hickle, 2020), and the American Convention on Human Rights (Nettheim, 1984). Open justice is also laid down in common law, notably in the 1913 leading English case of *Scott v Scott*, in which Lord Shaw described the principle as "a sound and very sacred part of the constitution of the country and the administration of justice" (*Scott v Scott* [1913] AC 417, 473). Its endorsement by the United Nations, through its Global Judicial Integrity Network, highlights the importance of judicial transparency and the need to demystify the judiciary to achieve effective open justice (United Nations Office on Drugs and Crime, 2020).

This network[3] points out how, globally, many jurisdictions promote open justice simply by publishing court records and other documentation, while other jurisdictions go further, proactively seeking contact with the public through outreach (United Nations Office on Drugs and Crime, 2020). International organizations such as the European Network of Councils for the Judiciary (ENCJ) endorse the need for judiciaries to develop public outreach that suits the needs of their citizens, especially if this relationship has been historically fragile (Sterk & Chis, n.d.). Accordingly, "It is important for the judiciaries to stay in contact with the public through various activities in order to have a platform to explain to citizens that the judiciary is a vital, and independent, part of any democracy" (Sterk & Chis, n.d.). Central to this process of proactive communication has been the development of the court-PR role, which is often described as a judicial assistance function. It is also, crucially, a media-assistance role (Davis, 1994; Johnston, 2012, 2018a; Moran, 2014). And, as the chapter now explores, this role has continued to evolve over its short history in support of open justice.

The development of public relations in courts

Modern legal thinking proposes that open justice requires transparent communication about the workings of the courts in order to maintain effective authority and social order and for the public to have trust and confidence in the administration of justice (Brennan, 1997; Australian Law Reform Commission, 2015; Johnston, 2018a; Rodrick, 2014). While the press was traditionally seen as the "primary linking mechanism between the courts and the public" (Davis, 1994, p. 6), the need for the courts to more proactively facilitate and assist this understanding became increasingly apparent during the 20th century. As media demands increased with television, for example, seeking camera access, and as the judiciary became subject to increasing media criticism (see Kirby, 1998; Moran, 2014; Schulz, 2008; Rodrick, 2014), there grew a need for the courts to work actively in both engagement with the news media and through their own communication channels. Thus, early court-PR roles were said to hold both public information and media liaison duties (Gleeson, 1998; Johnston, 2012, 2017, 2018a; Newland, 1964). Initiatives in the US Supreme Court noted how public understanding of the Court did not "float freely, in a seemingly aimless fashion" (Caldiera, 1986, p. 1223). In other words, the Court needed to help public understanding along. As US judicial historian Richard Davis noted: "The Court's objective for strategic communication efforts is . . . to perpetuate the image of the Court as a nonpolitical, independent institution that is a legitimate authority figure and endowed with a special expertise" (1994, p. 12). This understanding captured several key elements of the way court communication and PR was to evolve – that is, the need for it to be *strategic, nonpolitical, and authoritative*. It therefore also needed expertise, and this came with the appointment of professionals, now a core role within courts in many parts of the world.

These professionals fiercely differentiated themselves from PR in other fields. In the United States Davis (1994, p. 8) noted:

> the Court, unlike other institutions, cannot engage in the same public relations tactics as the Congress or the White House. Reticence to pursue these objectives in a similar fashion as other institutions is the product of distinctive characteristics of the Court and public expectations placed on the Court.

Davis further (1994, p. 47) noted how:

> Even the title of the court's press relations arm reflects its effort to disassociate itself from an image of media manipulation. While the title "press secretary" and "press office" have

acquired wide acceptance in the parlance of government public relations, the Court prefers the more benign term "Public Information Officer".

One of the earliest appointments in Australia described her job as "the supply of accurate information and service rather than a public enhancement or PR role" (Nelson, 1995, p. 34). Around the same time one US court-PR carefully differentiated her work from that of other government public relations departments, noting "we do not do spin" (House cited in Ginsburg, 1995, p. 2122). In this way, the courts set themselves apart from what they saw as other government and politically focussed communication. More than 20 years later, this sentiment continues. Those working in this environment see their role quite differently to others in government or elsewhere. After working for many years in the Supreme Court of New South Wales, one Australian court-PR noted: "it's a unique workplace unlike any other" (Zadel, 2018 in Johnston, 2018b, p. 1).

Elsewhere, the court-PR role has been highly distinguishable from others in the justice sector – notably police-PR. Research comparing these two consistently found that police have a higher profile and are "by far the most visible of all criminal justice institutions" (Chermak & Weiss, 2005, p. 502). Moreover, court-PR focusses on "information-out communication with an emphasis on access and accuracy" while in contrast police-PR focusses on "conversations and 'information-in' as well as promoting a positive police image" (Johnston & McGovern, 2013, p. 1682).

Job descriptions for the court-PR role vary from place to place, yet some elements remain consistent. For example, celebrated US Supreme Court Judge Ruth Bader Ginsberg wrote that the role was "indispensable as a supplier of documentary information and answers to process questions" (1995, p. 2122). In Australia, upon making its first appointment in 2002, the High Court described the role as:

> promoting understanding in the Australian community of the Court's role, including media liaison, preparing summaries of judgments, answering queries from students and the public, responding from time to time to comment and criticism of the Court, conducting tours of the Court for specialist groups, and addressing community groups.
> (High Court of Australia, 2003, p. 10)

In addition to the role of court-PR, courts in the Netherlands have appointed dedicated 'press judges' to work with the news media. Demand for press judges in that country was said to follow pressure from the emerging post-war generation, which identified justice as a public concern (de Rechtspraak, n.d.), plus a judiciary responding to an increasingly critical and inquisitive press (Gies, 2005). While the press judge role was something of a "sleeping institution" until the late 1980s (Gies, 2005, p. 45), by 2005 every Dutch court had a press judge (de Rechtspraak, n.d.). Their role is intended to translate legal, complex language to assist the public understanding of the background, context, and assumptions surrounding a legal case. "The judge also contributes to the development and implementation of communication policy, either aimed specifically at the media or at society in general" (de Rechtspraak, n.d., p. 2).

All these developments centred on bringing openness and publicness to the courts, calling for a modern response to this highly conservative environment, bounded by centuries of tradition, culture, and law-making. Canada's former Chief Justice Beverley McLachlin noted how the view from within the courts had changed little:

> Much has changed since Bentham's time. The courtroom scene, however, remains remarkably similar. An observer from the 19th Century would have no difficulty recognising the players in the modern courtroom. Behind the bench sits the judge. At the counsel table sit

the lawyers. The witness sits in the witness box and the parties listen from pews behind the bar. Sometimes members of the public . . . join the parties in the audience. And, occasionally, usually in the public seats but sometimes at a special bench to one side, one finds a member of the press. This is how things were in Bentham's time, and this is how, by and large, they remain.

(McLachlan, 2003, para 2)

As McLachlan notes, however, change has been profound elsewhere. Indeed, there have been seismic shifts in media, communication, and technology outside and surrounding the courts. Notably, this includes two major interconnected changes which have impacted on court-PR and its need for greater openness: "The first is the rapid and dramatic development of organisational communication management; the second are the radical and pervasive changes to media" (Johnston, 2018a, p. 534). And so, while courts must retain their primary purpose of administering justice and maintaining the rule of law, they have also needed to adapt their open justice agendas through public communication to work within the changed external environment. This has been achieved through a diverse range of media and communication tactics which have, for the most part, been facilitated by the professional communication practitioners (court-PRs and press judges) who now work within these institutions. Many of these are mainstream corporate or political communication tactics – each adapted and applied with attention to the specific needs of courts, as the chapter now explores.

Storytelling and court-owned media

When the president of the UK Supreme Court Lady Brenda Hale appeared in a feature article in *Vogue* magazine in 2019, the Court's media and communication team received full credit for the story. The Supreme Court's Annual Report that year noted how the dedicated communication team had secured high-profile interviews with justices with national and local media, including *Vogue, The Times, The Guardian*, and Radio 4 (Supreme Court of the UK, 2018/2019). The report explained:

> These interviews have enabled justices to demonstrate their independence and explain the work of the Court. . . . Justices are able to discuss their views on legal topics of interest outside the courtroom setting and give behind-the-scenes insight into how the court functions.
>
> (p. 19)

The interview with *Vogue* marked the 100th anniversary of the year in which women were first given the right to practise law in Britain and the 10th anniversary of the formation of the UK Supreme Court. Lady Hale brought a certain levity to the interview, telling the *Vogue* journalist: "A 73-year-old woman like me in Vogue? It's hilarious" (Pithers, 2019). This somewhat extraordinary example illustrates how storytelling about the courts has become a significant part of the court-PR agenda. While most behind-the-scenes stories of court actors and their activities will not garner the massive circulation of *Vogue*, the story illustrates a shift in attention to court communication and arguably a new direction for open justice, incorporating the *people* involved in courts and not just the *function* they carry out. Far from a traditional pathway to open justice, through the publication of court judgments via the news media, human interest feature stories such as this provide insights into the judiciary, breaking down the barriers to this mysterious sector of society. This reflects the focus of the United Nations (United Nations Office on Drugs and Crime [UNODC]), the ENCJ, the US Conference of Court Public Information Officers (CCPIO), the National Association of

Court Management (NACM) in the United States, and other institutions and bodies internationally which seek to demystify the judiciary and the processes of courts, with the aim of connecting courts and judges with the public. From the high-profile approach in *Vogue*, to local stories such as a Ukraine farmyard fable written by a local judge for school children, to the real-life story of a black and tan dog called 'Old Drum', commemorated in the Supreme Court of Missouri in the United States (CCPIO, 2019) – stories such as these are fundamental to the community-building agendas of courts in many parts of the world.

There is indeed "momentum amongst courts globally" to use the media and other outreach possibilities to speak directly to the public (Warren, 2014, p. 58). Coupled with the use of celebrity (e.g. Lady Hale has been given 'rock star' status by several media publications), plus other media tactics such as social media, live web-streaming, blogs, podcasts, court-TV, and a myriad of educational and community outreach initiatives, many courts have grown their modern publicity in quite profound ways. Leading among these has been social media. Following its first court-PR appointment in 2012, the UK Supreme Court positioned itself "as a world leader in judicial comms, using social media channels such as Twitter and Instagram to build engagement" (Owen, 2017). In Australia, a study by the author found that while courts were initially tentative about adopting social media in 2012 (Johnston, 2012; Johnston & McGovern, 2013), many had done so several years later (Johnston, 2017). Likewise, in the United States the first annual study by the CCPIO in 2010 found that a very small fraction of courts (6.7%) had developed social media profiles (Davey et al., 2014). By 2014–15, the transition to social media had become well advanced, with many courts incorporating it into their overall communication strategies (Davey et al., 2014; Meyer, 2014). One US court administrator wrote:

> For years courts have struggled with media relations. From whether to allow cameras in the courtroom to how to respond to a reporter's questions, the questions often outnumber the answers to issues that arise. With the explosion of social media, courts must now decide not if we will embrace social media but when and to what degree.
>
> (Slayton, 2011, p. 34)

Former Chief Justice of the Supreme Court of Victoria Marilyn Warren noted how new media technologies, with social media amongst them, were driving the courts to engage directly with the community to maintain the operation of open justice (2014, p. 45). And as social media has become increasingly pervasive, judicial guidance documents have been developed to assist the judiciary in how to use it – both for personal and institutional purposes. The ENCJ explains the rationale for assisting judges in using it as a personal medium: "Judges have a right to use social media, as an aspect of freedom of expression. By using social media judges share in modern life" (European Network of Councils for the Judiciary, 2019, p. 14).

Social media challenges to open justice

However, while the judiciary acknowledges that "new media has enabled the full and proper operation of the open justice principle" (Warren, 2014, p. 51), the flip side is that it can also undermine public confidence in the judicial system. The pervasive media environment has presented unprecedented challenges through unwelcome publicity brought about through its lack of filters and control and the immediacy and reach of these platforms. Though a utilitarian principle, open justice has always come with exceptions. As Bentham noted: "It is not proper to make the law of publicity absolute, because it is impossible to foresee all circumstances" (Bentham, 1843, p. 315). Following this principle, openness must be balanced with fair trials and the due administration of justice, and there are times courts must suppress or counterbalance external publicity to facilitate this process; sometimes this is at odds with the ease and breadth of modern media. Routinely, courts try to balance these two priorities in large part because of the adverse effect that 'pre-trial publicity' can have on trials. Indeed, research has found "social media use by jurors can damage the capacity of courts to maintain an appropriate balance between these rights and principles [of open justice and fair trial]" (Johnston et al., 2013, p. 3). This balance remains a key focus for courts as they move forward within the saturated, networked, and complex world of modern media and technology requiring, more than ever, communication expertise to assist in the process.

Court-PR working for open justice

The capacity for courts to achieve open justice, once reliant on the news media to act on the public's behalf, now has a vast array of communication options. However, these do not occur by chance; nor, as outlined earlier, is open justice simple or absolute. Courts have introduced proactive measures to achieve and manage open justice, and central to this has been the appointment of court-PRs. Not surprisingly, the judiciary has emerged as among the greatest supporters of this role and the people who successfully manage it. Court-PRs have been called "invaluable", "ground-breaking" (Teague, 1999, p. 117), and "indispensable" (Ginsburg, 1995, p. 2122). They have been thanked for "bringing the third branch of government [the judiciary] to the people" (Kirby, 2017). Overall, the function of PR has been described as a core part of courts and judicial accountability (National Association of Court Management, 2015).

Implicit in all the commentary is the underlying link between court-PR and open justice and the part this plays in maintaining public confidence and learning about the judicial arm of government. The NACM in the United States places a high priority on the role in the democratic process:

> Public relations involves effective external and internal communication to improve the understanding of court processes and the court's critical role in preserving the rule of law. The public's trust and confidence is vital for courts to fulfill their constitutional mandate to safeguard the rights of all.
>
> (NACM, 2015, p. 2)

With this acknowledgement, court-PR has often been afforded management status by the judiciary and courts administration. One former Victorian Supreme Court judge in Australia aligns the importance and value of "a good" court-PR (or PIO) with "a good CEO and a good [legal] counsel" (Teague, 2018 in Johnston, 2018b). That is, the three are equally important to courts and their role in society. Indeed, there is no shortage of plaudits for this role, the people who undertake it, and what it can achieve (Kirby, 2017; NACM, 2015; Teague, 1999; Supreme Court of the UK, 2018/2019). And in earning this status through its significant achievements, court-PRs have helped transition open justice into the 21st century. At the same time, court-PRs have also engaged directly with a centuries' old tradition centred on openness and public accountability. This, in turn, provides both practical and theoretical lessons to assist the professional growth and development of the professional communication and PR sector more broadly.

Acknowledgements

I would like to thank the many court public information officers in Australia, the United States, and the UK and press judges in the Netherlands, who have supported my research into court communication and open justice for over 25 years.

Notes

1 The term court-PR is used in this chapter to capture many titles, including public information officer (PIO), media manager, communication manager, public affairs manager, etc. Debate about the title is included in the chapter.
2 The UK Supreme Court was only established in 2005.
3 The network was established in 2018 by the United Nations Office on Drugs and Crime (UNODC).

References

Australian Law Reform Commission (2015, August). Open justice in traditional rights and freedoms – encroachments by Commonwealth laws. *Interim Report 127 (chapter 10)*. www.alrc.gov.au/publications/open-justice

Bentham, J. (1843). *The works of Jeremy Bentham* (Vol. 2) (Judicial Procedure, Anarchical Fallacies, works on Taxation) (J. Bowring, Ed.). Edinburgh. https://oll.libertyfund.org/titles/bentham-the-works-of-jeremy-bentham-vol-2

Brennan, G. (1997, April 22). *The third branch and the fourth estate*. Paper presented at the Broadcasting, Society and the Law, University College of Dublin. www.hcourt.gov.au/publications/speeches/former/speeches-by-the-hon-sir-gerard-brennan

Caldeira, G. (1986). Neither the purse nor the sword: Dynamics of public support for the United States Supreme Court. *American Political Science Review*, 80(4): 1209–1226.

Chermak, S., & Weiss, A. (2005). Maintaining legitimacy using external communication strategies: An analysis of police-media relations. *Journal of Criminal Justice*, 33(5), 501–512.

Conference of Court Public Information Officers (2019, August). Annual CCPIO Conference, Cleveland, Ohio.

Davey, C. J., Salaz, K., Hodson, T., & National Center for State Courts. (2010, August). *New media and the courts: The current status and a look at the future*. Presented at the Conference of Court Public Information Officers 19th annual meeting, Atlanta, Georgia. Retrieved from http://ccpio.org/wp-content/uploads/2012/02/2010-ccpio-report-summary.pdf

Davey, C. J., Salaz, K., Hodson, T., & National Center for State Courts. (2014, August 6). *CCPIO new media survey: A report of the conference of court public information officers*. Conference of Court Public Information Officers 23rd Annual Meeting, Las Vegas, Nevada. http://ccpio.org/wp-content/uploads/2014/08/CCPIO-New-Media-survey-report_2014.pdf

Davis, R. (1994). *Decisions and images: The supreme court and the press*, Prentice Hall.

de Rechtspraak (n.d.). Press judge profile. *The Netherlands, Council for the Judiciary*, 1–5.

Ericson, R., Baranek, P., & Chan, J. (1989). *Negotiating control: A study of news sources*. University of Toronto Press.

European Network of Councils for the Judiciary (2019). *Public confidence and the image of the judiciary: Individual and institutional use of social media within the judiciary*. ENCJ Report, Bratislava.

Fife-Yeomans, J. (1995). Fear and loathing: The courts and the media. *Journal of Judicial Administration*, 5, 39–42.

Gies, L. (2005). The empire strikes back: Press judges and communication advisers in Dutch courts. *Journal of Law and Society*, 32(3), 450–472.

Ginsburg, R. B. (1995). Communicating and commenting on the court's work. *The Georgetown Law Journal*, 83, 2119–2129.

Gleeson, M. (1998, November 10). First court information officer. Jan Nelson, Court Media Officer, 1945–1998. *The Australian*, 16.

Greenhouse, L. (1996). Telling the court's story: Justice and journalism at the Supreme Court. *Yale Law Journal*, 105(6), 1537–1561.

Hickle, J. (2020, October). Justice policy series part II, open justice. *The Open Government Partnership*. www.opengovpartnership.org/wp-content/uploads/2020/10/Open-Justice-OGP_Introduction.pdf

High Court of Australia. (2003). *Annual report 2002–03*. Halstead Press.

Johnston, J. (2012). Courts new visibility 2.0. In P. Keyzer, J. Johnston, & M. Pearson (Eds.), *Courts and the media in the digital age* (pp. 41–54). Halstead Press.

Johnston, J. (2017). Courts use of social media: A community of practice model. *International Journal of Communication*, 11, 1–15.

Johnston, J. (2018a). Three phases of courts' publicity: Reconfiguring Bentham's open justice in the twenty-first century. *International Journal of Law in Context*, 14, 525–538. https://doi.org/10.1017/S1744552318000228

Johnston, J. (2018b). *History of court public information officers in Australia 1993–2018*. Report commissioned for the Australasian Institute of Judicial Administration, Melbourne.

Johnston, J., Keyzer, P., Holland, G. Pearson, M., Wallace, A., & Rodrick, S. (2013). *Social media and juries*. Report commissioned by the Victorian Attorney General on behalf of the Standing Council on Law and Justice, Melbourne.

Johnston, J., & McGovern, A. (2013). Communicating Justice: A comparison of courts and police use of contemporary media. *International Journal of Communication*, 7. http://ijoc.org/index.php/ijoc/article/view/2029

Kirby, M. (1998, January 5). *Attacks on judges a universal phenomenon*. Speech delivered to the American Bar Association, Winter Leadership Meeting, Maui Hawaii.

Kirby, M. (2017, August 31). *Opening address: PIO forum*. AIJA Annual Conference, Federal Court Building, Sydney.

Luban, D. (1998). The publicity principle. In R. E. Goodin (Ed.), *The theory of institutional design* (pp. 154–198). Cambridge University Press:

McLachlan, B. (2003). Courts, transparency and public confidence – to the better administration of justice. *Deakin Law Review*, 8. www.austlii.edu.au/au/journals/DeakinLawRw/2003/1.html.

Meyer, N. (2014). Social media and the courts: Innovative tools or dangerous fad? A practical guide for court administrators. *International Journal for Court Administration*, 6, 1–27.

Moran, L. J. (2014). Managing the 'critical interdependencies' of the media and the judiciary in the United Kingdom. In M. Asimow, K. Brown, & D. R. Papke (Eds.), *Law and popular culture: International perspectives* (pp. 194–215). Cambridge Scholars Publishing.

National Association for Court Management. (2015). *Curriculum design: Public relations*. Training material. http://nacmcore.org/app/uploads/Public-Relations.pdf

Nelson, J. (1995). The Role of the Public Information Officer in New South Wales Courts, *Journal of Judicial Administration*, 5(1): 34–38.

Nettheim, G. (1984). The principle of open justice. *University of Tasmania Law Review*, 8(1), 25–45.

Newland, C. A. (1964). Press coverage of the United States Supreme Court. *The Western Political Quarterly*, 17, 15–36.

Owen, J. (2017, July 12). Back to university for former supreme court comms chief. *PR Week*. www.prweek.com/article/1438821/back-university-former-supreme-court-comms-chief

Peleg, A., & Bogoch, B. (2014). *Silence is no longer golden: Media, public relations and the judiciary in Israel* (pp. 819–835). Oñati Socio-legal Series [online] 4. http://opo.iisj.net/index.php/osls/article/viewFile/332/474.

Pithers, E. (2019). Meet Baroness Hale, the judge who presided over the Hammer Blow to Boris Johnson's premiership. *British Vogue*. www.vogue.co.uk/arts-and-lifestyle/article/baroness-hale-of-richmond-interview.

Postema, G. J. (2014). The soul of justice: Bentham on publicity, law and the rule of law. In X. Zhai & M. Quinn (Eds.), *Bentham's theory of law & public opinion* (pp. 40–62). Cambridge University Press.

Resnik, J. (2013). The democracy in courts: Jeremy Bentham, 'publicity', and the privatization of process in the twenty-first century. *No Foundations: An Interdisciplinary Journal of Law & Justice*, 10, 77–119.

Rodrick, S. (2014). Achieving the aims of open justice? The relationship between the courts, the media and the public. *Deakin Law Review*, 19, 123–162.

Schulz, P. (2008). Rougher than usual treatment: A discourse analysis of media reporting and justice on trial. *Journal of Judicial Administration*, 17, 223–236.

Scott v Scott [1913] AC 417.

Slayton, D. W. (2011). Social media: A new way to communicate that can no longer be ignored. In National Center for State Courts (Ed.), *Future trends for state courts*, 34. www.ncsc.org/~/media/Microsites/Files/Future%20Trends/Author%20PDFs/Slayton.ashx

Sterk, K., & Chis, A. (n.d.). *Reaching out to the general public*. European Network of Councils for the judiciary, UNODC. www.unodc.org/dohadeclaration/en/news/2019/04/reaching-out-to-the-general-public.html

Stoker, K., & Rawlins, B. L. (2005). The 'light' of publicity in the progressive era. *Journalism History*, 30, 177–188.

Supreme Court of the United Kingdom. (2018/2019, June 6). *The supreme court annual report and accounts 2018–2019*. Crown copyright. https://www.supremecourt.uk/docs/annual-report-2018-19.pdf

Teague, B. (1999). Access to the courts and its implications. In University of Technology Sydney (UTS) (Ed.), *The courts and the media* (pp. 112–118). Halstead Press.

United Nations Office on Drugs and Crime. (2020). *Open justice and public confidence*. Global Judicial Integrity Network. www.unodc.org/ji/en/knowledge-products/open-justice.html

Warren, M. (2014). Open justice in the technological age. *Monash University Law Review*, 40(1), 45–58.

Wilson, J. (2015). Open justice and the courts: From Fairfax to Fair Work. *Ethos*, 20–22.

3.7

SEMIOTIC ANALYSIS OF ENVIRONMENTAL COMMUNICATION CAMPAIGNS

Andrea Catellani

Introduction

Environmental communication studies are a wide research field, analyzed thoroughly from many different points of view (see for example Hansen & Machin, 2013; Evans et al., 2018; Pezzullo & Cox, 2018; Catellani et al., 2019; Catellani et al. in Takahashi et al., 2022). Environmental communication is defined by the International Environmental Communication Association (IECA) as "communication about environmental affairs. This includes all of the diverse forms of interpersonal, group, public, organizational, and mediated communication that make up the social debate about environmental issues and problems, and our relationship to the rest of nature".[1] Environmental communication "is also an interdisciplinary field of study that examines the role, techniques, and influence of communication in environmental affairs" (ibidem). We focus here on a specific part of this wide area, the one concerning nongovernmental organizations' (NGOs') communication and one specific approach: semiotics.

The methodology that is presented in this chapter is adapted to the analysis of all types of NGO communication activities (and all other types of organizations) and not only "campaigns".[2] Environmentalist NGOs like Greenpeace have been developing strategic communications for a long time. Strategic communications is defined in this chapter, following Hallahan et al. (2007), as "the purposeful use of communication by an organization to fulfill its mission", given that people develop "deliberate communication practice on behalf of organizations, causes, and social movements" (pp. 3–4). Oliveira et al. (2019) tend to enrich this definition, which is based on a functionalist approach, by integrating different approaches to the analysis of strategic communications in what they call "nonprofit communications" (including organizations like churches, unions, foundations, etc.). They also identify "environmental communications" as a specific sub-field of study of nonprofit communications, although this does not mean that businesses and governments are not also actors of environmental communications in the larger sense we identified earlier.

One of the approaches that Oliveira et al. (2019) cite is linked to the focus on the "performativity and emerging dimension of the language" (ibid., p. 4), linked to the work of Karl Weick. This attention to language is important, but it is also necessary to remember the role of other systems of signs, like the visual ones, in interaction with verbal texts (and a chapter of the book edited by Oliveira, Melo and Goncalves precisely analyzes examples of audiovisual narratives in NGO communications). From this point of view, approaches of meaning construction and production like semiotics have a real role to play concerning the analysis of nonprofit communications in general, and NGO communications in particular: they can indeed help in deepening the symbolic dimension of communication.

Consequently, this chapter aims at answering the following question: how has strategic environmentalist communication been studied, and where is the place for semiotics? Hansen (2011, p. 7), talking about research on environmental communications in general, identifies "three major foci of communications research on media and environmental issues: the production/construction of media messages and public communications; the content/messages of media communication; and the impact of media and public communication on public/political understanding and action with regard to the environment". Semiotic approaches, like other similar ones (rhetorical, discursive, pragmatic, multimodal, etc.), apply mainly to the analysis of content, even if concrete analysis can also include production and "impact".[3] So, it is time now to introduce this research area and its main features.

Semiotics and the use of semiotic categories to analyze purposeful communication

Semiotics is not a unified research field, and different traditions exist, which refer to different "founding fathers" (unfortunately, not "mothers", even if authors like Julia Kristeva have played an important role here): Charles S. Peirce and Ferdinand de Saussure in particular, and more recently Roland Barthes, Algirdas Julien Greimas, Umberto Eco, Thomas Sebeok, etc.[4] Semiotics can be defined as the science of signs and of the construction of meaning that is linked to the production and circulation of signs. Signs are all types of entities that have or can have meaning for someone. Signs can be produced and spread voluntarily, as in the case of words, images, gestures, etc., or non-voluntarily, including elements of the natural world that are interpreted by someone as meaningful (for example, smoke can be a sign of fire, a panorama can evoke certain meanings and emotions and be considered a sign, the whole world can be a sign of God the creator, etc.).

It is not possible here to introduce semiotics in a complete way. Interesting introductions or reference books are available in different languages: in English, for example, Chandler (2017), Hébert (2019) and Cobley (2010); in French, Bertrand (2000), Verhaegen (2010), Groupe MU (2015), Perusset (2020).

In this chapter we make reference to the school derived from the works of Algirdas J. Greimas and his disciples, like Jean-Marie Floch (2001) (see Greimas & Courtès, 1982; Berthelot-Guiet & Boutaud, 2015; Catellani, 2011a, 2011b, 2012a, 2012b, 2015, 2018; Fontanille, 2006). It is the so-called "Paris school", that provides a structured list of analytical tools. These researchers' aim is a *modelling* of the meaning that is probably linked (at least in a certain cultural and historical contexts that can be more or less specified in the analysis) to the text(s) under analysis. The notion of "text" is very wide here: it covers language but also images and any "portion of reality that is supposed to be meaningful for someone (an 'interpreter'), and that can be isolated and observed" (Catellani, 2018, p. 162). As Catellani wrote in 2018 (pp. 161–162), in a quite radical way:

> Semiotics cannot discover the real effects of texts on real social actors. It can only propose hypotheses on the most probable interpretations and results, basing this on the analysis of the internal configuration of texts. Semiotic analysis of multimodal texts can help in answering questions about the contribution of specific texts to a specific communication activity, like Greenpeace's campaigns.

But semiotics as the identification of probable meaning can be combined with specific strategies aimed at discovering the *real* meaning production of real people, like interviews, questionnaires, experiments, observations, etc. As we wrote in a previous paper, "The semiotic approach of this paper [focused on classical text analysis] is a form of 'epochè', a selective attention to texts that temporarily does not take into consideration the context and the social situation in which texts appear, are produced and interpreted" (Catellani, 2018, p. 162). But this temporary "epochè" is not the final stage of analysis: it is more a way of taking seriously the internal construction of texts, and it can be accompanied by other analytical phases in which the social and cultural context is explicitly considered. Texts are always a part of the global "fabric" of the culture and society in which they are produced and interpreted: they are the incarnation of cultural systems and habits, and they are inherently intertextual (each text is in dialogue and interaction with others). Semiotics can work on intertextuality (relations between different texts), on reactions and interpretations by real interpreters of texts, and on the relation between text and context, as is done in approaches like "socio-semiotics", the semiotics of culture, and cognitive semiotics. Comparing texts with comments or reactions to these texts is a way of doing this.

Semiotic tools can be applied also to the analysis of open-ended answers to interviews or reports of observations, as in the case of stakeholders' meetings (Catellani, 2019). As an example, Floch (2001) proposes a typology of different kinds of users' behaviors inside Paris metro stations that can lead to a survey aimed at quantifying these into different categories (the "sleepwalkers", the "surveyors", etc.). Meaning structures identified using the approach of Greimas (presented in the following pages) are a hypothesis on meaning that can be enriched, modified, and tested with different methodologies, including intertextual comparison, surveys, interviews, observations, etc.

The "generative model" as a source of inspiration

The methodology drawn from Greimas's semiotics is articulated in different levels of "structures", from the most sensible and specific to the most abstract and general; these series of levels form a "generative pathway" or "generative model" (Greimas & Courtés, 1982, pp. 157–160). Presented here is a simplified and slightly modified version of their original model. What the interpreter perceives is the sensible appearance of texts: written or spoken words, images, etc. In the case of visual images, this includes the "plastic" aspects like colors, types of forms, disposition and topology, effects of texture, specific techniques (drawing, painting, or infographics), types of framing, etc. All these aspects are signifiers of some "signified" or meanings that can be analyzed at the different levels of the generative model. For example, green can be a signifier of the abstract notion of environmental quality of a product, but it can also simply be the color of the socks of a character that has a certain narrative role in a story.

The first level of Greimas's original model is the one of "discursive structures" that include all aspects linked to the "*mise en discourse*", the fact that meaning comes to discourse: in particular, the presence of abstract themes (like nature or freedom), on one side, and of concrete "figures" (like people, objects, animals, buildings, etc.) on the other side. Concerning images, figures are represented inside the message (icons like the polar bear or melting glaciers are examples); as for verbal language, these figures are expressed through words. It also includes specific ways of enunciating, i.e. of creating a discursive world with actors, spaces, and times inside it. When someone says "yesterday I went to Brussels to meet Jean" she is creating a discursive world that includes specific themes, figures, places, times, and actors, and she creates a connection between her and this discursive universe (a form of direct implication). Rhetorical analysis of figures and tropes can be placed here, at this level.

The second level of the Greimas model includes the "semio-narrative structures": this is the most abstract level, the one of narrative forms and of basic "values" as they are present in texts. The focus here is on narration as a basic form of meaning that goes beyond the distinction of concrete forms of texts (narrative, argumentative, descriptive, etc.). The "deepest" level concerns values that are

Semiotic analysis of environmental campaigns

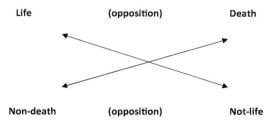

Figure 3.7.1 Example of a semiotic square.

incarnated into the text. Greimas proposed the (quite famous) "semiotic square", which visualizes the logical structure concerning a specific value by articulating it with its complementary, contrary, and contradictory positions, as in this example shown in Figure 3.7.1.

Life and death, but also not-life and not-death, are in a relationship of contrariety;
Life and not-death, but also death and not-life, are in a relationship of complementarity;
Life and not-life, but also death and not-death, are in a relationship of contradiction.

This square can be used to articulate the relationships that underpin the meaning of texts and to synthetize the basic textual dynamics. For example, a tale in the Bible can narrate the passage from the death of Christ (based on a previous negation of life, Passion and Crucifixion), via the negation of death (the Resurrection), to life (eternal life). Likewise, an environmentalist website can show that nature is in danger (negation of life, and death as possible result) and that the NGO is fighting against pollution (negation of death) to restore or preserve nature (life, again). Pro-nuclear discourses (see Catellani, 2012b) could try to put together values like the protection of the climate (nuclear power as a low-carbon energy source), national energy independence and low economic costs. On the other hand, anti-nuclear rhetoric can show that nuclear energy threatens essential goods and/or values, such as life and security.

Values and oppositions can be expressed not only by narratives (with heroes and opponents) but also by simple discursive figures (like logos and iconic animals – the panda for WWF – which represent basic values), or even at the "plastic" level, with colors (green) or light effects (light vs. darkness). To illustrate, the opposition between the green of Greenpeace and the black and yellow of the symbol of nuclear power is probably linked to an opposition between positive and negative values (environment and life vs. danger and death) (see Figure 3.7.2).

The superficial level of semio-narrative structures concerns narrative pathways and roles (or actants) in which value dynamics "incarnate". Greimas and his school identify here the basic articulation of "objects of values" and "actants" that look for, exchange, produce, give, etc., these valuable objects. For example, "the planet" or nature, or a specific forest, or an animal species can be seen as a valuable object that Greenpeace or the WWF tries to preserve, and the public is called to help this effort with its gifts and signatures.

Here is the origin of the quite famous "actantial model" of Greimas (at least, its original version) that identifies different abstract "roles" for the actors of texts: the valuable object, the subject (the heroes that acts to get the object or to take it to a receiver in need), the helper/"adjuvant" and the opponent (sometimes a real "anti-subject"), the sender (the actors that attribute the task to the subject), and the receiver (the actor that receives the task to be accomplished by the sender, or the recipient of the object itself). Values are incarnated in the valuable objects; the narrative subjects can be described as more or less "able" for their quests (more or less gifted in terms of knowledge, power, will, and duty).

Figure 3.7.2 Screenshot from the website of Greenpeace.

Actions can be described at this level also from the point of view of their logical development, following the "canonical narrative scheme" of Greimas. An action logically implies different phases:

> Competence, which includes the conditions that are necessary in order to accomplish the action (wanting-to-do, having-to-do, knowing-how-to-do, and being-able-to-do) and (3) performance, the actual accomplishment of the action, made possible by the acquisition of competence. (4) Manipulation is the component that deals specifically with wanting-to-do and having-to-do. (5) The last component, sanction, has to do with evaluating whether the action was in fact accomplished, and the corresponding retribution (reward or punishment) that the performing subject has incurred.
>
> (Hébert, 2019, p. 68)

Action and interaction always need these four different steps (competence, performance, manipulation, and sanction), even if the concrete texts can have complex discursive configurations and, for example, highlight one phase in relation to the others. This is the case for the "victories" that Greenpeace exhibits in its communication in which the "sanction" (a positive one) is in evidence.[5] These analytical categories improve the narratological toolkit, which also includes models like the traditional "quinary model" of initial situation, complication, action, resolution, and final situation (Adam, 1997).

The "structures" presented here in Table 3.7.1 (that are only a part of the whole analytical toolkit of the Paris school's model) are useful for making hypotheses on how meaning will probably appear in the concrete minds of the interpreters: they do not propose "the" meaning of a specific text. In a similar way as social semiotics, the approach presented here can be seen as focused on the analysis of the "semiotic potential" of "semiotic resources" (Van Leeuwen, 2005, p. 4). Authors like Paul Ricoeur have critiqued the formal nature of structural semiotics, but it keeps its usefulness as a structured toolkit, useful for modelling probable shared meaning.[6]

Table 3.7.1 A visualization of the different layers of the generative scheme of meaning

		Semantic aspect	Syntactic aspect (relations)	
The signified (meaning)	Deep semio-narrative structures	Basic values (life, death; nature, culture; etc.)	Logical relations inside the semiotic square (opposition, contradiction, complementarity)	More abstract and general
	Superficial semio-narrative structures	Basic values are seen as valuable objects in relation with other actants (subjects, etc.).	Logical relations are seen as relations between "actants" in a narrative program (subject, object, sender, receiver, adjuvant and opponent.)	
	Discursive structures	Themes/topics that incarnate semio-narrative structures Concrete figures (visual, verbal, etc.) recognizable in texts	Projection of actors, spaces, times that incarnate semio-narrative structures; specific enunciation strategies	
The signifier	The perceptible textual object	Incarnation of meaning (signified) into a concrete textual object (signifier): image, verbal text, video, object, tool, part of the world, etc.		More concrete and specific

Source: Based on Greimas & Courtés (1982).

This semiotic approach is, globally, a contribution to multimodal analysis (Kress, 2010), and it can also contribute to the identification of the ideological semiotic support of injustice and domination. There is a critical aspect with the semiotic tradition that creates a bridge, with approaches like the critical rhetorical analysis of public relations (Ihlen, 2016). In some articles, a semio-rhetorical approach was developed by focusing on the persuasive dimension of communication (Catellani 2011a, 2011b, 2012a, 2012b). This illustrates the fact that it is possible to create hybrid analytical approaches and devices based on this tradition, which is still evolving (see Perusset, 2020). It is particularly clear in the case of rhetoric: if semiotics has developed much later than rhetoric, this latter discipline can be considered a sub-genre of semiotics, focused on persuasive and argumentative texts, mostly verbal (even if semioticians like Roland Barthes have started studies of "visual rhetoric").

Applications: the construction of the environmental culprit

This second section presents some more examples of applications of the Greimas model of semiotics and of its hybridization with categories from other traditions, like discourse analysis and rhetoric, to the analysis of environmentalist communication campaigns.

"*L'emprise total*" (the hold of Total, but also total grip) is a recent campaign by Greenpeace France, commenting on the hold of the French petrochemical company Total on French society and culture. It is a good example of the rich and diversified way in which strategic communication is used by environmentalist NGOs, and in particular of a strategy that can be called "the construction of the culprit" (Catellani, 2011b).[7] From a semio-narrative point of view, Greenpeace is a subject (hero) that has the aim (the valuable object) of discovering truth and denouncing strategies used by Total in order to protect its image and its social acceptability, and its basic values are freedom and the protection of the environment. The "narrative program" of the hero is based on the analysis and criticism of the narrative journey of another actant, Total, which is depicted as an anti-hero, by accumulating examples, testimonies from authorities and experts, and judgements on the coherence between communication content and reality. It's a form of "epideictic rhetoric" (Catellani, 2011a), based on blame.

> For Total, preserving its image is a strategic and priority issue. [. . .] Except that the voices denouncing Total's cynicism and the impact of its industrial activity on the planet are increasingly numerous. To protect its image and maintain its power of influence, the oil and gas group no longer has a choice: it has to twist reality, skew perceptions, and to do this, be present everywhere.[8]

In relation to the narrative path of Total, Greenpeace takes the position of the "sender-judge": the NGO accumulates evidence of guilt to consolidate a negative sanction on the performance of Total. It is an example of strategic narrative framing.

From the point of view of the public, the valuable object is, of course, the truth about Total's practices: the episodes of the video series "*L'emprise total*" are offered to the public to obtain these values. The public is not *only*, as in traditional NGO communications, the receiver of a task from the NGO-sender (to help and participate in solving problems in order not to feel guilty or because we are able and strong) but also the recipient of a "gift", in the form of a spectacular, interesting media content, which is put as evidence on the website. The website of the campaign completes this interactive scheme by proposing to the public that they become an adjuvant of the subject in its fight against the anti-subject.

> In the near future, we will launch a campaign for the adoption of a European regulation banning partnerships of all European public institutions with the fossil fuel sector. Total's power is enormous. We need all of us to stop them from continuing to destroy the climate. Sign up now for a sneak preview.[9]

The tale of the villain (Total) creates an absorbing and entraining narrative experience, not far from the fictional ones (Schaeffer, 2010); the presence of multiple episodes creates a tension to complete the "trip". This entertaining and immersive experience (not far from what the poet Coleridge called "suspension of disbelief") is useful to compel the new information to modify the knowledge of the receiver. This can alter, or at least confirm and nourish, a specific vision of the world (and of an organization in this case), create premises to action, and increase familiarity and loyalty to the source of this cognitive experience, the enunciator.

This campaign, in which Greenpeace becomes a real *media content producer*, is an example of the blurring of boundaries between informative media content and promotion. The NGO can mobilize science, experts, and media and entertainment formats, like those of a TV series, journalistic investigation, and documentary, in order to offer cognitive and emotional support for its awareness-raising strategies. From a more anthropological point of view, this semiotic configuration looks like a typical gift/counter-gift scheme: the NGO offers a rich cognitive experience and asks in return for consideration, involvement, and help.

A specific aspect of this kind of communication (on the level of discursive structures) is intertextuality, and in particular the combination of different *genres* (documentary, journalism, fictional series). Genres are conventions concerning formats of texts that Fairclough (1995, p. 14) defined as "a socially ratified way of using language in connection with a particular social practice". Strategic mimetic mixing of genres and the blurring of frontiers between different discursive practices are typical of our time and of the digital world (see, for example, Markham, 2013), and strategic NGO campaigns are involved in this movement. Other examples of intertextuality are the well-known parodies of Greenpeace (see Catellani, 2012b). Parodies are defined as "an intertextual work, because it modifies a pre-existing textual universe; and it is also a form of attack and criticism" (Catellani, 2018, p. 168). Blame and criticism develop and are more attractive, via the coherent and strategic deformation of the pre-existing visual and textual world, such as that of the Volkswagen advertisements (based on the Stars Wars movies) or of the Barbie doll.

In both cases (the mimesis of documentaries and series or parodies), the underpinning semiotic strategy is always the same: to attack a crucial asset of businesses and organizations, to link their narrative world to their public image and reputation, and to move the business towards more sustainable choices. See, for example, the campaigns against Mattel (concerning the use of paper from deforestation in Indonesia) and Volkswagen (concerning vehicle carbon emissions). In the case of Total, the goals are to reduce its influence and to pressure the company for a change in its politics, to move it away from fossil fuels (see the campaign website). The discursive narrative world is constructed to impact and change the *real* one.

In a previous article, Catellani (2011b) proposed a list of some strategies that are used to build the image of the culprit, which can be combined in concrete NGO campaigns. *Semantic criticism* is focused on terms and their meaning, as in the case of the use of the adjective "natural" by businesses, which is very vague in its meaning.

Syntagmatic criticism addresses the internal articulation of messages: it "can focus on connotations of visual rhetoric associations of objects (cars and wild nature, for example, or a rural landscape and food)" (ibid., p. 288). This meta-semiotic operation, which reinterprets images and emotional texts like advertisements, can produce "a shift from the utopian and emotional to the rational and discursive" (ibid.).

Referential criticism is aimed at underlining "all the modifications and manipulations that occur between the fictional narrative world built by the firm, on one side, and the (supposed) real world, accessible through numbers and scientific information, on the other" (ibid.). This type of criticism is applied in the case of Total by Greenpeace, and it changes the narrative role of the firm from hero to villain, from subject to anti-subject, and Catellani (2011b) called it "actantial criticism", a form of accumulation of episodes and examples of negative behaviors.

The last type of criticism is *intertextual*: it compares strategic messages and symbols of the organization under attack with other texts, produced by the same organization (like financial reports or internal memos) or by other enunciators (like journalists or researchers). Let's take an example from the "Total grip" campaign used by Greenpeace:

> On 9 February 2021, Total chose to change its name to TotalEnergies. Behind this maneuver, the oil giant is trying to make people believe that it has the will to leave a model based mainly on fossil fuels. Except that this is not the case: Total expects that in 2030 hydrocarbons will still represent 80% of its investments. This communication sleight of hand shows that the group is still procrastinating when faced with the need to radically change its model and begin its transition.[10]

In this case, criticism is both intertextual (comparison of announcements with reports on investments) and referential (denying the reality of the company's narrative world by comparing it with what is shown as reality).

The videos of the "Total grip" campaign offer also a clear example of some other main rhetorical strategies used by NGOs: data, numbers, and infographics – which create an impression that they are using serious science; humanization through the use of real people and stories; the construction of a polyphonic enunciation with different experts and researchers that confirm the frame and narrative developed by the NGO and who contribute their legitimacy ("ethos") to the discursive strategy.

Michel Foucault (2001) proposed two quite useful analytical categories that can complement other semiotic tools at the discursive level, originally applied to spiritual exercises and meditation (Catellani, 2016): pedagogy and "psychagogy". The first is a communication practice focused on data and information and on instructions for treating these data (like the meta-discourse largely present in the "Total grip" campaign). The second, psychagogy, is focused on "draining" and "pulling" the soul by proposing an intense experience: reading or watching a video becomes an experience, and images and music have a role to play in this case (for applications to environmental campaigns, see Catellani, 2018). Both aspects are present in the "Total grip" campaign. The videos offer information and instruction on how to reframe and criticize the corporate discourse; this aspect is dominant. But music (often in a minor key, typically depicting evil and menace) and other aspects like colors and the construction of an entraining narrative structure that accumulates elements of menace, also offer aspects of psychagogy. The observer is invited to "elaborate" data, but also to feel emotions, to enter an affective state. The video entitled "A Vicious Circle", part of the campaign "Save the Arctic",[11] is an example in which psychagogy is dominant through music and visual (aesthetically beautiful) images (see Catellani, 2018 for more details). The two poles (psychagogy and pedagogy) can alternate or combine in different ways in concrete texts.

Some conclusions: exploring NGO campaigns using semiotic tools

The objective of this chapter was to introduce a specific semiotic approach to the analysis of environmentalist NGO communication campaigns. The aim of semiotics is to go beyond "impressions" and subjectivism concerning meaning production analysis by structuring it on different layers The generative scheme of Greimas and his school was presented briefly, and some examples of application and hybridization, specifically on a recent campaign by Greenpeace France against the Total company, were discussed. The examples given here were perhaps too short and sketchy to support claims of rigor and objectivity; indeed, a complete analysis, like that proposed by Floch (2001), would have been better suited for this. Nonetheless, this chapter attempted to show the basics of this approach and to underline its ability to integrate other contributions, like the categories elaborated by Foucault or other authors. These analytical tools remain useful, even outside their original cultural context (structuralism), and even if they need to be completed and perhaps modified. This tradition can inspire researchers to find new categories and tools as a response to the needs of new objects (like "forms of life", see Perusset, 2020). Semiotics, as a modeling of probable shared meaning, can contribute to the analysis of environmental communication campaigns by adapting its approaches to a changing environment and to the creativity of NGOs.

Notes

1 https://theieca.org/resources/environmental-communication-what-it-is-and-why-it-matters, retrieved on April 16, 2021.
2 According to Werder "A strategic communication campaign is a set of deliberate and purposive communication activities enacted by a communication agent in the public sphere on behalf of a communication entity to reach established goals that are informed by multiple perspectives" (2015, p. 81).
3 The term "impact" can have a strong positivistic and ballistic connotation. From a semiotic point of view, we would use also terms like "interpretation" or "sense making" to underline the fact that the impacts of

communication are not only direct and irreflexive but include a wide range of more or less conscious cognitive, emotional, and sense-making actions.
4 Social semiotics, an important international semiotic tradition, is based mostly on another important linguist of the 20th century, M. A. K. Halliday (see Van Leeuwen, 2005, 2010).
5 See for example the page "our history and successes" on the international website of Greenpeace, available at www.greenpeace.org/international/ and accessed on January 21, 2022.
6 As was suggested in Catellani (2018, p. 162), "there is a possible reconciliation between post-structuralism, based on the notions of enunciation and subjective experience, and the semiotics inspired by Charles S. Peirce, based on notions like the "interpretant, semiosis and abduction". In a similar way, contemporary narratologists like Baroni (2007) reinterpret the "quinary model" of Adam (1997) and other authors from the interpreter's point of view as a source of narrative tension and suspense.
7 Main website of the campaign: www.greenpeace.fr/emprise-total. The campaign's most prominent materials are YouTube videos. It is clear that the analysis of the influence of the format and device of specific media, like digital social media, is a crucial issue. NGO's communications adapt to different supports and devices, and it is important to take their influence into consideration. However, we will not develop this particular aspect in this chapter.
8 www.greenpeace.fr/emprise-total, accessed on January 7, 2022.
9 www.greenpeace.fr/emprise-total/total-reseau-d-influence/, accessed on 21 January 2022.
10 www.greenpeace.fr/emprise-total/total-l-influence-mise-a-mal/ (accessed on 21 January 2021).
11 www.youtube.com/watch?v=bL3luiNGshM

References

Adam, J.-M. (1997). *Les Textes, types et prototypes. Récit, description, argumentation, explication et dialogue*. Nathan.
Baroni, R. (2007). *La Tension narrative*. Seuil.
Berthelot-Guiet, K., & Boutaud, J. (2014, 2015). *Sémiotique, mode d'emploi*. Le bord de l'eau.
Bertrand, D. (2000). *Précis de sémiotique littéraire*. Nathan.
Catellani, A. (2011a). La justification et la présentation des démarches de responsabilité sociétale dans la communication corporate: notes d'analyse textuelle d'une nouvelle rhétorique épidictique. *Etudes de communication*, 37, 159–176.
Catellani, A. (2011b). Environmentalists NGOs and the Construction of the Culprit: Semiotic Analysis. *Journal of Communication Management*, 15(4), 280–297.
Catellani, A. (2012a). Critiques visuelles: Observations socio-sémiotiques sur quelques campagnes parodiques environnementalistes. *Communiquer dans un monde de normes. L'information et la communication dans les enjeux contemporains de la "mondialisation"*. Proceedings of the congress "Communiquer dans un monde de normes. L'information et la communication dans les enjeux contemporains de la 'mondialisation'". http://hal.univ-lille3.fr/hal-00823885
Catellani, A. (2012b). Pro-nuclear European discourses: Socio-semiotic Observations. *Public Relations Inquiry*, 1(3), 285–311.
Catellani, A. (2015). Visual aspects of CSR reports: A semiotic and chronological case analysis. In A. Duarte Melo, I. Somerville., & G. Gonçalves (Eds.), *Organisational and strategic communication research: European perspectives II* (pp. 129–149). CECS – Centro de Estudos de Comunicação e Sociedade Universidade do Minho.
Catellani, A. (2016). Écrire et instruire la méditation et la contemplation chrétiennes: les Exercices spirituels d'Ignace de Loyola. *Communication & Langages*, 2016, 85–106. https://doi.org/10.4074/S0336150016013053
Catellani, A. (2018). Environmentalist Multi-modal Communication: Semiotic Observations on Recent Campaigns. In S. Roberts-Bowman & S. Collister (Eds.), *Visual public relations: Strategic communication beyond text* (pp. 161–176). Routledge.
Catellani, A., Pascual Espuny, C., & Malibabo Lavu, P. (2022). Environmental communication research in the French-speaking world. In B. Takahashi, J. Metag, J. Thaker, & S. Evans Comfort (Eds.), *The handbook of international trends in environmental communication*. Routledge.
Catellani, A., Pascual Espuny, C., Malibabo Lavu, P., & Jalenques Vigouroux, B. (2019). Les recherches en communication environnementale. *Communication*, 36(2). http://journals.openedition.org/communication/10559. https://doi.org/10.4000/communication.10559
Chandler, D. (2017). *Semiotics: The basics*. Taylor & Francis.
Cobley, P. (ed.), 2010. *The Routledge companion to semiotics*. Routledge.
Evans Comfort, S., & Eun Park, Y. (2018). On the field of environmental communication: A systematic review of the peer-reviewed literature. *Environmental Communication*, 12(7), 862–875.
Fairclough, N. (1995). *Critical discourse analysis*. Longman.

Floch, J.-M. (2001). *Semiotics, marketing and communication: Beneath the signs, the strategies*. Palgrave (original version: 1990. *Sémiotique, marketing et communication*. PUF).

Fontanille, J. (2006). *The semiotics of discourse*. Peter Lang.

Foucault, M. (2001). *L'herméneutique du sujet. Cours au Collège de France 1981–1982*. Seuil/Gallimard.

Greimas, A. J., & Courtés, J. (1982). *Semiotics and language: An analytical dictionary*. Indiana University Press.

Groupe MU. (2015). *Principia Semiotica. Aux Sources du sens*. Les Impressions Nouvelles.

Hallahan, K., Holtzhausen, D., van Ruler, B., Vercic, D., & Sriramesh, K. (2007). Defining strategic communication. *International Journal of Strategic Communication*, 1(1), 3–35.

Hansen, A. (2011). Communication, media and environment: Towards reconnecting research on the production, content and social implications of environmental communication. *International Communication Gazette*, 73, 7–25. https://doi.org/10.1177/1748048510386739

Hansen, A., & Machin, D. (2013). Researching visual environmental communication. *Environmental Communication*, 7(2), 151–168. https://doi.org/10.1080/17524032.2013.785441

Hébert, L. (2019). *An introduction to applied semiotics: Tools for text and image analysis*. Routledge. www.routledge.com/9780367351120.

Ihlen, Ø. (2016). Critical rhetoric and public relations. In J. L'Etang, D. McKie, N. Snow, & J. Xifra (Eds.), *The Routledge handbook of critical public relations* (pp. 90–100). Routledge.

Kress, G. R. (2010). *Multimodality: A social semiotic approach to contemporary communication*. Routledge.

Markham, A. (2013). Remix culture, remix methods: Reframing qualitative inquiry for social media contexts. *Global Dimensions of Qualitative Inquiry*, 63, 81.

Oliveira, E., Melo, A. D., & Goncalves, G. (2019). *Strategic communication for non-profit organisations: Challenges and alternative approaches*. Vernon Press.

Perusset, A. (2020). *Sémiotique des formes de vie*. De Boeck.

Pezzullo, P., & Cox, R. (2018). *Environmental communication and the public sphere*. Sage.

Schaeffer, J.-M. (2010). *Why fiction?* University of Nebraska Press.

Van Leeuwen, T. (2005). *Introducing social semiotics*. Routledge.

Verhaegen, P. (2010). *Signe et communication*. De Boeck.

Werder, K. P. (2015). The integration of domains: Multidisciplinary approaches to strategic communication campaigns. *International Journal of Strategic Communication*, 9(2), 79–86. https://doi.org/10.1080/1553118X.2015.1010829

3.8
ECO-ART AS DISCOURSE DRIVER

Franzisca Weder and Denise Voci

Introduction

Organizations and forms of organized communication are one of the central structural elements of our society today (Castells, 2000, 2002). They are generators and facilitators of sense- and meaning making processes, reproducing society, culture and related normative frameworks. Generally, organizations are the result of – but are also initiators – of social change (Weder et al., 2021). Organizations are communicatively embedded in the society, and at the same time, they are constituted via communication (Berger & Luckmann, 1966; Weick, 1995; Taylor & van Every, 2000; Schoeneborn, 2011). From a media and communication perspective, public discourses are also a form of organized communication, potentially "stimulated" and "driven" by organizations. In this chapter, we take a closer look on movements, community groups and organized activism, as well as art projects and forms of "intermediaries" which act and communicate increasingly professionally as agents of social change (Hurst & Ihlen, 2018).

Today, sustainability is a new principle that guides strategies and action – not only on an individual level (sustainable consumption, see Fischer et al., 2017) but also on an organizational level (Weder, 2012; Weder et al., 2021). From a business and management perspective, sustainability is the central frame used in corporate social responsibility (CSR) communication (Rasche et al., 2017; Diehl et al., 2017). From a public relations (PR) and strategic communication perspective, nonprofit organizations, including the previously mentioned variations of "organizations," are more broadly linked to the UN Agenda for Sustainable Development (UN, 2015) and play an increasingly important role in realizing the 17 Sustainable Development Goals (UN, 2020). From a more general social constructivist and critical perspective, sustainability as a "societal norm," or guiding principle for action, needs to be negotiated in public discourses (Weder, 2021b; Weder, 2017). Here, nonprofit organizations have the possibility to lead the way on Sustainability Development Goals (SB, 2018). This goes beyond the more established strategic perspective on nonprofits as "good cause" organizations in partnerships helping businesses or political institutions to get the license to operate and shows the social impact of a business (Rasche et al., 2017; Golob & Bartlett, 2007). Instead, our new understanding of nonprofits is that they are drivers of discourses, are responsible for stimulating debate and negotiation processes of "new" norms like sustainability (Bäckstrand & Lövbrand, 2016; Pandey, 2015; Giorgetti, 1998), or for realizing transformation processes in local environments (McGregor et al., 2018) on a national (Quinn-Thibodeau & Wu, 2016) and international level (Allan & Hadden, 2017; Della Porta & Parks, 2014).

This implies various relational, structural, and rhetorical challenges – but also new possibilities to communicate about sustainability (Berny & Rootes, 2018; Newig et al., 2013). In this chapter, supported by a case study, we conceptualize the potential of problematization and agonistic deliberation through new ways of nonprofit communication, introducing art projects and artistic interventions questioning dominant paradigms (Belfiore & Bennett, 2007; Curtis et al., 2012) with the power to move people (Buckland, 2013, p. 367; Weintraub, 2012) by articulating (new) narratives and visions for the future (Roosen et al., 2018).

Sustainability as a point of contention

Sustainability is debated in many disciplines and on various levels, from individual action (sustainable consumption, see i.e., Fischer et al., 2017), institutionalization, and organizational communication (CSR, i.e., Rasche et al., 2017) and on a societal macro-level (education for sustainable development or transformation and social change, i.e., Hopkin & McKeown, 2002). However, sustainability is rather a principle or norm and as such a "moral compass" (Frank, 2017; Weder et al., 2019) or master narrative used and abused in corporate communication (Weder & Baker, 2021) and the media (Weder et al., 2019). From a communication perspective, sustainability works on a macro-level as a point of orientation for organization and structuration processes; individual, collective, and organizational action is related to it as well, and it is used to problematize certain (irresponsible or unsustainable) practices. Thus, sustainability is used to "make an issue out of" a certain practice or situation, it "requires society to develop a common course of action to deal with the (related) problems" (Buchholz et al. 1985; Buchholz, 1989), so sustainability stimulates sense- and meaning-making processes. In this chapter, we introduce a certain form of nonprofit communication (art and artistic interventions), which particularly act as a discourse driver and stimulator of problematization processes. Before we focus on eco-art, supported by a case study, we want to conceptualize nonprofit communication from two different perspectives, a CSR communication, complemented by a PR communication perspective.

The third way: a CSR perspective on nonprofits and their communication

In our contribution, we use the term nonprofit organizations as the wider framework compared to nongovernmental organizations (NGOs, Lecy et al., 2012; Martens, 2002); they are generally described as environmentally or socially concerned organizations pursuing nonprofit interests and motives, holding a "moral supremacy" and "cultural voluntaristic authority" (Boli & Thomas, 1999). There are approximately 10 million (nonprofit action, 2019) nongovernmental, and thus not-for-profit, operating organizations worldwide, sometimes labelled as the "third sector", which serve the public in either offering certain goods, contributing to society in international settings, and pointing out societal deficits and the necessity for change or transformation processes (Forbes, 2019; Anheier, 2014).

The literature shows that nonprofit organizations are often conceptualized as "in-between", as "intermediary" (communication focus) or "third parties" (business/management focus). The character as intermediary is, for example, described as being a mediator in trust relationships (i.e. between the consumer and a specific brand; Bentele & Nothhaft, 2011), as bridging the gap in (climate change/sustainability) communication between scientists and other actors (Vu et al., 2021; McNaught et al., 2014; Laestadius et al., 2013), or as "infomediary", influencing corporate CSR agendas with specific knowledge, social capital, and content (Grafström & Windell, 2011) or offering a reflection on corporate behavior (i.e. the Global Reporting Initiative or labels, Valor, 2008; Dubbink et al., 2008). The idea of nonprofits being a "third party" is discussed from a reputation or trust perspective (Eisenegger & Schranz, 2011) or external instance of moral control (Ihlen, 2011), as well as a facilitator of dialogues (Burchell & Cook, 2013) and providers and organizers of discourses. Therefore, next to nonprofit organizations which offer content, there are those who evaluate, label, and offer a license to operate and a third type that establishes new structures (resources as well as new norms and related narratives and communication processes) and therefore act as facilitators and multipliers of change (Weder & Egger, 2018). This third type needs to be further conceptualized by taking a closer look at the role of communication and discourses.

All about dialogue? Nonprofit communication from a PR perspective

An increase in professionalization, governance, management, and control have entered the nonprofit vocabulary, which leads to a different and more professional understanding of organizational communication and communication management in the nonprofit sector (Oliveira, 2019; Liu, 2012; Martens, 2002; Clarke, 1998). Professionalization means that the communicative persecution of goals aligned with movements on a larger scale (peace movement, environmental movement, or human rights movement) reaches a certain degree of organization to realize the mission and goals. However, still, nonprofits are mostly conceptualized as rather passive regarding their communication, as the "institutional environment" of political organizations and corporations, playing a key role in stakeholder communication processes (Den Hond & De Bakker, 2007). As mentioned in the introduction, the growing field of literature about social impact and CSR, including the engagement or involvement of nonprofits, sits at the core of related strategies (Brand et al., 2019; Rasche et al., 2017; Crane, 2000; Curbach, 2009), using mostly communication models from a corporate communication perspective (Bünzli & Eppler, 2019; Schwarz & Fritsch, 2015; Seo et al., 2009; Liu, 2012). Only recently, a new perspective captures nonprofit communication as integrated communication; as citizen participation, activism, or campaigns for change (Oliveira et al., 2016; Oliveira, 2011; Meneghetti, 2001); and lists specific communicative challenges of provocation and bottom-up communication. In looking at communication for change and transformation, for a "normalization" of a new norm like sustainability, we draw on Davidson (2016), who takes on this critique and introduces a normative position of communication management that he calls an agonistic critique of the established frameworks of dialogue and symmetry. He develops this idea with Mouffe's political theory (2005, 2013; Wenman, 2013; Parker & Parker, 2017), which we see being in line with a social constructivist perspective on communication, in particular the idea of the central role of communication in societal sense- and meaning-making processes.

Other critical PR theory also talks about the role of nonprofit organizations in public discourses, described as the space where ideas are exchanged, either in response to or *to perform and to facilitate change* (L'Etang, 2008, p. 17; see also Koschmann, 2012 and Murphy et al., 2012). This is complemented by the work of Weder (2021a), bringing in the concept of *problematization* as a core process of communicative engagement – especially in a sustainability context. We therefore see conflict, tensions, and discourse fields as part of nonprofit organizing processes – and thus communication processes. Following Davidson (2016), communication about pluralism in a conflict situation is constructive rather than destructive (Mouffe, 2013); problematization as the "driving power" can be perceived as the core process of permanent contestation or a stimulation of dissent. Problematization is organized in conversations (Weder, 2021a) and per se a process of (ethical) reflection and of critical thinking, led by the principle of reflexivity and intrinsic social values, which goes hand-in-hand with a demystification of common knowledge or common-sense issues (Weder & Voci, 2021; Callon & Latour, 1981; Weder, 2017).

Thus, problematization is the *communicatively performed and organized deconstruction of situations taken for granted* (Weder & Voci, 2021). It invites the transformation of situations and is basically an action that starts with the recognition of a situation (context), an issue (content), or idea as *problematic*, followed by an increasing level of involvement via conversations (Weder, 2021a; Crable & Vibbert,

Table 3.8.1 A third way of nonprofit communication: communicatively performed problematization

	A	B	C
Example	Communication *about* climate change and sustainability Top-down Universities, political institutions, Shareholder activism/ethical investment, investment in business from an ethical perspective with a "positive" influence on corporate behavior in mind, consulting; reporting, evaluation of corporates by NGOs, like the global reporting initiative or litigation, lawsuits and court proceedings of activists to fight against corporates/ their misbehavior (Earth Rights International)	Communication *of* the climate crisis Bottom-up Watchdog activism, investigation and disclosure of corporate misconduct (naming and shaming) like Greenpeace, as well as consumer activism and the fair trade movement, information about and boycott of "unsustainable"' or unethical products, like fair trade Critical research, public education, advocacy against misconduct on a larger scale (politics/ economy), like Amnesty International	Communication *for* sustainability Reflexive Friday-for-Future, Extinction Rebellion, Sunrise Movement, Eco-art Eclectic activism, mixed and diverse participation, initiating and stimulation of agonism, generating information and context related to a specific corporate or broader field of economic (or political) behavior
Problematization	Low (dialogue as ideal)	Reactive (provocation, disruption)	(Pro)active problematization (reflexivity)
Communication as organization	Construction of an issue	Deconstruction of an issue	Constitution, conversational through representation of an issue; emergence of new narratives
Constitutive potential	Research, innovation (technical, solutions), information and education	Popularization, orientation for action is given	Agonistic deliberation

1985). Thus, we introduce a "third way" of nonprofit communication (Type C, Table 3.8.1), which includes the "problematization" aspect, and thus, all communication processes *for* transformation and social change, which means all communication processes, where *dissensus is seen as important for the continuation of communication.*

With the categorization at hand, we differentiate between organizations that communicate climate change as threat and crisis, which is rather deconstructive (Type B, Table 3.8.1, an example would be Greenpeace), from a second type of nonprofit communication, described as communication *about* climate change communication and sustainability (Weder & Voci, 2021), which is done by scientific organizations, political institutions, or nongovernmental organizations, characterized as rather constructive communication (Type A, Table 3.8.1).

The third category (Type C, Table 3.8.1) is a category for organized action communicating *for* sustainability, for a better future. This new type are "communities of interpretation", which constitute entities of social change and thus are "natives of social change" (Oliveira, 2019, p. 93). Here the Friday-for-Future movement or Extinction Rebellion are examples that show the constitutive potential, the potential to instigate conversations by problematization, by introducing new narratives and arguments. This third category meets the theoretical implications of a new perspective on nonprofit communication as a performance of organized problematization. Art and art-based interventions are also types of nonprofit communication in the third category, which will be further explained in the next section.

Art-based interventions as organized problematization

Art and art-based interventions have been classified as one example of a new, third type of nonprofit communication. In this chapter, we focus on an environmental art project, standing for various forms of eco-art and "artivism" which represent this new type (Curtis et al., 2012; Giannachi, 2012). The literature describes art as a very effective "medium" to communicate *for* sustainability (Gabrys & Yusoff, 2012; Buckland & Wainwright, 2010; Munden, 2008; Weintraub, 2012; Davoudi, 2012; Thornes, 2008) by exposing and critiquing the ways in which humanity is connected to the earth. It "makes an issue out of" the limitedness and fragility of nature and the environment and highlights how the disconnectedness from earth causes social and ecological inequality and injustice (Wakeland, 2012; Darts, 2004; Weintraub, 2006, 2012; Thornes, 2008; Gabrys & Yusoff, 2012; Guy et al., 2015).

Today, environmental art projects are getting more radical, are rather disruptive, and represent an intervention in a specific natural environment, having a rather destructive character (Type B). Miles (2010) identified the two standpoints as either the art project is a *representation of* or *intervention in* an issue at hand. While *intervention* means the creation and strategic communication of meaning, the artists behind the *representation* projects engage people's minds and their imaginations – they initiate and stimulate change by being no longer interested in "just" an audience for their work but in a public *with whom they can correspond about the meaning and purpose* of their work. Thus, an intervention includes a deliberative process, an ongoing continuing sense-making process and reflexivity (Brand et al., 2019), as well as the contestation of cultural norms and emancipation (Weder & Milstein, 2021; Darts, 2004; Giroux, 1981), which will be further elaborated with a case study.

For Forest: an art-based intervention

"For Forest – the Unending Attraction of Nature" was an eco-art project conceptualized and realized as a temporary art intervention by Klaus Littmann, a Swiss artist and art manager. The intervention took place between 8 September and 27 October 2019 in the local stadium in Klagenfurt, a Central European city (100,000 inhabitants) in the southern part of Austria.

Going back to the pencil drawing of Max Peintner (1970/1971) (Figure 3.8.1), the idea for the intervention was this sarcastic and critical scenario of the future, where the human–nature relationship is deviated in such a way that we can only "watch" and observe nature in a stadium like we observe animals in a zoo. Now, 40 years later, the artist worked with landscape architect Enzo Enea; they planted 300 trees covering the entire playfield of the stadium in Austria with a mixed forest, characteristic of the forests in Central Europe; see Figure 3.8.2.

During the intervention, visitors were able to "watch" the trees and admire them day and night from the grandstands for free, reflecting on this rather unfamiliar experience and their related emotions. The disruption of a familiar sight (trees) placed in an entirely different context was meant to change our awareness of the human–nature relation in a – possibly more sustainable – future. From our perspective on finding an example for the third type of nonprofit communication, including problematizing, cracking existing norms, and establishing a meaning-making process in conversations, we picked For Forest as variation of *eclectiv activism* (Waddell, 2004) and art-based intervention. We captured conversations and the degree of problematization with a text-based media analysis of the project's Facebook page (287 posts, 2000 comments) and the media coverage of the project (284

Figure 3.8.1 "Die ungebrochene Anziehungskraft der Natur"/"The unending attraction of nature", Max Peintner, 1970/1971; source: www.forforest.net.

Figure 3.8.2 For Forest, Klagenfurt/Austria. Credit UNIMO.

articles) collected by a media observation agency, complemented by interviews with stakeholders ($n = 15$; political parties, project lead, journalists, lay people, sports union, neighborhood, and PR team; further methodological details are in Weder & Voci, 2021).

Problematization and deliberation

The media discourses around For Forest show three strains of problematization: The first discourse developed around the problematization of the purpose of the stadium and a financial loss that was expected due to the stadium not being used for sport events. The deliberation around art or sport was even more problematized by bringing in a historical conflict around the stadium being built against a massive opposition in a rather small city, criticized as megalomania. This is an interesting learning for the typology, conceptualized earlier, because while art itself is theoretically described as autotelic, eco-art seems not to be. Eco-art as a specific type of nonprofit communication is dependent on the location where it takes place, which can be supported by the case at hand.

The second discourse was about the funding for the project and public money that was "wasted" by the city council. This discourse again was highly politicized, which transformed a potential discourse on art per se and its potential into a political antagonism (right vs. left). At the end of September, at For Forest's halftime, the national polls in Austria changed the eco-art project into a political battlefield, so that even the artist himself has been met by a level of hostility such that he feared for his own safety and of being physically assaulted on the street.

However, the third discourse that we could detect with the findings of our explorative analysis of the data, further described in Weder and Voci (2021), was actually a great example for the previously conceptualized third way of disruptive and, as a consequence, agonistic nonprofit communication. While generally "liked" and "loved" by the local and international public, the intervention was questioned from an environmental perspective. One dominant argument, for example, brought up by people predominantly on social media was the transplantation of the trees, the trucks, and CO_2 emissions used for that, as well as transportation and the number of cars and buses getting visitors to the stadium. Furthermore, people questioned if the "ever-green" and "water- and forest-rich" region around Klagenfurt was the best place for the art installation: "Everywhere around me, everywhere I look, there are trees, there are mountains, there are massive forests – why would this art thing be a 'memorial' or moral pointing finger for me?" (Comment on Facebook).

Overall, mainly with the third stream of the discourse around For Forest, sustainability became a point of contestation. While the project itself did not intentionally and strategically "implement" a sustainability narrative from the beginning, For Forest fostered agonistic deliberation and acknowledged the conflicting voices and frames used by various actors. The narrative of sustainability emerged *within* the plurality of arguments and narratives and due to the breadth of the public discourse. Narratives – for example, sustainable development – offer the possibility to explore alternative choices that might lead to "feared" or "hoped-for futures" (Heidegger, 1965). If we can change narratives, then we create impact. So, it's not the art project itself, but rather the communicative constitution of a new narrative that happened throughout the intervention that offers learnings for future nonprofit communication: "If we change narratives, we change something fundamental in the moral and political constitution of the society; thus, it is in narrative(s) that new visions of sustainable living begin" (Frank, 2017, p. 312). And the eco-art intervention For Forest opened up the conversations and discourse streams where the new narrative could emerge. It was only through conversations that the event received social relevance and meaning. The discourse on For Forest was a constitutive communicative process event within the society. With sustainability as a point of contestation, we also show new research potential to not only study and theorize sustainability as moral compass or framework but much more as a framework for reflexivity and problematization.

Outlook

The chapter takes a critical perspective on nonprofit communication and theorizes a new type of nonprofit communication as active problematizing, as performing on agonism instead of antagonism and conflict. The given example, the eco-art project For Forest, was highly debated on a local level in an economic, social, and political dimension – staged in various discourse fields with divergent narratives. We conceptualized communication *for* change as *organizing* social change, as *doing social change, doing transformation via problematization*. Agonistic deliberation seems to sit at the core of doing transformation and is the potential innovative concept leading away from consensus- or compromise-focused concepts of communication management in a nonprofit setting (Weder & Voci, 2021).

Agonism means acknowledging the "right to dissent", where a new type of nonprofit communication can be further explored and theorized regarding its specific transformative potential (social impact) and communicatively created and constituted problematization processes.

References

Allan, J. I., & Hadden, J. (2017). Exploring the framing power of NGOs in global climate politics. *Environmental Politics, 26*(4), 600–620. https://doi.org/10.1080/09644016.2017.1319017

Anheier, H. K. (2014). *Nonprofit organizations: Theory, management, policy* (2nd ed.). Routledge.

Bäckstrand, K., & Lövbrand, E. (2016). The road to Paris: Contending climate governance discourses in the post-Copenhagen era. *Journal of Environmental Policy & Planning, 21*(5), 519–532. https://doi.org/10.1080/1523908X.2016.1150777

Belfiore, E., & Bennett, O. (2007). Rethinking the social impact of the arts: A critical-historical review. *International Journal of Cultural Policy, 13*(2), 135–151. https://doi.org/10.1080/10286630701342741

Bentele, G., & Nothhaft, H. (2011). Trust and credibility as the basis of corporate social responsibility: (Mass-) mediated construction of responsibility and accountability. In Øyvind Ihlen, Jennifer L. Bartlett & Steve May (Eds.), *The handbook of communication and corporate social responsibility* (pp. 208–230). Wiley.

Berger Peter, L., & Luckmann, T. (1966). *The social construction of reality. A treatise in the sociology of knowledge.* Penguin Books.

Berny, N., & Rootes, C. (2018). Environmental NGOs at a crossroads? *Environmental Politics, 27*(6), 947–972. https://doi.org/10.1080/09644016.2018.1536293

Boli, J., & Thomas, G. M. (1999). *Constructing world culture. International nongovernmental organization since 1875.* Stanford University Press.

Brand, T., Blok, V., & Verweij, M. (2019). Stakeholder dialogue as agonistic deliberation: Exploring the role of conflict and self-interest in business-NGO interaction. *Business Ethics Quarterly, 30*(1), 3–30. https://doi.org/10.1017/beq.2019.21

Buchholz, R. A. (1989). *Business environment and public policy. Implications for management and strategy formulation.* Englewood Cliffs.

Buchholz, R. A., Evans, W., & Wagley, R. (1985). *Management response to public issues. Concepts and cases in strategy formulation.* Englewood Cliffs.

Buckland, D. (2013). Climate is culture. In *World social science report 2013: Changing global environments* (pp. 365–367). OECD Publishing and UNESCO Publishing.

Buckland, D., & Wainwright, C. (2010). *Unfold: A cultural response to climate change.* Springer.

Bünzli, F., & Eppler, M. J. (2019). Strategizing for social change in Nonprofit contexts: A typology of communication approaches in public communication campaigns. *Nonprofit Management and Leadership, 29*(4), 491–508. https://doi.org/10.1002/nml.21346

Burchell, J., & Cook, J. (2013). Sleeping with the enemy? Strategic transformations in business – NGO relationships through stakeholder dialogue. *Journal of Business Ethics, 113*(3), 505–518.

Callon, M., & Latour, B. (1981). Unscrewing the Big Leviathan: How actors macrostruc-ture reality and how sociologists help them to do so. In K. Knorr-Cetina & A. V. Cicourel (Eds.), *Advances in social theory and methodology: Towards an integration of micro- and macro-sociologies* (pp. 277–303). Routledge and Kegan Paul.

Castells, M. (2000). Toward a sociology of the network society. *Contemporary Sociology, 29*(5), 693–699.

Castells, M. (2002). Local and global: Cities in the network society. *Tijdschrift voor economische en sociale geografie, 93*(5), 548–558.

Clarke, G. (1998). Non-governmental organizations (NGOs) and politics in the developing world. *Political Studies, 46*(1), 36–52.

Crable, R. E., & Vibbert, S. L. (1985). Managing issues and influencing public policy. *Public Relations Review, 11*(2), 3–15.

Crane, A. (2000). Culture clash and mediation exploring the cultural dynamics of business-NGO collaboration. In J. Bendell (Ed.), *Terms for endearment: Business, NGO and sustainable development* (pp. 163–177). Greenleaf.

Curbach, J. (2009). *Die corporate-social-responsibility-Bewegung*. VS Verlag.

Curtis, D. J., Reid, N., & Ballard, G. (2012). Communicating ecology through art: What scientists think. *Ecology and Society, 17*(2). http://dx.doi.org/10.5751/ES-04670-170203

Darts, D. (2004). Visual culture jam: Art, pedagogy, and creative resistance. *Studies in Art Education, 45*(4), 313–327. https://doi.org/10.1080/00393541.2004.11651778.

Davidson, S. (2016). Public relations theory: An agonistic critique of the turns to dialogue and symmetry. *Public Relations Inquiry, 5*(2), 145–167.

Davoudi, S. (2012). Climate risk and security: New meanings of "the environment" in the English planning system. *European Planning Studies, 20*(1), 49–69.

Della Porta, D., & Parks, L. (2014). Framing processes in the climate movement: From climate change to climate justice. In M. Dietz & H. Garrelts (Eds.), *Routledge handbook of climate change movements*. Routledge.

Den Hond, F., & De Bakker, F. G. A. (2007). Ideologically motivated activism. How activist groups influence corporate social change activities. *Academy of Management Review, 48*, 147–160.

Diehl, S., Karmasin, M., Mueller, B., Terlutter, R., & Weder, F. (Eds.). (2017). *Handbook of integrated CSR communication*. Springer.

Dubbink, W., Graafland, J., & Van Liedekerke, L. (2008). CSR, transparency and the role of intermediate organisations. *Journal of Business Ethics, 82*(2), 391–406.

Eisenegger, M., & Schranz, M. (2011). CSR – Moralisierung des Reputationsmanagements. In *Handbuch CSR* (pp. 71–96). VS Verlag für Sozialwissenschaften.

Fischer, D., Stanszus, L., Geiger, S., Grossman, P., & Schrader, U. (2017). Mindfulness and sustainable consumption: A systematic literature review of research approaches and findings. *Journal of Cleaner Production, 162*, 544–558.

Forbes Nonprofit Council. (2019). *12 nonprofit trends we're likely to see in 2020, according to experts*. www.forbes.com/sites/forbesNonprofitcouncil/2019/10/22/12-Nonprofit-trends-were-likely-to-see-in-2020-according-to-experts/#3f4448cf72af

Frank, A. K. (2017). What is the story with sustainability? A narrative analysis of diverse and contested understandings. *Journal of Environmental Studies and Sciences, 7*, 310–323.

Gabrys, J., & Yusoff, K. (2012). Arts, science and climate change: Practices and politics at the threshold. *Science as Culture, 21*(1), 11–21. https://doi.org/10.1080/09505431.2010.550139

Giannachi, G. (2012). Representing, performing and mitigating climate change in contemporary art practice. *Leonardo, 45*(2), 124–131.

Giorgetti, C. (1998). The role of nongovernmental organizations in the climate change negotiations. *Colorado Journal of International Environmental Law and Policy, 9*, 115.

Giroux, H. (1981). Hegemony, resistance, and the paradox of educational reform. *Interchange on Educational Policy, 12*(2), 3–26.

Golob, U., & Bartlett, J. (2007). Communicating about corporate social responsibility: A comparative study of CSR reporting in Australia and Slovenia. *Public Relations Review, 33*(1), 1–9.

Grafström, M., & Windell, K. (2011). The role of infomediaries: CSR in the business press during 2000–2009. *Journal of Business Ethics, 103*(2), 221–237.

Guy, S., Henshaw, V., & Heidrich, O. (2015). Climate change, adaptation and eco-art in Singapore. *Journal of Environmental Planning and Management, 58*(1), 39–54. https://doi.org/10.1080/09640568.2013.839446

Heidegger, M. (1965). *Being and truth*. Yale University Press.

Hopkins, C., & McKeown, R. (2002). Education for sustainable development: An international perspective. *Education and Sustainability: Responding to the Global Challenge, 13*.

Hurst, B., & Ihlen, O. (2018). *Corporate social responsibility and engagement: Commitment, mapping of responsibilities, and closing the loop*. Wiley Blackwell.

Ihlen, Ø. (2011). Rhetoric and Corporate Social Responsibility. In Ø. Ihlen, J. Bartlett, und S. May (Hg.), *The handbook of communication and corporate social responsibility*. Wiley-Blackwell.

Koschmann, M. A. (2012). Developing a communicative theory of the nonprofit. *Management Communication Quarterly, 26*(1), 139–146. https://doi.org/10.1177/0893318911423640

Laestadius, L., Neff, I., Barry, R., & Frattaroli, A. (2013). Meat consumption and climate change: The role of non-governmental organizations. *Climatic Change, 120*(1–2), 25–38. https://doi.org/10.1007/s10584-013-0807-3

Lecy, J. D., Schmitz, H. P., & Swedlund, H. (2012). Non-governmental and not-for-profit organizational effectiveness: A modern synthesis. *Voluntas: International Journal of Voluntary and Nonprofit Organizations, 23*(2), 434–457.

L'Etang, J. (2008). *Public relations: Concepts, practice and critique*. London: Sage.

Liu, B. (2012). Toward a better understanding of Nonprofit-communication management. *Journal of Communication Management, 16*(4), 388–404.

Martens, K. (2002). Mission impossible? Defining nongovernmental organizations. *VOLUNTAS: International Journal of Voluntary and Nonprofit Organizations, 13*, 271–285. https://doi.org/10.1023/A:1020341526691

McGregor, I., Yerbury, H., & Shahid, A. (2018). The voices of local NGOs in climate change issues: Examples from climate vulnerable nations. *Cosmopolitan Civil Societies: An Interdisciplinary Journal, 10*(3), 63–80. https://doi.org/10.5130/ccs.v10.i3.6019.

McNaught, R., Warrick, O., & Cooper, A. (2014). Communicating climate change for adaptation in rural communities: A Pacific study. *Regional Environmental Change, 14*(4), 1491–1503. https://doi.org/10.1007/s10113-014-0592-1

Meneghetti, S. B. (2001). *Comunicação e marketing: fazendo a diferença no dia-a-dia de organizações da sociedade civil*. Global.

Miles, M. (2010). Representing nature: Art and climate change. *Cultural Geographies, 17*(1), 19–35.

Mouffe, C. (2005). *On the political*. Routledge.

Mouffe, C. (2013). *Agonistics: Thinking the world politically*. Verso.

Munden, P. (2008). *Feeling the pressure – Poetry and science of climate change*. British Council.

Murphy, A. G., Dixon, M. A., Kirby, E. L., & Koschmann, M. A. (2012). Discourse, identity, and power in international nonprofit collaborations. *Management Communication Quarterly, 26*(1), 166–172. https://doi.org/10.1177/0893318911424374

Newig, J., Schulz, D., Fischer, D., Hetze, K., Laws, N., Lüdecke, G., & Rieckmann, M. (2013). Communication regarding sustainability: Conceptual perspectives and exploration of societal subsystems. *Sustainability, 5*, 2976–2990. https://doi.org/10.3390/su5072976.

Nonprofitaction. (2019). *Statistics*. http://Nonprofitaction.org/2015/09/facts-and-stats-about-ngos-worldwide/

Oliveira, E. (2011). *Comunicação estratégica integrada para a participação cívica, activismo e campanhas para mudanças em organizações sem fins lucrativos: Greenpeace, Amnistia e Ser+ em Portugal*. Universidade do Minho.

Oliveira, E. (2019). Outline of the instigatory theory of NGO communication. In *The Instigatory theory of NGO communication*. Springer VS.

Oliveira, E., Melo, A., & Gonçalves, G. (Eds.). (2016). *Strategic communication for Nonprofit organisations: Challenges and alternative approaches*. Vernon Press.

Pandey, C. L. (2015). Managing climate change: Shifting roles for NGOs in the climate negotiations. *Environmental Values, 24*, 799–824.

Parker, S., & Parker, M. (2017). Antagonism, accommodation and agonism in Critical Management Studies: Alternative organizations allies. *Human Relations, 70*(11), 1366–1387. https://doi.org/10.1177/0018726717696135.

Quinn-Thibodeau, T., & Wu, B. (2016). NGOs and the climate justice movement in the age of Trumpism. *Development, 59*, 251–256. https://doi.org/10.1057/s41301-017-0091-z

Rasche, A., Morsing, M., & Moon, J. (2017). *Corporate social responsibility. Strategy, communication, governance*. Cambridge University Press.

Roosen, L. J., Klöckner, A. K., & Swim, J. K. (2018). Visual art as a way to communicate climate change: A psychological perspective on climate change – related art. *World Art, 8*(1), 85–110. https://doi.org/10.1080/21500894.2017.1375002

SB. (2018). *NOGs leading the way on sustainable development goals*. www.sustainablesids.org/wp-content/uploads/2018/08/NGOs-leading-SDGs-Sustainable-Brands.pdf.

Schoeneborn, D. (2011). Organization as communication: A Luhmannian perspective. *Management Communication Quarterly, 25*(4), 663–689. https://doi.org/10.1177/0893318911405622

Schwarz, A., & Fritsch, A. (2015). Strategic communication practice of international non-governmental organizations. In D. R. Holtzhausen & A. Zerfaß (Eds.), *The Routledge handbook of strategic communication* (pp. 459–480). Routledge.

Seo, H., Kim, J. Y., & Yang, S.-U. (2009). Global activism and new media: A study of transnational NGOs' online public relations. *Public Relations Review, 35*(2), 123–126.

Taylor, J. R., & van Every, E. J. (2000). *The emergent organization. Communication as its site and surface*. Lawrence Erlbaum.

Thornes, J. E. (2008). A rough guide to environmental art. *Annual Review of Environment and Resources, 33*, 391–411.

UN. (2015). *Transforming our world: The 2030 agenda for sustainable development.* www.un.org/ga/search/view_doc.asp?symbol=A/RES/70/1&Lang=E

UN. (2020). *Sustainable development goals.* https://sustainabledevelopment.un.org/?menu=1300

Valor, C. (2008). Can consumers buy responsibly? Analysis and solutions for market failures. *Journal of Consumer Policy, 31*(3), 315–326.

Vu, H. T., Blomberg, M., Seo, H., Liu, Y., Shayesteh, F., & Do, H. V. (2021). Social media and environmental activism: Framing climate change on Facebook by global NGOs. *Science Communication, 43*(1), 91–115.

Waddell, S. (2004). *NGO strategies to engage business: Trends, critical issues and next steps.* Retrieved March 2, 2020, from http://networkingaction.net

Wakeland, R. G. (2012). Eco-art installation. *Experiential Nature, 160,* 119–124.

Weder, F. (2012). *Verantwortung 'als trendige Referenz der Wirtschaftsberichterstattung.* Oder: Der fehlende öffentliche Diskurs über Corporate Social Responsibility, Springer Verlag.

Weder, F. (2017). CSR as common sense issue. In S. Diehl, M. Karmasin, B. Mueller, R. Terlutter, & F. Weder (Eds.), *Handbook of integrated CSR communication* (pp. 23–36). Springer.

Weder, F. (2021a). Strategic problematization of sustainability reframing dissent in strategic communication for transformation. *Public Relations Inquiry,* 2046147X211026857.

Weder, F. (2021b). Sustainability as master frame of the future? Potency and limits of sustainability as normative framework in corporate, political and NGO communication. In *The sustainability communication reader: A reflective compendium* (pp. 103–119). Springer.

Weder, F., & Baker, T. (2021, July 11–15). *The evolution of the sustainability story in corporate communication.* International Association for Media and Communication Research 2021, Nairobi, Kenya.

Weder, F., & Egger, H. (2018). Unternehmen als Diskurs-Treiber? In *Handbuch NGO-Kommunikation* (pp. 405–424). Springer VS, Wiesbaden.

Weder, F., Krainer, L., & Karmasin, M. (2021). *The sustainability communication reader: A reflective compendium.* Springer.

Weder, F., Lemke, S., & Tungarat, A. (2019). (Re)storying sustainability: The use of story cubes in narrative inquiries to understand individual perceptions of sustainability. *Sustainability, 11*(19), https://doi.org/10.3390/su11195264

Weder, F., & Milstein, T. (2021, accepted for publication). Revolutionaries needed! Environmental Communication as a Transformative Discipline. In B. Takahashi, J. Metag, J. Thaker, & S. E. Comfort (Eds.), *ICA-Routledge handbook of international trends in environmental communication.* Routledge.

Weder, F., & Voci, D. (2021). From ignorance to resonance: Analysis of the transformative potential of dissensus and agonistic deliberation in sustainability Communication. *International Journal of Communication, 15,* 24.

Weder, F., Voci, D., & Vogl, N. C. (2019). (Lack of) problematization of water supply use and abuse of environmental discourses and natural resource related claims in German, Austrian, Slovenian and Italian media. *Journal of Sustainable Development, 12*(1), 39–54.

Weick, K. E. (1995). *Sensemaking in organizations* (Vol. 3). Sage.

Weintraub, L. (2006). Final thoughts: Eco-art in practice. *Art Journal, 65*(1), 81–82.

Weintraub, L. (2012). *To life! Eco art in pursuit of a sustainable planet.* University of California Press.

Wenman, M. (2013). *Agonistic democracy: Constituent power in the era of globalisation.* Cambridge University Press.

3.9
POSITIVE COMMUNICATION AND PUBLIC RELATIONS IN THE NONPROFIT SECTOR

José Antonio Muñiz-Velázquez and Alejandro José Tapia Frade

Introduction

Positive communication is a reference framework for human communication in its multiple scenarios or realities that is based on a model that imports and adapts the main postulates of positive psychology, as has been described elsewhere (Muñiz-Velázquez & Álvarez-Nobell, 2013).

Positive psychology is defined as a branch of psychology whose object of study and intervention is positive experiences, positive personal traits, psychological and subjective well-being, etc. In short, it focuses on human excellence, on living life to its fullest and the joy of being human (Seligman & Csikszentmihalyi, 2000). Institutions and organizations of all kinds are not exempt from such an approach. In fact, for Seligman (2002) himself, among others, the institutional or organizational dimension of well-being represents the third pillar of positive psychology (Gable & Haidt, 2005).

Thus, positive communication is both the study of and the intervention focused on communicative phenomena that help or enhance the subjective and psychological well-being of people, and it focuses in some way on the growth and excellence of human beings in any of their multiple dimensions. In summary, it is communication that "in all kind of human interactions, can be a very powerful tool to improve the world" (Muñiz-Velázquez & Pulido, 2019, p. 12), regardless of whether it also has other and more specific goals. Such interactions can include, of course, those that are mediated or performed by organizations, regardless of their type.

It should be emphasized that when we talk about positive communication and the well-being that is linked to it, we refer to a concept of well-being rooted in the eudaemonic tradition. That is, from a perspective of human happiness in which ethics and human virtues and values are essential. Therefore, it is a well-being or happiness that is not limited to an individual's satisfactory psychological state from the hedonic point of view; without denying this aspect, the happiness and well-being nature goes further and is closely linked to the exercise of virtues (Peterson & Seligman, 2004). In this sense, positive communication is related with communication ethics, but it is going beyond it.

On one hand, the ethical dimension is central to the authentic happy expression of human nature. On the other hand, something similar can be noted in organizational communication and public relations (PR) scholars. The current thinking in this professional field also emphasizes ethics, virtue and human values (Parsons, 2016). Regardless of whether we approach the issue in a more normative or descriptive way, the fact is that we refer to a central issue in the debate surrounding the very nature of PR (Bowen & Bhalla, 2021). Almost a century ago, Edward Bernays, one of the fathers of contemporary PR, alluded to this issue, pointing out that ethical principles and a practice adapted to an ethical code should always prevail in the daily praxis of the PR practitioner (Bernays, 1998).

Using a two-way model, Bernays proposes that the main objective of PR practitioners is to pursue an agreement or confluence of interests between a company or institution and its audiences. Thus, one of the functions of these PR practitioners is to "discover where the interests of the client coincide with those of other individuals or groups" (Bernays, 1998, p. 76). From there, the author insists, at least theoretically, on truth as the axis of construction for this confluence.

With these postulates, PR as an activity and as a profession was clothed in a certain air of ethics, responsibility and good practices (Tapia, 2015). Leaving aside the debate regarding whether Bernays himself was always faithful to his own ethical principles, the truth is that PR has not always remained within the deontological boundaries. McIntyre (2018) reminds us, for example, of the role that certain PR agencies had in the 1950s in the communicative and scientific battle, which could be said to be pseudoscientific, to dissociate the consumption of tobacco from its harmfulness to health. To an extent, the misinformative work of the agencies was such that more than a few authors consider that modus operandi a clear antecedent of the current emergence of post-truth as a widespread phenomenon (Villanueva, 2021).

Leaving this matter for another occasion, we will have to focus on the fourth of the canonical models of PR, the two-way symmetrical model, to consider, at least in North America–centered theory, the debate surrounding not only the praxis but the purposes of PR (Gruning & Hunt, 1984; Grunig & Grunig, 1992). We speak of a model under which the goals and interests of the two parties involved in all PR processes – organizations and the public – converge in a natural, sincere, honest and symmetrical way, mediated and facilitated by the PR practitioner. Here, ethics emerge intrinsically. The concept of positive communication or PR would be really close to this.

In other words, positive communication would have ethics and honesty as its backbone, without exception, but being covered with other hedonic and especially eudaemonic factors. According to that, we understand positive PR as that organizational communication that, apart from other objectives, consciously or unconsciously promotes happiness and psychological well-being of the publics to whom it is addressed (Muñiz-Velázquez & Álvarez-Nobell, 2013), mainly from a eudaemonic perspective. The greatest epitome of this paradigm described until now should be that of nonprofit organizations and, therefore, their PR. It is true that the fourth model has been criticized many times, qualified as idealistic or even as naïve (L'Etang & Pieczka, 1996). But if there is any sector where it shouldn't be like that, it is certainly the nonprofit sector.

Positive public relations in the nonprofit sector

Delving into the issue of positive communication in PR, it should be noted that, *prima facie*, the final objective of all communication in the nonprofit sector could be classified as positive in the sense that its ultimate and essential purpose is the improvement of some particular aspect of society or world. By defining a nonprofit or nongovernmental organization as an entity that expresses and defends the concerns, behaviors, thoughts or ideals of a group of individuals and presenting it as an expression of the civil community (Castillo Esparcia, 2007), everything communiated by this kind of organization will promote, at bottom, the conveyance of the values, strengths and virtues, all of which characterize positive communication (Muñiz-Velázquez & Álvarez-Nobell, 2013).

Studies of communication in the nonprofit sector are not lacking. In this regard, Pérez Sanz et al. (2019), in an analysis carried out in the field of social economy, specifically on cooperatives, showed relatively high compliance with socially responsible behaviors, as well as in communication. Thus, a framework bound by a constructive dialogic relationship was established in open agreement with different interest groups, making it profitable in terms of both commercial margin and profitability or economic viability.

If among these interest groups we focus on internal audiences, such as employees, for example, communicative work that favors their adjustment to the values and purpose of the organization is key (Park & Kim, 2016; Bilbao, 2018). This is an adjustment that we can describe as eudaemonic, when the values and purpose of the nonprofit organization nurture the personal values and life purpose of employees. This is interesting in itself, because it will determine employees' performance and satisfaction, as well as their commitment and loyalty (Alfes et al., 2016). Related to this, it should be remembered that a leadership style that prioritizes the sharing of knowledge in a context of positive moral standards is crucial to this process. As Lu and Li (2015) recall, if all this is important for all types of organizations (Yang &Grunig, 2005), for a nonprofit organization, it is a matter of unavoidable coherence.

Another stakeholder of capital importance for any nonprofit organization, as all kinds of organizations, is the media. Authors such as Lee and Desai (2014), among others, highlight the importance of the aforementioned dialogic direction in the relationship between entities to ensure that the relationship is truly one of quality, one that is nourishing and marked by mutual commitment, key elements in the idea of positive PR. In this sense, the integration, at least in this aspect, of the nonprofit management and PR literature can be said to be a reality today (Penning, 2015), although there are still problems to be solved in terms of the full professionalization of PR in many nonprofit organizations, as noted by Steyn and Puth (2000), Puertas Hidalgo et al. (2019) and Wiggill (2011), among others.

However, leaving these possible challenges aside, the proposal presented here aims to delve into the role that the communication of the nonprofit organization can play in contributing to the happiness of different stakeholders through or in collaboration with the mass media and also beyond them. The proposed challenge could well be to bring nonprofit PR into a positive communication framework in a double sense: not only because of the ultimate goal of nonprofit organizations, always pursued under a symmetrical model (Grunig et al., 1992), but because at the operational level, nonprofit organizations can help to promote hedonic and eudaemonic happiness among their audiences with their communication, as mentioned earlier. These changes at the operational level should occur without losing sight of the strategic level. Thus, once there is awareness of the position that the organization truly occupies among its stakeholders, coherent and realistic planning of positive PR for the organization is proposed. For this purpose, among the different positive psychology models available, the 24 human strengths of Peterson and Seligman (2004) may provide the greatest operational possibilities, as will be shown next.

Organizational signature strengths: a possible model

What is proposed here is the development of a simplified system of knowledge of the communicative reality in terms of positive organizational communication. This system is based on the 24-strengths model of Peterson and Seligman (2004), which is grouped around six virtues. Although this model, taken from positive psychology, is geared mainly toward the personal sphere, we offer an adaptation of it to the organizational sphere. This is done with an understanding of the organizational sphere as not just a mere ecosystem or space for individual interactions but as its own entity, as an organism in itself, with its own personality, one could say.

Thus, the first of the categories refers to the virtue of wisdom and knowledge, and it is composed of cognitive strengths (see Table 3.9.1). In organizational terms, it could be considered met if organization maintains a communication structure that tends toward symmetry and bidirectionality (Grunig et al., 1992). This would be reflected in a sincere interest in the demands of the stakeholders, the cultivation of critical thinking to propose solutions and the will to carry them out in a creative and original way.

Table 3.9.1 The six virtues and 24 character strengths, with short descriptions

Virtues	Character strengths
1) Wisdom and knowledge Cognitive strengths that entail the acquisition and use of knowledge.	1. Creativity: Thinking of novel and productive ways to do things. 2. Curiosity: Taking an interest in all ongoing experiences. 3. Open-mindedness: Thinking things through and examining them from all sides. 4. Love of learning: Mastering new skills, topics and bodies of knowledge. 5. Perspective: Being able to provide wise counsel to others.
2) Courage Emotional strengths that involve the exercise of will to accomplish goals in the face of opposition, external or internal.	6. Authenticity: Speaking the truth and presenting oneself in a genuine way. 7. Bravery: Not shrinking from threats, challenges, difficulty or pain. 8. Persistence: Finishing what one starts. 9. Zest: Approaching life with excitement and energy.
3) Humanity Interpersonal strengths that involve "lending and befriending" others.	10. Kindness: Doing favors and good deeds for others. 11. Love: Valuing close relations with others. 12. Social intelligence: Being aware of the motives and feelings of oneself and others.
4) Justice Civic strengths that underlie healthy community life.	13. Fairness: Treating all people the same according to notions of fairness and justice. 14. Leadership: Organizing group activities and seeing that they happen. 15. Teamwork: Working well as member of a group or team.
5) Temperance Strengths that protect against excess.	16. Forgiveness: Forgiving those who have done wrong. 17. Modesty: Letting one's accomplishments speak for themselves. 18. Prudence: Being careful about one's choices; not saying or doing things that one might later regret. 19. Self-regulation: Regulating what one feels and does.
6) Transcendence Strengths that forge connections to the larger universe and provide meaning.	20. Appreciation of beauty and excellence: Noticing and appreciating beauty, excellence and/or skilled performance in all domains of life. 21. Gratitude: Being aware of and thankful for the good things that happen. 22. Hope: Expecting the best and working to achieve it. 23. Humor: Liking to laugh and tease; making other people smile. 24. Spirituality: Having coherent beliefs about the higher purpose and meaning of life.

Source: Ruch and Proyer (2015), adapted from Peterson and Seligman (2004).

The second of the categories proposed by Peterson and Seligman (2004) refers to courage. Organizationally speaking, this category should be considered resolved if the organization is capable of setting goals and objectives that involve substantial progress, including in terms of communication. This task should require perseverance, diligence, integrity, honesty and moral rectitude. All of these connect with the confluence between saying, doing and being, something that is key to our happiness, as Gandhi said, and is increasingly applicable to PR.

The third of the categories proposed in the 24-strengths model refers to humanity. This category could be considered, a priori, less applicable if we think about an organization in general, or in a business company and its communication. But if we think about a nonprofit organization, it could be interpreted as a way of communicating with its stakeholders that is characterized by empathy and kindness as a result of the emotional, personal and social intelligence of an organization's employees, collaborators and other agents – all of which, after all, should be in the DNA of a nonprofit organization, as far as it works for others.

The fourth of the virtues refers to justice. In view of this circumstance, it could be considered applicable if the fundamental purpose of the organization's PR action is performed with loyalty, civility and equity toward its stakeholders. Similarly, a corporate culture based on teamwork and guided by positive, nurturing leadership that considers both results and people and their well-being in a symbiotic and balanced way should be considered important.

Temperance is the fifth category. We assert that to fulfill this category, an organization should communicate with its audiences symmetrically, proportionally, with modesty and prudence, and showing the ability to amend its possible errors before its stakeholders.

Finally, Peterson and Seligman (2004) allude to transcendence. A communicatively transcendent organization keeps and shows an existential attitude of gratitude towards its stakeholders with optimism, hope and a sense of the future, and it is also capable of conveying this attitude to its audiences.

This cataloging of human strengths offers the nonprofit organization a broad frame of reference from which to establish a healthy, constructive and nourishing relationship with its stakeholders. That is to say, *positive* in terms of human flourishing, according to Seligman (2011). However, just as not all people have the same preferences or dedication to each of the 24 human strengths, the same can happen with organizations, which will develop one or another to a greater extent. Thus, from this catalog, each organization, as individuals do, can rank the human strengths with respect to how central they are to it.

Most of us have a few core strengths, which Peterson and Seligman (2004) call "signature" strengths, that to a large extent reflect their identity (Niemiec & Pearce, 2021). In other words, there are usually about five strengths (Huber et al., 2020) that resonate more strongly with each individual that he or she exercises more frequently. In positive interventions with individuals, those who work to identify these signature strengths and then focus on them perform best (Harzer & Ruch, 2013). A similar process could be proposed for nonprofit organizations and their PR strategies. That is, starting with an in-depth study of the mission, purpose, vision, values and beliefs of the organization; its positioning; and its scope of action, it would be wise to analyze which organizational signature strengths are naturally better suited to these areas. From there, a profile is created, from which the nonprofit organization can deploy all its communicative actions. For example, if the organization in question is a museum, it seems clear that its strengths would be more closely related to the appreciation of beauty than to self-control. As with personal interventions, the goal is to define the pool of key strengths that the organization possesses that can be used to move the audience of interest. These would be considered strategic strengths of the first order; others are granted lower priority but are not dismissed in their entirety.

Essentially, the development of communication plans and actions entails analyzing the role of these strengths and how to foster them among different audiences. Thus, a working scheme for the implementation of a signature strengths model for an organization could begin by summarizing the existential parameters of the nonprofit organization: its mission, purpose, vision, values and beliefs – in short, its organizational culture and its *brand territory*.

As a second step, an audit of internal and external audiences could be performed to determine the association between the result of step one and each of the 24 human strengths. Through this process, the pool of five organizational signature strengths would be selected, as the third step, and these strengths would be ranked from most to least relevant or present in and for the organization (see Figure 3.9.1).

Conclusions

In this chapter, we propose an outline of one model of action that allows the incorporation of a positive communication perspective into a two-way symmetrical model of PR for nonprofit organizations. And we say *positive* in terms of both the ultimate ends of these organizations, and therefore the

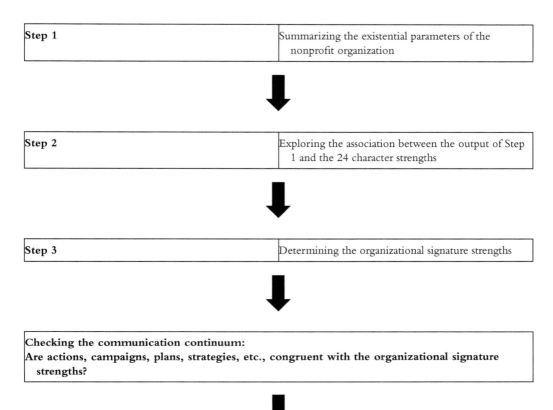

Figure 3.9.1 Scheme and workflow of the proposed organizational signature strengths model for nonprofit organizations (author's own elaboration).

ultimate end of their communication, and their PR strategies, actions, etc., because all this would try to encourage character strengths among the organization's audiences. To this end, we propose the application of the model of individual signature strengths to an organization, which the positive PR of a nonprofit organization can apply tactically and strategically.

Nonprofit organizations, more than any other type of organization, have an easier time following the parameters of what we can call positive organizational psychology, i.e., a framework focused on an effective and efficient management of organizational development in order to boost the well-being and health of the organization's people and other stakeholders (Salanova Soria et al., 2016). Positive PR can add to this paradigm by showing that the desire for well-being, as a core management principle, should not be limited to the inside of an organization. Thus, we can speak of organizations that are positive not only because they seek organizational excellence, in which financial success or sustainability is at least unavoidable, but also because they nurture human excellence, both in the people who compose the organization and those surrounding the organization.

In short, with the proposed model, we foster "positive communication" for two reasons. First, because its end in itself is already eudaemonic insofar as the nonprofit organizations have in general an intrinsically virtuous purpose, such as improving the world in some specific aspect. And second, because with their communication, nonprofit organizations could also help to exercise some character strengths. Therefore, we could speak about PR in the service of human happiness and flourishing in a deeper way and from several simultaneous fronts, having positive direct effects in the short, medium and long term.

References

Alfes, K., Shantz, A., & Bailey, C. (2016). Enhancing volunteer engagement to achieve desirable outcomes: What can non-profit employers do? *Voluntas*, 27(2), 595–617. https://doi.org/10.1007/s11266-015-9601-3
Bernays, E. (1998). *Cristalizando la opinión pública*. Gestión 2000.
Bilbao, M., Martínez-Zelaya, G., Pavez, J., & Morales, K. (2018). Burnout of NGO workers who implement social policy in Chile. *PsicoPerspectivas*, 17(3), 199–210. https://doi.org/10.5027/psicoperspectivas/vol17-issue3-fulltext-1454
Bowen, S. A., & Bhalla, N. (2021). 30 ethical theories and public relations: Issues and challenges. In C. Valentini (Ed.), *Public relations* (pp. 581–598). De Gruyter Mouton. https://doi.org/10.1515/9783110554250-030
Castillo Esparcia, A. (2007). Relaciones Públicas en las organizaciones no gubernamentales. *Sphera Pública*, 7, 193–210.
Gable, S., & Haidt, J. (2005). What (and why) is positive psychology? *Review of General Psychology*, 9. https://doi.org/10.1037/1089-2680.9.2.103
Grunig, J. E., Dozier, D. M., Ehling, W. P., Grunig, L. A., Repper, F. C., & White, J. (Eds.). (1992). *Excellence in public relations and communication management*. Erlbaum.
Grunig, J. E., & Grunig, L. (1992). Models of public relations and communication. In J. E. Grunig (Ed.), *Excellence in public relations and communication management* (pp. 285–325). Lawrence Erlbaum Associates.
Gruning, J., & Hunt, T. (1984). *Managing public relations*. Holt, Rinehart and Winston.
Harzer, C., & Ruch, W. (2013). The application of signature character strengths and positive experiences at work. *Journal of Happiness Studies*, 14, 965–983, https://doi.org/10.1007/s10902-012-9364-0
Huber, A., Strecker, C., Hausler, M., Kachel, T., Höge, T., &Höfer, S. (2020). Possession and applicability of signature character strengths: What is essential for well-being, work engagement, and burnout? *Applied Research in Quality of Life*, 15(2), 415–436. https://doi.org/10.1007/s11482-018-9699-8
Lee, S. T., & Desai, H. (2014). Dialogic communication and media relations in non-governmental organizations. *Journal of Communication Management*, 18(1). https://doi.org/10.1108/JCOM-07-2012-0059
L'Etang, J., & Pieczka, M. (1996). *Critical perspectives in public relations*. International Thomson Business Press.
Lu, M., & Li, G. (2015). A study on the effects of authentic leadership on psychological capital and knowledge in China association for NGO cooperation. *Acta Oeconomica*, 65(2), 115–129. https://doi.org/10.1556/032.65.2015.S2.9
McIntyre, L. (2018). *Post-truth*. MIT Press.
Muñiz-Velázquez, J. A., & Álvarez-Nobell, A. (2013). Comunicación Positiva: la comunicación organizacional al servicio de la felicidad. *Vivat Academia*, 124, 90–109. https://doi.org/10.15178/va.2013.124.90-109
Muñiz-Velázquez, J. A., & Pulido, C. (2019). *The Routledge handbook of positive communication*. Routledge.
Niemiec, R. M., & Pearce, R. (2021). The practice of character strengths: Unifying definitions, principles, and exploration of what's soaring, emerging, and ripe with potential in science and in practice. *Frontiers in Psychology*, 11, 3863. https://doi.org/10.3389/fpsyg.2020.590220
Park, Sung M., & Kim, M. (2016). Antecedents and outcomes of non-profit public service motivation in Korean NPOs. *International Journal of Manpower*, 37(5), 777–803. https://doi.org/10.1108/IJM-12-2014-0242
Parsons, P. J. (2016). *Ethics in public relations: A guide to best practice*. Kogan Page Ltd.
Penning, T. (2015). PR capacity on nonprofit boards. In R. D. Waters (Ed.), *Public relations in the nonprofit sector: Theory and practice*. Routledge.
Pérez Sanz, F. J., Gargallo-Castel, A. F., & Esteban-Salvador, M. L. (2019). CSR practices among co-operatives. Experience and results of case studies. *CIRIEC*, 97.
Peterson, C., & Seligman, M. E. P. (2004). *Character strengths and virtues: A handbook and classification*. Oxford University Press.
Puertas-Hdalgo, R., Camacho, J., & Altamirano-Benítez, V. (2019). Communication for development in Ecuador. In *14th iberian conference on information systems and technologies* (CISTI) (pp. 1–6). https://doi.org/10.23919/CISTI.2019.8760691
Ruch, W., & Proyer, R. T. (2015). Mapping strengths into virtues: The relation of the 24 VIA-strengths to six ubiquitous virtues. *Frontiers in Psychology*, 6, 460. https://doi.org/10.3389/fpsyg.2015.00460
Salanova Soria, M., Llorens Gumbau, S., & Martínez Martínez, I. A. (2016). Contributions from positive organizational psychology to develop healthy and resilient organizations. *Papeles del psicólogo*, 37(3), 177–184.

Seligman, M. E. P. (2002). Positive psychology, positive prevention, and positive therapy. In C. R. Snyder & S. J. Lopez (Eds.), *Handbook of positive psychology* (pp. 3–9). Oxford University Press.
Seligman, M. E. P. (2011). *Flourish: A visionary new understanding of happiness and well-being*. Free Press.
Seligman, M. E. P., & Csikszentmihalyi, M. (2000). Positive psychology: An introduction. *American Psychologist*, *55*(1), 5–14. https://doi.org/10.1037/0003-066X.55.1.5
Steyn, B., & Puth, G. (2000). *Corporate communication strategy*. Sandown.
Tapia, A. (2015). *Fundamentos de las Relaciones Públicas*. Pirámide.
Villanueva, D. (2021). *Morderse la lengua: Corrección política y posverdad*. Espasa.
Wiggill, M. N. (2011). Strategic communication management in the non-profit sector: A simplified model. *Journal of Public Affairs*, *11*(4), 226–235. https://doi.org/10.1002/pa.415
Yang, S. U., & Grunig, J. E. (2005). Decomposing organisational reputation: The effects of organisation-public relationship outcomes on cognitive representations of organisations and evaluations of organisational performance. *Journal of Communication Management*, *9*(4). https://doi.org/10.1108/13632540510621623

PART IV

Nonprofit communication, campaigns and case studies

The last part of this handbook assembles campaigns and case studies of different areas of practice, causes and geographies. One group of chapters presents actual work in the field of environmental advocacy, human rights campaigns, and grassroots movements. The other group of chapters reflect upon the merits and pitfalls of the digital media environment, in particular websites and social media as dialogic tools and networks of engagement. Taken together, several important themes emerge from these chapters. First the potential of communication; then, the role of mediated communication to achieve nonprofit missions, both at formal and informal levels; finally, the social impact of the different cases and campaigns. The chapters in this last part help to reflect the triality of the current circumstances and conditions as scholars, practitioners, and citizens (activists). It also illustrates the diversity within these fields, not only from the distinctive topics but also from the studies addressing possibilities.

The case study of a new food cooperative – Farming Communities, a grassroots initiative in the south of the Netherlands – opens this part of the handbook. In Chapter 4.1, Korien van Vuuren-Verkerk from Ede University of Applied Sciences, Noelle Aarts from the Radboud University in Nijmegen, and Jan van der Stoep from the Wageningen University in the Netherlands reflect about how communication can foster collective and connective action. They go even further by arguing that in a wider context, they contribute to agricultural transformation. Collective action is promoted by acknowledged vertical and horizontal interdependence and trust. Connective action – a concept introduced by the authors – entails interaction dynamics among individuals who share ideas and opinions via networked technologies. One main conclusion is that connective action can overcome the fragility of a single local initiative and is suitable for enhancing the transformative capacity of a grassroots initiative.

How environmental nongovernmental organizations (ENGOs) manage their e-communication in order to be heard by decision-makers is the question guiding the case study presented by Valentina Burksiene and Jarolav Dvorak from Klaipèda University, Lithuania (Chapter 4.2). Through a content analysis of ENGOs' digital presence, they conclude that due to limited financial and human resources and analytical skills, the e-communication capacity of ENGOs operating in Klaipeda, the third-largest city in Lithuania, is highly fragmented. More specifically, they advance that in this case, e-communication is limited to presenting information about a problem or feedback to a proposal that does not provoke a significant reaction from the population. Based on Goffman front-/backstage dichotomy, it is argued that ENGOs need to professionally employ an approach of managed e-communication in order to achieve their environmental goals. That is, to act in front-stage mode.

DOI: 10.4324/9781003170563-30

Chapter 4.3 discusses processes of mobilization and awareness of women around the issues of water to make them central stakeholders in water management interventions by a local NGO in India. Ram Awtar Yadav, from Jagran Lakecity University, Bhopal, and Kanshan Malik, from the University of Hyderabad, look at the efforts carried out in 96 villages of the three districts of Uttar Pradesh. Methodologically, this case study is built upon a qualitative approach collecting data through field visits, in-depth interviews and focus group discussions, and participant observation. It critically examines the project's success in transforming the villages from water-scarce to water-sufficient and the role of women associated with the water collectives in mobilizing other women for the cause.

The two following chapters (Chapters 4.4 and 4.5) have in common the pandemic context and the questioning about how it influences communication management in human rights NGOs. Sónia de Sá, from LabCom/University of Beira Interior, reviews communication strategies laid out by NGOs that provide support for domestic violence victims in Portugal within a lockdown context. From the qualitative interview-based approach to 15 NGOs, one conclusion stands out: the specialized staff working with the NGOs, who are exceedingly exhausted and on the verge of burnout, disregard the need for communication strategic planning that encompasses the different audiences – a relationship based on dialogue and horizontality.

In Chapter 4.5, Laura Visan investigates a fundraising campaign to purchase medical equipment and supplies for the local hospital, developed by a community foundation from Romania. According to a recent Eurobarometer survey, Romania ranks in the last position among the EU states for community engagement. Drawing from the content posted by the Țara Făgărașului Foundation on social media and from five ethnographic interviews, the researcher from the University of Toronto Scarborough concludes that interpersonal trust and the civic spirit are developing in Romania.

The role of communication and information practices in recent feminist activism is investigated in the chapter co-authored by Allessandra Farné and Eloís Nos-aldás, from Interuniversity Institute for Social Development and Peace at University Jaume I (Spain), and Carla Cerqueira, from Lusófona University (Portugal). Chapter 4.6 analyses the case of the 8M women's strikes in Spain and Portugal in 2019 adopting an activist communication perspective, based on the concept of "cultural efficacy." This concept refers to the shared premise that the core cross-cutting responsibility and main long-term aim is transformative communication above the private or management needs of movements and organizations. By applying a content and discourse analysis to the websites that coordinated the Iberian 8M strikes, the authors use cultural efficacy criteria to discuss how it contributed to the movement's communication and activist practices. Results indicate that both feminist activism experiences advocate enduring transformation with a nonviolent, transgressive, and intersectional approach, enhancing recognition of previous struggles and inspiring alliances.

Chapter 4.7 offers an innovative answer to the challenges faced by nonprofit organizations in creating value-informed communication activities. Birgit Breninger and Thomas Kaltenbacher from Paris-Lodron University Salzburg suggest that the concept of communication has to be redefined from an integrative, bio-social angle in order to be able to trigger humanitarian mindsets and action in individuals. Bio-social entails that individuals who consistently act on such values do not only effectuate progress on the sociocultural level but will ultimately experience a rewiring on the neurobiological level. Moreover, they defend that in multicultural societies, the perception of authenticity of values has to be founded on the neurobiological integration of cultural difference on an individual level in order to habitually trigger prosocial actions. An experimental eye tracking pilot is introduced as an example for a possible approach to analyze genuinely value-informed communication.

María Pallarés-Renau, Lorena López-Font, and Susana Miquel-Segarra from the University Jaume I de Castellón (Spain) propose a model to mapping nonprofit organizations' stakeholders (Chapter 4.8). The model is based on a content analysis of the annual reports published by five of the main organizations in Spain: Caritas (Spain), the Spanish Red Cross, Oxfam Intermon Foundation,

Save the Children Foundation (Spain), and the Spanish UNICEF Committee Foundation. Approximately 200 groups were extracted from the analysis and then reduced to 58 collectives that can be categorized by typologies into 12 key groups or parents' groups.

Two case studies from Greece are brought by Michael Nevradakis, from the Hellenic American University and College Year in Athens, to close this handbook. Chapter 4.9 interrogates the broader impact and longevity of new civil society initiatives formed during the crisis period, as well as the role of social media in bolstering Greek civil society. The discussion is illustrated with two Greek organizations – Boroume, a nonprofit organization whose mission is to reduce food waste and to fight malnutrition, and Radiobubble, an "alternative" online radio station with a strong level of involvement in activism and civil society. Findings demonstrate that, like many similar initiatives starting in Greece during the crisis, the enthusiasm with which they initially approached social media did not last. Their social media presence was deemphasized, and they increasingly replicated practices of well-established NGOs.

4.1
BALANCING COLLECTIVE ACTION AND CONNECTIVE ACTION IN NEW FOOD COOPERATIVES

Fertile ground for transformative change?

Korien van Vuuren-Verkerk, Noelle Aarts and Jan Van der Stoep

Introduction

Food is a prerequisite for human existence, as we all experience hunger on a daily basis. Globally, food and agricultural production has increased significantly, but it has also adversely impacted nutrient cycles, biodiversity, and climate change (Springmann et al., 2018). Transformation toward a future-proof, sustainable food system is one of the most significant challenges facing humankind. Understanding transformation processes that lead to sustainability is therefore a key interest in research on food and agriculture. Equally, this topic entails communication, because collectives and individuals shape transformation processes mainly through communication (Moore et al., 2014).

Communication that fosters collective action is indeed considered a key driver of transformational change (Aarts, 2018; Leeuwis & Aarts, 2011; Loorbach et al., 2020; Van Bueren et al., 2003). Furthermore, there is a strand of research that suggests that transformative change is often triggered at a local level through collective action or co-construction of local solutions (Avelino et al., 2020; Balvanera et al., 2017; Staggenborg, 2016; Wittmayer et al., 2019). Agricultural transformation is a multifaceted challenge and consists of changing interrelated social, cultural, economic, and ecological processes that together reproduce the current unsustainable food system (Leeuwis et al., 2021). It is therefore paramount to know whether and how people in a local context are able to make sense of this complex issue and mobilize other actors to self-organize around a different viewpoint or a new practice that addresses transformative change (Weick & Sutcliffe, 2011). Moore et al. (2014, p. 4) describe this sense-making process as "building 'collective action frames' in a local context, that contribute to a common story and purpose to motivate action" (building on Staggenborg, 2016; see also Wittmayer et al., 2019). This chapter aims to explore how insights into interaction dynamics can foster transformation by emergent new ways of doing, knowing, framing, and organizing (Pel et al., 2020). The focal point of the study is how communication processes of nonprofit cooperative forms of collective action (hereafter cooperatives) can optimize their transformative capacity and, in a wider context, foster agricultural transformation.

Before exploring how transformative change in food systems can occur through interactions at a local level, we need to understand how collective action comes about in local cultural and policy contexts (Balvanera et al., 2017). For this purpose, the case of Farming Communities – a grassroots initiative in the south of the Netherlands – is investigated. The Farming Communities (in Dutch: *Herenboeren*) case serves as an example of an innovative form of food production. Each community farm is a small-scale, sustainably operating mixed farm initiated and supported by a group of local residents. Their local farmlands are no longer used for large-scale intensive farming to produce low-cost export products with polluting production methods; instead, consumers invest collectively in the surrounding farmland. The participants are "prosumers": both producers and consumers, as the local organic products constitute about 50% of their food consumption. This study investigates whether such an initiative can develop into a fertile ground for transformative food-system change.

The chapter unfolds as follows. The next section elaborates on the concepts of transformative change, collective action, and connective action. Then, the Farming Communities case illustrates comprehensively how collective action and connective action in cooperatives come about through interaction. A discussion completes the study, reflecting on the communicational preconditions that need to be met for cooperatives to be a fertile ground for transformative change.

Theoretical considerations

Transformative change

Transformative change can be defined as "a fundamental, system-wide reorganization across technological, economic and social factors, including paradigms, goals and values" (IPBES, 2019, p. 14). A sustainable food system entails a global food production that maintains "favorable conditions for human and non-human flourishing across generations" (Pickering et al., 2022, p. 3).

Various schools of thought have different understandings of how transformative change toward sustainability happens. For example, the multilevel perspective describes how sustainable transformation can be brought about by "alternative 'niche' practices that manage to overthrow the dominance of 'mainstream' regime practices" (Hebinck et al., 2021, p. 1; Geels, 2020; Loorbach et al., 2020). Others consider sustainable transformation a merely technical issue: a synonym for a carbon-reduction strategy (Moragues-Faus & Morgan, 2015; Shove & Walker, 2010). In this approach, which emphasizes technological tools and innovations, there is a tendency to overlook the relevance of context-specific social and political dynamics (Labanca et al., 2020; Leeuwis & Aarts, 2011; Loorbach et al., 2020; Stacey, 2007;). We, however, follow those who alternatively work with grassroots interpretations, which have "a more capacious and multi-dimensional conception of sustainability transformation, embracing social, economic, and environmental values" (Moragues-Faus & Morgan, 2015, p. 1564; see also Van Bueren et al., 2003; Shove & Walker, 2010). Although we incorporate the multilevel perspective in this study, we delve further mainly into the previously mentioned grassroots interpretation, as this conception of transformation relates to the Farming Communities case elaborated on in the case analysis.

In this vein, Seyfang and Smith (2007, p. 585) emphasize the transformative role of grassroots initiatives, considering them "networks of activists and organizations generating novel bottom-up solutions for sustainable development; solutions that respond to the local situation and the interests and values of the communities involved". Transformative capacity then entails the embedding of these novelties in local structures, practices, and discourses. It also includes the resources to motivate wider acceptance and replication in order to challenge a dominant regime, such as an unsustainable food system (Hölscher et al., 2019).

This finding is in line with the transformation theory of small wins coined by organizational theorist Karl Weick (1984), who argues that changes cannot be simultaneously in-depth, large, and quick, "given cognitive limitations regarding complex problems and widespread conflict over values" (Termeer & Dewulf, 2019, p. 203; see also Weick & Quinn, 1999). Termeer et al. (2017, 2019) elaborate on the fact that, although small-win changes have a limited scope, this does not prevent them from amplifying and accumulating into large-scale transformative change (Termeer & Dewulf, 2019; Weick & Quinn, 1999). They contend that a sequence of small, deep changes may also accomplish a radical alteration in the status quo (Lindblom, 1979). The establishment of Farming Communities cooperatives may very well serve as an example of a small win, as explained in the forthcoming case analysis.

Following Aarts (2018), Moragues-Faus and Morgan (2015), and Termeer et al. (2017), this small-win approach emphasizes the importance of the analysis of discourse, interaction, and networks to gain insight into sense-making and decision-making processes toward transformation (Hovelynck et al., 2020; Weick & Quinn, 1999). Such analysis highlights the pivotal role played by communicating actors in a network or a cooperative in "generating, sustaining and overthrowing everyday practices" by social interaction and by the building and breaking of stories, using language as a vehicle (Shove & Walker, 2010, p. 476; see also Gray & Purdy, 2018; Leeuwis & Aarts, 2011). In other words, interactions for transformative change may be viewed as a "form of interchange that succeeds in transforming a relationship between those committed to otherwise separate realities (and their related practices) to one in which common and solidifying realities are under construction" (Gergen et al., 2001, p. 682). As these realities and their related practices are negotiated in social interaction, we take a closer look at interaction processes in cooperative forms of collective action, otherwise known as cooperatives.

Interaction for collective action

Collective action refers to settings where individual decisions are made independently but affect collective outcomes, generally in the hope that these decisions will impact the common good positively (Ostrom, 2010). Collective action is regarded as a challenging process because "actors involved in dealing with environmental problems often hold divergent perspectives on the issue at stake and related solutions" (De Vries et al., 2019, p. 3). Noncooperative behaviors like free-riding or powerplay may impact the effectiveness of the collective action process. Although collective action has the potential to produce strong cooperatives, not all collaborations realize this potential: many fail to produce innovative solutions or to balance the concerns of community members, and some even fail to generate any collective action whatsoever (Gray, 2004).

Recent work on collective action emphasizes that cooperatives are social and natural relationships "imbued with inequities and power relations that impact whether and how individuals choose to participate" (Zhang & Barr, 2019, p. 772). Collaboration processes typically involve power struggles and value conflicts (Patterson et al., 2016). However, interdependencies make it impossible for any one participant to resolve these struggles and achieve transformation by himself or herself. Hence, the adoption of a new behavior is linked with the performance of others' behaviors (Aarts, 2018; Leeuwis & Aarts, 2020).

The notion of people being faced with interdependencies when considering a change in behavior can in part be captured by the concept of trust (De Vries et al., 2019) – or more precisely, the expectation that others are trustworthy in terms of their legitimacy and credibility and that they are willing to perform the necessary complementary behaviors (Baldassarri, 2015). Several types of interdependence can be distinguished, such as *vertical* and *horizontal* interdependence (Leeuwis & Aarts, 2020). In a pandemic context, for example, *vertical trust* relates to whether citizens expect the national government to behave in a conducive manner. *Horizontal trust* then consists of the extent to which someone believes that fellow citizens will demonstrate the complementary behaviors on which the adoption of a new behavior depends ("if they don't keep their distance, why should I?"). Thus, the perceived experimental space to perform new framings or new doings is related to the extent to which participants accept their interdependencies and can expect other actors to be trustworthy. In sum, we can conclude that a certain level of trust and the recognition of interdependence are considered pivotal to collaboration and to the transformative potential of a cooperative (Leeuwis & Aarts, 2020).

Throughout the life of a cooperative, these mutual relationships are negotiated on a permanent basis. Hardy et al. (2005) state that, consequently, collaboration represents a complex set of ongoing communicative processes among the members of the cooperative. Successful collective action is strongly dependent on the nature, quality, and results of interaction, information, and communication (Cieslik et al., 2018; Ostrom, 1990, 2009). It involves "acknowledging differences, accepting that all actors have legitimate interests, and attempting to construct a complementarity of differences" (Hovelynck et al., 2020, p. 260). In order to examine how effective collaboration can be stimulated, Nobel laureate Elinor Ostrom (1990, 2009) identified communicational features that influence whether or not civil society organizations succeed in fostering effective cooperation while managing commons or creating public goods. Face-to-face communication, stable membership, and small groups facilitate commitment to collective action (Ostrom, 2010). In the same vein, Baldassarri (2015) adds that reciprocity, sustained interaction, and verbal commitment make cooperation more convenient and discourage free-riding.

In sum, creating a sort of discursive space where interdependencies are acknowledged is considered vital to both transformative potential and fruitful collective action. Deep change asks for the opportunity to discuss and negotiate strategies in order to create common ground and mutual trust (Damtew et al., 2021; Leeuwis & Aarts, 2011). Transformative capacity thus depends on sustained "interaction where the actors with a stake in the problem must manage to coordinate their perceptions, activities and institutional arrangements" (Koppenjan & Klijn, 2004, p. 9).

Connective action and transformative capacity

In recent years, numerous cooperatives that pursue collective action have also demonstrated an alternative communication style with distinctive features, called connective action. The concept was elaborated upon by Bennett and Segerberg (2012), following Castells (2007) in his analysis that the group ties of formal organizations are less attractive to individuals as understood in "late modernity", who tend to choose fluid social networks. Emergent network-based communities, which are merely self-organized, foster opportunities for communicative ways of organizing that are less reliant on formal organizational coordination (Bennett & Segerberg, 2012; Cieslik et al., 2018). Such communities use network technologies as important organizational agents, marking connective action. For example, the mass farmer protests in the Netherlands in 2019 – with tractors that blocked the capital's main roads – started with just one social media message that went viral (Van Vuuren-Verkerk et al., 2021). The social movement Agractie, which was formed as a consequence, is now considered a committed sparring partner of the government, but it is still mainly organized as an online network.

Network-based cooperatives, which combine collective action with connective action, differ from traditional cooperatives in four aspects: 1) the adoption of networked technologies; 2) the creation of loosely connected communities; 3) a typical "focus on individualized expressions of engagement" (Rosenbaum, 2020, p. 120); and 4) the strengthening of translocal linkages that enable cooperatives to exchange and create shared ideas, objects, and activities with distant like-minded people or initiatives (Loorbach et al., 2020). Cooperatives that look for empowerment or attempt to enhance their transformative capacity are dependent not only on a well-organized structure that shapes collaboration or on mainstream media to motivate people into action. The use of digital technologies has partially changed how people organize communication and collaboration. For instance, social media offers the opportunity to enlarge cooperatives' networks with new (loosely coupled) audiences. Networked technologies enable cooperatives to share ideas and opinions directly with known and unknown peers all over the world. In fact, sharing personal experiences in network-based cooperatives is a substantial factor in working toward a collective goal that contributes to the creation of a shared narrative (Rosenbaum, 2020). Wittmayer et al. (2019, p. 2) underline the transformative potential of connective action, as they state:

> The impact and reach of the narratives . . . [are] not to be underestimated, as modern information and communication technologies enable collaborative construction and broad sharing across networked individuals and initiatives at a global scale. Their stories, ideas and metaphors frame current problems, promise alternative futures and propose ways to get there.

Translocal linkages can also empower participants in the local initiative because the broader network reinforces self-efficacy, creativity, and adaptivity (Avelino et al., 2020). Moreover, the collectivity of loosely coupled networks enables cooperatives to expand their impact and increase their access to resources like funding (Avelino et al., 2020). This development can overcome the fragility of a single local initiative and includes the chance of similar initiatives spreading translocally: diffusion of philosophies and practices (new framings and new doings). Overall, connective action is particularly suitable for enhancing a cooperative's transformative capacity. It could facilitate wider acceptance of ideas and replication of practices in order to challenge, alter, or replace a mainstream system (Avelino et al., 2019).

Case analysis

In the following paragraphs, previously mentioned concepts such as the interactional dimensions of collective action and connective action are applied to the Farming Communities case. An illustrative case can be a useful gateway toward understanding how these actions materialize in practice. The empirical material used was collected from websites of various local Herenboeren farms, from the national Herenboeren website (Herenboeren.nl), and from the international website (Farmingcommunities.org). Furthermore, webinars concerning the Farming Communities' activities and issues, posts on social media (Twitter, Facebook, YouTube), and monthly newsletters were consulted. The lively discussions and updates on YouTube (more than 60 short videos) were highly informative because both participants and farmers appeared in these videos and reported on developments, issues, and daily business. Most of these contributions were vlogs made by one of the farmers and targeted at his local Herenboeren farm community, shedding light on internal affairs, interactions, and local cultural practices ("please close the door when you leave the greenhouse", "the fifth calf was born Sunday night in good health, it's a heifer!"). The analysis presented is based on a content analysis (local, national, and international websites and monthly newsletters), a social media analysis (Twitter, Facebook, and YouTube), and the transcripts of three one-hour webinars on the collaboration goals and practicalities of farming in accord with the Herenboeren concept.

Farming Communities: an introduction

Farming Communities (Herenboeren) started in Boxtel in the Dutch province of Brabant in 2015. The main principles of the new food cooperative are to work in a nature-driven, socially connected, and economically supported way. A group of local residents buys farmland and employs a professional farmer who produces their food. The residents participate in the farming activities and consult and cooperate on matters like the cropping plan. A Herenboeren farm feeds 500 people sustainably on an area of 20 hectares and provides the farmer with a fair, stable income paid by the participants. The farmer produces organic food for the cooperative's participants and aims to regenerate the ecosystem, including water, soil, flora, fauna, and other natural values. The movement has matured over the past years, and at time of writing (2022) there are 14 more farms and 10 initiatives to start a Herenboeren farm in various parts of the Netherlands, making Herenboeren a network of farming communities.

Collective action

New ways of knowing and framing. The instantiation of the new Herenboeren farming concept was also a new framing. Founder Geert van der Veer recounts that he aspired to design a novel communal food production format that would bypass the global food market and connect urban citizens to their surrounding farmland. Ownership as a citizen and as a consumer, taking responsibility for the local living environment, gives new meaning to the concept of citizenship. Furthermore, after the establishment of the farm, participants shaped and reshaped shared meanings about being a new community of prosumers and what it meant consequently for collaborating style, rules, and chores, for example, regarding cooperative farming and collective decision making. One of the cooperative's frames is: to bio or not to bio is not the question. The cooperative's aim is to produce nature inclusively. Although it might be tempting to go for the biological farmer quality label, the community decided not to engage in the application process because it serves as its own internal market: it does not need the label to attract customers. Nonetheless, it complies with the rules for biological production.

New ways of doing and organizing. The investment rules demonstrate a new way of doing: land is secured for seven generations, and its financial value is separated from the enterprise. This shows how frames and doings are intertwined: a central frame is to make land a common good again, and this is how it is done. Another example involves buildings: often a Herenboeren community is a farm without a farmhouse. Farming Communities can function effectively with only a large shed or a compact building to store some essential equipment. This innovative way of farming has made a farmhouse superfluous.

Vertical and horizontal interdependence. A supermarket consumer does not need to rely heavily on other customers. In the prosumers' case, this is different. Is everybody receiving an equal share of food? Is there transparency about the way the cropping plan comes about? Do we all have equal power in the decision-making process? Building trust slowly but surely is an essential process for a Herenboeren cooperative's future. Participants choose to be mutually interdependent. What makes it easier in this case is the professional farmer who bears final responsibility for the food production process. With regard to vertical interdependence, Farming Communities are hindered by the functional division that exists in land use. Current laws and regulations leave little or no room for hybrid, plural, or co-creative methods. Herenboeren works to tackle these issues organizationally and economically.

Discursive space. The community needs to decide about all kinds of agricultural and organizational aspects, for example, what crops to cultivate the next year, how much produce each member can take home, and so on. This means that this group of 500 people, in order to be successful as a farm, needs to negotiate on all kinds of financial, organizational, and agricultural issues. In regular meetings, participants discuss the cropping plan for the next season. Meat production is a common theme: people differ in their opinions about meat eating and animal welfare. Vegetarians and meat lovers decide together how to tackle this issue. As a possible compromise solution, the participants were negotiating the placing of a mobile slaughterhouse on the farm to prevent the animals suffering from transport stress. Another discursive space is Herenboerenstek, the Farming Communities' intranet. Third, the farm's central place also functions as a discursive space: community members stop by every week to collect their share of food and engage in informal conversations.

Connective action

Networked technologies. The Farming Communities make use of networked technologies such as podcasts, a local website for each farming community, webinars on land management, a forum to exchange Herenboeren recipes, crowdfunding initiatives, and an online knowledge center. From the start, but even more since Herenboeren has developed into a nationwide network with interest even from abroad, networked technologies are a common means of organizing.

Loosely connected communities. Farming Communities connect in numerous ways to diverse audiences and communities. Together with other organizations and 21 nature-conscious cooks, they initiated the launch of a manifesto called *Samen voor Grond* (Let's go for healthy soil together). Also, the Farming Communities network uses crowdfunding to collect money from society with the aim of acquiring land for new Farming Communities. Farming Community members were invited to participate in the Climate Walks social movement in the run-up to COP26. Whereas the connective action feature that entails the individual expression of engagement (see the theory section) is not emphasized, the collective vibe is all the more present. However, on the different Farming Communities' websites, the board members introduce themselves with quite detailed stories, and via social media channels members express their engagement with the cooperative via personal statements and pictures.

Translocal linkages. The initiators of Farming Communities are extremely competent in building alliances and networked partnerships. The established crowdfunding organization consists of a bank and another nature-driven land foundation. Conversations are held with local and national governments about adapting laws and regulations. Researchers and students work on projects with Herenboeren, farming experts participate in the knowledge center, and the Farming Communities' founder is a member of the Farmers' Council, a group of influential farmers who aspire to reroute the Dutch food system toward sustainability. One last example out of many is Herenboeren's linkage with the Community Supported Agriculture (CSA) network: an empowering network of various forms of food collectives.

In sum, Farming Communities cooperatives appear to be strong in both collective action and connective action. The way in which the initiative flourishes, the spreading of cooperatives around the country, and the abundance of translocal linkages mkae Herenboeren a shining example of applying collective action and connective action both substantially and fruitfully.

Discussion and conclusion

Having started with a thought experiment, Farming Communities has developed from a concept into a practice and finally into a movement that is currently spreading out over the Netherlands. The key question in this study is whether such a food cooperative – or, to extend the topic, whether any grassroots initiative – has the power to contribute to transformative change toward a sustainable food system. Given that we define transformative capacity as the extent to which an organization challenges, alters, or replaces dominant regimes (Avelino et al., 2019), we must assess the findings of the Farming Communities case in terms of transformative potential.

The Farming Communities approach aims to offer an alternative to the dominant unsustainable food system: an innovative, sustainable way of food production – innovative because it alters social relations and financial and economic structures (urban prosumers buy the surrounding farmlands for a Farming Community for seven generations, barely dependent on world markets); sustainable in the sense that the production and transport footprints are low and soil is regenerated without polluting methods. Everything needed for collective action seems to be in place: a discursive space is available where interdependent relationships are acknowledged and negotiated. New frames and narratives have come into being, as well as new ways of doing and organizing; and with the abundance of connective action, this Farming Community tucked away in the Dutch countryside has gained traction in the Netherlands and beyond. Connective action in this case serves as a highway to expand the narrative, raise funds, and replicate the cooperatives' practices throughout the Netherlands. These developments, specifically the diffusion of new framings and doings via translocal linkages, suggest a transformative capacity that at least challenges the regime.

However, Herenboeren cooperatives have so far not replaced the current food system right away. Although in crisis, on the lookout for new revenue models and aspiring towards circular agriculture, the regime predominantly holds on to the status quo while some elements are moving slowly. Some scientists who adopt the multilevel perspective argue that the expectation that niche initiatives can change a dominant regime is somewhat naive and idealistic, although according to Geels, a leading author on the multilevel perspective, (networks of) niche initiatives can make the regime slightly move or incrementally change the landscape in which the regime and the niches are embedded (Geels, 2011, 2020). Furthermore, transformation expert Loorbach does not refrain from emphasizing that the transformative capacity of bottom-up initiatives is underrated. Loorbach et al. (2020, p. 252) argues that the focus on policy-driven innovations "ignores other types of innovations that emerge more organically within society in which technology is a less dominant element such as novel lifestyles, business models or organizational forms". In this vein, Avelino et al. (2019) suggest speaking of "shades of change" brought about by social innovations, on the understanding that these diffuse transformational processes are too complex to indicate (short term) causal relations. Lastly, the "small wins" approach emphasizes that this kind of small, in-depth change, whilst easily overlooked, over the long run may appear as a micro-level continuous change that shapes the emergence of a recognizable shift in the process of transformative change (Termeer et al., 2017, 2019; Weick, 1984).

Although the Farming Communities case displays an exemplary interplay between the bonding and converging features of collective action and the connecting and diverging characteristics of connective action, the intricate balancing of both is a matter of concern. A risk exists that the two forms of action could undermine each other if an imbalance occurred. Robust collective action requires face-to-face communication, stable membership, and small groups. Connective action can hinder these bonding processes for collective action. Although loosely coupled audiences and linkages with distant peers can be beneficial to the cooperative (as discussed in the theory section), connective action also carries a risk of superficial commitments and shifting and messy relationships (Rosenbaum, 2020). Furthermore, sharing ideas and opinions via networked technologies can, as already discussed, lead to dissemination of a narrative, but it can also induce polarization (Stevens et al., 2021). Finally, a surplus of connective action could lead to disempowerment instead of empowerment, because prevalent superficial relationships with relative strangers can make actors lose commitment to the common goals or can make them feel less self-determined (Avelino et al., 2020); this counteracts the preconditions for collective action. Given the benefits of connective action, the challenge for actors (for instance, communication practitioners) is to carefully balance cooperatives' communication processes between collective action and connective action. The reward for this balancing act can be – as the Dutch Farming Communities vibrantly demonstrates – an empowered network with optimal transformative capacity. Or, to use an image from the agricultural field, the reward can be a fertile ground for transformative change.

References

Aarts, N. (2018). *Dynamics and dependence in socio-ecological interactions.* Inaugural address Radboud University. https://repository.ubn.ru.nl/bitstream/handle/2066/197147/197147.pdf

Avelino, F., Dumitru, A., Cipolla, C., Kunze, I., & Wittmayer, J. (2020). Translocal empowerment in transformative social innovation networks. *European Planning Studies, 28*(5), 955–977.

Avelino, F., Wittmayer, J. M., Pel, B., Weaver, P., Dumitru, A., Haxeltine, A., . . . O'Riordan, T. (2019). Transformative social innovation and (dis) empowerment. *Technological Forecasting and Social Change, 145*, 195–206.

Baldassarri, D. (2015). Cooperative networks: Altruism, group solidarity, reciprocity, and sanctioning in Ugandan producer organizations. *American Journal of Sociology, 121*(2), 355–395.

Balvanera, P., Calderón-Contreras, R., Castro, A. J., Felipe-Lucia, M. R., Geijzendorffer, I. R., Jacobs, S., & Gillson, L. (2017). Interconnected place-based social – ecological research can inform global sustainability. *Current Opinion in Environmental Sustainability, 29*, 1–7.

Bennett, W. L., & Segerberg, A. (2012). The logic of connective action: Digital media and the personalization of contentious politics. *Information, Communication & Society, 15*(5), 739–768.

Castells, M. (2007). Communication, power and counter-power in the network society. *International Journal of Communication, 1*(1), 238–266.

Cieslik, K. J., Leeuwis, C., Dewulf, A. R. P. J., Lie, R., Werners, S. E., Van Wessel, M., . . . Struik, P. C. (2018). Addressing socio-ecological development challenges in the digital age: Exploring the potential of Environmental Virtual Observatories for Connective Action (EVOCA). *NJAS – Wageningen Journal of Life Sciences, 86*, 2–11.

Damtew, E., Leeuwis, C., Struik, P. C., Cecchi, F., van Mierlo, B., Lie, R., . . . Cieslik, K. (2021). Communicative interventions for collective action in the management of potato late blight: Evidence from a framed field game experiment in Ethiopia. *Food Security, 13*(2), 255–271.

De Vries, J. R., Van der Zee, E., Beunen, R., Kat, R., & Feindt, P. H. (2019). Trusting the people and the system. The interrelation between interpersonal and institutional trust in collective action for agri-environmental management. *Sustainability, 11*(24), 7022. https://doi.org/10.3390/su11247022

Geels, F. W. (2011). The multi-level perspective on sustainability transitions: Responses to seven criticisms. *Environmental Innovation and Societal Transitions, 1*(1), 24–40.

Geels, F. W. (2020). Micro-foundations of the multi-level perspective on socio-technical transitions: Developing a multi-dimensional model of agency through crossovers between social constructivism, evolutionary economics and neo-institutional theory. *Technological Forecasting and Social Change, 152*, 119894. https://doi.org/10.1016/j.techfore.2019.119894

Gergen, K. J., McNamee, S., & Barrett, F. J. (2001). Toward transformative dialogue. *International Journal of Public Administration, 24*(7–8), 679–707.

Gray, B. (2004). Strong opposition: Frame-based resistance to collaboration. *Journal of Community & Applied Social Psychology, 14*(3), 166–176.

Gray, B., & Purdy, J. (2018). *Collaborating for our future: Multistakeholder partnerships for solving complex problems.* Oxford University Press.

Hardy, C., Lawrence, T. B., & Grant, D. (2005). Discourse and collaboration: The role of conversations and collective identity. *Academy of Management Review, 30*(1), 58–77.

Hebinck, A., Selomane, O., Veen, E., De Vrieze, A., Hasnain, S., Sellberg, M., . . . Wood, A. (2021). Exploring the transformative potential of urban food. *Urban Sustainability, 1*(1), 1–9.

Hölscher, K., Frantzeskaki, N., & Loorbach, D. (2019). Steering transformations under climate change: Capacities for transformative climate governance and the case of Rotterdam, the Netherlands. *Regional Environmental Change, 19*(3), 791–805.

Hovelynck, J., Craps, M., Dewulf, A., Sips, K., Taillieu, T., & Bouwen, R. (2020). Relational practices for generative multi-actor collaboration. In S. McNamee, M. M. Gergen, C. Camargo-Borges, & E. F. Rasera (Eds.), *The Sage handbook of social constructionist practice* (pp. 258–267). Sage.

IPBES (Intergovernmental Science-Policy Platform on Biodiversity and Ecosystem Services). (2019). *Global assessment summary for policy makers.* IPBES.

Koppenjan, J., & Klijn, E. H. (2004). *Managing uncertainties in networks: A network approach to problem solving and decision making.* Routledge.

Labanca, N., Pereira, Â. G., Watson, M., Krieger, K., Padovan, D., Watts, L., . . . Mehta, L. (2020). Transforming innovation for decarbonisation? Insights from combining complex systems and social practice perspectives. *Energy Research & Social Science, 65*. https://doi.org/10.1016/j.erss.2020.101452

Leeuwis, C., & Aarts, N. (2011). Rethinking communication in innovation processes: Creating space for change in complex systems. *Journal of Agricultural Education and Extension, 17*(1), 21–36.

Leeuwis, C., & Aarts, N. (2020). Rethinking adoption and diffusion as a collective social process: Towards an interactional perspective. In H. Campos (Ed.), *The innovation revolution in agriculture: A roadmap to value creation* (pp. 95–116). Springer.

Leeuwis, C., Boogaard, B. K., & Atta-Krah, K. (2021). How food systems change (or not): Governance implications for system transformation processes. *Food Security, 13*(4), 761–780.

Lindblom, C. E. (1979). Still muddling, not yet through. *Public Administration Review*, *39*(6), 517–526.

Loorbach, D., Wittmayer, J., Avelino, F., von Wirth, T., & Frantzeskaki, N. (2020). Transformative innovation and translocal diffusion. *Environmental Innovation and Societal Transitions*, *35*, 251–260.

Moore, M. L., Tjornbo, O., Enfors, E., Knapp, C., Hodbod, J., Baggio, J. A., . . . Biggs, D. (2014). Studying the complexity of change: Toward an analytical framework for understanding deliberate social-ecological transformations. *Ecology and Society*, *19*(4). http://dx.doi.org/10.5751/ES-06966-190454

Moragues-Faus, A., & Morgan, K. (2015). Reframing the foodscape: The emergent world of urban food policy. *Environment and Planning A: Economy and Space*, *47*(7), 1558–1573.

Ostrom, E. (1990). *Governing the commons: The evolution of institutions for collective action.* Cambridge University Press.

Ostrom, E. (2009). A general framework for analyzing sustainability of social-ecological systems. *Science*, *325*(5939), 419–422.

Ostrom, E. (2010). Analyzing collective action. *Agricultural Economics*, *41*, 155–166.

Patterson, M. (2016). The global city versus the city of neighborhoods: Spatial practice, cognitive maps, and the aesthetics of urban conflict. *City & Community*, *15*(2), 163–183.

Pel, B., Haxeltine, A., Avelino, F., Dumitru, A., Kemp, R., Bauler, T., . . . Jørgensen, M. S. (2020). Towards a theory of transformative social innovation: A relational framework and 12 propositions. *Research Policy*, *49*(8). https://doi.org/10.1016/j.respol.2020.104080

Pickering, J., Hickmann, T., Bäckstrand, K., Kalfagianni, A., Bloomfield, M., Mert, A., . . . Lo, A. Y. (2022). Democratising sustainability transformations: Assessing the transformative potential of democratic practices in environmental governance. *Earth System Governance*, *11*, 100131. https://doi.org/10.1016/j.gloenvcha.2021.102422

Rosenbaum, J. E. (2020). Twitter, social movements and the logic of connective action: Activism in the 21st century – An introduction. *Participation*, *17*(1), 120–125.

Seyfang, G., & Smith, A. (2007). Grassroots innovations for sustainable development: Towards a new research and policy agenda. *Environmental Politics*, *16*(4), 584–603.

Shove, E., & Walker, G. (2010). Governing transitions in the sustainability of everyday life. *Research Policy*, *39*(4), 471–476.

Springmann, M., Clark, M., Mason-D'Croz, D., Wiebe, K., Bodirsky, B. L., Lassaletta, L., . . . Willett, W. (2018). Options for keeping the food system within environmental limits. *Nature*, *562*(7728), 519–525.

Stacey, R. (2007). The challenge of human interdependence: Consequences for thinking about the day to day practice of management in organizations. *European Business Review*, *119*(4), 292–302.

Staggenborg, S. (2016). *Social movements.* Oxford University Press.

Stevens, T. M., Aarts, N., & Dewulf, A. (2021). Using emotions to frame issues and identities in conflict: Farmer movements on social media. *Negotiation and Conflict Management Research*, *14*(2), 75–93.

Termeer, C. J., & Dewulf, A. (2019). A small wins framework to overcome the evaluation paradox of governing wicked problems. *Policy and Society*, *38*(2), 298–314.

Termeer, C. J., Dewulf, A., & Biesbroek, G. R. (2017). Transformational change: Governance interventions for climate change adaptation from a continuous change perspective. *Journal of Environmental Planning and Management*, *60*(4), 558–576.

Van Bueren, E. M., Klijn, E. H., & Koppenjan, J. F. (2003). Dealing with wicked problems in networks: Analyzing an environmental debate from a network perspective. *Journal of Public Administration Research and Theory*, *13*(2), 193–212.

Van Vuuren-Verkerk, K., Aarts, N., & Van der Stoep, J. (2021). Meaning-making on the ground: (Re)discovering the competence of interactional framing in environmental conflicts. *Journal of Communication Management*, *25*(4), 368–384.

Weick, K. E. (1984). Small wins: Redefining the scale of social problems. *American Psychologist*, *39*(1), 40–49.

Weick, K. E., & Quinn, R. E. (1999). Organizational change and development. *Annual Review of Psychology*, *50*(1), 361–386.

Weick, K. E., & Sutcliffe, K. M. (2011). *Managing the unexpected. Resilient performance in an age of uncertainty* (2nd ed.). Jossey-Bass.

Wittmayer, J. M., Backhaus, J., Avelino, F., Pel, B., Strasser, T., Kunze, I., & Zuijderwijk, L. (2019). Narratives of change: How social innovation initiatives construct societal transformation. *Futures*, *112*, 102433. https://doi.org/10.1016/j.futures.2019.06.005

Zhang, J. Y., & Barr, M. (2019). The transformative power of commoning and alternative food networks. *Environmental Politics*, *28*(4), 771–789.

4.2

LOCAL NGO E-COMMUNICATION ON ENVIRONMENTAL ISSUES

Valentina Burkšienė and Jaroslav Dvorak

Introduction

Nongovernmental organizations (NGOs) play a significant role in modern public life. They can achieve changes due to active participation in solving social and environmental problems and the effective communication of these issues. Online communication is no doubt the primary channel in the modern world. According to Haselkorn (2007) and Pavlovic et al. (2014), the fourth industrial revolution has moved the world to a technological space where everyone can create and use various social networks to communicate and ask society, government and different stakeholders for support or to take actions to solve problematic issues.

NGOs actively operate internationally, regionally and locally – playing the role of intermediators between local communities and governments in the latter context. They indeed focus on public policy problems and launch appropriate missions, but their messages need to be managed in order to be effective and to reach the target audiences (Oliveira, 2019; Herranz de la Casa et al., 2018; Dvorak & Civinskas, 2018). Research (Rajhans, 2018; Herranz de la Casa et al., 2018; Raupp & Hoffjann, 2012) reveals the process of communication as a highly complex one and proposes that the management thereof should be strategically organized.

In this chapter we concentrate on local environmental problems and analyze the communication management of environmental NGOs (ENGOs) in the case of Klaipeda, the third largest city of Lithuania, answering the following research question: *how do environmental NGOs manage their e-communication in order to be heard by decision-makers?*

Research criteria were collected from the literature related to ENGOs and their e-communication. The research data were collected online; therefore, the chosen criteria also needed to be reached online. A deductive content analysis approach was used to analyze the information available on the websites of respected ENGOs, as well as on the Google platform, and to logically classify and categorize all data collected.

The research results revealed that communication requires structured management, as only in this way is it possible to engage all necessary stakeholders and governmental institutions in cooperative networking. Finally, we proposed a primary framework for effective e-communication by ENGOs.

Theoretical background

Modern governance focuses on involving citizens and stakeholders in decision-making. However, with the strengthening of active citizen groups in democratic societies, there is a redistribution

Table 4.2.1 Types of bottom-up communication

1. NGOs (formal organizations)	2. Unstructured civic initiatives
Formal and organized in initiatives and operation (Raupp & Hoffjann, 2012)	Corporations with a critical concern, which do not know about each other (Raupp & Hoffjann, 2012)
More general in their objectives; are of unlimited duration; and have a higher degree of institutionalization, transparency and trust (Herranz de la Casa et al., 2018)	Sporadic movements related to the problems addressed; unstructured operation (Herranz de la Casa et al., 2018)

of communicative weight, with nongovernmental actors promoting citizen involvement and the citizens themselves actively encouraging government officials to engage and participate in the communicative space they have created. This is especially evident in online communication – social networks. Digital media provide all the possibilities for this "bottom-up" communication (which originates from the initiative of NGOs and active individual citizens).

Various social networks suggest that bottom-up communication (i) can be professionally and constructively managed and administered using modern management principles or (ii) can become difficult to manage in the medium of disseminating a variety of individual opinions, which are often unsubstantiated (see Table 4.2.1).

Drawing on Goffman's dramaturgical perspective (see Kroll et al., 2019), the first type of communication can be perceived as a *frontstage mode* of communication and the second type as a *backstage mode*.

It may be assumed that ongoing communication in backstage mode should not be of great interest and attract formal city/municipal developers as well as other stakeholders relevant to the city (business, education, culture, etc.) because of citizens' communication being individual, more intuitive, straightforward and unmanaged (*low-profile communication*). In the case of frontstage mode, by contrast, the city authorities and those involved in creating the city's economic and social well-being should respond in a timely manner to bottom-up statements, comments and requests, among others. In such a type of communication, the citizens not only individually complain about existing problems but by acting in organized groups, they can also offer innovative ways to solve common problems.

In the scope of the European Union, NGOs are treated as the second most effective (after business associations) in terms of their pressure, lobbying and influence on citizens (Herranz de la Casa et al., 2018; Sidor & Abdelhafez, 2021). Therefore, NGOs could strategically focus on public policy problems, implementation activities, and cooperation areas based on the agreed dimensions of cooperation. These organizations can achieve positive changes in collaborative planning on a national and even a European Union (EU) level (Kilger et al., 2015). The outcome of such processes would be effective for collective actions.

NGOs can be classified into international, regional and local, the latter of whom play the role of intermediators between local communities and governments. They can control public institutions and influence the formation of a legal framework of civil society while representing the attitude of society to social and environmental issues (Tumulytė, 2012). Communication is especially important for this reason.

Communication experts highlight the importance of focusing on target audiences for releasing appropriate missions and sending effective messages (Dvorak & Civinskas, 2018; Oliveira, 2019; Vveinhardt et al., 2019). Communication strategy can foster partnership initiatives that drive joint actions. However, not a great deal of attention is paid to communication practices (Muszynska, 2015), as communicators spend more time as technicians than communication strategy developers

(Liu, 2012). Furthermore, there are also issues inherent in the communication networking process, which are difficult due to complications in the measurement of its progress or success (Rajhans, 2018) and because of the duality of internal and external communication activities. These aspects refer to the constant improvement of communication skills (Mihai, 2017).

The complexity of communication requires it to be treated not only as an instrument but also as a strategic process that is highly appropriate for interrelating all representing parties both vertically and horizontally (Herranz de la Casa et al., 2018) in order to better understand all issues concerned (Andres, 2011). Therefore, communication management, which is strategically organized and carried out, is proposed for effective communication (Rajhans, 2018; Herranz de la Casa et al., 2018; Raupp & Hoffjann, 2012) so as to ensure the right information reaches the right person at the right time and in a cost-effective manner (Muszynska, 2015).

Effective communication management raises awareness among citizens, generates notoriety in the media and generates spaces for meetings and debates (Herranz de la Casa et al., 2018); in other words, it refers to systemic and corporate initiatives that need to be planned, monitored and cover all communication channels (Rajhans, 2018).

The fourth industrial revolution (Industry 4.0) has provided technological space for communication and information sharing, where everyone (NGOs included) can create and maintain various types of social networks and give voice to their actions (Haselkorn, 2007) or communicate problematic messages in order to ask for public support in confronting issues (Pavlovic et al., 2014). Communication channels increase transparency and refer not only to local issues but to global issues as well, with most emphasis placed on challenges related to the environment and climate change – or in other words, related to sustainability. Coxas (2010, as quoted in Tumulytė, 2012) proposes the following components of environmental communication for sustainability: (i) perceptions of the environment, (ii) the relationship with nature and (iii) symbolic space suitable for analyzing environmental issues and evaluating different societal attitudes. Unfortunately, ENGOs still scarcely recognize the importance of online communication with their stakeholders and do not make much use of strategic online communication (Pavlovic et al., 2014). Although the ENGOs were thought to have a strong influence on the outcome of the Paris Agreement from COP21, they use social media platforms more for informational messaging rather than engaging society and government in dialogues or discussions (Comfort & Hester, 2019).

Problem formulation

There are many issues to be solved in cities. In the context of sustainability, many urban areas face environmental problems due to irresponsible business practices. Active residents of industrial cities, whether individually or in groups, are looking for ways to be heard, often by business representatives or even by city authorities. However, the success of bottom-up communication (whether it will turn into e-governance communication) will largely depend on its management.

Advanced technologies propose conditions for the rapid creation of social networks, so it is easy to find IT platforms in which citizens with low transaction costs can discuss issues relevant to them at any time and from anywhere (Sieber et al., 2016). We argue that *frontstage communication* on e-media platforms is an opportunity for the formation of democratically based e-governance communication. However, e-communication, like any process, must be managed. Professional communication management can have a positive effect and coerce the government to listen to the voices of citizens. According to Kroll et al. (2019), in this way, citizen participation would even ensure better political outcomes for the city authorities. The success of such communication would be determined by clear strategic priorities and components leading to effective communication management (Raupp & Hoffjann, 2012; Muszynska, 2015), which include the competences of individuals in public relations (PR) and marketing (Liu, 2012; Burksiene, 2019); relations with the media and the press (Liu, 2012;

Muszynska, 2015; Herranz de la Casa, 2018); social media (Haselkorn, 2007; Liu, 2012; Comfort & Hester, 2019); collaboration with politicians, governments and other stakeholders as well as lobbying (Liu, 2012; Tumulytė, 2012; Mihai, 2017; Herranz de la Casa, 2018); leadership and organizational culture (Mihai, 2017; Comfort & Hester, 2019); and gaining interdisciplinary expert skills (Burksiene, 2013), among others.

Klaipeda is the third-largest city in Lithuania, with a population of approximately 150,000, and has faced numerous environmental problems over the last three years. In most cases, those environmental issues have been identified or begun to be debated in the public sphere, not by local politicians, but by either active residents or local NGOs. Some of those problems have lasted since the Soviet era. After Lithuania regained independence in the early 1990s, the first green organizations began to organize protests against polluting companies, which had just been privatized. However, in the face of the first shocks of the market economy, when corporate bankruptcies and rising unemployment began, the arguments of green organizations were weakened in turn as society prioritized livelihoods instead of another "empty space". Later, with increased economic well-being, environmental issues have again returned to the forefront.

The formation of several active NGOs has begun to constantly draw the attention of residents, city authorities and businesses to the environmental problems in the city (i.e., hard particles in the air, port handling, constant odors in certain areas of the city) influencing climate change. Such NGO communication takes place starting from protest actions against the city authorities and/or companies and constantly urging the population to start acting on social networks or electronic media for the benefit of the city, families and children.

In the case of Klaipeda, we noticed that the population is not as active as it is supposed to be, nor is the local government quick to engage and participate in the solution of environmental issues. Therefore, we hypothesize that these NGOs need to professionally employ an approach of managed e-communication in order to achieve their environmental goals (to act in frontstage mode).

Methodology

The study aims to reveal how communication management is reflected in the online communication of Klaipeda ENGOs. Information available online was examined by means of specific criteria in order to explore the communication process of Klaipeda ENGOs. All criteria from the literature can be treated as benchmarks for effective communication management, but in our case, for the purposes of analysis of e-communication of environmental organizations, we decided to shorten the list and chose criteria which in the literature were (i) directly related to ENGOs, (ii) relevant to e-communication and (iii) could be reached online.

Content analysis has proven to be a suitable approach in similar studies (see Comfort & Hester, 2019; Herranz de la Casa et al., 2018; Rajhans, 2018) and was used in our case, as suggested by Krippendorff (2013) and Mayring (2014).

Deductive content analysis means that data were analyzed using categories and subcategories identified as components of effective communication management in existing literature. This approach helped us to analyze information available on the websites of respected NGOs,[1] as well as on the Google platform and to logically classify and categorize all data collected. As the basis for criteria (main categories and subcategories), we used elements of the Facebook profiles of ENGOs in the same vein as Pavlovic et al. (2014). The subcategories in Pavlovic (ibid) were compared with the characteristics (criteria) of communication management in existing literature, and similar definitions were configured to general subcategories (see Table 4.2.2).

Table 4.2.2 Elements of research content

Category	Subcategory	Literature source
Basic information/ strategy (C1)	Description, history (volume)	Pavlovic et al., 2014
	Size of the organization	Andres, 2011
	Strategy, including the mission	Mihai, 2017
	Communication strategy (plan and monitoring)	Muszynska, 2015; Raupp & Hoffjan, 2012
	Leadership and competences in PR/marketing	Burksiene et al., 2019; Mihai, 2017; Liu, 2012
	Employees and volunteers (number and competences in PR/marketing)	Liu, 2012
	Brand (logo)	Liu (2012); Pavlovic et al. (2014)
	Web page administrators/URL	Liu (2012)
Info about activities (C2)	News/press releases	Pavlovic et al. (2014)
	Progress reports/summaries	Muszynska (2015)
	Ability to subscribe to newsletters	Pavlovic et al. (2014)
	External links to news	Pavlovic et al. (2014)
	Info photos/video/audio	Pavlovic et al. (2014)
Interaction (C3)	Discussions/debates on the wall	Pavlovic et al. (2014); Tumulyte (2012)
	Web monitoring/announcements	Liu (2012)
	Other platforms/URL, multiple communication	Pavlovic et al. (2014); Muszynska (2015); Ruehl and Ingenhoff (2015)
	Participants (followers)	Comfort and Hester (2019)
	Joint actions with other NGOs and domination in coalition	Liu (2012); Mihai (2017)
	Cooperation with government institutions	Tumulyte (2012); Herranz de la Casa (2018)
	Photo/video/audio with stakeholders (proof of collaboration)	Pavlovic et al. (2014)
Engagement (C4)	E-mail of the organization	Pavlovic et al. (2014)
	Phone no.	Pavlovic et al. (2014)
	Volunteer opportunities	Pavlovic et al. (2014); Liu (2012)
	Donations	Pavlovic et al. (2014)

In order to check the benefit of the *frontstage communication mode* in practice, we decided to research a very well-known NGO in Lithuania – the Public Nature Conservation Association "Lašišos dienorastis"[2] (Salmon Diary), which is highly active in environmental issues in Lithuania with very diverse and successful communication (see annual reports for 2017, 2018, 2019 and 2020[3]), and to compare its e-communication to Klaipeda's NGOs. The research outcomes should prove the benefits of *frontstage* communication mode and reveal a framework for environmental e-communication for effective governance.

Results

The research revealed that the nationally active NGO Salmon Diary mostly fulfills our criteria for the 'frontstage communication mode'. The three remaining Klaipeda NGOs fulfill only a few of them and thus would represent 'backstage communication mode'.

Table 4.2.3 Differences between Salmon Diary and other NGOs

Salmon Diary	Other NGOs
Web monitoring with formal (protected rights) website administration and sufficient news reports (C3)	No individual URL
Links from their dedicated website to their Facebook, Instagram and YouTube pages (C3)	Only Facebook
A detailed description and history available on the website (C1)	No
Annual progress and financial reports since 2017 (C2)	Progress summaries
Sufficient communication (seen in photos/videos) with stakeholders that prove collaboration (C3)	Rare
Invitation on Facebook and the web page to become an active member; fill in form and procedure definition available (C4)	No public invitation but replies to e-messages (i) that there is such a possibility (KIDE and GA) or (ii) such a possibility is not offered at the moment (AoC)

There are some similarities in the communication of all four NGOs, mostly when *informing about activities (C2)*. All NGOs involved in the research have news or press releases and external links to news. They also publish photos and videos; however, none provide the ability to subscribe to newsletters. Only the possibility of following them on their Facebook page is available.

The phone number of each NGO can also be found for communication purposes *(C4)*. Naturally, all of them request donations, but Salmon Diary's tool is more developed for this purpose, as they only have an individual website. This NGO has more criteria that fulfill the *frontstage management model* and thus differ from the remaining three (see Table 4.2.3).

Other results of the research revealed differences among the NGOs in all subcategories, with some of them failing to fulfill certain categories (see Table 4.2.4).

According to Tumulytė (2012), there are some specific differences between green and local environmental NGOs. The Greens seem to be more radical in their protests and picket next to governmental institutions and national parks, while other local NGOs are mostly focused on the protection of community rights for a clean and healthy environment. They seek to unify local communities, politicians and the media in the scope of ecological actions. In our case, the Klaipeda Green Association does not match Tumulytė's (ibid) definition, acting much like other local ENGOs.

All the NGOs in question have their own logo (with the exception of the Greens) and, in this way, they wish to show their uniqueness from others because they compete for the attention of Klaipeda city residents and those who are interested in environmental protection in a broad sense. However, only the national NGO has a strategy with goals and objectives; two of the three Klaipeda city NGOs have presented their mission on social media. Furthermore, Klaipeda city NGOs do not have communication plans and describe their achievements, activities and positions in random articles in the local press. By contrast, national NGOs communicate rationally, carefully planning their messages. The current study found that NGO communication is structured according to specific topics. Clearly, only national NGOs see communication as a strategy and a tool, which is what scholars have emphasized (Herranz de la Casa et al., 2018; Raupp & Hoffjann, 2012).

The lack of staff clearly reflects the extent of communication. According to the official information provided in the registers, only one of the three Klaipeda city NGOs has an employee (and that person is also responsible for PR activities). By contrast, the national NGO has at least three employees (with one administrative staff member and another two to four regular professional reporters). MacIndoe and Sullivan (2014) argue that despite the emergence of ever more people involved

Table 4.2.4 Differences in communication management

Category	Subcategory	KIDE	Green Association (GA)	Association of Communities (AoC)	Salmon Diary
C1	Size (employees)	1	No	No	3
	Logo	Yes	No	Yes	Yes
	Strategy with a mission	Mission	Not available	Mission	Strategy with two goals and 19 objectives
	Communication strategy (plan and monitoring)	Not available	Occasional articles (though rare) on past events in local media	Occasional articles related to past events in local media	Structured communication with specific topics (important, actual, most popular, comments) in news pages with links to articles and video
	Employees/ volunteers with PR competences	1 (since fall 2020)	Not available	Not available	1 Admin of news (Adm2); 2–4 professional reporters (host of meetings, author of video reports, camera operators)
C3	Discussions/debates online	No	Occasional, brief discussions	Occasional, brief discussions	Sufficient/active discussions and debates
	Joint actions with other NGOs, dominance	Yes Dominance in coalition with stevedoring companies at the port and/or port development for the city	No	Yes Dominance in coalition: port development plan for the city	Yes, more with state or regional environmental institutions, international or national public bodies or famous people, science and education institutions Dominance in coalition: in terms of the mission (efforts to stop professional salmon fishing)
	Relations with government	Protests against state and local institutions, written requests. Discussions and debates with representatives of state-owned enterprises	Written requests to state institutions, state-owned enterprises. Discussions and debates with representatives of state-owned enterprises	Written requests, representation in local government commissions, committees. Discussions and debates with representatives of state-owned enterprises	Written requests; discussions and debates with state institutions and politicians, environmental agencies; influence on changes to the law: practical achievements in legal corrections (info links available in the progress reports)
Missing subcategories:		2 of 8	5 of 8	2 of 8	0 of 8

in NGOs, the organizations themselves already need help, as persistent economic instability often pushes financially weak NGOs into difficult situations where their very survival may be in question. Previous research (Dvorak et al., 2017) in Klaipeda discovered that financial support (resources) for NGOs is not permanent and provided only for specialized activities (projects).

When analyzing Tables 4.2.3 and 4.2.4, it was found that the dominant form of communication of Klaipeda NGOs is based on one-way communication, which actually corresponds to the evidence presented in the scientific literature (Comfort & Hester, 2019). This finding reflects the NGO's wish to inform, persuade the public through its messages and the desire for social network participants to share in and be attracted to the discussion of the e-message (Comfort & Hester, 2019). Of course, since their human resources are limited (if compared to the nationwide Salmon Diary), we see that the success of Klaipeda city NGOs' communication on social media is very limited, and in some cases only reaches a frequency of feedback of two or three times.

Klaipeda NGOs find it more difficult to develop discussions and debates after the information is provided on their Facebook profiles. These are usually brief multiple responses to the information provided, which rarely escalate into a discussion of up to ten posts. According to Tumulytė (2012), one of the most relevant and problematic areas in which civic initiatives are necessary is the environment and environmental protection. However, it is highly likely that Klaipeda city NGOs use social media platforms for unidirectional, informational messaging rather than engaging in dialogue with the population (Comfort & Hester, 2019). Klaipeda city NGOs provide various new pieces of information, pictures and videos related to the existing pollution in the city, but there is a lack of feedback from the supporters of these organizations because most of the information provided on the social network profile does not bring about discussions. It can be assumed that the lack of funding and human resources does not allow them to strategically exploit communication on Facebook in order to "engage members and encourage interaction with key stakeholders, local authorities, volunteers, the media, [and the] local community" (Pavlovic, 2014). By contrast, national NGOs develop sufficient and active discussions among different stakeholders.

Analyzing the e-communication of NGOs, it was found that two of the three Klaipeda city NGOs participate in joint actions with other NGOs. This is most often manifested in the planning of joint actions related to pollution caused by stevedoring companies operating in the port of Klaipeda. Very often the aims of communication are directed to provide scientific evidence and data collected by researchers from Klaipeda University. The effectiveness of knowledge sharing through digital media (especially in the field of environment issues) has been confirmed by previous research in Norway as well (Unander, Sørensen, 2020). On the other hand, there is evidence that environmentalists communicate scientific findings (Yearley, 2017). Klaipeda NGOs also organize joint actions against the expansion of the port into the city. In principle, it can be stated that the city's NGOs specialize in a limited number of environmental problems (for example, pollution by port stevedoring companies or pollution by other producers).

All respected NGOs aim to be heard by national or regional environmental institutions, but the capacity of Salmon Diary to operate at the national level is significantly greater due to communication management structures. This NGO also requests and receives the support of renowned scientists and celebrities (i.e., artists, TV producers and singers). The results of such cooperation are consistent with the argument of Liu (2012) that by properly using social media, NGOs can stimulate the interest of journalists and attract them to special events, leading to highly effective outcomes.

Finally, communication directed to the government is enthusiastically used by all organizations. When it comes to Klaipeda NGOs, they make an effort to show their frivolity, meaningfulness and the influence of the local population on the government. NGOs post comments on their social networks about how the government or a state-owned company has responded to one request or another. Information about upcoming meetings, debates and protests and invitations, as well as reports, are also communicated. It is obvious that Klaipeda NGOs cannot be classified as radical environmental movements as defined by certain authors (Tumulytė, 2012; Telešienė & Kriaučiūnaitė, 2008). In contrast, our case revealed the weakness of the Green association in terms of communication management.

Nationwide NGOs communicate much more actively and can make a real impact on legislative change and progress. The findings prove that NGOs with effective communication management can be heard by the government and have a real influence on solving environmental issues.

Limitations and conclusions

In our study, following Liu (2012), we provide communicators with some appropriate tools for more effective communication that could hopefully foster governance in environmental issues. Although our findings provide meaningful insights, the study has some limitations. The data available on web pages are limited; therefore, the qualitative approach was not used in its full depth. Also, our findings cannot be generalizable due to the small number of NGOs researched.

The argument of Comfort and Hester (2019) that environmental NGOs use social media platforms for informational messaging instead of for engagement of communities and governments in dialogues and debates was proven.

Communication that originates on the initiative of NGOs can engage governmental institutions and create cooperation networks, leading to real governance. Technological means are beneficial for the arrangement of e-communication that can reach a wider audience. To be successful, such communication requires structured management consisting of particular components.

The components for well-structured e-communication management can lead to the effectiveness of organization strategy, to the development of a wider space for sharing information and to strengthening the interaction and engagement of all stakeholders, which finally can form a frontstage mode of communication.

There are many components of communication management proposed and defined in literature sources, but few of them are directly related to the communication of environmental issues or adapted to e-communication. The proposed components for communication management can serve as the basic framework and may be expanded to include more components. Further studies are necessary in order to develop an overall e-communication management framework.

Notes

1. NGO 1: Klaipėdiečių iniciatyva už demokratiją ir ekologiją – KIDE www.facebook.com/KIDEKLAIPEDA
   NGO 2: Klaipėdos Žalieji asociacija. www.facebook.com/profile.php?id=100008449032535
   NGO 3: Klaipėdos bendruomenių asociacija. www.facebook.com/Klaipedosbendruomeniuasociacija
2. Salmon Diary (2021). http://lasisosdienorastis.lt/
3. Salmon Diary (2021). *Reports*. http://lasisosdienorastis.lt/ataskaitos/

References

Andres, S. (2011). Communication, the essence of management of a nonprofit organization. *Annals of Eftimie Murgu University Resita, Fascicle II, Economic Studies, 1*(1), 121–130.

Burksiene, V. (2013). Influence of personal competence in creation of organizational knowledge for sustainable development. *Socialiniai Tyrimai, 3*(32), 71–83. https://etalpykla.lituanistikadb.lt/fedora/objects/LT-LDB-0001:J.04~2013~1384620190862/datastreams/DS.002.1.01.ARTIC/content

Burksiene, V., Dvorak, J., & Duda, M. (2019). Upstream social marketing for implementing mobile government. *Societies, 9*(3), 54. https://doi.org/10.3390/soc9030054

Comfort, S. E., & Hester, J. B. (2019). Three dimensions of social media messaging success by environmental NGOs. *Environmental Communication, 13*(3), 281–286. https://doi.org/10.1080/17524032.2019.1579746

Dvorak, J., Burbulytė-Tsiskarishvili, G. A., & Barkauskaitė, B. (2017). Local governments and NGO's network cooperation: Lithuanian evidence. *Journal of the Belarusian State University, International Relations*, *1*, 21–27.

Dvorak, J., & Civinskas, R. (2018). The determinants of cooperation and the need for better communication between stakeholders in EU countries: The case of posted workers. *Polish Journal of Management Studies*, *18*(1), 94–106 https://doi.org/10.17512/pjms.2018.18.1.08

Haselkorn, M. (2007). *National research council strategic management of information and communication technology: The United States Air Force Experience with Y2K. Policy and global affairs*. The National Academies Press.

Herranz de la Casa, J. M., Alvarez-Villa, A., & Mercado-Saez, M. T. (2018). Communication and effectiveness of the protest: Anti-fracking movements in Spain. *Zer*, *23*(45), 35–56. https://doi.org/10.1387/zer.19543

Kilger, C., Reuter, B., & Stadtler, H. (2015). Collaborative planning. In H. Stadtler, C. Kilger, & H. Meyr (Eds.), *Supply chain management and advanced panning* (5th ed., pp. 257–277). Springer, Springer Texts in Business and Economics.

Krippendorff, K. (2013). *Content analysis: An introduction to its methodology*. Sage Publications.

Kroll, A., Neshkova, M. I., & Pandey, S. K. (2019). Spillover effects from customer to citizen orientation: How performance management reforms can foster public participation. *Administration &Society*, *51*(8), 1227–1253. https://doi.org/10.1177/0095399716687341

Liu, B. F. (2012). Toward a better understanding of nonprofit communication management. *Journal of Communication Management*, *16*(4), 388–404. https://doi.org/10.1108/13632541211279012

MacIndoe, H., & Sullivan, F. (2014). Nonprofit response to financial uncertainty: How does financial vulnerability shape nonprofit collaboration. *Journal of Management and Sustainability*, *4*(3). https://doi.org/10.5539/jms.v4n3p1

Mayring, P. (2014). *Qualitative content analysis: Theoretical foundation, basic procedures and software solution*. https://nbn-resolving.org/urn:nbn:de:0168-ssoar-395173

Mihai, R. L. (2017). Corporate communication management: A management approach. *Valahian Journal of Economic Studies*, *8*(22), 2. https://doi.org/10.1515/vjes-2017-0023

Muszynska, K. (2015). *Communication management in project teams – practices and patterns*. Managing Intellectual Capital and Innovation for Sustainable and Inclusive Society: Managing Intellectual Capital and Innovation; Proceedings of the MakeLearn and TIIM Joint International Conference. https://EconPapers.repec.org/RePEc:tkp:mklp15:1369-1366

Oliveira, E. (2019). Strategic communication and NGOs. In *The instigatory theory of NGO communication: Organisationskommunikation*. Springer VS. https://doi.org/10.1007/978-3-658-26858-9_4

Pavlovic, J., Dusan, Lalic, D., & Djuraskovic, D. (2014). Communication of non – governmental organizations via Facebook social network. *Inzinerine Ekonomika-Engineering Economics*, *25*(2), 186–193. https://doi.org/10.5755/j01.ee.25.2.3594

Rajhans, K. (2018). Effective communication management: A key to stakeholder relationship management in project-based organizations. *The IUP Journal of Soft Skills*, *XII*(4), 47–66.

Raupp, J., & Hoffjann, O. (2012). Understanding strategy in communication management. *Journal of Communication Management*, *16*(2), 146–161. http://doi.org/10.1108/13632541211217579

Ruehl, C. H., & Ingenhoff, D. (2015). Communication management on social networking sites: Stakeholder motives and usage types of corporate Facebook, Twitter and YouTube pages. *Journal of Communication Management*, *19*(3), 288–302. https://doi.org/10.1108/JCOM-04-2015-0025

Sidor, M., & Abdelhafez, D. (2021). NGO – public administration relationships in tackling the homelessness problem in the Czech Republic and Poland. *Administrative Sciences*, *11*(1), 24. https://doi.org/10.3390/admsci11010024

Sieber, R. E., Robinson, P. J., Johnson, P. A., & Corbett, J. M. (2016). Doing public participation on the geospatial web. *Annals of the American Association of Geographers*, *106*(5), 1030–1046. https://doi.org/10.1080/24694452.2016.1191325

Telešienė, A., & Kriaučiūnaitė, N. (2008). Trends of nongovernmental organizations' environmental activism in Lithuania. *Public Policy and Administration*, *1*(25), 94–103.

Tumulytė, I. (2012). Darnaus vystymosi komunikacija: Pilietinės iniciatyvos aplinkosaugos komunikacijoje. *Informacijos mokslai*, *62*, 7–17.

Vveinhardt, J., Stonkutė, E., & Sroka, W. (2019). Discourse on corporate social responsibility in the external communication of agricultural enterprises. *European Journal of International Management*, *13*(6), 864–879.

Unander, T. E., & Sørensen, K. H. (2020). Rhizomic learning: How environmental non-governmental organizations (ENGOs) acquire and assemble knowledge. *Social Studies of Science*, *50*(5), 821–833. https://doi.org/10.1177/0306312720908343

Yearley, S. (2017). Communication strategies of environmental NGOs and advocacy groups. In *Oxford research encyclopedia of climate science*. Oxford University Press. https://doi.org/10.1093/acrefore/9780190228620.013.402

4.3
THE GRASSROOTS WOMEN WATER COLLECTIVE IN INDIA

Ram Awtar Yadav and Kanshan Malik

Introduction

Spread across a geographical area of 70,000 square kilometers, Bundelkhand covers 14 districts of Uttar Pradesh and Madhya Pradesh. It comprises seven districts of Uttar Pradesh, namely Jhansi, Lalitpur, Jalaun, Banda, Chitrakut, Hamirpur and Mahoba, and seven districts of Madhya Pradesh, which are Tikamgarh, Chhatarpur, Sagar, Datia, Damoh, Panna and the newly formed Niwari district.

Bundelkhand is a semi-arid region characterized by unreliable rainfall. The rate of evaporation of water in the region is higher than the rate of moisture received through precipitation, ultimately resulting in unfertile and famine-prone land (Development Alternatives, 2012). Recurring droughts year after year have been a common feature of the Bundelkhand region, especially in the last two decades. The region is prone to deficient rainfall and consequent drought due to both changing climatic conditions and man-made reasons (Singh, 2014). The water crisis in the region is so acute that it often leads to tensions between "water haves and have-nots" (Dasgupta, 2016).

The deficient monsoon in consecutive years has made this region vulnerable to drought – making the living conditions extremely harsh, especially in the rural areas where the people mainly depend on incomes from agriculture for sustenance. As it can be gauged from several reports, issues like farmers' suicide, starvation, unemployment, large-scale migration and abandonment of cattle have become regular features of the region. The state of water resources is such that the women and girls in several rural areas have to travel several kilometers and spend hours collecting water for drinking and other purposes. Women and young girls are always at the receiving end due to the water crisis–like situation caused by droughts because of societal norms and structures.

Women's struggle for water

Even if gender equality is one of the central aspects of the Sustainable Development Goals (SDGs), as well as the Millennium Development Goals (MDGs), gender discrimination is still widespread in the rural hinterlands of the country. The deep-rooted patriarchal mindset and practices still dominate the rural way of living. According to a report of UNICEF (2007) on the state of women and children, women and girls have to face discrimination in every walk of life, be it access to resources, education, career opportunities and political power, etc. The discrimination is meted out in various forms like gender-based violence, oppression of girls and women, limited personal and professional choices

DOI: 10.4324/9781003170563-33

and denial of basic human rights (UNICEF, 2007). To tackle the issue of gender discrimination and ensure children's rights, it is important to make sure that both boys and girls get equal opportunities in terms of getting an education. However, the access to education for many of the girls in the rural areas of Bundelkhand is a distant dream, as they are supposed to share the burden of the household responsibilities of the mother, which may vary from cooking, washing utensils and cleaning home to fetching water or taking care of the younger siblings when their mothers go to collect water. For the families in rural Bundelkhand, there is a popular belief that even if the girl children are educated, they are not going to bring any economic benefits to the family, as they have to get married and go to another family.

Considering these disturbing realities in the rural settings of the region, many civil society organizations and nongovernmental organizations have come forward to work to address the situation according to their capacities. Different organizations are working in different ways for conserving water in the region to improve people's livelihood and stop migration. Parmarth Samaj Sevi Sansthan (PSSS) is one of such organizations working in the water management sector in the region in partnership with the local women with a view to address the issues of water and at the same time empower the women.

Parmarth Samaj Sevi Sansthan and women's 'right to water' project

PSSS is a voluntary organization registered under the Society Act of 1860 with its headquarters at Orai town located in the Jalaun district of Uttar Pradesh. It was established in 1995 to work for the upliftment and empowerment of vulnerable and marginalized sections of the society (which included people from the scheduled castes and women). It has been working in both Madhya Pradesh and Uttar Pradesh in the areas comprising the Bundelkhand region. In partnership with different government and nongovernment agencies, the organization is working on the issue of drought in six districts of Bundelkhand for vulnerability reduction. It works in sectors like reducing vulnerability in drought-affected areas, watershed development, livelihood promotion, women empowerment, etc.

Considering the everyday struggle of the women in terms of procuring water and men's attitudes to exploit the water resources for irrigating their farmlands, Parmarth decided to start a project to ensure women's right to water. The idea behind this project was to enable women to have their say in the decision-making processes in terms of using the available water resources. So, Parmarth started a project titled, *Establishing Women's First Right to Water Resources* in 2011 with financial support from the European Union in three districts of the Bundelkhand region of Uttar Pradesh, namely Jalaun, Hamirpur and Lalitpur. These three districts in the region are affected by drought almost every year. This affects the socioeconomic condition of these districts too. In Lalitpur, Hamirpur and Jalaun, the female literacy rate is 32.97%, 40.14% and 49.21%, respectively, as per the UP Human Development Report 2008. The main objective of the project was to reduce vulnerability of women through their participation in water management interventions. It also aimed at ensuring drinking water security for the rural populations and capacity building of the women through awareness and education and enabling them to assert their rights on the use of water resources and promote their role in water management initiatives and sustainable use of water for agriculture and household purposes.

The state coordinator of Parmarth for Uttar Pradesh, Manish Kumar, stated during one of the interactions at the Jhansi office that even after almost seven decades of the Indian Constitution coming into force, the idea of gender equality that it mandates remains far from being achieved. Kumar said,

> In a state like Uttar Pradesh and in one of its most backward regions i.e. Bundelkhand, gender and caste identities still have a very dominant impact in everyday lives of the people.

Here the feudal and patriarchal culture and practices still dictate terms in day-to-day affairs of the people in both public as well as private spaces, he pointed saying that "women have to cope with the issue of gender inequality in their everyday lives in such a way that they do not even realize that they are becoming a victim of the age-old traditions and beliefs, as for them it is common societal norms that they have to follow being women and girls.
(M. Kumar, personal interview, January 18, 2019)

Under such a circumstance, it was not easy for the Parmarth officials to talk to the women in rural areas who they wanted to mobilize and work with. Vineeta Yadav, the team leader of the project titled "Establishing Women's First Right to Water" based at Talbehat block of Lalitpur district, recalling her initial experiences, said, "It was quite challenging for her to talk to the women in the villages of the region during the beginning of the project as they would all be shy talking to the outsiders and remain head bowed with their faces covered with the *pallu* (veil) up to the neck" (V. Yadav, personal interview, December 28, 2018). Reflecting further on her assessment of the situation, she added,

For women it was a family culture to remain covered in their in-law's house especially before the father-in-law or other senior male members of the family and while moving out. The custom of covering the faces with *pallu* or *ghunghat*, as they call it locally, was not only among the communities belonging to the scheduled castes but also among upper castes. Most of the women in the rural areas of Bundelkhand faced similar kind of treatment in their in-law's house no matter which caste they came from.
(V. Yadav, personal interview, December 28, 2018)

During the beginning of the project in 2011, Yadav recalled,

The women would hardly open up when they would try to talk to them about their everyday experiences of life, their problems, issues related to water etc., if there were any male members of the families around. However, when there were no male members, they would talk freely and narrate their stories about the everyday challenges that they would face with no water source being present at their houses.
(V. Yadav, personal interview, December 28, 2018)

According to her, the feeling of being an inferior gender was so deeply entrenched in the minds of the women that they would have to seek permission from their husbands or other elder male members of the family in the absence of their husbands, even when going to the market for purchasing their personal items or going to their parental homes.

Talking about the need for such a project in Bundelkhand, Sanjay Singh, the secretary of Parmarth, said, "After a closer look at the everyday lives of the women in the region and the stress for water, one realizes the cruel realities of their lives. The struggle of pregnant and elderly women for fetching water is extremely concerning and needs serious attention of the society" (S. Singh, personal interview, December 19, 2018).

It was these realizations that made us resolve to work towards women empowerment and addressing the water-related issues so that they can enjoy their right to a dignified life. We felt that pushing for women's first right to water resources would help them be on board in the decision-making processes for managing water resources and creating new infrastructure for conserving water.
(S. Singh, personal interview, December 19, 2018)

Formation of *Pani Panchayat* and communication for and by women

Manvendra Singh, the coordinator for 'Ensuring Women's First Right to Water' project based at the Talbehat block of Lalitpur district, says,

> Having realized that women were the worst victims of the feudal and patriarchal system and the customary norms, and the situations of the water crisis, we decided to first reach out to them and mobilize them towards the issue. We thought of talking to them about their *adhikar* (rights) and *samman* (dignity) so that they could feel stronger and muster courage for moving out of their confined spaces and fighting for their rights and entitlements.
>
> (M. Singh, personal interview, December 21, 2018)

But that was going to be extremely challenging, as they were accustomed to a particular kind of lifestyle and societal customs that were ingrained in their minds. However, Singh said, "We knew that the need was to reach out to them on a regular basis and keep trying to convince them in the right manner and one day they will rise to assert their voice." On being asked what gave them this kind of confidence, he said that they had it in their mind that the women who were capable of silently coping with extremely stressful and strenuous situations every day were certainly very strong from within and could become great agents of change once they realize their potential as a significant change-making force. The project coordinator said,

> We knew for sure that initially, we needed only one or two women to come forward and show courage. Once that happens, others too will follow. Besides, we had a good team of female staff members and volunteers who knew their languages coming from the local settings and therefore, were able to get access to their households without major difficulties.

So, to begin with, the nongovernmental organization (NGO) decided to start mobilizing women and forming their groups at the village level. They decided to name the group *Pani Panchayat* (water collective). Singh went on, saying,

> People in rural areas understand the term *Panchayat* as it is used in *Gram Panchayat* which is the village-level governing body to which people are elected through voting. The word *Panchayat*, thus, signifies some sort of authority and respect. Generally, representatives of the *Panchayats* would be men and even if women are elected to the *Panchayats*, as *Gram Pradhan* (village head) it would actually be their husbands locally known as *Pradhan Pati* (husband of the village head) who would manage their day-to-day affairs on their behalf. No elected woman *Pradhan* would go to the block offices where they would get their funds for carrying out small development works or under various government schemes to be distributed to the beneficiaries.[1] Even after being elected they would remain inside their houses and let their husbands do the work on their behalf as it was about power which they think only men have the right to.
>
> (M. Singh, personal interview, December 21, 2018)

This was quite evident when Parmarth volunteers introduced one of the authors to many *Gram Pradhans* in the villages who would actually be working on their wives' behalf. Even if he wanted to meet some of the women representatives in some villages with the officials and volunteers of Parmarth, they would simply deny the meeting saying, "*Pradhan Ji ghar pe nahi hain*" (*Pradhan* is not at home), whereas they are the actual elected *Pradhans*.

Women becoming agents of change

The project coordinator said that even as women were undertaking the daunting task of procuring water, they had absolutely no role in the decision-making processes in the villages and communities. That, he said, gave them a sense of opportunity to reach out to the women and identify those with leadership qualities to spearhead the campaign for water management interventions by mobilizing other women. He said that having understood the value of water owing to their everyday struggle for it, the women were always going to be the better managers and decision-makers when it came to valuing water and conserving it.

> After regularly meeting the women for 4–5 times and telling them that if they came forward, the issue of water scarcity could be dealt with to a great extent, some women expressed their curiosity to understand the task they will have to perform. We told them that with voluntary services we would work for the rejuvenation of the old water bodies and create new ones to stop rain water run-off during the monsoon and to improve the ground water level that will minimize their efforts for procuring water and save them a lot of time and energy.
>
> (M. Singh, personal interview, December 21, 2018)

It appears to be what James (2011) called "pre-conditions" before beginning the actual work of water conservation, with the involvement of the local women and other actors after having understood the context of the problem which the NGO sought to address.

The idea clicked with some of the women, as it was evident in Motto village, where three women decided to dig an old well that was completely covered up with soil, and they kept digging despite people making a mockery of them. Later when they did not give in, other women and men joined them, after which they had dug the well in two months and got water in their own village. They went on to create two check dams in the village to stop the rainwater run-off that resulted in improving the ground water level, which saw the water level in the well improve. Similarly, the stories of women leading such initiatives started to emerge from other villages too like Kakradi, Vijrautha, Kalothra and others, and the campaign took off.

After the formation of the *Pani Panchayat* groups at the village level and building the cadres of the *Jal Sahelis* (women water warriors) to lead those groups, Parmarth officials realized that the work was only half done, and to ensure availability of water in the villages, it was crucial to bring the other stakeholders together. So they started leading the *Pani Panchayat* members and *Jal Sahelis* to the district administration offices, block development offices and *Panchayat* representatives so that they could be apprised of the gravity of the problems. The regular meetings with the officials and local public representatives helped Parmarth and *Pani Panchayat* groups to sensitize the officials and district and block administration offices, as well as the *Pradhans* and ward members at the village levels. With the passage of time, they too started extending the administrative support to their work of water management, providing them the benefits under various schemes which the villagers were entitled for, like employment under the Mahatma Gandhi National Rural Employment Guarantee Act (MNREGA), pensions, etc.

Through its constant efforts in terms of sensitization and conscientization, Parmarth formed *Pani Panchayat* collectives in 96 villages of the three districts of Hamirpur, Lalitpur and Jalaun after identifying them as 'vulnerable' based on a baseline survey that it conducted in 2011. Of these 96 *Pani Panchayat* groups, 26 were in Hamirpur district, 40 in Lalitpur and 30 in Jalaun. The most active ladies working in the groups were identified as the *Jal Sahelis*, who would informally lead them. A total of 172 women were recognized as *Jal Sahelis* in the 96 villages of three project districts for their active engagement with the work of the groups. The *Pani Panchayat* groups proved to be instrumental in creation of the new water resources, revival of the old ones and conservation of the natural water resources. Several check dams were constructed, ponds and wells were dug and new hand-pumps and rainwater harvesting structures were installed in the project villages with support from the local community members, government departments and *Panchayats*.

The members of the Pani Panchayat were given training for repairing hand-pumps and were provided with the kits, as a result of which the small problems of the hand-pumps were fixed by the women on their own without waiting for help from the local administration. In addition to that they were imparted with basic skills of writing applications for taking up their issues to the local administration by the Parmarth officials and volunteers during various capacity-building workshops.

In many programs that Parmarth would organize for training and capacity building of the *Pani Panchayat* members and the *Jal Sahelis*, they would make sure that the government officials like collector, sub-divisional magistrate (SDM), block development officer (BDO) and others came and participated. This would help Parmarth bridge the gap between the administration and rural population. Such events would also give women the confidence to interact and talk to the government officials with ease, which was otherwise completely in the realms of impossibility for them.

The 'Women's Right to Water' project started by Parmarth played a significant role in creating an enabling environment for the rural women in Bundelkhand, as a result of which they realized their potential and worked for change. The project brought the issues of 'water and women' to the center of the local discourses in the intervention areas. The women who were confined to their houses, taking care of household chores, started to assert their voice for their rights and rose to become the crusaders for addressing the issues related to water. In doing so, they not only made their lives more convenient but also helped other families have access to water in their own villages – a huge respite to those who had to commute several kilometers for water.

The women who became members of *Pani Panchayat* and *Jal Sahelis* not only helped the cause of water but they also worked for the social security of the women in their areas, as they started going to the local administration and demanding what they were entitled to like widow pensions, old-age pensions, funds for toilets, etc. While on one hand, they ensured work for many women and men who were facing a livelihood crisis due to declining agricultural production through MNREGA, on the other, the employment scheme helped them create new water conservation structures like check-dams and ponds and also revived the old water bodies whose water storage capacity was reduced due to silting and garbage dumping.

The government officials, who otherwise were apathetic to the hardships of the rural women owing to the water crisis, became concerned, and many of them provided administrative support for the cause through Parmarth, *Pani Panchayat* and the Panchayati Raj Institutions (PRIs). They started listening to the concerns of the villagers and made sincere efforts to help them using the administrative mechanisms and processes.

In this way the project led to the emergence of an environmental public sphere in the project areas of Bundelkhand as a result of environmental discourses engaging various stakeholders ranging from community members, women, farmers and local public representatives to the authorities from the government and administration, which is one of the important functions of the field of environmental communication, as mentioned by Yang and Calhoun (2007). As a part of this aspect of environmental communication, people not only engage in debating environmental problems but also share their concern about the threats of irresponsible behavior of humans towards nature. This aspect resonates in the functioning of *Pani Panchayat* groups, which work to educate people about not dumping waste materials in the water bodies or obstructing the channels through which water flows through the ponds and lakes during the monsoon season.

The activities being carried out under the project also appear to be in line with the idea of Milsten (2009) that environmental communication is vital in explaining the ecological damages caused due to human interventions in nature. In the many villages of Bundelkhand, the members of the

Pani Panchayat would interact with the villagers to sensitize them to not defecate along the water bodies; discharge any solid or liquid domestic waste into them; or dump plastic, cloth, glass, etc., as it would contaminate the water, which was harmful for the health of the water bodies as well as the humans. In consultation with the local public representatives and the community members, they would also plan rational use of water for irrigation from these water bodies so that they could have water in nearby hand-pumps and wells for drinking during the summer season. This way, the interventions of the Parmarth and *Pani Panchayat* also help in shaping local communities' understanding of the natural environment as well as their relationship with it, which according to Mishra (2013) and Cox (2012) is one of the main characteristics of environmental communication. The insights drawn from Parmarth's interventions in the regions around water resonate with Pezzulo and Cox (2018), who consider the NGOs significant sources of environmental communication with the ways in which they facilitated a discourse around water by bringing various actors together.

To conclude, this case study shows the role of the local civil society in Bundelkhand and women members of Pani Panchayat playing a significant role in building awareness among the local communities around issues of water and other environmental concerns, shaping what Yang and Calhoun (2007) and Cox (2012) a "green" public sphere. Through a strategic communication process, Parmarth carried out targeted interventions to address the water-related problems by sensitizing people, especially women, and motivating them to take actions to revive water resources like rivers and lakes; developing watersheds; and creating other water conservation structures like check-dams, stop-dams, farm ponds, etc.

Note

1 In Uttar Pradesh one-third of the total Gram Panchayat seats are reserved for women.

References

Cox, R. (2012). *Environmental communication and the public sphere*. Sage Publications.
Dasgupta, K. (2016, May 10). Don't blame nature for the drought in Bundelkhand. *Hindustan Times*. Retrieved February 18, 2017, from www.hindustantimes.com/editorials/don-t-blame-nature-for-the-drought-in-bundelkhand/story-4ZJjFLdYJ3Tq8pN1sJvrsO.html
Development Alternatives. (2012). *Sustainable civil society initiative to address global environmental challenges*. Development Alternatives.
James, C. (2011). *Theory of change review*. A report commissioned by Comic Relief. Comic Relief.
Kumar, M. (2019, January 18). Personal communication [Personal interview].
Milsten, T. (2009). Environmental communication theories. In S. W. Foss (Ed.), *Encyclopedia of communication theory* (pp. 344–348). Sage Publications Inc.
Mishra, M. (2013). Environmental communication in India: Lessons from Orissa. *Media Asia*, 85–95. https://doi.org/10.1080/01296612.2013.11689953
Pezzulo, P. C., & Cox, R. (2018). *Environmental communication and the public sphere*. Sage.
Singh, J. (2014, June 9). Bundelkhand's cycle of droughts: Is it man-made? *Down to Earth*. Retrieved February 15, 2017, from www.downtoearth.org.in/news/bundelkhands-cycle-of-droughts-is-it-manmade-44677
Singh, M. (2018, December 21). Personal communication [Personal interview].
Singh, S. (2018, December 19). Personal communication [Personal interview].
UNICEF. (2007). *Women and children: The double dividend of equality*. UNICEF.
Yadav, V. (2018, December 28). Personal communication [Personal interview].
Yang, G., & Calhoun, C. (2007). Media, civil society, and the rise of a green public sphere in China. *China Information*, *21*(2), 211–236. https://doi.org/10.1177/0920203X07079644

4.4
THE ROLE OF COMMUNICATION WITHIN A DOMESTIC VIOLENCE CONTEXT DURING A LOCKDOWN

Sónia de Sá

Introduction

Domestic violence[1] is formally framed in the Portuguese Penal Code by Articles 152 – *Domestic violence*, 152-A – *Abuse* and 152-B – *Violation of safety rules*, as well as 132 – *Aggravated case of intentional killing*, 145 – *Aggravated case of offense to physical integrity* and 69-A – *Statement of unworthiness to inherit* (AR, 2021). It has its roots in gender violence, i.e., in an imbalance of forces and power between genders, historically generated by evident and/or latent discrimination against the dominated elements – mostly women and children – by the dominant ones – mostly men (APAV, 2021; O'Toole et al., 2020). This form of violence has increased globally since the onset of the COVID-19 pandemic (UN, 2020; UN Women, 2021; WHO, 2021a; Fawole et al., 2021). Considering that the victim,[2] in addition to continuing to work remotely at home, assisting their children, organizing the house, meals and other household management tasks, became isolated and living continuously and closely with the aggressor, in a space that lacks easy access to the outside world and to aid organizations, the scenario became even more dangerous (CIG, 2020; Nigam, 2020; Kumar, 2020; Poiares, 2020).

In this context of great tension (Oliveira & Fernandes, 2020), in addition to the "anxiety, concern, fear and anger associated with COVID-19", the worsening of "dysfunctional relational dynamics and communication difficulties" led to the triggering of more moments of "violence" (OPP, 2020)[3] and, consequently, to the increase of cases of physical – even deadly – psychological, moral, and financial violence (Fornari et al., 2021b; Katana et al., 2021; Wong et al., 2021; Bastos et al., 2020): "This pandemic has generated several health consequences, hindering the access of the population and the creation and development of practices aimed at prevention and action on violence against women or children" (Barros et al., 2021).

Even though in the first months of the first lockdown[4], the number of reports decreased, given the circumstance of the aggressor's control over the victim, the data show us today that thousands of victims were prevented from asking for help, limited by fear and by the change in the logic of the organizations in the COVID-19 period. Thus, the pandemic crisis led to another crisis, that of violence, even though this had been largely ignored by the authorities of the various states, who were more primarily concerned with tackling COVID-19 (Pilipchuk, 2020). As a result, there were many survivors who came to more permanently experience aggression and abuse from domestic and intimate partners with whom they were forced to share a closed place for many more hours a day now (Ranee, 2021; Vieira et al., 2020).

If, on the one hand, governments that were more – or less – concerned with the value of human life that was in danger with the advancing waves of the pandemic (Kay & Wood, 2020), sent people home, in a generalized lockdown, often associated with incorrect and conspiratorial information (Ferreira & Borges, 2020), on the other hand, these measures – and these governments – did not meet the necessary conditions for the protection of the victim in the context of isolation with the aggressor (Gama et al., 2021; Wells, 2020). Although warned by the World Health Organization (WHO, 2021b) and the European Institute for Gender Equality (EIGE, 2021a),[5] governments in general have tended not to prioritize these warnings and focused on protection against the widespread contagion of the virus.

In the Spanish case, domestic violence mitigation measures, promoted through the *Contingency plan against gender violence in the face of the Covid-19 crisis*,[6] proved insufficient because they lacked financial support and economic impetus for women in situations of violence (Ruiz-Pérez & Pastor-Moreno, 2020, p. 393): "It is not possible to prevent gender-based violence in a comprehensive manner without considering the increase in unemployment, temporary employment and job instability, economic dependence or the overload of reproductive tasks, among other elements that facilitate it."

In Portugal, the Commission for Citizenship and Gender Equality (CIG) launched the *#EuSobrevivi* ("I am a survivor") campaign, which presents, as an alternative to the phone call for help and/or to report a case of violence, the sending of a silent phone message via text messages. The campaign – both offline[7] and online[8] – is framed by the following text: "If you are a victim or know someone who is a victim of domestic violence, ask for help. Call 112, or 800 202 148, or text 3060" (CIG, 2020). The campaign, which makes the general population co-responsible for warning and reporting cases of domestic violence, was extended by traditional media, namely free-to-air television, and disseminated massively in social media, in close coordination with 15 nongovernmental organizations (NGOs)[9] from all over the country.

Even so, as the study on Portuguese lockdown and representation of violence concluded (Gama et al., 2021), the campaign seems to have been insufficient, since out of 1,062 respondents, 13.7% indicated having suffered from some kind of domestic violence; however, more than 62.3% did not ask for help, in short, "playing down the significance of the abuse, feelings of shame and embarrassment, and sense of lack of support and distrust from the services, among others" (p. 39).

Globally, victims and survivors in situations of greater financial risk were the most affected by the pandemic (Silva et al., 2020), both due to the increase in episodes of recurrent violence, financial need, and domestic instability but also due to the lack of conditions for protection against the advance of the virus. As the Institute for Women's Policy Research (IWPR, 2020)[10] notes, this scenario has become more evident, and therefore worrisome, among nonwhite and poor women victims of violence, such as children and the elderly (Sobande, 2020; Phipps, 2021).

Here emerge the very strenuous – albeit limited – actions of NGOs as a task force in helping these victims, relegated by the various states to nonpriority plans (Oliveira et al., 2020). As we will further develop and substantiate through our empirical study, NGOs in various countries (Pilipchuk, 2020) and also in Portugal had the role of relieving the pressure on the victims, maintaining the emergency withdrawal support services, and ensuring support to the survivors and their children in most cases.

It is precisely these support organizations for victims and survivors of domestic violence that experience two equally worrying circumstances: the first has to do with the increase in the number of requests for help and the severity of the violence that this request frames, and the second deals both with the difficulty of communicating directly and effectively with the victims and with the lack of resources accompanied by the economic crisis that the pandemic triggered (EIGE, 2021a, 2021c).

The data from the EIGE reinforce the urgency of action by the various governments on the escalation of cases and violence in a search for local and global responses, even if the fight against COVID-19 has slowed the progress of measures for gender equality[11] in Europe, which may be implying an increase in the number of cases of violence since the beginning of the pandemic (EIGE,

2021b). This reality is all the more worrisome when it is known from experiences in other economic and public health crises (Kourti et al., 2021) that official statistics show only part of the gravity of the situation (Medel-Herrero et al., 2020). This increase in cases of violence – formally registered or not (UN Women & ILO, 2021) – has prompted the European Commission to propose more assertively to member states more effective measures[12] to protect victims and survivors[13], namely through "Awareness-raising campaigns related to intimate partner violence in the context of Covid-19 were identified in almost all member states" (EIGE, 2021a, p. 10)

These victims, however, more limited in their access to formal (legal and victim support organizations) and informal (family and friends) support networks, found themselves constrained in their actions – more so than before – so they needed to find communication alternatives, whenever possible, offered by support agencies (Marques et al., 2020), whether these were governmental or not (EIGE, 2021c; UN Women, 2020a, 2020b; Silva et al., 2020).

Because it is ubiquitous and mostly associated with the dominant gender of the couple – or former couple – violence, often dangerously romanticized by the media (Béres, 1999), is also associated with a growing toxic masculinity – male dominance – in the last two pandemic years (Harsin, 2020).

NGOs and communication during lockdown

The communication of most NGOs in Portugal is based on an idea of communication for dissemination and instrumental and less on communication for involvement and dialogue (Sá, 2020; Gonçalves & Lisboa, 2017). The reasons for this are, first and foremost, the lack of communication professionals in organizations and the overall lack of funding, always pegged to state- or European Union–funded projects, limited in time, and the vagueness of the role of communication in the overall strategy of organizations (Eiró-Gomes & Neto, 2017).

NGOs supporting victims and survivors of domestic violence, prevented from communicating regularly with their priority audience, had to find alternative ways of contact. Digital platforms, digital social media, and/or text messages became avenues of nonpresential communication (Fornari et al., 2021a), however, on an almost amateur basis, without the necessary technology education – in the NGOs and the audiences. Slakoff et al. (2020) propose that both public and private organizations should clearly invest in training for technological and digital literacy, empowering diverse audiences: "technologists could host educational webinars for victims and advocates to learn about technological advances in this space, or they could help create digital toolkits for people looking to learn more about IPV and safe online communication during COVID-19" (p. 2783).

This proposal touches on one of the most evident – albeit silent – inequalities of today, exacerbated by pandemic and remoteness: access to and mastery of networked digital technology. As far as the countries of the European Union are concerned, women represent just over 20% of the jobs in this area. When the analysis focuses on black women, the statistic is residual. This shows the lack of digital literacy and the disproportionality of gender, race, and social status (Cabral & Sá, 2021), which increasingly disenfranchises a very significant group of the population, who are often silenced.

Allied with this lack of knowledge and use of emerging networked technology, violence is a continuum, highlighted in periods of crisis, and that "the pandemic illuminates is embedded in broader systems of domination and exclusion" (Forester & O'Brien, 2020, p. 1150).

In a scenario of great weakness, the question was: "How can NGOs communicate with victims – the priority audience – effectively when they are prevented from leaving their homes and are in the permanent presence of the aggressor?" For the adopted strategy, we take into consideration Lucas and Landman's (2021) proposal on the relevance of NGO communication – and other organizations – that "(a) facilitate the identification of agenda proxies reflected in strategic communications used by [other] organizations, and (b) to provide insights into changing communication tactics deployed by these organizations in the context of mass-communication using social media as a result of the global pandemic" (p. 314).

Improving communication through strategic thinking and tactical action (Smith, 2017) appropriate to the pandemic situation has thus become one of the pressing needs highlighted by social workers, especially those dealing with domestic violence and other types of abuse (Pai & Ashok, 2020). But we find ourselves at a crossroads: if, on the one hand, NGOs have become crucial players in the fight against violence, especially during a lockdown, applying their knowledge in the field, on the other hand, they have not shown themselves fit for the development of new communication plans for the outreach and involvement of families – of the priority audiences – in a more vulnerable situation (Silva, 2018).

In a state of great vulnerability, intensified by the change in the organizations' pre-pandemic operating models, victims and survivors of violence have seen their perception of abandonment and loss of solutions intensified (Mahapatro et al., 2021), especially during the first lockdown in Portugal. This lack of face-to-face support, mixed with the pressure of domestic isolation and the confusion of work and leisure times, increased "gender inequality, making some women more invisible and [. . .] the victims of violence and others more ill" (Aires & Sales, 2020, p. 183).

López-Hernández and Rubio-Amores (2020) state, and we agree, that this form of information exchange between organizations and victims, clearly insufficient, is a sign of unpreparedness from government authorities and the victim rescue and assistance services:

> Son los gobiernos los llamados a tomar acción, pues son quienes deben garantizar a las víctimas eficacia ante sus denuncias y no solo eso sino propiciar el ambiente para que existan líneas y servicios de apoyo que brinden no solo información, sino asesoramiento legal y psicológico a la población cuando lo necesite, y que este pueda ser a través de distintos medios y no solo presencial, ya que esto puede obstaculizar los pedidos de ayuda en situaciones como la actual en la que nos encontramos en aislamiento obligatorio.[14]

Women have thus become more at risk, and organizations have become somewhat perilous in their possible responses in the context of a pandemic crisis. The woman at risk (Stark & Flitcraft, 1996) became the only priority of NGOs, insofar as she represents submission and hopelessness, fear and loss, an outcast that society had apparently forsaken.

The solution was to create alternative communication strategies for the resumption of support. Mahardika's (2020) proposal is that the strategy for (re)connecting organizations and priority audiences should involve the implementation of the relationship management model, based on constant exchanges between parties. Ultimately, what organizations continue to seek is the establishment of effective communication (MohdHanafiah et al., 2021) with their audiences, creating meaning in digital communication (abundant, confusing, and often contradictory) and providing tools for cautious and efficient use of emerging platforms (Servaes & Malikhao, 2020).

There are several proposals for improving NGO communication: the instigatory theory of NGO communication (Oliveira, 2019), the sustainability as normative framework in NGO communication (Weder, 2021), and the storytelling-based communication (Riley et al., 2021). The goal focuses on engaging diverse audiences from priority audiences – or beneficiaries or potential beneficiaries – to the media and broader populations. However, as exposed by (Grilo, 2018), NGO communication in general is as necessary as it is deficient, since it largely depends on volunteer work for its unstructured achievement.

The communication of these organizations is intended to be, in short, a daily operation for social change (Tufte, 2017), especially targeting vulnerable groups. When the context is one of violence in lockdown, the engagement of audiences becomes exclusively digital, and the "organization's ability to attract public attention on social media is contingent on its ability to fit its network position with the network structure of the communication context" (Yang & Saffer, 2021, p. 2902).

Zucco et al. (2021) also detected the centrality of digital communication in NGOs during the pandemic period and the strategies – more or less hasty, given the urgency of the actions – that involved almost exclusive contact with the public (internal and external) through social media, without time for adequate media literacy for the effective use of tools. The problem, as analyzed by Fröhlich and Jungblut (2018), who studied the strategic management of NGO communication in a conflict context, is that NGOs end up mixing two fields into one: communication and expertise; that is, they try to show themselves as experts in the area they deal with and as communication strategists. This crossroads can lead to confusion of various kinds, which, we would add, tends to increase possible entropies, aggravated in crisis situations.

In the pandemic situation we live in, NGOs are faced with so-called nonroutine processes, which combine the obstacles of interpersonal communication and communication without restrictions, either technological or in terms of the availability of public involvement. Demir et al. (2021) propose that more attention be paid to "strategic dimensions and managerial processes both separately and together, in a change in order to achieve the desired level of communication quality [. . .] during the pandemic process" (p. 14). In fact, even in a context of lockdown, and in order for adaptation to take place, communication must be participatory (even if limited), dialogical (even if disguised), conscious, emancipatory, and liberating.

This is the era of risk communication (Gonçalves et al., 2022), which was amplified during the pandemic period and is therefore critical for the design of effective, sustained, and safe strategies when the recipients are in a situation of fear and, therefore, of great vulnerability. "Effective risk communication means that all messages can be presented and shared with the population in a transparent, credible, and easily understood communication process" (Heras-Pedrosa et al., 2020, p. 18).

If a clear, transparent, and effective communication is expected from governments and political leaders, and such expectation has failed throughout the pandemic (Okviana et al., 2020), how should one demand a high-quality and expeditious level from NGOs that, for the most part, do not have public relations professionals or communication strategists for building communication plans in times of crisis (Riley et al., 2021)?

Empirical study

From the object of the study – the communication of NGOs supporting victims and survivors of domestic violence in a context of a lockdown – we set our goals: both general (to understand how NGOs supporting victims and survivors of domestic violence have adapted communication with their priority audiences) and specific (to analyze the communication strategies) (Smith, 2017, p. 155) used by NGOs and analyze the communication tactics (p. 311) applied by NGOs supporting victims of domestic violence, limited in their action by COVID-19.

By outlining goals, and through the theoretical framework, we will verify the following hypotheses: H1) NGOs supporting victims of domestic violence in Portugal have adopted new communication plans based on alternative strategies of access to priority audiences that resulted in the redefinition of specific communication tactics in a context of confinement and H2) NGOs supporting victims of domestic violence in Portugal have applied a set of sundry communication tactics, based on digital means and lacking strategic planning.

Method and materials

To verify the established hypotheses, the methodological option is qualitative (Seidman, 2006; May, 2002), and the semi-structured interview (Daymon & Holloway, 2011; Gillham, 2005; Boje, 2001) model was used, having been applied to 15 of the approximately 50 NGOs supporting victims of domestic violence in Portugal.[15] The interview request[16] was sent out to all NGOs from mainland Portugal and the archipelagos of Madeira and Azores. We received 15 answers,[17] which we will analyze next.

Data analysis

Interview

For the analysis of the interviews, we followed the structure proposed by Daymon and Holloway (2011), which presupposes the coding from the text of all the responses from all the organizations, through the labeling of ideas and themes that are most frequently repeated and the intentions of the research. From this, the following categories emerged: "communication", "NGO", "violence", "pandemic", "outreach", and "network".

The categories "communication", "NGO", and "violence" are directly related to the objectives of the research, outlined in the script, while the categories "pandemic", "proximity", and "network" emerged from the repetitions detected in the answers. From here on, the description of each of the categories is analytical and exhaustive.

C1:[18] violence

The NGOs almost unanimously relate that there has been a significant increase in the number of cases of violence and of requests for help, above all, by telephone and digital means. The situations of violence were "more serious" (organization 1)[19] and, therefore, there was a growing "instability and severity of domestic violence episodes" (organization 14). This scenario intensified after the end of the first lockdown period: "If in January or February 2020 the Office had about 60 monthly appointments, in April 2020, this number was north of 200" (organization 5). The increase in reported cases was recorded, essentially, in 2021, with a significant increase after the second lockdown period: "Since May 2021, we actually felt an increasing demand for our service, not only by the victims themselves, but also by referrals from local entities" (organization 10).

However, many victims during their confinement had "less chances to denounce". Therefore, "by the contingencies of the pandemic situation itself and the health and economic crisis that it generated", many households were left in a "precarious situation" and under "increased pressure when making the decision to leave a violent relationship" (organization 9).

C2: NGO

Being "proximity collectives", NGOs "play a pivotal role in supporting victims during the COVID-19 context" (organization 3). Therefore, these organizations decided to maintain at least one face-to-face support member, so that victims who were able to travel there could be attended to and immediately supported and referred to places of safety.

NGOs often replace the state in conditions almost always of great instability, "being key actors in victim support" (organization 2). The support to victims in Portugal is mostly provided by NGOs, so, they emphasize, "we never interrupted our services" (organization 7). However, "in crisis situations, namely when leaving home, the victims continued to be referred to Emergency Shelter/*Casa Abrigo*" (organization 4).

All, without exception, highlight their "crucial role in the proximity support" to victims and family members, who are also victims (organization 6), in a permanent cooperation with the Gulbenkian Institute of Science (IGC) and the "national network against violence" (organization 15).

One of the notes that was also highlighted by all the support structures has to do with the state of "absolute exhaustion" (organization 8) of the victim support staff and the other members of the organizations: "our team is at the limit of burnout since the beginning of the pandemic" (organization 10).

C3: communication

All organizations perceive communication as "extraordinarily important and central" (organization 12), "crucial" (organization 6), and an "asset" to "get the messages across" (organization 1) for "inter-institutional sharing and cooperation" that "allows for the safety and protection of victims" (organization 8). Moreover, "without careful, sensitive, attentive and flexible communication, it is very difficult to help those who need support" (organization 11). However, the perception of the role of communication is both limited and poorly defined: "as in everything, communication is the most effective way to train/inform, teach, evolve, therefore, to produce changes" (organization 1).

Although with limited but guaranteed face-to-face support, the support structures began to prioritize the support by telephone and by messages via "telephone, email, text messages and in private chats on social media". In an incipient resource without a strategic communication plan to support it: "it is only through publicity that [the victims] are aware of the support" (organization 12) or communication is important for the "coordination with the services and entities involved [. . .] in the process" (organization 13).

Communication, addressed institutionally, is understood as a means and not as a transversal element of the support process – from prevention to permanent follow-up of victims and survivors: "with instituted procedures at the level of dissemination of services" (organization 10); or the organizations "articulate [. . .] institutional efforts in the 24 entities that make up the Zero Violence Network for the signaling and referral of situations" (organization 7). Also, organization 12 acknowledges that "the dissemination and creation of ways to pass the message to victims [. . .] is very important". As does organization 10, which highlights that "communication of the situations and their signaling is essential to [. . .] act, namely in cases where the risk assessment is high".

However, the issue remains: "The sources of funding for victim assistance and reception structures do not foresee a specific field for external communication, so there is a lack of support for this commitment" (organization 7).

C4: pandemic

To the questions that related to the pandemic and the organizational adjustments of the victim support and assistance structures, the organizations' representatives give similar answers: reduction of the team in face-to-face context and priority to assistance by phone, text messages, social media, and video call when possible.

The teams stayed in separate places and, therefore, "the moments to discuss the cases were reduced" (organization 3); in addition, in the case of some mothers of the teams who, having their school-age children at home, "had to give support to the children", this added "difficulty in following up the cases" (organization 13) as effectively as it was done before the pandemic. The pandemic thus required an increase in the physical distance between the victims and the support structures; however, it led to the reinforcement of the attendances – more or less concealed when in the presence of the aggressor – by "telephone, [. . .] video calls and WhatsApp and Messenger" (organization 10) and of the "publications in social media, [. . .] communication channels we use in an attempt to reach people of different ages and social strata, who are potential victims of domestic violence" (organization 7).

C5: proximity

Almost paradoxically, the pandemic and the need to use digital and remote means to support victims have led organizations to frequently refer to the need to reapproach audiences: "The adoption of a proximity policy, through the different forms of communication, thus assumes a fundamental role in prevention and intervention in situations of greater risk" (organization 12). The centrality of the organizations' communicative action was the victim and her protection, making her close, even in the context of detachment: "we try that the communication with the person in a situation of victimization respects her protection, but also her privacy and confidentiality, [. . .], so as not to compromise her safety" (organization 10).

This idea of proximity is thus associated with the more "familiar use of digital platforms" (organization 8), so many of the consultations "were maintained" because "campaigns were strengthened in social media for contact alternatives in case of the presence of the aggressor" (organization 6). There was therefore an action to meet "the needs of users" (organization 11), especially those who were – and still are – in a more fragile economic situation since the beginning of the pandemic.

However, maintaining on-site appointments is another indicator of proximity in times of lockdown: "We did not stop supporting those who came to the office" (organization 2), because, almost always, it was "an important window of opportunity" for a victim and her children (organization 15).

C6: network

The idea of network was common in the answers from all the organizations, but with two distinct meanings: digital networks (social media) and the network for the fight against violence, which unites public, nongovernmental, and governmental entities, technically promoted by the IGC and politically by the Secretary of State for Citizenship and Equality.

The support and dissemination support via social media was implemented in all organizations: "The 24-hour emergency line of our structure always remained active, either by phone call, text messages or social media, proving to be essential in supporting victims in emergency situations" (organization 14); "we applied alternative ways to face-to-face contact, namely [by] using social media, such as Facebook, MSN, and other digital platforms, such as WhatsApp" (organization 12).

From this notion of a network, more or less structured, the NGOs started to define "the most pertinent times to make contact" with the victims "without jeopardizing their safety" (organization 4). These networks, which became primarily digital, included all organizations with the common goal of "informing, involving the media" (organization 5) and providing the most effective support possible in the context of confinement. However, these networks may not have been effective, and the issue is the often "amateurish" (organization 2) level of communication, not least because organizations report that alternative forms of contact may even today "not be known to all victims" and that they "have no specific funds" for communication (organization 8).

Discussion

Through the data, it is perceived that the communication of NGOs supporting victims of domestic violence was, on the one hand, essential to the mission of the organizations (Zucco et al., 2021; Fornari et al., 2021a); however, on the other hand, it was unstructured because it is reactive, emergent, and incipient.

As we perceive from the descriptions of the organizations, the perception of communication continues to be essentially one of publicity (Grilo, 2018) and institutional vehicles (MohdHanafiah et al., 2021; O'Toole et al., 2020). And even though the need for communicational involvement is pressing in these organizations, especially with the priority audience, it is not taken as structuring, but as a means to an end (victim support) and not so much as a process of co-development (Sá, 2020) or dialogic relationship (Gonçalves & Lisboa, 2017) between the parties involved.

At the strategic communication planning level, the analyzed organizations lack global, analytical, and systematic thinking about the actions, the objectives, and the audiences involved. While not dismissing the relevance of communication for the proper functioning of the office or structure, the organizations do not situate it as a transversal element to the victim support processes, nor to the NGO. It has, as we have seen, an institutional tendency to relate to the network and within, which results in an amalgam of actions without the necessary connection between them and in amateurish communication, given the lack of communication and public relations professionals in almost all the NGOs interviewed.

This appropriation of communication as a tool leads to the fact that the tactics applied by NGOs since the beginning of the pandemic have been ad hoc, because they do not emanate from strategic planning (Smith, 2017). It is perceived that organizations prioritize the care and support to victims through interpersonal communication, social media, and the telephone, but always in a functional aspect, of necessity, of means to. Or through the publication of information on the organizations' networks, in an organic way, in a top-down style, not involving the various publics (bottom-up option, for example).

The original reason for this nonplanned and instrumental communication may be related to the lack of funding from the funding entities of these offices (national and European governments) for the area of communication, as it is considered as essential as the expertise of the victim support staff.

Conclusions

To the increase in cases of domestic violence, documented or not (UN, 2020; UN Women, 2021a; WHO, 2021a), the COVID-19 pandemic has added the severity and dangerousness of violence (Vieira et al., 2020) in a scenario of great concern and need for intervention by NGOs supporting victims, mainly women, girls, and the elderly (CIG, 2020; Nigam, 2020; Kumar, 2020; Poiares, 2020).

Communication, both from NGOs, victims, and other publics directly or indirectly involved, has become as difficult as it is crucial (OPP, 2020; Barros et al., 2021). While governments were mainly concerned with the advancement of one virus, they did not anticipate the advance of another: that of domestic violence (UN Women, 2020b). Therefore, NGOs, supported by governmental or non-governmental structures, united through the IGC network, became the frontline for the protection and defense of thousands of victims and survivors who, due to the lockdowns, returned to the status of victims, as described by organization 7: "We recorded a 37.1% increase in victims accompanied in previous years who needed support again".

In this context, the organizations decided to maintain part of the face-to-face service and strengthen the service via social media and phone. A decision that arises from the emerging need to adapt to the circumstances that the pandemic has required was not accompanied by a strategic planning of communication, but rather, resulted from an amalgam of communication tactics that came to meet immediate needs, even if in an amateurish and unprepared way.

Our analysis indicates that the vast majority of these NGOs do not have any communication professional to assist them, nor even funds for hiring in this field that, in short, is transversal to all actions of prevention and support to victims and survivors of violence.

Thus, from the empirical study, which engages with the reviewed literature, three essential conclusions emerge: i) the communication of NGOs remains instrumental and institutional; ii) victim support staff in NGOs have a perception of communication as dissemination of their expertise; and iii) NGOs, where the staff is massively exhausted and on the verge of burnout, ignore the need for a strategic planning of communication that involves the various publics in a dialogical and horizontal relationship.

This study presents, even so, shortcomings in terms of the scope of the organizations, since only 30% were analyzed. For future research, we believe it would be useful to analyze the communication of governmental organizations of protection and support to victims of domestic violence.

Notes

1 See Law 59/2007 of September 4 (Portuguese Law).
2 Although we accept the argument used by several feminist approaches about the need to replace the term "victim" with "survivor" as a way to reduce the image of fragility of the woman-victim, we agree with Andrus (2015, p. 5) when she states that she applies the "term 'victim' to emphasize the fact that the law sees women who have been abused by domestic partners as victims", and therefore, "positioning women as 'survivors' potentially reduces the visibility of the crime as well" (p. 6).
3 www.ordemdospsicologos.pt/ficheiros/documentos/covid_19_violencia_domestica.pdf
4 In Portugal, the first nationwide lockdown period began on March 13, 2020, and the second nationwide lockdown began on January 15, 2021.
5 https://op.europa.eu/pt/publication-detail/-/publication/6af1ff62-82e8-11eb-9ac9-01aa75ed71a1/language-en/format-PDF/source-197868801
6 https://violenciagenero.org/noticias/plan-contingencia-contra-violencia-genero-ante-crisis-del-coronavirus
7 www.cig.gov.pt/area-portal-da-violencia/violencia-contra-as-mulheres-e-violencia-domestica/campanhas/campanha-eusobrevivi/
8 www.youtube.com/watch?v=tGHE9WbELaA
9 Associação de Mulheres Contra a Violência, Associação Mulheres Sem Fronteiras, Associação Ser Mulher, Associação Portuguesa de Apoio à Vítima, Associação de Planeamento da Família, Associação Plano I, Associação Portuguesa de Mulheres Juristas, CooLabora, Corações Com Coroa, Feministas em Movimento, Instituto de Apoio à Criança, Movimento Democrático de Mulheres, Plataforma Portuguesa para os Direitos das Mulheres, União das Mulheres Alternativa e Resposta e Quebrar o Silêncio Associação.
10 https://iwpr.org/media/press-releases/new-iwpr-report-highlights-the-systemic-challenges-young-women-of-color-are-facing-in-the-covid-19-pandemic/
11 https://eige.europa.eu/news/gender-equality-index-2021-fragile-gains-big-losses
12 Document available for public download. https://eige.europa.eu/sites/default/files/documents/20210224_mhna30566enn_pdf.pdf
13 https://eige.europa.eu/news/gender-based-violence-costs-eu-eu366-billion-year
14 Available at: http://cienciamerica.uti.edu.ec/openjournal/index.php/uti/article/view/319/580
15 www.guiaderecursosvd.cig.gov.pt/#/
16 The interview was conducted by e-mail and the contacts retrieved by the database made available by CIG.
17 The answers were received between September and November 2021.
18 C (category).
19 The organizations will not be identified. They will be coded as "organization 1", "organization 2", etc.

References

Aires, J., & Sales, C. O. (2020). Tempo e gênero na crise do covid-19. In C. Sales, E. Araújo, & R. Costa (Eds.), *Tempo e Sociedade em Suspenso/Time and society in the lounge* (pp. 173–190). CIES_Iscte. http://doi.org/10.15847/cies2020temposuspenso

Andrus, J. (2015). *Entextualizing domestic violence: Language ideology and violence against women in the Anglo-American Hearsay principle.* Oxford University Press.

APAV. (2021). *Associação Portuguesa de Apoio à Vítima.* Obtido de Folha informativa – violência de género. https://apav.pt/apav_v3/images/pdf/FI_VDG_2020.pdf

AR. (2021, October 18). *Assembleia da República.* Obtido de Legislação na área da Violência Doméstica. www.parlamento.pt/Legislacao/Paginas/Legislacao_AreaViolenciaDomestica.aspx#VDEP

Barros, A., Caldas, G., Sobrinho, S., Oliveira, W., Sousa, L., França, L., . . . Oliveira, R. (2021). COVID-19 X violence: What is your relationship? *Research, Society and Development, 10*(7), e15510616246. https://doi.org/10.33448/rsd-v10i7.16246

Bastos, G., Carbonari, F., & Tavares, P. (2020). *Obtido de Addressing violence against women under COVID-19 in Brazil*. World Bank Open Knowledge. https://openknowledge.worldbank.org/handle/10986/34379

Béres, L. (1999). Beauty and the beast: The romanticization of abuse in popular culture. *European Journal of Cultural Studies*, *2*(2), 191–207. https://doi.org/10.1177/136754949900200203

Boje, D. (2001). *Narrative methods for organizational and communication research*. Sage.

Cabral, M., & Sá, S. (2021). A representatividade da mulher negra na mídia social: O coletivo brasileiro "Pop Afro". *RCL – Revista Comunicação e Linguagens*, *54*, 193–214. https://rcl.fcsh.unl.pt/index.php/rcl/article/view/130

CIG. (2020, November). *Comissão para a Cidadania e a Igualdade de Género*. Obtido de Campanha #EuSobrevivi. www.cig.gov.pt/area-portal-da-violencia/violencia-contra-as-mulheres-e-violencia-domestica/campanhas/campanha-eusobrevivi/

Daymon, C., & Holloway, I. (2011). *Qualitative research methods in public relations and marketing communications* (2nd ed.). Routledge.

Demir, N., Özmutaf, N. M., Bank, R. B., Yılmaz, O. C., Sevgi, H., Coşkun, S., . . . Atay, T. (2021). *Academic studies in humanities and social sciences*. Livre de Lyon.

EIGE. (2021a, March 11). *European institute for gender equality*. Obtido de he Covid-19 pandemic and intimate partner violence against women in the EU. https://op.europa.eu/pt/publication-detail/-/publication/6af1ff62-82e8-11eb-9ac9-01aa75ed71a1/language-en/format-PDF/source-197868801

EIGE. (2021b, July 15). *European institute for gender equality*. Obtido de EU research shows COVID-19 poised to end progress on gender equality. https://eige.europa.eu/news/eu-research-shows-covid-19-poised-end-progress-gender-equality

EIGE. (2021c, October 28). *European institute for gender equality*. Obtido de gender equality index 2021: Fragile gains, big losses. https://eige.europa.eu/news/gender-equality-index-2021-fragile-gains-big-losses

Eiró-Gomes, M., & Neto, C. (2017). O Estatuto da "Comunicação" nas OSC em Portugal: Um primeiro retrato. Em *40º Congresso Brasileiro de Ciências da Comunicação*. Intercom – Sociedade Brasileira de Estudos Interdisciplinares da Comunicação. http://hdl.handle.net/10400.21/7421

Fawole, O., Okedare, O., & Reed, E. (2021). Home was not a safe haven: Women's experiences of intimate partner violence during the COVID-19 lockdown in Nigeria. *BMC Women's Health*, *32*, 21–32. https://doi.org/10.1186/s12905-021-01177-9

Ferreira, G. B., & Borges, S. (2020). Media and misinformation in times of COVID-19: How people informed themselves in the days following the Portuguese declaration of the state of emergency. *Journalism and Media*, *1*(1), 108–121. https://doi.org/10.3390/journalmedia1010008

Forester, S., & O'Brien, C. (2020). Antidemocratic and exclusionary practices: COVID-19 and the continuum of violence. *Politics & Gender*, *16*, 1150–1157. https://doi.org/10.1017/S1743923X2000046X

Fornari, L. F., Lourenço, R. G., Oliveira, R., Santos, D. L., Menegatti, M. S., & Fonseca, R. M. (2021a). Domestic violence against women amidst the pandemic: Coping strategies disseminated by digital media. *Revista Brasileira de Enfermagem*, *4*(1), 1–9. http://doi.org/10.1590/0034-7167-2020-0631

Fornari, L. F., Menegatti, M. S., Lourenço, R. G., Gessner, R., Santos, D. L., Oliveira, R. N., & Fonseca, R. (2021b). Violence against women at the beginning of the Covid-19 pandemic: The discourse of the digital media. *Revista Mineira de Enfermagem*, *25*, e-1388, 1–10. https://doi.org/10.5935/1415.2762.20210036

Fröhlich, R., & Jungblut, M. (2018). Between factoids and facts: The application of 'evidence' in NGO strategic communication on war and armed conflict. *Media, War & Conflict*, *11*(1), 85–106. https://doi.org/10.1177/1750635217727308

Gama, A., Pedro, A., Carvalhoc, M. J., Guerreiro, A., Duarte, V., Quinta, J., . . . Dias, S. (2021). Domestic violence during the COVID-19 pandemic in Portugal. *Portuguese Journal of Public Health*, *38*(1), 32–40. https://doi.org/10.1159/000516228

Gonçalves, G., & Lisboa, J. (2017). ONG e Comunicação dialógica: A AMI em estudo de caso. Em C. Cerqueira & S. Lamy (orgs.), *Vozes Plurais – A comunicação das organizações da sociedade civil* (pp. 49–64). Documenta.

Gonçalves, G., Piñeiro-Naval, V., & Sá, S. (2022). Risk communication and disinformation in Portugal: How media consumption affects the understanding of COVID-19 health-protective messages. Em R. Tench, J. Meng, & A. Moreno (Eds.), *Strategic communication in a global crisis*. Routledge.

Grilo, M. C. (2018). Terceiro Sector: Estratégias, dinâmicas e desafios de comunicação (resenha). *Questões Transversais – Revista de Epistemologias da Comunicação*, *6*(11), 58–60. http://revistas.unisinos.br/index.php/questoes/article/view/17214

Gillham, B. (2005). *Research interviewing. The range of techniques*. Open University Press.

Harsin, J. (2020). Toxic white masculinity, post-truth politics and the Covid-19 infodemic. *European Journal of Cultural Studies*, *23*(6), 1060–1068. https://journals.sagepub.com/doi/full/10.1177/1367549420944934

Heras-Pedrosa, C., Sánchez-Núñez, P., & Peláez, J. I. (2020). Sentiment analysis and emotion understanding during the COVID-19 pandemic in Spain and its impact on digital ecosystems. *International Journal of Environmental Research and Public Health, 17*. https://doi.org/10.3390/ijerph17155542

IWPR. (2020, November). *Institute for women's policy research*. Obtido de New IWPR Report Highlights the Systemic Challenges Young Women of Color Are Facing in the COVID-19 Pandemic. https://iwpr.org/media/press-releases/new-iwpr-report-highlights-the-systemic-challenges-young-women-of-color-are-facing-in-the-covid-19-pandemic/

Katana, E., Amodan, B. O., Bulage, L., Ario, A. R., Fodjo, J. N., Colebunders, R., & Wanyenze, R. K. (2021). Violence and discrimination among Ugandan residents during the COVID-19 lockdown. *BMC Public Health, 21*(1). https://doi.org/10.1186/s12889-021-10532-2

Kay, L., & Wood, H. (2020). Cultural commons: Critical responses to COVID-19, part 2. *European Journal of Cultural Studies, 23*(6), 1019–1024. https://doi.org/10.1177/1367549420952098

Kourti, A., Stavridou, A., Panagouli, E., Psaltopoulou, T., Spiliopoulou, C., Tsolia, M., . . . Tsitsika, A. (2021). Domestic violence during the COVID-19 pandemic: A systematic review. *Trauma, Violence, & Abuse*. https://doi.org/10.1177/15248380211038690

Kumar, A. (2020). COVID-19 and domestic violence: A possible public health crisis. *Journal of Health Management, 22*(2), 192–196. https://doi.org/10.1177/0972063420932765

Lucas, B., & Landman, T. (2021). Social listening, modern slavery, and COVID-19. *Journal of Risk Research, 24*(3–4), 314–334. https://doi.org/10.1080/13669877.2020.1864009

López-Hernández, E., & Rubio-Amores, D. (2020). Reflexiones sobre la violencia intrafamiliar y violencia de género durante la emergencia por COVID-19. *CienciAmérica, 9*(2), 312–321. http://dx.doi.org/10.33210/ca.v9i2.319.

Mahapatro, M., Prasad, M. M., & Singh, S. P. (2021). Role of social support in women facing domestic violence during lockdown of Covid-19 while cohabiting with the abusers: Analysis of cases registered with the family counseling centre, Alwar, India. *Journal of Family Issues 2021, 42*(11), 2609–2624. https://doi.org/10.1177/0192513X20984496

Mahardika, D. A. (2020). Communication strategy for women organizations in minimizing female violence during pandemic. *INJECT – Interdisciplinary Journal of Communication, 5*(1), 41–58. https://doi.org/10.18326/inject.v5i1.41-58

Marques, E., Moraes, C., Hasselmann, M., Deslandes, S. F., & Reichenheim, M. (2020). A violência contra mulheres, crianças e adolescentes em tempos de pandemia pela COVID-19: Panorama, motivações e formas de enfrentamento. *Cad. Saúde Pública, 36*(4), e00074420. https://doi.org/10.1590/0102-311X00074420

May, D. (2002). *Qualitative research in action*. Sage.

Medel-Herrero, A., Shumway, M., Smiley-Jewell, S., Bonomid, A., & Reidye, D. (2020). The impact of the great recession on California domestic violence events, and related hospitalizations and emergency service visits. *Preventive Medicine, 139*, 106186. https://doi.org/10.1016/j.ypmed.2020.106186

MohdHanafiah, K., Ng, C., & Wan, A. (2021). Effective communication at different phases of COVID-19 prevention: Roles, enablers and barriers. *Viruses, 13*(6), 1058. https://doi.org/10.3390/v13061058

Nigam, S. (2020). *COVID-19, lockdown and violence against women in homes*. SSRN. http://doi.org/10.2139/ssrn.3587399

Okviana, L., Nanda, S., & Fitriyah, P. (2020). *Analysis of public communication strategy during the Covid-19 pandemic*. 6th International Conference on Social and Political Sciences (ICOSAPS 2020), Advances in Social Science, Education and Humanities Research (Vol. 510, pp. 189–193, ISSN (Online): 2352-5398). Atantic Press.

Oliveira, E. (2019). Strategic communication and NGOs. In *The instigatory theory of NGO communication*. Springer VS. https://doi.org/10.1007/978-3-658-26858-9_4

Oliveira, M., & Fernandes, C. (2020). Managing the Coronavirus pandemic in Portugal: A step-by-step adjustment of health and social services. *American Psychological Association, 12*(5), 536–538, ISSN: 1942-9681

Oliveira, W., Magrin, J., Andrade, A., Micheli, D., Carlos, D., Fernández, J., & Santos, M. (2020). Violência por parceiro íntimo em tempos da covid-19: Scoping review. *Psicologia, Saúde & Doenças, 21*(3), 606–623. http://dx.doi.org/10.15309/20psd210306

OPP. (2020, March 30). *Ordem dos Psicólogos Portugueses*. Obtido de Covid-19: Isolamento com direitos – conter o vírus e a violência doméstica. www.ordemdospsicologos.pt/ficheiros/documentos/covid_19_violencia_domestica.pdf

O'Toole, L., Schiffman, J., & Sullivan, R. (2020). *Gender violence: Interdisciplinary perspectives* (3rd ed.). New York University Press. https://doi.org/10.18574/9781479801794

Pai, A. A., & Ashok, L. (2020). An outstanding contribution of NGOs was in developing communication strategies in different vernaculars which went a long way in taking awareness measures to the community level. *Adelaide Journal of Social Work, 7*(1), 5–16, ISSN2349-4123

Phipps, A. (2021). White tears, white rage: Victimhood and (as) violence in mainstream feminism. *European Journal of Cultural Studies*, *24*(1), 81–93. https://doi.org/10.1177%2F1367549420985852

Pilipchuk, M. (2020, September). A crisis ignored: Domestic violence and the COVID-19 pandemic. *Feminism and Philosophy*, *20*(1).

Poiares, N. (2020). *Violência Doméstica, Polícia e COVID-19*. *Polícia Portuguesa*. Direção Nacional da PSP. http://hdl.handle.net/20.500.12207/5270

Ranee, A. (2021). Covid-19 pandemic and related rise in domestic violence. *Academia Open Access*, 1–5.

Riley, A. H., Sangalang, A., Critchlow, E., Brown, N., Mitra, R., & Nesme, B. C. (2021). Entertainment-education campaigns and COVID-19: How three global organizations adapted the health communication strategy for pandemic response and takeaways for the future. *Health Communication*, *36*(1), 42–49. https://doi.org/10.1080/10410236.2020.1847451

Ruiz-Pérez, I., & Pastor-Moreno, G. (2020). Medidas de contención de la violencia de género durante la pandemia de COVID-19Measures to contain gender-based violence during the COVID-19 pandemic. *Gaceta Sanitaria*, *35*(4), 389–394. https://doi.org/10.1016/j.gaceta.2020.04.005

Sá, S. (2020). As RP em rede e o envolvimento dialógico em plataformas feministas ("A Coletiva" e "INMUNE"). *Revista Internacional de Relaciones Públicas*, *10*(20), 5–26. http://dx.doi.org/10.5783/RIRP-20-2020-02-05-26

Seidman, I. (2006). *Interviewing as qualitative research: A guide for researchers in education and the social sciences* (3rd ed.). Columbia University.

Servaes, J., & Malikhao, P. (2020). Communication for development and social change: Three development paradigms, two communication models, and many applications and approaches. In J. Servaes (Ed.), *Handbook of communication for development and social change* (pp. 64–90). Springer Nature. https://doi.org/10.1007/978-981-15-2014-3_110

Silva, V. F. (2018). As mídias sociais e sua contribuição na comunicação de ONGs. *Revista Especialize On-line IPOG*, *9*(1), 16, ISSN 2179-5568

Silva, A. F., Estrela, F. M., Magalhães, J., Lima, N., Morais, A., Gomes, N., & Lima, V. (2020). Marital violence precipitating/intensifying elements during the Covid-19 pandemic. *Ciênc. Saúde Coletiva*, *25*(9), 3475–3480. https://doi.org/10.1590/1413-81232020259.16132020

Slakoff, D., Aujla, W., & PenzeyMoog, E. (2020). The role of service providers, technology, and mass media when home isn't safe for intimate partner violence victims: Best practices and recommendations in the era of COVID-19 and beyond. *Archives of Sexual Behavior*, *49*, 2779–2788. https://doi.org/10.1007/s10508-020-01820-w

Smith, D. (2017). *Strategic planning for public relations* (5th ed.). Routledge.

Sobande, F. (2020). 'We're all in this together': Commodified notions of connection, care and community in brand responses to COVID-19. *European Journal of Cultural Studies*, *23*(6), 1033–1037. https://doi.org/10.1177/1367549420932294journals.sagepub.com/home/ecs

Stark, E., & Flitcraft, A. (1996). *Women at risk: Domestic violence and women's health*. Sage Publications.

Tufte, T. (2017). *Communication and social change – a citizen perspective*. Polity.

UN. (2020). UN chief calls for domestic violence 'ceasefire' amid 'horrifying global surge'. *un.org*. https://news.un.org/en/story/2020/04/1061052

UN Women. (2020a). *Tech giants partner with UN women to provide life-saving information to survivors of domestic violence during COVID-19*. www.unwomen.org/en/news/stories/2020/6/news-tech-giants-provide-life-saving-information-during-covid-19

UN Women. (2020b). *Trust fund assesses COVID-19 impact on violence against women and front line organizations*. www.unwomen.org/en/news/stories/2020/10/news-untf-report-shows-covid-19-impact-on-violence-against-women

UN Women. (2021a). *Facts and figures: Ending violence against women*. www.unwomen.org/en/what-we-do/ending-violence-against-women/facts-and-figures

UN Women & ILO. (2021). *United Nations entity for gender equality and the empowerment of women & international labour organization*. Obtido de The COVID-19 shadow pandemic: Domestic violence in the world of work: A call to action for the private sector. www.unwomen.org/en/digital-library/publications/2020/06/brief-domestic-violence-in-the-world-of-work

Vieira, P. R., Garcia, L. P., & Maciel, E. N. (2020). Isolamento social e o aumento da violência doméstica: O que isso nos revela? *Revista Brasileira de Epidemiologia*, *23*, e200033. https://doi.org/10.1590/1980-549720200033

Weder, F. (2021). Sustainability as master frame of the future? Potency and limits of sustainability as normative framework in corporate, political and NGO communication. In F. Weder, L. Krainer, & M. Karmasin (Eds.), *The sustainability communication reader*. Springer VS. https://doi.org/10.1007/978-3-658-31883-3_7

Wells, L. (2020). Media monitoring during COVID-19: Domestic violence, sexual violence, child abuse, women's rights, gender equality. *Sh!ft: The Program to End Domestic Violence*, 1–112. http://dx.doi.org/10.11575/PRISM/38329

WHO. (2021a, March 9). *Obtido de violence against women*. World Health Organization. www.who.int/news-room/fact-sheets/detail/violence-against-women

WHO. (2021b). *Obtido de levels of domestic violence increase globally, including in the region, as COVID-19 pandemic escalates*. World Health Organization. www.emro.who.int/violence-injuries-disabilities/violence-news/levels-of-domestic-violence-increase-as-covid-19-pandemic-escalates.html

Wong, J. Y., Wai, A., Wang, M. P., Lee, J. J., Li, M., Kwok, J., . . . Choi, A. (2021). Impact of COVID-19 on child maltreatment: Income instability and parenting issues. *International Journal of Environmental Research and Public Health*, *18*(4). https://doi.org/10.3390/ijerph18041501

Yang, A., & Saffer, A. J. (2021). Standing out in a networked communication context: Toward a network contingency model of public attention. *New Media & Society*, *23*(10), 2902–2925. https://doi.org/10.1177/1461444820939445

Zucco, F. D., Machado, J., Quadros, C. M., & Fiuza, T. F. (2021). Comunicación en el tercer sector antes y durante la Pandemia COVID 19: Estrategias de comunicación en las redes sociales de las ONG de Blumenau, Santa Catarina, Brasil. *Ámbitos. Revista Internacional de Comunicación*, *52*, 140–155. https://dx.doi.org/10.12795/Ambitos.2021.i52.09

4.5
FUNDRAISING STRATEGIES DURING PANDEMIC CHALLENGES

Laura Visan

"[These are] people who don't know much about medicine, but know a lot about community" (ARC, representative, personal communication, May 19, 2021). This is what a representative of the Association for Community Relations (ARC) in Romania commented about the resilience of the community foundations which, in a quick response to a crisis situation, conducted fundraising campaigns for medical equipment and supplies that were donated to hospitals in Romania. Such initiatives indicate that interpersonal trust and the civic spirit are developing in Romania, although civic initiatives are still scarce, according to a recent Eurobarometer survey that ranks Romania in the last position among the European Union (EU) states for community engagement (European Parliament, 2020).

To set the context, the chapter begins by explaining that the lack of inclination for civic participation in today's society is rooted in communism, when suspicion dominated interpersonal relations, state surveillance was omnipresent, and the mandatory community work was a form of keeping people's free time under control. The 1989 anti-communist revolution, with the shift from a totalitarian regime to a democratic one, did not bring a significant change in Romanians' civic participation practices and attitudes towards civic participation.

However, this gap begins to be addressed, thanks to the efforts of the local third sector. Building on a case study ethnographic method, the remainder of the chapter will present the fundraising campaign developed by the Community Foundation Țara Făgărașului (CFTF) in response to the COVID-19 pandemic. The case study will draw from content posted by the CFTF on social media, which consisted exclusively of updates on the fundraising campaign and on the actions undertaken in cooperation with the local authorities, and from five ethnographic interviews with two representatives of the ARC, a management representative of the CFTF, a volunteer from the local community, and a representative of the Social Services Department from the City of Făgăraș.

Romania before the 1989 anti-communist revolution: lack of interpersonal trust, fear of surveillance, and mandatory community work

The existence of social capital, the "glue that holds [people] together" (Huysman & Wulf, 2004, p. 1) depends on the trust manifested in interpersonal relations, as without trust, our various forms of association could hardly function (Putnam, 2000, p. 18; Hooghe, 2008; Fennema & Tillie, 2008). Social capital resources also lie at the core of civil societies as interfaces between the macro level of the state and the micro level of citizens (Nagle & Mahr, 1999, p. 64), but they can only develop in democratic regimes. This was not the case of Romania before 1989, as will be discussed next.

During communism, Central European countries had a thicker civil society fabric than the Eastern European ones: Romania, Bulgaria, and Albania. In Poland, the Catholic Church and the Solidarity movement insistently voiced their criticisms against the communist authorities (Smolar, 1996, pp. 26–31; Wallace et al., 2012, p. 4), while Czechoslovakia had the "Charter 77" advocacy group (Verdery, 1991, p. 310). In turn, the few civic organizations active in Romania offered in-kind incentives for their members, but were less than vocal in opposing Nicolae Ceaușescu's regime (Verdery, 1991).

During the last decade of communism, the Central European states began to introduce Mikhail Gorbachev's perestroika model, gradually allowing the existence of semi-private enterprises and various forms of association. (Gilberg, 1990, pp. 217–219; Tismaneanu, 2003; Chen, 2003, p. 187). In turn, Nicolae Ceaușescu subjected Romania to a "sultanistic" regime of power, reminiscent of North Korea (Linz & Stepan, 1996, p. 347), ostentatiously rejecting the social and economic reforms that were implemented in the neighbouring countries. Furthermore, during the late 1980s, the state intensified the surveillance of its citizens. Afraid to express their dissent towards authorities for fear of retaliations that could go from workplace demotions to police harassment or even to jail time, most Romanians developed a small personal network consisting of safe persons, i.e., trusted not to be informers of the secret police (Gilberg, 1990; Linz & Stepan, 1996; Mondak & Gearing, 2003; Howard, 2003, p. 174). "Wary of strangers" (Uslaner, 2003, p. 81) and "afraid to trust all but their closest friends" (Uslaner & Badescu, 2004, p. 38), people limited their interactions with persons outside this network.

Before 1989, Romanians had to attend muncă patriotică (patriotic work), helping with agricultural works, doing work on construction sites or sweeping sidewalks in the city. Many of these tasks were utterly useless, but they allowed the state to control people's free time and to prevent them from attending religious service. Missing patriotic work was sanctioned by steep fines or, in the case of students, by grade penalties. So vivid the memory of doing these chores was that, more than 10 years after the 1989 revolution, some persons were still reluctant to volunteer, although they acknowledged the difference between genuine civic participation and muncă patriotică (Vișan, 2013).

Romania after 1989: low appetite for civic engagement, with some promising signs

The decades of communism "bred atomized, amoral cynics good at doubletalk and 'working the system', but not at effective enterprise" (Smolar, 1996, p. 33), with "particularized trust" prevailing over "generalized trust" (Bădescu et al., 2004, p. 321; Sapsford & Abbott, 2006). Things did not significantly change after 1989, as the former party apparatchiks preserved their political and economic privileges, along with their network of ties that were inaccessible to ordinary citizens. Under these circumstances, Romanians' initial enthusiasm soon gave way to the discomfiting realization that the substantial change of regimes they had hoped for was more of a cabinet reshuffle.

Empirical evidence demonstrates that the stock of interpersonal trust has remained low after 1989, same as Romanians' interest in joining community organizations and engaging in civic matters (see Bădescu et al., 2004, p. 341 for a correlation between organization membership and the inclination to actively participate in community, and Pop-Eleches & Tucker, 2013, pp. 63–64). It has been suggested that during the 1990s Romanians did not feel represented by the civic organizations, many of them funded from the West (Chen, 2003, p. 199) and that "[t]he rule in post-89 Romania [was] non-participation" (Teodorescu & Sultănescu, 2015, p. 221). Furthermore, in 2020 only 4% of Romanians make donations to civic society organizations, and only 3% "regularly" volunteer, with Romania ranking the lowest among the EU states in these respects (European Parliament,

2020, p. 8). However, the civic engagement gap indicated by the mentioned research begins to be addressed, thanks to the efforts of the local third-sector organizations, such as community foundations, whose role will be presented next.

The role of community foundations in empowering the local leaders

In 2005, the ARC, whose mandate was to develop "an infrastructure for philanthropy" ("Programele noastre", 2019), created a pilot programme for developing community foundations. These organizations were intended to become key actors in their local communities, identifying projects and opportunities that required funding and know-how support, and bridging them with donors. As of 2021 there are 19 community foundations in Romania, most located in the geographical areas of Transylvania and Moldova, and in Bucharest, the capital city. Between 2008 and 2019 the foundations have raised a total of 8,837,933 USD that were distributed as grants for education, health, social inclusion, and environment and biodiversity. Two important factors that made community foundations a model of success are the capacity building through the involvement of local leaders and the complete transparency about the spending procedures. As an ARC representative shared in an interview conducted for this research,

> Foundations involve the communities in their projects. "Let's make a fund to repair a public square", but before shoveling the ground, they go to the square, talk to the people there, to understand their needs, work with them, involve them as much as they want to be involved. Foundations are successful because they involve people from the very beginning. . . . There is a bubble of trust that keeps growing.
>
> (ARC representative 2)

The ARC and the community foundations responded quickly to the crisis caused by the COVID-19 pandemic. Shortly after the first case of COVID-19 was announced in the territory of Romania, on 26 February 2020, the ARC created a National Emergency Fund. The fund raised almost 6,000,000 RON (the equivalent of 1,457,000 USD) from individual and institutional donors. The entire amount was directed to the local community foundations, which had already initiated fundraising campaigns in order to purchase medical equipment and supplies for the local hospitals. An example in this sense is the campaign Împreună pentru Făgăraș/Together for Făgăraș, developed by the CFTF, discussed next.

Împreună pentru Făgăraș/together for Făgăraș: a case study

The campaign implemented by the CFTF from March to April 2020 is presented here through a case study methodological approach. This initiative does meet the criteria of a case study, as it had clear time boundaries, and it was representative of a broader, yet unique phenomenon (Yin, 1989, p. 31, Merriam, 2002, p. 7). The broader framework is represented by the projects of Romanian not-for-profit organizations in areas where the resources of the local authorities are insufficient, such as public health, while the unique aspect comes from the particularities of the Făgăraș area.

The case study is not intended to be "all things to all people" (Flyvberg, 2006, p. 238). Generalization would be impossible, given the specifics of the local context. The attempt to generalize at all costs has its own caveats, Lincoln and Guba suggest, pointing instead to Stake's direction of a naturalistic generalization (2009, pp. 30–36). This recommends a detailed description of a particular case, programme, or event, so that the audiences find it relatable; in other words, readers should be able "to apply ideas from the natural and in-depth depictions presented in case studies to personal contexts" (Mills et al., 2010, p. 600). Instead, this case study aims to present the development of the anti-COVID campaign in the Făgăraș area and the ensemble of actors that made it possible: the foundation employees and volunteers who developed and coordinated the campaign, attuning it to the diverse voices of the community; the local authorities, challenged by an emergency situation they had not encountered before, yet willing to cooperate with local organizations and accept their local support; and the ARC representatives who supported the efforts of the Făgăraș foundation, supplementing the funds raised locally.

In a case study, setting the context is a necessary step (Yin, 1989, pp. 13–18; Flyvberg, 2006, p. 222; Lincoln & Guba, 2009, pp. 30–34), so a brief description of Făgăraș will precede the presentation of the CFTF. This region is situated in the centre of Romania, in Brașov County. The local economy is sluggish, although the authorities have made efforts to capitalize on the touristic potential of the area. After 1989 most state-owned factories closed, as they could not face the transition from a centrally planned economy to a market economy. The opportunities for professional reconversion were scarce, so many residents of Făgăraș moved to more prosperous areas of Romania or emigrated to Western Europe or North America.

Founded in 2013, the CFTF targets more than 140,000 persons in the urban and rural communities of Făgăraș with projects related to public health and education. According to the ARC representatives interviewed for this chapter, the sense of local pride is particularly powerful among the Făgăraș residents, nourishing their sense of community. There are, however, several characteristics that make the CFTF and the Făgăraș area unique. First, although there are two community foundations in the Brașov county, one in Făgăraș, the other in the city of Brașov, they cooperate rather than being in competition. Second, CFTF serves a community that is not affluent, differing thus from the pattern noticed by the ARC representatives: financial wealth correlates with civic vibrancy. Most of the Făgăraș residents are children, seniors, or youths who are also planning to leave, while the persons who are most likely to participate in the community – i.e., aged between 30 and 50 – have already left Făgăraș in search for better professional opportunities. And yet the CFTF is one of the most active foundations, with a strong enterprising spirit, whose success is due to the social cohesiveness of the area and to the supportiveness of the local authorities.

The presentation of the Împreună pentru sănătate (COVID-19)/Together for health (COVID-19) campaign will draw from the content that the CFTF posted on its Facebook page between March and April 2020, as this was the main platform used to document the development of the campaign, and from five ethnographic interviews conducted remotely between April and June 2021.

The research sample includes two representatives of the ARC, a management representative of the CFTF, a volunteer from the local community, and a representative of the Social Services Department from the city of Făgăraș. For confidentiality purposes, the respondents will only be identified through their professional roles. As far as the CFTF social media communication is concerned, it is important to mention that it consisted exclusively of updates on the fundraising campaign, with regular listings of the medical equipment and supplies purchased up to that moment, and on the actions undertaken in cooperation with the local authorities. It may be argued that, thanks to its transparency, this represents an example of effective organizational communication, much needed, given the often contradictory messages transmitted by the Romanian authorities in the first stage of the pandemic.

Launched on 17 March 2020, the campaign aimed to raise at least 100,000 RON (approximately 25,000 USD) to purchase a portable ventilator and a defibrillator for the Dr. Aurel Tulbure Municipal Hospital in Făgăraș. The CFTF staff and board members felt that it was their duty to initiate this campaign, considering that the hospital was "unprepared for everyday emergencies, let alone a pandemic" (CFTF management representative). Donations could be made via bank deposit or a dedicated short message service. On social media the campaign ran under the hashtag acumemomentul (#nowisthemoment). The status of donations was posted in a Google document that was regularly updated.

The foundation volunteers who were not involved in the fundraising activities helped in different ways, such as running errands for the seniors who could not leave their homes, with the support of the Social Services Division at the city of Făgăraș which coordinated all requests for help. The mobilization was exemplary: the CFTF volunteers were joined by volunteers from other organizations, including the Maria Brâncoveanu Church, the Partida Romilor associatio, representing the Roma ethnic group in the Făgăraș area, and an association that offers palliative care services.

Individual donations for the campaign came from many sources, including: the "internal diaspora", as the CFTF representatives call it: young people who had left the Făgăraș area but whose grandparents still live there; the residents of a village, who collected a little over 1,000 RON [250 USD]; the UNIREA Retirees' Association, with a 1,000-RON contribution "from [its] meagre budget"; and members of the Romanian diasporas donated 24,000 USD, reaffirming their attachment to the Făgăraș area.

The funds raised by the CFTF representatives were supplemented by a grant from the National Emergency Fund created by the ARC. The Făgăraș City Hall cancelled all the events scheduled for 2020 and redirected the amount of 787,000 RON [197,000 USD] to the municipal hospital. At the end of the campaign, the CFTF provided a detailed update of the donations raised since mid-March 2020: 446,292 RON [115,000 EUR] that helped purchase medical equipment and supplies, including two VG70 ventilators, a defibrillator, a ventilator, an oxygen redactor, a steel tank for medical oxygen, 285 hazmat suits, 150 boxes of gloves (Fundația Comunitară, April 15, 2020). All purchases were made after consultation with the management of the municipal hospital, and their complete list is still available on the Facebook page of CFTF.

All respondents agreed that the community mobilization was the most rewarding part of the Împreună pentru sănătate (COVID-19) campaign. "People felt very impressed by the fact that somebody cared about them and was able to help them" (volunteer from the local community). Reflecting on the CFTF campaign, the ARC representatives were pleased to notice the effectiveness of the philanthropy infrastructure they had been developing for 10 years. In some cases, local community foundations responded faster and more effectively to the pandemic crisis than the local authorities:

> We bought a PCR testing machine from a supplier in South Korea that Bogdan Tanase from the Iasi foundation had found. In 10–12 days the machine arrived in Romania, while the state needed a month or two to buy a machine like that.
> (ARC representative 1, personal communication, 19 May 2021)

Among the challenges of the campaign, the respondents mentioned the long delivery times of the medical equipment and the donors' reluctance to contribute money to other initiatives: "we couldn't ask for more money, because they told us, we've done enough" (CFTF management representative); the fear-inducing way in which the central authorities managed the pandemic: "those emergency acts only issued at night time that caused terrible anxiety to many people" (volunteer from the local community); and the authorities' lack of preparedness and resources: "the customs officers came and said 'we don't have masks, please give us some'" (ARC representative 1). The representative of the Social Services Department from the city of Făgăraș was disappointed to see that as soon as the crisis moment was over, people's willingness to volunteer diminished and that civic participation did not become a habit, as he had hoped: "we returned to our old routine, to our typical selfishness from before the pandemic".

Conclusion

This chapter presented the fundraising campaign of the CFTF in support of the local hospital during the first wave of the COVID-19 pandemic. Though implemented in just two months, March and April 2020, by a small number of people – the foundation employees and a group of volunteers – the campaign raised approximately 107,000 USD that was used to purchase medical equipment and supplies. This campaign represented an impressive mobilization of resources, attracting donations from individual donors, some of them with limited incomes, and from local and multinational companies. Members of Romanian diasporas also contributed to the fundraising, reasserting their emotional ties with the Făgăraș area and with their homeland. Aside from the funds raised, this campaign brought around the same table all the community stakeholders: donors, some of whom had never contributed with cash before; representatives of the local community; local authorities; and the hospital management. The social media communication of the CFTF campaign consisted exclusively of updates on the fundraising campaign, including listings of the medical equipment recently purchased and on the actions undertaken in cooperation with the local authorities. Further research is necessary, but it may be argued that this approach was a key factor in the success of the campaign by strengthening the trust of the community in the campaign and making people more willing to donate. The CFTF gave pre-eminence to factual information and communicated it in a straightforward manner, in contrast to the discourse of the central authorities, which was often contradictory, particularly in the first stage of the pandemic. This campaign, and the similar initiatives developed by community foundations in Romania, supported by the ARC National Emergency Fund, were necessary interventions, as the state authorities seemed overwhelmed in the first weeks of the COVID-19 pandemic. An important lesson of the last year was that "large-scale results are often best achieved through strong cross-sector coordination, rather than from the isolated intervention of individual organizations" (Gurescu, 2020). This is also a good indicator that the gap in civic participation between Romania and the other EU countries, particularly those in Western and Northern Europe, can be recuperated. A concerning tendency, though, is people's willingness to volunteer only at moments of crisis, as the Social Services Division representative mentioned in the interview cited earlier. If local communities are able to transform civic participation into a habit, as opposed to a one-time response to a crisis situation, it could be yet another successful initiative developed by the community foundations in Romania.

Acknowledgements

To the respondents who graciously accepted to be interviewed for this research: I am humbled by your dedication in support of the local community and wish you would receive more of the public recognition you deserve. This research is my token of gratitude for you.

Thank you to Dr. Gisela Gonçalves and Dr. Evandro Oliveira for bravely guiding us through the editorial process and to the anonymous reviewer for their valuable suggestions.

References

Bădescu, G., Sum, P., & Uslaner, E. M. (2004). Civil society development and democratic values in Romania and Moldova. *East European Politics and Societies*, *18*(2), 316–341. https://doi.org/10.1177/0888325403259915

Chen, C. (2003). The roots of illiberal nationalism in Romania: A historical institutionalist analysis of the leninist legacy. *East European Politics and Societies*, *17*(2), 166–201. https://doi.org/10.1177/0888325403017002002

European Parliament. (2020). *Civic engagement, flash eurobarometer, a public opinion monitoring study*. www.europarl.europa.eu/at-your-service/files/be-heard/eurobarometer/2020/civic_engagement/report/en-report.pdf

Fennema, M., & Tillie, J. (2008). Social capital in multicultural societies. In D. Castiglione, J. W. Van Deth, & G. Wolleb (Eds.), *The handbook of social capital* (pp. 349–370). Oxford University Press.

Flyvbjerg, B. (2006). Five misunderstandings about case-study research. *Qualitative Inquiry*, (12), 219–245. https://doi.org/10.1177/1077800405284363

Fundația Comunitară Țara Făgărașului. (2020, April 15). https://ro-ro.facebook.com/fundatiacomunitaratarafagarasului/

Gilberg, T. (1990). *Nationalism and Communism in Romania*. Westview Press.

Gurescu, G. (2020, September 7). Baptism by fire: How Romania's community foundations rallied in the face of COVID-19. *Global Fund*. https://globalfundcommunityfoundations.org/blog/pulling-together-for-the-national-good-lessons-from-romanias-community-foundations-covid-19-response/?fbclid=IwAR3smJ2lxKK_dzVJoEsl0wa0iZP_lYSe1tj5Eb9JUaeljXroSbphqQbm0BQ

Hooghe, M. (2008). Voluntary associations and socialization. In D. Castiglione, J. W. Van Deth, & G. Wolleb (Eds.), *The handbook of social capital* (pp. 568–593). Oxford University Press.

Howard, M. M. (2003). Why post-communist citizens do not join voluntary organizations. In G. Badescu & E. Uslaner (Eds.), *Social capital and the transition to democracy* (pp. 165–183). Routledge.

Huysman, M., & Wulf, V. (2004). Social capital and information technology: Current debates and research. In M. Huysman & V. Wulf (Eds.), *Social capital and information technology* (pp. 1–16). MIT Press.

Lincoln, Y., & Guba, E. (2009). The only generalization is: There is no generalization. In R. Gomm, M. Hammersley, & P. Foster (Eds.), *Case study method* (pp. 27–44). Sage Publications Ltd, https://www-doi-org.myaccess.library.utoronto.ca/10.4135/9780857024367

Linz, J. J., & Stepan, A. (1996). *Problems of democratic transition and consolidation: Southern Europe, South America, and post-communist Europe*. The Johns Hopkins University Press.

Mills, A. J., Durepos, G., & Wiebe, E. (2010). *Encyclopedia of case study research* (Vol. 1). Sage Publications, Inc. https://doi.org/10.4135/9781412957397

Merriam, S. B. (2002). *Qualitative research in practice: Examples for discussion and analysis*. Jossey-Bass.

Mondak, J. J., & Gearing, A. F. (2003). Civic engagement in a post-communist state. In G. Badescu & E. M. Uslaner (Eds.), *Social capital and the transition to democracy* (pp. 140–164). Routledge.

Nagle, J., & Mahr, A. (1999). *Democracy and democratization*. Sage.

Pop-Eleches, G., & Tucker, J. A. (2013). Associated with the past?: Communist legacies and civic participation in post-communist countries. *East European Politics and Societies, 27*(1), 45–68. https://doi.org/10.1177/0888325412465087

Programele noastre de filantropie responsabilă [Our programs for responsible philanthropy]. (2019). *ARC*. Retrieved May 25, 2021, from https://arcromania.ro/arc/programe/

Putnam, R. D. (2000). *Bowling alone: The collapse and revival of American community*. Simon & Schuster.

Sapsford, R., & Abbott, P. (2006). Trust, confidence and social environment in post-communist societies. *Communist and Post-Communist Studies, 39*(1), 59–71. https://doi.org/10.1016/j.postcomstud.2005.12.003

Smolar, A. (1996). Civil society after communism: From opposition to atomization. *Journal of Democracy, 7*(1), 24–38. https://doi.org/10.1353/jod.1996.0018

Teodorescu, B., & Sultănescu, D. (2015). The electoral Republic of Romania: Arguments about the need for an analysis regarding the Romanian participatory culture. Polis. *Journal of Political Science, III*(10), 219–233.

Tismaneanu, V. (2003). *Stalinism for all seasons: A political history of Romanian communism*. University of California Press.

Uslaner, E. M. (2003). Trust and civic engagement in East and West. In G. Badescu & E. M. Uslaner (Eds.), *Social capital and the transition to democracy* (pp. 81–94). Routledge.

Uslaner, E. M., & Badescu, G. (2004). Honesty, trust, and legal norms in the transition to democracy: Why bo Rothstein is better able to explain Sweden than Romania. In J. Kornai, S. Rose-Ackerman, & B. Rothstein (Eds.), *Creating social trust in post-socialist transition* (pp. 31–53). Palgrave.

Verdery, K. (1991). *National ideology under socialism: Identity and cultural politics in Ceausescu's Romania*. University of California Press.

Vișan, L. (2013). *Creating social capital resources: A case study of Romanian immigrants in Toronto and the greater Toronto area*. CERIS Working Paper, No. 93. CERIS.

Wallace, C., Pichler, F., & Haerpfer, C. (2012). Changing patterns of civil society in Europe and America 1995–2005: Is Eastern Europe different? *East European Politics and Societies, 26*(1), 3–19. https://doi.org/10.1177/0888325411401380

Yin, R. K. (1989). *Case study research: Design and methods*. Sage Publications.

4.6
COMMUNICATION AND ACTIVIST LITERACY FOR SOCIAL CHANGE IN FEMINIST MOVEMENTS

Alessandra Farné, Carla Cerqueira and Eloísa Nos-Aldás

Introduction[1]

In 2017, feminism worldwide was reinvigorated by the #MeToo and Latin American #NiUnaMenos [Not One Less] movements, with first stoppages called as part of the International Women's Day demonstrations on March 8 (8M); in Spain, the national movement organized partial shutdowns for a few hours that enjoyed some support but which inspired a bigger event the following year (Campillo, 2018). In 2018, for the first time in Spain, a major feminist strike was held that brought out tens of thousands of women in mobilizations across the country. It drew international headlines and inspired women in other countries, such as in Portugal, to call for a similar stoppage, although turnout was patchy. This success led to the calling of the 8M feminist strike in 2019, which gained greater adherence in both countries and therefore provides ample material for understanding the differences, similarities and evolution of this phenomenon in the Iberian context.

The objective of this chapter is to analyze the 2019 8M feminist strikes in Spain and Portugal to trace elements of cultural efficacy in their discourse and discuss how they contributed to the movements' communication and activist practices.

This study adopts an activist communication perspective (Pinazo-Calatayud & Nos-Aldás, 2016; Pinazo-Calatayud et al., 2020) that identifies in protest scenarios a series of practices that represent an advance for researchers and practitioners in relation to the traditional communication for development/communication for social change (CDSC) studies. Thus, theoretically, it is grounded in the interdisciplinary approach of transgressive communication (Nos-Aldás & Farné, 2020) as a feminist, cultural, postcolonial and critical step forward (hooks, 1994; Lagarde-y-de-los-Ríos, 2005) focused on the transformation of the symbolic and structural root causes of suffering, inequality and diversity and based on reframing representations through universal, inclusive and emancipatory values (Mesa et al., 2013).

Theoretical framework

Communication for social change has evolved as a field in recent decades, shifting from traditions of communication for development linked to institutional cooperation and charities (Melkote, 1991; Servaes, 2002) to more participatory perspectives (Marí-Sáez, 2020; Nos-Aldás & Farné, 2020; Tufte, 2017). Recent trends in "communicating for change" (Tacchi & Tufte, 2020) are based on critical perspectives from postdevelopment, cultural and feminist studies (Bachmann & Proust, 2020; De-Sousa-Santos, 2012) and the effects of the reactivation of social movements in the last decade since the emergence of the Arab Spring, Occupy and, particularly in Spain, the 15M movements (Bernal-Triviño & Sanz-Martos, 2020).

This CDSC paradigm is nurtured from the evolution of media and communication research and its cultural and social turn (Baú, 2016; Hemer & Tufte, 2016), as well as cross-reflections with the field of education for development (Riek, 2015; Skinner et al., 2016) to converge as a communication field understood as agency (Jacobson, 2016). Following this conceptual shift from an instrumental approach to the dialogic transformative potential of activist communication, this chapter relates to previous debates on how to define and assess the efficacy of a participatory, emancipatory communication for the nonprofit sector (Oliveira et al., 2016).

This study connects with the political implications of CDCS, understanding politics in terms of collective negotiations and decisions, resistance and change and culture and power (Durham & Kellner, 2012; Wilkins, 2014), together with trends focused on civil society, both structured (non-governmental organizations [NGOs] and formal associations) and fluid social movements (collectives and alliances). Nonprofit communication is not understood here as an instrumental campaigning tool, but as the synthesis of organic cultural and transformative responsibilities and the functioning of communication as social advocacy (Dogra, 2007).

Both contributions converge on the concept of cultural efficacy (Nos-Aldás, 2019; Nos-Aldás, 2020). This analytical criterion holds nonprofit organizations accountable for their narratives. It points at the salience of symbolic consequences as being the basis and legitimation for structural and direct effects. This theoretical model understands the communication of the nonprofit sector from its performativity (Nos-Aldás & Farné, 2020): the representations, relations and commitments that any communicative action establishes. Cultural efficacy, thus, situates cultural consequences in the center of the communicative process and connects every decision with the challenge of promoting discourses that are consistent with the core responsibility and main long-term aim of CDCS (aligned with the foundational principles of nonprofit organizations), which is its transformative ambition. That is, a broad understanding of communication (quality international information, awareness campaigns, intersectional narratives, fundraising, informal education, etc.) in continuous dialogue with educational, legal and formal political contexts oriented to the transformation of symbolic and structural violence.

This debate on CDSC runs parallel to another on global critical citizenship education, which also comes from the field of education for development (Torres, 2017). In current societies, media and information literacy play an important role in forming critical citizens and promoting democratic societies based on human rights (Carlsson, 2019; Kellner & Share, 2007; Singh et al., 2016). In fact, beyond the right to information and expression, all literacies – textual, media, audio-visual, digital and so on – converge to make citizens aware of social injustice issues (Murakami, 2019; Kibbey, 2011). To be effective citizens, people must acquire communication literacy (the ability to communicate effectively), which entails critical understanding of information and meaning (its sociocultural context and implications), and possess social skills to communicate and participate in ways that are socially responsible in a diverse global society (Nutbeam, 2000; Texas Tech University, 2020). Such communication literacy is related to social change and democratic process in a way that enables an activist literacy that includes "agency, coalition building and collaboration, an awareness of power structures, and the deliberate use and interpretation of language" (Crisco, 2005, n.p.).

Following these approaches, communication and activist literacies are understood as the ability to make effective communication for social change that contributes to transgressing oppressive hegemonic frames and promoting alternative discourses that engage citizens for equality and social justice.

Method

As an example of activist communication, this study addresses the 8M feminist strikes in Spain and Portugal in 2019 as the most recent large feminist demonstrations staged due to restrictions on the following marches imposed as a result of the pandemic.

The analysis focuses on the website of each platform that coordinated events around the 8M strikes:

- Portugal: *https://grevefeminista.wordpress.com/*
- Spain: *https://hacialahuelgafeminista.org/*[2]

The focus is on the websites/digital platforms because the present repertoire of feminist actions occurs in a scenario characterized by the widespread use of digital communication and the continuum of online activism to street activity (Núñez-Puente, 2018; Cruz & Cerqueira, 2017). Their social media networks were not included in the analysis because it exceeded the scope of this chapter and, especially, because the website was the main source for the information and materials disseminated through their social media accounts (Acosta & Lassi, 2020), in line with current trends in content curation as a gateway for social media (Stanoevska-Slabeva et al., 2012). Furthermore, the websites function as a repository of all the materials disseminated by the movement and allow activists to document unfolding protest events and share their emotions (Papacharissi & de-Fatima-Oliveira, 2012).

On the methodological level, content and discourse analysis was applied to the websites, first, in the form of a mixed content analysis of the web architecture to define the general structure, design and browsing elements (Sosa-Valcarcel et al., 2019) and then a discursive approach to explore the resignification of the subjects, transforming their role as victims to subjects with agency capable of transforming victimization into activism. The analysis addressed the discursive elements through criteria of the cultural efficacy of communication for social change (Nos-Aldás & Farné, 2020), identified and compared by the authors on previous international social movements (Table 4.6.1).

These are the results for each case, starting with general website content, then the discursive elements for the five criteria.

Table 4.6.1 Criteria of cultural efficacy of transgressive communication

Criteria	Description
1. Nonviolence	Avoid all types of violence, even symbolic. Care needs to be taken when dealing with stereotypes; avoid ridiculing, blaming, generalizing and adopting condescending attitudes, etc.
2. Recognition	Recognition and acknowledgement of the other person from a perspective of equality despite differences, with empathy based on universal, inclusive and emancipatory values.
3. Transgression	Transform hegemonic representation frames that perpetuate oppression; promote new imaginaries through creativity and innovation.
4. Intersectionality	Be aware of the crossovers and overlaps in questions of gender, ethnicity and origin, class, sexuality, age and functional diversity.
5. "Inspiraction"	Foment communication with proposals that provide reference models inspired by equality and an invitation to action and emancipation.

Source: Nos-Aldás and Farné (2020, p. 24).

Results

8M strike in Portugal

Website content

Greve Feminista [Feminist strike] was created by the *Rede 8 de Março*[3] [8th March Network] for the Portuguese 8M (hereafter P8M) in 2018 to prepare for the 2019 strike. The national platform brings together collectives, associations, political organizations and trade unions. The website emphasizes the international feminist strike and provides information on the strike projected for 2020, the last for which information exists, and which shows that, despite the pandemic, many initiatives and materials were created, several of which were available only online. The site menu presents seven sections, including how to contact the promoters/organizers and supporters of the strike, what the international strike is about, the specifics of the Portuguese context (protests in relation to consumption, care, students and labor), a manifesto, materials, press releases and agenda (indicating the geographical reach of the events).

The side menu presents news about the strike, the link to their Facebook account, e-mail and petition (signing the manifesto). The website's layout can be confusing, does not facilitate much information and mixes archive material of previous years' activities with other information, all of which is in Portuguese.

Nonviolence

The P8M discourse is a nonviolent approach that is consistent throughout the website. The press releases condemn femicides (one entitled: "No more silence on femicides!"[4]), racism and police violence in neighborhoods. The issue of nonviolence is also addressed in the manifesto, with reference to data on the Portuguese context:

> We are from the country where 6576 women and girls have been victim of genital mutilation. We are the survivors of gender violence in Portugal that kills two of us on average every month, 80% victims of domestic violence, 90.7% victims of sexual crimes.

Other material speaks bluntly on the issue: "Because we suffer multiple violence, so this strike we call will be multiple."

Recognition

The website acknowledges past achievements and the struggles that need to be pursued. Its online material signals an awareness of the need to act against violence: "To be a feminist is to be aware of all this [violence] and take action in defense of what we have already achieved, and fight for what we still do not have." This aspect is also very visible throughout the manifesto:

> We are heirs of the feminist struggles and of the workers, anti-colonial and anti-racist resistance. We claim the heritage of the struggles for the right to vote, to work for a fair wage, to a free and responsible sexuality, to maternity as a choice, to housing, to public education and health.

Transgression

P8M falls within this innovative type of protest. This was not a classic labor strike, but a fourfold demonstration, as expressed in the manifesto: "On 8 March, we will strike for wage labor, domestic and care workers, responsible consumption of goods and services, and for students." The strike called by the 8 March Collective did not only involve traditional actors in strikes but also other collectives and individuals.

In fact, their discourse aimed at mobilizing everyone:

"HOW TO MAKE YOUR OWN STRIKE"

- Talk to your union representative, and explain the importance of going on strike in your sector on 8 March;
- Inform your colleagues about the strike;
- The 8 March Network meetings are open for all to participate!

Intersectionality

The discourse has a clear intersectional approach, addressing multiple discriminations, and P8M defines itself as a force for "anti-colonial and anti-racist resistance." This is clearly expressed and emphasized several times over, for instance:

> For us, to be feminist is to be aware that we women are the poorest of the poor, the ones who work the hardest among the exploited, the ones who are excluded and exposed to violence; and in this equation, the color of our skin, the place where we come from or where we live, and our sexual orientation, are by no means irrelevant. To be a feminist is to be aware of all this and to act in defense of what we have already achieved and to fight for what we still do not have. All struggles unite and rise up together! ALIVE, FREE AND UNITED! 8 MARCH IS OUR DAY OF STRUGGLE!

"Inspiraction"

In the discursive elements that inspire action and emancipation, there is frequent mention of fomenting both local and international networking with other feminist movements, as manifested by the website's name, "International Feminist Strike." The call for individual and collective action is ever present in the material, and all women are invited to engage: "We know that stopping consumption for just one day will not make a big difference, so we invite you to think about more conscious and sustainable consumption of goods and services throughout the year."

The manifesto also uses a discourse that calls to action and draws inspiration from the historical memory of daily struggles:

> Every March 8th, we celebrate the union of women and mobilize in defense of our rights. We are heirs of the feminist struggles and of workers' anti-colonial and anti-racist resistance. We reclaim the heritage of the struggles for the right to vote, to work for a fair wage, to free and responsible sexuality, to motherhood as a choice, to housing, to public education and health.

When explaining what the feminist strike is about, this same discourse is present:

> The Feminist Strike is a proposal of the international feminist movement, which calls for a women's strike as a form of protest and revolt against the precariousness and violence that invade our lives. It is the biggest women's social strike movement in the world in recent decades, taking place on 8 March, International Women's Day.

8M strike in Spain

Website content

Hacia la huelga feminista [Towards the feminist strike] was created by the 8M Commission in Spain (hereafter S8M) in 2017 to prepare for the 2018 8M first feminist strike in Spain. The website carries information dating from its foundation to early 2021.[5] It has a clear, user-friendly layout, with a site menu organized in seven sections. First, the home page contains post miniatures, with the right sidebar providing links to information such as position statement, 8M radio, Google Map of local assemblies, Twitter account (@HuelgaFeminista) and a YouTube playlist (#HaciaLaHuelgaFeminista). The footer provides links to social media (Facebook, Twitter, YouTube, Instagram) and contact details. The second tab, 8M Commission, includes information on the national commission – code of ethics, guide on feminist practices, who they are and how they function, locations and e-mail addresses of 83 sections, a Google Form to add new sub-commissions, and a subsection with information on meetings. Third, the Materials tab offers "road maps to the 2019 strike" and calls for demonstrations. Fourth, the Territories tab provides 14 subsections on the local committees based in the main regions. The fifth tab, Migration and Anti-racism, gathers information on the committee for this area, position statement, demands and activities. Sixth, the International tab provides information in English on 2019 8M, its origin and meaning, demonstrations worldwide and the consumer strike. Finally, the 2018 tab is the archive of the first strike, with an international subsection with information in English.

Nonviolence

The movement's discourse is a nonviolent approach, starting with the manifesto. The denunciation of several forms of violence against women are contextualized to explain the root causes, rather than blaming individuals. They show awareness of the interconnections of violence and the importance of working to achieve direct, structural and cultural peace: "We denounce that being a woman is the main cause of poverty and that we are penalized for our diversity." Caring for people is essential, and the manifesto explicitly demands "that the defense of life is placed at the center of the economy and politics." The manifesto makes a clear connection between peace and nonviolence:

> We cry out: No to wars, no to weapons production! Wars are a product and extension of patriarchy and capitalism to control territories and people. The direct consequence of war is millions of displaced women around the world, women who are being forsaken, victimized and violated.

Recognition

Recognition is a clear, cross-cutting discursive feature with two elements that particularly stand out in the manifesto. First, explicit acknowledgment and gratitude towards the predecessors who fought to achieve rights for women: "There is a long genealogy of activists, suffragettes and trade unionist women who fought before us." Second, there is strong recognition for the women, mostly disregarded and underprivileged, who bear the burden of care:

> Domestic and care work done by women is essential to sustain life. The fact that it is mainly unpaid or undervalued is a trap perpetuated by capitalism. Today, with a strike by carers in the family and society, we shine a light on work that nobody wants to recognize, either unpaid at home, poorly paid or in the informal economy. We claim that care work be recognized as a first-order social good, and we demand the redistribution of these types of tasks.

Transgression

S8M explains that "one of the most important aspects for us has been the theoretical development of a new concept and its praxis: the feminist strike." This goes beyond the traditional forms of strikes because most women work in irregular or precarious conditions and are involved in work at home; therefore, the classical approach of a strike does not fit with their needs. "For this reason, the feminist strike is proposed so that women stop work in all spheres, labor, student, consumer, care, and go on strike." The care and consumer aspects are particularly transgressive in relation to hegemonic approaches. The consumer strike includes boycotts of products promoted by misogynistic advertising and, especially, a wider reflection on the economy and structure of production and how it affects women and their working conditions. The carers' strike highlights the role of women in sustaining life and relates to nonviolent and recognition criteria.

Other elements aimed at transgressing hegemonic and patriarchal frames refer to love. For example, the development of activities leading up to St. Valentine's Day, reframed as "Saint Violentin," a play on words "violent-valentine," to denounce the idea that romantic love often entails a toxic relationship that hinders the emotional and material independence of women and therefore sustains violence.

Intersectionality

The discourse has an intersectional approach, addressing several layers of discrimination suffered by women, and S8M defines itself as anti-colonial, anti-racist and anti-capitalist. The most visible issue is migration and anti-racism, with a dedicated section to highlight the additional discrimination that women face because of their ethnicity and origin. There are specific hashtags – #Migrantas8M [Migrants], #racializadas8M [racialized] and #refugiadas8M [refugees] – and posters such as one with drawings of ethnically and religiously diverse women under the slogan "Migrant woman: doubly resistant." Second, S8M showed its support for sexual diversity in the wake of the strike on Lesbian Visibility Day in April and Pride Day in July 2019 and claimed a space for women within the LGTBIQ+ movement, denouncing that it is still embedded in a patriarchal culture that relegates women. Third, S8M addresses class, focusing on underprivileged women, such as those involved in care and housework, with a Domestic Territory Conversation and actions against labor precarity. Finally, there is a cross-generational approach taking into account different types of violence contextualized by age range, for instance, harassment of young women, labor conditions or care work for adults and equitable pensions for the elderly.

"Inspiraction"

In the discursive elements that inspire action and emancipation, there are many references to promoting both local and international networking with other feminist movements. This is particularly visible in the bilingual manifesto (Spanish-English) "Beyond 8M: Towards the 'Feminist International'":

> the feminist movement is giving us hope and a vision for a better future in a crumbling world. [. . .] The new feminist wave is the first line of defense to the rise of the far-right. Today, women are leading the resistance to reactionary governments in a number of countries. [. . .] The feminist movement is also rediscovering the meaning of international solidarity and transnational initiative. [. . .] After the upcoming 8 March, the time has come for taking our movement a step further and calling for transnational meetings and assemblies of the movements: for becoming the emergency brake capable of stopping the capitalist train running at full speed, and hurtling all humanity and the planet we live in, toward barbarism.[6]

The website also provides global tracking of 8M abroad, with references to Honduras, Argentina, Andorra, Italy, Bolivia, Turkey, Kenya, United Kingdom, Switzerland, Germany and Portugal (the "*A Caminho Da Greve Feminista!*" campaign).

Following 8M, there are references to the activism around International Workers' Day (May 1), with the slogan "We take care, we work, we go back to the streets" – and the Swiss women's strike (June 14): "We want to be free, alive, feminist, combative and rebels! Feminist strike never ends, every day is 8M and 14J."

Discussion and conclusions

The analysis of the Portuguese and Spanish feminist strikes' websites shows that each initiative has its own particular characteristics, but they also share common discursive elements from protest communication models.

The preoccupation with providing information and communication is evident in both. This favors a discourse that connects with society and engages broader support. They combine info-activist literacy in terms of expertise in transforming information into action and a cultural-discursive awareness to enable effective communication to engage citizens in social change.

Regarding cultural efficacy criteria, both movements share discourse traits oriented to nonviolent activism and structural transformations:

1. Nonviolence: they denounce violence from a structural, interconnected and systematic perspective (femicides, poverty, sexual abuse), although nonviolence in itself is more salient in the Spanish manifesto.
2. Recognition: it is striking how both movements explicitly acknowledge their predecessors' achievements gained through feminist struggle and the additional burden of the reproductive work for women.
3. Transgression: the main contribution they have in common is the transformative frame of the global strike, not only for its international scope but also with innovative transgressions of traditional labor conceptions by introducing the elements of care and consumer strike.
4. Intersectionality: various actions are proposed to develop the diversity of contexts and identities, and intersectional approaches are observed in both initiatives (in terms of the actors involved and discourse projected). The range of organizations and collectives involved in organizing and supporting the strike demonstrate the integration of an intersectional approach, and both state their anti-colonial, anti-racist and anti-capitalist nature and focus. The photographs, press releases and the causes defended, such as the struggles against poverty and racism, clearly show that this activism is formed of intersecting struggles that characterize feminism today.
5. "Inspiration": both platforms call for participation and action and include an international approach. Moreover, there is a clear reference to the Spanish context in the Portuguese actions, with news items declaring that the strike in Spain has inspired the Portuguese movement.

This comparative study provides a perspective of the points in common between feminist activism in Spain and Portugal while referencing the particularities of each country's movement as seen in their messages. Police violence in neighborhoods, for instance, stands out as a cause for protest in Portugal, whereas efforts to bond with broad alliances and international networks are salient in Spain. These differences demonstrate the need to adopt situated knowledge (Haraway, 1988/1991) and take into account contexts of action (Gámez-Fuentes, 2015), so important for feminist movements. Overall, the information and communication strategies adopted with activist expertise are visible on the two websites, and they demonstrate the application of cultural efficacy criteria with a view to forcing onto the public agenda the major struggles that women need to fight in order to achieve equality and diversity.

Notes

1. This research is funded by the R+D projects "Social digital education" (PGC2018-095123-B-I00) of the Spanish Ministry of Science, Innovation and Universities and "Communication for social change and media education to stand up to hate speech on gender and immigration, through the analysis of public discourses in Spain between 2016–2019" (UJI-B2019-13), of the Universitat Jaume I.
2. During the research, this website's server had access problems; however, the information is available on the Internet archive. https://web.archive.org/web/20201126233449/https://hacialahuelgafeminista.org/
3. See https://rede8marco.wordpress.com/about/. The network originates from the organization of the March to End Violence against Women, which took place on November 25, 2011. It brings together feminist, anti-racist, LGBT, immigrant rights and anti-precarity associations. The network has a presence in several Portuguese cities, and it called for the 8M International Feminist Strike in Portugal.
4. This and the following quotes in English have been translated from Portuguese and Spanish by the authors.
5. The last 8M was organized in 2020, although already affected by the pandemic, as the following week Spain declared the national lockdown. In 2021, 8M demonstrations were prohibited due to the pandemic, and only minor events were permitted in some towns and virtual actions, which is reflected in the scarcity of information on this website in 2021.
6. This original text is in English.

References

Acosta, M., & Lassi, A. (2020). #8M 2019: La conversación digital durante la Huelga Internacional de Mujeres [#8M 2019: The digital conversation around the international women's strike]. *Revista Arbitrada Interdisciplinaria Koinonía, 5*(5), 86–109. http://dx.doi.org/10.35381/r.k.v5i9.516

Bachmann, I., & Proust, V. (2020). Old concerns, renewed focus and novel problems: Feminist communication theory and the global South. *Annals of the International Communication Association, 44*(1), 67–80. https://doi.org/10.1080/23808985.2019.1647445

Baú, V. (2016). Waving the flag for development communication: Why there is still hope for communication research. *The International Communication Gazette, 78*(7), 711–715. https://doi.org/10.1177/1748048516655733

Bernal-Triviño, A., & Sanz-Martos, S. (2020). Las Periodistas Paramos in Spain: Professional, feminist Internet activism. *European Journal of Communication, 35*(4), 325–338. https://doi.org/10.1177/0267323120903687

Campillo, I. (2018). 'If we stop, the world stops': The 2018 feminist strike in Spain. *Social Movement Studies, 18*(2), 252–258. https://doi.org/10.1080/14742837.2018.1556092

Carlsson, U. (Ed.). (2019). *Understanding media and information literacy (MIL) in the digital age: A question of democracy*. University of Gothenburg. https://jmg.gu.se/digitalAssets/1742/1742676_understanding-media-pdf-original.pdf

Crisco, V. (2005). *Activist literacy: Engaging democracy in the classroom and the community* [Dissertation, University of Nebraska]. https://digitalcommons.unl.edu/dissertations/AAI3176773

Cruz, R. V., & Cerqueira, C. (2017). SlutWalk goes glocal: Estratégias de difusão online no caso português. In R. Ribeiro, V. de Sousa, & S. Khan (Eds.), *A Europa no mundo e o mundo na Europa: Crise e identidade* [*Europe in the world and the world in Europe: Crisis and identity*] (pp. 213–236). Lasics. www.lasics.uminho.pt/ojs/index.php/cecs_ebooks/article/view/2793

De-Sousa-Santos, B. (2012). Public sphere and epistemologies of the South. *Africa Development, XXXVII*(1), 43–67. www.jstor.org/stable/24484031

Dogra, N. (2007). Reading NGOs visually: Implications of visual images for NGO management. *Journal of International Development, 19*(2), 161–171. https://doi.org/10.1002/jid.1307

Durham, M. G., & Kellner, D. (2012). *Media and cultural studies: Keyworks*. Wiley-Blackwell.

Gámez-Fuentes, M. J. (2015). Feminisms and the 15M movement in Spain: Between frames of recognition and contexts of action. *Social Movement Studies, 14*(3), 359–365. https://doi.org/10.1080/14742837.2014.994492

Haraway, D. (1988/1991). Situated knowledges: The science question in feminism and the privilege of partial perspective. In D. Haraway (org.), *Symians, cyborgs and women: The reinvention of nature* (pp. 183–202). Routledge.

Hemer, O., & Tufte, T. (2016). Voice + matter: Communication, development and the cultural return. In *Nordicom*. University of Gothenburg.

hooks, b. (1994). *Teaching to transgress: Education as the practice of freedom*. Routledge.

Jacobson, T. L. (2016). Amartya Sen's capabilities approach and communication for development and social change. *Journal of Communication, 66*(5), 789–810. https://doi.org/10.1111/jcom.12252

Kellner, D., & Share, J. (2007). Critical media literacy is not an option. *Learn Inquiry*, *1*(1), 59–69. https://doi.org/10.1007/s11519-007-0004-2

Kibbey, J. (2011). Media literacy and social justice in a visual world. *Counterpoints*, *403*, 50–61. www.jstor.org/stable/42981595

Lagarde-y-de-los-Ríos, M. (2005). *Para mis socias de la vida: Claves feministas para el poderío y la autonomía de las mujeres* [*To my life partners: Feminist keys to women's power and autonomy*]. Horas y Horas.

Marí-Sáez, V. M. (2020). Lessons on communication, development, and evaluation from a Freirean perspective. *Development in Practice*, *30*(7), 862–873. https://doi.org/10.1080/09614524.2020.1755232

Melkote, S. R. (1991). *Communication for development in the third world: Theory and practice*. Sage.

Mesa, M., Alonso-Cano, L., & Couceiro, E. (2013). *Visibles y transgresoras: Narrativas y propuestas visuales para la paz y la igualdad* [*Visible and transgressive: Narrative and visual proposals for peace and equality*]. CEIPAZ.

Murakami, K. (2019). Media literacy and social activism. In R. Hobbs & P. Mihailidis (Eds.), *The international encyclopedia of media literacy*. Wiley-Blackwell. https://doi.org/10.1002/9781118978238.iem10139

Nos-Aldás, E. (2019). From grassroots action to public discourses of cultural peace. In A. Iranzo & A. Farné (Eds.), *Comunicación para el cambio social: Propuestas para la acción* (pp. 25–45). Tirant Lo Blanc.

Nos-Aldás, E. (2020). Learning with 'generation like' about digital global citizenship: A case study from Spain. In D. Bourn (Ed.), *The Bloomsbury handbook of global education and learning* (pp. 246–261). Bloomsbury.

Nos-Aldás, E., & Farné, A. (2020). Transgressive communication for social change: Performative epistemologies and cultural efficacy. *Convergencia Revista de Ciencias Sociales*, *27*, 1–26. https://convergencia.uaemex.mx/article/view/12720/11471

Núñez-Puente, S. (2018). Femen in the current Spanish political context: Feminist activism and counterhegemonic modes of representation. *Journal of Spanish Cultural Studies*, *19*(1), 111–126. https://doi.org/10.1080/14636204.2018.1414368

Nutbeam, D. (2000). Health literacy as a public health goal: A challenge for contemporary health education and communication strategies into the 21st century. *Health Promotion International*, *15*(3), 259–267. https://doi.org/10.1093/heapro/15.3.259

Oliveira, E., Melo, A. D., & Gonçalves, G. (Eds.). (2016). *Strategic communication for nonprofit organisations: Challenges and alternative approaches*. Vernon Press.

Papacharissi, Z., & de-Fatima-Oliveira, M. (2012). Affective news and networked publics: The rhythms of news storytelling on# Egypt. *Journal of Communication*, *62*(2), 266–282. https://doi.org/10.1111/j.1460-2466.2012.01630.x

Pinazo-Calatayud, D., & Nos-Aldás, E. (2016). Developing moral sensitivity through protest scenarios in international NGDOs' communication. *Communication Research*, *43*(1), 25–48. https://doi.org/10.1177/0093650213490721

Pinazo-Calatayud, D., Nos-Aldás, E., & Agut, S. (2020). Positive or negative communication in social activism. *Comunicar*, *62*, 69–78. https://doi.org/10.3916/C62-2020-06

Riek, B. (2015). *From the aims to the achievements of development education: Stumbling blocks on the way to political transformation*. DEEEP.

Servaes, J. (2002). *Approaches to development communication*. UNESCO.

Singh, J., Kerr, P., & Hamburger, E. (Eds.). (2016). *Media and information literacy: Reinforcing human rights, countering radicalization and extremism*. UNESCO. https://unesdoc.unesco.org/ark:/48223/pf0000246371

Skinner, A., Smith, M. B., Brown, E., & Troll, T. (2016). *Education, learning, and the transformation of development*. Routledge.

Sosa-Valcarcel, A., Galarza Fernández, E., & Castro-Martinez, A. (2019). The collective cyber-activist action of "Las periodistas paramos" for the feminist strike of 8M in Spain. *Comunicación y Sociedad*, 1–24. https://doi.org/10.32870/cys.v2019i0.7287

Stanoevska-Slabeva, K., Sacco, V., & Giardina, M. (2012, April 20–21). *Content curation: A new form of gatewatching for social media?* [Conference presentation abstract]. 13th International Symposium on Online Journalism (ISOJ). https://libra.unine.ch/Publications/Marco_Giardina/16123/L-en

Tacchi, J., & Tufte, T. (Eds.) (2020). *Communicating for change: Concepts to think with*. Palgrave Macmillan.

Texas Tech University. (2020, January 13). *Communication literacy requirements*. www.depts.ttu.edu/provost/curriculum/communication-literacy/index.php

Torres, C. A. (2017). *Theoretical and empirical perspectives of critical global citizenship education*. Routledge. https://doi.org/10.4324/9781315452579

Tufte, T. (2017). *Communication and social change: A citizen perspective*. Polity Press.

Wilkins, K. G. (2014). Advocacy communication. In K. G. Wilkins, T. Tufte, & R. Obregon (Eds.), *The handbook of development communication and social change* (pp. 57–71). Wiley-Blackwell.

4.7
VALUE-INFORMED COMMUNICATION IN NONPROFIT CAMPAIGNS

Birgit Breninger and Thomas Kaltenbacher

Introduction

Few ambitious ventures have incited as much passion as the unfolding of 'true values' informing communication processes and the authentic enactment of such values. Especially in the realm of nonprofit communication, many controversial expressions of 'values' have stirred the feelings of people, companies and governments, and the smoothing of many a ruffled feather has cost small fortunes and commanded the price of many a 'good' reputation. Take, for example, the advertising campaign created by Saatchi & Saatchi for the South African nonprofit charity organization Amy Biehl Foundation Trust in 2003. The campaign featured underprivileged children from poverty-stricken backgrounds outlining their future criminal records if they do not receive an education. Kevin Roberts, then CEO of Saatchi & Saatchi, claimed to have aimed at making the South African public aware of the grim future the country could hold for these young children. With the help of this campaign, they tried to spur people into responsible actions. The South African government considered the advertising campaign racist, banned its airing and kicked Saatchi & Saatchi out of the country.

In trying to design creative strategies to establish an engaging dialogue with consumers, employees, politicians, etc., 'genuine ethical values' have often been perceived as vital to prompt actions and contribute to the 'common good'. In the 21st century, however, ethical qualms have become attached to the once unconditional credo of profit and progress, and the infamous 'rat race' seems to have been replaced with a so-called 'values race' (cf. Barrett, 2017, p. xxii). In enacting a social conscience, people have started to hold individuals as well as organizations and businesses ethically accountable for their work. Displaying humanitarian concerns and being perceived as authentic in 'doing good' has become increasingly important (Mukherjee, 2020). It is claimed here that the authentic enactment of a principled approach to do business rests on the successful integration of values such as integrity, trust and accountable actions in individuals. This demand for a responsible, ethical mindset has created a major challenge regarding the purposeful use of communication by organizations, companies and governments. Against this background of action-oriented communication based on authentic values in volatile, multicultural societies, we propose to devise communication for the nonprofit sector in order to stay relevant to current societies and their concerns. We suggest that in order to create genuinely value-informed communication activities for multicultural societies, individuals have to integrate certain values on an individual basis across the axis of (cultural) difference and consistently 'walk the talk' so that such values become embodied, by which we mean integrated in a socio-cultural context on a neurobiological level. In this chapter we outline this novel, action-oriented and value-infused approach to communication. Afterwards, selected visual data from an experimental eye tracking pilot is presented to introduce an innovative methodological approach of how 'truly' value-infused communication can be documented.

Reconceiving communication for the nonprofit sector

Since people have grown more and more sensitive to direct and indirect forms of discrimination, they seem to have become less willing to turn a blind eye towards humanitarian concerns. Particularly in current multicultural environments anchoring visual expressions and ensuring culturally sensitive, ethical values in meaning making on an individual level presents a novel challenge for nonprofit communication. Examining such entanglements lies at the heart of a more integrative approach towards communication activities, for which an action-oriented redefinition of the concept of 'communication' is inevitable. This redefinition needs to encompass perception, since how and what we see create the very basis of communication.[1]

The bigger picture of 'truly' value-informed communication activities, able to trigger social/humanitarian action in individuals, requires a thorough analysis of the interlinkedness of mental and social mechanisms on an individual as well as on a socio-cultural level (see e.g. Thagard, 2019). Nevertheless, in the social sciences, the individual 'brain-mind' perspective has been often neglected. We cast a bio-sociocultural angle on action-oriented communication processes in multicultural environments from an individual stance. The profound change in how we conceive communication in general, and of 'successful communication strategies' in particular, is based on the necessity of having to redefine integrated communication activities as genuinely value-informed and action-oriented in a context steeped in multiculturality. It is argued here that the individual level of integration of (cultural) difference provides the central axis, i.e. constitutes the required scaffolding, for effective, i.e. value-informed communication processes in multicultural environments. Against this backdrop we consider cultural expertise as indispensable for authentic, humanitarian communication. Hence effective communication activities must be infused with cultural expertise, meaning that 'cultural difference' has to be integrated as a value on an individual level, not simply on a societal level (i.e. it needs to be what you want, not just what society wants you to do) in order to be able to devise effective communication strategies for multicultural environments. Communication strategies regarding, for example, nonprofit marketing campaigns need not only to be perceived as authentic and trustworthy in multicultural societies but also have to trigger prosocial mindsets to prompt actions (e.g. buying, donating, changing 'unhealthy' behaviours, etc.). Therefore, we claim that what is needed for effective, strategic communication in multicultural, digital, volatile-uncertain-complex-ambiguous (VUCA) settings is the integration of 'new values' on an individual level in order to be perceived as authentic in global settings. New values, such as surpassing the banality of win-win by contributing to a 'common good' have to be individually 'hardwired' on a neurobiological level via 'walking the talk' in order to give rise to authenticity. This 'hardwiring' of emerging new values (such as being inclusive, 'true' collaboration and interconnectedness, responsible actions and accountability) is bound to habitual prosocial actions and has to happen via the axis of cultural difference in individuals (Breninger, 2021). For example, the value of 'contributing to a common good', for which an individual has to have a truly inclusive mindset, does not simply encompass the needs and wants of in-group members but also those of unfamiliar out-group members, such as the Indian women dyeing the fabric for the French haute couture company.

Especially in disciplines of management, leadership and marketing, however, communication has a long history of being instrumentalized. Bound to the unimpeachable idea to foster the 'purposeful' use of communication by an organization in order to fulfill its mission, communication has often been relegated to 'do's and don'ts' lists, representing a mere skill, shackled by the purpose of achieving mostly profit-oriented goals (see: Hallahan et al., 2007; Heath et al., 2018). But how do we redefine communication when the indisputable goal of profit is questioned by the value of contributing to the common good?

Such profit-oriented communication endeavours have been termed as 'noncommunication approaches' (Dervin, 1991) since they mostly view communication in terms of information and influence and are therefore rarely able to unlock the 'true' potential of communication: its ability to transform individual minds and actions. Even more multifaceted approaches to strategic communication (cf. Hallahan et al., 2007) that aim to integrate various avenues of specialist communications (e.g. management, marketing, public relations [PR], technical, political and information/marketing campaigns) are often trapped by a capitalist mindset rarely able to cover the importance of emergent 'new values' and the culturalization of the idea of strategy in a more complex manner. Against the backdrop of three insights we have to critically reconsider a profit-oriented information/influence approach to 'communication': the interdependence of encoding and decoding not in a sociocultural vacuum but in specific situative contexts, such as business negotiations in VUCA settings, that have to be considered in the acquisition and analysis of data.

The unintentional and uncontrollable nature of communication, for example, leakage, i.e. nonverbal behaviours, often reveal information about a speaker's 'true' feelings, values and beliefs (DePaulo & Rosenthal, 1979; Ekman & Friesen, 1969)

The 'meaninglessness of information' per se, as Beau Lotto states: "The 'reality' that our perceptions see is the meaning of the meaningless information that your brain receives. [. . .] The meaning your ecology gives it" (Lotto, 2017, p. 46). In that, individuals are attributing meaning from a very personal interpretation: the individual brain creates a meaningful perception of the world and it does not simply relay on obtained information.

With the current emphasis on embodying certain values and eliciting pro-social actions, however, we have to surpass profit-based, info-influencer approaches and analyze the idea of viewing communication as a process through which relationships are formed and behaviours are changed more carefully. Generally speaking, social changes always necessitate conceptual adaptations; hence, it is proposed here to consider communication as a culturalized, bio-social mechanism enabling the emergence of certain phenomena, such as trust. Communication as a culturalized bio-social mechanism is crucial for interactions among individuals and dependent upon selected, culturalized and interlinked (emotional and cognitive) properties and their relations. Bio-social mechanisms always operate in an environment and are shaped by their surroundings as well as by the habitual 'tasks' they engage in, i.e. they are culturalized. We can hence attempt to identify the connections, interactions and changes of parts and wholes that lead to the emergence of certain phenomena. Moreover, mechanisms are frequently multilevel, i.e. entities and activities at multiple levels ('lower-level' and 'higher-level' processes) are required. For decades, a clear distinction has been assumed between 'low-level' perceptual processes – how we see, hear, touch, taste and smell – and higher-level cognitive processes that allow us to integrate and interpret our senses. Yet pertinent interdisciplinary research shows that the line between perception and cognition, in particular the distinction between bottom-up and top-down processes, is much blurrier than previously thought (Cichy et al., 2016; Fast & McGann, 2017; Firestone & Scholl, 2016). Top-down cognitive processes appear to influence even the most basic components of perception, affecting how and what we see constituting the very basis of communication. One of the pivotal questions for communication research in the future is therefore how to include 'lower-level' data and analyze, for example, perception in tandem with cognition.[2] The idea that the biological mode of 'seeing' and the culturalized, social mode of 'seeing' are intricately interwoven in the phenomenon of perception is pivotal, as there is a pivotal link between perception and action. Joaquin Fuster, for example, suggests a perception–action cycle and claims that the hierarchy of perceptual knowledge is paralleled by the hierarchy of action knowledge (Fuster, 2003, p. 74). Additionally, the idea that 'perception is for action' is fundamental to reconceiving communication as a bio-social mechanism for which more action-based approaches are required that do not view action and cognition as separate. The theory of sensorimotor contingencies (SMCs; O'Regan & Noë, 2001), for example, highlights the intimate link between perception and action systems, claiming that the cognitive processing of a living organism does not originate from a stimulus, but rather from an action (usually an intention). Another important link tying perception and action comes from expert research: expertise substantially relies on perception (cf. Gobet, 2015). It is perception that allows experts to rapidly categorize a problem and therefore 'see' more or different cues than a novice. It is pivotal to consider the key role of perception when reconceiving communication as value-infused, for valorization of an organism happens through enactment of the respective values (Thompson, 2007).

The role of values has to be redefined as well when taking a bio-social stance on communication, as values must be considered not as mere verbal constructs: "Values and attitudes result from the binding of concepts and emotions. [. . .] Values are not just verbal behaviors, social constructions, or abstract entities, but rather brain processes that combine a representation of something with an emotional assessment" (Thagard, 2019, p. 31). In referring to values as brain processes, combining a representation[3] with an emotional assessment, Thagard touches upon the importance of emotions for value-infused communication (Thagard, 2019, p. 31). This is where complexity goes 'full circle', since for an adequate analysis of value-infused communication, we also have to consider that perception and cognition are steeped in emotions. Emotional significance is made up of valence and intensity, and intensity goes with arousal, prompting people to act (Thagard, 2019, p. 37). Therefore, we suspect that if communication by an individual is truly value-infused, the individual would 'see' and act differently in certain situations and contexts. Take, for example, the value of 'embracing cultural diversity'. If an individual genuinely holds this value, it should mediate not only their utilization of intelligence but infuse perception and inform their actions. Hence we should be able to document this 'value' in perception and elicit whether individuals are genuinely able to design communication activities that truly encourage the value of inclusiveness and celebrate diversity.

Value-infused perception informing communication: an experimental pilot

Based on the suggestion of a perception–action link outlined earlier, we consider it necessary to add visual documentation to distinguish between genuinely value-infused communication and what has been outlined as 'noncommunication'. Whereas 'noncommunication' is believed to simply produce 'all talk and no action', it is assumed here that truly value-infused communication is able to prompt pro-social actions on a societal level. To show how it is possible to document this distinction, we introduce selected visual protocols from our perceptual-cognitive pilot offering promising initial results for the documentation of the communication of individuals 'truly' embracing the value of cultural diversity. We propose that value-infused communication activities are enabled by the individual level of integration of (cultural) difference. This complex integration process entails the frequency, valence and intensity of (culturalized) experiences in terms of exposure, experience, interaction and interaffection with a stimulus in a specific situative context (cf. Breninger, 2021).

In order to grasp such a manifold phenomenon as value-infused communication, we must not reduce complexity but improve experimental designs to combine different types of data for a more profound analysis. We propose an interrelated multilevel analysis based on the correlation of first-person data (relying on an observational stance), second-person (data is generated in interactions, such as open questions) and third-person data (recording brain and bodily activity, such as functional magnetic resonance imaging [fMRI]), able to take into account context, situation and time. Colombetti (2017, pp. 148–163), for example, advocates such an integrative approach to data. In our perceptuo-cognitive pilot we attempted to correlate perceptual data (third-person data), obtained by eye tracking technology, and 'cognitively penetrated' data (second-person data), gained from a questionnaire. The underlying idea was to document truly value-infused communication (answers provided) and to predict action, i.e. 'walking the talk'.

The entire perceptuo-cognitive experiment consists of 40 visual items (affectively charged and culturalized): 16 main stimuli and 24 distractors. We designed all 40 naturalistic and situated visual test items (comprising advertisements, campaigns and real-life photographs of events and people) with culturalized affective value. 'Affective items', as we call them, refer to the meaning that has been acquired by an object or event through culturalized experience and iterative encounter judgments (cf. affect-laden images Slovic et al., 2007). The 34 subjects (mean age was 30.3 years) were informed that their accuracy in assessing situations of a multicultural workplace was tested. In terms of embracing cultural diversity as a value, we expected the following three response styles:

> Ethnocentric (EC) responses more often prompting answers which can be clustered as egocentric and unappreciative or ignorant of cultural differences.
> Ethnorelative (ER) responses more often prompting answers which can be clustered as ethnorelative and aware of cultural differences often 'talking the talk'.
> Intercultural responses (IC) more often prompting answers which can be clustered to reveal cultural expertise and holding the value of cultural diversity by regularly 'walking the talk'.

and the following gaze types:

> Ethnocentric gaze (ECG): eliciting shorter and very few fixations on culturally coded items; no fixation on culturally relevant items; no or very few paths to culturally relevant items; very fast preference decisions and gaze cascade effect.
> Ethnorelative gaze (ERG): eliciting longer and more fixations on culturally coded items; considers culturally relevant items; few paths to culturally relevant items; preference decisions take longer and gaze cascade effect.
> Intercultural gaze (ICG): eliciting longer and more fixations which are equally distributed on culturally coded items; considers culturally relevant items; many paths to culturally relevant items; preference decisions take significantly longer and no gaze cascade effect.

The fixation protocol in Figure 4.7.1 depicts what we call an ethnocentric gaze (EC): no fixations on culturally relevant symbols (as e.g. in stimulus 22, on the Christian crucifix), shorter and very few fixations on racially and/or religiously coded items (e.g. the headscarf) and resulting in very fast preference decisions (decision time: 4.98 sec.). Upon display the subject was asked: "After recruiting for the position of receptionist in an Austrian hospital, these four candidates are left from a large pool of applicants. They all present with the same qualifications, competences and skills, whom do you give the job to?" and upon the decision: "Why have you decided this way?" As elicited by the question accompanying the stimulus presentation, the answer provided by this EC subject was: "She fits the working context best" (use of system justification motives and familiarity preference decision). In all EC subjects the displayed preferences were exclusively made in favour of the prototypical 'mousy personality type' in the top row left. According to more implicit cultural knowledge shared by some Austrians, she seems to 'fit' the set of culturalized (Austrian) expectations associated with this particular position best. The cultural knowledge underpinning this decision is that up to very recently, the majority of Austrian hospitals was exclusively Christian in denomination; therefore certain 'untraditional' candidates (e.g. the 'dolled up' blonde and the woman wearing a headscarf) are considered unfit.

Birgit Breninger and Thomas Kaltenbacher

Figure 4.7.1 Stimulus 22 receptionist: on the left hand side of the stimulus, a reception desk of an Austrian hospital is depicted and on the right, the four faces of potential candidates for the job are shown. On the images a prototypical ethnocentric (EC) gaze is plotted presenting short and few fixations on aspects of the stimulus that are racially or religiously coded.

Figure 4.7.2 Stimulus 22 receptionist: on the left hand side of the stimulus a reception desk of an Austrian hospital is depicted and on the right, the four faces of potential candidates for the job are shown. On the images a prototypical ethnorelative (ER) gaze is plotted displaying more and longer fixations on all candidates, as well as on culturally relevant aspects of the picture. The distribution of these fixations still isn't equally distributed.

Figure 4.7.2 shows a prototypical example of an ethnorelative (ER) gaze. As hypothesized, the ER gaze had fixations on culturally relevant symbols (in stimulus 22: the Christian crucifix) and had longer and more fixations on all faces, which were more or less equally distributed: cumulative fixation duration within the areas of interest (AIs) was distributed equally across the four face AIs. Decision-making time was insignificantly longer (7.12 sec.) but not biased towards the prototypical 'mousy person', who, interestingly enough, was not once chosen by any of the ER subjects. The ER subjects did not present with system justification motives, but stereotypical thinking was still employed (although not with all stimuli). The ER subject discussed here chose the Asian woman: "The Asian girl is young, competent and efficient". This is a commonly distributed stereotype of Asian people in the health profession in Austria.

Figure 4.7.3 shows a gaze protocol clustered as an intercultural (IC) gaze. As expected, the IC subjects did not only consider culturally relevant symbols but had significantly longer and more

Value-informed communication

Figure 4.7.3 Stimulus 22 receptionist: on the left hand side of the stimulus a reception desk of an Austrian hospital is depicted and on the right, the four faces of potential candidates for the job are shown. On the images a prototypical intercultural (IC) gaze is plotted displaying significantly longer and evenly distributed fixations on all relevant aspects of the image.

fixations on all the candidates (equally distributed), and preference decisions took significantly longer (26.34 sec.). The answer of the IC subject accompanying the gaze depicted here was:

> I choose the woman wearing the headscarf, because Muslim women are underrepresented in such public positions. And since Austria considers itself a very "homogenous" society, it is time to disrupt the convenience and complacency of the "normal" and accustom the public eye to diversity in key positions. This would also empower the Muslim community, since the job offers the opportunity to create a competent, public image for the Muslim woman.

Another stimulus from the qualitative experimental pilot that shows how one can approach visual data and perceptual change experimentally is from two campaigns: UNICEF (2004) and Mama Africa (2007). Two campaign posters were translated into a visual stimulus (no. 11). Due to the cultural relevance of this stimulus around the time of the experiment, we hoped to elicit culturalized, affective response styles. The UNICEF billboard is from the 'Schools for Africa' campaign and reads "In Africa, children are never late for school, they don't turn up at all" (own literal translation). The UNICEF mission was to ensure that every child in Africa has a chance for an education. The intention was to show German children displaying solidarity with African children, which was visualized by the minstrel-like face painting of the German children alongside various sarcastic remarks. The intended message was that African children may look different but are equal and all want to go to school.

The Mama Africa poster, on the other hand, promises a spectacle that is wild, erotic, exotic and authentically African. Mama Africa was marketed as giving African artists a chance in life by enabling them to earn 'an honest wage'. In attending the show you support this 'good cause'.

In the visual stimulus, we placed the two posters next to each other and asked: "Would you consider one of these campaigns racist? (Why, why not?) Do you think that the organizations behind these campaigns have a 'true' pro-social concern?" Interestingly enough, a tendency to doubt the 'true' concern of the organization was higher in individuals who considered the campaign racist. Hence it seems pivotal to assess the individual integration of the value of 'cultural diversity' in international marketing teams. Figure 4.7.4 displays an ethnocentric reading style (answer of the

Figure 4.7.4   Stimulus 11 UNICEF: on the left hand side of the image a UNICEF campaign is depicted showing a blonde girl with a blackened face, and on the right side the billboard Mama Africa portrays the head of a black woman surrounded by snakes. An ethnocentric (EC) gaze is plotted on the two images. Few and short fixations on stereotypical aspects reflect the ethnocentric answer.

Figure 4.7.5   Stimulus 11 UNICEF: on the left hand side of the image a UNICEF campaign is depicted showing a blonde girl with a blackened face and on the right side the billboard Mama Africa portrays the head of a black woman surrounded by snakes. An intercultural (IC) gaze is plotted on two images. Long fixations and the 'taking in of all aspects' go hand in hand with an intercultural response.

EC subject: "Of course not. They are helping these poor people") and Figure 4.7.5 an intercultural reading style of decoding the campaigns (answer of the IC subject:

> Oh my gosh, what an unfortunate campaign! Yes, both are racist, face-painting children black rings a colonialist bell and is more than disrespectful . . . does draw attention in a most negative way. And what is with the ironic remark it is so pathetic to "make fun" from a privileged point of view. So is the "wild & exotic" marketing of cultural difference . . . most problematic in it's Orientalizing fashion and deeply racist.

The two selected stimuli from the perceptuo-cognitive pilot already foreshadow the complexity of combining bio-cultural data for an improved analysis of human communication. More multimethod research paradigms based on theories with explanatory power for apparently incongruent implicit and explicit data sets will have to be developed. This will ultimately change how the next experiments in communication are designed – affecting data analysis and presentation as well. A special emphasis has to be placed on the detailed description of the real-life stimuli in order to be able to document relevant differences on an individual level. For a detailed analysis of the perceptuo-cognitive stimulus set and a discussion of the complex interactions of the previously mentioned intricately intertwined perception-action systems see Breninger (2021).

Conclusion

It has been suggested to reconceive communication as a culturalized, bio-social mechanism in order to capture the vigour and vitality of this concept for the 21st century and be able to account for genuinely value-informed communication activities that change perceptions and prompt certain actions in multicultural settings. Based on the idea of shared influences between biological and social factors in determining behaviour, emotions and cognition, the dynamisms of the micro developmental systems (e.g. genetics, hormonal system) must be analyzed in tandem with the ecological and social systems, considering their culturalization. This is why communication for the nonprofit sector in current multicultural VUCA environments:

> Needs to be redefined from a culturalized bio-social angle, since in order to 'walk the talk' not only change on a socio-cultural level but also a rewiring on an individual, neurobiological level is necessary;
> Needs to be individually 'hardwired' on a bio-social level in order to be perceived as genuinely value-infused and hence trustworthy;
> Requires interrelated, multilevel analyses based on the correlation of different data sets able to take into account context, situation and time.

We proposed that truly value-infused communication is hardwired, since 'genuinely held values' suffuse perception, cognition and actions (e.g. decision making) of the individuals. Through considerable experiences enacted and reflected upon in many diverse situations (predominantly professional) and contexts over time, value-informed processes emerge and are implemented as a specific perceptual architecture. We may be able to document the respective functional (i.e. fully integrated), perceptual architecture in individuals in order to assess whether certain values, e.g. 'cultural diversity' have successfully been integrated as core values to inform communication activities by the individual. The perceptuo-cognitive experimental pilot revealed promising initial avenues for documenting different perceptual architectures and is a first attempt to come to terms with complex real-life data in communication.

Notes

1 In this context 'perception' is to be understood in its broadest sense: the subjective experience that results from stimulation of the senses by the environment.
2 In neuroscience, perception is commonly treated as the product of an intricately intertwined, multilevel visual processing: the low-level visual processing, which is in charge of the detection of various types of contrasts in images; the intermediate-level visual processing, which is responsible for the identification of visual primitives such as contours, fields of motion and the representation of surfaces; and the high-level visual processing, which integrates information from a variety of sources, leading to conscious visual experience (cf. chapters 25–28, Hudspeth et al., 2013).
3 Our conception of communication as a culturalized bio-social mechanism, however, is based on an enactive stance, able to account for the complexities of living organisms such as emergence, embodiment and sense-making (Di Paolo et al., 2010). Hence we follow the enactive suggestion to abandon the concept of 'representation' and substitute it with the more enactive term 'directive' in order to adequately characterize the functioning of dynamic neural patterns of interactions in a cognitive system (Engel, 2010, pp. 228–229).

References

Barrett, R. (2017). *The values-driven organization: Cultural health and employee well-being as a pathway to sustainable performance*. Taylor & Francis.

Breninger, B. (2021). *A perceptual architecture of intercultural competence: Avenues for tracking cultural expertise*. Cambridge Scholars Publishing.

Cichy, R. M., Pantazis, D., & Oliva, A. (2016). Similarity-based fusion of MEG and fMRI reveals spatiotemporal dynamics in human cortex during visual object recognition. *Cerebral Cortex, 26*(8), 3563–3579.

Colombetti, G. (2017). *The feeling body: Affective science meets the enactive mind*. MIT Press.

DePaulo, B. M., & Rosenthal, R. (1979). Telling lies. *Journal of Personality and Social Psychology, 37*(10), 1713.

Dervin, B. (1991). Information as nonsense; information as sense: The communication technology connection. In H. Bouwman & M. Voojis (Eds.), *Tussen vraag en aanbod* (pp. 44–59). Cramwinckel.

Di Paolo, E., Rohde, M., & De Jaegher, H. (2010). *Horizons for the enactive mind: Values, social interaction, and play enaction: Towards a new paradigm for cognitive science*. MIT Press.

Ekman, P., & Friesen, W. V. (1969). Nonverbal leakage and clues to deception. *Psychiatry, 32*(1), 88–106.

Engel, A. K. (2010). Directive minds: How dynamics shapes cognition. In J. Stewart, O. Gapenne, & E. A. Di Paolo (Eds.), *Enaction: Towards a new paradigm for cognitive science* (pp. 219–243). MIT Press.

Fast, C. D., & McGann, J. P. (2017). Amygdalar gating of early sensory processing through interactions with locus coeruleus. *Journal of Neuroscience, 37*(11), 3085–3101.

Firestone, C., & Scholl, B. J. (2016). Cognition does not affect perception: Evaluating the evidence for "top-down" effects. *Behavioral and Brain Sciences, 39*.

Fuster, J. M. (2003). *Cortex and mind: Unifying cognition*. Oxford University Press.

Gobet, F. (2015). *Understanding expertise: A multi-disciplinary approach*. Palgrave Macmillan.

Hallahan, K., Holtzhausen, D., Van Ruler, B., Verčič, D., & Sriramesh, K. (2007). Defining strategic communication. *International Journal of Strategic Communication, 1*(1), 3–35.

Heath, R. L., Johansen, W., Hallahan, K., Steyn, B., Falkheimer, J., & Raupp, J. J. (2018). Strategic communication. *The International Encyclopedia of Strategic Communication*, 1–24.

Hudspeth, A. J., Jessell, T. M., Kandel, E. R., Schwartz, J. H., & Siegelbaum, S. A. (2013). *Principles of neural science*. McGraw-Hill.

Lotto, B. (2017). *Deviate: The science of seeing differently*. Weidenfeld & Nicolson.

Mukherjee, A. S. (2020). *Leading in the digital world: How to foster creativity, collaboration, and inclusivity*. MIT Press.

O'Regan, J. K., & Noë, A. (2001). A sensorimotor account of vision and visual consciousness. *Behavioral and Brain Sciences, 24*(5), 939–973.

Slovic, P., Finucane, M. L., Peters, E., & MacGregor, D. G. (2007). The affect heuristic. *European Journal of Operational Research, 177*(3), 1333–1352.

Thagard, P. (2019). *Mind-society: From brains to social sciences and professions*. Oxford University Press.

Thompson, E. (2007). *Mind in life: Biology, phenomenology, and the sciences of mind*. The Belknap Press of Harvard University Press.

4.8
IDENTIFYING AND CLASSIFYING STAKEHOLDERS IN SPANISH NONPROFIT ORGANIZATIONS

María Pallarés-Renau, Lorena López-Font and Susana Miquel-Segarra

Introduction[1]

In the reputation economy, communication is considered a strategic value and is defined as the main reason for the existence of nongovernmental organizations (NGOs) (Vernis et al., 1998 in Balas, 2010). Recent reports consider that "corporate responsibility is the way to move towards a fairer and more equitable citizenship, constructed collaboratively through stable commitments" (Corporate Excellence & Canvas, 2018, p. 48). However, NGOs have been unable to clearly communicate the importance of their work to their stakeholders, beyond awareness and fundraising campaigns. They have also failed to associate their acronyms with the transparency implied in gaining the trust of their publics, despite their social nature and codes of conduct.

In recent years, the presence of the third sector has notably increased in the media, the social imagination, and public life (Maracuello & Maracuello, 2000). The digital environment has provided a forum for encouraging conversation and for accountability (Santolino, 2010; Baamonde-Silva et al., 2017). But communication must go beyond purely economic interests (Herranz de la Casa, 2007) and consider the stakeholders offering and receiving transparency. "Reputation not only works with actions carried out well, but also proper communication of them" (PwC, 2018, p. 102). Dialogue must be established, but for this to take place, knowledge of the other party is required.

This chapter aims to show the results of research that analyses in depth which institutions, groups, and NGOs consider to be their stakeholders in order to propose a classification of these publics. The works of Araque and Montero (2006), Balas (2010), and Maguregui et al. (2019) are reviewed and an analysis is made of the annual reports published in 2018 by five of the main organizations in Spain: Caritas Spain (Caritas), the Spanish Red Cross, the Oxfam Intermon Foundation, the Save the Children Foundation Spain, and the UNICEF Foundation Spanish Committee (UNICEF).

Nongovernmental organizations' relationships with stakeholders

NGOs have taken on fighting inequality and providing solutions to achieve social balance as part of their work, but their stakeholders demand higher levels of transparency (Baamonde-Silva et al., 2017). They use awareness-raising strategies appealing to society's sense of responsibility, which is why communication is a determining factor in achieving their goals. María Tejada, head of the Campaigns and Communication Department of Accem, states that "at NGOs, communication means raising awareness" (Dircom, 2019, p. 140). But for this communication to be effective, it is essential to identify "any individual or entity that has some kind of direct or indirect relationship with the organization as a stakeholder, with the power to demand transparent information" (Maguregui et al., 2019, p. 81).

It is essential that NGOs identify their stakeholders and make them the focus of their communication strategy. As with any type of organization, it is necessary for NGOs to pay attention to and relate to the various "individuals or interest groups that may affect or be affected by the achievement of business objectives" (Freeman, 1984, p. 24). Proper management of conversations with different stakeholders will bring benefits associated with notoriety and visibility, but an inadequate selection will damage the organization's image and reputation, together with its social work, leading to the risk of instrumentalization by the publics (Araque & Montero, 2006).

Communication is a fundamental aspect for NGOs, since, as Nos-Aldás points out, "Communication is the scenario that develops social relations" (2019, p. 10), the basis and central point of this type of organization. Communication departments began appearing in NGOs in the 1990s, although "whether or not they are established depends on the organization's budget" (Soria, 2011 as cited in Gómez et al., 2018, p. 29). Meanwhile, the online environment has democratized NGOs in economic terms, offering plenty of platforms for conveying messages. Baamonde-Silva et al. (2017) present social media and the internet as a space for conversations, making NGOs accountable for their activities and encouraging the public to take part in actions for solidarity. The conversations must be begun to generate a climate of trust and integration with stakeholders and to offer them clear, truthful, reliable, objective information that is also complete, useful, and concise (Maguregui et al., 2019).

To do this, it is essential for them to find the people with whom they want to have these conversations. Araque and Montero set out 11 profiles: supplier, donor, intermediary, employee, volunteer, competitor, partner, influencer, consumer, beneficiary, and target adopter (2006, p. 120). Balas (2010) points out 12 groups: internal public (employees, managers, volunteers), ambivalent public (patrons, associates), third-sector entities (cooperatives, mutual societies), authorities (central, regional, local, European), politicians (parliamentarians, members of European parliament), business environment (companies, employer), trade unions (e.g UGT & CCOO), financial publics (banks, securities), media, opinion leaders (think tanks, gurus), users (disadvantaged groups), and public opinion (2010, p. 764). Maguregui et al. (2019) identify 11 groups: partners, patrons or donors, users, volunteers, employees, debtors, creditors, competitors, collaborators, pressure groups towards the NPO, and pressure groups from the NPO (p. 77).

Methods and discussion of data

To locate and classify the stakeholders, a qualitative research is proposed that uses the content analysis of the selected documents as a technique, considering them as informative products (Wimmer & Dominick, 1996). For this purpose, a systematic, objective, and replicable reading has been carried out in which stakeholders have been extracted according to two basic criteria: the express identification of the groups as stakeholders and those others that are repeatedly mentioned in the documents (to whom actions, communications, aid, etc., are addressed and about whom data and information are offered) but do not appear identified in the previous group. We therefore classify stakeholders into two levels.

At the first level (see Table 4.8.1), there are those that are openly mentioned. In the annual reports they are presented with figures, and the groups that compose them are specified. This is a determining criterion in the structure of the document.

Stakeholders in Spanish nonprofit

Table 4.8.1 Groups detected in the reports (2018) and order of appearance of the items covered

Groups in the reports (in order of appearance)			
Caritas	Participants and people supported in Spain		
	International cooperation participants		
	Volunteers		
	People hired		
	Interdiocesan Fair Trade Network (RICJ)	Diocesan Caritas	Shops and points of sale
	Integration initiatives	Lines of business	
	International confederation		
	Diocesan Caritas	Parish Caritas	
Red Cross	Beneficiaries	Spain, international and awareness-raising	
	Employees		
	Volunteers[2]		
	Members		
	Activity points[3]	Assemblies and offices and local presence points	
	Government	General assembly (elected members), national committee (elected members)	
	Collaborating companies		
	Other entities we work with		
	Society	Students on the International Humanitarian Law course	
Intermon Oxfam	Oxfam confederation organizations		
	Citizen action teams		
	Shops	Fair trade and second chance	
	Equipment	Volunteers and people hired	
	Support staff	Trailwalker organization and translators	
	Board of trustees (independent professionals)		
	Executive council		
	Members and donors		
	Fair trade purchasers		
	Activists		
	Signatories		
	Teams taking part in Trailwalker		
	Personalities from sports, journalism and culture		
	People who make up Empresas que Cambian Vidas (setting up and developing sustainable SMEs in Bolivia, Paraguay, and Burkina Faso)		
	Producer groups in 47 countries		
	Group of women cereal producers in Mali, Niger, Burkina Faso, and Chad		
	Organizations from the "Venid ya" platform		
	Refugees and migrants (relocated from Greek islands to Spain)		
	Families affected by hurricanes in Cuba, Dominican Republic, and Haiti		
	People supported by the humanitarian crisis in Yemen		
	Women domestic workers in Guipuzcoa		
	Tax haven–free territories in Spain (municipalities, provincial councils, and regional governments)		
	Partner organizations of Oxfam and Oxfam Intermon		
	Fair trade organizations		
	Beneficiaries for Oxfam and Oxfam Intermon		
	Public donors		
	Donor companies, foundations, and private entities		

(Continued)

Table 4.8.1 (Continued)

Groups in the reports (in order of appearance)		
Save the Children	Beneficiaries	Children cared for in emergencies
		Children in health programmes
		Healthcare workers
		Children in education programmes
		Children in protection programmes
		Children at risk of social exclusion
		Families at risk of social exclusion
		Children participating in prevention workshops
		Refugee or migrant children cared for
	Schools	Teachers and male and female students
	Companies and foundations that support them	
UNICEF	Beneficiaries	Children vaccinated against deadly diseases (45% of all those in the world)
		Children <5 years of age treated for malnutrition
		Children and their families with safe drinking water
		Children and their families with adequate sanitation
		Children with education in emergencies
		Children with psychological help in emergencies
		Children involved in child labour with assistance
		Child soldiers released and reintegrated
	United Nations Children's Fund Committees	
	Partners and donors	
	Companies, foundations, and sports bodies	
	Institutions and public authorities	
	Ambassadors, friends, and collaborators	
	Media	
	Spanish regional governments with pacts for childhood	
	Volunteers	
	Social media followers	

Source: Own creation

The second level shows other groups to explain the lines, projects, and objectives presented in the documents. These are collaborators, participants in initiatives, beneficiaries, and recipients (see Table 4.8.2). They specify sources of funding, reinforce the perception of the organization's character, and make certain actions more specific.

Discussion and conclusion

The research by Araque and Montero (2006), Balas (2010), and Maguregui et al. (2019) classify publics in the for-profit or business sector, the nonprofit sector, the public sector, and civil society. This makes it possible to understand the type of relationship and define the information demands in order to extract the basic stakeholders for the NGOs.

The classification by levels in the reports reveals repetition, or overlapping data; missing groups; and convergence between lines of action. Caritas presents its economic resources invested by programme. Red Cross determines its stakeholders considering the impact they have on the organization

Table 4.8.2 Other groups mentioned in the reports (2018)

Caritas – groups	
Organization chairman's office	Individuals and families seeking support
Victims of trafficking or exploitation	Spanish Caritas Confederation
Children, teenagers, and families	Ethical banking
Church Platform for Decent Jobs	International Labour Organization (ILO)
Refugee camps	Communities affected by earthquakes
Pan-Amazonian Ecclesiastical Network (REPAM)	Spanish Development Cooperation Agency

Global Trade Union Movement and Global Labour Movement
Social inclusion companies, cooperatives, special employment centres, and other social economy organizations

Victims of armed conflicts	Confederation of observatories of reality

Donors and collaborators (particularly individuals, private and public bodies, and religious institutions)

Parliamentary groups	DESC Platform
Migrants with Rights network	Common Future platform

Catholic Church and Episcopal Conference
Groups mentioned in the programmes (gypsy community, immigrants, elderly people, women, people with disabilities, homeless people, people deprived of their liberty [prisoners and former prisoners] and drug addiction, HIV-AIDS, and mental health)

Companies and institutions	Third-sector platform	
Local, regional, and central government	European Union	Social economy organizations
Christian community	Third-sector organizations	

Red Cross – groups
Sea rescue
Treasury and social security

Suppliers	Round table for civil dialogue	State council for social action NGOs	Committees
Third-sector platforms and coordinators		Protection council	Media

European Social Fund

Spanish Ministry of Health, Social Services and Equality	Spanish Federation of Municipalities and Provinces
Spanish Association of Social Responsibility Managers	CSR Observatory
Spanish Fundraising Association	Social Action NGO Platform (POAS)
Excellence in Management Club	Children's Organization platform
Spanish Youth Council	Third0Sector Platform
Spanish Council of Social Action NGOs	NGO Coordinating Group for Development
Institute for NGO Quality	Volunteering Platform
European Network for the Fight against Poverty and Social Exclusion	Spanish Network for the United Nations Global Compact

Spanish Ministry of Defence (legal advisers and officers of the armed forces, students from the Military Legal Corps, and peace mission observers; also staff from the Naval War College on promotion and adaptation courses and armed forces personnel)

Intermon Oxfam – groups

International governments	Civil society organizations in Spain

Local and feminist organizations
Euronews (media)
Spanish government, European Union, public and local authorities, multilateral organizations
Women's agricultural cooperatives

(Continued)

Table 4.8.2 (Continued)

Caritas – groups
Catalan government umbrella organization for foundations
Save the Children – Groups
Sports personalities
Government and political groups
Immigrant assistance centers in Melilla   CETI (Temporary Residence Centre for Immigrants)
Public institutions
UNICEF – groups
Educators, communities, and other agents and institutions
Government and all   Communities, municipalities, and professional groups (Spain) parties
Health personnel

Source: Own creation

and links action plans with the number of beneficiaries. Intermon Oxfam presents the benefits of specific actions and at year-end displays its expenditure items by programmes, revealing previously unconsidered groups (the Spanish government, the European Union, public and local authorities, and multilateral organizations) as sources of funding. UNICEF (the only one to consider social media followers) and Save the Children associate actions and beneficiaries; the latter lacks information on partners, donors, and volunteers.

There are 200 groups, which are difficult to characterize. This makes it difficult to extract parent groups, but it is beneficial to detect the collectives that make them up. Twelve key stakeholder or parent groups are established for NGOs, covering 58 groups (see Table 4.8.3).

Management refers to members and/or patrons. Balas (2010) defines it as an ambivalent public, and Maguregui et al. (2019) separates partners, as a group, from patrons. The associations have management teams that are accountable to members, and the foundations have boards of trustees (chair, secretary, and members) which establish their lines of action and ensure the fulfilment of the purpose for which they were established.

Although they are identified separately by Araque and Montero (2006) and Maguregui et al. (2019), Balas (2010) suggests considering workers and volunteers together, because they are an "internal public". Both are essential so that NGO activity can continue. It is important to know those in charge at local activity points (e.g., Caritas parishes or local regional councils assemblies).

Collaborators, partners, and influencers are considered by Araque and Montero (2006), Balas (2010) and Maguregui et al. (2019), but the time factor in the relationships and the fact that the agents are extremely diverse mean the proposal must be reconsidered in this research. In addition, the Spanish Fundraising Association's (AEFr's) 2016 Donor Profile Study shows that, of 9.5 million people, 24% were donors to NGOs in Spain and 12% of them were members (AEFr, 2017). This invites us to differentiate between long-term partners and donors for specific projects.

With their financial and/or in-kind contributions, members and collaborators are a key source of resources for carrying out the organization's activities. Moreover, "there is a tendency to argue that the importance of an NGDO is directly proportional to the number of members it has" (Maracuello & Maracuello, 2000, p. 106).

If the action for which the organization requires support is one-off or specific, the donors' and participants' parent public is involved. The term donor refers to individuals, companies, or organizations that contribute or pay for a one-off operation during a specific period or for the purchase of products. And participants are those who, through their actions, contribute to implementing and carrying out actions on the ground.

Table 4.8.3 Proposed stakeholder reputational evaluators for the social action third sector (SATS)

Parent groups	Composition
1- Management	• Trustees and members of the organization's management committees
2- Workers and volunteers	• Hired by the organization • Volunteers
3- Partners and collaborators	• Long-term collaborators (individuals, businesses, entities or institutions offering support on an ongoing basis) • Members of the entities (those making periodic contributions – monthly, quarterly, or annually – accepting more of a link with the organization and its activity)
4- Donors and participants	• Individuals who make one-off contributions • Customers (purchasers of fair trade and solidarity products)[4] • Signatories • Companies or organizations that contribute or pay for a one-off operation • Support staff (promoters and teams participating in specific events) • Employees of the public treasury and social security organization • Maritime rescue and armed forces personnel • Staff of the Spanish Ministries of Health, Social Services, and Equality • Members of the immigrant assistance centres • Educators and school staff (teachers and pupils) • Health personnel • Ethical banking members • Managers of special employment centres • Heads of producer groups and cooperatives
5- Beneficiaries	• Attendees at workshops, awareness-raising courses, and training • Refugees and migrants • Families affected by natural disasters • People supported in humanitarian crises • Vulnerable groups: gypsy community, people deprived of their liberty (prisoners and ex-prisoners), people with disabilities, homeless people, women, and the elderly • People and families supported/assisted • Victims of trafficking or exploitation • Workers in special employment centres, producer groups, and cooperatives • Children[5]
6- Suppliers and creditors	• Permanent services (structural) • Nonpermanent services (specific services associated with the activity) • Subcontracted services (ad hoc and subject to public procurement regulations)
7- Competition	• Legal representatives of the organizations carrying out the activity and seeking to raise funds and secure support for their causes
8- Government	• Members of government, administration, and parliamentarians at different levels of representation
9- Specialists in SATS	Representatives of: • Spanish Agency for Development Cooperation • NGO Coordinating Group for Development • Social Action NGO Platform (POAS) • Third-sector platform (TSP) • Children's organization platform • Spanish regional government umbrella organization for foundations • Spanish Association of Foundations • Spanish Fundraising Association • Third-sector observatory

(*Continued*)

Table 4.8.3 (Continued)

Parent groups	Composition
10- Opinion leaders	• Volunteering platform • Institute for NGO Quality • Excellence in Management Club • Activists • High-profile personalities from sports, journalism, and culture as the organization's ambassadors • Followers of organization's social media accounts with strong influence (influencers)
11- Media and communications	• Representatives of general and specialized media
12- Civil society	• Trade union representatives • Members of the university community • Spanish Federation of Municipal and Provincial Councils • Spanish Youth Council • Feminist Coordinator – Spanish Federation of Feminist Organizations • Spanish Platform of Organizations for Elderly People and Pensioners • Organization of Consumers and Users (OCU) • Social media users with average influence

Beneficiaries, also called users by Maguregui et al. (2019), are individuals or legal entities receiving aid from NGOs. Suppliers and creditors are included because, as suppliers of (commercial or financial) resources, they should receive adequate information so they can assess the organization's ability to meet its obligations and commitments.

Competition among the social action third sector (SATS) requires an understanding that NGOs do not perceive other NGOs as competition because "they carry out their mission without feeling the need to compete against anyone, so they do not perceive competitors as stakeholders, because, from their point of view, they simply do not have any" (Maguregui et al., 2019, p. 81). But they must be looked at like a collective because of the great efforts NGOs have to make to attract members or donors, bring in collaborators, and win the support of leaders or public figures to champion their causes.

The relationship of dependency and need that NGOs maintain with governments makes them a decisive stakeholder. Although "they do not feel as if they are a group that generates pressure in itself, merely an organization carrying out its activities" (Maguregui et al., 2019, p. 81), "the very income structure of the coordinating body's NGDOs shows the relationship of dependency on public funds" (Maracuello & Maracuello, 2000, p. 107) that has always existed for them. Balas (2010) also mentions authorities and politicians and attributes credibility for their behaviour, their conception of reality, and their ability to motivate and encourage society to opinion leaders, defined as "think tanks, trendsetting units, university lecturers, business schools and gurus – personalities [. . .] relevant in different scenarios, such as culture, sports, the church, art or science" (p. 760). But when the influence of these leaders is exerted on nonprofit bodies, Araque and Montero (2006) call them influencers. For the many different groups in the reports, we propose, firstly, specialists in SATS as experts in studying and managing it and, secondly, opinion leaders as catalysts of the NGO's values. These are considered to be any leading activists and influencers (individuals with a large number of social media followers) who follow the NGO's accounts.

The media are an essential group which must be served. NGOs must consider not only the so-called traditional mass media but also social media, since they generate an informative impact and favour interaction.

Finally, civil society is proposed as a platform suitable for citizens to influence public decision-making affecting NGOs. This group is made up of citizens who organize themselves collectively (outside government structures) to influence decision-making in the public sphere.

The heterogeneity of the third sector (foundations, associations, singular entities, etc.) and its social purpose force entities to be more transparent and to clearly transmit their true nature. To this end, it is essential to adapt the form and content of the message to each specific group and to be aware that the incorporation of discourses that prioritize social values and solidarity imply a high emotional charge. However, it must be considered that communication in the third sector has a double function: to inform about what the organization itself does, but also to give a voice to those who do not have one. Therefore, identifying stakeholders and actively listening to them will be essential, not only to inform and raise awareness but also to incorporate social demands into their speeches. Only in this way will NGOs be able to legitimize their role as collaborating, lobbying, and denouncing agents and their social recognition.

Notes

1. This study is linked to the Research Promotion Plan (2018–2021) project of the Universitat Jaume I in Castellón (18I417/UJI-B2018-27) entitled: "Medición de la Reputación Corporativa de Cruz Roja Española, creación de un modelo para el Tercer sector de acción social".
2. On page 11 of the report it says there are 197,619, alluding to the Volunteering and Participation Plan. There is a discrepancy of 558 people, which may refer to participants.
3. The sum does not tally: there is a discrepancy of 100 activity points.
4. Organizations such as Intermon Oxfam act as intermediaries to place fair-trade products in retail outlets. These initiatives are commercial but seek to raise funds to help the communities in which the projects are carried out, rather than making a profit for the organization.
5. Children are among the main beneficiaries of NGOs. Obtaining information from this public is difficult because they lack the ability to respond to certain requests for information. It is proposed to obtain information from groups 2 and 4 in the table because they feel the benefits as part of their work.

References

AEFr (Asociación Española de Fundraising). (2017). *Asociación Española de Fundraising: Trabajando para el desarrollo de la Captación de Fondos en España.* www.aefundraising.org

Araque, R., & Montero, M. J. (2006). *Corporate social responsibility under debate.* Icaria Editorial.

Baamonde-Silva, X., García-Mirón, S., & Martínez-Rolán, X. (2017, May 10). Solidaridad y transparencia digital: Webs y redes sociales de las ONGs españolas de acción social. *El profesional de la información, 26*(3), 438–446. https://doi.org/10.3145/epi.2017.may.10

Balas, M. (2010). *Communication management in the third sector: Analysis of the perceived image of third sector organizations* [Doctoral Thesis, Universitat Jaume I].

Corporate Excellence & Canvas (2018). *Approaching the future 2018.* Tendencias en reputación y gestión de intangibles. Retrieved July 10, 2019, from https://canvasconsultores.com/wpcontent/uploads/2018/06/Approaching%20the%20Future%202018_.pdf

Dircom. (2019). *Anuario de la comunicación 2018. La era de los bots con inteligencia emocional.* Published by the author.

Freeman, R. E. (1984). *Strategic management: A stakeholder approach.* Pitman.

Gómez, B., Soria, M. M., & Concejo, B. (2018). La comunicación en el Tercer Sector: El caso vallisoletano. *Vivat Academia, 143*, Forum XXI. https://doi.org/10.15178/va.2018.143.25-44

Herranz de la Casa, J. M. (2007, April). La gestión de la comunicación como elemento generador de transparencia en las organizaciones no lucrativas. *CIRIEC-España, Revista de Economía Pública, Social y Cooperativa, 57*, 5–31. ISSN: 0213-8093

Maguregui, M. L., Corral, J., & Elechiguerra, C. (2019). La identificación de los grupos de interés de las entidades sin fines de lucro en la emisión de información transparente. *Revesco, 131*, 65–85. http://doi.org/10.5209/REVE.62814

Maracuello, C., & Maracuello, C. H. (2000). Las organizaciones no gubernamentales para el desarrollo (ONGD) en España. *Revista Internacional de Sociología, 58*(25), 99–119. https://doi.org/10.3989/ris.2000.i25.784

Nos-Aldás, E. (2019). *Transgressive communication for social change*. Publications of the Universitat Jaume I. Castellón de la Plana: Sapientia Collection, no. 158. http://doi.org/10.6035/Sapientia158

PwC. (2018). *Radiografía del Tercer Sector Social en España: Retos y oportunidades en un entorno cambiante*. PwC Fundation. www.pwc.es/es/publicaciones/tercer-sector/fundacion-pwc-tercer-sector-social-2018.pdf

Santolino, M. (2010). Recuperando la esencia: Las ONGD como agentes de comunicación para el cambio social. *Plataforma Voluntariado*, 221–256. https://plataformavoluntariado.org/wp-content/uploads/2018/10/recuperando-la-esencia-las-ongd-como-agentes-de-comunicacion-para-el-cambio-social.pdf

Vernis, P., Iglesias, A., Sanz, M., Solernou, B. Urgell, M., & Vidal, J. (1998). *La Gestion de las organizaciones no lucrativas*. Deusto.

Wimmer, R. D., & Dominick, J. R. (1996). *La investigación científica de los medios de comunicación: Una introducción a sus métodos*. Bosch.

4.9
ACTIVISM AND SOCIAL MEDIA
Case studies from Greece's economic crisis

Michael Nevradakis

Introduction

Social movements fueled by social media garnered global attention in the preceding decade, exemplified by Occupy Wall Street, the Arab Spring, and the Spanish 'Indignados'. Greece was no exception to this trend, as evidenced by Greece's own 'Indignants' movement in 2011. These protests were said to have been precipitated by invitations which went 'viral' on social media, and they followed in the footsteps of widespread social unrest in December 2008, following the shooting death of a 15-year-old boy in Athens by police. Social media, such as Twitter, were utilized as a primary means of communicating and organizing among protesters (see Bresta, 2011; Clarke, 2015).

Greece has been regarded by many scholars as a country where the public sphere and civil society institutions have not developed as robustly as in many other western countries. Here, we can define the public sphere as encompassing the entire sphere of public discourse involving key societal issues, including the government and state, political parties and movements, public institutions such as the judicial system, mass media, and public spaces of all sorts where discussion and deliberation occur – including public squares and cafés (Nevradakis, 2018, p. 25). In turn, civil society can be defined here as encompassing nongovernmental organizations (NGOs), trade unions, professional organizations, grassroots and activist organizations of all kinds, volunteer groups, community and neighborhood organizations, academia, private voluntary organizations, religious groups, and foundations (Nevradakis, 2018, p. 25).

The Greek public sphere has been described by multiple scholars as lacking in independence from the state and leading societal institutions. Contogeorgis, for instance, argues that Greece's long-standing partisan system has taken 'ownership' of the political system and transformed public discourse into private discourse (2013, p. 48). He further argues that Greece's public intellectuals themselves reproduce the hegemonic discourse of the state and the political apparatus, describing these figures as "organic legitimizers" of the incumbent system (2012, p. 53). Panagiotopooulou has pointed out that counter-public spheres and oppositional public spheres in Greece have historically been marked by their ephemeral nature, lacking in longevity (2013, pp. 453–454). This highly politicized public sphere is also significantly polarized due to historic left-right cleavages that have never been resolved but which returned to the surface during the years of the economic crisis. These cleavages are reproduced by the incumbent political and media system (Boukala, 2014, pp. 492–493).

In turn, Greek civil society has been characterized as dominated by political and partisan interests. These characteristics have been highlighted as factors which have contributed to the relative

DOI: 10.4324/9781003170563-39

underdevelopment of civil society in Greece (see also Contogeorgis, 2013; Huliaras, 2015; Nevradakis, 2021, pp. 8–10; Pantazidou, 2013; Simiti, 2015; Sotiropoulos, 2004; Vathakou, 2015). For example, Contogeorgis argues that Greek civil society today consists of interest groups that hold a position of authority in society, and in particular within the political system. According to Contogeorgis, the interests represented by such groups are contradictory to those of society at large, while the groups themselves are dependent on clientelistic relations with the state and a system of patronage (2012, p. 111). Komninou identified this intense party-based clientelism as an obstacle for the formation of a strong, autonomous civil society (2001, pp. 55–62). Danopoulos points out that Greek civil society organizations exhibit a lack of autonomy due to their frequent financial dependence on the state (2015, pp. 128–129). Similarly, Greece's economic crisis could be said to also have contributed to a concurrent institutional credibility crisis. Public opinion surveys have consistently found low levels of public trust towards major societal institutions, including NGOs (see DiaNEOsis, 2017; Eurobarometer, 2015; European Commission, 2016; HumanGrid, 2013; Kalogeropoulos et al., 2016; Kapa Research, 2016; Nevradakis, 2021, pp. 10–12; Organization for Economic Co-operation and Development, 2017).

The transformations which took place in Greek society during the economic crisis largely occurred in parallel with the significant rise in usage of social media. Despite Greece's relatively low levels of broadband penetration, which has remained below the European Union average, Greeks continue to rank among the world's biggest consumers of news from online and social media sources (Kalogeropoulos, 2021). It is significant that this growth has occurred during a period of economic difficulty for many Greeks.

Therefore, this chapter is guided by the following research questions:

RQ1: How and to what extent were a new generation of civil society initiatives, which developed during the years of the Greek economic crisis, active on social media and operating in a more flexible manner than traditional NGOs, have a permanent or long-lasting impact on Greek society and the broader civil society sphere in Greece?

RQ2: To what extent did the new civil society initiatives borne during the years of the Greek economic crisis themselves demonstrate longevity? Was their existence ephemeral, like so many Greek civil society initiatives had been in the past, or were they able to overcome this trend and also to maintain their autonomy, perhaps with the help of their social media presence?

RQ3: To what extent did social media continue to play an ongoing and significant role in the operations of the Greek civil society initiatives that developed during the Greek economic crisis?

This chapter is derived from a broader longitudinal research project performed in Greece between 2012 and 2017 that encompassed over 120 interviews with a diverse range of individuals active within the Greek public sphere and civil society. What makes Greece a notable case is that it is a European country (and European Union [EU] member state) regarded as having a less-than-robust public sphere and civil society sector, where a severe economic crisis resulted in major political and social change, where low levels of credibility in major institutions are consistently measured, and where there is a particularly high usage of social media.

Two illustrative examples will be presented: Boroume (an NGO established during the economic crisis, which heavily utilized social media for public outreach and to recruit volunteers) and Radiobubble (an 'alternative' online radio station with a strong level of involvement in activism and civil society. For these illustrative examples, a series of detailed, semi-structured interviews were conducted during the aforementioned period of study, involving multiple volunteers from each entity and focusing on how those organizations viewed their position within Greece's civil society ecosystem and how they utilized social media tools as part of their operations.

As the findings will demonstrate, while there was some evidence that Greek civil society initiatives grew in number and prominence during the period studied, much of this expansion was ephemeral and lacked longevity. Boroume remains active as of June 2021, but by 2017, it had deemphasized its usage of social media tools and operated in a manner akin to established NGOs. Similarly, several of the civil society initiatives that Radiobubble had helped launch, such as Hackademy and Tutorpool, were inactive, while Radiobubble's social media presence had significantly declined.

Illustrative example: Boroume

During the Greek economic crisis, many new initiatives developed within Greek civil society. One such initiative is Boroume ('We Can'), founded in 2011, whose mission is to limit food waste by operating as an intermediary between organizations which possess a surplus of food and groups in need of food donations. Boroume attained a reputation for having been 'founded' on social media, due to its early emphasis placed on its Facebook presence. The organization's co-founder, Alexander Theodoridis, described the Greek public as "the most energetic users of Facebook" worldwide (personal communication, December 18, 2012) and explained the importance of social media for Boroume during its inception:

> From the beginning we realized that social media can be a very powerful tool for what we are doing. . . . We set up a Facebook page from the beginning and a Twitter . . . and right now, in 11 months, we have almost 8,000 'likes' in our Facebook page. [We have reached] 1.4 million people on Facebook and our website [has] several thousand unique visitors per month. . . . [Social media] got us known. Then it helped us communicate, to a broader public, specific needs.
>
> (Personal communication, December 18, 2012)

Fellow Boroume co-founder Xenia Papastavrou added:

> We were discovered by many journalists from our presence on Facebook and Twitter . . . I didn't have to advertise our message anywhere, other than social media and our website. . . . It helped, it just triggered companies donating food, volunteers as well as institutions, coming into contact with us. . . . It provided a body of people interested in supporting this idea.
>
> (Personal communication, April 15, 2013)

Social media applications also helped Boroume develop a "Map of Need". Volunteer Vicky Foteinou described this as "a map in which all the institutions which are in need, which have a lack of food, are presented, connected through Google Maps" (personal communication, December 14, 2012).

Theodoridis described the tangible impact of Boroume's social media presence and the interaction between the organization and the public via such mediums:

> We also use [the public's] suggestions in order to contact other possible donors. For example, what we have done is that we have taken several emails and posts [on] Facebook about the food waste in military camps . . . to the chief of staff of the Greek military and we showed him that people are talking about this. . . . He was very fond of the idea to get started with that.
>
> (Personal communication, December 18, 2012)

Boroume's social media presence also helped the organization attract volunteers. Theodoridis estimated that out of 20 to 25 volunteers, 5 or 6 had discovered Boroume via social media (personal communication, December 18, 2012). Foteinou described her experience:

> I had heard about Boroume . . . I [visited] the Facebook page of Boroume and from that time I [contacted] them and now I am a volunteer for over a year. I liked all the activities of Boroume and all the articles they had on their Facebook page, and this was something that caught my attention from the first time. The main reason why I found Boroume was through Facebook.
>
> (Personal communication, December 14, 2012)

In summarizing the overall impact of Boroume, Papastavrou stated:

> [W]e've helped raising awareness about the problem of hunger. We've helped the institutions become more extroverted as they [have started] voicing their needs instead of having problems and not knowing how to present them. We are getting more people actively involved and wanting to help, because actually we are presenting them a way to help . . . I think it's reinforcing a sentiment of . . . things will be alright, because so many good things are happening around us.
>
> (Personal communication, April 15, 2013)

In turn, volunteer Athinais A. connected Boroume's impact to the wider economic crisis:

> This attempt [operates] outside more traditional routes and governmental associations to take matters in their own hands and to do something about it, and I think that is something you see from the current crisis. There is a much greater activity and awareness about both the problems people are facing but also about how people are creating movements and organizations to deal with them . . . I think years ago we used to rely on the state, we used to rely on our family, but now you see that third sector alliance a lot more than you did years ago.
>
> (Personal communication, February 11, 2013)

Illustrative example: Radiobubble

While Boroume ultimately adopted practices more akin to 'official' and well-established NGOs, despite its substantial early reliance on social media, online radio station Radiobubble developed informally and took years to establish itself officially. Founded in 2007, Radiobubble was both an online radio station and activist hub, featuring 'alternative' radio programming and a significant news presence centered around its highly visible Twitter account and its *#rbnews* hashtag, which served as a point of reference during protests and social movements. However, Radiobubble also served as the catalyst for the launch of homegrown, grassroots civil society initiatives, such as Hackademy and Tutorpool.

Producer Panagiotis Oikonomou characterized Radiobubble as an attempt to re-create what had been known in Greece as 'free radio' during the early years following broadcast deregulation (Nevradakis, 2020, p. 244), stating: "We've made an attempt, through the opportunity provided to us by new media, to establish a free internet radio station", adding that its self-organized nature, collective decision-making, and commercial-free philosophy distinguished it from other media (personal communication, February 13, 2013).

Radiobubble's 'alternative' nature was reflected in its programming and perspectives. According to producer Petros Papathanasiou, anybody could join the station and produce a show, provided they loved radio and were willing to commit to a schedule (personal communication, December 17, 2012). Volunteer Theodora Oikonomides characterized Radiobubble as a station where "the basic rule is that there is no rule". No editorial policy or musical restrictions were imposed, while Oikonomides stated that diverse opinions were welcome: "[w]e are called a left-wing station or an anarchist station, and we would like to have a bigger diversity of opinions to be presented here than what we already have" (personal communication, December 17, 2012).

Greece's 'café culture' has long been a prominent part of the country's public sphere (Nevradakis, 2011, pp. 169–170, 2021, p. 16). Therefore, it is notable that Radiobubble was, for several years, operating out of a physical space, the Radiobubble Café, located in the Exarchia district of Athens, a neighborhood with a longstanding reputation as a hub for activism. Papathanasiou characterized the station's café space as "a catalyst" for the Radiobubble community to meet and to discuss matters pertaining to politics, economics, and communications (personal communication, December 17, 2012). Oikonomides added that "many of the most interesting initiatives in Greece over the past year started inside Radiobubble. Tutorpool started inside Radiobubble. Hackademy . . . is a Radiobubble project. This is a place, that not only physically, but even virtually, ideas develop" (personal communication, December 17, 2012).

Radiobubble was closely connected to activist and social movements in Athens and across Greece. It was during the December 2008 unrest that the station's *#rbnews* Twitter hashtag was established (Nevradakis, 2020, p. 247). In Papathanasiou's words, "an ecosystem developed surrounding this hashtag, through which the individuals who developed our news department" (personal communication, December 17, 2012). Oikonomou, for example, stated that he joined the station following the December 2008 riots, noting that Radiobubble "was the only medium . . . which managed to relay the truth about what was happening on the streets of Athens" (personal communication, February 13, 2013).

Indeed, during the years of the Greek economic crisis, Radiobubble's news programming was one of the most visible and prominent features of the station (Nevradakis, 2021. p. 13). As explained by Papathanasiou:

> The news department does not invite political figures. Systematically though we invite ordinary people, people who are involved in activism, people who are involved in the health or education sectors, and we prefer to speak to them even about politics, rather than with government representatives.
>
> (Personal communication, December 17, 2012)

Oikonomides characterized the *#rbnews* hashtag as the station's most powerful tool, as it was utilized by the public to tweet reports of incidents occurring on the ground in real time. These tweets would then undergo a verification process conducted by Radiobubble's news team, with verified reports officially reposted online and announced on air (Nevradakis, 2021, p. 14). As explained by Oikonomides, "[w]e are very conscious about putting the news on our feed, on our curation tool, because we need to be sure what is happening" (personal communication, December 17, 2012). Indeed, *#rbnews* captured the attention of *The Guardian*, which embedded the feed from the hashtag in its live Twitter feed of the June 2012 Greek parliamentary elections (Nevradakis, 2021, p. 15).

In describing the extent of Radiobubble's Twitter presence, volunteer Panos Kounenakis claimed that "[t]he Greek Twitter started practically by the community of Radiobubble. It was one of the pioneers", adding that in 2011, *#rbnews* was the most popular Twitter hashtag in Greece, due to its popularity during the 'Indignants' movement (personal communication, June 13, 2017).

Furthermore, according to Oikonomou, over half of the individuals who were involved with Radiobubble since 2008 were "well-known on Twitter" (personal communication, February 13, 2013), while Twitter itself was emphasized by the station over other mediums, such as Facebook, because, as stated by Papathanasiou, "Twitter is more immediate and more expressive than Facebook" (personal communication, December 17, 2012).

As previously mentioned, Radiobubble and its café served as a hub for civil society initiatives. One such endeavor borne out of this space was Hackademy, a project that provided professional, citizen, and aspiring journalists with training on new media (Nevradakis, 2021, p. 17). Papathanasiou described Hackademy as "a civil society initiative but not a solidarity initiative" and as an "innovative lab for new media" (personal communication, December 17, 2012). Zaira Konstantopoulou, a volunteer with Hackademy, stated that this initiative was borne out of the station, acted "as a branch of Radiobubble," was self-organized and nonprofit in nature, and was "probably the first [initiative] of its kind in Greece" (personal communication, February 15, 2013).

Another civil society endeavor that developed out of the Radiobubble ecosystem was Tutorpool, an initiative linking volunteer tutors to families who could not afford private tutoring. Tutorpool was characterized by Papathanasiou as "one of the first, if not the first, online solidarity movements in the field of education" (personal communication, December 17, 2012) and which reportedly began with a single tweet, posted in December 2011. Christina Lardikou, a Tutorpool volunteer, explained that the initiative was a product of individuals active in that year's 'Indignants' movement, who maintained an active Twitter presence and utilized the Radiobubble café as a meeting space (Nevradakis, 2021, pp. 17–18).

Similar to Boroume, Tutorpool utilized Google Maps to link tutors with families in need. As of 2013, according to Lardikou, between 600 and 700 educators offered services to approximately 500 families (personal communication, February 20, 2013). Tutorpool also produced its own monthly program on Radiobubble, focusing on educational issues (Nevradakis, 2021, p. 18).

Notably, another NGO, Doctors Without Borders, also produced a monthly show on Radiobubble during this period. Sophia Apostolia, the web editor for the Greek branch of Doctors Without Borders, stated that she discovered Radiobubble through the station's #rbnews hashtag and via Hackademy – which had presented a seminar on #rbnews that Apostolia attended (Nevradakis, 2021, p. 19). In Apostolia's words, she was "very impressed by the fact that #rbnews was a tool that had a proper scientific background behind it and guidelines" (personal communication, March 6, 2013). Apostolia, who co-hosted the radio program, stated that the station had developed "a community that is very close to our mentality" while serving as an example of "citizen journalism, safeguarded with guidelines" (personal communication, March 6, 2013).

Social media and civil society in Greece: was there an impact?

Based on findings from the broader study conducted between 2012 and 2017 (Nevradakis, 2018), social media was generally viewed as having a positive impact on civil society in Greece. Apostolia stated that social media enabled previously obscure activist movements, such as the initiative opposing controversial gold mining activities in the Skouries region, to attain visibility and "[cross] over to the mainstream" (personal communication, March 6, 2013). Fotinaki described an empowering effect for those previously "resigned to not being heard", with social media acting as a "game changer, [activating] people who may have been indifferent in the past . . . to become more actively involved in society and issues of concern to society" (personal communication, July 5, 2013). Papastravrou emphasized social media's role in helping citizens bypass the state: "[w]hat we have seen is that the crisis has made the people start to get more interested in what was happening around them . . . as people take things into their own hands instead of waiting for them to be solved by the state" (personal communication, April 15, 2013). Oikonomides added her view that traditional civil society organizations were also being bypassed: "people are going for something entirely different now . . . bypassing the traditional structures, not only the state, but also all the traditional structures that you would expect to fulfill that role" (personal communication, December 17, 2012). Theodoridis, however, noted that NGOs still "had a very negative stigma" in Greek society and that "the majority [still] associates NGOs negatively", adding that "[in Greece] we are still far away from even the most modest, low levels [of civil society involvement] of other countries . . . this has to do with people's attitudes and people's attitudes do not change in such important issues overnight" (personal communication, January 27, 2017).

What can be observed is that the early momentum of organizations such as Boroume and Radiobubble, and the enthusiasm with which they initially approached social media, did not last. In his 2017 follow-up interview, Theodoridis stated that while Boroume had grown as an organization, social media become less important to its operations compared to 2012:

> Facebook is not important any more to us in terms of general projection of what we are doing. . . . We thought it was really important to post every day on a permanent basis. Now we don't think that it's so important anymore. We think it's better to post fewer but better posts . . . and we have learnt that it's really difficult to make out what post brings the most views and likes. . . . We are still keen on posting on Facebook . . . I would say 3 or 4 times a week.
> (Personal communication, January 27, 2017)

Nevertheless, Theodoridis characterized Facebook as the organization's "most important source of volunteers" (personal communication, January 27, 2017).

Significant changes had occurred at Radiobubble by 2017. These included the station's formation as a legally registered cooperative, the closure of its café and its subsequent relocation to the interior of a theater, and the deemphasizing of news programming and social media in favor of music programming. Radiobubble volunteer Ioanna Paraskevopoulou explained that "there is a greater emphasis being placed on radio rather than Twitter", adding that "radio was always the heart of Radiobubble. It was never social media, even if this impression always existed because it became widely known on Twitter". Paraskevopoulou added that news was deemphasized, while the *#rbnews* hashtag was split, becoming "more journalistic" while a new hashtag, *#antireport*, was created with a focus on "counter-reporting and the anarchist world" (personal communication, February 2, 2015).

Foreshadowing future changes at Radiobubble, Paraskevopoulou shared her concerns that the station may lose its oppositional edge following the election of the left-wing SYRIZA party in Greece's January 2015 national parliamentary elections:

> [P]reviously the lines were drawn. There were those who did what they did, supporting the system, and there were the alternative media, which were far-left and which opposed the government. What will those far-left outlets do now though with a leftist government? . . . As a journalist you have to be . . . scrutinizing them. Here it will become apparent to what extent those sites that are friendly to the left will scrutinize the government or will be obliged to spread propaganda.
> (Personal communication, February 2, 2015)

Kounenakis detailed an internal schism which occurred at Radiobubble, arising from the station's decision to legally establish itself as a cooperative:

> [W]e reached a limit when financially it couldn't go on. There was the big question, how do we continue? A significant part of the Radiobubble community didn't want to go the way we did. The majority wanted to go the way we did, so there was a split around 2014.
> (Personal communication, June 13, 2017)

Kounenakis described some additional changes at the station, stating that:

> Radiobubble doesn't contribute much in the public sphere . . . we are not covering news the way we did. We take initiatives in some campaigns, but . . . through Twitter, which was our basic tool, we don't use it for news broadcasting . . . we focus more on Facebook as the Radiobubble central account . . . Facebook attracts more attention at the moment . . . and this has to do with the power of texts and images and interaction. Facebook is more friendly in general . . . and doesn't have so many constraints.
> (personal communication, June 13, 2017)

The *#rbnews* and *#antireport* hashtags were deemphasized in favor of a new Twitter hashtag, *#rbdata*, focusing on data journalism. These changes were reflective of a broader shift away from news, politics, and social media. Instead, asynchronous broadcasting, focusing on music and culture, was emphasized (personal communication, June 13, 2017).

Moreover, Radiobubble's civil society initiatives, Hackademy and Tutorpool, did not last. For instance, Hackademy "worked for three seasons, but it collapsed due to financial pressures", in the words of Kounenakis, who also questioned Radiobubble's ongoing viability: "we are not committed to continue. We have said that there is no stress, we don't owe anyone anything, we will continue only if we like it and if we are useful and if we contribute to society" (personal communication, June 13, 2017).

The Greek public today is one of the largest consumers of news and information content from social media (Kalogeropoulos, 2021, pp. 82–83). While this may appear counterintuitive at first glance, there is likely a direct connection between the demise of alternative news and information initiatives that were active on social media during the years of the financial crisis and the high degree of social media news consumption recorded in Greece today. Trust in news, including news found online or via social media, ranks among the lowest levels in countries worldwide, while the preferred online sources for news are themselves web versions of 'traditional' media outlets or are closely affiliated with such entities (Kalogeropoulos, 2021, pp. 82–83; Nevradakis, 2018, pp. 445–446).

The illustrative examples presented here are indicative of the ephemerality which was characteristic of many of the civil society initiatives that launched in Greece during the economic crisis. Radiobubble was still operating as of late 2019 but was barely active by June 2021: the station's social media accounts were largely inactive during 2020 and 2021, its Mixcloud page had not been updated in over a year, and the station's live web stream operated intermittently.

The other trend that can be identified here is replication, or mirroring. Many initiatives born during the crisis, initially at least, had positioned themselves as 'alternatives' to incumbent societal institutions. Many such entities, however, ultimately replicated the 'mainstream'. Boroume, though still active in the Greek nonprofit sphere as of June 2021, has shifted away from social media and could now be said to be operating similarly to established NGOs. Radiobubble, with its turn towards music-oriented content, arguably departed from what had made it almost unique among Greece's numerous online radio stations, few of which offer any news or information programming (Nevradakis, 2020, pp. 247–248). On the contrary, while the internet and social media are now prominent sources of news and information for a significant section of the Greek public, studies have shown that it is outlets operated by or associated with 'traditional' media outlets and mainstream journalists that are the most popular (Kalogeropoulos, 2021, pp. 82–83).

Finally, this ephemerality and mirroring were noted by several interviewees. As noted by Kounenakis, there was a period of change in Greece, but ultimately, it was one that was fleeting:

> [W]hat is called "movement" by many people, doesn't exist anymore or it has died out. It has turned into either passiveness or isolation or people trying to survive in these terms, trying to make it through the day, but the political involvement has dropped significantly.
> (Personal communication, June 13, 2017)

Scholars such as Bailey et al., Lievrouw, and Rodríguez highlighted the danger of co-optation faced by social movements, civil society, and alternative media. Bailey et al. proffered a conceptualization of alternative media as rhizomatic, meaning that they operate in a nonlinear, nomadic fashion, with a high degree of contingency wherein they may be considered 'alternative' at one time and 'mainstream' at some other point in time (2008, pp. 25–29). Lievrouw discussed the cycles of "capture and co-optation" experienced by alternative media outlets, which may leave no place for grassroots or independent organizations or forms of expression separate from the market and the hegemonic system (2011, pp. 2–3, 82–83). Rodríguez identified obstacles faced by community and grassroots groups, including frequently short life cycles and the risk they face of being corrupted and co-opted by their finding sources or by dependencies upon central authorities and/or commercial interests (2001, pp. 22, 55, 183).

The ephemeral nature of many of the initiatives which arose within Greek civil society and the country's public sphere during the years of the Greek economic crisis could be described, to various extents, as being representative of the capture and co-optation described by the aforementioned scholars. The decline of Radiobubble as a hotbed of activism and the move of Boroume towards the operating standards of an established NGO both appear to represent a continuation of a longstanding trend in Greece, identified by multiple scholars, where such initiatives were ephemeral in nature or were ultimately co-opted by the prevailing sociopolitical system and ended up reproducing, or mirroring, its characteristics, including a high degree of partisanship and dependence on the state (see Nevradakis, 2018, pp. 414–457).

References

Bailey, O. G., Cammaers, B., & Carpentier, N. (2008). *Understanding alternative media*. Open University Press.
Boukala, S. (2014). Waiting for democracy: Political crisis and the discursive (re)invention of the "national enemy" in times of "Grecovery". *Discourse & Society, 25*(4), 483–499.
Bresta, M. (2011). Oli i Ellada mia plateia (?). In C. Giovanopoulos & D. Mitropoulos (Eds.), *Dimokratia under construction: Apo tous dromous stis plateies* [*Democracy under construction: From the streets to the squares*] (pp. 91–100). A. Synechia.
Clarke, J. (2015). Solidarity and survival: A multidisciplinary exploration of volunteering during the Greek crisis. In D. A. Sotiropoulos (Ed.), *Austerity and the third sector in Greece: Civil society at the European frontline* (pp. 67–84). Ashgate.
Contogeorgis, G. (2012). *Kommatokratia kai dynastiko kratos: Mia ermineia tou Ellinikou adiexodou* (tetarti ekdosi) [*Partyocracy and the dynastic state: One interpretation of the Greek dead end* (4th ed.)]. Ekdoseis Pataki.
Contogeorgis, G. (2013). *Oi oligarhes: I dinamiki tis ypervasis kai i antistasi ton sigkatanevsifagon* [*The oligarchs: The ability to overcome and the resistance of the yes-men*]. Ekdoseis Pataki.
Danopoulos, C. P. (2015). Accountability and the quality of democracy in Greece. *Mediterranean Quarterly, 26*(4), 110–131.
DiaNEOsis. (2017). *Politismikoi paragontes tis oikonomikis autarkeias kai epiheirimatikotitas, Neoi ilikias 18–35, hristes diadiktuou* [*Cultural factors in economic independence and entrepreneurship: Youth aged 18–35, internet users*] [Data file]. www.dianeosis.org/wp-content/uploads/2017/07/anergia_neoi_17.7.2017_updated_final.pdf
Eurobarometer. (2015, Autumn). *Media use in the European Union* [Data file]. http://ec.europa.eu/COMM FrontOffice/publicopinion/index.cfm/ResultDoc/download/DocumentKy/72667
European Commission. (2016). *Flash Eurobarometer 437: Internet users' preferences for accessing content online* [Data file]. https://ec.europa.eu/commfrontoffice/publicopinion/index.cfm/ResultDoc/download/DocumentKy/74564
Huliaras, A. (2015). Greek civil society: The neglected causes of weakness. In J. Clarke, A. Huliaras, & D. A. Sotiropoulos (Eds.), *Austerity and the third sector in Greece: Civil society at the European frontline* (pp. 9–28). Ashgate.
HumanGrid. (2013). *Ethelontismos, syllogikes draseis allileggiyis: Anodikes taseis, para tin hamili ekkinisi* [*Volunteerism, collective actions of solidarity: Upward trend despite the low starting point*]. http://blog.HumanGrid.gr/εθελοντισμός-συλλογικές-δράσεις-αλλ/
Kalogeropoulos, A. (2021). Greece. In N. Newman, R. Fletcher, A. Schulz, S. Andi, C. T. Robertson, & R. K. Nielson (Eds.), *Reuters institute digital news report* (10th ed., pp. 82–83). Oxford University.
Kalogeropoulos, A., Panagiotou, N., & Dimitrakopoulou, D. (2016). *Reuters institute erevna gia tis psifiakes eidiseis 2016 (Ellada)* [*Reuters institute survey on digital news 2016 (Greece)*]. iwrite.gr Publications.

Kapa Research. (2016, October). *I krisi ton thesmon kai i apohi* [*The crisis of the institutions and abstention*] [Data file]. http://kaparesearch.com/index.php?option=com_k2&view=item&task=download&id=76_841eb3 12a5e458cbd1cec8bf65ba7928&Itemid=137&lang=el

Komninou, M. (2001). *Apo tin agora sto theama: Meleti gia ti sigrotisi tis dimosias sfairas kai tou kinimatografou sti sighroni Ellada, 1950–2000* [*From the market to spectacle: A study on the formation of the public sphere and cinema in modern Greece, 1950–2000*]. Ekdoseis Papazizi.

Lievrouw, L. (2011). *Alternative and activist new media*. Polity Press.

Nevradakis, M. (2011). From assimilation to Kalomoira: Satellite television and its place in New York City's Greek community. *Global Media Journal – Canadian Edition, 4*(1), 163–178.

Nevradakis, M. (2018). *From the polis to Facebook: Social media and the development of a new Greek public sphere* [Doctoral dissertation, The University of Texas]. https://repositories.lib.utexas.edu/bitstream/handle/2152/65842/NEVRADAKIS-DISSERTATION-2018.pdf?sequence=1

Nevradakis, M. (2020). Reproducing analog pathologies in the digital radio landscape: The case of Greece. In J. A. Hendricks (Ed.), *Radio's second century: Past, present, and future perspectives* (pp. 231–254). Rutgers University Press.

Nevradakis, M. (2021). Radio's role as an alternative online medium and site of activism during a time of crisis: The case of Greece's radiobubble. *Journal of Radio and Audio Media*, 1–27.

Organization for Economic Co-operation and Development (2017). *Government at a glance – 2017 edition: Serving citizens* [Data file]. https://stats.oecd.org/Index.aspx?QueryId=78415

Panagiotopoulou, R. (2013). www.real-democracy.gr: Oi epikoinoniakes praktikes tou kinimatos ton Aganaktismenon [www.real-democracy.gr: The communications practices of the movement of the Indignants]. In G. Pleios (Ed.), *I krisi kai ta MME* [*Crisis and the mass media*] (pp. 422–461). Ekdoseis Papazizi.

Pantazidou, M. (2013). Treading new ground: A changing moment for citizen action in Greece. *Development in Practice, 23*(5–6), 755–770.

Rodríguez, C. (2001). *Fissures in the mediascape: An international study of citizens' media*. Hampton Press.

Simiti, M. (2015). "Social need" or "choice"? Greek civil society during the economic crisis. *Hellenic Observatory Papers on Greece and Southeast Europe, 95*, 1–37.

Sotiropoulos, D. A. (2004). I koinonia politon stin Ellada: Atrofiki i afanis? [Civil society in Greece: Atrophic or invisible?] In D. A. Sotiropoulos (Ed.), *I agnosti koinonia politon* [*The unknown civil society*] (pp. 117–162). Potamos.

Vathakou, E. (2015). Citizens' solidarity initiatives in Greece during the financial crisis. In J. Clarke, A. Huliaras, & D. A. Sotiropoulos (Eds.), *Austerity and the third sector in Greece: Civil society at the European frontline* (pp. 167–192). Ashgate.

INDEX

#FFF Fridays for Future 165
#MeToo 142, 150, 165, 307
#NiUnaMenos 307
8M 256, 307, 309–314
15M 308

Aarts, Noelle 255, 259–268
abuse 79, 182, 286, 287, 289, 314
accountability 4, 5, 14, 34, 37, 66, 67, 70, 76, 112, 143, 144, 145, 146, 147, 221, 318, 327
actantial model 227
actatial criticism 231
activism 13, 16, 19, 32, 33, 35, 37, 50, 57, 67, 70, 145, 150–157, 198, 235, 237–239, 256, 257, 309, 314, 337, 338, 341, 345
activist 2, 3, 4, 33, 34, 43, 61, 75, 76, 150–157, 168, 196, 197, 238, 255, 256, 260, 307–312, 314, 329, 334, 337, 340–342; literacy 307, 308, 314
advocacy 13, 16, 19, 32, 33, 35, 37, 50, 57, 67, 70, 145, 150–157, 198, 235, 237–239, 256, 257, 309, 314, 337, 338, 341, 345; communication 28, 162, 196, 197, 198, 199
aid agencies 14, 66, 67, 68, 69, 70, 72
aid organizations 1, 68, 70, 71, 286
algorithmic filtering 90
Almansa-Martínez, Ana 162, 203–214
alternative media 343, 345
annual giving 3, 115, 117, 118, 119, 120, 121
annual reports 119, 257, 273, 327, 328
Arab Spring 42, 308, 337
Aristotelian rhetoric 185
articulation 78, 80, 88
association(s) 136, 144, 150, 152, 157, 166, 203–205, 208–210, 300, 301, 304, 308, 310, 332, 335, 340
associationalism 13, 15, 16, 17, 18, 19, 20
asynchronous broadcasting 344
Auger, Giselle 4, 76, 125–132
Avaaz 37

Back, Les 85
backstage communication model 273
Bailey, Olga Guedes 345
Barrett, R. 317
Barthes, Roland 225, 229
Bassel, Leah 88
behavioral insights 89, 111
behavior change 27, 29, 71, 109, 151
Bennett, W. Lance 34, 42, 90, 94, 176, 179, 236, 262
Bentele, Günter 5, 46, 51, 236
Bentham, Jeremy 57, 216, 218, 219, 220
Bernays 246, 247
Bickford, Susan 86, 90
bio-social 256, 319, 320, 325
Bodie, Graham 86, 87, 88
Boroume 257, 338–340, 342–345
bottom-up 13, 27, 28, 29, 30, 39, 101, 146, 166, 237, 238, 260, 266, 270, 271, 294, 319; communication 237, 270, 271
branding 4, 96, 97, 98, 101, 102, 136, 161, 174, 175, 176, 177, 178, 179, 180; internal 102, 161, 174, 175, 176, 177, 178, 179, 180
Breninger, Birgit 256, 317–326
Bruhn, Manfred 76, 94–103
Bucholtz, Barbara 143
BudgIT 105, 112
Bundelkhand 279, 280, 281, 284, 285
bureaucratization 16, 33, 34, 68, 204
Burksienė, V. 255, 269–279
business-like 3, 66, 81, 82, 136
business model 32, 182, 183, 186, 266

campaigns 7, 36, 37, 41, 68, 71, 110–111, 120, 129, 154, 170, 207, 209, 225, 227, 230, 231, 232, 251, 255, 283, 288, 293, 302–305, 308, 317, 321, 323, 324, 328, 344; advertising 317; advocacy 20; for change 237; communication 95, 110, 162, 205,

Index

207, 224, 229, 232; cross media 195; disinformation 60; fundraising 2, 66, 256, 300, 302–304, 327; marketing 318, 319; online 4; social marketing 6; social media 119, 195, 206; transmedia 195, 200
Campos, Ioli 162, 203–214
capacity building 29, 71, 112, 129, 228, 280, 284, 302
Caritas 257, 327, 329, 330, 331, 332
Castells, Manuel 18, 51, 235, 262
Castillo-Esparcia, António 162, 203–214, 247
Cattelani, Andrea 162, 224–234
CCO theory 6, 78, 87, 172
CDSC 13, 24, 27, 28, 30, 307, 308
Cerqueira, Carla 256, 307–316, 329
character strengths 163, 249, 251, 252
charities 1, 18, 70, 76, 127, 128, 176, 180, 307
chat bots 90
citizen 6, 13, 32, 35–37, 41, 42, 47–49, 52, 57–59, 70, 75, 89–91, 105, 110, 112, 113, 143–147, 151, 166, 168–172, 204–209, 212, 217, 255, 261, 264, 269–271, 301, 308, 329, 335, 342; association 204, 205; councils 59; engagement 32, 35, 308, 314; journalism 342; journey 172; mobilization 112; participation 1, 26, 32, 47, 147, 205, 237, 271; perception 142; private lives 32; social networks 208; voices 35
citizenship 47–49, 52, 143, 178, 205, 264, 287, 293, 308, 327; brand 174, 180
civic engagement 1, 33, 129, 301, 302
civic participation 36, 144, 300, 301, 304, 305
civic relations 14, 35, 37, 47, 50, 52, 166, 167, 169, 171
civil society 1, 2, 4, 5, 6, 7, 13, 14, 15, 18, 19, 20, 28, 32, 33, 34, 35, 36, 37, 39, 40, 46, 47, 49, 50, 51, 52, 53, 55, 59, 62, 63, 66, 67, 68, 70, 112, 142, 143, 144, 145, 146, 147, 148, 150, 158, 161, 165, 166, 167, 171, 172, 195, 257, 262, 270, 280, 285, 301, 308, 330, 331, 334, 335, 337, 338, 339, 340, 342, 343, 344, 345; organizations 1, 5, 6, 32, 35, 37, 46, 50, 51, 52, 161, 165, 172, 195, 262, 280, 331, 338, 342
co-creation 168, 169, 170, 171
collective action 14, 39, 42, 46, 47, 48, 51, 59, 80, 146, 157, 165, 166, 197, 255, 259, 260, 261, 262, 263, 264, 265, 266, 270, 311
collective coping 198
common good 1, 14, 32, 37, 46, 47, 48, 49, 50, 52, 57, 126, 143, 165, 166, 167, 261, 264, 317, 318, 319
communication actions 42, 113, 205, 207, 58, 100, 205, 212
communication content 99, 108, 185
communication dynamics 46, 76, 133, 169, 172
communication evaluation 106, 109, 208
communication for change 237, 242
communication for development 13, 23, 24, 27, 29, 41, 307
communication for social change 27, 40, 41, 151, 307, 308, 309, 315
communication goals 3, 107, 169, 170
communication management 1–3, 7, 8, 46, 75–76, 94, 98, 112, 161, 163, 165–166, 168–169, 172, 219, 237, 242
communication monitoring 76, 104
communication objectives 99, 105–106, 108, 109, 110, 111, 112, 206
communication perspective 4, 5, 78, 80–83, 166, 168, 235, 236, 237, 250
communication professional 6, 35, 168, 288, 294
communication strategies 5, 24, 27, 35–36, 41, 42, 91, 99, 121, 136, 137, 143, 146, 154, 155, 161, 162, 186, 195, 196, 198, 200, 206, 209, 220
communicative action 6, 41, 46, 52, 78, 168, 250
communicative constitution of organization *see* CCO theory
communicative constitution *see* CCO theory
community 1, 13, 17, 24, 26–29, 34, 42, 47, 48, 57–62, 75, 76, 102, 110, 112, 118, 119, 125, 126, 129, 131, 154, 155, 162, 166, 167, 168, 175, 185, 196–198, 211, 212, 215, 218, 220, 235, 247, 249, 256, 260–266, 274, 276, 323, 331, 333, 334, 337, 341–345; behavior 28; international 69; media 27–29; members 91, 136, 261, 264, 284, 285; mobilization 30, 128, 304; needs 182, 264; values 62
competence 36, 169, 188, 228, 271, 273, 275, 321
conceptual model 161, 168, 169, 172, 186, 331
consensus 6, 23, 27, 52, 55, 57, 62, 75, 86, 96, 242
constitutive approach 75, 77, 78, 80, 81, 82
constitutive communication 78, 80, 169
content analysis 89, 109, 255, 257, 263, 269, 272, 309, 328
contextual turn 191
corporate activism 150, 152
corporate communication 98, 187, 236, 237
corporate political advocacy (CPA) 150, 151, 157
corporate social responsibility (CSR) 150, 187, 235, 236, 237, 242, 331
corruption 28, 49, 68, 97, 144, 145, 146, 147
Costa, Bruno F. 76, 142–149
Couldry, Nick 85, 88
court-PR 215, 217, 218, 219, 220, 221
courts 162, 196, 215, 216, 217, 218, 219, 220, 221
COVID-19 20, 23, 40, 61, 130, 144, 150, 153, 198, 286, 287, 288, 290, 291, 294, 300, 302, 303, 304, 305
Craig, Robert 55, 58, 62, 77, 85
critical citizenship education 308
critical school of public relations 151
cross-media 102, 162, 195, 196, 198, 200
Cruz Roja *see* Red Cross
cultural expertise 318, 321
culturalized 319, 320, 321, 323, 325
cultural peace 312
customer journey mapping 89
cybernetic 161, 168, 171, 172

data analysis 154, 178, 291, 324
Davies, Thomas 1, 13, 15–22, 39, 49–51, 166
Deetz, Stan 79.8
deliberative democracy 60, 58, 59, 60
deliberative inquiry 58
deliberative polling 89
democracy 1, 7, 13, 18, 20, 32, 35, 47, 52, 58, 60, 76, 85, 90, 142, 143, 144, 145, 146, 147, 148, 166, 167, 217
Dewey, John 55, 56, 58, 59, 60, 62
dialogue 30, 42, 43, 69, 70, 71, 75, 86, 89, 91, 175, 176, 226, 237, 238, 256, 271, 276, 277, 288, 308, 317, 327, 331
DiaNEOsis 338
digital age 14, 39, 40, 41
digital media 36, 198, 199, 255, 270, 276
digital surveillance 90
Di Paolo, E. 325
discourse analysis 186, 229, 256, 309
discourse arenas 56, 59, 60, 61, 62
discursive structures 226, 229, 230
diversity 1, 2, 4, 15, 19, 27, 35, 42, 57, 75, 91, 94, 95, 105, 118, 129, 130, 136, 139, 166, 167, 203, 255, 259, 302, 307, 309, 312, 313, 314, 320, 321, 323, 325, 341
Dobson, Andrew 87, 90
Doctors Without Borders 342
domestic violence 256, 286, 287, 288, 289, 290, 291, 292, 293, 294, 295, 310
donations 36, 41, 67, 68, 97, 115, 118, 122, 167, 182, 204, 273, 274, 301, 303, 304, 305, 339; mismanagement 97
Donor Bill of Rights 256, 286, 287, 288, 289, 290, 291, 292, 293, 294, 295, 310
Donor Pyramid 15, 17, 19, 196, 199
donors 256, 286, 287, 288, 289, 290, 291, 292, 293, 294, 295, 310
Dreher, Tanja 15, 17, 19, 196, 199
Dvorak, Jaroslav 255, 269–279

echo chamber 32, 90
eco-art 162, 236, 238, 239, 241, 242
e-communication 255, 256, 269, 271, 272, 273, 276, 277
economic crisis 287, 291, 337, 338, 339, 340, 341, 344, 345
education for development 308
Eliantonio 204
emotion 67, 76, 117, 161, 176, 177, 182, 185–188, 197, 225, 230–233, 239, 249, 301, 305, 309, 313, 319, 320, 325, 335
empathy 185, 197, 199, 200, 249, 309
empowerment 27, 30, 37, 43, 137, 138, 143, 185, 198, 262, 266, 280, 281
enactment 168, 169, 170, 187, 317, 320
engagement 1, 4, 14, 32, 33, 35, 36, 47, 60, 66, 68, 70, 75, 82, 86, 89, 91, 97, 107, 108, 110, 112, 113, 116, 120, 129, 138, 145, 147, 150, 157, 158, 162, 167, 169, 170, 171, 174, 176, 179, 205, 217, 220, 237, 255, 256, 262, 265, 273, 277, 283, 289, 300, 301, 302
entrepreneurial ecosystem 191
environmental communication 162, 224, 232, 271, 284, 285
environmental issues *see* environmental communication
environmental NGOs 4, 5, 37, 269, 274, 277
ethical 3, 14, 33, 46, 55, 66, 67, 68, 69, 70, 72, 122, 153, 199, 216, 237, 238, 246, 247, 317, 318, 331, 333
ethics 26, 86, 118, 151, 199, 246, 247, 312
eudaimonia 47, 52
euergetic 47, 48, 52
eurobarometer 146, 256, 300
European Commission 106, 107, 209, 212, 288, 338
European Union 35, 162, 209, 210, 211, 212, 270, 280, 288, 300, 331, 332, 338
evaluation 4, 25, 29, 34, 71, 75, 76, 104, 105, 106, 107, 108, 109, 110, 111, 112, 113, 162, 183, 185, 196, 199, 206, 207, 208, 238
evaluation framework 25, 106
eyetracking 113, 256, 318, 321

Facebook 42, 71, 153, 195, 239, 241, 263, 272, 274, 276, 293, 303, 304, 310, 312, 339, 340, 342, 343, 344
Farné, Alessandra 256, 307–316
feminism 19, 40, 41, 256, 307, 308, 309, 310, 311, 312, 313, 314, 331, 334; activism 256, 314; movements 307, 311, 313
feminist *see* feminism
feminist strike 307, 310, 311, 312, 313, 314
Fogarty, E. 204
Forester, S. 288
Foucault, Michel 162, 232
foundations 1, 4, 6, 40, 41, 105, 125–130, 145, 168, 188, 189, 124, 329, 330, 332, 333, 335, 337; community foundations 76, 125, 128, 255, 300–305; micro-foundations 188, 189
Freire, Paulo 197–199
functionalism 5, 6, 78, 79, 80, 81, 191, 224
fundraising 2, 4, 5, 14, 66, 67, 69, 71, 75, 76, 77, 115, 116, 117, 118, 119, 120, 121, 122, 130, 165, 166, 171, 172, 199, 256, 300, 302, 303, 304, 305, 308, 327, 331, 332, 333
fundraising life cycle 76, 116, 119, 120, 121

gender equality 1, 279, 280, 287
generative path of meaning 226
genre 229, 230, 231
global governance 143, 144
globalization 20, 24, 39, 144, 147, 166
goals 3, 7, 32, 34, 35, 47, 59, 80, 100, 105; charitable 126; collective 145; environmental 256, 272; millennium development goals 279; social change goals 34; storytelling goals 196; strategic goals 169, 170; sustainable development goals 107, 108, 126, 150, 158, 197, 235, 279

Goffman's dramaturgical perspective 270; frontstage and backstage communication mode 273
Gonçalves, Gisela 1–11, 13–14, 42, 75, 76, 142, 149, 161–163, 224, 255–257, 288, 290, 294, 305
Google Maps 339, 342
Gorin, Valerie 14, 66–74
governance 2, 4, 17, 20, 33, 35, 56, 77, 127, 136, 143, 144, 147, 148, 168, 169, 177, 237, 269, 271, 273, 277
government relations 142, 148
granting 76, 125, 126, 127, 129, 130, 131
grassroots 13, 27, 42, 144, 145, 146, 197, 208, 209, 255, 259, 260, 265, 279, 337, 340, 345
grassroots movement 197, 255
Greece 48, 85, 257, 337, 338, 340, 341, 342, 343, 344, 345
Greek economic crisis 338, 339, 341, 345
Greenpeace 162, 165, 224, 225, 227, 228, 229, 230, 231, 232, 238
Greimas, Algirdas Julien 162, 225, 226, 227, 228, 229, 232
Grenfell Tower 3, 7, 32, 34, 35, 47, 59, 80, 100, 105, 107, 108, 112, 126, 135, 137, 143, 145, 150, 151, 155, 158, 161, 166, 167, 168, 169, 170, 171, 187, 191, 196, 231, 235, 237, 246, 247, 249, 256, 260, 263, 266, 272, 274, 275, 279, 290, 318, 328
Grunig, James 5, 46, 117, 163, 247, 248
Gutterman, Ellen 146, 147

Habermas, Jürgen 51, 52, 55, 56, 58, 60, 62, 166
Hackademy 339, 340, 341, 342, 344
Hale, Lady Brenda 219, 220
Harsin, J. 288
hedonic 246, 247, 248
Herranz de la Casa, J. 37, 269, 270, 271, 272, 273, 274, 327
Honneth, Axel 86, 88
human flourishing 250, 260, 277
human rights 1, 2, 4, 19, 32, 36, 50, 57, 63, 67, 70, 72, 75, 76, 129, 142, 150, 152, 153, 157, 158, 165, 168, 170, 196, 216, 237, 255, 256, 280, 308
humanitarian 13–15, 17, 19, 41, 66–72, 256, 317, 318, 329, 333
humour 197, 200
Husband, Charles 86, 88
hybrid 29, 150, 151, 157, 182, 183, 187, 229

identity 4, 25, 36, 37, 68, 69, 70, 97, 98, 101, 102, 118, 136, 167, 168, 170, 176, 177, 183, 184, 187, 188, 189, 190, 200, 250
impact 2, 4, 14, 24, 28, 68, 70, 72, 102, 104, 108, 113, 117, 118, 122, 129, 130, 134, 136, 144, 178, 179, 180, 186, 187, 191, 197, 198, 219; aid 68; big-data 71; branding 179; campaigns 71; communication 106–108, 111, 112–113, 207, 208, 225, 241, 257, 259, 261; integrated communication 101; media 39; political 14, 39, 40; public relations 46, 219; social 127, 182, 183, 185, 186, 235, 237, 242, 255

indicators 36, 150; communication 104, 106–113; democratic 76, 144
indignados 42, 337
indignants 337, 341, 342
information 28, 29, 30, 37, 42, 43, 52, 63, 72, 85, 86, 87, 88, 90, 97, 104, 110, 111–112, 118, 119, 120, 122, 127, 129, 130, 134, 138, 139, 148, 151, 152, 153, 176, 178, 183, 184, 185, 187, 195, 196, 197, 206, 209, 218, 219, 230, 232, 238, 255, 256, 262, 263, 272, 273, 276, 277, 285, 287, 289, 294, 305, 308, 310, 312, 314, 319, 325, 328, 330, 334, 335, 344; analysis 111, 269, 272; disinformation 60; dissemination 28, 42, 71, 137, 138, 271, 276, 309; official 274; public 217, 221; scientific 231; sharing 3, 24, 30, 116, 137, 271, 277; transmission 42, 75, 77, 78, 79, 82, 91; trusted 72; use 71
inputs 106–109, 112–113, 166, 176
inspiration 309, 311, 313, 314
instigatory theory 5, 161, 165, 166, 167, 168, 169, 172, 289
institutionalization 40, 46, 236, 270
integrated communication 96, 97, 98, 99, 100, 101, 102, 112, 318
integrated marketing communication management 75, 76, 94, 95
integrity warriors 145, 148
intercultural gaze 321–324; process 152; responses 321
internal relations 146, 169, 170, 171
International Association for Measurement and Evaluation of Communication (AMEC) 104, 106
interpersonal 1, 23, 27, 28, 8, 86, 87, 88, 90, 91, 117, 118, 120, 121, 161, 177, 224, 249, 256, 290, 294, 300, 301
intersectionality 309, 311, 313, 314
interview 89, 110, 111, 139, 143, 145, 147, 148, 152, 153, 155, 157, 162, 168, 187, 197, 199, 205, 219, 225, 226, 241, 256, 281, 282, 283, 285, 290, 291, 294, 295, 300, 302, 303, 305, 338, 343
investment 36, 95, 112, 120, 128, 184, 185, 186, 187, 238, 264
Ireland's marriage equality referendum 59
Isbell, Matthew 75, 77–84
ITNC *see* instigatory theory

Jal Saheli 283, 284
Jenkins, Henry 91, 195
Jensen, Inger 51
Johnston, Jane 5, 14, 55–65, 162, 215–223
journalism 41, 46, 67, 199, 216, 230, 329, 334, 342, 344

Kalogeropoulos, Antonis 338, 344
Kaltenbacher, Thomas 256, 317–326
Kapa Research 338
Kelly, Kathleen S. 115, 117, 118, 120
Klaipeda 255, 269, 272, 273, 274, 276, 277
Koschmann, Matthew 3, 4, 5, 6, 75, 77–84, 166, 237

Index

labor unions 1, 224
Lang, Sabine 1, 13, 14, 32–38, 39, 166
legitimacy 3, 6, 34, 35, 68, 69, 71, 95, 97, 147, 169, 170, 183–188, 190, 191, 216, 232, 261
Lewis, Laurie 4, 76, 133–140
LGBTQ 34, 195
LGBTIQ+ activism 198
LGBTIQ+ rights 61, 62, 151, 154
liberal democracy 20, 33, 144, 215, 216; courts in 216; illiberal democracy 36; illiberal discourses 144; illiberalism 32
linguistic turn 79, 80, 185
listening 62, 91, 138–139, 284, 335; competency 87; seven canons 86, 88; systems 88, 90; technologies 88–90
literacy 286, 288; media literacy 290, 308
Liu, Gordon 4, 102, 161, 174–181
lobby *see* lobbying
lobbying 5, 19, 58, 62, 70, 143, 154, 157, 161, 162, 203, 209, 211, 270, 272, 335
local NGO 256, 269–275, 277
lockdown 256, 286, 287, 288, 289, 290, 291, 294, 295
Lopes, H. F. 76, 142–149
López Font, L. 256, 327–336

Macnamara, Jim 75, 85–93, 104–106, 107, 109, 111
macro level 6, 7, 13, 14, 24, 41, 171, 188, 236, 301; Macrosocial 39, 40, 46
major gifts 119–121
Malik, Kanchan 256, 279–285
management 6, 7, 30, 55, 94, 96, 101, 104, 105, 107, 112, 113, 127, 130; collaborative 30; humanitarian 70; human resource 133, 174; natural resource 24, 34; relationship 116, 117; responsible 151; strategic 60, 161
management logic 168, 169, 172
management of intangibles 95, 96, 182, 187
manipulation 217, 228
Marí-Sáez, Victor M. 14, 39–45, 307
market relations 169–171
marketing 67, 85, 95, 97–98, 102, 116, 119–120, 145–146, 161, 174, 175–176, 178, 180; internal 102, 174–179; relationship 116, 117
marketplace 2, 182
measurement 104–106, 112, 113, 114, 206, 207, 271
media access 195, 198, 199
media campaign 60, 119, 162, 195, 196, 198, 200
media outlets 67, 69, 72, 344, 345
media relations 4, 5, 106, 165, 215, 220
media trend 195, 196
membership organization 33, 136
meme 42, 161, 162, 195–200
meso 6, 7, 14, 24, 46, 48, 188
metrics 104, 106, 108
micro 7, 17, 24, 35, 41, 43, 46, 48, 150, 152, 171, 185, 188, 189, 242, 266, 301, 325
Miquel-Segarra, S. 256, 327–336
modern society 1, 62

monitoring 76, 88, 96, 104, 105, 107, 108, 110, 110, 112–113, 145, 153, 274, 305
monitoring & evaluation (M&E) 76, 104–112
Muller, Naíde 76, 150–160
multimodal analysis 162, 225, 229
multistakeholder 26, 139
Muniz-Velazquez, J.A. 163, 246–253

narrative 60, 61, 101, 182, 195, 196, 198–200, 236–238, 241, 242, 263–266; canonical scheme 228; dominant narrative 15, 17, 19, 196, 199; program 229, 230; in social entrepreneurship 161, 162, 183–191; social venture narrative 161, 162, 183–191; transportation 184, 185
National Association of Court Management (NACM) 220, 221
neoliberal 33, 37; humanitarianism 68; logic 67
neoliberalism 14, 39, 40, 42, 43
networked technologies 255, 262, 265, 266, 288
Nevradakis, Michael 257, 337–346
new media 69, 195, 220, 340, 342
new public management 34
NGO activation 169–171
NGO communication 5, 35, 36, 161, 166–169, 224, 232, 272, 274, 288–290
NGO dual management dynamic 168, 169, 172
NGO-ization 1, 13, 14, 33–37, 39–43
NGO loop 169–171
nongovernmental organizations 1, 18, 39, 46, 147, 165, 167, 204, 224, 236, 238, 255, 269, 280, 327, 337
nonprofit communication 1, 77
nonprofit sector 3, 85, 104, 174, 203, 246
Nos-Aldas, Eloísa 256, 307–316, 328

Occupy Wall Street 42, 308, 337
OECD 104, 105, 111, 112–113, 145, 242, 338
Oliveira, Evandro 1–11, 13–14, 35, 37, 46–54, 75–76, 105, 142, 161–173, 224, 237, 238, 255–257, 269, 270, 289, 305, 308
O'Neil, Glenn 4, 76, 104–114
ontological principles 161, 167
ontos 47, 52
open justice 161, 162, 215–217, 219–221
operational model 161, 168, 171, 172
oppressed 19, 197, 198, 199
organizational change 76, 83, 133, 134, 135, 137, 14
organizational communication 4, 6, 68, 77, 78, 83, 168, 183, 236, 246–248, 303
organizational listening 75, 85, 87–90; architecture of listening 87, 88; formal and informal methods 75, 88, 89, 90, 91, 105; the organizational listening project 87–89
organizational signature strengths 248, 250, 251
outcomes 28, 55, 57, 72, 75, 83, 106–110, 112, 113, 118, 133, 139, 162, 175, 178–180, 182–184, 187, 189–191, 207, 272, 276; behavioral 6; collective 261; emotional 76, 117; marketing 175, 178, 179; political 271; social venture 189

351

outputs 106–110, 207
OXFAM Intermón 257, 327, 329

Pallarés-Renau, M. 256, 327–336
pandemic 7, 23, 40, 72, 76, 130, 131, 144, 150, 153, 256, 261, 286–295, 300–305, 309, 310
Pani Panchayat 282–285
participatory action research 89
participatory communication 24, 28, 29, 30, 36, 42, 70, 162, 190, 197, 199, 290, 307, 308
Pavlovic 269–273, 276
peace 1, 19, 24, 50, 51, 71, 72, 129, 256, 312, 331
pedagogy 199, 232
Peirce, C. S. 225, 233
perception 26, 46, 69, 71, 97, 102, 113, 114, 134, 135, 137, 142, 146, 154, 174, 175, 183, 184, 195, 200, 203, 204, 206, 207, 230, 256, 271, 289, 292, 293, 294, 318–320, 325, 330
perception-action 319, 320, 325
performance 5, 109, 175–179, 182, 216, 228, 230, 239, 248, 249, 261
Peterson, C. 48, 150, 163, 246, 248–250
philanthropic 17, 19, 51, 71, 127; sector 13, 15, 16
philanthropy 15–17, 20, 72, 125, 126, 131, 302, 304; e-philanthropy 115, 118
planned giving 120, 121
Plato 48, 85
plot 183, 184, 185, 322, 323, 324
polis 47, 48, 189
political communication 6, 39, 41, 70, 72, 166, 212
political institutions 76, 143, 144, 146, 147, 235, 238
polyphonic 6, 7, 169, 232
positioning 56, 76, 94, 96, 98, 100, 102, 155, 157, 169, 170, 250, 295
positive communication 163
positive psychology 161, 163, 246, 247, 248, 249, 251
pragmatism 55, 57, 58, 63, 87
press judges *see* court-PR
professional organizations 337
professionalization 2, 19, 33, 40, 66, 94, 95, 165, 208, 237, 248
proximity 67, 197, 291, 293
psychagogy 232
public arenas *see* discourse arenas
Public Dialogue Consortium 91
Public Information Officer *see* court-PR
public interest 2, 5, 13, 14, 16, 52, 55–63, 142, 157
public interest communication 5, 14, 55, 56, 57, 59, 61, 63, 142
publicness 35, 60, 62, 216, 218
public relations 2–4, 14, 28, 35, 46, 51, 59, 66, 67, 69, 85, 87, 88, 98, 101, 113, 114, 116, 117, 125, 131–152, 155, 157, 158, 162, 163, 169–171, 208, 212, 215, 217, 218, 221, 229, 235, 246, 247, 271, 290, 294, 319
publics 4, 5, 7, 32, 34–37, 56–59, 62, 63, 75, 88, 95, 106, 163, 165, 168–170, 198, 247, 294, 295, 327, 328, 330

public sphere 2, 6, 7, 13, 35, 40, 42, 46, 50, 51, 52, 71, 142, 143, 147, 152, 161, 165, 166, 169–171, 232, 272, 284, 285, 335, 337, 338, 341, 344, 345

quality of democracy 13, 143, 146, 345

Radio 219, 257, 312, 338–345
Radiobubble 257, 338, 339, 340, 341, 342, 343, 344, 345
raising awareness 69, 191, 205, 328, 340
recipients 70, 90, 128, 135, 169, 198, 209, 290, 330
recognition 17, 33, 58, 63, 86, 87, 88, 112, 113, 117, 118, 191, 237, 256, 261, 305, 309, 310, 312, 313, 314, 335
Red Cross 19, 70, 71, 257, 327, 329, 330, 331
relationships 1, 4–6, 24, 34, 50, 52, 60, 70, 71, 75, 77, 82, 96, 102, 114, 115, 117, 119, 120, 122, 131, 134, 147, 151, 169, 170, 188, 203, 204, 212, 215, 227, 236, 261, 262, 265, 266, 319, 327, 332
religious 14, 15, 16, 17, 18, 23, 49, 50, 52, 68, 82, 125, 126, 131, 210, 301, 313, 321, 322, 331, 337; religion 28, 50
reporting 34, 36, 66, 69, 72, 89, 111, 117, 118, 135, 207, 236, 238, 343
reproduction 34, 36, 41, 169, 170, 171, 200
reputation 4, 6, 7, 37, 75, 91, 97, 134, 150, 169, 170, 175, 185, 231, 236, 317, 327, 328, 333, 339, 341; strategic goals 169–171
rhetoric 58, 85, 91, 162, 185, 186, 187, 225, 226, 227, 229–232, 236
rhizomatic media 345
Roundy, Philip 161, 182–194

Sá, Sónia de 256, 286–299
Saussure, F. de 225
Save The Children 69, 70, 257, 327, 330, 332
Scott v Scott 216
Seligman, M. 163, 246, 248, 249, 250
semio-narrative structures 226, 227, 229
semiotic square 227, 229
semiotics 67, 161, 162, 224, 225, 226, 228, 229, 232; signs 162, 225, 225
sensemaking 37, 137
Servaes, Jan 13, 23–31, 41, 289, 307
shared vision 145, 170
SMART objectives 106, 112
social action 24, 63, 81, 167, 256, 318, 319, 320, 331, 333, 334
social capital 4, 68, 198, 236, 300, 305
social change 6, 13, 14, 23, 24, 26–29, 34, 40–43, 56, 60, 62, 105, 107, 108, 148, 151, 153, 157, 167, 168, 187, 196, 235, 236, 238, 242, 289, 307–309, 314, 319, 338
social entrepreneur 63, 162, 182, 183, 184, 185, 186, 187, 188, 189, 190, 191
social impact 182, 185, 186, 235, 237, 242, 255
social marketing 6, 29, 66, 72, 91, 94

Index

social media 4, 27, 28, 34, 36, 43, 60, 67, 86–89, 102, 104, 108–109, 113, 116, 119, 121, 122, 152, 153, 158, 162, 190, 195, 196, 200, 204, 206, 215, 220, 221, 241, 255–257, 262, 263, 265, 271, 272, 274, 276, 277, 287–294, 300, 303, 305, 309, 312, 328, 330, 332, 334, 337–345
social mission 75, 182, 183, 185, 188
social movements 19, 33, 40–42, 58, 62, 144, 151, 153, 157, 162, 166, 224, 262, 308, 309, 337, 340, 341, 345; climate walks 265; feminist 40, 307, 311, 313
social networks 162, 197, 203, 208, 262, 269–272, 276
social reality 52, 78, 79, 82, 171
socio-communicative 14, 46, 47, 52, 161
solidarity 1, 14, 17, 19, 35, 39, 40–43, 67, 69, 70, 94, 155, 166, 167, 301, 313, 323, 328, 333, 335, 342, 345
stakeholders 3, 4, 6, 7, 30, 34, 35, 42, 61, 68, 76, 82, 87–89, 91, 94–106, 117, 118, 133–139, 151, 153, 162, 167, 168–177, 182–191, 196, 200, 215, 226, 241, 248–251, 256, 269–277, 283, 284, 305, 327–334
stewardship 117, 118
Stoep, J. Van der 255, 259–277
Stonewell riots 61
storytelling 91, 135, 162, 195–200, 215, 219, 289
strategic communication 4, 6, 95, 98, 99, 106, 114, 143, 148, 151, 158, 161–163, 165, 167, 169, 171, 172, 209, 215–217, 224, 229, 232, 235, 239, 285, 288, 292, 294, 318
strategic marketing 102, 161
strategic planning 256, 317, 318, 319, 321, 323, 325
strategic positioning 76, 98, 102
surveillance 36, 90, 168, 300, 301
sustainable development 25, 26, 28, 30, 76, 126, 150, 235, 241, 260, 277, 279
Sydney Gay & Lesbian Mardi Gras 60, 61, 62, 64

Tapia-Frade, A. J. 163, 246–253
textual analysis 88, 89, 90
theory of change 107, 111, 285
third sector 7, 113, 151, 158, 236, 300, 327, 333–335, 340, 345
trade unions 210, 310, 328, 337
transformative communication 39, 256
transformative power 197
transgression 36, 309, 310, 313, 314
transmedia 162, 195, 196, 198, 200
transmission of information model of communication 75, 77–79, 81, 82, 85
transnational associations 18, 19, 20
transparency 3, 5, 24, 97, 105, 113, 117, 144, 146–148, 216, 264, 270, 271, 302, 303, 327
Transparency International 76, 143, 145
Transparency Register 209–212
trust 1, 4–6, 23, 25, 37, 48, 68, 71, 72, 75, 76, 90, 91, 96, 97, 116–118, 126–128, 131, 138, 144, 146, 147, 157, 191, 215, 217, 236, 242, 255, 262, 264, 270, 287, 302, 305, 317, 319, 327–344; distrust 25, 48, 68, 157, 287; interpersonal 256, 300, 301; public trust 169, 170, 338; trustworthy 261, 318, 325
trustees 332, 333
Tumulyte 273, 274
Tutorpool 339, 340, 341, 342, 344
Twitter 66, 158, 220, 263, 312, 337, 339–344

UK Supreme Court 215, 219, 220
UNICEF 29, 71, 199, 257, 279, 280, 285, 323, 324, 327, 330, 332
United Nations 33, 68, 76, 145, 150, 162, 165, 199, 216, 217, 219, 330, 331

value-informed communication 256, 317, 318, 319, 321, 323, 325
victim 199, 256, 281, 282, 286–295, 309, 310, 312, 331, 333
violence 23, 61, 70, 200, 256, 279, 286, 287, 288, 289, 290, 291, 292, 293, 294, 295, 308, 309, 310, 311, 312, 313, 314
virtues 246, 247, 248, 249, 250
Visan, Laura 256, 300–306
Voci, Denise 162, 235–245
voices 30, 32, 33, 35, 37, 59, 60, 62, 63, 68, 70, 72, 83, 85, 87, 88, 89, 90, 102, 108, 109, 113, 118, 119, 130, 138, 151, 157, 195, 199, 230, 241, 271, 282, 284, 301, 303, 335
voluntary 2, 3, 4, 7, 13, 15, 16, 17, 18, 20, 48, 49, 83, 94, 126, 142, 150, 151, 157, 158, 167, 179, 180, 280, 283, 337
volunteering 3, 102, 331, 334, 335, 345
volunteer management 77
volunteers 2, 3, 5, 36, 68, 69, 71, 75, 76, 81, 95, 97, 99, 101, 115, 117, 133–139, 169, 170, 174, 176, 178–180, 182, 185, 196, 273, 275, 276, 282, 284, 303–305, 328–333, 338–343
Vuuren-Verkek, K. 255, 259–268

water crisis 279, 282, 284
water management 256, 280, 283
Waters, Richard D. 4, 42, 76, 115–124, 219
Weder, Francisca 5, 162, 289, 235–245
well-being 91, 108, 153, 246, 247, 250, 251, 270, 272
women 1, 26, 32, 47, 205, 237, 271
women's strike 256, 311, 314
World Bank 39, 107, 109, 114

Yadav, R. Awtar 256, 279–285
Yearbook of International Organizations 1, 50

Zimmermann, Anja 76, 94–103
Zoon Politikon 47, 52

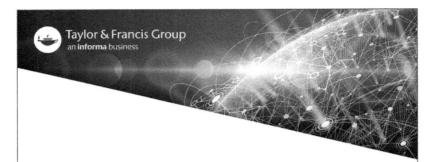

Milton Keynes UK
Ingram Content Group UK Ltd.
UKHW050047270524
443136UK00005B/76